Whitworth College Library

0 0068 0204313

S0-EMA-236

DISCARD

A
WOMAN OF THE CENTURY

FOURTEEN HUNDRED-SEVENTY BIOGRAPHICAL SKETCHES
ACCOMPANIED BY PORTRAITS

OF

LEADING AMERICAN WOMEN

IN ALL WALKS OF LIFE

EDITED BY

FRANCES E. WILLARD AND MARY A. LIVERMORE

ASSISTED BY A CORPS OF ABLE CONTRIBUTORS

In Two Volumes:
VOLUME ONE

GORDON PRESS

NEW YORK
1975

First published 1893

Library of Congress Catalog Card Number: 74-27501

International Standard Book Number: 0-87968-183-7

GORDON PRESS—Publishers
P.O. Box 459
Bowling Green Station
New York, N.Y. 10004

Printed in the United States of America

PREFACE.

Among all cyclopædias and books about famous women, this is intended to be unique and to supply a vacant niche in the reference library. The nineteenth century is woman's century. Since time began, no other era has witnessed so many and so great changes in the development of her character and gifts and in the multiplication of opportunities for their application. Even to those best informed on this subject, we believe that a glance at these pages will bring astonishment at the vast array of woman's achievements here chronicled, in hundreds of new vocations and avocations. Few eminent names and faces will here be missed, while many worthy names, which can not be found elsewhere, are strung upon this rosary of nineteenth-century achievement. Every department of life and work is here represented. One branch of philanthropic work, that of the missionary, is less numerously represented than its importance deserves, only because an adequate showing would require the addition of nearly every missionary society in our country since missionary societies began to be. This book is not alone a book of record of famous names, but one which aims to show what women have done in the humbler as in the higher walks of life. It is a record of American women offered, at the close of four centuries of life in the New World, to the consideration of those who would know what the nineteenth century of Christian civilization has here brought forth, and what are the vast outlook and the marvelous promise of the twentieth century.

Frances E. Willard

Mary A. Livermore

Christmas, 1892.

VOLUME 1

A

WOMAN OF THE CENTURY.

ABBATT, Miss Agnes Dean, artist, born in New York City, 23rd June, 1847. She still resides in her native city. Her paternal ancestors were English, and she is of French Huguenot descent on her mother's side. Her great-grandfather and his family came from England to this country in the latter part of the last century. They settled in what is now Pleasant Valley, Dutchess county, N. Y., where William D. Abbatt, the father of Agnes, was born. He passed his life in business in Poughkeepsie, Philadelphia and New York. Miss Abbatt's grandmother, Mrs. Dean, an English woman, was an art amateur of unusual talent and accomplishments. Of her children, nearly all possessed the talent for painting, but of all the descendants Agnes alone has adopted art as a profession. She showed in early childhood a marked talent for drawing, but it was not till 1873 that she took up the study of art as a profession. In that year she entered the Cooper Union art-school. She won a medal for a head of Ajax in the first year of her studies, and on the merit of that achievement she was admitted to the art-school of the National Academy of Design in New York. So decided was her progress that, at the end of the first year in that institution her first full-length drawing was one of those selected for exhibition. As it was not her intention to become a figure-painter, she left the Academy and devoted herself to the study of landscape painting. That branch of art she studied for several years under R. Swain Gifford, N. A., and James D. Smillie, N. A., constantly showing new powers and making rapid progress. At the same time she was gratifying her tastes in another direction, and she won distinction as a water-colorist and also as a flower-painter. Her first pictures, two panels of flowers, were shown in the exhibition of the Brooklyn Art Club in 1875, where they attracted much attention and found purchasers. Her next picture, "My Next Neighbor," was shown in New York, and was the subject of much favorable comment. In the Water Color Society's exhibition, in 1880, she showed a composition named, "When Autumn Turns the Leaves," which was one of the most conspicuous features of the exhibition. In the same year Miss Abbatt was elected a member of the American Water Color Society, at once taking high rank in that somewhat exclusive organization of artists. She is the second woman on its list of members. She has given especial attention to the painting of chrysanthemums. Besides the picture entitled "When Autumn Turns the Leaves," she has painted others that are noteworthy, among which are "The Last of the Flowers," "Flowers of the Frost," "Our Japanese Cousins," "From the Land of the Mikado," "Autumn Colors," and "A Japanese Embassy," all devoted to the royal chrysanthemum. In the landscape field she has confined her work mostly to the rural scenes in Westchester, county, N. Y., the picturesque nooks of the eastern end of Long Island, and the coast of Maine and Massachusetts Bay. Among her notable productions in landscape are "Near Barnstable, Cape Cod," "The Noisy Geese that Gabbled o'er the Pool." "A Summer Afternoon on the New England Coast," and "In Lobster Lane, Magnolia, Mass." The last named picture won for her a silver medal in the exhibition of the Charitable Mechanics' and Tradesmen's

AGNES DEAN ABBATT.

Association of Boston, Mass. She works with equal facility and success in oil and water colors, and she has also made a study of pastel work. In addition to her own extended creative work, she has been a successful art-teacher, in studio and in field. Aside from her home studio, she has taught classes in Washington, D. C., Troy, N. Y., and in New Haven, Conn., while her field instruction has been given in New York, Massachusetts and Maine. She is a genuine enthusiast in art, both as creator and instructor, and in these two fields, calling for so widely differing powers, she has been equally at home. Her work is distinct in character, in outline and tone in shades and lights, and her proud position among the painters of the United States is a one legitimately won and successfully held.

ABBOTT, Mrs. Elizabeth Robinson, educator, born in Lowell, Mass., 11th September, 1852. Her maiden name was Elizabeth Osborne Robinson. She is the youngest daughter of William S. and Harriet H. Robinson. Through the writings and conversations of Miss Elizabeth P. Peabody she became interested, in her girlhood, in the kindergarten method of teaching, and would gladly have taken up that branch of educational work at the time when the death of her father made it necessary for her to become self-supporting. But circumstances prevented, and she therefore sought other ways of earning her living. Successively, she taught a district school in Maine and "boarded

ELIZABETH ROBINSON ABBOTT

round," kept a little private school of her own, tried bookkeeping and learned to set type. After giving three months to learning type-setting, she hardly earned enough to pay her board out of the low wages given to women compositors. About that time two positions were open to her, one to "'tend store" and the other as "second assistant" in Mrs. Shaw's charity kindergarten and nursery at the North End in Boston. The latter position meant simply to be the kitchen-maid or cook, and nothing more; but, preferring this position to that of shop-girl, and thinking it might eventually lead or open the way into higher kindergarten work, she accepted the offer. While there, Miss Phœbe Adam, the manager, became interested in the "second assistant" and, knowing her desire to become a kindergartner, with money helped her to carry on her studies, and kindly allowed her the privilege of taking time for her lessons out of the afternoon hours of her work. She was one of the

early pupils of Miss Lucy H. Symonds, of Boston, and was a graduate of the class of 1883. So, after waiting seven years for the fulfillment of her cherished desires, Mrs. Abbott began her work as a kindergartner. Her first teaching was done in a summer charity-school in Boston. She then went to Waterbury, Conn., and introduced this method into the Hillside Avenue school. There she taught until her marriage, in 1885, to George S. Abbott, of that city. After her marriage Mrs. Abbott did not lose her interest in kindergarten work, but continued her class until most of her little pupils were graduated into primary schools. Since that time she has encouraged and helped others to keep up the work she so successfully began, having for two years given part of her home for use as a kindergarten. Thus Mrs. Abbott has created and maintained in the city where she now lives a lasting interest, and she may be considered a pioneer of kindergarten work in Connecticut. She is now secretary of the Connecticut Valley Kindergarten Association, an association of kindergartners embracing western Massachusetts, Connecticut and Rhode Island. Mrs. Abbott is not well known as a writer or speaker, but she is interested in and works for all that relates to the advancement of women. She is chairman of the correspondence committee for Connecticut of the General Federation of Women's Clubs, one of the founders of Old and New, the woman's club of Malden, Mass., and the chief founder of the Woman's Club of Waterbury, Conn.

ABBOTT, Emma, prima donna, born in Chicago, Ill., in 1850. Her father was a music teacher, and he encouraged her and her brother George to develop the musical talents that each showed at a very early age. Emma was a singing child, and under her father's training she sang well and became a proficient performer on the guitar. Professor Abbott moved from Chicago to Peoria, Ill., in 1854. There his patronage was so small that his family was in straitened circumstances. He gave a concert in 1859, in which the young Emma was prima donna and guitar player, and her brother was her support. The entertainment was a success, and Professor Abbott and his two talented children gave a large number of concerts in other towns and cities, with varying fortunes. In 1866 the finances of the family were at a low ebb, and Emma took a district school to teach in order to assist in supporting the household. Emma's early lessons on the guitar and her brother's on the violin were not entirely paid for until she had become a successful concert singer in New York. At the age of thirteen she taught the guitar with success. Her education was acquired in the Peoria public schools. When she was sixteen years old she sang in the synagogue in Peoria. At that age she joined the Lombard Concert Company, of Chicago, and traveled with them in Iowa, Illinois, and Wisconsin. When the company disbanded Emma found herself in Grand Haven, Mich., friendless and moneyless. With her guitar she started out alone and gave concerts in Michigan and the neighboring States, and thus worked her way to New York City, where she gave parlor concerts in the hotels in which she staid, and in that way earned the money for her expenses. Failing to gain notice in New York, she borrowed money and returned to the west. She tried a concert season in Chicago and Milwaukee, but was unsuccessful. She then tried a number of smaller towns and ended her tour in a failure in a hotel in Toledo, Ohio. Among her hearers in that slimly attended concert was Clara Louise Kellogg, who recognized her merit and gave her money enough to go to New York, with a letter to

Professor Errani. In 1870 she began to study with him, and was engaged to sing in Dr. Chapin's church at a salary of $1,500 a year. In 1872 Mr. Lake, with the aid of Dr. Chapin's congregation,

EMMA ABBOTT.

raised $10,000 to send her to Europe for musical training. She went to Milan and studied with San Giovanni, and afterwards to Paris, where she studied under Wartel for several years. She studied with Delle Sadie also. While in Paris, she suffered an illness that threatened the destruction of her voice. She made a successful début, however, and she had there a warm friend in the Baroness Rothschild. Numerous enticing offers were made to her by European managers. She made an engagement with Manager Gye in London, but refused, on moral grounds, to appear in the opera, "La Traviata." In this she was supported by Eugene Wetherell, her husband. He was a member of Dr. Chapin's church and had followed her to Europe, where they were secretly married. Her refusal to sing that rôle ended in the cancellation of her engagement with Mr. Gye. In 1876 she returned to the United States, and with C. D. Hess organized an opera company. She appeared in the Park Theater, Brooklyn, N. Y., in her famous rôle of Marguerite. Soon after she became her own manager, and her husband and Charles Pratt attended to her business until Mr. Wetherell's sudden death in Denver, Col., in 1888. Miss Abbott, for she always retained her maiden name, was successful from the start. In spite of abuse, ridicule and misrepresentation, she drew large audiences wherever she appeared. The critics at first derided her in every possible way, but the public did not heed the critics and crowded to hear the courageous little woman who could maintain her good temper under a shower of ridicule, the like of which never before fell upon the head of a public personage. She grew artistically every year, and her stainless character, her generosity to her com-

pany, her gifts to charity, and her industry and perseverance at length won over the critics, who had simply made manifest their inability to write down a really meritorious artist. Miss Abbott sang throughout the United States, and in an incredibly short time she had amassed a fortune of several millions of dollars. Her voice was a pure, clear, long-range soprano of great flexibility. Her rôles included Norma, Semiramide, Elvira, Martha, Lucia, and Marguerite, and in her last years she appeared in costumes more magnificent than any other singer had ever worn. She died in Ogden, Utah, 4th January, 1891, after an illness of less than a week. Her funeral was held in Chicago on 9th January, her body was cremated, in accordance with a provision of her will, and its ashes were deposited in the magnificent mausoleum she had built in Gloucester, Mass. Her large fortune was divided by her will among her relatives and friends, and various churches and charitable societies.

ACHESON, Mrs. Sarah C., temperance worker, born in Washington, Pa., 20th February, 1844. She is descended on the paternal side from English and Dutch families that settled in Virginia in 1600, and on the maternal side from Col. George Morgan, who had charge of Indian affairs under Washington, with headquarters at Fort Pitt, and of whom Jefferson, in a letter which Mrs. Acheson has in her possession, says, "He first gave me notice of the mad project of that day," meaning the Aaron Burr treason. Among her ancestors were Col. William Duane, of Philadelphia, editor of the Philadelphia "Aurora" during the Revolution. Her girlhood was spent in the town of her birth, where she was married, in 1863, to Capt.

SARAH C. ACHESON.

Acheson, of the same place, then on Gen. Miles's staff, the marriage taking place while the Captain was on furlough with a gunshot wound in the face. He left for the front ten days after, encouraged by his young wife. Dr. and Mrs. Acheson moved to Texas in 1872. During their residence in Texas Mrs. Acheson has been a moral force. Her influence has been strongly felt, not only in the city where she resides, but throughout the State. Her generous nature has been shown in heroic deeds of a kind which the world seldom sees. When a cyclone struck the village of Savoy, many of its inhabitants were badly wounded, some were killed, others made homeless. Mrs. Acheson reached them as speedily as a train could take her, doing duty as nurse and special provider for the suffering. She gave three years of active service to the Woman's Christian Temperance Union. She was State president at a time when a strong leader was greatly needed, guiding their bark into a haven of financial safety. Her life is active along all lines of duty. She is abreast of the advanced thought of the age. The world's progress in social, scientific and religious reform is not only an open, but a well-read book, to her. Her home is in Denison, Tex.

ACKERMANN, Miss Jessie A., president of the Woman's Christian Temperance Union of Australasia, born in Boston, Mass.,4th July, 1860. As befits a Fourth-of-July child, she has the ring of American independence. She is a descendant of the Pilgrim Fathers on her mother's side, and is of German extraction on her father's. Her inherited virtues and talents have been developed by liberal educational advantages. She was instructed in law, and spent much time in the study of elocution. She took a private course of study in theology, while drawing and painting and instruction in household matters were not neglected. She had the advantage of extensive travel through her native land and spent much time in the Southern States, immediately after the close of her schooldays. At twelve years of age she was taken to a Good Templars' Lodge, where she received her first temperance teaching, and gave her first temperance talk. She began public work as grand lecturer and organizer for that society in 1881, and continued until, in 1888, the wider scope and higher spiritual tone of the Woman's Christian Temperance Union, with its special opportunities for work among women, won her heart, and she began to serve in its ranks. She succeeded amid extraordinary difficulties in organizing unions at Sitka and Juneau, in Alaska She also traveled and organized in British Columbia with success. She gladly responded to the call to go round the world, and receiving her appointment at the National Convention held in New York, in October, 1888, she sailed from San Francisco for the Sandwich Islands on 29th January, 1889. She reached Honolulu on 6th February, and was cordially welcomed at the residence of the W. C. T. U. president. The Japanese Consul-General, a cultivated Christian gentleman, president of a temperance society of 1,400 members, was much interested in her work and acted as interpreter at the meetings she held among the Japanese residents, the other foreigners and the native Hawaiians. She spent some time in the Islands. The history of her mission in New Zealand and the Australian colonies was recorded in the "Union Signal" by her letters during 1889. Successful and enthusiastic missions were held in the North and South Islands of New Zealand and in the Island of Tasmania. She visited Melbourne on the way for Adelaide. She remained two months in South Australia, traveled over the greater part of the colony, organized twenty-four local unions, called a convention in Adelaide, formed a Colonial Union, and left a membership of 1,126. Workers responded to her call in every place, and money was forthcoming for all needs. Finding the work in Victoria well

organized under the care of Mrs. Love, of America, she stayed only a few days, in which she spoke in the crowded meetings of the Victorian Alliance, which is very influential in Melbourne. Her stay in New South Wales was very brief, for she found that outside help was not at that time welcomed in that oldest and most conservative colony, although a good work was doing by the several local unions. She was most cordially welcomed to Queensland, but stayed only long enough to attend their annual convention, as the way to China and Japan seemed open before her. A sense of duty rather than inclination took Miss Ackermann to China, but from the time she landed in Hong Kong she was well received everywhere. As there seemed no opportunity to organize in Hong Kong, she decided to proceed to Siam, by way of Swatow. Her visit to Bankok was prolonged through an attack of malarial fever, which greatly reduced her strength. While in that city, she obtained an

JESSIE A. ACKERMANN.

audience with His Royal Highness, Prince Diss, who is at the head of the department of education in Siam. She was also presented to His Majesty, the King of Siam, who received her graciously. She returned again to Hong Kong, on the way to Canton, which she reached by river. The northern ports of China being closed, Miss Ackermann proceeded to Japan, going to Yokohama. There she did much work and formed a union. She next visited Tokio. A very successful mission was held at Numadza, where a union of forty members was formed. Meetings were held in Nagoya, and also under the auspices of the temperance society in Kioto, where Miss Ackermann addressed the Congregational Conference, then in session. There she also spoke in the theater to six hundred Buddhist students, on "What Christianity has done for the World." She addressed nine hundred students in the Doshisha school. Osaka was visited at the invitation of the Young Men's Christian

Association. Returning to Shanghai, she enjoyed the privilege of attending and making an address before the General Missionary Conference of China. The last was held thirteen years earlier. At that time a woman was called upon to bring her work before the conference, at which the chairman vacated the chair, and many left the meeting in sore grief and indignation. On this occasion, however, all women delegates present, including missionaries' wives, were made voting members of the conference with all the privileges of the floor, amid storms of applause. Miss Ackermann was able to form a National Woman's Christian Temperance Union for China. Successful missions were conducted in Cooktown, Townsville, Mount Morgan, Rockhampton and Brisbane, and she again went into New South Wales. The work was very hard. In the first month she traveled seven-hundred miles, held forty-two meetings, and made more than one-hundred calls in search of leaders for the work. The results were gratifying, being twenty new unions, a reorganized Colonial Union, and fifteen Colonial superintendents. The Good Templars were her faithful friends in that colony, and she spoke in the annual meetings of the Grand Lodge, where about three-hundred delegates were present. She called a convention in Melbourne for May, 1891, which was attended by forty-nine delegates. Miss Ackermann was elected president. A constitution was adopted providing for a triennial convention, the next to be held in Sydney in 1894, and Miss Ackermann was elected president of the Woman's Christian Temperance Union of Australasia for the ensuing term of three years. Since October, 1888, she has traveled more than forty-thousand miles, spoken through interpreters in seventeen different languages, formed more than one-hundred unions, taken five thousand pledges, and received over four thousand women into the union. The suppression of the opium traffic and of gambling, and the religious education of the young are questions to which she is devoting much thought. Since the Australasian convention she has traveled and organized in Victoria and South Australia. Miss Ackermann writes modestly of her platform ability, but she is really a speaker of no mean order. Her audiences are held by her addresses and fascinated by her lectures.

ADAMS, Mrs. Abigail, wife of John Adams, second President of the United States, born 22nd November, 1744, in Weymouth, Mass. She was a daughter of the Rev. William Smith, for forty years minister of the Congregational church in Weymouth. Her mother was Elizabeth Quincy, a great-great-granddaughter of Rev. Thomas Shepard, an eminent Puritan clergyman of Cambridge, and a great-grandniece of the Rev. John Norton, of Boston. Abigail Adams was one of the most distinguished women of the Revolutionary period. She was in delicate health in youth and unable to attend school, but she became a far better scholar than most of the women of her day. She read widely and wrote in terse, vigorous and elegant language. Her youth was passed in converse with persons of learning, experience and political sagacity. She was married on 25th October, 1764, to John Adams, then a young lawyer practicing in Boston. During the next ten years her quiet and happy life was devoted to her husband and her four children, three sons and one daughter. Then came the troubled times that were marked by the disputes between the Colonies and England. Mrs. Adams seconded her husband in his opposition to the English oppression, and encouraged him in his zeal and determination in urging the Colonies to declare their independence. She remained in Braintree,

Mass., while Mr. Adams was absent as a delegate to the Continental Congress and afterwards on diplomatic missions in Europe. In 1784 she joined her husband in France, and in 1785 they went to London, whither Mr. Adams was sent as Minister Plenipotentiary to the Court of Great Britain. Remembering the patriotic zeal and independence of Mrs. Adams during the Revolution, George III and his queen, still smarting over the loss of the American Colonies, treated her with marked rudeness. Mrs. Adams remembered their rudeness, and afterwards wrote: "Humiliation for Charlotte is no sorrow for me." After spending one year in France and three in England, Mrs. Adams returned to the United States in 1788. In 1789, after her husband was appointed Vice-President of the United States, she went to reside in Philadelphia, Pa., then the seat of government. In 1797 Mr. Adams was chosen President. In 1800, after his defeat, they retired to Quincy, Mass., where Mrs.

ABIGAIL ADAMS.

Adams died 28th October, 1818. She was a woman of elevated mind and strong powers of judgment and observation. Her letters have been collected and published with a biographical sketch by her grandson, Charles F. Adams, in a volume entitled "Familiar Letters of John Adams and his Wife, Abigail Adams, During the Revolution."

ADAMS, Mrs. Florence Adelaide Fowle, dramatic reader and teacher, born in Chelsea, Mass., 15th October, 1863. Her maiden name was Fowle. Her father's family, originally from England, have been for many generations residents of the old Bay State. On her mother's side she is descended from the Earl of Seafield, who was her mother's great-grandfather, and from the Ogilvies, Grants, Gordons and Ichmartins of Scotland, tracing their ancestry back to 1300. She was graduated from the Chelsea public school and afterwards attended the girl's Latin school in Boston. She learned readily, making particularly rapid progress in the study of the languages. During childhood she gave promise of great dramatic power. This, combined with her pretty childish face and happy disposition, won her much

FLORENCE ADELAIDE FOWLE ADAMS

attention, while it held out flattering prospects for the future. She was graduated from the Boston School of Oratory in 1884, under the late Prof. Robert R. Raymond. In June, 1888, she was married to George Adams, a direct descendant of the statesmen and presidents. Her marriage has not interfered with her chosen line of work. Naturally of a sympathetic disposition, she has devoted much time and talent to charities. Having had from time to time many pupils to instruct, she felt the need of a text-book that should set forth the principles of the Delsarte system in a form easily grasped by the student. This led to the publication of her book "Gestures and Pantomimic Action" (Boston, 1891). Mrs. Adams was her own model for the numerous illustrations used in the volume, and in this, as throughout the work, she had an invaluable critic in the person of her mother, who is also a graduate of the Boston School of Oratory. One distinguishing trait of Mrs. Adams' character is her great love for animals, not confined to a few pampered pets, but extended to the whole brute creation. Her personal appearance is pleasing. She is youthful looking and is fond of society in which she has ever been a general favorite.

ADAMS, Miss Hannah, the first woman in the United States to make a profession of literature was born in Medfield, Mass., in 1755, and died in Brookline, Mass., 15th November, 1832. Her father was a well-to-do farmer of considerable education and culture. Hannah was a delicate child fond of reading and study. In childhood she memorized most of the poetical works of Milton, Pope, Thomson, Young and others. Her studies were varied, including Greek and Latin,

in which she was instructed by the divinity students who made their home with her family. In 1772 her father lost his property, and the children were forced to provide for themselves. Hannah supported herself during the Revolutionary War by making lace and by teaching school. After the war she opened a school to prepare young men for college, in which she was very successful. Her principal work, a volume entitled "A View of Religious Opinions," appeared in 1784. The labor necessary for so great a work resulted in a serious illness that threatened her with mental derangement. That book passed through several editions in the United States and was republished in England. It is a work of great research and erudition. When the fourth edition was published, she changed the title to "A Dictionary of Religions." It was long a standard volume. Her second work, "A History of New England," appeared in 1799, and her third, "Evidences of Christianity," in 1801. Her income from these successful works was meager, as she did not understand the art of making money so well as she knew the art of making books. Her reputation extended to Europe and won her many friends, among whom was Abbé Grégoire, who was then laboring to secure the emancipation of the Jews in France. With him she corresponded, and from him she received valuable aid in preparing her "History of the Jews," which appeared in 1812. Her next book, "A Controversy with Dr. Morse," appeared in 1814, and her "Letters on the Gospels" in 1826. All her books passed through many editions. Miss Adams was a woman of great modesty and simplicity. Her life was very quiet; her only journey

HANNAH ADAMS.

by water was the ten-mile trip from Boston to Nahant and her longest land journey was from Boston to Chelmsford. The closing years of her life she spent in Boston, supported by an annuity settled upon her by three wealthy men of that city.

She was buried in Mount Auburn, being the first one to be buried in that cemetery. Her autobiography, edited with additions by Mrs. Hannah F. Lee, was published in Boston in 1832.

ADAMS, Mrs. Jane Kelley, educator, born in Woburn, Mass., 30th October, 1852. Her father was a member of a prominent firm of leather manufacturers. Her family had gone from New Hampshire,

JANE KELLEY ADAMS.

her mother being a descendant of the Marston family that came over from England in 1634. Mrs. Adams as a child showed great fondness for the schoolroom and for books. When three-and-one-half years old she "ran away" to attend the infant school, of which she became a regular member six months later. From that time her connection with school work, either as student, teacher, or committeewoman, has been almost continuous. As a student, she worked steadily, in spite of delicate health and the protests of physician and friends. She was graduated from the Woburn high school in 1871, and from Vassar College in 1875. In 1876 she became a teacher in the high school from which she was graduated, leaving in 1881 to become the wife of Charles Day Adams, a member of the class of 1873 in Harvard, and a lawyer practicing in Boston. Since her marriage, as before, her home has been in Woburn, and, although a conscientious housekeeper and the mother of two children, she has found time within the last ten years, not only to have occasional private pupils, but also to identify herself fully with the public work of her native city. In 1886–7 she was president of the Woburn Woman's Club. Within that time she organized three parliamentary law clubs among her women friends. Later, she was one of the founders of the Woburn Home for Aged Women and was one of its vice-presidents. She has served as a director and an auditor of the Woman's Club, as president of a church society, and as chairman of the executive committee of the Equal Suffrage League. In 1888 she was elected to a position on the Woburn school board, and in 1890 served as its presiding officer. In the spring of 1891, feeling from her work on the board of education the great need the students had of instruction in manual training, she was instrumental in establishing classes in sewing, sloyd and cooking, which were largely attended. Besides her work in her native town, Mrs. Adams has found time to be active in the various societies for college-bred women in the neighboring city of Boston. She is of a social nature, has a great interest in her husband's work, and it is not impossible that she will become a student of law.

ADAMS, Mrs. Louise Catherine, wife of John Quincy Adams, born in London, England, in 1775. She was a daughter of Joshua Johnson, of Maryland, but passed her early years in England and France. Her father's house in London was the resort of Americans in England. She was married to Mr. Adams in 1797. Mr. Adams had been resident minister at The Hague, and when his father was elected President of the United States, he went as minister to Berlin, Germany. There the young wife sustained herself with dignity in social and political life. In 1801 she returned with her husband to the United States. Mr. Adams was elected to the United States Senate, and they passed their winters in Washington, D. C., and their summers in Boston. In 1808 Mr. Adams was appointed by President Madison the first accredited minister to Russia. Mrs. Adams accompanied him to Russia, and she was the first American woman presented at the Russian court. She made an eminently favorable impression on Russian society. She passed one winter alone in St. Petersburg, while Mr. Adams was in Ghent negotiating a

LOUISE CATHERINE ADAMS.

treaty between the United States and England. In the spring, accompanied by her eight-year-old son and servants, she set out to travel to Paris by land. The journey was a memorable one to her, as the times were troublous, the traveling very bad and the country full of soldiers. She reached Paris in March, 1815. There she witnessed all the momentous affairs that preluded the famous "Hundred Days." Mr. Adams was next appointed Minister to England, and they made their home near London. In 1817 they returned to the United States. Mr. Adams served as Secretary of State for eight years, and Mrs. Adams did the honors of their home in Washington. When her husband was elected President, she became the mistress of the White House. There she displayed the same quiet elegance and simplicity that had distinguished her in so many prominent situations. Failing health forced her into semi-retirement. She ceased to appear in fashionable circles, but still presided at public receptions. After the expiration of President Adams' term of office, her retirement was complete. The closing years of her life were spent in the care of her family and the practice of domestic virtues. She died on 14th May, 1852, and was buried by the side of her husband in the family burying ground at Quincy, Mass.

ADAMS, Mrs. Mary Mathews, poet, born 23rd October, 1840. She is of Irish birth and parentage, but having come to this country when she was a mere child, she may easily claim America as her mental birthplace. Her father was a devout Protestant, and her mother an ardent Catholic; but

MARY MATHEWS ADAMS.

with fine breeding and a sincere and tender affection between them, the religious inheritance of the sons and daughters of John Mathews and his wife is rich in faith and tolerance. Their American home was in Brooklyn, N. Y., and there Mary, their oldest daughter, was educated, mainly at Packer Institute, from which she passed into a graded school, where for nine years she was a successful teacher. Her well-equipped mind and her winsome personality proving a rare combination of endowments for the work. After that period of successful effort

Miss Mathews was married to C. M. Smith, and for five years her life was passed in a western city. At the end of that time she returned to Brooklyn, a childless widow, and again entered her favorite field of labor. Her enthusiasm as a student, which she always has been, finds its best result in her Shakespearian study. She has for years gathered about her, in her own home and elsewhere, classes of ladies, and her method of leadership is at once unique and inspiring. The refined literary appreciation manifested in this work reveals itself in her poems. The "Epithalamium" is perhaps the best known. Her verse is largely lyrical, and her themes include romance, heroism, and religion. In 1883 she became the wife of A. S, Barnes, the well-known publisher. He lived but a short time, and in London, in 1890, Mrs. Barnes was married to Charles Kendall Adams, the President of Cornell University, and at once assumed a position of intellectual, social, and moral responsibility for which her special mental gifts, her cultivation and her noble ideals of manly and womanly character fit her in a marked manner. There she has opportunity to impress the height and largeness of her standards upon college students of both sexes, from all points of the country and remote lands. Mrs. Adams is one of the highest types of her race. That she has written less than the public craves is partly due to her own under-estimation of her poetic gifts, and partly because she lives a religion of true hospitality and is an earnest home-maker, which talent is more time-consuming than that of a housekeeper. Above and beyond all charms of pen and speech, she is a practical and sincerely tolerant woman who transforms much of the prose of everyday life into poetry by her devotion to all beautiful works and things.

ADKINSON, Mrs. Mary Osburn, temperance reformer, born in Rush county, Ind., 28th July, 1843. Her husband, the Rev. L. G. Adkinson, D. D., is President of New Orleans University. She has illustrated what an earnest worker can accomplish in the fields lying within reach of one busied with the cares of domestic life. She is the daughter of Harmon Osburn, who was a prominent farmer in Rush county, Ind. Her mother was a woman of great force of character and often entertained ministers, teachers and other guests of refinement in her home. Miss Osburn was educated in Whitewater College, Centerville, Ind. She began her married life as a pastor's wife in Laurel, Ind. There, by teaching a part of the time, she supplemented the small salary received by her husband and added many valuable books to their library. Removing to Madison, she was persuaded to take a leading part in organizing the Woman's Foreign Missionary Society of the Methodist Episcopal Church in that city. For ten or twelve years she did much successful work; she was four times unanimously elected president of the Madison district association, she was the association's delegate in 1883 to the State convention, and in 1884 to to the branch meeting in Kalamazoo, Mich. In 1873 she united with the temperance women of the city in the woman's crusade and has since been actively engaged in temperance work. She is now superintendent of the Woman's Christian Temperance Union among the colored people in the State of Louisiana and is working with much success. Many societies have been organized and hundreds of young people have taken the triple pledge of abstinence from intoxicating drink, tobacco and profanity. Mrs. Adkinson is also matron in New Orleans University and teacher of sewing and dressmaking. While thus active in philanthropic work, she has been eminently a "keeper at home." Of her family of five children, the oldest daughter, a graduate of Moore's Hill College, Indiana, is the wife of Dr. E. G. Conklin, of the chair of biology

MARY OSBURN ADKINSON.

in the Ohio Wesleyan University. The second daughter and son are teachers in New Orleans University, and a younger daughter and son are students in the same institution.

ADSIT, Mrs. Nancy H., art-lecturer, born in Palermo, Oswego county, N.Y., 21st May, 1825. She is of New England Puritan lineage, is descended from the Mayflower Robinsons on the mother's side, and from the patriotic Warrens of Massachusetts on the father's side, her father being a clergyman and missionary. Her early life was a discipline in self-dependence, which aided and stimulated the development of an inherited force of character, enabling her to combat and conquer adverse conditions, overcome obstacles and from childhood mark out for herself and pursue steadily a career that has been crowned with success. At the age of thirteen years she assumed entire charge of herself and her fortunes. The expenses of a collegiate course, in Ingham University, were met by teaching and journalism. She was a regular contributor to the columns of the New York "Baptist Register," the Boston "Recorder," the New York "Tribune" and the "Western Literary Messenger." This earlier work was mostly in the line of poetic effusions and several series of "Lay Sermons" under the signature of "Probus." These sermons aroused intense antagonism in clerical circles, on account of their latitudinarianism on theologic questions. Heated and prolonged discussions followed each publication. "Probus," the unknown, was adjudged by a general council "guilty of heresy," and the sermons were denounced and condemned. The series was completed, however, and her identity was held sacredly between herself and the editor,

and not until many years later, by her own voluntary confession, was the writer identified. Meanwhile the thought of the clergy, as of the world at large, had broadened, and the sermons were no longer under proscription. Mrs. Adsit was married to Charles Davenport Adsit, of Buffalo, N. Y., 13th December, 1862. Her home during the next three years was at 11 North Division street, in that city. Alternating literary, charitable and church work with her domestic duties, she developed an ideal home. They removed to Milwaukee, Wis., in 1865, where Mr. Adsit died in 1873, leaving the erstwhile happy wife charged with large responsibilities in a hitherto unexplored field. Mrs. Adsit immediately assumed the entire charge and management of a general insurance agency, at once meeting every requirement of its multiform duties in person. She was the first woman in general insurance in this country, and, so far as is known, in the world. Protests from family friends and jealous antagonisms on the part of business competitors met her at the threshold of the work, but she won public favor as she gave assurance of ability, until the work was crowned with such success as to leave no cause for its further prosecution. Accordingly, Mrs. Adsit sold the business, with her good will, and resumed the pen as a more congenial exponent of her taste. Her range of work was many sided, reaching from the political questions of the day to science and art. Her contributions to the London "Art Journal," many years since, brought a request for a series of articles on the "White and Black in Art," or "Etching and Engraving." Finding no satisfactory data for thorough investigation in books, she visited the studios of artists as well as the workshops of engravers, gathering at first

NANCY H. ADSIT.

hands the necessary information, even to the practical use of the tools of each craft. An entire year was consumed in this preparatory work. Months before the articles were completed the demand for parlor conversation on the topics which so absorbed her induced Mrs. Adsit to open her home to groups of ladies and gentlemen, who cared to take up the study in earnest. The field of her labor gradually broadened, and during the last thirteen years she has given her lecture courses in nearly all the principal cities east and west. Her name is now prominently identified with art education, both in this country and abroad. While Mrs. Adsit disclaims being an artist, she is yet a most competent and thorough critic and elucidator of art. Her criticisms of prints, especially, are sought by connoisseurs and collectors. The secret of her success lies in the fact that her work is simply the expression of her own personality. Her abounding enthusiasm carries her audiences on its forceful tide. In a recent report of its Wisconsin secretary to the Association for the Advancement of Women, of which Mrs. Adsit is one of the vice-presidents, the writer says: "To Mrs. C. D. Adsit's work is due, directly or indirectly, most of the art interest in our State as well as the entire West." Her own adverse experiences have quickened and enlarged her sympathies toward all working women, to whom she gives not only wholesome advice, but also substantial aid. Her pleasant home in Milwaukee is a center of art and of delightful social interchange.

AGASSIZ, Mrs. Elizabeth Cabot, naturalist. She is the daughter of Thomas Graves Cary of Boston, Mass. She was married to Professor Louis Agassiz in 1850. She accompanied her husband on his journey to Brazil in 1865-6 and on the Hassler expedition in 1871-2; of the second she wrote an account for the "Atlantic Monthly," and was associated with him in many of his studies and writings. She has published "A First Lesson in Natural History" (Boston, 1859), and edited "Geological Sketches" (1866). Her husband died in 1873, and Mrs. Agassiz edited his "Life and Correspondence" in two volumes (Boston, 1885), a very important work. Mrs. Agassiz resides in Cambridge, Mass, and has done much to further the interest of the Harvard "Annex."

AHRENS, Mrs. Mary A., lawyer and philanthropist, born in Staffordshire, England, 29th December, 1836. When she was fifteen years of age her father, the Rev. William H. Jones, brought his family to America and settled in Illinois. Mary was a pupil in the seminary in Galesburg for several years, and a close student until her first marriage, in 1857. Two sons and a daughter were born to her from this union. For eighteen years she was engaged in home duties and horticulture, and in the seclusion of this home she took up the study of medicine and earned her diploma. She felt impelled to labor for the elevation of the recently emancipated colored race, and was the first woman teacher in southern Illinois for that ignorant and long-neglected people. For years after her removal to Chicago Mrs Ahrens devoted herself largely to the lecture field, for which she is well qualified. Soon after her marriage to Louis Ahrens, an artist of ability, this woman of many talents entered the Chicago Union College of Law, and was graduated with honors in 1889. Her success as a practitioner has been marked. True to a high womanly standard, she adopted as a principle of action that, so far as the interests of her clients allowed, her aim should be to adjust differences outside of the courts. Naturally, many of her clients were women, poor and friendless. As vice-president of the Protective Agency for Women and Children, Mrs. Ahrens has been of great service to that benevolent organization. Recently, at the annual banquet of the State Bar Association held in Springfield, Ill, Mrs. Ahrens responded to the toast, "Woman in the Learned Professions." Mrs. Ahrens was made chairman of the Woman's School Suffrage Association, of Cook county, and her efforts to secure to the women citizens their legal right to vote at school elections entitle her to the gratitude of every woman in the State. She is a

MARY A. AHRENS.

member of the Illinois Woman's Press Association, and a paper prepared for the club, in 1892, entitled "Disabilities of Women before the Law," was a masterful presentation of the need of the ballot-power for woman. She has been a suffrage advocate for more than twenty years. Her home is in Chicago.

AIKENS, Mrs. Amanda L., editor and philanthropist, born in North Adams, Mass., 12th May, 1833. Her father's name was Asahel Richardson Barnes. Her mother's maiden name was Mary Whitcomb Slocum. Mrs. Aikens was reared under deeply religious influences. Much of her education was received in Maplewood Institute, Pittsfield, Mass. Since her marriage to Andrew Jackson Aikens she has lived in Milwaukee, Wis., where she has been for many years a leader in local charities, church work and efforts for the intellectual development of women. She has one daughter, Stella, who is a poet of wide reputation. In November, 1887, Mrs. Aikens began to edit "The Woman's World," a special department of "The Evening Wisconsin," of which her husband is one of the proprietors, published in Milwaukee. Up to that time she was best known for her active interest in, and intimate connection with, numerous benevolent societies. She was at one time president of the Board of Local Charities and Corrections, two years president of the Woman's Club of Milwaukee, two years chairman of the Art Committee, and has been vice-president of the Wisconsin Industrial School for Girls, and for ten years the chairman of its executive committee. During the Civil War she was an indefatigable worker. It was she who made the public appeals and announcements through the press when the question of a National Soldiers' Home was agitated. In the history of Milwaukee, published in 1881,

AMADA L. AIKENS.

there is a long account of her various labors for suffering humanity in that time of strife and bloodshed, the War for the Union. She has traveled extensively in Europe, and her newspaper letters were really art criticisms of a high order. She was one of the most enthusiastic and successful of those who raised money in Wisconsin for the Johns Hopkins Medical School in Baltimore, for the purpose of admitting women on equal terms with men. She helped largely in organizing the first Woman's Republican Club of Wisconsin, and was a State delegate to the National Conference of Charities when it met in Baltimore. In 1891 she read a paper before the State Conference of Charities in Madison, Wis. Mrs. Aikens had much to do with the introduction of cooking into the public schools of Milwaukee. She has been identified for fifteen years as an officer or director with the Art Science Class, a literary organization for the purpose of developing a taste in architecture, painting, sculpture, and science. One-hundred-fifty ladies belong to this class, and it has done more for the direct education of women in the arts and sciences than any other society in the State. There are few, if any, interests of importance in the matter of advancement for women in her city or her State with which Mrs. Aikens has not been more or less identified. She is known to be a talented woman in the literary sense of the word, a loyal wife, a devoted mother, and a philanthropist of the truest and tenderest type.

ALBANI, Mme. Emma, operatic singer, born in Chambly, near Montreal, Province of Quebec, Canada, in 1851. Her maiden name was Marie Emma La Jeunesse. Her parents were French-Canadians, descendants of Frenchmen that settled

in Canada long before the conquest. Her father was a musician, a professor of the harp, and he conducted her early musical studies. In 1856 the family removed to Montreal, where Emma entered the convent school of Notre Dame de Sacré Cœur. There she studied singing. In 1863, when she was twelve years old, she went on a starring tour with her sister. She made her first appearance in Albany, N. Y., and displayed the vocal and dramatic endowments that have since made her famous. In 1864 her family removed to Albany, where she was engaged to sing in the Roman Catholic cathedral. The bishop was so impressed by her talent that he urged her father to send her abroad for training. A public concert was given in Albany to raise money to enable her to go to Europe. Accompanied by her father, she went to Paris, remaining two years with the Baroness Lafitte, to study under Duprez, and next went to Milan, Italy, where she was trained by Lamperti. In 1870 she sang in Messina with success, and was at once engaged for Malta. She adopted the stage-name "Albani," in remembrance of Albany, whose citizens had been her generous friends and patrons. In 1871 she sang at the theater La Pergola, in Florence, Italy, where she created successfully the rôle of Mignon in Ambroise Thomas's opera, which had been condemned in four Italian theaters. In 1872 she made her first appearance in England, at the Royal Italian Opera in London, where she made an extraordinary success as Amina in "La Sonnambula." She strengthened her reputation by her presentation of Lucia, Marta, Gilda, and Linda. In November, 1872, she sang as Amina in Paris with marked success. She returned to London and was enthusiastically received. There she

EMMA ALBANI.

added Ophelia to her list of triumphs. In 1874 she revived Mignon. In the winter of 1874-5, she made a successful tour of the United States. In May, 1875, she was again in London,

England, where she sang the rôle of Elsa in "Lohengrin," brought out by manager Gye in Covent Garden theater. In Nice, in 1876, she made a deep impression. In Paris she revived the fortunes of the Théâtre Ventadour by her rendition of Lucia and of Gilda in "Rigoletto." In 1877, in the Royal Italian Opera in London, she sang the rôle of Elizabeth in "Tannhäuser," scoring a great success in that majestic character. In August, 1878, she was married to Ernest Gye, the oldest son of Frederick Gye, director of the Royal Italian Opera in London, England. During the winter of 1878 she sang in the Imperial Opera in St. Petersburg, Russia, and afterwards in Moscow, Milan and Brussels, always with increasing popularity. In 1879 and 1880 she appeared in Covent Garden, London, as Gilda, Amina, Marguerite, Elvira, Elsa, Mignon, and Ophelia. In the last-named rôle she has no rival. In 1883 she sang in "Faust" and "Rigoletto" in Washington, D. C., and closed her operatic tour in Philadelphia in April of that year in "The Flying Dutchman." On 3d April, 1884, she sang in Gounod's "Redemption" in the Trocadéro, Paris, where that composer conducted his own work. In March, 1884, she sang in the Royal Opera house in Berlin. Her operatic career has been one long line of successes. Her voice is a pure soprano of great flexibility and wide range, and her dramatic powers are of the highest order. She is equally successful in concert and oratorio. Her repertoire includes most of the famous rôles. In May, 1886, at the opening of the Colonial Exhibition in London, she sang the ode written for the occasion by Tennyson. Among her acquaintances in Europe is Queen Victoria, who visits her at Mar Lodge, Albani's home in the Scotch Highlands, and meets her as a friend. Madame Albani-Gye is unspoiled by her successes.

ALBRIGHT, Mrs. Eliza Downing, church and temperance worker, born in Philadelphia, Penn., 13th March, 1847. She is descended from Puritan ancestry, dating back to that goodly company of 20,000 emigrants, Englishmen of the adventurous and thrifty class, whose sails whitened the Atlantic between 1630 and 1640. At the age of eleven years Eliza Downing was graduated from the public schools of Philadelphia, and later she studied under private teachers and in some of the institutes in which the city at that time abounded. In 1867 she was married to the Rev. Louis M. Albright, D. D., a graduate of the Ohio Wesleyan University and a minister of the Methodist Episcopal Church. After marriage she was engaged with her husband in teaching mathematics and natural sciences in the Ohio Wesleyan Female College, in Delaware, Ohio. Later she was a teacher of mathematics in Lewis College, Glasgow, Mo., and De Pauw Female College, of which Dr. Albright was president. More recently, in the itinerancy in Ohio, Mrs. Albright has been occupied in good work as a pastor's wife in connection with the churches and districts in which her husband has successively served. For the last six years they have resided in Delaware, Ohio. When the temperance crusade began, Mrs. Albright threw herself into that new movement. She became corresponding secretary of the Ohio Woman's Christian Temperance Union at its organization, in 1877, and for three years, until family cares made necessary her resignation, she did a large amount of work in the way of correspondence and public speaking. She has been identified with the Woman's Foreign Missionary Society of the Methodist Episcopal Church, as district secretary and speaker. At present she is one of the national officers of the Woman's Home Missionary Society and is also chairman of the State executive committee of the Young Woman's Christian Association. A clear and effective speaker, she is in constant demand for public addresses in the interest of these and other causes.

ELIZA DOWNING ALBRIGHT.

While in sympathy with every movement for reform, Mrs. Albright counts her duties to her family first and highest. Naturally a student, with strong physique and great energy, she turns to account every opportunity for personal improvement.

ALCOTT, Miss Louisa May, author, born in Germantown, Penn., 29th November, 1832. Her birthday was the anniversary of the birth of her father, the late A. Bronson Alcott, the "Sage of Concord." Louisa was the second of four daughters, only one of whom, Mrs. J. B. Pratt, is now living. Surrounded in childhood by an atmosphere of literature, she began to write at an early age, her reading including Shakespeare, Goethe, Emerson, Margaret Fuller, Miss Edgeworth and George Sand. Her first poem, "To a Robin," was written when she was eight years old. In 1838 the Alcott family removed to Boston, and she lived in or near that city until her death. Concord was longest her home. Their life in this latter town was interrupted by a year spent in an ideal community, "Fruitlands," in the town of Harvard, where they abstained from meat as food. The experience Miss Alcott described in an amusing sketch, "Transcendental Wild Oats." Returning to Concord, the Alcotts lived for a while in a house that was afterwards Hawthorne's home. Her father, a distinguished lecturer and teacher of his time, was one of the first to insist that gentleness was more influential than the rod, and to show that education should bring out the best that was in a child's nature, not simply cram a young mind with facts. Miss Alcott received her instructions chiefly from Henry Thoreau. Emerson was Mr. Alcott's most intimate friend, and very early in her life Miss Alcott became his favorite. When she was fifteen, Mr. Emerson loaned her a copy of "Wilhelm Meister," from the reading of which dated her life-long devotion to Goethe. At the age of sixteen Miss Alcott began to teach a little school of twenty members, and continued to do work of this kind in various ways for fifteen years, although it was extremely distasteful to her, and at the same time she began to write stories for publication. Her first published book was "Flower Fables" (Boston, 1855). It was not successful. She continued to write for her own amusement in her spare hours, but devoted herself to helping her father and mother by teaching school, serving as nursery governess, and even at times sewing for a living. Many of the troubles of those early years have been referred to in the sorrows of Christie in her volume called "Work," published after her

LOUISA MAY ALCOTT.

name was widely known. After awhile she found there was money in sensational stories, and she wrote them in quick succession and sent them to many papers ; but this style of writing soon wearied her and she had conscientious scruples about continuing it. In 1862 she became a nurse in the Washington hospitals and devoted herself to her duties there with conscientious zeal. In consequence, she became ill herself and narrowly escaped death by typhoid fever. While in Washington she wrote to her mother and sisters letters describing hospital life and experience, which were revised and published in book-form as "Hospital Sketches" (Boston, 1863). In that year she went to Europe as companion to an invalid woman, spending a year in Germany, Switzerland, Paris and London. Then followed "Moods" (1864); "Morning Glories, and Other Tales" (1867); "Proverb Stories" (1868). She then published "Little Women," 2 volumes, (1868), a story founded

largely on incidents in the lives of her three sisters and herself at Concord. This book made its author famous. From its appearance until her death she was constantly held in public esteem, and the sale of her books has passed into many hundred thousands. Most of her stories were written while she resided in Concord, though she penned the manuscript in Boston, declaring that she could do her writing better in that city, so favorable to her genius and success. Following "Little Women" came "An Old-Fashioned Girl" (1870); "Little Men" (1871), the mere announcement of which brought an advance order from the dealers for 50,000 copies; the "Aunt Jo's Scrap-Bag" (1871), 6 volumes; "Work" (1873); "Eight Cousins" (1875); "A Rose in Bloom" (1876); "Silver Pitchers and Independence" (1876); "Modern Mephistopheles," anonymously in the "No Name Series" (1877); "Under the Lilacs" (1878); "Jack and Jill" (1880); "Proverb Stories" a new edition revised (1882); "Moods" a revised edition (1884); "Spinning-Wheel Stories" (1884); "Jo's Boys" (1886). This latest story was a sequel to "Little Men." "A Garland for Girls" (1887). With three exceptions her works were all published in Boston. Miss Alcott did not attempt a great diversity of subjects; almost everything she wrote told of scenes and incidents that had come within her personal knowledge. The sales of her books in the United States alone amount to over a half-million. Her "Little Women" reached a sale of 87,000 copies in less than three years. She wrote a few dainty poems, but never considered that her talents lay in versifying. Her death occurred 6th March, 1888, just two days after the death of her father. She was buried on 8th March in the old Sleepy Hollow graveyard in Concord, the funeral being a double one and attended only by the immediate relatives. Miss Alcott's will directed that all her unfinished manuscripts, including all letters written by her, should be burned unread.

ALCOTT, Miss May, see NIERIKER MME. MAY ALCOTT.

ALDEN, Miss Emily Gillmore, author and educator, born in Boston, Mass., 21st January, 1834. In infancy her parents removed to Cambridge, and her education was pursued in the public schools of that city, and in Mt. Holyoke Seminary, South Hadley, Mass. Her career has been chiefly that of a teacher in Castleton, Vt., and in Monticello Seminary, Godfrey, Ill. In this latter institution she now has charge of the departments of history, rhetoric, and English literature, and of senior classes for graduation. Her literary work, stimulated probably by the scope of her teaching and her experience as an enthusiastic and truly artistic educator, has been the recreation of her years, and her poems have the delicacy and spontaneity that belong to genius. Miss Alden comes of Pilgrim ancestry, being of the eighth generation in lineal descent from the Mayflower. She is singularly retiring in manner, courts no admiration for her work, and holds ever her daintiest verses in most modest estimation. She shrinks from publicity, and her first efforts were offered under a pen-name. An early critic, detecting an artistic touch in her poetic fancy, insisted that the mask should be dropped, and since then her poems have reached a very appreciative circle of readers under her own signature.

ALDEN, Mrs. Isabella Macdonald, author, born in Rochester, N. Y., 3d November, 1841. Her maiden name was Macdonald. While she was still a child, her father moved to Johnstown, N. Y., and afterwards to Gloversville, in the same State. Her pen-name "Pansy," by which she is known so widely, was given to her by her father on the occasion when Isabella, a mere child, had plucked every blossom from a treasured bed of pansies grown by her mother. As the child showered the

ISABELLA MACDONALD ALDEN.

blossoms in her mother's lap, she said they were "every one for her," and Mr. Macdonald gave her the name which has become so famous. Her father and mother, both persons of intellect and education, encouraged her in every way in her literary work, and her progress was very rapid. When she was only ten years old, she wrote a story about an old family clock which suddenly stopped after running many years, and her father had it published. As a girl, Isabella was an aspiring and industrious author. She wrote stories, sketches, compositions, and a diary in which she recorded all the important events of her life. Her articles were accepted and published in the village papers, and "Pansy" began to be known. Her first book was published when she was yet a mere girl. A publishing house offered a prize for the best Sunday-school book upon a given subject. She wrote "Helen Lester," a small book for young people, partly to amuse herself, and sent the manuscript to the publishers, not expecting to hear from it again. To her surprise the committee selected her book as the best of those received. From that time her pen has never been idle. More than sixty volumes bear the name "Pansy," and all are good, pure books for young and old alike. Miss Macdonald was married in May, 1866, to the Rev. G. R. Alden, and she is a success as a pastor's wife. She composes easily. Her mornings are given to literary work. Some of her books are: "Esther Reid," "Four Girls at Chautauqua," "Chautauqua Girls at Home," "Tip Lewis and His Lamp," "Three People," "Links in Rebecca's Life," "Julia Reid," "Ruth Erskine's Crosses," "The King's Daughter," "The Browning Boys," "From Different Standpoints," "Mrs. Harry Harper's Awakening,"

and "The Pocket Measure." Story-writing by no means is all her work. She writes the primary lesson department of the "Westminister Teacher," edits the "Presbyterian Primary Quarterly" and the children's popular magazine "Pansy," and writes a serial story for the "Herald and Presbyter" of Cincinnati every winter. Mrs. Alden is deeply interested in Sunday-school primary teaching, and has had charge of more than a hundred children every Sunday for many years. She is interested in temperance also, but delicate health and a busy life hinder her from taking an active part in the work. She gives liberally to the cause, and four of her books, "Three People," "The King's Daughter," "One Commonplace Day," and "Little Fishers and their Nets," are distinctively temperance books, while the principle of total abstinence is maintained in all her writings. Mrs. Alden is a constant sufferer from headache, which never leaves her and is often very severe, but she refuses to call herself an invalid. She is a model housekeeper in every way. Her physician limits her to three hours of literary work each day. The famous Chautauqua system of instruction is warmly advocated by her. She has been prominently identified with that movement from its beginning. Her books are peculiarly adapted to the youth of this country. Most of them have been adopted in Sunday-school libraries throughout the United States. Rev. and Mrs. Alden are now pleasantly located in Washington, D. C.

ALDEN, Mrs. Lucy Morris Chaffee, author, born in South Wilbraham, New Hampden, Mass., 20th November, 1836. She is a daughter of Daniel D. and Sarah F. Chaffee. Among her maternal ancestors was Judge John Bliss, of South

LUCY MORRIS CHAFFEE ALDEN.

Wilbraham, who on the eighth of April, 1775, was appointed sole committee "to repair to Connecticut to request that Colony to co-operate with Massachusetts for the general defense," and who, under the constitution was chosen to the first and several succeeding senates. Miss Chaffee spent a year at Monson Academy, twenty years in teaching school, and three years as a member of the school

ANNE REEVE ALDRICH.

board of her native town. She was left alone by the death of her mother in 1884, and was married in July, 1890, to Lucius D. Alden, an early school-mate but long a resident on the Pacific coast, and she still occupies her father's homestead. Her poetic, and far more numerous prose, writings have appeared in various newspapers of Springfield, Boston, Chicago, and Minneapolis, in several Sunday-school song-books, and in quarterly and monthly journals. One doctrinal pamphlet of hers has lately been translated by a British officer and missionary in Madras into the Hindustani tongue, and many copies printed. Copies of another were voluntarily distributed by a county judge in Florida among members of his State legislature. Two years ago, under an appropriation, made by an association whose conferences reach from Maine to California, of a sum to be distributed among writers of meritorious articles, Mrs. Alden was selected to write for Massachusetts.

ALDRICH, Miss Anne Reeve, poet and novelist, born in New York City, 25th April, 1866. From her earliest childhood she showed a fondness for composition, spending hours from the time she learned to print in writing stories and verses, although she had the usual healthy childish tastes for romping and all out-of-door sports. At the death of her father, which occurred in her eighth year, her mother removed to the country, where she at first took charge of her daughter's education, which was afterward carried on by competent tutors. Miss Aldrich displayed remarkable proficiency in compostion and rhetoric, which was counterbalanced by what she herself calls an amusing inaptitude for mathematics, so that, while she was translating French and Latin authors for amuse-

ment, she was also struggling over a simple arithmetic, whose tear-blotted leaves she still preserves. In her fifteenth year a friend suggested to her to send a poem to "Scribner's Magazine." Although the verses were returned, with them she received a friendly note of encouragement and praise from the editor, who from that time often criticized the young girl's work. She wrote constantly and voluminously, usually destroying her work from month to month, so that but few of her earlier verses are extant. She also read widely, her taste inclining to the early English poets and dramatists and to mediæval literature. When she was seventeen, her first published poem appeared in "Lippincott's Magazine," followed by others in the "Century" and various periodicals. In 1885 Miss Aldrich's mother moved back to New York, where they now reside. Her first book was "The Rose of Flame and Other Poems of Love" (New York, 1889), and she has published one novel, "The Feet of Love" (New York, 1890). Miss Aldrich dislikes country life and is fond of society. Her family is of English extraction. Her ancestors were Tories in Revolutionary days, and their large estates were confiscated by the American government because of their allegiance to the crown.

ALDRICH, Mrs. Flora L., doctor of medicine, born in Westford, N. Y., 6th October, 1859. Her maiden name was Southard. Her father was a farmer, and her childhood was spent on a farm known as "Sutherland Place." Her paternal ancestors were among the original Dutch settlers of the Hudson river valley at Kinderhook and Hudson. Among them are the names of Hoffman and Hubbard. Of the Southard family little is known, as the great-grandfather was an adopted child of a

FLORA L. ALDRICH.

Hudson merchant and could remember only that his name was Southard, and that he was stolen from a port in England. From all that can be gathered he is believed to be of good English family, and probably Southworth was the original name. Her maternal ancestors were of the Sutherland family, who have a clear connection with the nobility of England and Scotland. Her early education was

JOSEPHINE CABLES ALDRICH.

conducted almost entirely by her mother, who ranked among the educated women of her day. Before Flora was eleven years old she could trace nearly every constellation of stars, and knew the names and characteristics of flowers, insects, and birds in that section of her native State. When she was in her twelfth year her mother died, and her education subsequently was academic and by instruction under private teachers. When eighteen years old she was an advanced scholar in many branches. Interest in the sick and suffering was uppermost in her mind, and her chosen life-work would have been that of a missionary. Her marriage with Dr. A. G. Aldrich, of Adams, Mass., in 1883, resulted in her beginning immediately the study of medicine and surgery. A year later they removed to Anoka, Minn., where they now reside. She was graduated in 1887 from the old Minnesota Medical College, now the Medical Department of the State University, and has since taken postgraduate courses in the best schools in this country. She is now preparing for a course of study in Europe. In addition to her professional attainments, Dr. Aldrich has talent as a writer, and has nearly ready for publication a volume of almost twohundred poems. In religious belief she is Episcopalian. Though exceedingly busy in her profession, both as physician and surgeon, in social life and the literary and scientific world, she is at the head of several literary and social organizations, and is greatly interested in charitable and philanthropic work.

ALDRICH, Mrs. Josephine Cables, author and philanthropist, born in Connecticut She was but a few years old when her mother died, leaving her in the care of two Puritan grandmothers of the

most severe school, strict in the observance of what they considered their religious duties. They believed that a free use of the rod was necessary to save the child's soul from destruction. This severe treatment taught her that the Golden Rule was by far the best maxim for morality and happiness, and no sooner was she in control of a home of her own in Rochester, N. Y., than she gave such instruction for the betterment of humanity by word and deed that her home became a sort of Mecca for advance thinkers, not only of America, but pilgrims came from Europe, Asia and Africa to confer with her. In 1882 she began in Rochester, N. Y., the publication of "The Occult World," a little paper devoted to advanced thought and reform work. Her editorials taught liberality, justice and mercy. Her greatest work has been in private life, and her influence for good over the individual was remarkable. She was at one time secretary of the Theosophical Society of the United States, and president of the Rochester Brotherhood. She is now in affluent circumstances in a home in Aldrich, Ala., a mining town named for her husband Mr. Aldrich fully sustains his wife in all her work, and she is in turn assisting him to carry out a plan of his, whereby persons accused of crime shall be defended before the court, at the public expense, as diligently and ably as such persons are now prosecuted. The town of Aldrich is a quiet, peaceful, moral and refined community, where the rights of all are respected, and where drink and tobacco are almost unknown. Mrs. Aldrich is vice-president of the Woman's National Industrial League, vice-president of the Woman's National Liberal Union, and one of the founders of the Woman's National University and School of Useful and Ornamental Arts.

ALDRICH, Mrs. Julia Carter, author, born in Liverpool, Ohio, 28th January, 1834. She was

JULIA CARTER ALDRICH.

the fifth in a family of seven children. Her maiden name was Carter. Her paternal ancestors were New

Englanders of English stock. Her mother's parents, born and reared in Richmond, Va., were of Scotch and German descent. Miss Carter began to write when quite young, making a successful attempt at the age of fourteen years. Her school-days were marked by thorough and rapid proficiency. At the age of seventeen years she began to teach in a large village school, following that vocation for four years. During all the busy period of study and teaching, frequent contributions from her pen, both of verse and prose, found place in various periodicals and won for her much encouragement from high sources. In October, 1854, she was married to Joseph Aldrich, of New York. During the earlier years of her married life literary work was somewhat neglected, but out of the joy of her own home sprang a desire to carry sunshine and happiness to others. Believing that many fountains of evil had their origin in bad home management, for several years she did much earnest work for the home circle in many periodicals, and under various pen-names, "Petresia Peters" being the best known. Reformatory measures have always received her aid, and her articles written in the interests of humanity would make volumes. Poetry has been to Mrs. Aldrich its own reward, but she has neglected to make any collection of her poems. She is the mother of three sons. Her husband died in 1889, at their country place, "Maple Grove Home," near Wauseon, Ohio.

ALDRICH, Mrs. Mary Jane, temperance reformer, born in Sidney Plains, N. Y., 19th March, 1833. Her home was on a tract of land purchased before the Revolutionary War by her paternal great-grandfather, the Rev. William Johnson, a Scotch-Irish Presbyterian minister who, with her grandfather, Col. Witter Johnson, was in the Revolutionary army. Her father, Milton Johnson, was a farmer possessing uncommon intellectual ability. Her mother, Delia Hull, was a well educated woman of deeply religious nature. Beyond attending a select school in early childhood, and later in the public school, three terms in Franklin Academy supplied the school privileges of Miss Johnson. Ever since her eighteenth year she has been deeply interested in Christian and philanthropic work. She is a member of the Presbyterian Church, but is in cordial fellowship with all Christians. She was married in 1855 to John Aldrich and removed soon after to Nebraska, where the first ten years of her married life were full of pioneer experiences. In 1866 she removed with her husband and two children, a son and daughter, to Cedar Rapids, Iowa, her present home, where her youngest child, a son, was born. Her uneventful life was spent in caring for her husband and children and in Sabbath school and missionary work. From childhood, a "total abstainer" and in full sympathy with prohibitory law, she was never a temperance worker, not even a member of any temperance society, until the Crusade. That movement touched the deepest springs of her being. It fanned a latent interest into a flame of enthusiasm, brought out the hitherto undeveloped powers of an intense nature, and wedded her to a work for all homes. Quick in thought, fertile in expedients and prompt in action, she soon became a recognized worker. In all her labor she has had the consent and co-operation of her husband and children. At the organization of the Woman's Christian Temperance Union of Iowa, 3d and 4th November, 1874, the Raising of Lazarus was her text for more earnest temperance work by Christian people in restoring to a better life and nobler manhood those who are

morally dead through drink. Later, at a county Woman's Christian Temperance Union convention, she took the place of a college professor, who had failed to appear, and delivered her first address. Made a vice-president of the National Woman's Christian Temperance Union at its organization, 18th and 20th November, 1874, she visited different localities to enlist women in the work of that society, and some of the unions then formed are still doing good service. Chosen corresponding secretary of the Woman's Christian Temperance Union of Iowa in 1875, she held the office for one year only, leaving it in order to spend more time in the field. In different positions she has been a member of the executive committee of the Iowa union to the present time, and there are few counties in Iowa in which she has not spoken. Elected president of her State union in 1883, she declined re-election in 1885 because unable to give to the work all the time

MARY JANE ALDRICH.

it required. She was elected corresponding secretary by the union, which office she still holds. When the National Union, at the St. Louis Convention in 1884, declared in favor of political temperance work by the union, Mrs. Aldrich, with the majority of the Iowa delegation, voted against the resolution. Subsequently, as corresponding secretary, she was, from her own intense conviction as well as from her official position, the efficient co-worker of Mrs. J. Ellen Foster, the president, who represented the Woman's Christian Temperance Union of Iowa in its open opposition to political Woman's Christian Temperance Union work, and final withdrawal from the auxiliaryship to the National, on that account in October, 1890. As a temperance worker she is sanguine and practical. As a speaker she is bright, forceful, entertaining and logical. She attended the convention held in Cleveland, Ohio, 22–24 January, 1890, at which time the Non-partisan National

Woman's Christian Temperance Union was organized. As secretary of the department of evangelistic work she has been a member of the executive committee from its organization.

ALDRICH, Miss Susanna Valentine, author, born in Hopkinton, Mass., 14th November,

SUSANNA VALENTINE ALDRICH.

1828. She is the only child of Willard and Lucy (Morse) Aldrich. From her earliest years she showed that fondness for putting her thoughts on paper which seems to be the unerring indication of the possession of literary talents. When other children were satisfied with dolls and playthings, the little Susan was always asking for paper and pencil to use in "writing letters," as she then called her work. In her schooldays she always found it far easier to write compositions than it was for her to commit lessons to memory, and she was generally permitted to choose her own subjects for the regular "composition day" in school. Her studies were interrupted by a severe illness which lasted for several years. She was long a victim to insomnia, and she always kept paper and pencil within reach in order to be able to jot down the fancies that thronged upon her in long hours of wakefulness. The Rev. J. C. Webster, her pastor, also one of the directors of the academy which Miss Aldrich attended, being struck with the merit and quality of her compositions, selected some of them to offer to a magazine for publication. These were accepted, and Mr. Webster, who later became a professor in Wheaton College, Illinois, had the satisfaction of knowing that the author whom he had introduced to the literary world had shown herself capable of holding a high rank among literary workers. For many years Miss Aldrich contributed both prose and poetry to a number of papers and magazines. Some years ago her health became impaired, and since that time she has confined her literary work to the preparation of articles appropriate to occasions in which she and her intimate friends are

interested. Since 1879 she has made her home in the Roxbury District of Boston, Mass.

ALEXANDER, Miss Jane Grace, pioneer woman-banker, born in Winchester, N. H., 26th October, 1848. She is a daughter of Edward and Lucy Capron Alexander, highly respected people of Puritan ancestry and of sterling qualities. Miss Alexander was educated in the Winchester schools, and finished her course in Glenwood Seminary, Brattleboro, Vt. After graduating she taught school for a time, and then accepted the position she now holds in the Winchester National Bank. For twenty years or more she has pursued the path of her choice, until now she is the long-time assistant cashier of the National bank, and the treasurer of the savings bank of her native town. In 1881, at the time of the incorporation of the Security Savings Bank, Miss Alexander was elected treasurer, being the first woman to fill such a position. She has been a successful business woman and has always made it a point to enjoy her success. She drives her own horses and indulges in a flower garden. The bank is made cheery and bright with blossoms of her own growing, and through all the details of her official duties the woman's presence shines out, glorifying and beautifying the whole place. As superintendent of a Sabbath school and president of a Chautauqua class, she has long been

JANE GRACE ALEXANDER.

a leading spirit in the village, and she has abundantly shown what a true-hearted, earnest woman may attain in the line of business.

ALLEN, Mrs. Elizabeth Akers, poet, born in Strong, Franklin county, Maine, 9th October, 1832. She inherited mental and physical vigor from her father, and delicacy and refinement from her mother, who died when Elizabeth was yet an infant. After her mother's death her father made his home in Farmington, Maine, where the poet's girlhood was passed. A weekly newspaper published in Farmington gave her poems to the public.

over the pen-name "Florence Percy." Her verses were received with marked favor and were widely copied. Her earliest verses, written when she was only twelve years old, were sent without her

ESTHER LAVILLA ALLEN.

knowledge to a Vermont paper, which promptly published them. In 1847 she began to publish over her own name. In 1855 she became assistant editor of the Portland, Maine, "Transcript." In 1856 she published her first volume of poetry, "Forest Buds from the Woods of Maine." The volume was a success financially, and she was able to go to Europe, where she spent some time in Italy, France and Germany. In 1860 she was married to her first husband, Paul Akers, the sculptor, a native of Maine. He died in Philadelphia, Pa., in the spring of 1861, at the age of thirty-five years, just as a brilliant career was opening to him. Their only child, Gertrude, died shortly afterwards, and Mrs. Akers, after rallying from a long mental and physical prostration, returned to Portland and took her old situation in the "Transcript" office. In 1863 she received an appointment in the War Office in Washington, D. C., at the suggestion of the late Senator Fessenden. She was in Ford's Theater on the night of President Lincoln's assassination. In 1866 she brought out her second volume of verse, "Poems by Elizabeth Akers," which was successful. In the fall of 1866 she was married to E. M. Allen, and went with him to Richmond, Va. While living in that city there arose the famous discussion of the authorship of her poem, "Rock Me to Sleep, Mother." That now celebrated poem was written by Mrs. Allen, in 1859, and sent from Rome to the Philadelphia "Post," and that journal published it in 1860. In 1872 her husband engaged in business in New York City. After making their home in Ridgewood, N. J., for several years, she has recently removed to New York, and is engaged in literary work. She is a member of Sorosis.

ALLEN, Mrs. Esther Lavilla, author, born in Ithaca, N. Y., 28th May, 1834. While she was a child, her parents removed to Ypsilanti, Mich., where her youth was passed, and she was educated in the seminary of that town. In 1851 she was married, and for the past few years her home has been in Hillsdale, Mich. She wrote verses in her youth but study first and then domestic cares occupied her attention. She began her literary career in earnest in 1870, when her powers were fully matured. She wrote stories, sketches and poems for publication, and her productions were of that character which insures wide copying. She contributed to the "Ladies' Repository," the "Masonic Magazine," the "Chicago Interior," the "Advance," the "Northwestern Christian Advocate" and other prominent periodicals. Much of her work has been devoted to temperance and missionary lines, but she writes countless poems for all kinds of occasions. Besides her work as a writer, she is a fine reader and she has often read her poetical productions in public, mainly before college societies. Recently she has done less of this work. Mrs. Allen has never collected her productions, although there are enough of them to fill a number of volumes. At present she is engaged in literary work of a high order.

ALLEN, Mrs. Esther Saville, author, born in Honeoye, Ontario county, N. Y., 11th December, 1837. Her parents were Joseph and Esther Redfern Saville, natives of England. Her father was a man of refined literary taste and well cultivated, as is shown by his contributions to British journals of his time. Mrs. Allen at an early age gave proof of a strong and ready mind and a passion for letters. Both were fostered by her appreciative

ESTHER SAVILLE ALLEN.

father, whose criticism and counsel gave her mind a proper impetus and direction. Before she was ten years old she made her first public effort in a poem, which was published. At the age of twelve years she wrote for Morris and Willis a poem which they published in the "Home Journal." Her father judiciously, so far as possible, repressed all precocious display, but the passion was her master, and while a pupil in the common schools of western New York, and in the academy in Rushford, N. Y., she wrote and published many poems under the pen-name of "Winnie Woodbine." She became a teacher in the public schools of western New York and continued to write for eastern papers, assuming her proper name, Etta Saville. Moving to Illinois in 1857, she taught in the public schools until 1859, when she was married to Samuel R. Allen, a lawyer in Erie, Ill. Since her marriage all her literary productions have appeared under the name of Mrs. S. R Allen. Since 1872 she has resided in Little Rock, Ark. She is probably the author of more productions, both in prose and verse, than any other woman of her State. Much of her work has been widely copied and recopied. Devoted to charity, organized and practical, her writings in that cause have promoted the institution and development of much useful work, or revived and reinvigorated it. Though retiring by nature and disposition, she is fearless and vigorous in action when occasion calls and the right demands it. Her life-work, by her own choice, has been the faithful and efficient discharge of every duty in her home and social relations. She is a true outgrowth and exemplification of the greatness of American women, to whose devotion to duty and rich display of intellect and truth in domestic relations is owing a great proportion of the might of the Nation in the past and present, and its hope for the time to come.

ALLEN, Mrs. Mary Wood, physician, author and lecturer, born in Delta, Ohio, 19th October, 1841. She is the daughter of George Wood, who emigrated from his English home when just of age, and in the wilds of southern Michigan met and married Miss Sarah Seely. The young couple settled where the village of Delta now stands, but at that time there were but two dwellings in the place. In one of these Mary was born, and there her childhood was passed. Even in those early days her future was shadowed forth, for she never played with dolls except to doctor them in severe illnesses. They often died under her treatment, and then she enjoyed having a funeral, in which she figured as chief mourner, preacher and sexton, as she had neither brother nor sister, and her playmates were few. At fourteen she had exhausted the resources of the village school. She manifested a love for study, especially of music, and before fifteen years of age had established herself in central Ohio as a music teacher with a class of twenty pupils. Her talent in music was a direct inheritance from her mother who had a remarkable voice. As a music teacher Mary earned money to begin her college course in Delaware, Ohio, where she proved an ardent student, putting four years work into three and, as a result breaking down in health. After graduation she taught music, French and German in a collegiate institute in Battle Ground, Ind., continuing there until her marriage to Chillon B. Allen, a graduate of the classical department of the Ohio Wesleyan University in Delaware, Ohio, and of the Ann Arbor Law School. Her own delicate health led her into the investigation of many therapeutical measures, and after the death of her first child in infancy she, with her husband, began the study of medicine, first in her own country and then in Europe, where she spent three years, returning to graduate in medicine from Ann Arbor in 1875. In Newark, N. J., where she settled and practiced her profession, her first important literary work was done. This was the beginning of the "Man Wonderful and the House Beautiful" (New York, 1884), an allegorical physiology. The first ten chapters appeared in the "Christian Union," and received such a recognition that their expansion into a book was began, and she and her husband united in completing the volume. Dr. Allen has also been a contributor of both prose and poetry to many leading periodicals, her poem entitled "Motherhood" having won for itself immediate fame. It is, however, as a lecturer that Dr. Allen has won her brightest laurels. A paper upon heredity which she presented at the State convention of the Woman's Christian Temperance Union in Cortland, N. Y., was both eloquent and logical and aroused the interest of the whole convention, and as a result Dr. Allen was appointed national lecturer of the Woman's Christian Temperance Union in the departments of heredity and

MARY WOOD ALLEN.

hygiene. Since then she has received calls from various parts of the United States to lecture upon these and kindred topics. A demand soon arose for her instruction in teachers' institutes and normal colleges upon the subject of temperance physiology. Her presentation of the topic gave general satisfaction. At present Dr. Allen has her home in Toledo, Ohio, whence she goes forth into the lecture field. Glorious as has been her work for temperance, that which she has done, and is doing, for social purity is more beautiful. Upon this subject, so difficult to handle, she has spoken Sabbath evenings in many pulpits, and has received the unqualified praise of such noted clergymen as Dr. Heber Newton, Dr. Theodore Cuyler and Dr. Pentecost in the East, and Dr. McLean upon the Pacific coast. She manifests a peculiar fitness for giving wise counsel to girls, and has done acceptable work in this line in schools and colleges. During several winters, by invitation of Miss Grace

Dodge, she has spoken to the Working Girl's Clubs of New York City. It is a scene of absorbing interest when, with rare tact and delicacy, she addresses large audiences of young men on the work of the White Cross. Her mission in the work of reform and philanthropy demands a peculiar talent which she possesses in an unusual degree; a scientific education which enables her to speak with authority; a winning presence; a musical voice which makes itself heard in the largest building with no apparent effort, and which by its sympathetic quality arrests attention and touches the heart, while her words appeal to the reason, and a gentle womanly manner which converts the most pronounced opposer of woman's public work. To those who hear her on the platform or in the pulpit, she is a living voice, alluring her hearers to lives of truth and purity, and to those who know her personally she is a sweet womanly presence, the embodiment of those graces which are the power in the home.

ALLERTON, Mrs. Ellen Palmer, poet, born in Centerville, N. Y., 17th October, 1835. Her ancestors were of Knickerbocker blood. She received a district-school education and afterwards spent a few terms in academies, but never graduated. Her marriage to Alpheus B. Allerton, took place in 1862, soon after her removal to Wisconsin. Mr. and Mrs. Allerton were both invalids in Wisconsin, but in 1879, traveled to Kansas in a wagon, cooking their own meals and getting health and happiness out of the journey. They selected for a home an unimproved farm, a-quarter section, on very high land in Brown county, in sight of Padonia, Hamlin, Falls City and Hiawatha. They now have a handsome home and every com-

ELLEN PALMER ALLERTON.

fort that prosperity brings in its train. Mrs. Allerton composed and recited verses before she could write, but offered little to the press until she was past thirty years of age. Her first poems were pub-

lished in "The Jefferson County Union," Ex-Governor Hoard's paper. Later she contributed to Milwaukee and Chicago papers, and was at one time book-reviewer for the Milwaukee "Sentinel." She has published one volume, "Poems of the Prairies," (New York, 1886). She is considered one of the leading authors of Kansas. As a woman and as a writer she is quiet and sensible. At her home in Padonia she has a wide circle of loving friends, and throughout the West the hearts that hold her dear are legion.

ALLYN, Mrs. Eunice Eloisae Gibbs, author, born in Brecksville, a suburb of Cleveland,

EUNICE ELOISAE AILYN.

Ohio. Her father, Dr. Sidney Smith Gibbs, was a native of Schoharie county, N. Y., and her mother, Eunice Lucinda Newberry, was a native of St. Lawrence county, in the same State. Dr. Gibbs was practicing in Brecksville when he married Miss Newberry, who was a cultured and successful teacher. He was a relative of Sidney Smith, and was naturally of a literary turn. Mrs. Gibbs possessed similar talents, and many articles from their pens were published in the press of the day. Their family consisted of four children, of whom Eunice was the third. After various changes of climate in search of health, Dr. Gibbs died in comparatively early manhood, leaving his wife with three young children to provide for. The devoted mother most nobly filled her trust. After his death the family moved from Jackson, Mich., to Cleveland, Ohio, where Eunice was graduated with honors from the high school. She intended to become a teacher, but her mother dissuaded her and she remained at home, going into society and writing in a quiet way for the local papers. Her articles were signed by various pen-names in order to avoid displeasing one of her brothers, who did not wish to have a "blue-stocking" in the family. Her first published poems appeared in the Cleveland "Plain Dealer," when she was only thirteen years old. Besides composing poems for recitation in school, she often wrote songs, both words and music, when she could not find songs suited to various occasions. In 1873 she was married to Clarence G. Allyn, of Nyack, N. Y. After spending several years at Nyack, New London, Conn., and Auburn, N. Y., they moved to Dubuque, Iowa, where they now live. Mrs. Allyn is a prominent member of the Dubuque Ladies' Literary Union, and for eight years she has served as president of the Dubuque Woman's Christian Temperance Union. She has been connected with the local press at times, and she has also won distinction as an artist. She is a member of the Episcopal Church, is broad in her views, while strictly orthodox, and is an ardent admirer of Oriental philosophy. Before her marriage she gained valuable experience as Washington correspondent of the Chicago "Inter-Ocean," a position which she filled for a year, during which time she also wrote numerous articles for the St. Louis "Globe," the New York "World," and before and since then for various New York, Boston, Indianapolis, Philadelphia and Chicago journals. She is a pointed, incisive writer, and all her work, prose or poetry, has an aim, a central thought. In her own city she has quietly inaugurated many reforms and educational movements, doing the work, not for notoriety, but prompted by her inborn desire to do something towards lifting up humanity.

ALRICH, Mrs. Emma B., journalist, author and educator, born in Cape May county, N. J., 4th April, 1845. She was the first child of fond parents, and no attempt was made to guard against

EMMA B. ALRICH.

precocity. At the age of three years a New Testament was given her as a prize for reading its chapters, and at five years she picked blackberries to buy an arithmetic. At twelve years of age she joined the Baptist Church. At that time she began to write for the county paper. At sixteen she

taught the summer school at her home. In 1862 she entered the State Normal School in Trenton, N. J., going out for six months in the middle of the course to earn the money for finishing it. She was graduated in June, 1864, as valedictorian of her class. She began to teach in a summer school on the next Monday morning after her graduation. In 1866 she was married to Levi L. Alrich, who had won laurels as one of Baker's Cavalry, or 71st Pennsylvania Regiment. Her first two years of married life they spent in Philadelphia, Pa. In 1876 the Centennial opened up new possibilities and Mr and Mrs. Alrich moved to the West and settled in Cawker City, Kans. There she again entered the school-room, was the first woman in Mitchell county to take the highest grade certificate, and the only woman who has been superintendent of the city schools. She was a warm supporter of teachers' meetings, church social gatherings, a public library and a woman's club. In 1883 her husband's failing health compelled a change in business. He bought the "Free Press," and changed its name to the "Public Record." All the work of the office has been done by their own family, and each can do every part of it. Besides her journalistic work, she served two years on the board of teachers' examiners. She was one of the forty who organized the National Woman's Relief Corps, one of the three who founded the Woman's Hesperian Library Club, and was the founder of the Kansas Woman's Press Association. Her busy life leaves her but little time for purely literary work.

AMES, Mrs. Eleanor M., author, born in 1830. She now lives in Brooklyn, N. Y. She has written a number of books, under the pen-name "Eleanor Kirk" designed to assist young writers, and she publishes a magazine entitled "Eleanor Kirk's Idea," for the same purpose. Her works include "Up Broadway, and its Sequel" (New York, 1870), "Periodicals that Pay Contributors" (Brooklyn), "Information for Authors" (Brooklyn, 1888); and as editor, "Henry Ward Beecher as a Humorist" (New York, 1887), and "The Beecher Book of Days" (New York, 1886).

AMES, Mrs. Fanny B., industrial reformer, born in Canandaigua, N. Y., 14th June, 1840. In her childhood she was taken with her father's family to Ohio, where she was for some time a student in Antioch College, under the presidency of Horace Mann. Her first experience in practical work was gained in military hospitals during the war. For five years she was a teacher in the public schools in Cincinnati. She was married in 1863 to the Rev. Charles G. Ames, and during his ministry in Philadelphia she engaged in the work of organized charity, was president of the Children's Aid Society, traveled widely in Pennsylvania, assisting in the organization of county branches of that society, visiting almshouses, and getting up the provisions by which dependent children were removed from almshouses and placed in private families under the supervision of local committees of women. Under State authority she was for five years one of the visitors of public institutions, with power to inspect and report to the Board of State Charities. She thus became familiar with the methods, merits and abuses of those institutions, her knowledge of which not only qualified her to prepare the reports of the Philadelphia Board of Visitors, but led her into wide and careful study of the causes of poverty and dependence, quickening her natural sympathy with the struggling classes, at the same time elevating her estimate of the social service rendered by wisely-used capital and fairly-managed industries. She was for two years president of the

New Century Club of Philadelphia, one of the most active and influential women's clubs of this country. Mrs. Ames now resides in Boston, her husband presiding over the Church of the Disciples. She read a paper before the National Council of Women in 1891 on the "Care of Defective Children." She was appointed Factory Inspector in Massachusetts, 8th May, 1891, by Governor Russell, in accordance with an act passed by the State legislature.

AMES, Miss Julia A., editor and temperance reformer, born near Odell, Livingston county, Ill., 14th October, 1861. She was the daughter of a well-known wealthy citizen of Streator, Ill. She was a graduate of Streator high school, the Illinois Wesleyan University, and of the Chicago School of Oratory. Her work in the Woman's Christian Temperance Union began in Streator, where she proved herself a most valuable and efficient helper to Mrs. Plumb, the district president of the Woman's Christian Temperance

JULIA A. AMES.

Union. Her peculiar talents for temperance work soon brought her into prominence, and she was drawn into the central union in Chicago. There, in addition to her elocutionary talents and executive capacity, she showed herself the possessor of the journalistic faculty, and she was soon placed where she could make good use of that faculty for the noble organization of temperance workers. The first of the Chicago daily newspapers to publish a Woman's Christian Temperance Union department was the "Inter-Ocean." In her first interviews with the editors, Miss Ames received many charges and cautions, all of which she tried faithfully to heed. Yet, in spite of her care, everything she sent was sharply scanned and often mercilessly cut. At first only a few inches of space were given to her. This was gradually increased as the editors learned they could trust her, till, before she gave the department into other hands, she usually occupied nearly a column, and editors ceased to

cut her manuscript. Other and more important work soon came to her hand. The national superintendent of press-work, Mrs. Esther Housh, found her labor too great for her strength, and Miss Ames was appointed her assistant. She performed all the necessary work in this field until her duties on the "Union Signal" forced her to give the work into other hands. Her connection with the central union brought her into intimate contact with many noble women, among whom were Helen Louise Hood, Mrs. Matilda B. Carse, Mrs. Andrew and Miss Willard. Her intercourse with them molded her views and life visibly, and her progress was rapid. Position after position called her, and in each she did earnest, noble work without stint. When Mrs. Andrew felt that, on account of her health, she must give up her work on the "Union Signal," the question of her successor was earnestly discussed. The thoughts of the leaders at once turned to Miss Ames, and despite her youth, she justified the choice of those who urged her to follow Mrs. Andrew. Up to 1889 her special province was the difficult one of news from the field and children's department. She originated the department of illustrated biography and the queen's garden. In all her work she showed a thoroughness, patience and courtesy absolutely indispensable to success, yet seldom found united in one person. Her forte was not so much writing, though she was ready with her pen, as it was that higher faculty which instinctively told her what to choose and what to reject of others' writing, and the winning power to draw from them their best thoughts. In 1889 she had sole charge of the "Union Signal" in the absence of the editor. She took a vacation trip to Europe in 1890, spending a month in London, England, and visiting Lady Henry Somerset at Eastnor Castle. Miss Ames was received with honor by the British Woman's Temperance Association. While in London, she organized the press department of that society on lines similar to those of the American organization. She traveled through Europe with a chosen party conducted by Miss Sarah E. Morgan, under the auspices of Mrs. M. B. Willard's school for girls. She witnessed the Passion Play at Oberammergau, visited Rome and other famous cities and returned to the United States refreshed in mind and body to resume her editorial duties on the "Union Signal." She attended the Boston convention in November, 1891, in her editorial capacity. She assisted in editing the daily "Union Signal," prepared the Associated Press dispatches each night, and was the chairman of one or two committees. She was not well when she left Chicago, and she contracted a severe cold, which through the pressure of her work developed into typhoid pneumonia, of which she died 12th December, 1891. Miss Ames was a member of the Woman's Temperance Publishing Association Circle of King's Daughters and was president of that organization when she left Chicago for her European tour. The silver cross and the white ribbon were the symbols of her life. She was an efficient worker, a thorough organizer and the possessor of more than ordinary executive capacity. She was direct, positive, earnest, amiable and indefatigable.

AMES, Miss Lucia True, author, born in Boscawen, N. H., 5th May, 1856. She has written two books, "Great Thoughts for Little Thinkers" (New York, 1888), and "Memoirs of a Millionaire" (Boston, 1889), a work of fiction. The first is an attempt to present modern and liberal thought on scientific and religious questions in a simple form which shall supplement home and Sunday-school instruction. The second volume treats of experiments in modern social reforms. Miss Ames has been to Europe several times and traveled extensively. She has for some years conducted numerous large adult classes in Boston and vicinity in studies in nineteenth century thought, taking Emerson, Lowell, Carlyle, Webster and Bryce as the bases for study. She has been a contributor to various periodicals. She is a woman suffragist and an earnest worker in furthering measures that shall promote good citizenship. She is a niece of Charles Carleton Coffin, the author of books for boys. Her home is in Boston, Mass., in which vicinity she has spent the greater part of her life.

AMES, Mrs Mary Clemmer, see HUDSON, MRS. MARY CLEMMER.

AMIES, Mrs. Olive Pond, educator and lecturer, born in Jordan, N. Y. She was two weeks old when her father died, and the mother and child went to the home of the grandparents in New Britain, Conn. There the mother worked

OLIVE POND AMIES.

untiringly with her needle for the support of herself and her two children. The older child, a boy, was placed in the care of an uncle, and to Olive the mother took the place of father, mother, brother and sister. When Olive was four years old, the mother and child left the home of the grandmother and went to the village to board, that Olive might be sent to school. Soon after this the mother married Cyrus Judd, a man of influence in the town of New Britain. Olive continued in school for many years. She passed through the course of the New Britain high school, was graduated from the State Normal School, and later, after several years of teaching, was graduated from the Normal and Training School in Oswego, N. Y. She was always a leader in school and became eminent as a teacher. She has for many years given model lessons at conventions and institutes. For five years in the State of New York and two in the State of Maine she was in constant demand in the county teachers' insti-

tutes. She founded the training school for teachers in Lewiston, Maine, and graduated its first classes. In 1871 she was married to the Rev. J. H. Amies, pastor of the Universalist Church, Lewiston, Maine, though she had been brought up a Methodist and had become, in later years, an Episcopalian. In 1877 she began to edit the primary department of the "Sunday School Helper," published in Boston, the exponent for the Universalist Church of the of the International Lessons. Since January, 1880, she has never failed with a lesson, excepting two months in 1884, during a severe illness. The Rev. Mr. Amies is a student, a man of original thought, and in full sympathy with the advanced questions of the day. Mrs. Amies feels that his encouragement and assistance have been the moving power in her work. They have constantly studied together and stood side by side in sympathy and work whether in the pulpit, on the lecture platform, or in the home. She holds State positions in the Woman's Christian Temperance Union · and the Woman Suffrage Association, and delivers lectures on the different themes connected with those two organizations. She also speaks on kindergarten and object-teaching, and her "Conversations on Juvenile Reforms" have been exceedingly popular wherever given. Her home is now in Philadelphia, Pa. She has had a family of six children, three girls and three boys, of whom one son and one daughter died while young.

AMORY, Mrs. Estelle Mendell, educator and author, born in Ellisburgh, Jefferson county, N. Y., 3d June, 1845. She is better known as a writer by her maiden name, Estelle Mendell. Her childhood was passed on a farm. In 1852 her family moved to Adams, a near-by village, where her father, S. J. Mendell, engaged in mercantile business. The Mendell home was a home of refinement and culture, and Colonel and Mrs. Mendell entertained many prominent persons, among whom were Henry Ward Beecher, Thomas Starr King, Edwin H. Chapin, Frederick Douglass and Gerrit Smith; and intercourse with those brilliant men and others did much to inspire the young girl with a desire to make a mark in literature. When the Civil War broke out, Mr. Mendell raised a company of soldiers, took a commission as captain and went to the South. He served throughout the war, rising to the rank of colonel by brevet. Estelle had developed meanwhile into a studious young woman, and had taught her first school. She studied in the Hungerford Collegiate Institute in her home town, and in Falley Seminary, Fulton, N. Y. In 1866 the family moved to Franklin county, Iowa. There Estelle continued to teach. In 1867 she returned to the East and re-entered Falley Seminary, from which institution she was graduated with honors in 1868. Her family—there were eight brothers and sisters—had been placed in financial straits by the war, and Estelle was obliged to earn the money, aided by some devoted friends, with which to complete her seminary course. Then followed seven years of earnest work as a teacher, she holding successively the positions of governess in a family in Chicago, and principal and preceptress of seminaries in the East. In 1875 she became the wife of J. H. Amory, of a prominent family of Binghamton, N.Y., and they went to Elgin, Ill., to live. During all those years Mrs. Amory had written much but done little in the way of publication. At length she began to offer her work. Ready acceptance encouraged her, and soon she became a regular contributor to standard periodicals. Her literary productions consist mainly of domestic articles, short stories for children, essays on living themes and occasional poems. Her well-known "Aunt Martha Letters," published in the Elmira "Telegram," in 1882, and later the more famous "Aunt Chatty" series in the Minneapolis "Housekeeper," have made her name a household word. Among the journals that have given her articles to the public are the "Ladies' Home Journal," "Mail and Express," "Epoch," Cincinnati "Enquirer," "Journalist," "Union Signal," "Babyhood," "Golden Days" and a score of others. In addition to her family cares and literary work, Mrs. Amory has often had classes at home and in the school-room, besides classes in music. Her family consists of two children, a son and a daughter, and her home is now in Belmond, Iowa. From her mother Mrs. Amory has inherited qualities of soul and mind that have endeared her to a large circle of friends; and from her public-spirited, talented father, a broad, enthusiastic nature, that allies her actively with the advance thought and movements of the day.

ANDERSON, Mary, Mme. Navarro, actor born in Sacramento, Cal., 28th July, 1859. Her maiden name was Mary Antoinette Anderson. Her mother was German descent, and her father was the grandson of an Englishman. In January, 1860, her parents removed from Sacramento to Louisville, Ky., where she lived until 1877. Her father joined the Confederate army at the beginning of the Civil War, and was killed at Mobile, Ala., in 1862. Her mother was married again, in 1864, to Dr. Hamilton Griffin, a practicing physician in Louisville. Mary and her brother Joseph had a pleasant home. Mary was a bright, mischievous child, whose early pranks earned her the name of "Little Mustang." Afterwards, when her exuberance was toned down and she had settled seriously to study, she was called "Little Newspaper." In school she was so careless of books and fond of mischief, that at the age of thirteen years she was permitted to study at home. There, instead of the usual studies, she spent her time on Shakespeare. Fascinated by the world that the poet opened to her she began to train her voice to recite striking passages that she committed to memory. The desire to become an actor was born with her. At the age of ten she recited passages from Shakespeare, with her room arranged to represent the stage scene. Her first visit to the theater occurred when she was twelve years old. She and her brother witnessed the performance of a fairy piece, and from that moment she had no thought for any profession but the stage. Her parents attempted to dissuade her from this choice, but she pursued her studies with only her inborn artistic instincts as teachers. She was known to possess dramatic talent, and friends urged her parents to put her in training for the stage. In her fourteenth year she saw Edwin Booth perform as Richard III in Louisville, and the performance intensified her desire to become an actor. She repeated his performance at home, and terrified a colored servant girl into hysterics with her fierce declamation. The performance was repeated before an audience of friends in her home, and in it she achieved her first success. Her interrupted course in the Ursuline Convent school of Louisville was supplemented by a course of training in music, dancing and literature, with the idea of a dramatic career. By the advice of Charlotte Cushman she made a thorough preparation, studying for a time with the younger Vanderhoff in New York. That was her only real training — ten lessons from a dramatic teacher ; all the rest she accomplished for herself. Her first appearance was in the rôle of Juliet, on 27th

November, 1875, in Macauley's Theater, Louisville, in a benefit given for Milnes Levick, an English stock actor, who was in financial straits. Miss Anderson was announced on the bills simply as "Juliet, by a Louisville Young Lady." The theatre was packed, and Mary Anderson, in spite of natural crudities and faults, won a most pronounced success. In February, 1876, she played a week in the same theater, appearing as Bianca in "Fazio," as Julia in "The Hunchback," as Evadne, and again as Juliet. Her reputation spread rapidly, and on 6th March, 1876, she began a week's engagement at the opera house, in St. Louis, Mo. She next played a week in Ben de Bar's Drury Lane Theater in New Orleans, and scored a brilliant triumph. She next presented Meg Merrilies in the New Orleans Lyceum, and in that difficult rôle she won a memorable success. Prominent persons overwhelmed her with attentions, and when she left New Orleans a special

MARY ANDERSON.

engine and car bore her to Louisville. She now passed some time in study and next played a second successful engagement in New Orleans. Her first and only rebuff was in her native State, where she played for two weeks in San Francisco. The press and critics were cold and hostile, and it was only when she appeared as Meg Merrilies the Californians could see any genius in her. In San Francisco she met Edwin Booth, who advised her to study such parts as "Parthenia," as better suited to her powers than the more somber tragic characters. Her Californian tour discouraged her, but she was keen to perceive the lesson that underlay ill success, and decided to begin at the bottom and build upward. She made a summer engagement with a company of strolling players and familiarized herself with the stage "business" in all its details. The company played mostly to empty benches, but the training was valuable to Miss. Anderson. In 1876 she accepted an offer from

John T. Ford, of Washington and Baltimore, to join his company as a star at three-hundred dollars a week. Accompanied by her parents, as was her invariable custom, she went on a tour with Mr. Ford's company and everywhere won new triumphs. The management reaped a rich harvest. On this tour Miss Anderson was subjected to annoyance through a boycott by the other members of the company, who were jealous of the young star. She had added Lady Macbeth to her list of characters. The press criticisms that were showered upon her make interesting reading. In St. Louis, Baltimore, Washington and other cities the critics were agreed upon the fact of her genius, but not all agreed upon her manner of expressing it. Having won in the West and Southwest, she began to invade eastern territory. She appeared in Pittsburgh in 1880, and was successful. In Philadelphia she won the public and critics to her side easily. In Boston she opened as Evadne, with great apprehension of failure, but she triumphed and appeared as Juliet and Meg Merrilies, drawing large houses. While in Boston, she formed the acquaintance of Longfellow, and their friendship lasted through the later-life of the venerable poet. After Boston came New York and in the metropolis she opened with a good company in "The Lady of Lyons." Her engagement was so successful there that it was extended to six weeks. During that engagement she played as Juliet and in "The Daughter of Roland." After the New York engagement she had no more difficulties to overcome. Everywhere in the United States and Canada she was welcomed as the leading actor among American women. In 1879 she made her first trip to Europe, and while in England visited the grave of Shakespeare at Stratford-on-Avon, and in Paris met Sarah Bernhardt, Madame Ristori and other famous actors. In 1880 she received an offer from the manager of Drury Lane, London, England, to play an engagement. She was pleased by the offer, but she modestly refused it, as she thought herself hardly finished enough for such a test of her powers. In 1883 she also refused an offer to appear in the London Lyceum. In 1884-5 she was again in London, and then she accepted an offer to appear at the Lyceum in "Parthenia." Her success was pronounced and instantaneous. She drew crowded houses, and among her friends and patrons were the Prince and Princess of Wales, Lord Lytton and Tennyson. She played successfully in Manchester, Edinburgh and other British towns. During that visit she opened the Memorial Theater in Stratford-on-Avon, playing Rosamond in "As You Like It." Her portrait in that character forms one of the panels of the Shakespeare Theater. In 1885-6 she played many engagements in the United States and Great Britain. In 1889 a serious illness compelled her to retire from the stage temporarily. In 1890 she announced her permanent withdrawal from it, and soon after she was married to M. Antonio Navarro de Viano, a citizen of New York. They now live in England.

ANDREWS, Miss Alice A., composer and director, born in St. Peter, Minn. She is a member of the musical Andrews family, now grown into the well-known Andrews Opera Company. It has been said of her that she could sing before she could lisp a word, as she began to sing at the early age of two years. When she was nine years of age, she started out with her brothers and sisters as one of the family concert troupe, giving sacred concerts in the churches throughout the State. After a few musical seasons she left the concert stage for the school-room, where she spent her time for sev-

eral years, taking a trip with the family now and then in the summer vacations. As a child she had a remarkably strong voice, but at twelve years of age it failed completely, and for six years she did not sing a note. After that time she regained it in a measure, but not in its completeness, and she has since turned her attention more to instrumental music, being for eight or nine years the

ALICE A. ANDREWS.

pianist and musical director of the company. She has composed several vocal pieces, which she is now having published. She has a remarkable talent for transposition, and could transpose music as soon as she could read it. The Andrews family is of Spanish descent by the line of the father who was a man of much intellectual ability. The paternal grandfather came to this country when quite a young boy, leaving his parents upon large landed estates to which he, the only child, would one day be heir. Here he married, and his wife would never consent to his returning to look after his interests in far-away Spain. Much of the musical and dramatic talent of his grandchildren is doubtless an inheritance, brought to them by him from the land of the vine and the olive, of sunshine and song.

ANDREWS, Miss Eliza Frances, author and educator, born in Washington, Ga., 10th August, 1847. Her father was Judge Garnett Andrews, an eminent jurist and the author of a book of amusing sketches entitled "Reminiscences of an Old Georgia Lawyer." Among others of her immediate family who have distinguished themselves are her brother, Col. Garnett Andrews, a brave Confederate officer and the present mayor of Chattanooga, and her niece, Maude Andrews, of the Atlanta "Constitution." Soon after the death of her father, in 1873, his estate was wrecked by one of those "highly moral" defaulters, whose operations Miss Andrews has vividly portrayed in her novel, "A Mere Adventurer" (Philadelphia,

1879). The old homestead was sold, and Miss Andrews was reduced to the necessity of toiling for her daily bread. Though wholly unprepared, either by nature or training, for a life of self-dependence, she wasted no time in sentimental regrets, but courageously prepared to meet the situation. Journalism was hardly at that time a recognized profession for women in Georgia, and Miss Andrews, whose natural timidity and reserve had been fostered by the traditions in which she was reared, shrank from striking out into a new path. She did a little literary work secretly, but turned rather to teaching as a profession. For six months she edited a country newspaper, unknown to the proprietor himself, who had engaged a man to do the work at a salary of forty dollars a month. The pseudo-editor, feeling himself totally incompetent, offered Miss Andrews one-half of the salary if she would do the writing for him, and, being in great straits at the time, she accepted the un-

ELIZA FRANCES ANDREWS.

equal terms, doing all the actual work, while the duties of the ostensible editor were limited to taking the exchanges out of the post-office and drawing his half of the pay. After a few months the senior member of this unequal partnership, finding employment elsewhere, recommended Miss Andrews as his successor, a proposition to which the proprietor of the paper would not hear, declaring in his wisdom that it was impossible for a woman to fill such a position. Even when assured that one had actually been filling it for six months, he persisted in his refusal on the ground that editing a paper was not proper work for a woman. This, with exception of a few news letters to the New York "World," written about the same time, was Miss Andrews' first essay in journalism, and her experience on that occasion, together with similar experiences in other walks, has perhaps had something to do with making her such an ardent advocate of a more enlarged sphere of action for

women. In spite of this unpromising beginning, she has been successful both as writer and teacher, and had gone far towards retrieving her shattered fortunes when her health failed. She spent eighteen months under treatment in a private hospital, and for two years more was compelled to withdraw from active life. Even under these adverse circumstances her energetic nature asserted itself, and "Prince Hal," an idyl of old-time plantation life, was written when she was so ill that she often had to lie in bed with her hands propped on a pillow to write. After a winter in Florida, in which she wrote a series of letters for the Augusta "Chronicle," she recovered her strength so far as to be able to accept an important position in the Wesleyan College in Macon, Ga., where she has remained for six or seven years, and in that time has added to her literary reputation that of a successful platform speaker. Her lectures on "The Novel as a Work of Art," "Jack and Jill," and "The Ugly Girl," delivered at the Piedmont Chautauqua, Monteagle, Tenn., and other places, have attracted wide attention. Besides being a fine linguist, speaking French and German fluently, and reading Latin with ease, she is probably the most accomplished field botanist in the South. Her literary work has been varied. From the solemn grandeur that marks the closing paragraphs of "Prince Hal" down to such popular sketches as "Uncle Edom and the Book Agent," or "The Dog Fight at Big Lick Meetin' House," her pen has ranged through nearly every field of literary activity. It is, perhaps, in what may be called the humorous treatment of serious subjects that her talent finds its best expression, as in her witty reply to Grant Allen on the woman question ("Popular Science Monthly"), or her "Plea for the Ugly Girls" ("Lippincott's Magazine"). "A Family Secret" (Philadelphia, 1876) is the most popular of her novels. This was followed by "How He was Tempted," published as a serial in the Detroit "Free Press." "Prince Hal" (Philadelphia, 1882), is the last of her works issued in book form. Her later writings have been published as contributions to different newspapers and periodicals. Her poems have been too few to warrant a judgment upon her as a writer of verse, but one of them, entitled "Haunted," shows how intimately the humorous and the pathetic faculties may be connected in the same mind.

ANDREWS, Mrs. Judith Walker, philanthropist, born in Fryeburgh, Maine, 26th April, 1826. She was educated in Fryeburgh Academy with the intention, so common with New England girls, of becoming a teacher. Her brother, Dr. Clement A. Walker, one of the first of the new school of physicians for the insane, having been appointed to the charge of the newly established hospital of the city of Boston, his sister joined him there. Although never officially connected with the institution, which had already gained a reputation as a pioneer in improved administration of the work for the insane, Miss Walker interested herself in the details of that administration, and by her personal attention to the patients endeared herself to them. No better school of training could be found for the activities to which she has given her life. She was married while in the institution, on 15th January, 1857, to Joseph Andrews, of Salem, a man of generous public spirit, who gave much time and labor to the improvement of the militia system of the commonwealth, both before and during the Civil War. He died in 1869. They had three children, all boys, to whose early education Mrs. Andrews gave the years, only too few, of a happy married life. Removing to Boston in 1863, she became a member of the South Congregational Church (Unitarian), and in 1876 was elected president of its ladies' organization, the South Friendly Society. Her service of sixteen years in that office

JUDITH WALKER ANDREWS.

is only one of five such terms in the history of the society. Under the influence of its pastor, Dr. Edward Everett Hale, the South Congregational Church has had wide relations both inside and outside denominational lines, and these relations have brought to Mrs. Andrews opportunities for religious and philanthropic work to which she always has been ready to respond. While most of these, though requiring much work and thought, are of a local character, two lines of her work have made her name familiar to a large circle. Elected, in 1886, president of the Women's Auxiliary Conference, she was active in the movement to enlarge its scope and usefulness, and in 1889, when the National Alliance of Unitarian and Other Liberal Christian Women was organized, she became its first president, declining re-election in 1891. Since 1889 she has been a member of the Council of the National Unitarian Conference. Having become interested in the child-widows of India, through the eloquence, and later the personal friendship, of Pundita Ramabai, she was largely instrumental in the formation of the Ramabai Association, to carry out the plans of Ramabai and to systematize the work of her friends throughout the country. To the executive committee of that association, of which Mrs. Andrews has been chairman from the beginning, is entrusted the oversight of the management of the school for child-widows, the Shâradâ Sadana at Poona and the settlement of the many delicate questions arising from a work so opposed to the customs, though fortunately not to the best traditions, of India.

ANDREWS, Mrs. Marie Louise, story writer and journalist, born in Bedford, Ind., 31st October, 1849. She was the second daughter of

the late Dr. Benjamin and Louise A. Newland, who were educated and intellectual persons. Her early life was spent in Bedford. She was educated mainly in private schools. She was a student in St. Mary's-of-the-Woods, in St. Agnes' Hall, Terre Haute Ind., and in Hungerford Institute, Adams, N. Y. The last-named institute was destroyed by fire shortly before commencement, so that Miss Newland was not formally graduated. She was married on 15th May, 1875, to Albert M. Andrews, of Seymour, Ind. In 1877 they removed to Connersville, Ind., where Mr. Andrews engaged in the drug business. They had one child, a son. Mrs. Adams died on 7th February, 1891, in Connersville, Ind. She was thoroughly educated. She spoke French and German and was familiar with Latin and the literature of the modern languages. Her literary tastes were displayed in her earliest years. She wrote much, in both verse and prose, but she never published her productions in book form. She was the originator of the Western Association of Writers, and served as its secretary from its organization until June, 1888, when she insisted on retiring from the office. Among her acquaintances were many of the prominent writers of the West, and at the annual conventions of the Western Association of Writers she was always a conspicuous member. She foresaw the growth of literature in the West, and her ideas of that growth and of the best means of fostering it are embodied in the organization which she founded. That association has already been the means of introducing scores of talented young writers to the public, and

MARIE LOUISE ANDREWS.

it alone is a worthy monument to Mrs. Andrews. She was a brilliant conversationalist and an effective impromptu speaker.

ANDREWS, Mrs. Mary Garard, Universalist minister, born in Clarksburgh, Va., 3rd March, 1852. She is of good old Pennsylvania ancestors in whom the best Quaker and Baptist blood mingled. Her maiden name was Garard. Always fondly proud of the home of her adoption, Iowa, she calls herself a thoroughly western woman. She was left motherless at the age of five

MARY GARARD ANDREWS.

years and her father was killed in the service of his country a few years later. Thus early left to struggle with the adverse elements of human life, she developed a strong character and marked individuality, and overcame many difficulties in acquiring an education. In spite of ill health, the discouragement of friends and financial pressure, she maintained her independence and kept herself in school for eight years. She spent two years in the academy in Washington, Iowa, three years in the Iowa State Industrial College, and three years in Hillsdale College, Mich. While in the last-named place she completed the English Theological course with several elective studies, having charge of one or two churches all the time and preaching twice every Sunday during the three years. She says: "I never spent much time over the oft controverted question, 'Shall woman preach?' I thought the most satisfactory solution of the problem would be for woman quietly, without ostentation or controversy, to assume her place and let her work speak for itself." After five years of faithful, fruitful service in the Free Baptist Church, convictions of truth and duty caused her to sever ties grown dear and cast her lot with a strange people. For eight years she was engaged in the regular pastoral work of the Universalist Church, during which time she was a close and thorough student, keeping well informed on the questions of the day. Never satisfied with present attainments, she pursued a more advanced theological and philosophical course, in which she passed an examination and received the degree of B. D. from Lombard University, Illinois. She has been an interesting, successful and beloved pastor. Besides doing well and faithfully her parish work,

she was an enthusiastic temperance and Grand Army worker, and for two years was National Chaplain of the Woman's Relief Corps. In April, 1888, she was married to I. R. Andrews, a prosperous attorney of Omaha, Neb., where she now resides.

ANGELINI, Mme. Arabella, evangelical worker, born in Elton, Md., 8th July, 1863. Her maiden name was Chapman. On her mother's side she is descended from a Huguenot family, the De Vinneys, who settled in Maryland over a century ago. Her father died when she was only four years old and Arabella was taken to Europe at the age of eight years, by Miss Mary Gilpin, of Philadelphia, for the ostensible purpose of learning music and languages. On reaching Germany, Miss Gilpin developed a strange mania for abusing her little charge. They spent several months in Germany and Switzerland and passed on to Italy, stopping first at Verona. In that city the police were instructed to watch Miss Gilpin closely, as her erratic behavior attracted attention. In Florence her cruelty to her charge caused the police to interfere. They took charge of Arabella, who was less than nine years old, and Miss Gilpin left her to her fate among strangers, whose language she did not understand. She found shelter in the Protestant College in Florence and was there cared for until her health was restored. She remained in the institution nine years and at the end of that time was married to the Rev. Luigi Angelini, a minister of the Evangelical Church of Italy. After their marriage they settled in a small village in northern Italy, Bassignana. In 1884 the board of the Evangelical Church of Italy nominated Dr. Angelini as its representative in the United States, and thus,

ARABELLA ANGELINI.

after a long absence, Mme. Angelini returned to her native land only to find herself quite as much a foreigner as though born in Italy. When brought face to face with her mother, she could not speak her native language. Long disuse had not effaced the English language from her memory, however, and the words soon came back to her. Mme. Angelini is aiding her husband to arouse an interest in the churches of America, and in organizing undenominational societies for the support of the native Evangelical Church of Italy. She looks forward to a career of usefulness in Italy, aiding the women of her adopted country in their struggle for elevation.

ANTHONY, Miss Susan B., woman suffragist, born in South Adams, Mass., 15th February, 1820. If locality and religious heritage have any influence in determining fate, what might be predicted for Susan B. Anthony? Born in Massachusetts, brought up in New York, of Quaker father and Baptist mother, she has by heritage a strongly marked individuality and native strength. In girlish years Susan belonged to Quaker meeting, with aspirations toward "high-seat" dignity, but this

SUSAN B. ANTHONY.

was modified by the severe treatment accorded to her father, who, having been publicly reprimanded twice, the first time for marrying a Baptist, the second for wearing a comfortable cloak with a large cape, was finally expelled from "meeting" because he allowed the use of one of his rooms for the instruction of a class in dancing, in order that the youth might not be subject to the temptations of a liquor-selling public house. Though Mr. Anthony was a cotton manufacturer and one of the wealthiest men in Washington county, N. Y., he desired that his daughters, as his sons, should be trained for some profession. Accordingly they were fitted, in the best of private schools, for teachers, the only vocation then thought of for girls, and at fifteen Susan found herself teaching a Quaker family school at one dollar a week and board. When the financial crash of 1837 caused his failure, they were not only teaching and supporting themselves, but were able to help their father in his

efforts to retrieve his fortunes. With a natural aptitude for the work, conscientious and prompt in all her duties, Susan was soon pronounced a successful teacher, and to that profession she devoted fifteen years of her life. She was an active member of the New York State Teachers' Association and in their conventions made many effective pleas for higher wages and for the recognition of the principle of equal rights for women in all the honors and responsibilities of the association. The women teachers from Maine to Oregon owe Miss Anthony a debt of gratitude for the improved position they hold to-day. Miss Anthony has been from a child deeply interested in the subject of temperance. In 1847 she joined the Daughters of Temperance, and in 1852 organized the New York State Woman's Temperance Association, the first open temperance organization of women. Of this Mrs. Elizabeth Cady Stanton was president. As secretary Miss Anthony for several years gave her earnest efforts to the temperance cause, but she soon saw that woman was utterly powerless to change conditions without the ballot. Since she identified herself with the suffrage movement in 1852 she has left others to remedy individual wrongs, while she has been working for the weapon by which, as she believes, women will be able to do away with the producing causes. She says she has "no time to dip out vice with a teaspoon while the wrongly-adjusted forces of society are pouring it in by the bucketful." With all her family, Miss Anthony was a pronounced and active Abolitionist. During the war, with her life-long friend and co-worker, Elizabeth Cady Stanton, and other coadjutors, she rolled up nearly 400,000 petitions to Congress for the abolition of slavery. Those petitions circulated in every northern and western State, served the double purpose of rousing the people to thought and furnishing the friends of the slave in Congress opportunities for speech. In Charles Sumner's letters to Miss Anthony we find the frequent appeals, "Send on the petitions; they furnish the only background for my demands." The most harrassing, though most satisfactory, enterprise Miss Anthony ever undertook was the publication for three years of a weekly paper, "The Revolution." This formed an epoch in the woman's rights movement and roused widespread thought on the question. Ably edited by Elizabeth Cady Stanton and Parker Pillsbury, with the finest intellects in the Nation among its contributors, dealing pungently with passing events, and rising immediately to a recognized position among the papers of the Nation, there was no reason why there should not have been a financial success, save that Miss Anthony's duties kept her almost entirely from the lecture field, and those who were on the platform, in the pulpit and in all the lucrative positions which this work was opening to women, could not and did not feel that the cause was their own. After three years of toil and worry a debt of $10,000 had accumulated. "The Revolution" was transferred to other hands but did not long survive. Miss Anthony set bravely about the task of earning money to pay the debt, every cent of which was duly paid from the earnings of her lectures. Miss Anthony has always been in great demand on the platform and has lectured in almost every city and hamlet in the North. She has made constitutional arguments before congressional committees and spoken impromptu to assemblies in all sorts of places. Whether it be a good word in introducing a speaker, the short speech to awaken a convention, the closing appeal to set people to work, the full hour address of argument or the helpful talk at suffrage meetings, she always says the right thing and never wearies her audience. There is no hurry, no superfluity in her discourse, no sentiment, no poetry, save that of self-forgetfulness in devotion to the noblest principles that can actuate human motive. A fine sense of humor pervades her arguments, and by the *reductio ad absurdum* she disarms and wins her opponent. The most dramatic event of Miss Anthony's life was her arrest and trial for voting at the presidential election of 1872. Owing to the mistaken kindness of her counsel, who was unwilling that she should be imprisoned, she gave bonds, which prevented her taking her case to the Supreme Court, a fact she always regretted. When asked by the judge, "You voted as a woman, did you not?" she replied, "No, sir, I voted as a citizen of the United States." The date and place of trial being set, Miss Anthony thoroughly canvassed her county so as to make sure that all of the jurors were instructed in a citizen's rights. Change of venue was ordered to another county, setting the date three weeks ahead. In twenty-four hours Miss Anthony had her plans made, dates set, and posters sent out for a series of meetings in that county. After the argument had been presented to the jury, the judge took the case out of their hands, saying it was a question of law and not of fact, and pronounced Miss Anthony guilty, fining her $100 and costs. She said to the judge, "Resistance to tyranny is obedience to God, and I shall never pay a penny of this unjust claim," and she glories in never having done so. The inspectors, who received the ballots from herself and friends, were fined and imprisoned, but were pardoned by President Grant. Miss Anthony has had from the beginning the kindly sympathy and cöoperation of her entire family, all taking deep interest in the reforms for which she has labored. Especially is this true of her youngest sister, Miss Mary S. Anthony, who has freed her eldest sister from domestic responsibilities. A wonderful memory which carries the legislative history of each State, the formation and progress of political parties, the parts played by prominent men in our National life, and whatever has been done the world over to ameliorate conditions for women, makes Miss Anthony a genial and instructive companion, while her unfailing sympathy makes her as good a listener as talker. The change in public sentiment towards woman suffrage is well indicated by the change in the popular estimate of Miss Anthony. Where once it was the fashion of the press to ridicule and jeer, now the best reporters are sent to interview her, and to put her sentiments before the world with the most respectful and laudatory personal comment. Society, too, throws open its doors, and into many distinguished gatherings she carries a refreshing breath of sincerity and earnestness. Her seventieth birthday, celebrated by the National Woman Suffrage Association, of which she was vice president-at-large from its formation in 1869 until its convention in 1892, when she was elected president, was the occasion of a spontaneous outburst of gratitude which is, perhaps, unparalleled in the history of any living individual. Miss Anthony is still of undiminished vigor and activity, and, having in a most remarkable degree the power to rally around her for united action the ever-increasing hosts of the woman suffrage organization, of which she is now the head, she is a powerful factor in molding public opinion in the direction of equal rights and opportunities for women. She is one of the most heroic figures in American history. The future will place her name with the greatest of our statesmen, and in

her life-time she enjoys the reward of being esteemed by men and loved by women.

ARCHIBALD, Mrs. Edith Jessie, temperance reformer, born in St. Johns, Newfoundland, 5th April, 1854. She is the youngest daughter of Sir Edward Mortimer Archibald, K. C. M. G., C. B., late Her Britannic Majesty's Consul-General in New York. Her parents were both Nova Scotians. Her father's family were descendants of Loyalists who emigrated from Massachusetts during the Revolution and settled in Truro, N. S., which township they helped to organize. Her grandfather on her father's side was one of the historic personages of the Province. He was called to the bar, where he displayed great talent. He entered public life and became successively a member for his county, Attorney-General of Nova Scotia, Judge of the Supreme Court of Prince Edward's Island, and Speaker of the House of Assembly of Nova Scotia He was an eloquent orator of broad mind and lib

EDITH JESSIE ARCHIBALD.

eral views. Her father, after a residence of twenty-five years in St. John's, Newfoundland, where he was successively Attorney-General and Judge of the Supreme Court, received the appointment of British Consul in New York. In 1857 he removed with his family to New York, where he held the consulship during twenty seven years, making a record of public life of over fifty-two years. His daughter, Mrs. Archibald, was educated in New York and London. In London she studied two years. She is passionately fond of art, music and literature. She was married at the age of twenty years to Charles Archibald, a son of the Hon. Thomas D. Archibald, senator, of Sydney, Cape Breton, where her husband is an extensive property owner and the manager of one of the largest collieries in the island. Their residence is at Gowrie Mines, Cow Bay. Living in a country so isolated and surrounded by the cares of family and home, Mrs. Archibald has still endeavored to keep in touch with culture and literature. Until recent years she found scant time for indulging her tastes and talents. She has recently given more time to letters, and has published a number of poems and magazine articles. She is devoted to reforms and is an enthusiastic member of the Woman's Christian Temperance Union of the Dominion. Her four children take much attention but she is collecting materials for a more extensive work than she has yet given to the public.

AREY, Mrs. Harriett Ellen Grannis, author and editor, born in Cavendish, Vt., 14th

HARRIETT ELLEN GRANNIS AREY.

April, 1819. Her father's family had settled in New Haven, Conn., previous to 1655, among the earlier immigrants to New England. A hundred years later her grandfather removed from New Haven to Claremont, N. H., taking up a section of land included between the Connecticut and Sugar rivers and the township boundary on the north. There he married a daughter of Dr. William Sumner, who had removed thither from Boston. The seventh child of this family was the father of Harriet E. Grannis. Being of a studious turn of mind, he was destined for the Church, and while his studies were in progress, the older brothers engaged in extensive business enterprises. The war of 1812 came with its ruinous effects upon the country, followed from 1815 by the two or three cold seasons so well remembered in New England, in which crops were cut off. The business of the country had been unsettled since the first demonstrations of war, and her father was called from his studies to assist in saving the crippled business in which his brothers were engaged. The last blow of ruined crops brought about a disastrous failure, so that Harriett first saw the light in the midst of a depression quite as serious, probably, as that which followed the War of the Revolution. When she was three years of age, her father removed to Woodstock, Vt., and a year or two later to Charles-

ton in the township of Hatley, Province of Quebec. In her fifteenth year she had the misfortune to lose her mother. Through this loss the family became separated, her father being at the time a member of the Provincial Parliament and obliged to be in Quebec a portion of the year, and the young girl was under the care of relatives in Claremont for the next three or four years. At the end of that time she joined her father at Oberlin, Ohio, whither he had removed when released from his official duties. There she resumed the school work that had been laid by and spent some years in uninterrupted study, at the close of which time she found a position as teacher in a ladies' school in Cleveland, Ohio, and from that place she removed, on her marriage, to Buffalo, N. Y. She had been from early girlhood a contributor to various papers and magazines, and not long after her marriage, she became editor of the "Youth's Casket" and the "Home Monthly." Active as she was in sound movements for reform, this work prospered in her hands, until, under the double burden of a growing family and her editorial responsibilities, her health failed, and it had to be given up. Soon afterwards her husband, who had charge of the central high school in Buffalo, was called to the principalship of the State Normal School in Albany, N. Y., and they removed to that city, where she spent a few pleasant years. A serious illness and a railroad accident following close upon it had prostrated her husband, and he was obliged to give up active duties for a year or more. When his health began to improve, he accepted the principalship of the State Normal School, then opening in Whitewater, Wis. Thinking that with his frail health her duty was at his side, Mrs. Arey went into the school with him, holding the position of lady principal. That occupation was congenial to her, and for nine or ten years she enjoyed the work. A few years later she found herself in her old home in Cleveland, where for some years she edited a monthly devoted to charitable work, at the same time holding a position on the board of the Woman's Christian Association. She was one of the founders and still holds her position as first president of the Ohio Woman's State Press Association. She has been for many years president of an active literary and social club. Her principal writings are "Household Songs and Other Poems" (New York, 1854).

ARMBRUSTER, Mrs. Sara Dary, business woman and publisher, born in Philadelphia, Pa., 29th September, 1862. Her early years were passed in luxury, and she had all the advantages of thorough schooling. When she was seventeen years old, reverses left her family poor and she was made partly helpless by paralysis. Obliged to support herself and other members of her family she took the Irving House, a hotel of ninety-five rooms, in Philadelphia, and by good management made it a successful establishment and lifted herself and those dependent upon her above poverty. She was married at an early age. Of her three children, only one is living. She has been a business woman, and a successful one from the day on which she was thrown upon her own resources. She originated in Philadelphia the Woman's Exchange. Her present enterprise is to furnish a house for the infants of widows and deserted wives in her native city. She is the publisher of the "Woman's Journal," a weekly paper devoted to the cause of women. Her interest in philanthropic movements is earnest and active.

ARNOLD, Birch, see BARTLETT, MRS. ALICE ELOISE.

ARNOLD, Mrs. Harriet Pritchard, author, born in Killingly, Conn., in 1858. She was the only child of her parents. Her father was the Rev. B. F. Pritchard, a New England clergyman of Scotch and English descent, and her mother, Celia Handel Pritchard, was a lady of much refinement and culti-

HARRIET PRITCHARD ARNOLD.

vation. Mrs. Arnold in her childhood evinced no particular fondness for books, evidently preferring outdoor recreations, which she enjoyed with keenest zest. While wandering among the wooded vales and hills near her home in a suburb of the beautiful city of Portland, Maine, where the greater part of her life was passed, she perhaps unconsciously developed the latent poetry in her nature, and when in 1882 a lingering illness afforded her many hours of leisure, the hitherto unencouraged desire for work of a literary nature found expression. Since that time poems and sketches from her pen have appeared in various magazines and periodicals under the signature H. E. P., and her maiden name, Harriet E. Pritchard. In the year 1886, Miss Pritchard became the wife of Ernest Warner Arnold, of Providence, R. I., which city has since been her home. There in the companionship of her husband, son and little daughter she displays a modest and home-loving nature.

ARMSTRONG, Mrs. Ruth Alice, national superintendent of heredity for the Womans' Christian Temperance Union, born near Cassopolis, Cass county, Mich., 30th April, 1850. Her father, Amos Jones, was from Georgia, and her mother, Rebecca Hebron, was from Yorkshire, England. Both parents were distinguished for their helpfulness to others. From them Ruth received a wise home training. She was educated in the public schools of her native State. At the age of eighteen she commenced to teach, while she was herself a student in the higher branches. Becoming impressed with the injustice done to women in the smaller salaries paid to them than were paid to men for like services, she left her native State for California, but not until she had made an effort to

bring about a better state of affairs for coming generations by aiding in the organization of the first woman suffrage society of her native county. As a teacher she was successful. In 1874 she was married to Thomas Armstrong, a stock-raiser of Trinity county, Cal. He, believing in the social and civil equality of man and woman, and that a wife should be a companion not only in the joys and sorrows of a home, but in business also, bestowed upon her the same privileges and responsibilities as he himself bore. Their life on their mountain stock ranch was idyllic, spent in hard work and pleasant recreations. For four years they lived in isolation, with no society except that furnished by a well-selected library. Just before the birth of their only child, Ruth, they moved to Woodland, Cal. There Mrs. Armstrong organized a Shakespeare Club, which has reached its eighth year of work with a large membership. She organized a lecture bureau and was its first president. She assisted in the organization of a literary society for the study of literature of all nations. She was the first woman ever elected to the office of trustee in the Congregational Church of Woodland, of which she was for many years a worthy member. She left that denomination in 1891 and united with the Christian Church. Desiring to aid in moral reform, she united with the Woman's Christian Temperance Union and has given to that society her time and resources, organizing the county and several local unions. Her boundless enthusiasm and common-sense make her a leader and inspirer in that society. The department of heredity had its share of her attention. She began to plan for the education of women in maternity and other allied subjects. She

RUTH ALICE ARMSTRONG.

was made the superintendent of heredity for the town of Woodland, next for the county, and afterwards for the National Union. From her pen go out over all the Nation leaflets and letters of instruction to aid in the development of the highest physical, mental, moral and spiritual interest of mankind. Her lectures on "Heredity" and "Motherhood" carry the conviction that, for the

SARAH B. ARMSTRONG.

highest development of manhood and womanhood, parentage must be assumed as the highest, the holiest and most sacred responsibility entrusted to us by the Creator. At present she is helping to plan and put into execution a womans' building, to contain a printing office, lecture hall and a home for homeless women and girls. Mrs. Armstrong's helpfulness in the town, in the church, in the Woman's Christian Temperance Union and in the world comes from her belief in the powers of the unit and from the fact that her education has been assimilated into her character, producing a culture which has ministry for its highest aim. Possessed of keen and critical acumen, she ever makes choice of both word and action, endeavoring to say and do what is true, honest and pure, holding herself responsible to God and God alone.

ARMSTRONG, Miss Sarah B., physician and surgeon, born in Newton, near Cincinnati, Ohio, 31st July, 1857. Her early education was acquired in the schools of Cincinnati. Her family removed to Lebanon, Ohio, in 1865. She took a course of study in the university located in that town. She became a teacher at the age of sixteen years. In 1880 she took the degree of B.S. in the Lebanon University having graduated with the highest honors in a class of sixty-six members. In 1883 she returned to the university as a teacher and took charge of the art department. While thus engaged, she completed the classical course taking the degree of B.A. in 1887. In 1890 the degree of M. A. was conferred upon her as honorary. In 1886 she took her first degree in regular medicine. She was appointed matron and physician to the college, serving in that capacity while continuing to teach. In 1888 she was appointed

assistant to the chair of theory and practice in the Homœpathic College of Michigan, in Ann Arbor. She remained there two years and took a postgraduate degree in 1889. She then returned to Lebanon to serve as a member of the medical faculty of the university. She soon resigned her position and went to New York, where she spent a year in the hospitals, making a special study of surgery. She removed to Bay City, Mich., 1st January, 1891, and has successfully established herself in practice in that city. Dr. Armstrong is a musician and is engaged as a soprano singer in the Baptist Church in Bay City. Her professional duties have not kept her from public work. She was elected a member of the city school board in 1891. She is an active worker in the cause of woman's advancement. Her literary talents are displayed in poetical productions of a high order of merit. Dr. Armstrong inherits her liking for the profession of medicine from her maternal greatgrandmother, who was the first woman to practice medicine west of the Alleghany mountains. She was not, of course, permitted to take a degree in those early days, but took her preceptor's certificate and bought her license to practice. Dr. Armstrong has been well received as a physician, and her success is positive.

ATWOOD, Miss Ethel, musician, born in Fairfield, Maine, 12th September, 1870. Her parents were Yankees, and possessed sterling thrift and independence. The first fifteen years of Miss Atwood's life were passed in a quiet, uneventful way in her native town, but the desire to branch out and do and be something led her to migrate to Boston, where she has since resided. She began the study of the violin when eight years old, but

ETHEL ATWOOD.

lack of means and competent teachers in her native place prevented her from acquiring any great proficiency as a soloist. After going to Boston she turned her attention to orchestral work. Two years study and experience determined her to have an orchestra of her own. Securing a young woman whose reputation as a violinist and thorough musician was well established in the city, she organized the Fadette Ladies' Orchestra, with four pieces. Then it was that her Yankee shrewdness began to serve her well. She immediately had the name of her orchestra copyrighted and, hiring an office, put out her "shingle." Finding that prompting was essential to success in dance work she went to one of Boston's best prompters and learned the business thoroughly. An elocutionist taught her to use her voice to the best advantage, and now she stands as one of the best prompters in the city and the only lady prompter in the country. Business has increased rapidly in the past few years, and now there are thirteen regular members of the orchestra who are refined young women of musical ability.

AUSTIN, Mrs. Harriet Bunker, author, born in Erie, Pa., 29th December, 1844. She is a daughter of Mr. and Mrs. John F. Bunker, descending from New England stock. Her great-grandfather, Benjamin Bunker, was a soldier of the Revolution, and was killed in the battle of Bunker Hill. The hill from which the battle was named comprised part of the Bunker estate. On her mother's side she is related to the Bronson Alcott and Lyman Beecher families. When quite young, she removed with her parents to Woodstock, McHenry county, Ill., where she has since resided. Her education was received in the Woodstock high school and Dr. Todd's Female Seminary. At the close of her seminary life she was married to W. B. Austin, a prosperous merchant of that city. She has been a prolific writer, many of her poems having been set to music and gained deserved popularity. She has always taken an active

AUSTIN, Mrs. Helen Vickroy, journalist and horticulturist, born in Miamisburg, Montgomery county, Ohio, in 1829. She is a daughter of Edwin Augustus and Cornelia Harlan Vickroy.

HELEN VICKROY AUSTIN.

Her family on both sides are people of distinction. Her mother was a daughter of the Hon. George Harlan, of Warren county, Ohio. Her father was a son of Thomas Vickroy, of Pennsylvania, who was a soldier in the Revolution under Washington and an eminent surveyor and extensive land-owner. When Mrs. Austin was a child, the family removed to Pennsylvania and established a homestead in Ferndale, Cambria county. There her early life was passed. With an inherent love of nature, she grew up amid the picturesque scenes of the foot-hills of the Alleghany mountains, a poet in thought and an ardent lover of the beautiful. She was married in 1850 to William W. Austin, a native of Philadelphia, at that time residing at Richmond, Ind., in which delightful city they lived until, in 1885, the family went East, taking up their residence at Vineland, N. J. Although Mrs. Austin is a domestic woman, she has taken time to indulge her taste and promptings and has done considerable writing. Some of her best work has been for the agricultural and horticultural press, and her essays at the horticultural meetings and interest in such matters have given her a fame in horticultural circles. As a writer of sketches and essays and a reporter and correspondent Mrs. Austin has marked capacity. She is accurate and concise. Much of her work has been of a fugitive nature for the local press, but was worthy of a more enduring place. One of the marked characteristics of her nature is benevolence. She has given much time and used her pen freely in aid of philanthropic work. She has for many years been identified with the cause of woman suffrage, and the various institutions for the elevation and protection of woman have had her earnest help. Long before the temperance crusade she was a pronounced

HARRIET BUNKER AUSTIN.

interest in every scheme for the advancement of women, and is ever ready to lend her influence to the promotion of social reforms.

advocate of temperance and while in her teens was a "Daughter of Temperance." Her philanthropic spirit makes her a friend to the negro and Indian. She is a life member of the National Woman's Indian Rights Association. Mrs. Austin is the mother of three children. One of these, a daughter, is living. Her two sons died in childhood.

AUSTIN, Mrs. Jane Goodwin, author, born in Worcester, Mass., in 1831. Her parents were

JANE GOODWIN AUSTIN.

from Plymouth in the Old Colony, and counted their lineage from the Mayflower Pilgrims in no less than eight distinct lines, besides a common descent from Francis Le Baron, the nameless nobleman. Believers in heredity will see in this descent the root of Mrs. Austin's remarkable devotion to Pilgrim story and tradition. Her father, Isaac Goodwin, was a lawyer of considerable eminence, and also a distinguished antiquary and genealogist. Her brother, the Hon. John A. Goodwin, was the author, among other works, of "The Pilgrim Republic," the latest and best of all histories of the settlement of Plymouth. Her mother, well-known as a poet and song-writer, was furthermore a lover of the traditions and anecdotes of her native region, and many of the stories embodied in Mrs. Austin's later works she first heard as a child at her mother's knee, especially those relative to the Le Barons. Although Mrs. Austin's pen has strayed in various fields of poesy and prose, it has now settled down into a course very marked and very definite, yet capable of great development. This daughter of the Pilgrims has become a specialist in their behalf and has pledged her remaining years to developing their story. Her four books last published, namely: "Standish of Standish," "Betty Alden," "The Nameless Nobleman" and "Dr. Le Baron and his Daughters," cover the ground from the landing of the Pilgrims upon Plymouth Rock, in 1620, to the days of the Revolution, in 1775, and a fifth volume

is to succeed, which will complete the series. She has written a great number of magazine stories and some poems. Her principal books with the date of their publication are as follows: "Fairy Dreams" (Boston, 1859); "Dora Darling" (Boston, 1865); "Outpost" (Boston, 1866); "Tailor Boy" (Boston, 1867); "Cypher" (New York, 1869); "The Shadow of Moloch Mountain" (New York, 1870); "Moon-Folk" (New York, 1874); "Mrs. Beauchamp Brown" (Boston, 1880); "The Nameless Nobleman" (Boston, 1881) "Nantucket Scraps" (Boston, 1882); "Standish of Standish" (Boston, 1889); "Dr. Le Baron and his Daughters" (Boston, 1890); "Betty Alden" (Boston, 1891). Although a prolific writer, she has always written carefully and in finished style, and her contributions to the literature of early New England possess a rare value from her intimate knowledge of the pioneers of the eastern colonies gained from thorough reading and tradition. Her work is distinctly American in every essential. Mrs. Austin was married in 1850 to Loring H. Austin, a descendant of the fine old Boston family which figured so largely in the Revolution. She has three children. She is instinctively gracious, and those who know her not only admire her work, but give her a warm place in their affections. Her home is with a married daughter in Roxbury, although she passes a part of the winter in Boston, in order to be near her church, and every summer finds her ready to return to Plymouth, where she constantly studies not only written records, but crumbling gravestones and oral tradition.

AVANN, Mrs. Ella H. Brockway, educator, born in Newaygo, Mich., 20th May, 1853. Her father, the Rev. G. W. Hoag, born in Charlotte,

ELLA H. BROCKWAY AVANN.

Vt., was of Quaker parentage and a pioneer in the Methodist Episcopal Church in Michigan, having gone to that State in boyhood. Her mother, Elizabeth Bruce Hoag, from Rochester, N. Y., was gifted with pen and voice, and was a high official in the Woman's Foreign Missionary Society of her church. At the age of twelve Ella went to Albion College, Albion, Mich., and was graduated in 1871. In 1873 she was married to L. Hamline Brockway, of Albion, where they lived for fifteen years, when his election as county clerk caused their removal to Marshall. Mr. Brockway died in August, 1887, and Mrs. Brockway with her son, Bruce, aged twelve, and daughter, Ruth, aged six, returned to Albion. In January, 1889, she became preceptress of the college. In that position she displayed great executive ability. Wise in planning, fertile in resources and energetic in execution, her undertakings were successful. She had great power over the young women of the college and exercised that power without apparent effort. She won the friendship of every student, and they all instinctively turned to her for counsel. She had the department of English literature, and also lectured on the history of of music. Her earnestness and enthusiasm were contagious, and her classes always became interested in their studies. Her addresses to the young ladies were especially prized. For ten years she was president of the Woman's Foreign Missionary Society of Albion district. In June, 1891, she resigned her position in Albion College and on 11th August was married to the Rev. Joseph M. Avann, of Findlay, Ohio. As a speaker she is pleasing and fascinating. Occasionally she gives a literary address or speaks in behalf of some benevolent cause away from home. She makes frequent contributions to the religious press, and is connected with various literary, social and benevolent societies, holding official positions.

AVERY, Mrs. Catharine Hitchcock Tilden, author and educator, born in Monroe, Mich., 13th December, 1844. She is the daughter of Hon. Junius Tilden, formerly a prominent lawyer of that State. She was educated in the Framingham Normal School, in Massachusetts, graduating in 1867. In 1870, she was married to Dr. Elroy M. Avery. He was for several years principal of the East high school and City Normal School, of Cleveland, Ohio, in which positions his wife was his most able assistant. Dr. Avery is the author of many text-books, notably a series on natural philosophy and chemistry. He is now engaged in historical research and writing, in which Mrs. Avery is his efficient helper. She is president of the East End Conversational, a club organized in 1878 and comprising many of the bright women of the city. She is a member of the executive committee of the Art and History Club and also of the Cleveland Woman's Press Club. She was a delegate from the latter club to the International League of Press Clubs, 1892, and took part in the journey from New York to the Golden Gate. Her letters descriptive of the trip were published in the Cleveland "Leader and Herald." She is the regent of the Cleveland Chapter of the Daughters of the American Revolution. Four of her ancestors served in the Continental Congress and the cause of freedom. Col. John Bailey, of the Second Massachusetts Regiment, was at Bunker Hill and Monmouth, crossed the Delaware with Washington, and was at Gates's side in the northern campaign which ended in Burgoyne's surrender. The Gad Hitchcocks, father and son, served as chaplain and as surgeon. The elder Gad, in 1774, preached an election sermon in which he advocated the cause of the Colonies and brought forth the wrath of Gage and the thanks of the Massachusetts General Court. Samuel Tilden, private from Marshfield, and member of the Committee of Safety, completes the list of her Revolutionary ancestors. Descended from six

of the "Mayflower" band, she is proud of the Pilgrim blood that flows in her veins. She has been for twenty years a member of the Euclid Avenue Congregational Church of Cleveland. Mrs.

CATHERINE HITCHCOCK TILDEN AVERY.

Avery's father died in the spring of 1861. Her husband, when a boy of sixteen years, went to the war, in 1861, with the first company that left his native town. He was mustered out of service in August, 1865.

AVERY, Mrs. Rachel Foster, woman suffragist, born in Pittsburgh, Pa., 30th December, 1858. Her father was J. Heron Foster, of the Pittsburgh "Dispatch." Her mother was a native of Johnstown, N. Y., the birthplace of her Sunday-school teacher and life-long friend, Elizabeth Cady Stanton. When Rachel was a child, Mrs. Stanton lectured in Pittsburgh. Shortly after, a suffrage meeting was held in Mrs. Foster's house, and a society was formed of which she was made vice-president. Thus the young girl grew up in an atmosphere of radicalism and advanced thought. That she is a woman suffragist comes not only from conviction, but by birth-right as well. In 1871 the family, consisting of her mother, her sister, Julia T., and herself, the father having died shortly before, moved to Philadelphia, where they at once identified themselves with the Citizens' Suffrage Association of that city, in which Lucretia Mott, Edward M. Davis, M. Adeline Thompson and others were leading spirits. Her sister, Julia, was for many years a most efficient secretary of that society as well as recording secretary of the National Woman Suffrage Association, and seconded warmly the more active work of her sister, Rachel G., as did also their mother, Mrs. Julia Foster. Both mother and sister have passed away, but their works live after them. When about seventeen years old, Miss Foster began to write for the news-papers, furnishing letters weekly from California and afterward from Europe to the Pittsburgh

"Leader." Later she took part in the Harvard examinations, traveled extensively in Europe with her mother and sister, and studied political economy in the University of Zurich. In the winter of 1879 she attended for the first time a Washington, D. C., convention of the National Woman Suffrage Association, the eleventh, and the impression she there received determined her career, for she has ever since held high official positions in that powerful association.   With her characteristic promptitude she began at once to plan the series of conventions to be held in the West during the summer of 1880, including the great Farwell Hall meeting in Chicago, during the week of the Republican national nominating convention, the gathering in Cincinnati at the time of the Democratic nominating convention, and the two-day conventions in Bloomington, Ill., in Indianapolis, Terre Haute, and Lafayette, Ind., in Grand Rapids, Mich., and in Milwaukee, Wis.   In the spring of 1881 she planned the series of ten conventions to

RACHEL FOSTER AVERY.

be held in the different New England States, beginning with the annual meeting of the National Woman Suffrage Association in Tremont Temple, Boston, during the May anniversary week.   In 1882 she conducted the Nebraska amendment campaign, with headquarters in Omaha, making all the appointments for the twelve speakers to be employed by the National Association during the last six weeks before the election.   To secure the best leaflet possible, she engaged Gov. John W. Hoyt, of Wyoming, to give a lecture in Philadelphia on "The good results of thirteen years experience of woman's voting in Wyoming Territory," had the lecture stenographically reported, collected the money to publish 20,000 copies, and scattered them broadcast over the State of Pennsylvania.   On the morning of 22nd February, 1883, Miss Foster sailed for Europe with "Aunt Susan," as she always affectionately called Miss Anthony, and with her

superior linguistic attainments she served as ears and tongue for her companion in their journeyings through France, Italy, Switzerland and Germany. Miss Foster's management of the International Council of Women, held in Washington, D. C., in February, 1888, under the auspices of the National Woman Suffrage Association, was the crowning effort of her executive genius. There were forty-nine official delegates to that council, representing fifty-three different societies from seven distinct nationalities. The expense of this meeting made a grand total of fourteen-thousand dollars, the financial risk of which was beforehand assumed by Miss Anthony, supported by Miss Foster. Although Mrs. Foster-Avery devotes her best energies to the suffrage cause, she does not confine to that one channel her "enthusiasm of humanity." She is a philanthropist in the broadest sense. Of her independent fortune she contributes most liberally, of course, to her best loved work, but she also gives largely to numerous reforms and charities that commend themselves to her interest and approbation. In 1887 she adopted a baby girl of five months and gave her the name of Miriam Alice Foster. In her marriage with Cyrus Miller Avery, which took place 8th November, 1888, Miss Foster entered a life companionship full of sympathy with her special aims and interests, for of Mr. Avery it may be said as surely as of herself that he is "a woman suffragist, not only by conviction, but by birthright as well." Mr. Avery had accompanied his mother, Mrs. Rosa Miller Avery, president of the Anthony Club, of Chicago, to the International Council, and his association with Miss Foster there furnished the romance of the occasion which culminated in their union a few months later. In strict accordance with the past life of the bride was the ceremony which was performed by the Rev. Charles G. Ames, pastor of the First Unitarian Church, Chicago, assisted by Rev. Anna H. Shaw, the only woman in holy orders in the Methodist Protestant church of the United States. Immediately after their marriage, Mr. Avery took legal steps to add his name to that of his wife's adopted child. They have two children of their own, Rose Foster Avery and Julia Foster Avery. Mrs. Foster-Avery at present holds the office of corresponding secretary, not only of the National Suffrage Association, but also of the National and of the International Councils of Women, each of which three bodies is to hold a convocation in Chicago in 1893. The "Transactions of the National Council of Women of the United States, assembled in Washington, D. C., February 22nd to 25th, 1891" (Philadelphia 1891), was edited by Mrs. Foster-Avery.

AVERY, Mrs. Rosa Miller, reformer, born in Madison, Ohio, 21st May, 1830. From her maternal grandfather, James McDonald, she inherited a strong love of animals. Cattle-shows and horse-fairs are a special delight to her, and the name of Henry Bergh is immortalized in her calendar of saints. Her father, Nahum Miller, was an insatiable reader of Biblical and political history and a man of broad humanitarian views. His love of children was the ruling passion of his life, and he adopted two in addition to five children of his own. His wife cheerfully bore the burden his benevolence imposed upon the household, only hinting, now and then, that "the laws pertaining to property and the holding of children were as oppressive for women as for negroes." Rosa pondered these sayings in her heart, and always speaks of her mother as her inspiration to work for woman's advancement. Reared in the atmosphere of such a home, she went forth to radiate the light she had received, and bless the world, but her anti-slavery sentiments and essays met with derision and abuse. Years later two class students confessed to her that her anti-slavery papers induced them to

ROSA MILLER AVERY.

give up their ambition for the pulpit to study law and politics. They became famous on the battle-field and did signal service throughout the Civil War. She never charged the sin of slavery to the door of the Southern people, but maintained that the spirit of slavery was everywhere present in any and every form of injustice. It was confined and sectional in the case of the poor blacks, because "Cotton was King" and so controlled New England manufactories, and the manhood of the entire nation paid tribute. Rosa was married 1st September, 1853, to Cyrus Avery, of Oberlin, Ohio. During their residence in Ashtabula, Ohio, she organized the first anti-slavery society ever known in that village, and not a clergyman in the place would give notice of its meetings so late as two years before the war; and that, too, in the county home of Giddings and Wade, those well-known apostles of freedom. The leading men of wealth and influence were so indignant because the churches would not read a notice of her missionary effort for our black heathen, that they counseled together and withdrew from their respective churches and built a handsome brick church edifice for the congregational sentiment of the town, which was decidedly anti-slavery. During the years of the war Mrs. Avery's pen was actively engaged in writing for various journals on the subject of union and emancipation, under male signatures, so as to command attention. Her letters and other articles attracted the notice of Gov. Richard Yates, of Illinois, James A. Garfield, James Redpath and Lydia Maria Child, all of whom sent her appreciative letters, with their portraits, which are still preserved as sacred souvenirs of those stormy days. During ten years' residence in Erie, Pa.,

besides writing occasional articles for the newspaper world, she disseminated her views on social questions, love, matrimony and religion in romance to the high-school graduates, of which her son was a member, in their organ, the "High School News," over the pen-name, "Sue Smith." work which produced much and rich fruition in the years following. About that time her husband was appointed by the Young Men's Christian Association of Erie as visitor to the criminals confined in the city prison. Mrs. Avery usually assisted her husband in this work and became much interested in the underlying motives and allurements to crime. As the result of her investigation, she has ever since maintained, "that there is not a criminal on this broad earth but that there lies back of him a crime greater than he represents and for which he, we, and everyone suffers in a greater or less degree." For the last fourteen years Mr. and Mrs. Avery have resided in Chicago. Mrs. Avery's special labors have been largely for social purity and suffrage work. The many and ably written articles and responses to the opponents of franchise for women, which have appeared from time to time in the Chicago "Inter-Ocean" under her signature, have sown much seed broadcast in favor of equal suffrage and have borne much fruit in favor of municipal and school suffrage. Mrs. Avery is very domestic in her tastes, and few can equal her as a caterer or excel her in domestic economy. Her "Rose Cottage," facing Lake Michigan, is an ideal home.

AYER, Mrs. Harriet Hubbard, business woman and journalist, born in Chicago, Ill., in 1852. Her maiden name was Hubbard. The Hubbard family tree extended back without a break to 1590. About 1844 its then youngest offshoot

HARRIET HUBBARD AYER.

left New England for Chicago and there his youngest daughter was born. She was educated in the Convent of the Sacred Heart, where she was graduated at fifteen years of age, and soon after was married to Mr. Ayer. Her social life was distinguished. Her husband's wealth enabled her to train and gratify her taste and love for beauty, and her home became a house famous for its refinement and hospitality. She was then, as now, a many-sided woman. Her husband depended upon her and owed much of his fortune to her guidance. In every philanthropic effort her name was in the forefront of those who gave and those who did. An indefatigable student always, her reading covered the literature of all time. In painting and in plastic art, in crystal and in porcelain, in fabrics and in form, her judgment acquired a mathematical exactness. Her frequent trips abroad made London, Paris, Vienna and Rome second homes to her. She speaks a half-dozen languages. Reverses came in 1882 and Mr. Ayer failed for several millions. Disheartened by the blow, he became a wreck. Mrs. Ayer gave up to her husband's creditors much that she might have legally claimed as her own. Without a dollar and with two little daughters dependent upon her, she went from a home of luxury into the arena in which men fight for bread. There she fought and won the fight. She became a business woman of the highest type of the present, without ceasing to be the gentlewoman of the past. A few weeks after the failure she was a saleswoman in a leading shop in New York. For eight hours a day, and sometimes for fourteen, she worked behind the counter, returning to the tiny apartment where she, her mother and her children were attended by a solitary maid-of-all-work, to write letters, sketches, essays and editorials by the weary hour. Within a year she had an income from her salary in the shop, from the agreed-upon commissions on her sales, from her pen, and from a successful real estate operation, devised and carried out by herself, of more than ten-thousand dollars a year. Such a success is almost beyond belief, as it is almost without a parallel. The strain upon her health was too great. A change became inevitable. She decided to leave the shop and begin to buy goods and furnish houses for her friends upon commission. She succeeded in this departure also, and was soon able to take a house of her own. In an unfortunate moment for herself she offered the Récamier toilet preparations to the public. An unfortunate moment, first, because within a month the house was filled from top to bottom with women trying to manufacture them fast enough to meet the public demand, so that the home ceased to be a home. An unfortunate moment again, because the rapidity with which the Récamier preparations began to make her fortune excited the avarice of some of the assistants whom she had gathered about her, and led to a conspiracy to capture the Récamier Company. The careless generosity with which she had given away some shares of her stock in the company was abused. A desperate, determined fight was made to wrest the control of the company from her and to deprive her of all share in the profits of her industry and her brain. Mrs. Ayer discovered this conspiracy while in Europe. She returned to find her business in the possession of her foes, her offices barricaded against her, and her money used to hire lawyers to rob her of her rights. Alone, ill, reduced to absolute poverty a second time, this undaunted woman showed that the blood of the Hubbards, which had flowed through soldiers' veins in 1776, in 1812, in 1846 and in 1861, was fighting blood still. At once she began the fight, one against many, a pauper against millionaires, and won. The court found that she was absolutely right and her adversaries absolutely wrong. Every claim she made was conceded. At the close of the litigation she was again in possession as sole owner of the business, the offices and the money. Since that victory Mrs. Ayer has devoted herself to extending and increasing the work of the Récamier Company, of which she is the president and chief owner. The company occupies a five-story building on Fifth avenue and a factory on Thirty-first street, New York, and employs about fifty people. The Récamier toilet preparations are bought and sold as standard pharmaceutical compounds in the United States and over all the world. The company stands as a monument to a fight won by a woman. Mrs. Ayer is in the prime of life and superintends personally every department of her great business.

BABCOCK, Mrs. Elnora Monroe, woman suffragist, born in Columbus, Pa., 11th January, 1852. Her maiden name was Monroe. She was married at the early age of eighteen to Prof. John W. Babcock, of Jamestown, N. Y., who for the last

ELNORA MONROE BABCOCK.

twelve years has been city superintendent of public schools in Dunkirk, N. Y., where they now live. From early girlhood she felt the injustice of denying to woman a voice in government, which concerned her the same as a man, but as her time was taken up to a great extent in household affairs, and she lived in a community where but few sympathized with that feeling and none were ready to come out and take a stand for freedom, she took no very active part in the reforms of the day until 1889, when, owing mainly to her efforts, a political equality club was organized in Dunkirk, of which she was made president. This club flourished remarkably under her management, and before the close of her first year as president of the Dunkirk club, she was elected president of the Chautauqua County Political Equality Club, the most thoroughly organized county in the United States, having twenty-five flourishing local clubs within its borders and a membership of 1,400. At the close of her first year as president of that club she was unanimously re-elected. That office she still holds. On 25th July, 1891, she had the honor of presiding over the first woman suffrage meeting ever held at the great Chautauqua Assembly, where, through the request of the county club, the subject was allowed to be advocated. Aside from the presidency of these clubs, she has served upon a number of important committees connected with suffrage work. Although deeply interested in all the reforms of the day tending to the uplifting of humanity, she has devoted most of her time to the enfranchisement of woman believing this to be the most important reform before the American people to-day, and one upon which all other reforms rest.

BABCOCK, Mrs. Emma Whitcomb, author, born in Adams, N. Y., 24th April, 1849. She is now a resident of Oil City, Pa., in which town her husband, C. A. Babcock, is superintendent of schools. As a writer, Mrs. Babcock has been before the public for years, and has contributed to journals and magazines, besides doing good work as a book-reviewer, but is probably best known through her series of unsigned articles which during five years appeared in the New York "Evening Post." She was a contributor to the first number of "Babyhood" and also of the "Cosmopolitan." She has published one volume, "Household Hints" (1891), and is about to issue another, "A Mother's Note Book." At present she is conducting a department in the "Homemaker." Mrs. Babcock has written a novel, which embodies many distinctive features of the oil country. Her husband's profession turned her attention to educational subjects, and she has published many articles in the technical journals on those subjects. She is

EMMA WHITCOMB BABCOCK.

interested in home mission work and is president of a literary club which is known throughout western Pennsylvania, and which has founded a public library.

BABCOCK, Mrs. Helen Louise B., dramatic reader, born in Galva, Ill., 13th August, 1867. Her maiden name was Bailey. She early displayed a marked talent for elocution and on reaching

HELEN LOUISE B. BABCOCK.

woman's estate she decided to make dramatic reading her profession. With that aim she became a pupil in the Cumnock School of Oratory of the Northwestern University, and, being an earnest student, she was graduated with the highest honors. Afterwards she became an assistant instructor in the same oratorical school and was very successful in the delicate and difficult work of developing elocutionary and dramatic talents in others. Perfectly familiar with the work, she was able to guide students rapidly over the rough places and start them on the high road to success. After severing her connection with the Cumnock school, she taught for a time in Mount Vernon Seminary, Washington, D. C. After the death of her mother, in 1890, she accompanied her father abroad and spent some time in visiting the principal countries of Europe. In 1891 she was married to Dr. F. C. Babcock, of Hastings, Neb., where they now live.

BAER, Mrs. Libbie C. Riley, poet, born near Bethel, Clermont county, Ohio, 18th November, 1849. Her ancestors on the paternal side were the two families Riley and Swing. From the original family of the former descended the distinguished poet and humorist, James Whitcomb Riley, and from the latter the eminent philosopher and preacher, Prof. David Swing, of Chicago. On the maternal side Mrs. Baer is a descendant of the Blairs, an old and favorably known family of southern Ohio. It is not surprising, therefore, that through early associations, combined with a natural taste and aptitude for literary work, her genius for poetry was shown during childhood. Her first poem, written when she was scarcely ten years of age, was a spontaneous and really remarkable production for one so young. In November, 1867, she was married to Capt. John M. Baer, an officer with gallant military record. She went with her husband to Appleton, Wis., where they still reside. Upon the organization of the Woman's Relief Corps, as allied with the G. A. R., Mrs. Baer took an important part in the benevolent work of that order, and has held various responsible positions connected therewith, devoting much time and energy to the cause, solely as a labor of love. Though always proficient in poetical composition, she really began her literary career during the last decade, and the favor with which her poems have been received proves the merit of her productions.

BAGG, Miss Clara B., pianist and music teacher, born in New York City, 26th September, 1861. Her life has been passed in her native city with the exception of a brief residence in Orange, N. J., and a residence in Brooklyn, N. Y., where her family spent several years. She showed remarkable musical talents at an early age, and as a child she was a skillful pianist, playing difficult classical music with correct expression and great taste. When she was eleven years old, she was placed under training with competent teachers of the piano, and her progress in that art has been rapid and remarkable, her technical and expressional talents seeming to burst at once into full flower. Enthusiastic in her love of music, she has studied earnestly and thoroughly. From the last of her instructors, Rafael Joseffy, she absorbed much of that artist's power, technical skill, fire, force and delicacy. To this she adds her own talent, equipping her for success as a concert performer and as a teacher. She has become well known in the metropolis in both capacities. Although she does not intend to make concert playing her profession, she has appeared

ALICE BAGGETT.

BAGGETT, Mrs. Alice, educator, born in Soccapatoy, Coosa county, Ala., 184-. Her maiden name was Alice Phillips. On her mother's side she is descended from the Scotch families of Campbell, McNeill, Wade, and Hampton, of Virginia. On her father's side her ancestors were the Dowds and Phillipses, of North Carolina. Her father, James D. Phillips, was a Whig who clung to the Union and the Constitution, doing all that lay in his power to avert the Civil War. Alice, just out of school, was full of the secessionist spirit, but a strong advocate of peace. Her early desire to enter the profession of teacher was opposed by her parents, but she resolved to follow her inclination, when, at the close of the Civil War, her family shared in the general desolation that lay upon the South. She became a teacher and for several years made successful use of her varied attainments. In 1868 she was married to A. J. Baggett, continuing her school work after marriage. In a few years her husband became an invalid and Mrs. Baggett then showed her mettle. She cared for her family of three children and assisted her brothers and sisters to get their education. Her husband died in 1875. Since that time she has served mainly as principal of high schools in Alabama. She has done much work for the orphans of Freemasons, to which order her husband had belonged. Wherever she has worked, she has organized, systematized and revolutionized educational matters. She now resides in St. Augustine, Fla., where her work is highly successful. Her family consists of one surviving daughter.

BAGLEY, Mrs. Blanche Pentecost, Unitarian minister, born in Torquay, England, 19th January, 1858. Her father is the Rev. R. T. Pentecost, a Unitarian minister, now of Salem, Mass. Miss Pentecost received her early education partly in private schools in London, England, where her family then resided, and partly in a French

CLARA B. BAGG.

with success in Orange, N. J., in Brooklyn, N. Y., and during the winter of 1891-92 in New York City. As a teacher she is quite as enthusiastic as she is in the rôle of a performer.

college in Avenches, Canton Vaud, Switzerland, from which she was graduated. In 1882 the family came to this country and made their home in Chicago, where three of her brothers, architects, still

BLANCHE PENTECOST BAGLEY.

reside. Blanche Pentecost, like the rest of her family, was brought up in the Established Church of England, but she became a Unitarian while visiting a sister, whose husband, the Rev. F. B. Mott, was then studying for the Unitarian ministry. By them she was induced to enter the Meadville Theological School, from which institution she was graduated in 1889. She had first met her future husband, the Rev. James E. Bagley, in Meadville, where they had entered and left school together. Her first experience of preaching, outside of the college chapel, was in Vermont, in the little town of Middlesex, where she spent the summer of 1887. After her graduation she took up work as a minister in Reedsburg, Wis. There she continued until her marriage, on 4th September, 1889, when she accompanied her husband to All Souls Church, Sioux Falls, S. D., to which he had received a call. Mr. and Mrs. Bagley were ordained and installed together there as joint pastors on 17th November, the same year, the ceremony being the first of that kind in the history of the world. It was, however, only returning to the New Testament custom of sending the disciples out two by two. During their residence in South Dakota Mrs. Bagley took an active interest in all public questions and moral reforms in that State. She usually conducted the evening services in the church and occasionally assisted in the morning service. She was also assistant superintendent of the Sunday-school, chairman of the executive board of the Unity Club a literary organization, a charter member of the board of directors of the Woman's Benevolent Association, a member of the Minister's Association, and with her husband, joint chairman of the executive committee of the Equal Suffrage Association.

She was a member of the Relief Corps, of which, a short time before she left the city, she became chaplain. While in Sioux Falls she made the acquaintance of Susan B. Anthony, and the Rev. Anna Shaw, and had the honor of introducing both of these speakers to Sioux Falls audiences. During the first year of her married life she took part in the ordination of two other woman ministers, the Rev. Helene Putnam and the Rev. Lila Frost-Sprague, both of whom had been college friends. Her home is now in Haverhill, Mass., where her husband in 1890 was installed pastor of the First Parish Church. They have two children, and Mrs. Bagley is naturally much occupied, as she feels that home duties have the first claim upon her, but she finds time for some outside work, occasionally taking her husband's pulpit and conducting the afternoon service at a little church in the outskirts of the city. She is also local superintendent of the department of scientific temperance instruction in connection with the Woman's Christian Temperance Union. Mrs. Bagley is an accomplished pianist and has an inherited gift for painting which she has found time to cultivate. She has a vigorous constitution and an unusually strong, clear contralto voice, with a distinct articulation, which makes it easy for her to be heard by the largest audiences.

BAILEY, Mrs. Ann, scout, said to have been born in Liverpool, England, about 1725, died in Hamson township, Gullia county, Ohio, 23rd November, 1825.

BAILEY, Mrs. Anna Warner, patriot, born in Groton, Conn., 11th October, 1758, and died there in 1850.

BAILEY, Miss Ellene Alice, inventor, born in Pond Fort, St. Charles county, Mo. She is

ELLENE ALICE BAILEY.

the third daughter of the late Judge Robert Bailey and Lucinda Zumwalt. Pond Fort was founded by her grandfather, Robert Bailey. Her father was a man of liberal thought with an appreciative interest in all new ideas. An owner of slaves, through the force of circumstances rather than from inclination, he and his son Robert were among the first to advocate their freedom. Her father's ancestors were English, her mother's German. Miss Bailey's first invention was the "Pond Fort" boot, a high boot reaching to the knee and close-fitting about the ankle, on which she obtained an American and a Canadian patent in 1880. The next thing was to put it upon the market and that led her to remove to New York. Her second invention was the "Pond Lily powder puff," patented in 1882. Later she invented another puff, the "Thistledown." An interest in this she sold for a fair price. In the spring of 1889 she improved and simplified these two puffs, bringing out the "Floral" puff. In the summer of 1891 she invented and patented the very best of all, the "Dainty" powder puff. These all proved of commercial value. One of her principal inventions is the "Dart" needle for sewing on shoe and other buttons, patented in 1884, 1886 and 1888. The man who undertook the setting up of her machinery and the manufacture of the needle, departed abruptly about the time things were ready for business, leaving no one who understood the mechanism. The inventor rose to the occasion and made the first sixty-thousand needles herself. There was more than one crisis to meet, and she met them all in the same business-like way. For the past three years the needles have been made by a well-known New England firm, and are staple goods. Another patented article, which is successful, is a device for holding on rubber overshoes. One of the ways in which she increased her resources was by designing useful articles for a novelty-loving public. The list includes a silver whisk-broom, patented in 1887, and several other novelties filled with perfume; a music roll which was used first as a Christmas card and then as an Easter card; a shaving case; a manicure case; a wall album for photographs; a desk holder for stationery; a work box; a perforated felt chest protector; a sleeve holder; a corset shield, patented in 1885; copyright photographs of Martha Washington and Mrs. Cleveland; odd novelty clocks; chains for holding drapery; ornamental tables, inkstands, screens, easels and unique boxes for holding candies, a hand pinking device (1892); a leg protector made of water-proof cloth, a combination of legging and over-gaiter (1892). She has also taken several crude designs of other inventors and improved them so as to make them salable and profitable. Miss Bailey enjoys the friendship of many of the most womanly women of the country, and she has the respect and confidence of the largest business houses. Her inventions have proved not only useful and practical, but of commercial importance. She is a member of Grace Episcopal Church, New York, and also a member of the Young Woman's Christian Association, in which she is greatly interested. She finds time to keep in touch with whatever is newest and best, and writes an occasional article for the press.

BAILEY, Mrs. Hannah J., philanthropist and reformer, born in Cornwall-on-the-Hudson, N. Y., 5th July, 1839. Her maiden name was Hannah Clark Johnston, and she was the oldest of a family of eleven children. Her parents were David and Letitia Johnston. Mr. Johnston was by occupation a tanner, but in 1853 he became a farmer, locating in Plattekill, Ulster county, N. Y. He was a minister in the Society of Friends, and on Sundays the family worshiped in the quiet little church near their home. Hannah passed her busy and studious girlhood on the homestead, and in

1858 she began to teach school. She continued to teach successfully until 1867. In that year she accompanied a woman preacher on a mission to the churches and institutions for criminals and for charity, within the limits of the New England Yearly Meeting of Friends. While on that mission, she met Moses Bailey, a noble and active Christian, to whom she was married in October, 1868. A peaceful, useful train of years followed until his death, in 1882, and she was left with one son, Moses Melvin Bailey, then twelve years of age. At the time of her husband's death Mrs. Bailey was very ill, but afterwards rallied to gather up the threads of his life-work and her own, and since then she has carried them steadily forward. Her husband's oil-cloth manufactury, and also a retail carpet store in Portland, Maine, was carried on under her management until, in 1889, she sold the manufacturing establishment, and in 1891 her son assumed the care and possession of the business in

HANNAH J. BAILEY.

Portland. For thirty years she has been a Sabbath-school teacher, and she continually adds new branches to her church work, holding positions on the Providence and Oak Grove Boarding School committees, and on other important committees of the church and other philanthropic organizations. She is treasurer of the Woman's Foreign Missionary Society of the New England Yearly Meeting of Friends and is always active in its interests. In 1883 Mrs. Bailey joined the Woman's Christian Temperance Union and entered heartily into its work of reform. She was always a strong advocate of peace principles, and in 1887, when the department of peace and arbitration was created, she was appointed superintendent of it. In 1888 she was made the superintendent of that department for the World's Woman's Christian Temperance Union. With active brain, willing heart and generous hand, she prosecutes this work, employing a private secretary, editing and publishing two monthly papers, "The Pacific Banner" and "The Acorn," besides millions of pages of literature. She is State superintendent of the Sabbath observance department of the Maine Woman's Christian Temperance Union, and is also working diligently in the interests of securing a reformatory prison for women in her State. She is the author of "Reminiscences of a Christian Life" (1884). In every branch of philanthropic work she is found to be interested. For the church, for the school, for the young man or woman who is striving for an education, her heart and purse are always open. Her home is in Winthrop Center, Maine.

BAILEY, Mrs. Lepha Eliza, author and lecturer, born in Battle Creek, Mich., 21st January,

LEPHA ELIZA BAILEY.

1845. Her maiden name was Dunton. Her father was of Scotch descent. Both parents were born and reared in Georgia, Vt., and their family consisted of nine children, all born in Georgia, Vt. except Mrs. Bailey, the youngest. From Vermont her parents removed, with their entire family, to Battle Creek in the fall of 1840. Michigan was at that time an unbroken wilderness. In early life Miss Dunton became a contributor to local papers. On 21st October, 1873, she was married to Lewis Bailey, of Battle Creek. Four children were born to them, two of whom died in infancy. Mrs. Bailey was a useful member of many local organizations, including the Woman's Christian Temperance Union, Sovereigns of Industry, Independent Order of Good Templars, and Grangers, and was an officer of each. When the red-ribbon movement became prominent Mrs. Bailey took an active interest in its development, and she dates her present work as a speaker from her local labor for the Woman's Christian Temperance Union and red-ribbon clubs. At that time Mrs. Bailey edited a department in "Our Age," published at Battle Creek, this she continued for three years. In 1876–77 she wrote much for the "Grange Visitor," and gave talks

upon the labor question before assemblies of Grangers, at that time flourishing in Michigan. In 1878 she was invited by the State amendment committee, to canvass her own county on the question of a prohibitory amendment submitted to the people. She gave two-hundred lectures, speaking in every city, village and school district. For two years previous Mrs. Bailey had been speaking occasionally upon the temperance question and woman suffrage, but her active public work began with the amendment campaign in her own State, since which time she has been constantly in field service, having been actively engaged in every State where an amendment campaign has been inaugurated. In 1880 Mrs. Bailey was invited to speak under the auspices of the National Prohibition Alliance. She responded, and worked in the East until that society disbanded, and finally merged with the Prohibition Party, under whose auspices she is at present employed.

BAILEY, Mrs. Sara Lord, elocutionist and teacher of dramatic elocution, born in Tottington, near Bury, England, 9th September, 1856. She is the only child of Mr. and Mrs. Daniel Lord, her parents bringing her to the United States the year following her birth and making their home in Lawrence, Mass., where they now reside. She early showed a fondness and talent for dramatic elocution, and it was developed by her participation in amateur plays given in Lawrence under the auspices of the Grand Army posts. She was educated in the Oliver grammar school, passing thence to Lasell Seminary, Auburndale, Mass., where she studied two years. She afterwards studied under the best teachers of elocution in Boston, and was graduated in 1888 from the Boston School of Ora-

SARA LORD BAILEY.

tory. A few years ago she was married to Elbridge E. Bailey, and in 1882 to benefit Mr. Bailey's health they went to the Sandwich Islands where they lived for nearly two years. They were present at the coronation ceremonies of the king and queen in Iolani palace, 12th February, 1883. In 1884 they returned to the United States, and Mr. Bailey went into business in St. Louis, Mo., where Mrs. Bailey taught elocution most successfully in the Mission School for the Blind. They afterwards removed to Kansas City, where Mr. Bailey has built up a flourishing business. Mrs. Bailey for some time taught elocution and voice-culture in the school of oratory there, but was obliged to return to Massachusetts on account of her failing health. She is devoted to her profession, having several large classes in elocution in Lawrence, besides fulfilling engagements to read in various cities.

BAKER, Mrs. Charlotte Johnson, physician, born in Newburyport, Mass., 30th March, 1855. Her maiden name was Charlotte Le Breton Johnson. She was graduated from the Newburyport high school in 1872, spent a year in teaching, and entered Vassar College in 1873. She was grad-

CHARLOTTE JOHNSON BAKER.

uated from that institution in 1877 with the degree of B.A. During the college year of 1877-78 she served as instructor in gymnastics in Vassar. In 1878 and 1879 she was assistant to Dr. Eliza M. Mosher, surgeon in the Woman's Reformatory Prison in Sherbourne, Mass. In the fall of 1879 she entered with advanced standing the medical department of the University of Michigan, from which institution she was graduated in 1881 with the degree of M.D. She returned to Newburyport and in 1882 was married to Dr. Fred Baker and they went to Akron, O. Threatened failure of health caused her to go to New Mexico, where she lived in the mountains for five years. Early in 1888 she and her husband moved to San Diego, Cal., where both are engaged in successful practice as physicians. Their family consists of two children. In 1889 Dr. Charlotte received the degree of A.M. from Vassar College for special work in optics and ophthalmology done after graduation.

Besides her professional work, Dr. Baker has always identified herself with the Woman's Christian Temperance Union and with all other movements for the advancement of women individually, socially and politically.

BAKER, Mrs. Harriette Newell Woods, author, born in Andover, Mass., in 1815. She has published, under the pen-name "Mrs. Madeline Leslie," nearly two-hundred moral and religious tales. She has also written under her own name or initials, and under that of "Aunt Hattie."

BAKER, Miss Ida Wikoff, business woman, born in Decatur, Ill., 31st July, 1859. Her father, Peter Montfort Wikoff, was a native of Warren county, Ohio, who removed with his father to Illinois while quite young. He was a descendant of Peter Cloesen Wikoff, who came from Holland in 1636 and settled on Long Island, where he held a position under the Dutch Government. He married Margaret Van Ness. Mrs. Baker's mother, whose maiden name was Elizabeth Fletcher, was born near Crotches' Ferry, Md. On 25th April, 1878, Ida was married to Joseph N. Baker, then a merchant of Decatur, and now connected with the Citizens' National Bank. Of two children born to them, one, a daughter aged nine, is living. In 1889 Mrs. Baker's sister, Miss Laura B. Wikoff, set on foot a plan to organize a stock company composed of women only, for the purpose of promoting the industrial, educational and social advancement of women, and for literary, scientific and musical culture in the city of Decatur. Articles of incorporation were issued to the Woman's Club Stock Company 15th August, 1889, and a building was finished and occupied by the first tenant 1st November, 1890. Mrs. Baker was named one of the nine directors at the first annual meeting, was elected secretary of the stock company 12th January, 1891, and has served in that capacity ever since. In December, 1889, the Woman's Exchange was established as a branch of the Industrial and Charitable Union. Mrs. Baker was elected president and served until forced by illness to resign. After partly regaining her health, she served as treasurer and business manager. She is a member of the Woman's Club, of the Order of the Eastern Star, and of the Woman's Christian Temperance Union. Her life is one of constant activity.

BAKER, Miss Joanna, linguist and educator, born in New Rochelle, Ogle county, Ill., 14th February, 1862. She is professor of Greek, language, literature and philosophy in Simpson College, Indianola, Iowa. Her name has come conspicuously before the public on account of her early and unusual proficiency in ancient and modern languages. Her parents, Orlando H. and Mary C. Ridley Baker, were both teachers and linguists, and began to instruct her in Greek and Latin as soon as she could speak English clearly. Her father for her amusement taught her, instead of Mother Goose melodies, the conjugation of the verb in Greek and Latin, which she learned merely from the rhythm. It was in her fourth year she was put to the systematic study of three languages, one lesson each day except Sunday. Mondays and Thursdays it was Greek, Tuesdays and Fridays, Latin, and Wednesdays and Saturdays, French. This system of instruction was continued with only the variation of oral exercises, and with scarcely ever an intermission, for several years. The lessons assigned were short, but the standard was perfection. She learned her lessons so easily that it took but a small part of the morning, and she seemed to have as much time for voluntary reading and childish amusements, of which she was very fond, as those children who had no studies. Before she was eight years old, she had thoroughly finished the primary books in Greek, Latin and French. She had read, besides, in Greek the first book of Xeno-

President Berry tutor of Greek. This was the occasion of the first public notice taken of her early linguistic attainments. The notice made of her in the Indianola "Herald" was copied with comments and variations all over America and in many countries of Europe. At eighteen years of age she published an original literal translation of Plato's Apology, which received commendation from eminent Greek scholars. Some years before she had begun the study of music and German. This language became a favorite and she soon acquired a speaking knowledge of it. In 1881 she entered Cornell College, Iowa, and in 1882 graduated, receiving the degree of A.B. She entered DePauw University in 1886, for special instruction in Greek, German, French and music. After two years of study, during which she acted as tutor of Greek, she received the degree of A.M. *pro merito*, was admitted an alumna of that university, *ad eundem gradum*, and was elected instructor of Latin by the board of trustees, in which position she served for one year. She was re-elected the second year, but, having received an offer of the chair of Greek in Simpson College, a position her father had filled twenty years before, she accepted the latter. A year after she lost her mother to whom she was affectionately attached. She has three younger sisters. The older, Myra, is now professor of German and French in Napa College, California, and the other two are still at home, students in college. Miss Baker is a clear, forcible writer and a ready speaker. Her public lectures are well attended. She is an interesting conversationist, has a pleasing address and is unassuming. She is popular with her students and imbues them with her own enthusiasm and love for the Greek language and its literature.

JOANNA BAKER.

phon's Anabasis and three books of Homer's Iliad. In Latin she had read Harkness' Reader entire, the first book of Cæsar, and two books of Virgil's Æneid. She took daily grammar lessons in Hadley's Greek grammar and Harkness' Latin, and all the grammatical references and notes annexed to the texts both of Latin and Greek. She had read in French a book of fables and stories, and learned Fasquelle's French course. Homer, Virgil and Fasquelle were recited with college classes. These were her studies in language before her eighth birthday. Her parents removed to Algona, Iowa, where she became a student in Algona College. At the age of twelve years, besides the above studies, she had read other books of Homer and Virgil, Herodotus, Memorabilia, Demosthenes de Corona, Sallust, Cicero de Senectute et Amicitia, Orations against Catiline, with frequent exercise in Latin and Greek composition. It is not to be supposed that she was wholly occupied with classical studies. She was initiated early into the mysteries of practical housekeeping, from the kitchen up. She read history, biography and such current literature as fell into her hands, and was always ready to take her place with girls of her age in excursions and sports. At twelve years of age she began to study arithmetic and finished it so far as the subject of interest in three months. She took up algebra, geometry and trigonometry in rapid succession, and showed as much ability in mathematics as in languages. Before her fourteenth year she had read several times over Œdipus Tyrannus in Greek, and made a complete lexicon of it, with critical notes on the text. At sixteen she had read most of the Greek and Latin of a college course and, having returned to Simpson College, was appointed by

JULIE WETHERILL BAKER.

She organized all students of Greek in the college into a club called "Hoi Hellenikoi," especially for the study of Greek home life and customs, mythology and civil polity; and to gain familiarity with choice passages from the best authors in the original Greek. Miss Baker is fond of company, plays the piano and violin, and sings. She is a devoted Christian, a member of the Methodist Church, and an enthuiastic worker in the Epworth League and the Sunday-school.

BAKER, Mrs. Julie Wetherill, author, born in Woodville, Miss., in 1858. Her birthplace was the home of her distinguished grandfather, Cotesworth Pinckney Smith, chief-justice of the State of Mississippi. Her maiden name was Julie K. Wetherill. Born in Mississippi and reared partly in that State, and partly in Philadelphia, Pa., the home of her Quaker ancestor, Samuel Wetherill, she shows in her writings the dual influence of her early surroundings. Five years ago she became the wife of Marion A. Baker, literary editor of the New Orleans "Times-Democrat." Mrs. Baker writes over the unassuming disguise of three initials, "J. K. W.," mainly for the New Orleans "Times-Democrat," in its Sunday issue, and is a keen, cultured critic. The "Bric-a-Brac" department of the "Times-Democrat" is an authority in the South on all matters of current literature. Mrs. Baker is not only a literary authority in New Orleans, but is a general favorite in its most refined circles.

BAKER, Miss Louise S., Congregational minister, born in Nantucket, Mass., 17th October,

LOUISE S. BAKER.

1846. Her parents were Arvin and Jerusha Baker, the latter of Quaker descent, and the former a Methodist in faith and a man of broad spirit. Louise was the only daughter among five sons. She was educated in Nantucket and was graduated from the high school in 1862. While well versed in mathematics, her specialty showed itself as linguist and elocutionist. She began to teach at eighteen, and at twenty-two was assistant in the high school in Pawtucket, R. I. Later, on account of her mother's semi-invalidism, she remained with her parents at home, receiving private pupils in the languages and

English literature. From 1877 to 1880 she spent much time in Boston, speaking in the interest of the Massachusetts Woman's Christian Temperance Union. She was chosen to read a paper before the Suffolk County Medical Society, calling attention to the lessening of the use of alcohol in medical prescriptions. The paper was well received, and a large edition was printed for circulation. On one of her visits home she was invited to preach in the Baptist church, and subsequently supplied that pulpit many times when the society was without a pastor. In November, 1880, Miss Baker was invited to preach in the First Congregational Church in Nantucket, for one Sunday. She was the acting pastor of the Old North Church for more than seven years, being ordained by that body in 1884. She was a member of the church, having united with it in 1866. Repeated family bereavements caused her to quit active work for a time, and in 1888 she withdrew from pastoral labors. She still responds to frequent demands for pulpit and public service, and the record of her work shows attendance at nearly two-hundred funerals, twenty-one marriages and a number of baptisms. She has preached by invitation in other cities, and is very active in her own community. In the pulpit her manner is earnest, reverent and impressive. She has done considerable literary work in essays and lectures. As a writer, her style is terse and condensed. She has published a volume of poems under the title of "By the Sea." Her home is in Nantucket.

BALDWIN, Mrs. Esther E., missionary, born in Marlton, N. J., 8th November, 1840. Her father, the Rev. M. Jerman, was for many years an honored and successful member of the New Jersey Annual Conference of the Methodist Episcopal Church. Esther was constitutionally frail, sensitive and studious. Her first schooling was given her at home, where was laid the foundation of all her future usefulness. To this was added instruction in the public schools and in an excellent private school in Salem, followed by a full course in Pennington Seminary, New Jersey. She was graduated from that institution in 1859, taking the highest honors. During the next year she became a teacher of higher mathematics, Latin and French in a seminary in Virginia. At the beginning of the Civil War her sympathies were with the North, and she resigned her position and returned home. Mrs. Baldwin became a Christian when only ten years old and united with the church of her parents. In 1862 she was married to the Rev. Dr. S. L. Baldwin, a missionary to China. After her marriage she accompanied her husband to Foochow, China, and at once entered heartily into her work. Besides her domestic responsibilities, she was soon entrusted with the supervision of several day schools and of a class of Bible women who were sent out to read the Bible to their country-women. In her thoughtful survey of the condition of woman and childhood in China, quickened by her personal observation and experience, she became deeply impressed with the need of educated Christian woman physicians. She saw that through this means access and confidence could be gained and the way opened for missionary work. Her voice was the first to ask for a medical woman to be sent to China. When the hospital for women and children was opened in Foochow, the first for such a purpose founded in that great empire, she gave it her coöperation. For several years she translated the Berean Lessons into the Chinese language for the use of the Methodist Mission and of the American Board. For two years she edited in the same language the "Youth's Illustrated Paper." She had the pleasure of seeing the missions grow from small beginnings into strong churches of intelligent and self-sacrificing Christians. In the midst of her usefulness sickness came to her of such a character that her physician declared that a change of climate and entire rest were essential to the preservation of her life, and, after eighteen years of earnest, patient, hopeful service in the foreign field, she turned her face homeward. The American pulpit was freely open to Dr. Baldwin, and his pastoral services were eagerly sought. For some years he has been the recording secretary of the Board of Missions of the M. E. Church. Mrs. Baldwin's health has been largely restored since her return to this country, and she spends the full measure of her strength in active benevolence. She has been extensively employed in the interests of the Woman's Foreign Missionary Society, being president of the New York branch of that society in the Methodist Church, of the Woman's Christian Temperance Union, in lectures on various subjects, and

ESTHER E. BALDWIN.

in many charities. She is an ardent advocate of the equality of women with men, both in the State and in the Church. The Chinese question in all its aspects has her sympathies. The misrepresentation and abuse of the Chinese have kindled her indignation. She has been called to speak before large audiences in many places on the Chinese question and has contributed numerous articles on the subject to various city papers. She has carefully collected and forcibly stated both the laws and the facts bearing on the subject, and has published them in a small volume entitled "Must the Chinese Go?" which has had three editions. It is especially addressed to the thoughtful and ruling minds of America. She has won the distinction of being the "Chinese Champion." Mrs. Baldwin is the mother of seven children, two of whom died in Foochow. She now resides in Brooklyn, N. Y.

BALL, Mrs. Isabel Worrell, pioneer woman journalist of the West, born in a log cabin near

Hennepin, Putnam county, Ill., 13th March, 1855. She is of Scotch-Irish parents. Her father was James Purcell Worrell. Her mother's maiden name was Elizabeth McClung. Mrs. Ball was always a self-reliant individual, even in childhood preferring to investigate and judge for herself. She was educated in public schools and academies, and was the leader in her classes, except in mathematics, for which science, in all its branches, she felt and showed the deepest aversion. Her favorite study was history. Her father was a lawyer, and at the age of thirteen years she began to study with him, gaining a fair knowledge of law. When she was sixteen years old, a weakness of the eyes forced her to leave school. In 1873 her family removed to western Kansas. There she rode over the prairies, assisting in herding her father's stock, learning to throw a lasso with the dexterity of a cowboy and to handle a gun with the skill of a veteran. The outdoor life soon restored her health. She taught the first public school in Pawnee county, Kans., and her school district included the whole immense county. She spent the next year as clerk in a store situated three miles from her home, riding back and forth on her pony. She was the second woman to be appointed a notary public in Kansas. She held positions in committee clerkships in sessions of the Kansas legislature from 1876 to 1886 and served as a press reporter from 1877 to 1890. She is a pronounced Republican in politics, for which she has always had a fondness, and through her positions in the legislature she has become acquainted with all the prominent politicians of the West. Her journalistic work began in 1881 on the Albuquerque "Journal" in New Mexico, and as correspondent of the Kansas City "Times." While living in New Mexico and Arizona she had many experiences with the Indians and gathered much interesting material for future work. There, as she says, she practically "lived in a little gripsack." The Atlantic and Pacific Railroad was being built from Albuquerque to the Needles, and she was special correspondent for the Albuquerque "Daily Journal." Her husband was a member of the construction party, but was with her only a part of the time, for, was there a washout, an Indian outbreak, or a wreck, she was expected to be on hand. Her life was often in danger from the Indians, both Navajoes and Apaches being belligerent at that time. Once the boarding train was surrounded by the Indians, and escape entirely cut off by washouts. The little dwelling, a box car, was riddled with bullets, and two men were killed, but Mrs. Ball escaped unhurt. For two years she lived in that wild country, seeing no woman's face, save that of a squaw, for three months at a time. In 1882 she returned to Kansas and acted for three years as editor of the Larned "Chronoscope," then the leading and official Republican journal in western Kansas. She removed to Topeka in 1886 and was made assistant secretary of the State Historical Society by legislative enactment. The Commonwealth Publishing Company engaged her as editor of their patent one-side publications, issued for State and county papers, handling one-hundred-sixty-two newspapers. She afterwards filled an important editorial position on the "Daily Commonwealth." In 1888 she became literary critic of the Kansas City "Daily Times," and editor of the weekly issue of that journal. In 1889 she took a position on the Kansas City "Star," which she held until the fall of 1891, when she removed to Washington and entered upon special journalistic work. Besides all this regular newspaper writing she has contributed many sketches to eastern periodicals. In 1889, in conjunction with others, she called together by correspondence a number of the most prominent writers in the West, and the meeting resulted in the formation of the Western Authors' and Artists'

ISABEL WORRELL BALL.

Club, which meets annually in Kansas City. Mrs. Ball is the secretary and master spirit of the organization. In 1887 she was married to H. M. Ball, a man of high scholarship and extensive reading and information. They have had but one child, which died at the age of three years. Mrs. Ball says she does not lay claim to any accomplishments. The only music she knows is the barking of the hounds on the trail of deer or antelope. She is a deal more familiar with a picket pin than with a needle, and with a lariat rope than with zephyr. While her husband thinks her a pretty good housekeeper, she can handle a gun with as much ease as she can handle a broom, and a hall full of angry politicians does not disconcert her half as much as a parlor or drawing-room full of chattering society dames. Though a leader among women, she is not a woman suffragist.

BALL, Miss Martha Violet, educator and philanthropist, born in Boston, Mass., 17th May, 1811. She was educated in the public schools and by private tutors. She was a school teacher for thirty years and a Sunday-school teacher for forty years. In 1838, under the auspices of the New England Moral Reform Society, she commenced her labors for fallen, intemperate women and unfortunate young girls. That association has rescued thousands from lives of intemperance, and thousands of young girls have been sought out and sheltered in the temporary home of the society. Miss Ball served on "The Home Guardian," a monthly periodical published by the society, for twenty-seven years, ten years as assistant and seventeen years as editor. She resigned in 1890, on account of the illness of her sister. She was one of the women who in 1833 assisted in forming the

Boston Female Anti-Slavery Society in the parlor of Mrs. J. N. Barbour, and was recording secretary of the society when the mob, in 1835, designated as "gentlemen of property and standing," entered the hall at number 46 Washington street and broke up a quarterly meeting. She continued to labor for the overthrow of slavery until it was abolished. In 1836, assisted by a few friends, she opened an evening school for young colored girls in the west part of Boston. In 1842 Miss Ball was sent as a delegate to an anti-slavery convention of women held in Philadelphia. Pennsylvania Hall, where the convention met, was attacked by a mob of several thousands, the women were driven out and pelted with stones, mud and missiles of various kinds, and Miss Ball was struck in her chest by a piece of brick. The hall was shortly after burned to the ground by the mob. Miss Ball aided in forming the Ladies' Baptist Bethel Society and was secretary for a time; she was then elected president, and retained that office for thirty years. The society became a large and influential body, laboring under the auspices of the Boston Baptist Bethel Society. In 1860 Miss Ball, with a few other women, organized The Woman's Union Missionary Society for Heathen Lands.

BALLARD, Miss Mary Canfield, poet, born in Troy, Pa., 22nd June, 1852. On her mother's side Miss Ballard is related to Colonel Ethan Allen, of Revolutionary fame. Her father was a self-made man and accumulated considerable property in Bradford county, Pa. She was sent to the State Normal School when about fourteen years old, but, growing homesick, she returned to her home in Troy where she finished her education. She is the youngest of a large family, but, her brothers and

MARY CANFIELD BALLARD.

sisters being married and her father and mother dead, she lives alone. She is devoted to painting, music and literature and has been a prolific contributor to periodicals under the name Minnie C.

Ballard ever since she sent her first poem to William Cullen Bryant, who gave it a place in the "Evening Post." Her early literary efforts were very ambitious ones. When she was only thirteen years old, she wrote a continued story about a hairpin, managing to introduce an elopement, an angry father, tears, repentance and forgiveness. She also wrote an essay on Sappho. She began to write poems at the age of sixteen, but her first published productions made their appearance when she was twenty-one years old. Since her bow to the public in the poets' corner of the "Evening Post," she has contributed occasionally to some thirty periodicals. She has published "Idle Fancies" (Troy, Pa., 1883), for private circulation, and a new edition for the general public (Philadelphia, 1884).

BALLOU, Miss Ella Maria, stenographer, born in Wallingford, Vt., 15th November, 1852, and has spent her life in her native State. She was educated in the Wallingford high school and immediately after leaving school began life as a teacher, in which vocation she was successful, but was rebellious over what she considered the injustice of requiring her to accept for equal service a much smaller compensation than was paid to a man of equal or less ability. After a few years of labor as a teacher, she learned shorthand and adopted it as a life-work. The persistence and thoroughness that had been a characteristic of her girlhood manifested itself in her work, and she went into the courts and wrote out evidence and argument until she became noted for accuracy and skill, and in 1885, upon the unanimous application of the Rutland County Bar, Hon. W. G. Veazey, Judge of the Supreme Court, appointed her the official reporter of Rutland County Court. Hers was the first appointment of a

ELLA MARIA BALLOU.

woman as official stenographer in Vermont, if not in the United States. Her success in her work has been marked and she has also been appointed official reporter of the adjoining county of Addison.

When not in court, Miss Ballou does general work in her profession. She has also done some literary work in the line of essays and addresses. Miss Ballou is a practical example of what may be done by women, and while she earnestly claims all her rights as a woman and her full right to have as much pay for her labor as is paid to a man for the same service, she makes no claim to be allowed to vote or hold office. She honors her sex and exalts it to an equality with the other, and yet believes it to be a distinct order of human life.

BANCKER, Miss Mary E. C., author, known by her pen-name, "Betsey Bancker," born

MARY E. C. BANCKER.

in New York City, 1st September, 1860. She is a lineal descendant of that old and historical Knickerbocker family whose name she bears, which came from Holland in 1658. The Bancker family intermarried with the De Puysters, Rutgers, Ogdens and Livingstons. The maternal grandfather of Miss Bancker was Michael Henry, one of the leading merchants of New York, as well as patron of art, and founder and owner of the once famous picture gallery at Number 100 Broadway. Mr. Henry was of Huguenot extraction. His ancestors, driven out of France after the revocation of the Edict of Nantes, during the reign of Louis XIV, established themselves at Henry's Grove, Armaugh, Ireland. Mr. Henry's father, John Sinclair Henry, came to America with the idea of founding a colony in South Carolina. Homeward bound, he stopped in New York, where he met Leah, of the old Brevoort family, of that city, and, wooing and wedding her, he remained and established a shipping business between this country and Newry, Ireland. Miss Mary, daughter of F. J. Bancker, began to write early. Her maiden efforts were a series of sketches descriptive of outdoor life, appearing in the "Turf, Field and Farm." These articles were well received and extensively copied. Miss Bancker corresponded for the Cincinnati "Enquirer" during several years, and now represents the Montreal "Herald" in New York, her present home, as staff correspondent for that Canadian journal. She is known from Quebec to British Columbia. Miss Bancker produced the Indian Opera "Dovetta" in April, 1889, in the Standard Theater in New York, in conjunction with Mrs. E. Marcy Raymond. Miss Bancker was librettist with Charles Raynaud. She is constantly writing upon a variety of topics, that find their way to American as well as Canadian periodicals. Miss Bancker began her education in New York, and at a very impressionable age traveled extensively in Europe and in the tropics of America. She has a knowledge of the French and Spanish languages.

BANKS, Mrs. Mary Ross, author, born in Macon, Ga., 4th March, 1846. On her father's side she is from Scotch ancestry. Her grandfather, Luke Ross, was a man of large wealth for his day, and had a sumptuously appointed home, the furniture of which was hauled in wagons from New York City to North Carolina. A man of unblemished integrity, having stood security for a friend and lost, he sacrificed all his possessions and moved to Jones county, Ga., when the present beautiful city of Macon was a small trading port. Mrs. Banks' father, John Bennett Ross, was one of seven brothers and three sisters. The Ross brothers clung together and established themselves in trade about the year 1832. A talent for business and the clannish Scotch blood that kept them together resulted in a splendid commercial success. There were changes in the course of time, some of the brothers embarking in other kinds of business, but John B. Ross continued in the wholesale and retail dry goods and planters' supply business till the end of his days and made so

MARY ROSS BANKS.

large a fortune that he was known as "the merchant prince of the South." His home was the center of elegant entertainment, and his children were reared in luxury. He was married three times.

His first wife was a Miss Holt; his second, Martha Redding, descended from the Lanes and Flewellens, was the mother of Mrs. Banks; his third wife, a charming woman who still survives him, is a sister of Judge L. Q. C. Lamar, of the Supreme Court of the United States. Mrs. Banks was educated in Wesleyan Female College, in Macon, Ga., and in the private school of Mrs. Theodosia Bartow Ford. She was married at seventeen years of age to Edward P. Bowdre, of Macon, at that time a captain in the Confederate army. She went to the army with her husband and did noble service in the hospitals. At twenty-five years of age she was a widow with three sons, and much of the fortune that should have been hers dissipated by the hazard of war and the scarcely less trying period of reconstruction. In June, 1875, she was married to Dr. J. T. Banks, of Griffin, Ga., a gentleman of high standing socially and professionally and lived with him in unclouded happiness for four years, when she was again a widow. Crushed by her grief, she realized that her only hope for peace of mind lay in employment and as soon as she had partly recovered from the shock, she went courageously to work to help herself and her boys. With no training for business, and no knowledge of labor, frail in body, but dauntless in spirit, she accomplished wonders in many lines. She was a successful farmer and turned many of her talents and accomplishments into money-making. After raising her sons to the age of independence, she accepted a position in the Department of the Interior at Washington, where she has been assigned to important work in the office of the Secretary, a position she finds both lucrative and agreeable. Her literary fame came to her suddenly and is the result of one book, "Bright Days on the Old Plantation" (Boston, 1882), and a number of sketches and short stories published in various newspapers and periodicals.

BANTA, Mrs. Melissa Elizabeth Riddle, poet, born in Cheviot, a suburb of Cincinnati, O., 27th March, 1834. Her father, James Riddle, was of Scotch descent, and her mother, Elizabeth Jackson, a Quaker, was of English origin. Melissa Elizabeth is the sole daughter of the house. She attended the Wesleyan Female Institute in Cincinnati until her fourteenth year, when, on the removal of the family to Covington, Ky., she was placed in the Female Collegiate Institute of that city, where she was graduated at the age of seventeen years. The same year she made a romantic marriage with Joseph I. Perrin, of Vicksburg, Miss. The young couple lived in Vicksburg, where the bride was a teacher in the public schools. A few days after the first anniversary of the wedding day, 11th September, 1853, Mr. Perrin died of yellow fever. That was the year when the fever was epidemic in the South. Mrs. Banta's recollections of that time are vivid. Her poem, "The Gruesome Rain," embodies a grief, a regret and a hint of the horrors of that season. Mrs. Sophia Fox, hearing of her situation, sent her carriage and servants a distance of twenty-five miles to carry the young widow to her plantation at Bovina, Miss. There she remained for two months, until her parents dared to send for her. Mrs. Fox, with characteristic southern warm-heartedness, had supplied all her needs and refused all proffered remuneration on the arrival of Dr. Mount, the old family physician. After the death of Mr. Perrin, a little daughter was born, but in a few weeks she faded from her mother's arms, and the child-widow took again her place in her father's house. For the sake of an entire change of scene her father disposed of his home and business interests in Covington, temporarily, and removed to Bloomington, Ind. It was there Mrs.

Perrin met David D. Banta, to whom she was married 11th June, 1856. Soon after the wedding they went to Covington, Ky., and in October, 1847, to Franklin, Ind., where they have since lived. They

MELISSA ELIZABETH RIDDLE BANTA.

have a beautiful home, and this second marriage is an ideal one. Mrs. Banta is the mother of two sons and one daughter. She has been twice to Europe and has visited all the notable places in the United States. Her letters of travel are only less charming than her poetry. She inherits her literary talent from her maternal grandmother, who, though not a writer, was a highly intellectual woman.

BARBER, Mrs. Mary Augustine, educator, born in Newton, Conn., in 1789; died in Mobile, Ala., in 1860. She entered the Visitation Convent in Georgetown, D. C., in 1818, with her four daughters. She founded a convent of visitation in Kaskaskia, Ill., in 1836, remaining there till 1844. She taught in a convent in St. Louis, Mo., from 1844 till 1848, and in Mobile until the time of her death.

BARBOT, Mme. Blanche Hermine, musical director and pianist, born in Brussels, Belgium, 28th December, 1842. She is the daughter of Victor and Marie Therese Petit, and inherits her great musical talents from her father, who was a musician and composer of ability and a fine performer on several instruments, but especially noted for the perfection of his playing on the clarinet. From infancy Hermine gave evidence of a decided talent for music. She received from her father the most careful training. At the age of seven she was already so accomplished a pianist that the celebrated French musician, Mme. Pleyel, complimented her most warmly on her playing and predicted for her a brilliant future upon the concert stage, for which her father destined her. Her first appearance in concert was in the Theatre Italien-Francais, in Brussels, in February, 1851. This first success of the little Hermine

was followed by many others during a tour she made with her father through the various large cities of Belgium and Holland. While in Holland, she was invited to play before the Queen, who was so delighted by the child's performance that she gave her a beautiful watch as a token of her admiration. The family removed to New York in the spring of 1852, where several concerts were given by the father and daughter. Mons. Petit was induced to visit the South and finally to settle in Charleston, S. C., where he was successful as a music teacher. While still a young man, he fell a victim to yellow fever in the epidemic of 1856, leaving his family in such straitened circumstances that all thought of a musical career for his daughter had to be renounced, and she became a teacher at the age of thirteen. When Thalberg visited Charleston, in 1857, he called upon Mlle. Petit, and was so delighted with her playing that he invited her to render with him a duo on two pianos at his concert. In 1863 Mlle. Petit was married to P. J. Barbot, a merchant of Charleston, who died in 1887, leaving six children. Her marriage in no way interfered with her musical work. Although Mme. Barbot is a brilliant pianist with fine technique and great force and delicacy of expression, she has always shrunk from appearing in public as a solo performer, except in response to the calls of charity, to which she has always given her services freely, irrespective of denomination, although she is herself an earnest Roman Catholic. Her peculiar gift is in training and directing large musical forces. She has for years given cantatas, oratorios and operas with the amateurs of the city. To her Charleston is indebted for most of the fine music it has had of late years, as her taste inclines to the serious and clas-

BLANCHE HERMINE BARBOT.

sical. In 1875 Mme. Barbot was chosen director of the Charleston Musical Association, a society of about a hundred voices, with which she has since given many important works. She has been organist in St. Mary's and St. Michael's churches, and is now organist of the Cathedral.

BARNES, Miss Annie Maria, author and editor, born in Columbia, S. C., 28th May, 1857. Her mother was a Neville and traced her descent in a direct line from the Earl of Warwick. Miss

ANNIE MARIA BARNES.

Barnes's position in literature depends upon no family prestige or any adventitious circumstances in life, but upon her own genius and industry. She knows what it is to struggle for recognition in the literary world and to suffer the inconveniences and embarrassments of poverty. Her family was left at the close of the Civil War, like most Southerners, without means. Under the impulse of genius she persevered and by her energy overcame the disadvantages of her situation and the discouragements that usually beset the path of the young writer. Before reaching the meridian of life she has won foremost rank in the one particular line wherein she has sought recognition, that of southern juvenile literature. Miss Barnes developed early in life a taste for literary work, and when only eleven years of age wrote an article for the Atlanta "Constitution," which was published and favorably noticed by the editor, and at fifteen she became a regular correspondent of that journal. She has been a frequent contributor to leading journals north as well as south. In 1887 she undertook the publication of a juvenile paper called "The Acanthus," which, with one exception, was the only strictly juvenile paper ever published in the South. In literary character it was a success, but financially, like so many other southern publications, it was a failure. Many of Miss Barnes's earlier productions appeared in the "Sunday-school Visitor," a child's paper published by the Methodist Episcopal Church, South, in Nashville, Tenn. Her first book was "Some Lowly Lives" (Nashville, 1885); then followed "The Life of David Livingston" (1887), and "Scenes in Pioneer

Methodism" (1889). Later she wrote "The Children of the Kalahari," a child's story of Africa, which was very successful in this country and in England. Two books from her pen were to be issued in 1892, "The House of Grass" and "Atlanta Ferryman: A Story of the Chattahoochee." Miss Barnes is at present junior editor for the Woman's Board of Missions, Methodist Episcopal Church, South, having charge of its juvenile paper and of all its quarterly supplies of literature. In that capacity she has done her most telling and forceful work.

BARNES, Miss Catharine Weed, photographer and editor, born in Albany, N. Y., 10th January, 1851. She is the eldest child of the Hon. William Barnes and Emily P. Weed, daughter of the late Thurlow Weed. After receiving an academical education in Albany she entered Vassar College, but was obliged to give up the idea of graduating because of illness resulting from overwork. In 1872 she accompanied her parents to Russia, where Mr. Barnes was an official delegate from this country to the International Statistical Congress in St. Petersburg. She has traveled much in this country and abroad, and is a close student and hard worker. She took up photography in 1886, having previously given much time to music and painting. On her mother's death, in 1889, she assumed charge of her father's household in Albany but gave all her spare time to camera work. After contributing many articles to various periodicals devoted to photography she went on the editorial staff of the "American Amateur Photographer" in May, 1890. She is an active member of the Society of Amateur Photographers of New York, of the New York Camera Club, and the Postal Photographic Club, an honor-

CATHARINE WEED BARNES.

ary member of the Chicago Camera Club and of the Brooklyn Academy of Photography, and has won prizes at various photographic exhibitions as an amateur. She is a member of the National

Photographers' Association of America, a professional organization. Miss Barnes is also connected with several literary and musical associations and belongs to the Sorosis Club of New York. She has a special portrait studio carefully planned, in a building separate from her residence, but is continually altering it for her favorite work of making illustrations and character studies. She does all the work in studio, laboratory and printing-room herself and is a thorough reader of everything bearing on camera work. Her great desire is to encourage women to take up this work as a regular profession. Her own preference is for figures and interiors rather than for landscapes. She makes lantern-slides from her own negatives and shows them in her oxyhydrogen lantern, and has read several papers before societies in different cities, besides recording her camera experiences in her own magazine. In 1888 she received a diploma for the excellence of her work exhibited at Boston and a silver medal in 1891 for lantern-slides. She entered the Enoch Arden prize competition in the Washington convention of the Photographers' Association of America for 1890 with three pictures, which were judged entitled to second place by an eminent art critic who examined all the photographs exhibited, and entered the Elaine competition in Buffalo in 1891. She is the first woman amateur photographer who has ventured to compete with professionals and was invited to read a paper in their Buffalo convention. Her new studio and laboratory are well fitted for photographic work, and owe most of their excellence to contrivances of her own designing. Her editorial work on the "American Amateur Photographer" at first covered the ladies' department only, but she has recently became associate editor. She is editing the woman's photographic department in "Outing," and has contributed a series of articles to "Frank Leslie's Weekly." Some of her pictures have been reproduced in art journals, and her reputation as a photographer is national. She was invited to address the Photographic Convention of the United Kingdom at Edinburgh in July, 1892, during her camera trip through England and Scotland.

BARNES, Mrs. Frances Julia, temperance reformer, born in Skaneateles, Onondaga county, N. Y., 14th April, 1846. Her maiden name was Allis. Her parents and ancestry were members of the orthodox society of Friends, of which she is a member. She received her early education in the schools of her native village and was finally graduated at the Packer Institute in Brooklyn, N. Y. After her graduation her family resided in Brooklyn, during which time she became interested in church and Sunday-school and mission work. On 21st September, 1871, she was married to Willis A. Barnes, a lawyer of New York, and made her home for a time in that city. In the fall of 1875 professional business called Mr. Barnes to Chicago, Ill. Mrs. Barnes accompanied him, and they remained there five years. During that time she became associated with Miss Frances E. Willard in conducting gospel temperance meetings in lower Farwell Hall and meetings in church parlors in the Newsboy's Home, and in visiting jails, hospitals, printing offices and other places. It was while the temperance movement was confined to the object of "rescuing the perishing" the attention of Mrs. Barnes and her co-workers was drawn to the necessity of not merely seeking to reform the fallen, but also of directing efforts to implant principles of total abstinence among young men and women, and enlisting their coöperation while they were yet on life's threshold. In 1878, in the national convention held in Baltimore, Mrs. Barnes was made a member of the committee on young women's work, and in the next convention, held in Indianapolis, in 1879, she made a verbal report, and was at that time made chairman of the committee for the following year, and at its expiration made the first report on young women's work, which appeared in the National Minutes. In 1879 and 1880 twenty Young Women's Christian Temperance Unions were organized in the State of New York, and of the twenty-five unions in Illinois, with a membership of seven-hundred, two-thirds had been formed during the year. In 1880 young women's work was made a department of the National Woman's Christian Temperance Union, and Mrs. Barnes was appointed superintendent. In 1890 she was appointed fraternal delegate to the annual meeting of the British Women's Temperance Association, held in London, 21st and 22nd May, at which time she so acceptably presented the subject that the department of young

FRANCES JULIA BARNES.

women's work was immediately organized, and Lady Henry Somerset accepted the superintendency. As an outgrowth of that interest sixteen branches were organized in Great Britian the first year. In 1891 Mrs. Barnes was made the superintendent for the World's Young Women's Christian Temperance Union work. Under her care it has so grown that there is a membership of 30,000 in the United States alone. The members distribute literature, form hygenic and physical culture clubs, have courses of reading, flower missions, loan-libraries, jail visiting, Sunday-school work, in all covering forty different departments of philanthropic and religious labor. During the year she travels extensively through the country, delivers addresses at public and parlor meetings and organizes new local unions. Not only is her voice heard in the cause of temperance, but practical sentiments flow from her ready pen. Mrs. Barnes has edited a manual on young women's temperance work and is a regular contributor both of prose and poetry to the "Oak and Ivy Leaf," the organ of the National Young Women's Christian Temperance Union. She has been president of the Loyal Legion Temperance Society of New York City for ten years, under whose care a free reading-room for working boys has been maintained during that length of time, the attendance aggregating over two-hundred-thousand boys.

BARNES, Mrs. Mary Sheldon, educator and historian, born in Oswego, N. Y., 15th September, 1850. Her father was E. A. Sheldon, the principal of the Oswego Normal School. As a child she had a passion for study. After going through the high and normal schools and preparing for college with boys and girls who were bound for Harvard and Yale, she decided to go to college, and Michigan University was her choice. She entered that institution in 1871, as a classical sophomore in a class of eighty boys and eight girls. She

MARY SHELDON BARNES.

was graduated in the classical course in 1874. She then went to teach history, Latin and Geeek in the Oswego State Normal School, but was soon called to Wellesley College, where she organized the department of history. She was at the head of that department from 1st January, 1877, to June, 1879. She next went to Europe for two years' study and travel, each of which had for her a strictly historical aim. She visited France, Italy, Egypt and Germany. The second year she spent as a student in Newnham College, Cambridge University, England, where she devoted the time to the study of modern history, under the direction of Prof. J. R. Seeley, regius professor of modern history. On her return to the United States she taught history and literature in the Normal School in Oswego, N.Y. Meanwhile she had been gathering materials for a text-book on general history which should present the subject on a more scientific method than the mere giving of ·a narrative.

While in that school she met Earl Barnes. In 1885 they were married, and in that year her first book was published, under the title "Studies in General History" (Boston). It met an immediate and sympathetic welcome from those who understood her plan. It has come rather slowly into popular use, on account of its originality. Her publishers, however, felt warranted in urging her to make an American history on the same plan, which she accordingly undertook. In 1888 that work was interrupted by a literary engagement which took her husband and herself to Europe, where they spent a year in the libraries of London, Paris and Zürich, collecting historical materials. The second book has recently been published under the title "Studies in American History" (Boston, 1892), and is the joint work of herself and her husband. In 1892 Mr. Barnes was called to the Leland Stanford Junior University, at the head of the department of education. Mrs. Barnes has received an appointment as assistant professor of modern history, an appointment obtained without any sort of solicitation, and it is one of the first appointments of the kind made in an institution of that rank. Her "Studies in American History" is having an immediate success. The home of Mrs. Barnes is now in Palo Alto, Santa Clara county, Cal.

BARNEY, Mrs. Susan Hammond, evangelist, was born in Massachusetts. Her father, Dr. John A. Hammond, was a prominent physician. She was a contributor to the local press when thirteen years old. It was her desire to become a foreign missionary, but, owing to ill-health and the strong opposition of friends, she reluctantly gave over her purpose. She was married to Joseph K. Barney, of Providence, R. I., in 1854, and has ever since resided in that city, with the exception of several years spent on the Pacific Coast. Her first public speaking was done in the interest of the Woman's Foreign Missionary Society of the Methodist Episcopal Church. She was one of the founders of the Prisoners' Aid Society of Rhode Island, and has always been interested in prison and jail work. She was the first president of the Rhode Island Woman's Christian Temperance Union, a position she held for several years. She is now a national evangelist. The enactment of constitutional prohibition in Rhode Island in 1886 was largely due to her executive ability. She has had much to do with securing police matrons for the station-houses of large cities, her work in that direction being second to none. She is an able platform speaker. Mrs. Barney contributed a chapter on the "Care of the Criminal" to "Woman's Work in America" (New York, 1891).

BARR, Mrs. Amelia E., novelist, born in Ulverstone, on Morecombe Bay, in the district of Furness, Lancashire, England, in 1832. Her maiden name was Amelia E. Huddleston. She was the daughter of Rev. William Huddleston, a representative of the Huddlestons of Millom, a family of ancient and pure Saxon lineage, who furnished a large number of well-known ecclesiastics and of daring navigators. Amelia was a child of precocious intellect. Brought up in an atmosphere of refined culture, she early turned to books for recreation, and later became a thorough student. Her father was a learned and eloquent preacher, and he directed her studies for years. When she was only six years old, she had memorized many of the "Arabian Nights" stories, and was familiar with "Robinson Crusoe" and Pilgrim's Progress." When she was nine years old, she became her father's companion and reader. Necessarily that work obliged her to read books of a deep nature and beyond her comprehension ; however, the sentiments they contained did much towards her mental development. When twelve years old, she read to her father the well-known "Tracts for the Times" and became an adherent of the religious movement they originated. Her education was conducted in an unmethodical manner, and the principal part was derived from reading instructive books. When Miss Huddleston was seventeen, she attended a celebrated school in Glasgow, Scotland, but she derived very little knowledge from that source. When about eighteen she was married to Robert Barr, the son of Rev. John Barr, of Dovehill Kirk, whose writings are still published. Mr. and Mrs. Barr came to America a few years after their marriage and traveled in the West and South. When the yellow fever broke out in 1856, they were in New Orleans, but, fearing to remain there, they left for Texas, settling in Austin, where Mr. Barr received an appointment in the comptroller's office. After the Civil War

AMELIA E. BARR.

they removed to Galveston. In 1876 the yellow fever broke out there, and Mr. Barr and their four sons were stricken and died. Mrs. Barr and her three daughters were spared, and, as soon as it was safe, they went to New York. Mrs. Barr took a letter of introduction to a merchant, who directly engaged her to assist in the education of his three sons. She instructed them in ancient and modern literature, music and drawing. When her pupils went to Princeton, Mrs. Barr sought advice from Rev. Henry Ward Beecher, who was then editor of the "Christian Union." He was very encouraging, and she began to write for that paper and has continued to write for its columns. Mr. Beecher introduced her to Dr. Lyman Abbott, through whom she met the Harper Brothers, for whose periodicals she wrote for a number of years. In 1884 she was confined to her chair by an accident, which seemed to be a fortunate one, however, for during that time she wrote her first novel, "Jan

Vedder's Wife." In 1885, it was bought and published by a New York house, who have since published her novels. Her first book attracted general notice and gave her an instantaneous success. It ran through many editions and has been widely read on both sides of the sea, and in more than one language. Since 1885 Mrs. Barr has published numerous stories. Scotland has furnished the scene of four of them ; two have dealt with life in the English manufacturing districts. "The Border Shepherdess" (1887) lived in a long-debated territory between Scotland and England. "Feet of Clay" (1889) carried its readers to the Isle of Man. "Friend Olivia," a study of Quaker character, which appeared in 1890 in the "Century," recalled the closing years of the Commonwealth in England. "The Bow of Orange Ribbon" (1886) is a charming picture of life in New York in the days when Dutch manners and habits were still in their prime. "Remember the Alamo" (1888) recalls the stirring episode of the revolt of Texas against the Mexican rule. "She Loved a Sailor" combines pictures of sea life with darker scenes from the days of slavery. It will be seen from this brief catalogue that Mrs. Barr's sympathies are with life rather than with classes of people. Her other works are "A Daughter of Fife" (1886), "The Squire of Sandle-Side," "Paul and Christina" (1887), "Master of his Fate" (1888), "The Last of the Macallisters" (1886), Between two Loves" (1886), "A Sister to Esau" (1890), and "A Rose of a Hundred Leaves" (1891). There is no other writer in the United States whose writings command so wide a circle of readers at home and abroad as Mrs. Barr's, and yet she is so much of a hermit that her personality is almost a mystery to the hundreds of thousands who are familiar with the creations of her intellect. Most of her time is spent at Cherry Croft, her home on the top of Storm King Mountain, at Cornwall-on-the-Hudson, N. Y. There she lives with her daughters, happy in her literary work and her social surroundings, and almost worshiped by the dwellers on the mountain, who are frequent visitors at the hermitage. Her career has been an admirable illustration of the capacity of woman, under stress of sorrow, to conquer the world and win success.

BARROW, Mrs. Frances Elizabeth, author born in Charleston, S. C., 22nd February, 1822. She is widely known by her pen-name, "Aunt Fanny."

BARRY, Mrs. Flora Elizabeth, concert and opera singer and musical educator, born in Paris, Maine, 19th September, 1836. Mrs. Barry is descended on the paternal side from William Harlow, who came to this country from England prior to 1637, and Richard Thayer, who immigrated into Massachusetts among the earliest Puritans. On her mother's side, the Watermans claim a direct line of descent from Alfred the Great, while the Maxims were of Spanish origin, dating back to the time of Philip and Mary. Mrs. Barry's father, Isaac Harlow, was a cultured gentleman of musical tastes. Her mother possessed talent as a writer and a musician. Mrs. Barry received a superior education and is still an earnest student in every department of learning, French, Italian, Spanish and German receiving careful attention. Her musical talent was the dominant one, and she early began the study of that art that she might make herself proficient as a vocalist and teacher. Her first appearances in public were with the Mendelssohn Quintette Club and the Händel and Haydn Society of Boston, in 1863. Later she studied with Luigi Vannucini, of Florence, Italy. Sacred music is her especial work, although successful in classical music, pathetic ballad singing and opera. Mrs. Barry has sung successfully throughout her native country, and from Halifax to the interior of Mexico. She has appeared in many elaborate

FLORA ELIZABETH BARRY.

rôles of the standard operas, has sung in the grand oratorios in all the large cities, and has held prominent places in church choirs in Boston since her twelfth year. She is a member of Trinity Church, Boston. She has been twice married. Her first husband was John S. Cary, son of Dr. N. H. Cary, of Maine, and brother to Annie Louise Cary, the noted contralto. Her second husband was Charles A. Barry, an artist, from whom she was divorced in 1873. Since her father's death, in 1877, Mrs. Barry has devoted her musical efforts to her pupils. At her home in Boston she dispenses a large hospitality.

BARRY, Mrs. Susan E., army nurse, born in Minisink, Orange county, N. Y., 19th March, 1826. Her maiden name was Hall. Her parents were natives of Orange county, and after forty years' residence on the old farm the family removed to Tompkins county, N. Y., near Ithaca. The care of the home fell upon Susan from the age of eighteen to thirty. When the farm was given up, after her mother's death, because her father was too infirm to care for it she went to New York City and became a medical student. She attended the lectures and studies in the college of a four-year course, graduating in the spring of 1861, just at the breaking out of the war. A mass meeting was called at Cooper Union to devise ways and means to help the Union soldiers. The Sanitary Commission was formed. The Ladies' Central Relief Association of New York had been organized. Women were called to volunteer as nurses. Miss Hall gave in her name. The volunteers were required to pass strict examination, then they were admitted to Bellevue and the city hospitals to receive practical instructions. Miss Hall's two

months spent in preparatory instruction proved invaluable in her army work. The volunteer nurses received orders 22nd July, 1861, to proceed to Washington and report to Miss Dorothy Dix for duty. When they arrived, all was confusion in the city, with many conflicting reports of the battle and defeat at Bull Run. Miss Hall and her companions received a kind welcome from the surgeon in charge of the Seminary Hospital in Alexandria. These women took turns in doing all the watching at night, with no help except a few contrabands to wait on the men. The nurses who had most experience in wound dressing and in the treatment of surgical cases were always hurried off to the front after battles. Miss Hall and her associate, Miss Dada, after eight months in Alexandria, were sent to Winchester, Va. Later they were sent to Strasburg, and thence they were transferred to Harper's Ferry, next to Annapolis Naval Hospital, then to Georgetown, D. C., Warehouse Hospital, which was filled with wounded from the battle of Cedar Mountain. After that came the battle of Antietam, and Miss Hall and six other women nurses, with Miss Dix, were on hand before the dead were buried. Later Miss Hall was again called to Harper's Ferry. The hospitals were crowded, and she remained during the winter. She was next ordered to Gettysburg, immediately after the terrible battle. After several months in that busy field, she was transferred to the Western Department and was assigned to duty in Nashville, and later sent to Murfreesborough. She stayed there seven months, and then went to Chattanooga where she remained till the close of the war, having served the entire period without a furlough. Miss Hall's health was permanently impaired by her long con-

SUSAN E. BARRY.

tinued labors, and returning home she spent the winter in Dr. Jackson's Sanitarium in Dansville, N. Y., for rest and treatment. In May, 1866, she was married to Robert Barry, of Chicago. After their marriage they went to California, making their permanent home in San Francisco. Mrs. Barry has not regained strength sufficient to engage in professional or public work.

BARTLETT, Mrs. Alice Eloise, author, born in Delavan, Wis., 4th September, 1848. Her maiden name was Bowen, and she is widely known

ALICE ELOISE BARTLETT.

by her pen-name, "Birch Arnold." "The Meeting of the Waters," her first poem, was published in the Madison "Democrat." With all its crudities, it was unique and poetic, and the encouragement received determined her to enter the field of literature as a profession. In 1877 she published her first novel, "Until the Daybreak," which at once gave her a rank among story writers. In 1872 she began to write for the Toledo "Blade" and "Locke's National Monthly." Her articles attracted a great deal of attention, and D. R. Locke (Petroleum V. Nasby) told a friend that he intended to "adopt that promising young man." His (Nasby's) chagrin on learning that the young man was a girl can be imagined. It has often afforded her amusement to find her utterances commented on as the "vigorous ideas of a thinking man." To the world at large she still remains, and is often addressed as, "Birch Arnold, esq." Ill health for several years prevented the continuous effort necessary to pronounced success, but lyrics, essays and miscellaneous writings have from time to time appeared under her signature. In 1876 she was married to J. M. D. Bartlett, of Quincy, Ill., and they have two children. As a conversationalist she is interesting, and she is an elocutionist of no ordinary ability. She is extremely sincere and earnest in her life as well as her writings, and her heart is in the work of elevating her sex and humanity in general. Her latest work is a novel entitled "A New Aristocracy" (Detroit, 1891), dealing with women and the labor question. Her home is in Detroit, Mich., where she is engaged in literary labor.

BARTLETT, Miss Caroline Julia, Unitarian minister, born in Hudson, St. Croix county, Wis., 17th August, 1858. She is a daughter of Lorenzo Dow and Julia A. Brown Bartlett. When she was sixteen years old, she heard a sermon which led her to make the liberal ministry her life-work. After she was graduated at Carthage College, in Illinois, the disapproval of her relatives and friends kept her from entering the ministry at once, and she turned her attention to newspaper work. For about three years she was on the staff of the Minneapolis "Tribune," and later was city editor of the Oshkosh "Daily Morning Times." As a newspaper writer and editor Miss Bartlett was a success. After spending a short time in special study, Miss Bartlett entered on her new calling as pastor of a little Unitarian flock in Sioux Falls, S. Dak. During the three years she remained there, her efforts were greatly prospered. A handsome stone church was built, and the membership increased to many times the number that made up her charge when she undertook the work. The fame of her labors at Sioux Falls brought her an urgent call from the First Unitarian Church of Kalamazoo, Mich., which she was induced to accept, as it would give her better opportunity for special study than she could have in South Dakota. Miss Bartlett has been in Kalamazoo three years, and the church of which she is pastor has flourished greatly during that time. Study clubs have been formed under her direction, and the church is an active and important factor in all good work in the community. Miss Bartlett spent the summer of 1891 abroad and preached in many of the Unitarian churches in England. She was received with great kindness, but a woman preacher was such a novelty that it was only

CAROLINE JULIA BARTLETT.

by showing the portraits of a dozen other women ministers that she could get the people there to realize that she was not solitary in her vocation. By special invitation she visited the great philosopher and theologian, Dr. James Martineau, in his Scottish highland home. When looking into different lines of philanthropic work while she was abroad, Miss Bartlett went about with the slum officers of the Salvation Army. Miss Bartlett is a fluent orator. Her conversion to the cause of woman's political enfranchisement did not come until after some years of public work, but she had only to be convinced in order to become an ardent supporter of the political, as well as the social, educational and legal advancement of women. She preached the sermon before the National Woman Suffrage Convention in Albaugh's Opera House, in Washington, in March, 1891.

BARTLETT, Mrs. Maud Whitehead, educator, born in Gillespie, Ill., 10th September, 1865. Her maiden name was Whitehead, and herself and one brother were the only children in her family. With her parents she removed to Ohio in 1879, and to Kansas five years later. She studied music under Prof. Cutler, of Pana, Ill., and later under

MAUD WHITEHEAD BARTLETT.

Prof. Fuehring, of Shelbyville, Ill. Fascinated with music, she left school before she was graduated that she might, by teaching, be able to finish her musical education. After teaching both day school and music, she finally adopted the former as a profession, and for nine years, the last three of which were spent in the El Dorado, Kans., schools, she devoted herself to the duties of the schoolroom, meanwhile steadily pursuing her musical studies. A member of the Methodist Episcopal Church, her life for years has been one constant sacrifice to the happiness of those about her. On 10th September, 1891, she was married to Harry Bartlett, of Denver, Col., which place has since been her home.

BARTON, Miss Clara, philanthropist, was born in North Oxford, Worcester county, Mass., about 1830. Her father was a soldier with General Anthony Wayne. She received a good education in the public schools of her native town. When

she was sixteen years old, she became a teacher. After teaching for some years she took a course of study in Clinton, N. Y., and then went to Trenton, N. J., where she engaged in teaching. She taught for a time in Bordentown, N. J., and in that place she established a free school, which, in spite of all opposition, grew to large proportions. Overwork there in 1853 caused her health to fail, and she went to Washington, D. C., to visit relatives and rest. There was at that time much confusion in the Patent Office, growing out of the treachery of clerks, who had betrayed secrets of inventors applying for patents, and Miss Barton was recommended to the Commissioner of Patents as a person qualified to take charge of affairs. She was employed, and the male clerks tried to make her position uncomfortable, employing direct personal insult at first, and slander at last. Instead of driving her out of the Patent Office, her abusers themselves were discharged. She remained in the Patent Office three years, doing much to bring order out of chaos. Under the Buchanan administration she was removed on account of her "Black Republicanism," but she was recalled by the same administration. When the Civil War broke out, she offered to serve in her department without pay, and resigned her position to find some other way in which to serve her country. She was among the spectators at the railroad station in Washington when the Massachusetts regiment arrived there from Baltimore, where the first blood had been shed. She nursed the forty wounded men who were the victims of the Baltimore mob. On that day she identified herself with army work, and she shared the risks and sufferings of the soldiers of the Union army to the close of the great struggle. Visits to the battle-fields revealed to her the great need of provision for the nursing and feeding of the wounded soldiers. She made an attempt to organize the work of relief, but women held back, and Miss Barton herself was not allowed at first to go to the battle-fields. She gathered stores of food and supplies, and finally she prevailed upon Assistant Quartermaster-General Rucker to furnish transportation facilities, and she secured permission to go wherever there was a call for her services. She at once went to the front, and her amazing work under the most distressful conditions, her unwearying devotion, and her countless services to the soldiers earned for her the name of "Angel of the Battlefield." During the last year of the war she was called to Massachusetts by family bereavements, and while there she was appointed by President Lincoln to attend to the correspondence of the relatives of missing prisoners after the exchanges. She went to Annapolis, Md., at once, to begin the work. Inquiries by the thousand poured in, and she established a Bureau of Records of missing men of the Union army, employing several assistants. Her records are now of great value, as they were compiled from prison and hospital rolls and burial lists. At Andersonville she was able to identify all but four-hundred of the thirteen-thousand graves of buried soldiers. In her work she used her own money freely, and Congress voted to reimburse her, but she refused to take money as pay for her services. She managed the bureau for four years, and her connection with the great conflict has given her a permanent and conspicuous place in the history of the country. In 1869 she went to Europe to rest and recover her wasted energies. In Geneva she was visited by the leading members of the International Committee of Relief of Geneva for the care of the wounded in war, who presented to her the treaty, signed by all the civilized nations excepting the United States, under which all who wore the badge of their society were allowed to go on the battle-fields to care for the wounded. Miss Barton had not heard of the society, although its principles were familiar to her from her service in connection with the Sanitary Commission. The society was the Society of the Red Cross. Miss Barton was at once interested in it and began to advocate its extension to cover the United States. In 1870, while she was in Berne, the war between France and Prussia broke out. Within three days Miss Barton was asked, by Dr. Appia, one of the founders of the Red Cross Society to go to the front and assist in caring for the wounded. Although herself an invalid, she went with her French companion, the "fair-haired Antoinette," and the two women were admitted within the lines of the German army. They there served after the battle of Hagenau, and Miss Barton realized the enormous value and importance of the Red Cross work, in having supplies of all

CLARA BARTON.

sorts ready and trained help to do everything required to save life and relieve suffering. Returning to Berne, Miss Barton was called to the court in Carlsruhe by the Grand Duchess of Baden, who wished her to remain with her and give suggestions concerning relief measures. She remained in Carlsruhe until the siege of Strasburg, and, when the gates of that city at last opened to the German army, Miss Barton entered with the soldiers. For her services she received a Red Cross brooch from the Grand Duchess of Baden, the Gold Cross of Remembrance with the colors of the Grand Duchy of Baden from the Grand Duke and his wife, and the Iron Cross of Merit with the colors of Germany and the Red Cross from the Emperor and Empress of Germany. Everywhere in the ruined cities Miss Barton did most valuable work. In Paris, in the closing days of the Commune, she did much work. Monsieur Thiers himself honored her in signal ways, and she was debarred from receiving

the cross of the Legion of Honor only by her refusal to solicit it, as, according to the laws governing its bestowal, it must be solicited by the would-be recipient. In 1873, utterly broken in health, she returned to the United States, and for several years she was unable to do any work. As soon as she was able to do so, she began to urge the Washington government to accept the Geneva treaty for the Red Cross Society. President Garfield was to have signed the treaty, but his untimely death prevented, and it was signed by President Arthur in 1882. In 1877 an "American National Committee of the Red Cross" was formed in Washington, and it was afterwards incorporated as "The American Association of the Red Cross." Miss Barton was appointed to the presidency by President Garfield, and she has since devoted herself to carrying out its benevolences. In the United States Miss Barton's society has done noble work among the fire sufferers in Michigan, and flood sufferers in Louisiana, Mississippi and Johnstown, Pa. During 1891 and 1892 the society worked for the famine sufferers in Russia, the American branch having made large collections of food and money for that purpose. In 1883 Miss Barton was appointed superintendent of the Reformatory Prison for Women in Sherburne, Mass., and she divided her time between that work and the work of the Red Cross. She has made that beneficent organization known throughout the United States by its services in times of suffering from fire, flood, drouth, tempest and pestilence. Miss Barton is spending her years in Washington, D. C., where, as a central sun, she diffuses energy, radiance and vitality throughout her world of philanthropy and of noble endeavor. Her long years of arduous labor have left their marks upon her, but she is still in the ranks, doing good service in the present and planning greater for the future.

BASCOM, Mrs. Emma Curtiss, woman suffragist and reformer, born in Sheffield, Mass., 20th April, 1828. She was the second daughter of Orren Curtiss. From earliest childhood she found occasion for that domestic watchfulness and care-taking that have marked her later life. New England ancestry and New England associations gave their distinct quality and color to her childhood. She was, through her mother, Caroline Standish Owen, a direct descendant of Miles Standish. Her early education was received in the Great Barrington Academy, in Pittsfield Institute, Massachusetts, and in Patapsco Institute, Maryland. Entering at once the one open vocation for women, that of instruction, she became a teacher in Kinderhook Academy, New York, and later in Stratford Academy, Connecticut. In 1856 she was married to John Bascom, at that time professor in Williams College. For years her husband was wholly deprived of the use of his eyes, and she thus had occasion, during a long period, to share his studies and render him daily assistance in reading and writing. She became the mother of five children and cherished a lively interest in all that pertained to the discipline, amplitude and pleasure of the home. By native tendency and life-long habit she has been an interested observer and eager advocate of those marvelous changes which have, in the rapid movement of recent years, opened the doors of opportunity to woman in the social, economic and political world. Her sense of the inner fitness and reconstructive power of this transformation of sentiment concerning the true relation of man and woman to each other has been deep, untiring and most sanguine. She was a charter member of the Association for the Advancement of Woman and for many years was one of its board of officers.

She has been an officer of the National Suffrage Association. She was secretary of the Woman's Centennial Commission for the State of Wisconsin. A zealous white-ribboner, she has been active in

EMMA CURTISS BASCOM.

the Woman's Christian Temperance Union almost from its first organization. While she has been especially earnest in claiming for woman a full participation in the larger outer circle of political action, this feeling has in no way weakened her loving hold on the center of life in the family. The two have been one in her thought.

BATEHAM, Mrs. Josephine Penfield Cushman, temperance reformer, born in Alden, N. Y., 1st November, 1829. She is descended from a godly New England ancestry. The attractions of Oberlin College and the desire to help the infant colony and educate their children drew her parents from New York State to Oberlin, Ohio, when Josephine was five years old. Her father died in a few years, and her mother was married to Prof. Henry Cowles, author of "Cowles' Bible Commentaries," and became a member of the Ladies' Board of Managers of the college. Josephine, soon after graduation, was married to the Rev. Richard S. Cushman, of Attleboro, Mass., and went on a foreign mission to St. Marc, Hayti. After eleven months of laborious service Mr. Cushman died, and unable to carry on the new mission single-handed, Mrs. Cushman reluctantly resigned the work and returned home, a widow at nineteen years of age. After teaching a short time in Oberlin College, she was married to M. B. Bateham, editor of the "Ohio Cultivator," and removed to Columbus, Ohio. There they resided fourteen years, spending part of their summers in travel in the old world and the new, and jointly editing the "Cultivator," afterward the "Ohio Farmer." Always foremost in church and reform work and widely known by her writings, her hospitable home was ever a center of attraction. In 1864 they removed to

Painesville, Ohio, for the benefit of Mr. Bateham's health. There for sixteen years Mrs. Bateham devoted herself to her growing family, to writing, to missionary and temperance work, and was then bereft of her husband, who had always encouraged her literary and reform efforts. Thenceforward she did the work of both parents. One child, twelve years old, had died. At the opening of the temperance crusade in Ohio, in 1874, Mrs. Bateham became the leader of the Painesville crusade band, and later one of the leaders in the State Woman's Christian Temperance Union. In 1884 she was made national superintendent of the Sabbath observance department of that organization, and her eldest daughter, Minerva, was her secretary till her death, in 1885, after eighteen years of invalidism. Mrs. Bateham removed to Asheville, N. C., in 1890, where she devotes her time to the work of the Woman's Christian Temperance Union. During 1890 she traveled sixteen-thousand miles, in nearly every State and Territory and through the Hawaiian Islands, and gave nearly three-hundred lectures. She has written a long line of valuable leaflets on Sabbath questions, of which she sends out more than a million pages every year. A natural leader and organizer, and acceptable both as a writer and speaker, she is now one of the foremost

JOSEPHINE PENFIELD CUSHMAN BATEHAM.

workers in the interest of a protected civil and a well-kept Christian Sabbath in our land.

BATEMAN, Isabel, actor, born near Cincinnati, Ohio, 28th December, 1854. Her family removed to England in 1863, and she first played a juvenile part in 1865 in her sister Kate's farewell benefit at Her Majesty's Theater. She began active theatrical work in 1869. She took leading parts with Henry Irving for six years. She has been very successful in many leading rôles.

BATEMAN, Kate, actor, born in Baltimore, Md., 7th October, 1842. She made her début in Louisville, Ky., at the age of five years. In 1850, as one of the Bateman Children, she appeared in the principal cities of Great Britain. She retired from the stage in 1856, but reappeared in 1860. In 1862 she made her first pronounced success as Julia in "The Hunchback," in the Winter Garden, New York. For several years she played leading parts in Great Britain as well as in the United States. In 1866 Miss Bateman became the wife of Dr. George Crowe, and took up her permanent residence in England. She has appeared in every city of importance in this country as well as in Great Britain.

BATES, Miss Charlotte Fiske, SEE ROGÉ, MRS. CHARLOTTE.

BATES, Mrs. Clara Doty, author, born in Ann Arbor, Mich., in 185-. She is the second daughter of Samuel Rosecrans Doty and Hannah Lawrence, who were among the pioneers of Michigan. Mrs. Bates comes of stalwart stock, mingled Dutch and English blood. Her great-grandfather,

CLARA DOTY BATES.

a Rosecrans, was ninety years old when he died, and the legend goes that at the time of his death "his hair was as black as a raven's wing." Another ancestor was with Washington at Valley Forge. On the mother's side are the Lawrences, and Hannah Lawrence, the great-grandmother, was famous for her gift of story-telling. Clara had a rhyming talent from her earliest days. She wrote verses when she could only print in big letters. Her first poem was published when she was nine years old. The most of her published work has been fugitive, although she has written several books, chiefly for children. Among these are "Æsop's Fables Versified," "Child Lore," "Classics of Babyland," "Heart's Content," and several minor books, all published in Boston. Her life up to her marriage was passed in Ann Arbor. The homestead, "Heart's Content," was well known for its treasures of books and pictures. The location of the State University in Ann Arbor

gave better facilities for education than were offered in the usual western village. It was before the admission of women to equal opportunities with men, but it was possible to secure private instruction in advanced studies. This the little flock of Doty girls had in addition to private schools, while the son had the university. Clara Doty was married in 1869 to Morgan Bates, a newspaper man and the author of several plays. Her home is in Chicago, Ill. She is a member of the Fortnightly literary club. She is upon the literary committee of the Woman's Branch of the World's Congress Auxiliary. All her manuscript and notes were destroyed by the burning of her father's house several years ago. Among them were a finished story, a half-completed novel and some other work. Mrs. Bates is fond of outdoor life and is a woman of marked individuality.

BATES, Miss Katharine Lee, author and educator, born in Falmouth, Mass., 12th August, 1859. Her father was Rev. William Bates of the Congregational denomination; his father was the Rev. Joshua Bates of the same denomination, and also president of Middlebury College, Vermont. Her mother was Cornelia Lee, daughter of Samuel Lee, tinsmith, Northampton, Mass. Her father died in 1859, within three weeks of her birth, leaving four children. The family remained in Falmouth until 1871, removing then to the neighborhood of Boston. Miss Bates was educated in the Falmouth primary and grammar schools; the Needham high school, graduating in 1874; the more advanced Newton high school, graduating in 1876; and Wellesley College, graduating in 1880, having been throughout the course president of her class. After graduation she taught mathematics, classics and English in the Natick high school, and then for four years mathematics and classics, gradually concentrating her work on Latin, in the leading preparatory school for Wellesley, Dana Hall. In 1885 she was called to the college as instructor in English literature, in 1888 was made associate professor, and in 1891 professor in charge. In 1890 she went abroad for rest, travel and study. In connection with educational work, she has edited Coleridge's "Ancient Mariner" (Boston, 1889), and a collection of "Ballads" (Boston, 1890), published by an educational firm in their series of English classics. Her general literary work has been always subordinate to the demands of a life closely busied with educational concerns. She has published prose and verse from her undergraduate days to the present time, but irregularly and often too hastily. In prose she wrote stories and sketches as an undergraduate for the Springfield "Republican" and a few other papers, has since contributed to the "Chautauquan," "Independent," "Christian Union," "Congregationalist," "Youth's Companion," and other publications. She took the first prize, $700, offered by the Congregational Publishing Society for a young people's story, to be published in book form, with "Rose and Thorn" (Boston, 1889). This volume was followed by another juvenile story, "Hermit Island" (Boston, 1890). In verse she took a college prize for a Latin boat-song, another for an English poem, was class poet, and has since served as commencement poet. Outside of college she took a prize offered by the Congregational Publishing Society for the children's poem, "Sunshine," since issued as an illustrated booklet (Boston, 1887). The same publishers have since issued her two similar booklets, "Santa Claus' Riddle" and "Goody Santa Claus." Her first book venture was a compilation known as the "Wedding Day Book" (Boston, 1882). In 1889 she won a prize of $30 for a quatrain contributed to the "Magazine of Poetry." She has published verses in the "Century," "Atlantic," "Independent," "New England Magazine," "Wide Awake" and many other publications, and has issued two small volumes for private sale in aid of one of the college funds which is under the control of the Wellesley alumnæ.

BATES, Mrs. Margaret Holmes, author, born in Fremont, Ohio, 6th October, 1844. Her maiden name was Ernsperger, and after five generations on American soil the name preserves its original spelling and pronunciation. Mrs. Bates' father was born and bred in Baltimore, Md. He went with his father's family some time after he had attained his majority and settled in northern Ohio. From Ohio he removed to Rochester, Ind., in the fall of 1858. The mother's family, as purely German as the father's, were Pennsylvanians. As a family, they were scholarly and

MARGARET HOLMES BATES.

polished, running to professions, notably those of law and theology. In Mrs. Bates' childhood she showed great fondness for books, and, as a schoolgirl, the weekly or fortnightly "composition" was to her a pleasant pastime, a respite from the duller, more prosaic studies of mathematics and the rules of grammar. It was her delight to be allowed, when out of school, to put her fancies into form in writing, or to sit surrounded by her young sisters and baby brother and tell them stories as they came into her mind. In June, 1865, she was married to Charles Austin Bates, of Medina, N. Y., and since that time her home has been in Indianapolis, Ind. Fascinated for several years after her marriage with the idea of becoming a model housekeeper, and conscientious to a painful degree in the discharge of her duties as a mother, she wrote nothing for publication, and but little, even at the solicitations of friends, for special occasions. This way of life, unnatural for her,

proved unhealthful. Her poem, "Nineveh," is an epitome of her life, and when health seemed to have deserted her, she turned to pencil and tablet for pastime and wrote much for newspapers and periodicals. Her first novel, "Manitou" (1881), was written at the urgent request of her son. It embodies a legend connected with the beautiful little lake of that name in northern Indiana, in the vicinity of which Mrs. Bates lived for several years before her marriage. "The Chamber Over the Gate" (Indianapolis, 1886), has had a wide sale. Besides her gifts as a writer of fiction, she is a poet, some of her poems having attracted wide attention.

BATTEY, Mrs. Emily Verdery, journalist, born in Belair, near Augusta, Ga., about the year 1828. She began her career as a journalist soon after the close of the Civil War, writing first for several Georgia newspapers, and traveling and corresponding for the "Ladies Home Gazette" of Atlanta, under the editorial guidance of her brother-in-law, Col. John S. Prather, an ex-confederate cavalry officer. Mrs. Battey went to New York in 1870, securing editorial positions at once on the "Tablet," the "Home Journal" and the "Telegram" and occasionally writing for the "Star," the "Democrat," the "Herald" and "Harper's Magazine." The "Sun," under the management of Hon. Amos J. Cummings and Dr. John B. Wood, frequently printed reports, special articles and editorials from Mrs. Battey's facile pen. In 1875 she became a salaried member of the staff of the "Sun," which position she held until 1890. While filling that position Mrs. Battey wrote for several syndicates, as well as special articles for newspapers in various parts of the country, signing various pen-names. She is not and never has been one of those workers who desire to acquire notoriety. Her aim has always been to do earnest work, and that work has always been excellent. The story of her career she tells in a lecture "Twenty Years on the Press." Her long experience on the New York press has made her well acquainted with leading women of the world, social, literary, political and religious. No woman knows better than she the history of the founding and progress of the various important women's clubs, guilds, temperance and religious societies and associations of the United States. The fruit of this wide knowledge has ripened for the delectation of those audiences that have heard her lecture, "The Woman's Century." She is a highly cultured and charming woman. Her home is now in Georgia and Alabama, with her relatives of the Verdery family. Childless herself, she has devoted her earnest life to her family ties and the study and assistance of her own sex.

BAXTER, Mrs. Annie White, business woman, born in Pittsburgh, Pa., 2nd March, 1864. She is of American parentage and of English and German extraction. She spent her early school-days in Newark, Ohio. Her parents removed to Carthage, Mo., in 1877, where her education was finished. She was graduated from the high school department of the Carthage public schools in 1882, and in July of the same year, she went to work as an assistant in the county clerk's office under George Blakeney, then clerk of the county court of Jasper county, Mo. She continued to perform the duties of that position with increased efficiency and remuneration under Mr. Blakeney's successor until November, 1885, when she was appointed and sworn as a regular deputy clerk of the county court, with power and authority to affix the clerk's signature and the county seal to all official documents, and to perform all other official acts under the law. The elevation of a woman to a position of so much responsibility attracted no small amount of attention. The statutes of Missouri required that a deputy should have all the qualifications of a clerk, and the opinion of the attorney-

ANNIE WHITE BAXTER.

general of the State was necessary before the county court would approve the appointment. The duties of this office are by far the most complicated and laborious of any office in the county, embracing the entire tax levy and extension, in a county of more than 50,000 people, the custody, computation and collection of interest on a public school fund of over $225,000 loaned out to citizens of the county, and keeping accounts and making settlements with the state treasurer, state auditor, county treasurer, county collector and all county and township officers entrusted with the collection and custody of state and county revenues, as well as writing the records and executing the acts and orders of the county court. Miss White shrank from no duty, and her keen perception, intuitive acumen, mathematical precision, untiring application, energy and directness, and her pleasing address and manners won for her the esteem and confidence of the entire population. She was found equal to every occasion and served so well that under the next incumbent of the clerkship she was again appointed and qualified as principal deputy. She was married to C. W. Baxter, of Carthage, Mo., 14th January, 1888, and withdrew from official duty to attend to the more pleasant tastes of domestic life, but, the county clerk becoming partly disabled by paralysis, she was induced again to take charge of the office. In 1890, she was placed in nomination for county clerk by the regular Democratic county convention for county clerk. Jasper county had for years polled a large Republican majority, but, although her rival was regarded as a popular and competent man, Mrs. Baxter received a majority of 463 votes at the polls. She took charge of the office as clerk under a commission signed by Gov. D. R. Francis. She

is the first woman in the United States elected by the people and qualified under the law to fill the office of clerk of a court of record. Mrs. Baxter retains all her womanly refinement and modesty, maintains a popular position in social life, and bears her honors and responsibilities with unconcious ease and natural grace.

BAXTER, Mrs. Marion Babcock, lecturer and author, born on a farm in Litchfield, Hillsdale county, Mich., 12th April, 1850. Her father, Abel E. Babcock, was an Adventist minister in the times when it required courage to preach an unpopular doctrine. Her mother, Mary Babcock, was a gracious woman, to whose love and tender teaching Mrs. Baxter owes all that she is. Mrs. Baxter traces her lineage back to the Reformation in England. Her early childhood was spent in poverty and self-denial, and she was familiar with work, for which she has ever been thankful. In childhood she had few companions, for the Adventist doctrine was so unpopular and the persecution so pointed that even the children caught the spirit and were accustomed to tease her. Many a time she has climbed a tree to avoid their persecution. In her girlhood she developed a very fine voice and was much in demand for concert singing, but she lost her voice suddenly, and turned to the lecture platform. Her first lecture was given in Jonesville, Mich., where she had lived since she was five years old. Her subject was "The Follies of Fashion," quite appropriate for one whose life had been spent in comparative poverty. On that occasion the opera-house was packed, a band furnished music, and all the world of Jonesville was there. Her first effort was a success in every way, and she eventually became widely known as a lecturer. She was mar-

MARION BABCOCK BAXTER.

ried at the age of twenty-two years to C. E. K. Baxter, a son of Levi Baxter, the head of one of the oldest and most respected families in the state. She is at present the State president of the White

Rose League. She has been a member of the Woman's Christian Temperance Union since its organization and has for years been a member of the Congregational church.

BAYLOR, Miss Frances Courtenay, author, born in Fayetteville, Ark., 20th January,

FRANCES COURTENAY BAYLOR.

1848. She is descended from an old Virginian family of English strain. Her childhood was spent in San Antonio and New Orleans, where her father, an army officer, was stationed. She was educated principally by her mother and her aunt, in her own home. After the Civil War was ended, she went to Europe and spent the years 1865 to 1867 in travel and residence in England and on the Continent. She spent 1873-74 in Europe, and during her sojourn there she gathered the materials for her literary work. Since 1876 she has lived in an old home near Winchester, Va. Her literary career began with articles in various newspapers, and she contributed to "Lippincott's Magazine," the "Atlantic Monthly" and the "Princeton Review." Among her earlier productions was a play, "Petruchio Tamed." She won a prominent position by her novel, "On Both Sides" (Philadelphia, 1885), in which she contrasts the American and English characters, manners and social creeds. Her second book was "Juan and Juanita" (Boston, 1886). Her third was "Behind the Blue Ridge" (Philadelphia, 1887). All these volumes were highly successful, passing through many editions in a short time. The first, "On Both Sides," was republished in Edinburgh. Miss Baylor deservedly ranks high as an author of remarkable powers of observation, of judgment, of humorous comment, and of philosophic generalization.

BEACH, Mrs. H. H. A., composer, born in Henniker, N. H., 5th September, 1867. Her parents were Charles Abbott and Clara Imogene Cheney. Mrs. Cheney, born Marcy, was well known as an excellent musician, and it is due to

her careful supervision and fostering care that Mrs. Beach's early musical development was so systematic and judicious. The earliest evidences of her musical powers were manifested before she was a year old, and as she was so situated as to hear much good music, she soon acquired the habit of catching the songs that were sung to her. When three years old, to play the piano was her chief delight, and soon she could play at sight any music that her hands could grasp. At the age of four years she played many tunes by ear. She improvised much and composed several little pieces. Among her earliest musical recollections is that of associating color with sound, the key of C suggesting white, A flat, blue, and so on. The exact pitch of sounds, single or in combination, produced by voice, violin, piano, bells, whistles or birds' songs, has always been perfectly clear to her, making it possible for her to name the notes at once. When she was six years old, her mother began a course of systematic instruction, which continued for two years. At the age of seven she played in three concerts. She continued to compose little pieces. Among these were an air with variations and a setting of the "Rainy Day" of Longfellow, since published. Regular instruction in harmony was begun at the age of fourteen. For ten years, with various interruptions, Mrs. Beach received instruction in piano playing from prominent teachers in Boston. She made her first appearance before a Boston audience as Miss Amy Marcy Cheney on 24th October, 1883, at sixteen years of age, playing the G minor concerto of Moscheles with grand orchestra. That performance was succeeded by various concerts and recitals in Boston and other places, in association with distinguished artists. In December,

MRS. H. H. A. BEACH.

1885, she was married to Dr. H. H. A. Beach, and since then has frequently contributed her services for the benefit of the charitable and educational institutions of Boston, in recitals and performances with orchestra. Her talent in composition has shown itself in the following list of published works : A grand mass in E flat, a graduale for tenor voice, an anthem for chorus and organ, three short anthems for quartet with organ accompaniment, a four-part song for female voices, three vocal duets with pianoforte accompaniment, nineteen songs for single voice with a pianoforte accompaniment, a cadenza to Beethoven's C minor concerto, and a valse caprice for piano. She has in manuscript other compositions, a ballad, several short pieces for the piano or piano and violin, and songs. The mass was performed on 7th February, 1892, by the Händel and Haydn Society of Boston, with the Symphony Orchestra and a quartet of soloists assisting.

BEASLEY, Mrs. Marie Wilson, elocutionist and dramatic reader, born in Silver Creek, a suburb of Philadelphia, Pa., about 1862. When she was seven years old, her father removed to the West and settled on a farm near Grand Rapids, Mich. Marie lived on the farm until she was fourteen years old, when her father died, leaving the family to make their own way. Bearing good credentials from the citizens of Paris, Kent county, Marie removed to Grand Rapids. She became a member of the Baptist Church at the age of fourteen years, but is liberal in sentiment towards all creeds that teach Christ and his works. In her youth, while striving to secure an education, she made her needle her support, earning by hard work enough money to enable her to attend Hillsdale College, Hillsdale, Mich., for a year. She afterwards studied under Professor Walter C. Lyman, of Chicago, and since 1883, when she made her début as an elocutionist and reader, and also as an instructor in the art of elocution, she has taught

MARIE WILSON BEASLEY.

many who are already prominent in that field, and her readings have brought her a reputation in many States. She was married in January, 1889, to J. H. Beasley, of Grand Rapids, where they now reside. They spent one year in San Francisco and other points in California. Besides her work as an elocutionist and instructor, she has been a successful lecturer, taking an active interest in the relation of women to law and society. The theme of one of her most successful efforts on the lecture platform is "Woman's Rights, or the XVIth Amendment to the Constitution of the United States of America." She is a woman of amiable disposition, much force and decided powers of intellect.

BEAUCHAMP, Miss Mary Elizabeth, educator and author, born in Burleigh, England,

MARY ELIZABETH BEAUCHAMP.

14th June, 1825. The family removed to this country in 1829, establishing themselves in Coldenham, Orange county, N. Y. In 1832 they removed to Skaneateles, N. Y., where Mr. Beauchamp went into the book business, to which seven years later he united a printing office and the publication of a weekly newspaper, which still maintains a healthy existence. In 1834 he established a thoroughly good circulating library, of nearly a thousand volumes, which was very successful for many years. His daughter had free range of its carefully selected treasures and early acquired an unusual familiarity with the best writers of the language. The little girl wrote rhymes when she was ten years old, acrostics for her schoolmates and wildly romantic ballads. Before she entered her "teens" she had become a regular contributor to a juvenile magazine, for which, in her fourteenth year, she furnished a serial running through half a volume. From that time she wrote under various pen-names for several papers and had achieved the honor of an illustrated tale in "Peterson's Magazine" before she was twenty. Then her literary career was checked by ill-health, and for ten years her pen was laid aside almost entirely. What she published during that time appeared in religious papers under the pen-name "Filia

Ecclesiæ,'' and some of these pieces found their way into cotemporary collections of sacred poetry. In 1853, accompanied by a younger brother, she visited England, where she remained nearly two years. At the desire of her uncle, a vicar in Wells, she prepared a "Handbook of Wells Cathedral," which was published in different styles with illustrations. After returning home she wrote a series of papers entitled "The Emigrant's Quest" which attracted for a year attention and were republished in a modest little volume some years later. Her mother died in 1859, and the death of her father in 1867 broke up her home in Skaneateles, and in the ensuing year she took the position of teacher in the orphan ward of the Church Charity Foundation, in Buffalo, N. Y., remaining there twelve years. In 1879 she went to Europe for a year accompanied by a lady who had been happily associated with her in church work. Soon after returning to this country Miss Beauchamp learned that the Mission of the Protestant Episcopal Church to the Onondaga Indians was in temporary need of a teacher. She offered her services and was delighted with the work. She next purchased a residence in Skaneateles, where she conducted a school for the children of summer residents, organized a literary society for young ladies, and had adult pupils in French and drawing. She took her full share in parochial and missionary work and wrote for religious papers. In March, 1890, she was prostrated for some months by cerebral hemorrhage, and has since resided with a married sister in Skaneateles.

BEAUMONT, Mrs. Betty Bentley, author and merchant, born in Lancastershire, England, 9th August, 1828. She was the only child of Joseph Bentley, the great educational reformer of

BETTY BENTLEY BEAUMONT.

England. Mr. Bentley organized and conducted a society for "the promotion of the education of the people," and wrote and published thirty-three books to improve the methods of education, but he presents

another example of the neglect, by public benefactors, of those bound to them by the closest ties of nature. He allowed his child to acquire only the elements of an education, and took her from school in her tenth year and employed her in his business to copy his manuscripts, correct proof and attend lectures. The independent spirit of the little girl was roused by a strange act on the part of her father. He showed her a summing up of the expenses she had been to him in the ten years of her life. To a child it seemed a large amount, and having set her young brain to devise some plan by which she might support herself so as to be of no further expense to her father, she surreptitiously learned the milliners' trade. She loved her books, and her propensity for learning was exceptional, but her opportunity for study was extremely limited. At a very early age she was married to Edward Beaumont, and came to America seven years after her marriage. They lived in Philadelphia for five years and, on account of Mr. Beaumont's feeble health, removed to the South, going to Woodville, Miss. The coming on of the Civil War and the state of feeling in a southern town toward suspected abolitionists are most interestingly described in Mrs. Beaumont's "Twelve Years of My Life." (Philadelphia, 1887). The failing health of her husband and the needs of a family of seven children called forth her inherent energy, and she promptly began what she felt herself qualified to carry on to success, and became one of the leading merchants of the town. Her varied experiences during a period of historical interest are given in "A Business Woman's Journal" (Philadelphia, 1888). That book graphically explains the financial state of the cotton-growing region of the South during the years immediately succeeding the Civil War, the confusion consequent upon the transition from the credit system to a cash basis, and the condition of the suddenly freed blacks. Mrs. Beaumont's books are valuable because they have photographed a period that quickly passed. Her style is simple and unpretending. She is one of the hard-working business women of to-day. She has shown independence of spirit, self-sacrificing courage and remarkable tenacity of purpose. She has a kind and sympathizing heart, and a nature susceptible to every gentle and elevating influence.

BECK, Miss Leonora, educator, born near Augusta, Ga., in 1862. At an early age she showed an unusual aptitude for linguistic study, speaking several modern languages when nine years old. She was well grounded in Latin and Greek when fifteen years old. Oxford College, Ala., having thrown open its doors to young women, and being the only college for men in the South which received them, Miss Beck entered and received a careful and thorough training for her chosen profession. At the age of sixteen years she was graduated with A.M. distinction and at once accepted the position of young lady principal in the Bowden, Georgia, College, which she held for two-and-one-half years. During her connection with that institution Miss Beck instructed in metaphysics, Latin and Greek about one-hundred students, ranging from the ages of fifteen to thirty years. Her success as an educator becoming more generally known, she was urged to accept many positions of trust and honor, but declined them. The Jackson Institute was her next field of labor, and that now famous school owes its popularity and success in a great measure to the energy of thought and action which characterized her work while connected with it. In 1889 Miss Beck removed to Atlanta to engage in founding a first-class school for girls. That college, first known as the Capital Female College, is now known as the Leonora Beck College. The success of the school has been remarkable. Under the principalship of Miss Beck, with a board of trustees

LEONORA BECK.

selected from the best-known educators of the land, and with a corps of seventeen assistant teachers in all the various branches of learning and fine arts, the school has taken rank with the foremost colleges for young women in the South. Socially Miss Beck is very popular. The amplitude of her mind and the generosity of her nature make her a desirable friend and interesting companion. In everything she does there is an earnest purpose, which illustrates a strong mental and spiritual law. Her sympathies are acute, and the sincere interest which she manifests in all of humanity makes her at once a power for good. Miss Beck is an occasional contributor to the periodical press. A series of essays on Robert Browning is, perhaps, her most enduring contribution to literature.

BECKWITH, Mrs. Emma, woman suffragist, born in Cincinnati, Ohio, 4th December, 1849. Her maiden name was Knight. Her father was born and reared near Baltimore, Md. Her mother is a direct descendant of the Sherman family, and to that fact Mrs. Beckwith probably owes her political tendencies and, we might say, her fighting propensities as well, for it is said that from her earliest childhood she was always befriending the weak and helpless, if they proved worthy of her support. She received a thorough common-school education, graduating at the age of seventeen years from the high school in Toledo, Ohio, whither her parents went when she was four years old. Her ambition was to earn money enough to cultivate her exceptionally fine musical talent. The only avenue open was a store clerkship, but the opposition of schoolmates and friends dissuaded her from making the attempt. At that time it was not considered respectable for a young lady to

stand behind a counter and measure off dry-goods and ribbons for women, and possibly men customers. It was the remembrance of that keen disappointment in her early life which led her to sympathize with the educational features of nationalism. At the age of nineteen years she was married to Edwin Beckwith, of Mentor, Ohio. After residing in Pleasantville, Iowa, a number of years, during which time she had ample opportunity to observe the necessity of more freedom for women, they removed to Brooklyn, N. Y. Her sympathies with women have always been on the alert. In her early life she found it inadvisable to read the journals devoted to their cause, on account of the extended knowledge of their grievances they gave her, and, not being in a position to help, she preferred not to feed her aforesaid fighting propensities. Upon locating in the East she began to put to practical use her knowledge of bookkeeping, after obtaining the permission of the owner of a building in Nassau street, New York, by promising to be good and not demoralize the men employed in the several offices in the building. She began work in April, 1879. Feeling assured that other women would soon follow in her footsteps, she fully realized that by her acts they would be judged. She was the pioneer woman bookkeeper in that part of the city and established a reputation for modesty and uprightness that has helped many another to a like position. Her business education of five years' duration gave her an insight into many matters not general among women. After leaving business life she turned her attention towards acquainting others with the knowledge thus gained and urging young women to become self-supporting. She believed that by working in that direction the vexed

EMMA BECKWITH.

question of marriage would eventually be settled. About that time she became acquainted with Mrs. Belva A. Lockwood and, having become disgusted with the vast amount of talk and so little practical work among the advocates of woman suffrage, felt that Mrs. Lockwood had struck the key-note of the situation when she became a candidate for the presidency of the United States. When she realized Mrs. Lockwood's earnestness of purpose, her ambition was roused to the point of emulation; hence her candidacy for the mayoralty of Brooklyn, as the representative of the equal rights party for that office, for she believes that a local treatment is best for any disease. The result testified to the correctness of her belief. The campaign of ten days' duration with but two public meetings, resulted in her receiving fifty votes regularly counted, and many more thrown out among the scattering, before the New York "Tribune" made a demand for her vote. Mrs. Beckwith has compiled many incidents relating to that novel campaign in a lecture on the subject. She believes thoroughly that women should take an active part in the political as well as the religious and social field, thus becoming broader and more charitable, and none the less loving, kind and womanly. Free from jealousy of any sort, believing in individualism, she is naturally an earnest advocate of the cause of the oppressed of all classes. She has entered the regular lecture field and is an able and entertaining speaker, enlivening her earnestness with bright, witty sayings.

BEDFORD, Mrs. Lou Singletary, author, born in Feliciana, Graves county, Ky., 7th April, 1837. She comes of a good and distinguished

LOU SINGLETARY BEDFORD.

family on both sides. Her father, Luther Singletary, was of English descent and a native of Massachusetts, born in 1796. He was educated and spent his early manhood in Boston. Her mother, Elizabeth Hamilton Stell, was born in 1802, in Dinwiddie county, near Petersburg, Va. Mrs. Lou Singletary Bedford is the fifth child and third daughter of Mr. and Mrs. Singletary. Her father was a teacher, and his little daughter was placed in his school at six years of age. She had no special

love for books, except for reading, spelling and grammar, but her ambition kept her at the head of most of her classes. Nearly all of her education was received under her father's instruction in a country school, though she completed her course of study in Clinton Seminary. After leaving school she taught for a year or two. In 1857 she became the wife of John Joseph Bedford, a friend and associate of her childhood. There were six children born to them four of whom are living. The father, a grown daughter, and a son are dead. Of the three living sons two are married. The other lives in El Paso, Texas, and is assisting to educate the youngest and only remaining daughter. Mrs. Bedford's literary career has in a great measure become identified with Texas, her adopted home. Her first poems were offered for publication when she was in her sixteenth year, appearing under a pen-name. She continued to write until her marriage, from which time her pen was silent for nearly fifteen years. When home cares to some extent were lifted, the accumulated experience and deep thought of years of silence found vent in song. The result was two volumes, "A Vision, and Other Poems" (Cincinnati and London, 1881), and "Gathered Leaves" (Dallas, 1889). Mrs. Bedford has for many years contributed to various periodicals, and her influence is felt in social circles embracing many southern States. Her present home is in El Paso, Texas, where she fills the position of social and literary editor of the El Paso "Sunday Morning Tribune."

BEECHER, Miss Catherine Esther, author and educator, born in East Hampton, L. I., 6th September, 1800, died in Elmira, N. Y., 12th May, 1878. Catherine was the oldest child of Lyman Beecher and Roxana Foote Beecher, and the first nine years of her life were spent in the place of her nativity, where she enjoyed the teaching of a loving mother and a devoted aunt, the latter of whom was a woman of great beauty, elegance and refinement, and to whose early instructions Miss Beecher often recurred as having a strong and lasting influence upon her life. In her ninth year Catherine removed with her parents to Litchfield, Conn., a mountain town, celebrated alike for the beauty of its scenery and the exceptional cultivation and refinement of its inhabitants. There, in the female seminary, under the care of Miss Sarah Pearse, Miss Beecher began her career as a schoolgirl. At an early age she showed talent for versification, and her poetical effusions, mostly in a humorous vein, were handed about among her school-mates and friends, to be admired by all. In her sixteenth year her mother died, and Miss Beecher's later writings carried an undercurrent of sadness in place of the happy, frolicsome poems of earlier days. As the oldest of the family, her mother's death brought upon her the cares and responsibilities of a large family. After a suitable period of mourning had elapsed, her father was married again to a woman of culture and piety, under whose organization the parsonage became the center of a cultivated circle of society, where music, painting and poetry combined to lend a charm to existence. Parties were formed for reading, and it was that fact which led Miss Beecher again to take up her pen, in order to lend variety to the meetings by presenting original articles occasionally. One of her poems, "Yala," written at that time, possessed no mean poetic merit as the composition of a girl of seventeen, and was extensively circulated among literary circles, especially in New Haven. At that time her father, who had risen into the front ranks of influence in Connecticut, in conjunction with literary men connected with Yale College, projected the idea of a monthly magazine of literature and theology, to be called the "Christian Spectator." To that magazine Miss Beecher was a frequent contributor under the initials "C. D. D." Those poems attracted the attention of a young professor of mathematics in Yale College, Alexander M. Fisher, who, after making the acquaintance of Miss Beecher, in due time became her betrothed husband. The wedding was arranged to take place immediately upon the return from Europe of Professor Fisher, who had gone abroad in pursuance of his educational ideas. Again was Miss Beecher to feel the hand of fate. The young lover never returned to claim his promised bride, having perished in a storm which struck the vessel off the coast of Ireland. For a time Miss Beecher could see no light through the clouds which overshadowed her, and it was feared that even her religious faith would forsake her. She was sent to Yale, in the hope that the companionship of Professor Fisher's relatives might have a beneficial effect upon the stricken mind. Shortly after her arrival there, she was induced to begin the study of mathematics under the guidance of Willard Fisher, a brother of her late lover. After a time she went back to Litchfield, united with her father's church, and resolved to let insoluble problems alone and to follow Christ. Shortly after that, Miss Beecher, in conjunction with her sister, opened a select school in Hartford, Conn. Such was the success of that school, that in four years' time there was not room for the scholars who applied for admittance. She had always enjoyed the friendship of the leading women of Hartford, and when she began to agitate the subject of a female seminary in that town, it was through their influence that the prominent men of Hartford became interested in the project and subscribed the money to purchase the land and erect the buildings, which afterward became known as the Hartford Female Seminary. With Miss Beecher as principal and a band of eight teachers of her selection, the school grew rapidly in influence and popularity. She published "Suggestions on Education," which was widely read and drew attention to the Hartford Seminary from all parts of the United States. With all the cares of a school of between one and two hundred pupils, her influence was felt, even to the minutest particular. She planned the course of study, guided the teachers, overlooked the boarding-houses and corresponded with parents and guardians. With all those cares on her mind, she yet found time to prepare an arithmetic, which was printed and used as a text-book in her school and those emanating from it. About that time the teacher in mental philosophy left the institution, and Miss Beecher not only took charge of that department, but wrote a text-book of some four or five-hundred pages, entitled "Mental and Moral Philosophy, Founded on Reason, Observation and the Bible." She kept up her piano practice, and now and then furnished a poem to the weekly "Connecticut Observer." After seven years of incessant activity her health gave out, and she was obliged to relinquish the school into other hands. Shortly after that the family removed to Cincinnati, Ohio, and, in connection with a younger sister, Miss Beecher commenced a school in that city. Although she did not personally labor in that institution, the teaching was all done by instructors of her own training. In connection with other women she formed a league for supplying the West with educated teachers, and, as the result, many teachers were sent West and many schools founded. During the latter years of her life, she devoted her time to authorship. Her first work, a treatise

on "Domestic Economy" (1845), was designed as a text-book for schools. That was followed by "Duty of American Women to Their Country" (1845), "Domestic Receipt Book" (1846), "Miss Beecher's Address" (1846), "Letters to the People" (1855), "Physiology and Calisthenics" (1856), "Common Sense Applied to Religion" (1857), "An Appeal to the People" (1860), "The Religious Training of Children" (1864), "The Housekeeper and Healthkeeper" (1873). In her sixty-first year she united with the Episcopal Church by confirmation, in company with three of her young nieces. She lived to be seventy-eight years of age, and although crippled by sciatica for the last ten years of her life, the activity of her mind and her zeal in education continued to the last.

BEHAN, Miss Bessie, social leader, born in New Orleans, La., 5th March, 1872. She is a daughter of Gen. W. J. Behan, a prominent southern merchant and an extensive sugar planter. She

BESSIE BEHAN.

was educated at home by skilled governesses, and had all the advantages of much travel. Her associations in the quaint Anglo-French city of New Orleans made the acquisition of the French language easy and natural, and she is thus master of two languages. Her education was completed, and she made her début in society in New Orleans in 1891, at once taking rank as a belle and winning general popularity. Her type of beauty has nothing of what is commonly called "creole." The most coveted of all social honors in New Orleans is to be chosen queen in the Mardi Gras Carnival. That honor fell to Miss Behan in the carnival of 1891, and, was made the occasion of a memorable display of the regard felt for her by the people of her native city. She bore the festival honors easily and regally. She was not yet out of her teens when she was chosen Carnival Queen, and she was the youngest woman yet selected for coronation in that characteristic festival.

BELCHER, Mrs. Cynthia Holmes, journalist, born in Lunenburgh, Vt., 1st December, 1827. She is a daughter of the Hon. George E. and Mary Moore Holmes. Her father served

CYNTHIA HOLMES BELCHER.

as a member of the State Senate and as judge in Essex county. Miss Holmes was educated in the academy in St. Johnsbury, Vt. Her father removed his family of seven daughters from St. Johnsbury to Port Byron, Ill., when she was eighteen years old. In her twentieth year she was married to Nathaniel Belcher, a descendant of prominent New England people and one of the pioneers in the settlement of Illinois. He held various offices of trust and was a member of the Whig party that nominated General Winfield Scott for the presidency, and was a prolific political writer. Mr. and Mrs. Belcher traveled extensively. In 1881 they visited Colorado, and in 1882 went to California, where they passed a pleasant year. Their tour included all parts of the Union. On one of their visits to Washington, D. C., they were received by President Franklin Pierce, and on a later occasion visited President Grant in the White House. After the death of her husband and two children Mrs. Belcher returned to New England and settled in Boston, that she might indulge and develope her literary, artistic and musical talents. She studied singing in the New England Conservatory of Music and gradually became known also as a contributor to leading newspapers. In 1889 she visited Europe and contributed letters on her travels through the different countries, also describing the Paris Exposition. She is a member of the New England Woman's Press Association. Besides her literary work, she has always been identified with all works of reform, and with church and temperance work, the woman suffrage movement in particular receiving much thought and labor from her. All her thought has been in the line of elevating the individual and the community.

BELL, Mrs. Caroline Horton, philanthropist, born in Windham, Green county, N. Y., 28th December, 1840. Her father, Rev. Goodrich Horton, was a minister of the Methodist Episcopal Church, a descendant of the Goodriches, one of those earnest, pious, old colonial families. Her mother, whose maiden name was Lydia Fairchild, was a granddaughter of John Fairchild, an officer in the war of the Revolution, and also of Joseph Woodworth, a soldier in the same war. She received a liberal education in a seminary in Springfield, Mass. Miss Horton was married 11th October, 1866, to Samuel R. Bell, and they settled in Milwaukee, Wis., where they have since resided. Mr. Bell was a soldier of the Rebellion, enlisting in the 28th Wisconsin Regiment and winning an honorable record. Soon after the formation of the department of the Wisconsin Woman's Relief Corps Auxiliary of the Grand Army of the Republic, Mrs. Bell became prominently connected with the order and has filled a number of positions in that organization. The work she has been enabled to accomplish in that line is important. She was a charter member of E. B. Wolcott Corps, served two years as its chaplain, and nearly two as its president, at which time she was also elected department president. Aside from the work of the Woman's Relief Corps, she has been prominently connected with various other charities of Milwaukee. She was a member of the Benevolent Society upon its organization, and afterward of the Associated Charities. She was one of the founders of the first kindergarten established in that city, and for a long time was one of the directors of the Home of the Friendless, and has been a director of the Home

CAROLINE HORTON BELL.

of the Aged since its organization. She was president of the aid society of Calvary Presbyterian Church for several years, during which time she assisted in raising money for the Young Men's

Christian Association building, and assisted in establishing a mission kindergarten on the west side of Milwaukee.

BELL, Miss Orelia Key, poet, born in Atlanta, Ga., 8th April, 1864. Her birthplace was

ORELIA KEY BELL.

the Bell mansion, a stately Southern home in the heart of the city. The house has become historic, as it was, soon after Orelia's birth, the headquarters of General Sherman's engineering corps, and the room in which she was born and spent the first three months of her life was that used by General Sherman as a stable for his favorite colt. Miss Bell is of gentle birth on both sides of her house, and is very thoroughly educated. A poem by her father, "God is Love," has been the key-note to some of her highest and sweetest songs. She suffered loss of home and property but met her reverses with a brave front and a song in her heart, and her spirit, strong in courage and purity, has voiced itself in countless melodies that have won for her both fame and money. She writes always with strength and grace. Power and melody are wedded in her poems. Her warmest recognition from the press has come from Richard Watson Gilder of the "Century," Page M. Baker, of the New Orleans "Times–Democrat," Charles A. Dana, of the New York "Sun," Mrs. Frank Leslie, Henry W. Grady, and Thaddeus E. Horton, and her own home papers the "Constitution" and the "Journal." Her poem "Maid and Matron" has been used by Rhea as a select recitation. To the instructions of her friend, Mrs. Livingston Mimms, leader of the Christian Science movement South, and founder of the first Church of Christ (Scientist) in Georgia, Miss Bell owes the inspiration of her most enduring work, the International Series of Christian Science Hymns, to the writing of which she gave much time.

BELLAMY, Mrs. Emily Whitfield Croom, novelist, born in Quincy, Fla., 17th April, 1839.

She was educated in Springer Institute, New York City. She taught in a female seminary in Eutaw, Ala., for several years. Mrs. Bellamy has written under the pen-name "Kampa Thorpe" "Four Oaks" (New York, 1867), and "Little Joanna" (New York, 1876). Besides her novels she has written many short prose articles and poems for the periodical press. Mrs. Bellamy now resides in Mobile, Ala.

BENEDICT, Miss Emma Lee, author and educator, born in Clifton Park, Saratoga county, N. Y., 16th November, 1857. The daughter of a quiet farmer, she early gained from the fields and woods a love for nature as well as the foundations of robust health and a good physique. Always fond of books, at the age of twelve years she had read nearly everything in her father's small but well-selected library. At school she was able to keep pace with pupils much older than herself, besides finding time for extra studies. Her first introduction to science was through an old school-book of her mother's, entitled "Familiar Science," and another on natural philosophy, which she carried to school and begged her teacher to hear her recite from. At seventeen she began to teach, and the following year entered the State Normal College at Albany, from which she was graduated in 1879. After a few more years of successful teaching, she began to write for educational papers and was soon called to a position on the editorial staff of the New York "School Journal," where she remained for more than three years. A desire for more extended opportunities for study and a broader scope for literary work led her to resign that position and launch on the sea of miscellaneous literature. A very successful book by her, "Stories of Persons and

EMMA LEE BENEDICT.

Places in Europe" (New York, 1887), was published in the following year, besides stories, poems and miscellaneous articles which appeared in various standard publications. Miss Benedict

was a member of the first class in pedagogy that
entered the now thoroughly established pedagogical course in the University of the City of New
York. Through contributions to the daily papers

IDA WHIPPLE BENHAM.

and interviews with leading educational people
she was an active factor in bringing about the general educational awakening in New York City, in
1888, which resulted in the formation of a new society for the advancement of education. Just at
that time she was sent for by Mrs. Mary H. Hunt,
national and international superintendent of the
department of scientific temperance instruction of
the Woman's Christian Temperance Union, to go to
Washington and assist in the revision of temperance physiologies, which had then been submitted
to Mrs. Hunt for that purpose by several of the
leading publishers of temperance text-books. In
Washington Miss Benedict spent a number of
months in the United States Medical Library, occupied in investigating and compiling the testimony
of leading medical writers concerning the nature
and effects of alcohol upon the human body. The
researches there begun have since been carried on
in Boston and New York libraries and by correspondence with leading medical and chemical authorities. There is probably no other person more
familiar than she with the whole subject of the nature and effects of alcohol upon the human system.
At present Miss Benedict is with Mrs. Mary H.
Hunt, in the home of the latter in Hyde Park,
Mass., assisting in laying out courses of study for
institute instructors and preparing manuals for the
use of teachers on the subject of physiology and
hygiene and the effects of narcotics. Miss Benedict is a pleasant, logical and forcible speaker and
writer in her special line of educational and scientific topics, and is in frequent demand as an
instructor at teachers' institutes.

BENHAM, Mrs. Ida Whipple, peace advocate, born in a farmhouse in Ledyard, Conn., 8th

January, 1849. She is a daughter of Timothy and
Lucy Ann Geer Whipple, and comes from a Quaker
family. At an early age she began to write verses.
At the age of thirteen years she taught a country
school. She was married 14th April, 1869, to
Elijah B. Benham, of Groton, Conn. She was
early made familiar with the reforms advocated by
the Quakers, such as temperance, anti-slavery, and
the abolition of war. She has lectured on peace
and temperance. She is a director of the American
Peace Society, and a member of the executive
committee of the Universal Peace Union. She
takes a conspicuous part in the large peace conventions held annually in Mystic, Conn., and she holds
a monthly peace meeting in her own home in Mystic. She has contributed poems to the New York
"Independent," the Chicago "Advance," the
"Youth's Companion," "St. Nicholas" and other
prominent periodicals.

BENJAMIN, Mrs. Anna Smeed, temperance worker, born near Lockport, Niagara county,
N. Y., 28th November, 1834. Her father and
mother were the oldest children of their respective
families, both bereft of their fathers at an early
age, and both from circumstances, as well as
by inheritance, industrious, energetic and self-
reliant in a remarkable degree. A clear sense
of right with an almost morbid conscientiousness
characterized both. All those traits are markedly
developed in their daughter, who, too, was the
oldest child. She was educated in the Lockport
union school, in Genesee Wesleyan Seminary, and
in Genesee College, now Syracuse University. In
each of those institutions she ranked among the
first in her classes. In 1855 she was married to G.
W. Benjamin, a thorough-going business man, who

ANNA SMEED BENJAMIN.

has constantly aided her work for God and home
and native land. One child, a son, was born to
them. In due time Mrs. Benjamin was drawn into
the work of the Woman's Foreign Missionary

Society. From that she naturally passed into the Woman's Christian Temperance Union, founded in 1874 as the systematized form of the great Ohio crusade. In that society her abilities at once marked her as a leader. Suffering from a morbid shyness which, as a school-girl, made the simple reading of an essay a most trying ordeal, she sought nothing more eagerly than the privilege of working in obscurity, but circumstances pushed her to the platform, where her own natural abilities have won for her a foremost place. At the convention held in Grand Rapids, Mich., in 1874, she was made chairman of a committee to draft a constitution and by-laws for the newly organized Woman's Christian Temperance Union of the Fifth Congressional District. She is now the superintendent of the national department of parliamentary usage, and the drills which she conducts in the white-ribboners' "School of Methods" and elsewhere are attended by persons of both sexes. At the Chautauquas, where she has had charge, these drills, attended by hundreds, have met an ever increasing need and have been among the most popular meetings held. Mrs. Benjamin has for years been a victim to neuralgia, but her remarkable will power has carried her on until she has become one of the leaders in State and national work. She is a logical, convincing, enthusiastic speaker with a deep, powerful voice and urgent manner. She has been elected president of the Woman's Christian Temperance Union for the fifth district of Michigan for thirteen consecutive years, and has built up white-ribbon interests in the Bay View Assembly, until that foremost summer camp has become a model for all others in that particular. Mrs. Benjamin is a notably excellent presiding officer and a skilled parliamentarian.

BENNETT, Mrs. Adelaide George, poet, born in Warner, N. H., 8th November, 1848. Her childhood was passed under the shadow of the famed Kearsarge Mountain. She is the daughter of Gilman C. and Nancy B. George and a sister of H. Maria George, who is also well-known in literary circles. She was educated in Contoocook Academy and under private tutors. She taught several years in the public schools of Manchester, N. H. In October, 1887, Miss George was married to Charles H. Bennett, of Pipestone City, Minn. Their marriage was quite a romantic one and was noticed by many papers of the country. The fascinating glamour of legend, woven into poetry by the master hand of Longfellow in his "Song of Hiawatha," led her to covet a piece of the "blood-red mystic stone" for her cabinet of geological curiosities, and she wrote to the postmaster of Pipestone City, then a paper town surveyed within the precincts of the sacred quarry, for a specimen of the stone. The specimen was forwarded by Mr. Bennett, accompanied by a set of views of the quarry and surrounding region, and a correspondence and acquaintance followed, which resulted in their marriage. On their bridal tour, while calling upon Mr. Longfellow, they informed him that he had unwittingly been a match-maker. As they went down the steps of the old colonial mansion, the venerable figure of the immortal poet was framed in the wide doorway as he beamed a benediction upon them and wished them much joy at their "hanging of the crane." Mrs. Bennett wrote no poems for the press until after her marriage. When she did write for publication, it was at the solicitation of her husband. She is a botanist of distinction. During the season of 1883 she made a collection of the flora of the Pipestone region for Prof. Winchell's report on the botanical resources of Minnesota. That collection was, at the request

ADELAIDE GEORGE BENNETT.

of Prof. Winchell, exhibited in the New Orleans World's Exposition in 1884. She is an active member of the Woman's Relief Corps, and during 1888-89 she held the office of National Inspector of Minnesota. She has quite a reputation throughout the West for the writing and rendition of poems on public occasions. Possessing rare qualifications for literary work, she has principally confined herself to poetry. She has an elegant prose style, as is shown in her correspondence and a number of fugitive newspaper and magazine articles.

BENNETT, Mrs. Alice, doctor of medicine, born in Wrentham, Mass., 31st January, 1851. She was the youngest of six children born to Francis I. and Lydia Hayden Bennett. She was educated in Day's Academy, in her native town, and taught in the district schools there from her seventeenth to her twenty-first year. During that period she prepared herself for the step which, at that place and time, was a sort of social outlawry, and at the age of twenty-one she entered the Woman's Medical College of Pennsylvania, from which she was graduated in March, 1876. One of the intervening years was spent as interne in the New England Hospital, Boston, under Dr. Susan Dimock. After her graduation Dr. Bennett went into dispensary work, living in the slums of Philadelphia for seven months. In October, 1876, she became demonstrator of anatomy in the Woman's Medical College of Pennsylvania and during four years devoted herself to the study and teaching of anatomy, in connection with private practice. At the same time she was pursuing a course of scientific study in the University of Pennsylvania, and received the degree of Ph.D. from that institution in June, 1880. Her graduating thesis upon the anatomy of the fore-limb of the marmoset received honorable mention. In the same month she was elected to the important position she still occupies as superintendent of the department for women of the State

Hospital for the Insane, in Norristown, Pa. The trustees of that hospital, then just completed and about to be opened, did a thing without precedent in placing a woman physician in absolute and inde-

ALICE BENNETT.

pendent charge of their women insane, and dire predictions were made of the results of that revolutionary experiment. At the end of twelve years that hospital is the acknowledged head of the institutions of its kind in the State, if not in the country, and from its successful work the movement, now everywhere felt, to place all insane women under the care of physicians of their own sex, is constantly gaining impetus. Since Dr. Bennett entered upon her work, with one patient and one nurse, 12th July, 1880, more than 2,825 insane women have been received and cared for, new buildings have been added, and the scope of her work has been enlarged in all directions. In 1892 there were 950 patients and a force of 95 nurses under her direction, subject only to the trustees of the hospital. Dr. Bennett is a member of the American Medical Association, of the Pennsylvania State Medical Society, of the Montgomery County Medical Society, of which she was made president in 1890, of the Philadelphia Neurological Society, of the Philadelphia Medical Jurisprudence Society, and of the American Academy of Political and Social Science. She has twice received the appointment to deliver the annual address on mental diseases before the State Medical Society, and she was one of the original corporators of the Spring Garden Unitarian Church of Philadelphia, established by Charles G. Ames. She has recently been appointed by Governor Pattison, of Pennsylvania, one of the board of five commissioners to erect a new hospital for the chronic insane of the State.

BENNETT, Mrs. Ella May, Universalist minister, born in Stony Brook, N. Y., 21st April, 1855. She was the twelfth child of a family of

fourteen, of whom all save two grew to manhood and womanhood. Her father's name was Daniel Shaloe Hawkins, and her mother's maiden name was Harriet Atwood Terry. Two of her brothers have been very prominent in political life. When a very small child, Mrs. Bennett thought deeply upon religious matters. She would often ask her mother to go and pray, especially when her mother seemed troubled in any way. From the very first God seemed to her a friend and comforter. When the doctrines of the church which she had always attended were explained to her, she rejected them. When about thirteen years of age, she visited a cousin in northern Pennsylvania, and for the first time listened to a sermon by a Universalist minister. She recognized her early ideas of God and heaven. On her return home she was told the Bible gave no authority for such a doctrine. She accepted that statement, gave up all interest in religious matters, and would not open a Bible, and tried to become an atheist. For years she groped in a mental darkness that at times threatened her reason. When about thirty years of age, Mrs. Bennett's mother, a devout woman, who had long been deeply concerned about her daughter's state of mind, presented her a Bible, begging her for her sake to read it. She gave the book with an earnest prayer that the true light from its pages might shine upon her mind. Mrs. Bennett reluctantly promised. She had only read a few pages when, to her surprise, she found authority for the Universalist faith. The Bible became her constant companion, and for months she read nothing else. Mrs. Bennett became anxious for others to know the faith which had so brightened her own life and readily consented, at the request of Edward Oaks,

ELLA MAY BENNETT.

to read sermons afternoons in Union Hall in Stony Brook. The sermon reading gradually changed to original essays, and finally Mrs. Bennett found herself conducting regular and popular sermons.

Rev. L. B. Fisher, of Bridgeport, Conn., became interested in her work. She united with his church in May, 1889. Her pastor presented her a library of books and assisted in procuring her a license to preach. On 25th September, 1890, she was ordained in Stony Brook. Mrs. Bennett entered the ministry with the determination never to accept a good position and stated salary, but to labor where the faith was new and for the free-will offering of the people, and, although tempted by large salaries, she has never wavered in that determination. Mrs. Bennett published verses at the age of eleven years, and she has through life given a portion of her time to literary work. In 1875 she was married to William Bennett, and they have three children. She divides her time between her home duties and her ministerial labor, doing full justice to both.

BENTON, Mrs. Louisa Dow, linguist, born in Portland, Maine, 23rd March, 1831. She is the daughter of Neal Dow and Cornelia Durant Maynard. She was educated in the best schools of her native city, the last and chief of which was the Free Street Seminary for young ladies, Master Hezekiah Packard, teacher. She had, besides these, teachers in French. On 12th December, 1860, she was married to Jacob Benton, of Lancaster, N. H. She passed four seasons in Washington, D. C., while Mr. Benton was member of Congress. She was physically as well as intellectually strong and active. In the fall of 1887 she contracted rheumatism, of which she thought little at first, but it soon assumed a serious form, when most energetic measures were adopted to throw it off, but all in vain. She went several times to mineral springs in Canada, and to Hot Springs in Arkansas, but

LOUISA DOW BENTON.

derived no benefit from any of them. At last she could not walk nor even stand, and was confined to her chair, where she passed the time away with books, pen, drawing and painting. But her hands and arms were so greatly and increasingly affected by the disease that drawing and painting were soon given up, and she devoted herself to the acquisition of languages, a study which was always especially attractive to her. She learned to read freely Italian, Spanish, German, Greek and Russian, all with no teacher except for Greek. After that she took up the Volapük and mastered it easily. She is so well known as a Volapük scholar that correspondence has come to her from several prominent linguists in Europe, and several European Volapük associations have elected her corresponding member. During her pains and aches from the disease, she has always been cheerful, never discouraged.

BERG, Miss Lillie, musician and musical educator, was born in New York City. Her father

LILLIE BERG.

was a German of noble birth, and her mother was a New England woman with a proud English ancestry. Miss Berg passed her childhood in Stuttgart, Germany, where she was thoroughly trained in piano, organ and harmony by professors Lebert, Faisst and Stark. She was graduated from the Royal School in Stuttgart, attending at the same time the Conservatory of Music. Professors Lebert and Stark complimented her by sending to her pupils to prepare in piano and harmony for their classes, while under the direction of the organ teacher, Dr. Faisst, she was organist and choir director of one of the most prominent churches in that city. Her precociousness caused such musical authorities as Julius Benedict and Emma Albani to advise her to devote her attention to her voice, predicting for her a brilliant future. Mme. Albani directed her to her own master, Lamperti. Lamperti, soon perceiving the ability of his new pupil, gave her the position of accompanist, which she held for three years, enabling her to note the artistic and vocal training of many of the most famous artists on the operatic and concert stages. In America she holds the position of the foremost exponent of the Lamperti school and she studies every season indefatigably with the famous artists and great teachers of the Old World. Among these have been Theresa Brambilla, Mme. Filippi,

CORNELIA M. BERGEN.

Stockhausen, the late Mme. Rudersdorf, Mme. Marchesi, and Della Sedie, of Paris, William Shakespeare and Randegger. She has developed a "method" which is distinctively her own, and she has an extraordinary knowledge of the art of song. She has the friendship of the majority of modern composers of note, and she aims to combine modern progressiveness and dramatic interpretation with strict adherence to purity and beauty of tone production. She passes the spring season of each year in London, England. Miss Berg possesses a clear soprano voice. She is constantly engaged in arranging concerts and classical recitals in and out of New York. She has also organized quartets and choruses. To Miss Berg belongs, it is believed, the honor of being the first woman musician in America to wield the baton at a public performance. In April, 1891, she conducted Smart's cantata, "King René's Daughter," before an audience which crowded the new Carnegie Hall, New York. The amount of artistic work which she accomplishes is the more astonishing, as she personally instructs an extraordinarily large number of private pupils, professionals and distinguished amateurs, conducts and leads classes and choruses in her private music school, and is in constant demand at social gatherings. Miss Lillie Berg is more widely versatile in her intellectuality than is usual with musicians. She is well versed in philosophy, art, history, poetry, political science and social lore, has traveled extensively, and can speak five languages with fluency.

BERGEN, Mrs. Cornelia M., philanthropist, born in Brooklyn, N. Y., 12th July, 1837. Her education was begun in the school of the Misses Laura and Maria Betts, to be continued in the school

of Miss Sarah Demorest, and to be finished, when she was eighteen years old, in the well-known institution kept by Alfred Greenleaf. From the time of her graduation, in 1855, until the present she has been actively engaged in philanthropic work, mostly of a private character. She believes that to succeed, to gain the best results in that field of work, it is necessary to give close and earnest personal effort. She has never associated herself with any particular institution of a charitable nature, but she has every year given generously to a number of philanthropic and charitable enterprises. Her life has been devoted to aiding and encouraging worthy ones, to whom she was attached by bonds of regard and friendship. Her main idea of life is to make lighter, brighter and happier the lives of those less fortunate than herself. Her substantial gifts have been accompanied by personal attention, comforting ministrations and cheering words. Her home life has been varied. She was married 22nd September, 1858, to Jacob I. Bergen, who died in 1885. He was well known in Brooklyn having served as surrogate of Kings county. Their family numbered five children, only three of whom are living. Mrs. Bergen is to-day a youthful woman in appearance, and she has reaped a harvest of love and respect for her benevolence. In 1886 she became a member of Sorosis and of the Society for the Advancement of Women. Later she joined the Seidl Club, and in 1890 she became a member of the Brooklyn Institute. In those societies her influence has been felt in many ways, and her membership in them has greatly widened her field of philanthropic labor.

BERGEN, Miss Helen Corinne, author and journalist, born in Delanco, N. J., 14th October,

HELEN CORINNE BERGEN.

1868. She belongs to the Bergen family that came from Norway and settled in New Jersey in 1618, in the place they called Bergen. Her mother was the daughter of the Rev. Isaac Winner, D. D., one of the most eloquent preachers in the New Jersey Conference of the Methodist Episcopal Church. Her father was Colonel George B. Bergen. Helen is the oldest child and only daughter. She has written for the press ever since she was a child. She passed her youth in Michigan, and later moved to Washington, D. C. She has lived in Louisiana and Texas, and has traveled much. She wrote first for home papers in Michigan and then for papers in the South. She has served on the Washington "Post," and is that journal's free-lance, and children's department editor. She acts as reporter when necessary, and is an all-round newspaper woman. She writes poetry, sketches, criticisms and stories. She has a wide circle of acquaintances among the prominent people of the day. She believes in equal pay for equal work by men and women. She holds high rank as a musical and dramatic critic. She is building a permanent home in Washington.

BERRY, Mrs. Adaline Hohf, author, born in Hanover, Pa., 20th December, 1859. She removed with her parents, at the age of four years, to Maryland, where she spent her childhood days amid the rural sights and sounds along the quiet Linganore. In 1870 her family removed to Iowa, where, as a school-girl in her teens, she first attempted verse. A talent for composition began its development about that time, and sketches from her pen, in the form of both poetry and prose, found their way into the local papers. She gave no particular evidence of a tendency to rhyme until 1884, at which time she resided in Illinois, when the death of a friend called forth a memorial tribute, which received such commendation from personal friends as to encourage her to

ADALINE HOHF BERRY.

continue to work in verse, and poems were frequently written by her afterward. She completed the academic course of Mt. Morris College (Illinois) in 1882, and about six months after

graduation entered a printing office as compositor. She worked at the case more than four years and in May, 1885, undertook the editing of "The Golden Dawn," an excellent but short-lived magazine published in Huntingdon, Pa. On 20th June, 1888, she was married to William Berry, an instructor in vocal music, and soon after rendered him valuable assistance in compiling an excellent song-book, "Gospel Chimes," writing hymns and some music for it. She and her husband are at present happily located in Huntingdon, and Mrs. Berry is editing a child's paper known as "The Young Disciple." Her family consists of one child, a son, born in February, 1891. She is of mixed ancestry. Her father, Michael Hohf, was of Dutch extraction, and her mother, whose maiden name was Elizabeth Bucher, was of Swiss blood. Born in a community of "Pennsylvania Dutch," that language was the first she learned to speak.

BERRY, Mrs. Martia L. Davis, political reformer, born in Portland, Mich., 22nd January,

MARTIA L. DAVIS BERRY.

1844. Her parents were born in New York State. Her father was of Irish and Italian descent. He was a firm believer in human rights, an earnest anti-slavery man and a strong prohibitionist. Her mother was of German descent, a woman far in advance of her times. Martia wished to teach school, and to that end she labored for a thorough education. She began to teach when she was seventeen years of age and taught five years in the public schools of her native town. At the close of the Rebellion she was married to John S. Berry, a soldier who had given to his country four years of service. In September, 1871, she removed with her husband and only child to Cawker City, Kans., and has since resided there. For twelve years she did a business in millinery and general merchandise. During eight years she was a superintendent of the Methodist Episcopal Sunday-school and a steward of the church. She organized the first Woman's Foreign Missionary Society west of the Missouri river, in April, 1872. The idea of the Woman's Club in her town originated with her and the club was organized 15th November, 1883. It is a monument to the literary taste and business ability of its founders. On 29th October, 1885, she was elected to the office of State treasurer of the Kansas Equal Suffrage Association, to which office she has every year since been re-elected. On 14th April, 1887, she was placed at the head of the sixth district of the Kansas Woman's Christian Temprance Union. On 28th February, 1889, she was elected to the office of State treasurer of the Union, and her yearly re-election proves her faithfulness.

BERT, Mabel, actor, born in Australia in 1862. Her father was A. C. Scott. The family came to this country in 1865, settling in San Francisco, Cal. Miss Bert was educated in Mills Seminary, Oakland, Cal. She left school when seventeen years old, was married and made her début on the stage the following year. For two years she played with various companies throughout California, and in 1885 joined a stock company in San Francisco, for leading parts. For fourteen months she took a new part every week, including Shakespeare's plays, old comedies, melodramas, society plays and burlesques. In 1887 she went east and joined one of Frohman's companies in "Held by the Enemy." Since that time Miss Bert has taken

MABEL BERT.

leading parts in various plays, and has appeared in all of the important cities of America.

BEST, Mrs. Eva, author, born in Cincinnati, Ohio, 19th December, 1851. She is a daughter of the late John Insco Williams and Mrs. Mary Williams, now of Chicago, Ill. Her father was an artist and painted the first bible panorama ever exhibited in the United States. Her mother was also an artist of merit and a writer of excellent verse and prose. The daughter inherits the talents

of both parents. In 1869 she was married to William H. Best, of Dayton, Ohio, and her home is now in that city. Mrs. Best began her literary career as a poet. Her first short story appeared in one of the Frank Leslie periodicals. That was

EVA BEST.

followed by stories in other publications. In 1882 her services were sought by the editor of the Detroit "Free Press," and now Mrs. Best is editor of the household department of that paper. She is also a regular contributor to A. N. Kellogg's Newspaper Company and has written several dramas. The first, "An American Princess," is now in its sixth season. A comedy drama, "Sands of Egypt," is in the hands of Miss Elizabeth Marbury, of New York. "A Rhine Crystal" is being used by Miss Floy Crowell, a young New England artist, and her other plays, "The Little Banshee" and "Gemini," the former in Irish dialect, the latter a two-part character piece, were written for Miss Jennie Calef. In all these plays the music, dances, ballads and all incidental scores are distinctively original. A number of ballads have also added to the author's fame. She has devoted some attention to art. She has two children, a son and a daughter, and the latter is already an artist of some reputation.

BETHUNE, Mrs. Louise, architect, born in Waterloo, N. Y., in 1856. She is of American parentage. Her maiden name was Blanchard. Her father's ancestors were Huguenot refugees. Her mother's family went to Massachusetts from Wales in 1640. Being a delicate child, she was not sent to school until the age of eleven. Meantime she had acquired habits of study and self-reliance which led her through school life to disregard the usual class criterions. In 1874 she was graduated from the Buffalo, N. Y., high school. A caustic remark had previously turned her attention in the direction of architecture, and an investigation, which was begun in a spirit of playful self-defense, soon became an absorbing interest. For two years she taught, traveled and studied, preparatory to taking the architectural course in Cornell University. In 1876 she received

LOUISE BETHUNE.

an offer of an office position as draughtsman and relinquished her former intention of college study. The hours were from eight to six, and the pay was small, but her employer's library was at her service. In 1881 she opened an independent office, thus becoming the first woman architect. She was afterward joined by Robert A. Bethune, to whom she was married in December of the same year. During the ten years of its existence the firm has erected fifteen public buildings and several hundred miscellaneous buildings, mostly in Buffalo and its immediate neighborhood. Mrs. Bethune has made a special study of schools and has been particularly successful in that direction, but refuses to confine herself exclusively to that branch, believing that women who are pioneers in any profession should be proficient in every department, and that now at least women architects must be practical superintendents as well as designers and scientific constructors, and that woman's complete emancipation lies in "equal pay for equal service." Because the competition for the Woman's Building of the Columbia Exposition was not conducted on that principle, Mrs. Bethune refused to submit a design. The remuneration offered to the successful woman was less than half that given for similar service to the men who designed the other buildings. In 1885 Mrs. Bethune was elected a member of the Western Association of Architects. She is still the only woman member of the American Institute. In 1886 she inaugurated the Buffalo Society of Architects, from which has grown the Western New York Association. Both were active in securing the passage of the Architects' Licensing Bill, intended to enforce rigid preliminary examinations and designed to place the profession in a

position similar to that occupied by medicine and law. In the last five or six years a dozen young women have been graduated from the different architectural courses now open to them, and Mrs. Bethune has ceased to be the "only woman architect."

BICKERDYKE, Mrs. Mary A., philanthropist and army nurse, born near Mount Vernon, Knox county, Ohio, 19th July, 1817. She is the daughter of Hiram and Anna Ball. The mother died when Mary was only seventeen months old. The little one was reared by her grandparents. Her grandsire was a Revolutionary soldier named Rogers and a descendant of the Rogers who landed on Plymouth Rock. While young, she was married to Mr. Bickerdyke, and in a few years was left a widow, with helpless little ones to rear. When the Civil War came, she left home and loved ones to offer her services as nurse to the soldiers, who were dying by scores for lack of food and care. When the supplies to the army were sent from Galesburg to Cairo, Mrs. Bickerdyke accompanied them as delegate. After the battle of Belmont she was assigned as nurse to the field hospital. Fort Donelson brought her in sight of battle for the first time. She obtained supplies sometimes by visiting the North and superintending fairs, by a simple note to a pastor at sermon time, and by her famous "cow and hen" mission, by which she furnished the wounded soldiers with a hundred cows and a thousand hens, to provide fresh dainties for the sufferers. During the winter of 1863–64 she made a short visit home, and returned and took part in the establishment of Adams Block Hospital, Memphis, Tenn. This accommodated about 6,000 men, and from this she became

MARY A. BICKERDYKE.

the matron of Gayoso Hospital, in which were more than 700 wounded men brought in from Sherman's battle of Arkansas Post. She took charge in Memphis, Tenn., of a small-pox hospital and cleansed and renovated it with her own hands, when nine men lay dead with the disease. Through the battles at Vicksburg, Lookout Mountain, Missionary Ridge and Chattanooga Mrs. Bickerdyke nursed friend and foe alike, and when, in 1864, Sherman started on his memorable March to the Sea, always devoted to the Army of the Tennessee, "Mother" Bickerdyke, as the soldiers used to call her, accompanied the 100,000 men who marched away. Resaca, Kingston, New Hope, Cassville, Allatoona, Dallas and Kenesaw Mountain furnished her with 13,000 of those brave men as subjects for her care. When Sherman cut his base of supplies, Mrs. Bickerdyke went to the North and collected immense sanitary stores for the soldiers. When Sherman entered Savannah, she sailed for the South, to take care of the liberated Union prisoners at Wilmington. At Beaufort, Averysboro and Bentonville she pursued her mission, and at the request of General Logan and the 15th Army Corps she marched into Alexandria with the army. At the final review in Washington Mrs. Bickerdyke, mounted upon a saddle-horse, dressed in a simple calico dress and sun-bonnet, accompanied the troops. This dress and bonnet were sold as relics of the war for $100. Since the rebellion Mrs. Bickerdyke has spent her life in procuring homes and pensions for the "boys." She resides with her son, Prof. Bickerdyke, in Russell, Kansas.

BIERCE, Mrs. Sarah Elizabeth, journalist, born in Sweden, Maine, in 1838. Her maiden name was Holden, one well-known in New England. While a school-girl, her essays and poems attracted attention, many of them finding place in the columns of eastern journals. Her early education was received in New England. Removing to

plays, which were first used at entertainments given by her pupils and afterwards published. From the time of her marriage, in 1866, to her husband's death, in 1881, Mrs. Bierce wrote little

BELLE G. BIGELOW.

for the press. In 1885 she accepted a permanent position in connection with the Cleveland "Plain Dealer," contributing stories, sketches and special articles to the Sunday issue. Her stories and sketches of home life and pioneer incidents were especially popular. While most inclined to fiction, she has written numerous letters of travel. Her descriptions of life and scenery in California, Arizona, Nevada and Utah were unusually entertaining. She has given much time to the investigation of certain phases of the working-woman problem, and has also written special articles on art subjects. She is a member of the Ohio Woman's Press Association and is at present (1892) corresponding secretary of that body. In 1891 she was chosen delegate to the International League of Press Clubs, formed in Pittsburgh. Mrs. Bierce is, perhaps, most widely known outside of Ohio through her efficient management of the woman's literary and journalistic department of the Ohio Centennial, held in Columbus in 1888. Through her efforts was secured a full representation of the literary women of Ohio, past and present, editors, journalists, authors and poets, scattered far and wide, sending the fruits of their work to the exposition of their native State. She has a family consisting of a daughter and two sons.

BIGELOW, Mrs. Belle G., woman suffragist and prohibitionist, born on a farm in Gilead, Mich., 16th February, 1851. Her education was confined to the district school. She has been from early childhood an omnivorous reader. Her mother died when Belle was ten years old. At the age of eighteen she began to teach. In 1869 she was married to George R. Bigelow, of Ravenna,

SARAH ELIZABETH BIERCE.

Michigan, she was graduated in 1860 from Kalamazoo College. During the next six years she taught in both public and private schools. While engaged in school work, she wrote numerous

Ohio. They removed and settled in Geneva, Neb., being the first residents of that place. After eight years of quiet home life, the question of the woman suffrage amendment being brought before

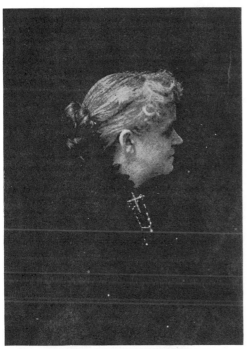

ELLA AUGUSTA BIGELOW.

the people, she entered into its advocacy. Soon becoming known as a talker and writer on that subject, she was elected president of the county Equal Suffrage Association and sent as a delegate to the State convention in Omaha. There she made her first appearance as a public speaker and her reception encouraged a continuance of work in that line. The next winter, in Lincoln, she was elected to the office of State secretary and traveled over the State in the interest of the amendment, making effective speeches where opportunity offered and awakening much interest in the subject. She was twice a candidate for county superintendent of instruction on the prohibition ticket, and represented the State in the national convention of that party held in Indianapolis in 1888. She has served for five years as secretary of the Lincoln Woman's Christian Temperance Union, being a member of the union in its infancy. She is superintendent of foreign work for the State union, and was elected delegate to the national convention in Boston in 1891. She is known as an interesting writer for the press on both religious and secular topics. She has been the mother of seven children, four of whom are living.

BIGELOW, Mrs. Ella Augusta, musician, born in Malden, Mass., in 1849. Her father, Lewis Fisher, and mother, Ruth Benchley, are both of good old English descent. For many years her home was in the town of Milford. Her parents being in good circumstances, the best of instruction was given her. Developing a taste for music, she was placed under the care of the most advanced teachers in Boston. As a church singer she has been well known in Fitchburg and various other cities, singing at intervals with such artists as

Carlyle Petersilea and Eichberg with his "Germania Orchestra." In 1873 she went to Germany, residing while there chiefly in Berlin. There she studied with Ferdinand Sieber, court professor of music, and Fräulein Ress, both of whom gave her strong encouragement to choose a musical career. Becoming acquainted with Mr. and Mrs. George Bancroft, he being minister to Berlin at that time, the opportunity was given her, through their kindness, of meeting many celebrities and making many friends. Before returning to America she traveled through Europe. At a later period she was married to Edward L. Bigelow, of Marlboro, Mass., where she now resides in an old Colonial house, full of antiques and souvenirs of travel. There she devotes her time to the education of her three children, making home-life attractive and giving to the public frequent helps to intellectual improvement. She has published "Prize Quotations" (Marlboro, 1887), "Venice" (Marlboro, 1890), "Old Masters of Art" (Buffalo, 1888), and "Letters upon Greece" (Marlboro, 1891). She has for years contributed articles for papers both in the East and the West, and has been president of numerous literary clubs as well as musical ones. Full of sympathy for those who are striving for education and true culture, the doors of her home are ever open to pupils of all classes in life.

BIGELOW, Miss Lettie S., author, born in Pelham, Mass., in 1849. She is the daughter of the Rev. I. B. Bigelow, an itinerant minister, for more than half a century an honored member of the Methodist Episcopal Church. Her early education was in the public schools of the cities and towns where her parents lived, as they were removed from place to place every two or

LETTIE S. BIGELOW.

three years by the decrees of the presiding bishops, according to the economy of their church. In 1866 she entered Wesleyan Academy in Wilbraham, Mass., and remained a student there two years.

Failing health compelled her to relinquish her course of study in that institution before the completion of the regular course, and she has since made her home with her parents at their various appointments. Four years ago her father left the active work of the ministry and made for himself and family a permanent home in Holyoke, Mass., where Miss Bigelow now lives, tenderly caring for an invalid mother. She has done considerable literary work, being always a close student of books and events. She has published no book of poems, but her verses have appeared quite frequently in the New York "Christian Advocate," "Zion's Herald" of Boston, the New York "Independent," the Boston "Journal" and other papers. Her prose writings, consisting of sketches, newspaper articles, and a serial story, have been for the most part under a pseudonym. A few years ago she wrote a book of Sunday-school and anniversary exercises, published in New York, which had a large sale. Miss Bigelow is also an interesting platform speaker. Her lecture on "Woman's Place and Power" has found special favor and most hearty commendation wherever it has been delivered. Her manner on the platform is easy and her delivery pleasing.

BIGGART, Miss Mabelle, educator and dramatic reader, born in New York City, 22nd February, 1861. She comes of Scotch and English ancestry and is descended from a long line of teachers, authors and collegians. Her great-grandmother on her father's side was named Porter, and was a sister of Commodore Porter, of Revolutionary fame, and a cousin of Jane Porter, the author of "Scottish Chiefs." Her great-grandfather married into the clan of McKies. Thomas Carlyle and Jane Welsh Carlyle were closely related. Her

college course in the State Normal School in Fredonia, N. Y., and an oratorical and literary course in Philadelphia. Her professional education has been mainly in Philadelphia and New York, and

JENNIE M. BINGHAM.

she is still a constant student of dramatic elocution and of languages. Her parents died when she was only a child, and her life has been varied and eventful. She is of an intense, highly strung nature, and not robust, and her close application to her profession and her studies has more than once forced her to rest. She has held several important positions in colleges and seminaries, and for five years she had charge of rhetoric and elocution in the West high school, Cleveland, Ohio. A bronchial trouble sent her to Denver, Col., where she was instrumental in building up an institution called the Woman's Polytechnic Institute. She gave part of each week to that work, and the remainder was employed in the State College in Fort Collins, seventy-two miles from Denver. During the summer of 1891 she filled a number of Chautauqua engagements in the East. For about two years the Colorado climate proved beneficial to her, but at length the high altitude caused extreme nervous troubles and necessitated another change. She entered upon a new line of dramatized readings from her own interpretations of French, German and English masterpieces. A tour of the United States was undertaken, accompanied by her friend, Miss Marie Louise Gumaer, contralto. Miss Biggart's literary productions are numerous, including a yet unpublished volume of miscellaneous poems and "Songs from the Rockies," short stories and sketches of western life, a book on "Educational Men and Women and Educational Institutions of the West," "Sketches of Popular Living American Authors," a series of "Supplementary Reading Leaflets," recently published, and a work of fiction, nearly completed. Some of her poems have been set to music.

MABELLE BIGGART.

grandfather on her mother's side was Sir Richard Bond, of London, England. Her father was born in Glasgow, Scotland, and her mother was a native of New York. Miss Biggart took a preparatory

BINGHAM, Miss Jennie M., author, born in Fulton, N. Y., 16th March, 1859. She is the daughter of Jane Mills and the Rev. Dr. I. S. Bingham. Her father has been for forty-eight years in the ministry of the Methodist Episcopal Church. When poor health shut off the possibility of teaching, Miss Bingham turned to her pen for a livelihood. Her first article offered for publication was a little story entitled "A Hospital Sketch," which appeared in the "Christian Union." Among her early productions was a missionary story, "A Grain of Mustard Seed" (1881). Eight-thousand copies were sold during the first six months after publication, the proceeds of which founded a home in Japan. She works in every department of literature, book-reviewing, essay writing, fiction, poetry, Sunday-school helps and art criticism. Some of her short stories have appeared in "Harper's Young People." She is the author of two books, "Annals of the Round Table" (1885), and "All Glorious Within" (1889), the latter a story embodying the origin and work of the King's Daughters. She has been specially interested in the charities of New York City, and part of her labor has been in visiting them and writing concerning them. The Newsboys' Lodging-house, Five Points Mission, Flower Mission, Florence Night Mission, and Children's Aid Society are among her subjects. Her life has been a busy one, in which literature has only been incidental. Her home is in Herkimer, N. Y.

BIRKHOLZ, Mrs. Eugenie S., author, born in Garnavillo, Clayton county, Iowa, in 1853. She is the daughter of Dr. F. Andros, who was the first physician and surgeon, regularly licensed to practice, who settled west of the Mississippi river

and sent many literary contributions to the periodicals and papers of the day. In 1881 she was married to John Birkholz, of Chicago, Ill, in which city they both resided, and whence they emi-

EMILY MULKIN BISHOP.

grated to Grand Forks, N. Dak., where she has since made her home. Mrs. Birkholz devotes considerable time to literary work.

BISHOP, Anna, singer, born in London, England, in 1814; died in New York City, 18th March, 1884. Her father was a drawing-master named Rivière. She studied the piano-forte under Moscheles, became distinguished for her singing, and in 1831 became the wife of Sir Henry Rowley Bishop. She eloped with Bochsa, the harpist, in 1839, and soon after went on a tour through the principal countries of Europe, which extended down to 1843. From that time until 1846 she remained in Italy, and was at one time prima donna at the San Carlo, Naples. After her stay in Italy she returned to England. In 1847 she came to this country, remaining here until 1855, when she sailed for Australia. She then again made a brief visit to England, and in 1859 came to this country for the second time. Her stay was prolonged to 1866, with a brief visit to Mexico and Cuba, when she sailed for the Sandwich Islands, visited China, India, Australia, Egypt and England, arriving in the United States again about 1869. Probably no other singer traveled so much or sang before so many people. She visited nearly every country on the globe, and the most of them repeatedly. In 1858 she was married to Martin Schultz, an American, and made it her permanent home in New York City. Her last public appearance was in a concert in New York in the spring of 1883.

BISHOP, Mrs. Emily Mulkin, Delsartean lecturer and instructor in dress, expression and physical culture, born in Forestville, Chautauqua county, N. Y., 3rd November, 1858. After leaving school she taught four years, serving as assistant

EUGENIE S. BIRKHOLZ.

and north of Missouri. He settled in Dubuque, Iowa, in 1830. Mrs. Birkholz was educated in the school of the Catholic sisters in Benton, Wis., and was in her early life a woman of original thought

principal of the union school in Silver Creek, N.Y. She afterwards gave several years to the study of Delsarte work in various cities. In 1884 she became the wife of Coleman E. Bishop, editor of the "Judge," New York. They soon went to Black Hills, Dak., to live. Mrs. Bishop was elected superintendent of public schools in Rapid City, S. Dak., being the first woman thus honored in the Territory. In the following year she was invited to establish a Delsarte department in the Chautauqua School of Physical Education, in the Chautauqua Assembly, New York. She has had charge of that department for four seasons, and it has steadily grown in popularity. In 1891 it was the largest single department in the Assembly. From the Chautauqua work has grown a large public work in lecturing and teaching. She has written a number of articles for various magazines and has published one book, "Americanized Delsarte Culture." At present Mrs. Bishop's home is in Washington, D. C.

BISHOP, Mrs. Mary Agnes Dalrymple, journalist, born in Springfield, Mass., 12th August,

MARY AGNES DALRYMPLE BISHOP.

1857. She is the only child of John Dalrymple and his wife, Frances Ann Hewitt. She has always been proud of her old Scotch ancestry and her ability to trace the family back from Scotland to France, where, early in the twelfth century, William de Darumpill obtained a papal dispensation to marry his kinswoman, Agnes Kennedy. It is scarcely a century since her grandfather came to this country. On her maternal side she traces her ancestry to the Mayflower, which brought over her several-times-removed grandmother May. In local papers her childhood poems were printed readily, but the reading of Horace Greeley's "Recollections of a Busy Life," in which he has some good advice for youthful writers, caused her to determine not to be tempted to allow her doggerel to be published, and for years she adhered to her determination. When she was less than two years old, her

parents removed with her to Grafton, Worcester county, Mass., and at the age of sixteen years she became the local editor of the Grafton "Herald." Beginning the week following her graduation, she taught in the public schools of Grafton and Sutton for many years. During that time she gave lectures quite frequently in the vicinity and often appeared in the home drama, making her greatest success as "Lady Macbeth." Miss Dalrymple was a frequent contributor to the 'Youth's Companion" and other publications, never adopting a pen-name and rarely using her own name or initials. In 1887 she accepted an editorial position on the "Massachusetts Ploughman." The position offered her had never been taken by a woman, and, indeed, the work that she did was never attempted previously, for she had the charge of almost the entire journal from the first. A few months after she accepted the position, the proprietor died, and the entire paper was in her hands for· six months. In the autumn the paper was purchased by its present owner, but the chief editorial work remained in her hands. The paper was enlarged from four to eight pages in the meantime and, as before, was published each week. In the autumn of 1889 she became the wife of Frederick Herbert Bishop, a Boston business man. Together they engage in literary pursuits and the work and pleasure of life along its varied lines. Their home is located on Wollaston Heights. Mrs. Bishop does not content herself with editorial work, but is interested in literature in general. She is one of the few newspaper women who is a practical reportorial stenographer. She is a member of the executive committee of the New England Woman's Press Association, of which she was one of the first members.

BISLAND, Miss Elizabeth, journalist, born in Camp Bisland, Fairfax plantation, Teche county, La., in 1863. Her family, one of the oldest in the South, lost its entire property while she was a child and Miss Bisland became impressed, at an early age, with the necessity of doing something toward the support of herself and relatives. Having shown a talent for writing, this, naturally, was the line of work along which she began her career. Her first sketches, published at the age of fifteen, were written under the pen-name B. L. R. Dane, and were favorably received by the New Orleans newspapers to which they were sent. Miss Bisland did considerable work for the New Orleans "Times-Democrat" and, later, became literary editor of that paper. After a few years' work in New Orleans she decided to enter the literary field in New York and for a time did miscellaneous work for newspapers and periodicals in that city. In a short time she was offered the position of literary editor of the "Cosmopolitan Magazine" which she accepted. It was while engaged upon that magazine that Miss Bisland undertook her noted journey around the earth in the attempt to make better time than that of Nellie Bly, who was engaged to perform the same journey in the interest of the New York "World"; Miss Bly going east while Miss Bisland took the western direction. Although she did not succeed in defeating her rival, Miss Bisland made such time as to command the admiration of the civilized world.· In May, 1890, she went to London, Eng., in the interest of the "Cosmopolitan," and her letters to that magazine, from London and Paris, have been widely read and appreciated. In addition to her journalistic work, she has also written, in collaboration with Miss Rhoda Broughton, a one-volume novel; also a romance and play in conjunction with the same author. She became the wife of Charles W. Wetmore of New York, 6th October, 1891, and they reside in that city.

BITTENBENDER, Mrs. Ada M., lawyer and reformer, born in Asylum, Bradford county, Pa., 3rd August, 1848. Her mother's ancestors were New Englanders, and her father's family were partly of New England and partly of German stock. Her father served as a Union soldier throughout the Civil War and died soon after from exposures then endured. Her maiden name was Ada M. Cole. Her early education was acquired mainly in private schools near her home. In 1869 she was graduated from a Binghamton, N. Y., commercial college. In January, 1874, she entered as a student the Pennsylvania State Normal School at Bloomsburg, where she was graduated in the normal class of 1875. After graduation she was elected a member of the faculty, and taught in the school one year. She then entered the Froebel Normal Institute in Washington, D. C., and was graduated there in the summer of 1877. On the same day of her graduation she

ADA M. BITTENBENDER.

received a telegram announcing her unanimous call back to her Alma Mater normal school, to the position of principal of the model school. She accepted that position and taught there until nearly the end of the year's term, when, being prostrated from overwork, she resigned and retired to her mother's home in Rome, Pa., for recovery. On 9th August, 1878, she was married to Henry Clay Bittenbender, a young lawyer of Bloomsburg, Pa., and a graduate of Princeton College. In November, 1878, they removed to Osceola, Neb. Mrs. Bittenbender taught school during their first winter in Nebraska, and Mr. Bittenbender opened a law office. In 1879 Mr. Bittenbender and Clarence Buell bought the "Record," published in Osceola, and the only paper in Polk county. Mrs. Bittenbender was engaged as editor, and for three years she made it an able, fearless, moral, family and temperance newspaper, Republican in politics. She and her husband were equally pronounced in

their temperance views. She strenuously opposed the granting of saloon licenses in the town or county. Mr. and Mrs. Bittenbender reorganized the Polk County Agricultural Association, and Mrs. Bittenbender served as secretary, treasurer, orator and in 1881 as representative at the annual meeting of the State Board of Agriculture. She was the first woman delegate ever received by that body. When the Nebraska Woman Suffrage Association was organized in 1881, she was elected recording secretary. She with others worked with the legislature and secured the submission of the woman suffrage amendment to the constitution in 1881. At the first suffrage convention following the submission she was made one of the three woman campaign speakers. At the following annual meeting she was elected president of the association, and the last three months of the campaign was also chairman of the State campaign committee. She retired from the editorship of the "Record" in 1881, and became the editor of the first Farmers' Alliance paper started in Nebraska. That was a journal started in Osceola by the Polk County Farmers' Alliance. While she was editing the "Record," she read law with her husband, and in 1882 passed the usual examination in open court and was licensed to practice law. She was the first woman admitted to the bar in Nebraska. On the day of her admission she and her husband became law partners under the style of H. C. and Ada M. Bittenbender. The firm still exists. They removed to Lincoln, Neb., in December, 1882. Mrs. Bittenbender prefers court practice to office work. She ranks as a very successful lawyer, and only once has she lost a case brought by herself. She has had several cases before the Supreme Court, the highest court of the State, which in every instance she has won. She has been admitted to the United States District and Circuit courts for Nebraska. She secured the passage of the scientific temperance instruction bill, the tobacco bill, secured a law giving the mother the guardianship of her children equally with the father, and several other laws. She is the author of the excellent industrial home bill which was enacted by the Nebraska legislature in 1887, which establishes an industrial school as well as home for penitent women and girls, with a view to lessen prostitution. At the International Council of Women held in Washington, D. C., in March, 1888, she spoke on "Woman in Law." During several sessions of Congress she remained in Washington, representing the National Woman's Christian Temperance Union as its superintendent of legislation and petitions. She was an indefatigable worker, constantly sending out to the local unions and the press as her base of operations, for petitions, paragraphs, help in the way of influence with Congress to grant prohibition to the District of Columbia and the Territories, protection to women, constitutional prohibition and other measures called for by the national convention. She drafted the bill to accompany the great petition for the protection of women, offered by Senator Blair. That involved much hard work, as she was obliged to go over all the laws of Congress from the first, to learn precisely what had been done already and to make her bill harmonious with existing legislation. It was mainly through her efforts Congress passed the protection bill. She spoke briefly, but with clear, convincing argument, at hearings before the committees of Senate and House in the interest of prohibition in the District of Columbia. On 15th October, 1888, she was admitted to practice in the Supreme Court of the United States. The motion for her admission was made by Senator Blair, of New Hampshire. In 1888 she was elected attorney for the National Woman's Christian Temperance Union, which position she still holds. She is the author of the chapter on "Woman in Law" in "Woman's Work in America" (New York, 1891). In September, 1891, she was placed in nomination on the prohibition ticket in Nebraska for Judge of the Supreme Court of that State. She received 7,322 votes out of a total of 155,000 cast in the State in 1891, the largest vote in proportion ever given for the head of the prohibition ticket. Her practice has been large, and her activity has been incessant. She has spent much time in Washington, D. C. Mrs. Bittenbender is the author of the "National Prohibitory Amendment Guide," a manual to aid in obtaining an amendment to the Federal Constitution which shall outlaw forever the traffic in alcoholic beverages. The "plan of canvassing" contained in her manual has been quite generally indorsed. She is preparing a treatise on the law of alcoholic liquors as a beverage, showing the unconstitutionality of license laws, as deduced from judicial decisions, including procedures in testing the matter and in enforcing prohibition. She and her husband will bring such test cases in the courts to secure decisions. Mrs. Bittenbender has for years borne a wonderful burden of work, showing the capacity of woman to endure the strain of deep thinking and of arduous professional labor. She is a member of the Presbyterian Church and has been an earnest Sabbath-school teacher.

BLACK, Mrs. Fannie De Grasse, singer and pianist, born in Nisouri, Canada, 21st November, 1856. Her maiden name was De Grasse. She moved with her parents to the United States

FANNIE DE GRASSE BLACK.

and made her home in Milwaukee, Wis., where she was educated in the high and normal schools, graduating in 1874. At ten years of age she began the study of piano and sight singing, continuing

until her sixteenth year, when she became a pupil of Prof. William Mickler, formerly director in court to the Duke of Hesse, Germany, studying with him for four years. She sang in public when she was only six years old, and made her début in classic music at the age of eighteen, under the direction of Professor Mickler, in the concerts of the Milwaukee German Musical Society, and has since sung successfully in opera and oratorio. Later on she took up the study of the pipe organ and is now (1892) organist of the Presbyterian church, El Dorado. In 1881 she was married to Judge S. E. Black, of El Dorado, Kan. Mrs. Black is a thorough scholar, and she believes that only a thorough scholar and student can become a fine musician. She sings equally well in English, German and Italian, and her pleasant El Dorado home is a center of music and refinement.

BLACK, Mrs. Mary Fleming, author and religious worker, born in Georgetown, S. C., 4th

MARY FLEMING BLACK.

August, 1848. Her father, Rev. W. H. Fleming, D. D., was a distinguished member of the South Carolina Conference of the Methodist Episcopal Church South, and died while pastor of Bethel Church, Charleston, S. C., in 1877. Her parents were both Charlestonians. Her mother, born Agnes A. Magill, was the daughter of Dr. William Magill, a prominent physician of that city. The education of Mrs. Black was begun in one of the city schools of Charleston. She was afterward graduated with honor in Spartanburg Female College, and later took a special course under the instructions of the faculty of Wofford Male College, of which Rev. A. M. Shipp, D.D., LL.D., was president. Soon after the completion of her studies she was married to Rev. W. S. Black, D. D., then a member of the South Carolina Conference. Mrs. Black soon displayed ability as a writer, her prose and verse productions appearing in various newspapers and periodicals. In 1882 she became the editor of the children's department of the Raleigh "Christian Advocate," of which her husband was one of the editors and proprietors. In that relation she continued until the Woman's Missionary Society of the North Carolina and Western North Carolina Conferences established a juvenile missionary paper, the "Bright Jewels," of which she was elected editor. That position she now holds, and she is known by the children as "Aunt Mary." She is superintendent of the juvenile department and corresponding secretary of the Woman's Missionary Society of the North Carolina Conference, and is a member of the Woman's Board of Missions of the Methodist Episcopal Church South. She is a prominent and influential member of the Woman's Christian Temperance Union and of the King's Daughters of her State. She has three sons, two of whom have reached majority while the third is still in college, and one daughter, just entering womanhood. As the wife of one of the most able and popular ministers of the conference, she faithfully discharged the many and delicate duties of that position, with great acceptability to her husband's congregation. In addition to many duties and labors, she is rendering her husband valuable aid in the management of the Oxford Orphan Asylum, of which he is superintendent.

BLACK, Mrs. Sarah Hearst, temperance reformer, born on a farm near Savannah, Ashland county, Ohio, 4th May, 1846. Her father's family removed from Pennsylvania to that farm when he was a boy of fourteen years, and Mrs. Black there grew to womanhood. Her ancestors were Scotch-Irish people, all of them members of the Presbyterian Church. Her mother's maiden name was Townsley.

SARAH HEARST BLACK.

Miss Hearst first attended school in a typical red school-house situated on a corner of her father's farm. At thirteen years of age she began to attend school in Savannah Academy, where she completed a regular course of study. She made a public profession of religion in her fifteenth year and soon after became a teacher in the Sabbath-school, and has continued in that work ever since. After completing her course of study, she entered the ranks as a teacher, and that was her employment for more than ten years. In 1878 she was married to Rev. J. P. Black, a minister of the Presbyterian Church, and went with him to his field of labor in Pennsylvania. They removed to Kansas in 1880, and since that time she has borne the labor and self-denial incident to the life of a home missionary's wife in Kansas, Nebraska and now in Idaho. She became actively engaged in Woman's Christian Temperance Union work in 1885, in Nebraska, and was elected president of the fifth district of that State for two years in succession. After her removal to Idaho she was chosen president of the Woman's Christian Temperance Union in that State. Her home is in Nampa.

BLACKALL, Mrs. Emily Lucas, author and philanthropist, born in Salem, Ind., 30th June, 1832, and died in New York City, 28th March, 1892. The first ten years of her life were spent in her birthplace amid picturesque surroundings. Her early school days were marked by a quickness of apprehension and an appreciative literary taste that gave indication of the life that was to be in later years. Her parents were Virginians of English descent. During a considerable period, including the years of the late Civil War, her residence was in Louisville, Ky., where she was identified with the Baptist Orphans' Home from its beginning until she left the State, and also was treasurer of the Kentucky branch of the Woman's Missionary Society, founded by the late Mrs. Doremus of New York. Removing to Chicago, she became identified with the woman's temperance crusade and aided in forming the Woman's Christian Temperance Union. She was one of a committee of women who appealed in person to the city council to restrain the liquor-saloon influence, and one of a special committee of three appointed to visit the mayor and urge him to carry out a plan for the protection of homes against the saloon. She was one of the founders of the Woman's Baptist Foreign Missionary Society of the West, and was treasurer of that organization until she left Chicago. She was largely instrumental in the formation of the Women's Baptist Home Mission Society, located in Chicago, with which she was actively engaged at the time of her death. In 1882 she became a resident of Philadelphia, Pa., where she was identified with various benevolent enterprises. A member of the Philadelphia Women's Council, a member of the Women's International Congress in 1887, and a delegate to the Woman's National Council in 1891, she showed a depth of sympathy and touch with progressive ideas that proved the breadth of her character and her influence. As a presiding officer and public speaker Mrs. Blackall always gave satisfaction and pleasure. As an author she was successful. Her first story, "Superior to Circumstances" (Boston, 1889), was followed by "Melodies from Nature" (Boston, 1889), and "Won and Not One" (Philadelphia, 1891). Short stories and biographical sketches have frequently appeared in various periodicals, and missionary literature has had numerous contributions from her pen. In collaboration with her husband, the Rev. C. R. Blackall, she was joint author of "Stories about Jesus" (Philadelphia, 1890). Her literary style is marked by purity, vigor and correctness. She dealt with social and economic problems in a practical, common-sense manner, writing from experience and broad observation rather than as an idealist, yet always with tenderness and in a spirit of helpfulness. In the various relations of wife, mother, and home-maker, she was eminent

EMILY LUCAS BLACKALL.

for the sweetness of her disposition, the unfailing accuracy of her judgment, and the purity of her life.

BLACKWELL, Miss Alice Stone, journalist, born in Orange, N. J., 14th September, 1857. She is the daughter of Lucy Stone and Henry B. Blackwell. She was graduated from Boston University with honors in 1881, and has been on the staff of the "Woman's Journal" ever since. During the last few years she has also edited a small weekly paper devoted to woman suffrage, called the "Woman's Column."

BLACKWELL, Mrs. Antoinette Brown, author and minister, born in Henrietta, Monroe county, N. Y., 20th May, 1825. She is a daughter of Joseph Brown, of Thompson, Conn., and Abby Morse, of Dudley, Mass. Her parents were descendants of early English colonists and Revolutionary soldiers, many of whom were prominent in the early days of New England. Miss Brown joined the Congregational Church when she was only nine years old, and sometimes spoke and prayed in meetings. She taught school when sixteen years old, and later taught several branches in a seminary in order to pay the expenses of a collegiate course. Even her vacations were devoted to extra study, so ambitious was she and so untiring in the pursuit of knowledge. She was graduated from Oberlin College, where she completed the literary course in 1847 and the theological course in 1850. She bears the degree of M.A. Her attention was engaged early in theological questions. In 1848 she published her first important essay, an exegesis of St. Paul on women, in the "Oberlin Quarterly Review." At the completion of the theological course she could not obtain a license, as was customary with students, but

was told she must preach or be silent on her own responsibility. That she was not afraid to assume, since ability and responsibility belong together. Without regard to sect, she preached whenever and wherever a place offered, but not always did she do this under favorable circumstances. Obstacles melted away under the powerful personality of such a speaker as Antoinette Brown, and, in spite of the objections to women preachers as a class, she finally became the ordained pastor, in 1852, of a Congregational church in South Butler, Wayne county, N. Y. In 1853 she was ordained by the council called by the church. After preaching for the society awhile she began to have distressing doubts concerning certain theological doctrines, and on that account she resigned her charge in 1854. She was married to Samuel C. Blackwell, a brother of Dr. Elizabeth Blackwell, 24th January, 1856. She began the study of some of the great questions concerning vice and crime and published the result under the title of "Shadows of Our Social System." Her life as a preacher, lecturer and writer has been a very useful one. In the latter direction she has done work that reflects great credit upon her sex, having received much praise for her logical methods of thought. "Studies in General Science" (New York, 1869), "A Market Woman" (New York, 1870), "The Island Neighbors" (New York, 1871), "The Sexes Throughout Nature" (New York, 1875), and "The Physical Basis of Immortality" (New York, 1876), are some of her various works. The most prominent fact to be recorded in the history of Mrs. Blackwell's life, and the one which speaks loudly for her present honorable place among the eminent women of our country, is her love of effort; only

ANTOINETTE BROWN BLACKWELL.

by persistent work has she been able to accomplish so much for herself and others. Although a wife and the mother of several daughters, she has kept abreast of the times on the questions of science, art and literature. She has by no means allowed the luster of intellectual gifts to grow dim from disuse. Amid scenes of domesticity she has found even fresh inspiration for public work. Not wholly preoccupied with home cares and duties, she has yet given faithful attention to them, and this fact, in connection with her success as a speaker and writer, should be chronicled. Mrs. Blackwell has always been actively interested in reformatory subjects and has spoken in behalf of the temperance cause. In 1854 she was a delegate to the World's Temperance Convention in New York, but a hearing was refused to her in that body, not because she was not an able representative, but simply because she was a woman. The change in the condition of women is plainly shown in the reminiscences of such women as Mrs. Blackwell. Mr. and Mrs. Blackwell have five children, and now live in Elizabeth, N. J. Mrs. Blackwell still preaches occasionally and has become a Unitarian.

BLACKWELL, Miss Elizabeth, physician and author, born in Bristol, England, 3rd February, 1821. Her father, Samuel Blackwell, was a wealthy sugar refiner, a man of broad views and strong benevolence. At the political crisis of 1830-31 commercial affairs in England were thrown into confusion, and Mr. Blackwell was among those whose fortunes were swept away at that time. He removed with his family to the United States in August, 1832, and settled in New York, where he started a sugar refinery. He was rapidly amassing wealth when the financial crash of 1837 in the United States swept away his fortune through the wreckage of the weaker houses with which he had business relations. He turned his eyes to the West, and in 1838 removed his family to Cincinnati, Ohio. There he was stricken by fever and died at the age of forty-five years, leaving a family of nine children to their own resources among strangers. Every cent of indebtedness left by the father was paid by his children. The three older daughters, of whom Elizabeth was the third, placed themselves at once at the head of the family. Two sons in school left their studies and took clerkships. The four younger ones were still in the nursery. The older sisters opened a boarding school for young women, and their liberal culture and enterprise won them a large patronage. The sisters felt the restrictions placed upon women in the matter of earning a livelihood, and they became convinced that the enlargement of opportunities for women was the one essential condition of their well-being in every way. After six years of hard work, when all the younger members of the family had been placed in positions to support themselves, the sisters gave up the school. Elizabeth resolved to study medicine, although she had to overcome a natural aversion to sickness of all kinds. She wrote to six different physicians for advice, and all agreed that it was impossible for a woman to get a medical education. She thought differently, however, and in 1844 she took charge of a Kentucky school to earn money for her expenses. In 1845 she went to Charleston, S. C., to teach music in a boarding-school, and there added a good knowledge of Latin to her French and German. There she entered the office-student class of Dr. Samuel Henry Dickson. In May, 1847, she applied for admission to the Philadelphia Medical School, but both college and hospital were closed to her. She applied to all the medical schools in the United States, and twelve of them rejected her application and rebuked her for temerity and indelicacy. The college faculty in Geneva, N. Y., and that in Castleton, Vt., considered her application, and the students in Geneva decided to

favor her admission. In 1847 she entered the college as 'No. 417' on the register. In January, 1849, she was graduated with the Geneva class. A large audience witnessed the granting of the first medical diploma to a woman. Immediately after graduation, Dr. Elizabeth Blackwell went to Paris, France, where, after months of delay, she was admitted to the great lying-in hospital of the Maternité as a resident pupil, and several other schools permitted her to visit. She also studied under able private tutors. In 1850 and 1851 she "walked" St. Bartholomew's hospital in London, England, studying in the Women's Hospital and under private teachers. She returned to the United States, and in the autumn of 1851 she opened an office in New York City. She succeeded in building up a large practice, in spite of social and professional antagonism and ostracism. The Society of Friends were the first to receive her warmly and support the new movement, and she soon became known as

ELIZABETH BLACKWELL.

a reliable physician. In 1853, with her sister, Dr. Emily Blackwell, she established in New York the New York Infirmary for Women and Children, which was incorporated and was for some years the only woman's hospital. In 1858 and 1859 she visited England and lectured in London, Birmingham and Liverpool on the connection of women with medicine. In 1859 she was placed on the register of English physicians. Returning to America, she entered with the warmest interest into the questions of the Civil War, and the sisters organized in the parlors of the Infirmary the Ladies' Central Relief Association, sending off the first supplies to the wounded. That association was soon merged in the Sanitary Commission, in which the sisters continued to take an active part. In 1869 Dr. Elizabeth lectured in the Medical College of the New York Infirmary, which had been chartered as a college in 1865. At the close of 1869 she went to England and settled in London, where she practiced for some years. There she founded the National Health Society and worked in a number of social reforms. She aided in organizing the London School of Medicine for Women, in which she served as the first lecturer on the diseases of women. In 1878, after a serious illness, she settled in Hastings, England, continuing her consultation practice only and working energetically for the repeal of the unjust Contagious Diseases Acts. Up to the present time she has continued to work actively for the promotion of equal standards of morality for men and women. Of late she has become an active opponent of vivisection, regarding it as an intellectual fallacy, misleading research and producing moral injury. She gives close attention to municipal affairs, as she feels the responsibility involved in the possession of a vote, which she possesses as a householder of Hastings. She knows in advanced age no diminution of her zeal for right over wrong. In addition to her long and arduous labors as a teacher, as a student and as the pioneer woman physician, Dr. Elizabeth Blackwell has been a prolific author. Naturally, her works lie in the field of her profession. Between 1852 and 1891 she wrote the following important medical and scientific works: "The Laws of Life in Relation to the Physical Education of Girls," "How to Keep a Household in Health," "The Moral Education of the Young in Relation to Sex," "Wrong and Right Methods of Dealing with the Social Evil," "Christian Socialism," "The Human Element in Sex," "The Corruption of New Malthusianism," "The Purchase of Women a Great Economic Blunder," "The Decay of Municipal Representative Government," "The Influence of Women in the Medical Profession," "Erroneous Methods in Medical Education," and "Lessons Taught by the International Hygienic Conference." Besides these are to be counted her numerous lectures, addresses and pamphlets on many branches of her profession. She is a woman of unbending will and a courage that never recognized defeat as possible. She opened the gate to the medical profession for women in the United States, in France and in Great Britain, and she has lived to see that profession made as easily accessible to women as to men. Dr. Blackwell is a profound thinker, a clear and logical reasoner, and a scientific controversialist of eminent ability. Her career, her achievements, her literary and scientific productions, and her work as a practicing physician make her a standing refutation of the easy-going assumption that women have neither the endurance, nor the intellect, nor the judgment, nor the requisites to serve in the medical profession. She owns a house in Hastings, England, where she resides, with an office in London for occasional work.

BLACKWELL, Miss Emily, physician, born in Bristol, England, in 1826. She is a younger sister of the well-known Dr. Elizabeth Blackwell. The story of her early life is similar to that of her famous sister. In 1848 Emily began the study of medicine, taking a course of medical reading and dissection with Dr. Davis, the demonstrator of anatomy in the medical college in Cincinnati, Ohio. Like her sister, she was endowed with great determination, good health, high ideals, quick perceptions and an exceptionally strong memory. Her early studies made her thoroughly familiar with French, Latin and German, and in Greek and mathematics she was well versed. She worked as a teacher to earn the funds to pay for her medical education. Dr. Elizabeth Blackwell had graduated at the Geneva Medical College in 1849, and at her graduation the professors had testified that her presence in the school "had

exercised a beneficial influence upon her fellow-students in all respects," and that "the average attainments and general conduct of students, during the period she passed among them, were of a higher character than those of any other class which has been assembled in the college since the connection of the president with the institution." The college professors having been severely criticised for making such an innovation, when her sister Emily, in 1851, applied for admission, she was met with the discouraging declaration that they were not ready to look upon the case of Dr. Elizabeth Blackwell as a precedent, and that the admission, training and graduation of one woman did not mean the permanent opening of the doors of the Geneva Medical College to women. Emily made application to ten other colleges, and each of the ten refused to permit her to enter. She then went to New York City, where she was admitted to study in the free hospital of Bellevue Medical Col-

EMILY BLACKWELL.

lege. In 1852 she was admitted to Rush Medical College in Chicago, Ill. The following summer she spent in New York in hospital work in Bellevue and study and experiment in the chemical laboratory of Dr. Doremus. Returning to Chicago to begin her second term, she was dismayed to learn that Rush College had closed its doors against her. The authorities of the college had been censured by the State Medical Association of Illinois for having permitted a woman to enter the institution as a student. She next went to Cleveland, Ohio, where the medical school admitted her. She studied earnestly and was graduated after passing triumphantly a most searching examination. She then went to Edinburgh, Scotland, where she studied under the eminent Dr. Simpson in the lying-in hospital. Then she went to Paris, where she attended clinics under the great physicians of that city in the Hotel Dieu, the Beaujou, the St. Louis and the Hospital des Enfants Malades, living and working in the Hospital of the Maternité. After Paris, she went to London, England, where she "walked" the wards of St. Bartholomew and other hospitals. In 1856 she returned to the United States, bringing the highest testimonials of training, study and acquirement. On her return she discovered that the popular sentiment seemed to have turned against women physicians more strongly than ever before. After the graduation of the Doctors Blackwell, several other schools had graduated women, but the faculties were determined that no more women should be admitted. Then separate schools sprung up. One of the immediate results of this revulsion of sentiment was the establishment of the hospital in New York by the Doctors Blackwell, in connection with a cultured Polish woman, Dr. M. E. Zakrzewska. In 1865 the legislature conferred college powers upon that institution. The new college extended the course of study to three years and was the first college to establish a chair of hygiene. Dr. Emily Blackwell has been from the first, and still is, one of the professors of that college, and the medical head of the infirmary for women and children established by the joint efforts of herself and her sister. The success of the college is a matter of history. The graduates number hundreds, and many of them have won distinction. It has been a "woman's college" throughout, owned, maintained, officered and managed by women. Dr. Emily Blackwell has also a large and lucrative practice and an honorable standing in her profession. She is interested in all the reform questions of the day and has written and published much in connection with her profession. She is one of the vice-presidents of the Society for the Promotion of Social Purity and the better protection of the young, and has written some of the leaflets published by that society, among them "The State and Girlhood," the "Need of Combination among Women for Self Protection," and "Regulation Fallacies — Vice not a Necessity." She is deeply loved and revered by her numerous friends and pupils. Her character is one of rare wisdom, disinterestedness and undeviating principle.

BLACKWELL, Miss Sarah Ellen, artist and author, the youngest daughter of Samuel and Hannah Lane Blackwell, born in Bristol, England, in 1828. She came to America with her parents at four years of age. Her father dying shortly afterwards, she was educated by her older sisters in Cincinnati, Ohio. She began to teach music at a very early age, while pursuing her studies. When nineteen years old, she went to Philadelphia to pursue the study of art in the newly opened School of Design, and while there received her first literary encouragement. "Sartain's Magazine" having advertised for ten prize stories, to be sent in under fictitious names, Miss Blackwell sent in a story of her own under the name "Brandon," and another by one of her sisters that happened to be in her possession. She received an award of two out of the ten prizes. That led to further literary work. Concluding to continue the study of art in Europe, she secured an engagement for weekly letters for two leading Philadelphia papers. She spent four years in Europe. She entered the government school of design for girls in Paris, then under the care of Rosa Bonheur and her sister, Mme. Julie Peyrol, and afterwards entered the studio of Mr. Leigh in London, and painted in the National Gallery, spending the summer on sketching from nature in Wales, Switzerland and the Isle of Wight. Returning to New York, she opened a studio and established classes in drawing and painting, but finally gave up her studio to assist

her sisters, the Doctors Blackwell, then greatly burdened with work connected with the New York Infirmary for Women and Children, and the medical college established by them. For several years she was occupied with domestic duties and the care of children in whom she was interested. As these duties lightened, she resumed artistic and literary work, writing occasional articles for magazines and newspapers and republishing the writings of Dr. Elizabeth Blackwell, then in England. A

SARAH ELLEN BLACKWELL.

series of letters written by her for the "Woman's Journal," of Boston, concerning Miss Anna Ella Carroll, author of the plan of the Tennessee campaign, having excited much interest, it was followed by an open letter on the same subject published in the "Century" for August, 1890. That increased the interest, and in the Woman's Council and suffrage meetings in the early spring of 1891, in Washington, D. C., a large number of subscribers were obtained, and Miss Blackwell was deputed to write a biography of Miss Carroll and an account of her remarkable work. After careful research, she printed, 21st April, 1891, the biography and sketch entitled "A Military Genius: Life of Anna Ella Carroll, the Great Unrecognized Member of Lincoln's Cabinet." Miss Blackwell spends her summers in an old farm-house at Martha's Vineyard, and her winters in New York or Washington, engaged in literary work. Her especial subjects of interest are land and labor reform, woman's suffrage and anti-vivisection, sympathizing as she does with Dr. Elizabeth Blackwell in her opposition to all cruel and demoralizing practices.

BLAIR, Mrs. Ellen A. Dayton, temperance organizer, born near Vernon Center, Oneida county, N. Y., 27th December, 1827. She was graduated in the classical course from Fort Edward Institute, N. Y., in 1837, and in the same year accepted the position of preceptress in Upper

Iowa University, Fayette, Iowa. She remained in that institution one year, having charge of the art department. Soon after she was married to Emery H. Blair, of Iowa, at one time professor of mathe-

ELLEN A. DAYTON BLAIR.

matics in Clinton Liberal Institute, N. Y. Both were strong in anti-slavery and prohibition sentiments. During the Woman's Crusade Mrs. Blair discovered her ability as a temperance speaker. Loving the cause and zealous in its behalf, she has ever since been one of its faithful workers. She is the mother of five sons, three of whom are living. Young men were her special care during the Crusade and in Sunday-school work. Moving to Wisconsin in 1881, she began her illustrative talks to children, on the invitation of Mrs. Mary B. Willard, and later was made superintendent of the juvenile department for Wisconsin. In 1885 she was elected to her present position as national organizer and "chalk talker" of the juvenile department of the Woman's Christian Temperance Union. In fulfillment of her duties she has visited nearly every State and Territory, as well as Canada, and has been a member of nearly every national convention. Since she removed to Creighton, Neb., she has continued her work in the same field. During the prohibitory amendment campaign in that State she was one of the leaders. As superintendent of the Demorest medal contests, which has occupied much of her time and that of several assistants, under her care Nebraska leads the world in that line of temperance work. Mrs. Blair's greatest influence as a temperance worker lies in her illustrative talks, by which she interests young and old. In her hand the piece of chalk becomes a power. She is a natural artist and, when not engaged in public duties, devotes herself to teaching oil painting, drawing and crayon work.

BLAKE, Mrs. Alice R. Jordan, lawyer, born in Norwalk, Ohio, 10th October, 1864. She bears the distinction of being the first and so far the

only woman to be graduated with a degree from Yale College. She received her high-school education in Coldwater, Mich., where from childhood she was considered a prodigy in learning. After graduating from the high school, the youngest of her class, she entered the University of Michigan at the age of sixteen years, being at that time the youngest pupil who had ever entered the course. After graduating from the literary department at the end of four years, Miss Jordan decided to study law, and she entered the law department of the University, then under Judge Thomas M. Cooley. So diligently did she prosecute her studies that, at the end of the first year, before she had even entered the senior class, she passed a most rigid examination in open court and was admitted to practice in all the courts of Michigan. Being ambitious that the foundation of her future work should be thoroughly assured, Miss Jordan wished to continue her studies, and with that view she applied for admission to the Law Department of Columbia College, but admission was refused because she was a woman. Not daunted by refusal, she applied to Harvard, but with like result. The authorities there were, if anything, more hostile even than those of Columbia had been. Then she opened correspondence with the authorities of Yale, but with the same discouraging reply that the constitution forbade the granting of a degree to a woman. So it did, but by perseverance against every obstacle, the door was finally opened to her, and she entered the senior class. So strange was it to see a young lady passing to and fro in those halls, dedicated only to young men, and to be reciting in the classes, that a few of the more conservative professors anticipated dire results, but in less than a fortnight

ALICE R. JORDAN BLAKE.

the refining influence was felt in hall and class-room, much to the satisfaction of the faculty. At first a few of the young men felt that their prerogatives had been invaded and their standard lowered by admitting a young woman to equal standing with themselves, but it was not for long. That feeling soon changed to one of respect and admiration, and cordial relations existed with every member of the class. As the college year drew to a close and Miss Jordan had with great credit passed the final examination, came the question whether the corporation could exceed the powers granted by the constitution and confer the degree of LL.B. They offered a compromise sort of certificate, but it was declined. The exitement was intense. How hard it had been to overcome the prejudice and drive the entering wedge for woman's admission may best be comprehended in the remark of its retiring president, Noah Porter: "Would that I had never lived to be called upon to sign a Yale College degree granted to a woman." A special session of the corporation was called and, notwithstanding the opposition of the president, it was voted to grant the degree with full honors. The result of this decision was almost electrifying. A banquet followed, and it was thought at that time that the battle for women to enjoy equal advantages in the college had been fought and won, and that one more progressive step had been taken in the history of the age. After leaving college, Miss Jordan continued her studies in California for two years, when she was married to George D. Blake, an attorney and former class-mate, and since her marriage she has resided in Seattle, Wash.

BLAKE, Mrs. Euphenia Vale, author and critic, born in Hastings, England, 7th May, 1825. Her father, Gilbert Vale, removed with his family to New York when the daughter was about seven years of age. Mr. Vale was well known as an author, publisher, inventor, public lecturer and a professor of astronomy and other branches of mathematics, making a specialty of navigation. He died in Brooklyn in 1866. In 1842 Mrs. Blake went to Massachusetts to reside, her husband, Dr. D. S. Blake, being a native of that State. Almost immediately Mrs. Blake began to write for the leading local paper, in Essex county, Mass., the Newburyport "Herald," taking the editorial duties whenever the chief was absent. She also edited a weekly literary paper the "Saturday Evening Union," and supplied leading articles for the "Watch Tower." In 1854 she wrote and published the history of the town of Newburyport, and a scientific work on the use of ether and chloroform applied to practical dentistry. At that time she was also writing for the "North American Review" and "Christian Examiner," all the editorials for the "Bay State," a weekly published in Lynn, with occasional articles in the Boston daily journals, the "Transcript," "Traveller," "Atlas" and others. It was in the "Atlas" one of her articles in 1853 started the movement for revising the laws of Massachusetts and causing the adoption of that law which now prevails, limiting the franchise to those capable of reading the Constitution of the United States. In 1857 Mrs. Blake returned to Brooklyn, N. Y., where she has ever since resided. She furnished a series of "Letters from New York" to the Boston "Traveller" and wrote essays for the "Religious Magazine." Then for the "New York Quarterly" she did much book reviewing. She also wrote for the "Constellation," edited by Park Benjamin. In 1859 to 1861 she regularly supplied the "Crayon," an art magazine published in New York, with elaborate articles on literature and art. To settle a wager between two friends, one of whom bet that no one "could impose on the New York "Herald," and the other thinking it might be possible, Mrs. Blake wrote a "Great Manifesto! Declaration of Independence by the States of South Carolina, Georgia, Alabama, Florida and Mississippi. Copy of the Instructions sent to France! etc." This the then editor-in-chief, the astute Hudson, accepted as genuine. It was printed 14th November, 1860, and paid for, and it was a nine-day wonder why the other papers never had it. In 1871 Mrs. Blake furnished historical articles to the "Catholic World" on the "Milesian Race." Next followed articles for the

EUPHENIA VALE BLAKE.

"Christian Union," and, at the request of Mr. Beecher, a few short stories. A little later she contributed essays to the "Popular Science Monthly." One of her productions was printed in the Brooklyn "Eagle" of 23rd November, 1871, discussing the riparian rights of Brooklyn to her own shore line. It was a historical resumé of all the legislation on the subject, from colonial times to the date of publication. The late Chief Justice Nielson, of the city court, remarked that "the argument was unanswerable." In 1874 she published "Arctic Experiences" (New York), to give a correct history of the Polaris Expedition and Captain Tyson's wonderful ice drift, and containing also a sketch of all the preceding expeditions, both American and foreign. In 1879, and subsequently, she wrote regularly for the "Oriental Church Magazine." Mrs. Blake wrote several lectures on historical and social topics for a literary bureau in New York, which have since been repeatedly delivered by a man who claimed them as his own. She has also written a book on marine zoölogy and a series of articles on "The Marys of History, Art and Song." She occasionally writes in verse.

BLAKE, Mrs. Lillie Devereux, woman suffragist and reformer, born in Raleigh, N. C., 12th August, 1835. Her father was George Pollok Devereux, and her mother was Sarah Elizabeth Johnson. Mr. Devereux was a wealthy southern gentleman, of Irish descent on his father's side. His mother, Frances Pollok, was a descendant of Sir Thomas

Pollok, one of the early governors of North Carolina under the Lords Proprietaries. Mrs. Devereux was the daughter of Judge Samuel William Johnson, of Stratford, Conn., and a granddaughter of the Hon. William Samuel Johnson, member of the Stamp Act Congress, of the Fourth and Fifth Continental Congresses and of the Federal Convention, Senator from Connecticut, and president of Columbia College, his father, the Rev. Samuel Johnson, D. D., having been the founder and first president of that university, when it was called King's College. Both Mr. and Mrs. Devereux were descended from the Rev. Jonathan Edwards, D. D. Mr. Devereux died in 1837, and his widow removed to New Haven, Conn., where she was widely known for the generous hospitality which she dispensed from her beautiful home, "Maple Cottage." Lillie received every advantage of education, taking the Yale College course from tutors at home. She grew up to be a beautiful and brilliant girl and was an acknowl-

LILLIE DEVEREUX BLAKE.

edged belle until she was married, in 1855, to Frank G. Q. Umsted, a young lawyer of Philadelphia. With him she made her home in St. Louis, Mo., and New York City until 1859, when she was left a widow with two children. She had already begun to write for the press, one of her first stories, "A Lonely House," having appeared in the "Atlantic Monthly." She had also published "Southwold," a novel, which achieved a decided success. The handsome fortune she had inherited was largely impaired, and the young widow began to work in real earnest, writing stories, sketches and letters for several leading periodicals. She made her home most of the time with her mother in Stratford, Conn., but spent some winters in Washington and New York. In 1862 she published a second novel, called "Rockford," and subsequently wrote several romances. In 1866 she was married to Grinfill Blake, a young merchant of New York, and since that time has made her home in that city. In 1869 she

became actively interested in the woman suffrage movement and devoted herself with all her energies to pushing the reform, arranging conventions, getting up public meetings, writing articles and occasionally making lecture tours. A woman of strong affections and marked domestic tastes, she has not allowed her public work to interfere with her home duties, and her speaking outside of New York City has been almost wholly done in the summer, when her family was naturally scattered. In 1872 she published a novel called "Fettered for Life," designed to show the many disadvantages under which women labor. In 1873 she made an application for the opening of Columbia College to young women as well as young men, presenting a class of girl students qualified to enter the university. The agitation then begun has since led to the establishment of Barnard College. In 1879 she was unanimously elected president of the New York State Woman Suffrage Association, an office which she held for eleven years. During that period she made a tour of the State every summer, arranged conventions, and each year conducted a legislative campaign, many times addressing committees of the senate and assembly. In 1880 the school suffrage law was passed, largely through her efforts, and in each year woman suffrage bills were introduced and pushed to a vote in one or both of the branches of the legislature. In 1883 the Rev. Morgan Dix, D. D., delivered a series of Lenten discourses on "Woman," presenting a most conservative view of her duties. Mrs. Blake replied to each lecture in an able address, advocating more advanced ideas. Her lectures were printed under the title of "Woman's Place To-day" (New York), and have had a large sale. Among the reforms in which she has been actively interested has been that of securing matrons to take charge of women detained in police stations. As early as 1871 she spoke and wrote on the subject, and through her labors, in 1881 and 1882, bills were passed by the assembly, failing to become laws, however, because of the opposition of the police department in New York City. She continued to agitate the subject, public sentiment was finally aroused, and in 1891 a law was passed enforcing this much-needed reform. The employment of women as census takers was first urged in 1880 by Mrs. Blake. The bills giving seats to saleswomen, ordering the presence of a woman physician in every insane asylum where women are detained, and many other beneficent measures were presented or aided by her. In 1886 Mrs. Blake was elected president of the New York City Woman Suffrage League, an office which she still holds. She has attended conventions and made speeches in most of the States and Territories and has addressed committees of both houses of Congress and of the New York and Connecticut legislatures. She still continues her literary labors. She is a graceful and logical writer, a witty and eloquent speaker and a charming hostess, her weekly receptions through the season in New York having been for many years among the attractions of literary and reform circles.

BLAKE, Mrs. Mary Elizabeth, poet, born in Dungarven, county Waterford, Ireland, 1st September, 1840. Her father's name was McGrath, a man of wide reading and much originality of thought. When Mary was six years old, the family came to America, settling in Quincy, Mass. Her education was acquired in the public and private schools of Boston and the Convent of the Sacred Heart, Manhattanville, N.Y. In June, 1865, she was married to Dr. John G. Blake, who has long held a prominent position among Massachusetts medical men. Up to the present time she has published the following works: "Poems" (Boston, 1881), which has passed to a second edition; "On the Wing" (Boston, 1883), a volume of letters of western travel, in its fifth edition; "Mexico" (Boston, 1888), a volume of travel, written in collaboration with Mrs. Margaret Sullivan; "A Summer Holiday" (Boston, 1890), an account of her European impressions; and "Verses Along the Way" (Boston and Dublin, 1890). Mrs. Blake has for many years contributed at frequent intervals to the Boston "Journal," the "Rambling Talks" by "M. E. B." being one of its most valued features. Much of her work in essays and poems has appeared in the "Catholic World," "Lippincott's Magazine," the "Independent," "St. Nicholas" and "Wide Awake." On the invitation of the Boston city government she wrote the poem read on the occasion of the Wendell Phillips Memorial Service in that city, and also the poem read on the occasion of similar honors paid to the memory of Admiral Porter. Mrs. Blake's verse is lyrical rather than epic or dramatic, and its quality deepens and strengthens as time goes on.

BLANCHARD, Miss Helen Augusta, inventor, born in Portland, Maine, is a lineal de-

HELEN AUGUSTA BLANCHARD.

scendant of the celebrated Huguenot exile, Sir Thomas Blanchard. Her father, Nathaniel Blanchard, was one of the most prominent and honored business men of Portland. In girlhood Miss Blanchard began to show that inventive power which has made her name famous. The death of her father and the embarrassment of his estate called forth her latent energies and developed the ability and ingenuity which determined her course as an inventor. She applied her powers to the intricacies of machinery, and in 1876, by the results of her inventions, she established the Blanchard Over-seam Company, of Philadelphia, which was the originality of what is now called zigzag sewing,

both inside and outside of material sewed, and which achieved a signal success. A number of great industries have sprung from that company, and the benefits of that invention have spread through the country. The ambition and energy that have marked her life were stimulated by the numberless annoyances and obstacles that always beset the pathway of a persevering inventor, in the shape of Patent Office delays, mercenary infringement of her rights and unscrupulous assaults upon the products of her brain. Among her numerous inventions are the Blanchard over-seaming-machine, the machine for simultaneous sewing and trimming on knitted fabrics, and the crocheting and sewing machine, all of which are in use by immense manufactories and are ranked among the most remarkable mechanical contrivances of the age. For many years Miss Blanchard lived in Philadelphia, managing and directing her business in that city, but for the last few years she has made her home in New York. In all the rush and publicity that have surrounded her she has preserved those qualities of gentleness, dignity and modesty which adorn her character and secure her a grateful welcome into the social life of the metropolis. Aiding with open-hearted generosity the meritorious efforts of struggling women wherever she has found them, she has distinguished herself as a benefactor of her sex.

BLAVATSKY, Mme. Helene Petrovna, theosophist and author, born in Russia in 1820, and died in London, Eng., 8th May, 1891. She was the oldest daughter of Colonel Peter Hahn, of the Russian Horse Artillery, and granddaughter of Lieut.-Gen. Alexander Hahn von Rallenstern-Hahn, a noble family of Mecklenburg, settled in Russia. Her mother was Helene Fadeef, daughter of Privy Council Andrew Fadeef and his wife, Princess Dolgouriki. Mlle. Hahn became the wife of General Nicole V. Blavatsky at the age of seventeen, but, the marriage proving an unhappy one, they separated after three months of married life. Mme. Blavatsky began the studies of mysticism and the languages at an early age, and became very proficient in the latter, speaking nearly forty European and Asiatic tongues and dialects. She was also a great traveler, having visited almost every part of Europe, and living for more than forty years in India. She spent a great deal of time in Canada and the United States, studying the Indian race and traditions, and also the mystic sects among the negroes. Mme. Blavatsky endeavored several times to penetrate the mysteries of Buddhism in India, but did not succeed till 1855, when, with the aid of an oriental disguise, she succeeded in entering a monastic house of the Buddhists, in Thibet. She afterwards embraced that religion and her book, "Isis Unveiled," which was published in 1877, is the most remarkable work of the kind in existence. In 1878 she organized the Theosophical Society in America, and the following year she returned to India to disseminate its tenets among the natives. She established a society in Egypt for the study of modern spiritualism. She was a naturalized citizen of the United States, and her third and last husband was an American, Henry S. Olcott, who assisted her in her various psychical researches and publications. It was believed by many that she was a Russian spy, and that her theosophical ideas were only subterfuges to hide her real purposes. Among her esoteric works are "The Secret Doctrine," "Synthesis of Science, Religion and Philosophy," "Key to Theosophy" and "Voices of Silence." She at one time published in London, a paper called "Lucifer," the organ of Theosophy.

BLOEDE, Miss Gertrude, poet, born in Dresden, Germany, 10th August, 1845. Her father and mother were among the refugees who fled from Germany in consequence of the revolu-

GERTRUDE BLOEDE.

tion of 1848. In this country they were intimate friends of Bayard Taylor, at whose house they met Stedman, Stoddard, Aldrich and other well-known American poets and authors. Miss Bloede was naturally impelled, by her surroundings and her talents, to literary effort, and in 1878 she published "Angelo." Miss Bloede used the pen-name "Stuart Sterne" in her first works, and even after that name had become widely known, very few readers were aware that its owner was a woman. Before the appearance of "Angelo," she had published a small volume of short poems, which bore no publisher's imprint. The little volume was favorably reviewed at great length in the New York "Times," and she learned, after much inquiry, that the notice was written by Richard Grant White, who was greatly impressed by the quality of the work. That was her first critical recognition, and she dedicated "Angelo," which she had already finished, to Mr. White. That eminent critic read the manuscript, and on his representations a prominent Boston house published it. Its success was instantaneous. Since its appearance, in 1878, it has passed through sixteen editions. Since that year she has published three notable volumes, "Giorgio" (Boston, 1881), a long poem, "Beyond the Shadows and Other Poems" (Boston, 1888), and "Pierod da Castiglione" (Boston, 1890), a story in verse of the time of Savonarola. In all her books she has used her pen-name, "Stuart Sterne," which, she says, she adopted, as many other female writers have done, because men's work is considered stronger than women's, and she wished her work to be judged by the highest standards and to stand or fall on its own merits. She has lived in Brooklyn since 1861, making her home with her

sister, the wife of Dr. S. T. King. She recently summed up her work and personality thus briefly and modestly: "There is very little to tell. I have published five volumes of poems, and that is all. I live very quietly. I go into society but little, and I do not belong to anything." Miss Bloede professes to find in the city the seclusion which pastoral poets find in rural life. She is an artist in human passions, not in mere word and scene painting. She is dramatic in instinct, and that quality illumines all her work, though none of her productions have been cast in dramatic form. Although she goes into society but little, she numbers among her friends the most prominent literary people of New York. She is not a member of any of the women's organizations in Brooklyn, as she feels that the artwork of societies from which men are excluded amounts to little. She is interested in art and music and is a lover and student of languages, speaking English, French and German with fluency, and reads Dutch, Italian and Latin with ease. Among her latest productions is a novel, "The Story of Two Lives" (New York, 1892).

BLONDNER, Mrs. Aline Reese, musician and educator, born in Georgia. She received a classical education from her father, Rev. Augustus Reese, a graduate of Oxford College. Her first musical instruction was given to her by her mother, Celeste Dewel Reese, who was educated in Troy Female Seminary, Troy, N. Y. Aline played at first sight, when eight years of age, with facility and skill, memorizing with rapidity and exciting the admiration of all who heard her play, when, as a tiny child, she appeared in many public exhibitions, executing on the piano compositions which required technical skill and ability. She re-

ALINE REESE BLONDNER.

ceived further musical education from Prof. George Briggs on piano, violin and guitar, and on the organ from Prof. Charles Blondner, of Philadelphia. In 1878 she took lessons from Prof. Asger Hamerik, of Baltimore. In 1879 she went to Leipsic, Germany, where she took private lessons from Herr Carl Reinecke for two years. In the summer of 1881 she went to Weimar, where Liszt received her as a pupil. Mrs. Blondner is now teaching in her own studio in Nashville, Tenn. She has a class in the Nashville College for Young Ladies. She is organist in the First Baptist Church and is widely known as pianist, organist and teacher.

BLOOMER, Mrs. Amelia, woman suffragist, born in Homer, Cortland county, N. Y., 27th May, 1818, of New England parentage. When six years of age, she removed with her parents to Seneca county in the same State, where in 1840 she was united in marriage to D. C. Bloomer, of Seneca Falls, and for fifteen years following resided in that place. In 1842 she became a member of the Episcopal Church and has ever since remained a sincere and devoted communicant of that body. She was first attracted to public life

AMELIA BLOOMER.

through the temperance reform, which began to be seriously agitated in 1840 and was continued for some years under the name of "Washingtonian." The agitation of that question soon led her to understand the political, legal and financial necessities and disabilities of woman, and, when she saw the depth of the reform needed, she was not slow to espouse the cause of freedom in its highest, broadest, justest sense. At that early day no woman's voice had yet been heard from the platform pleading the rights or wrongs of her sex. She employed her pen to say the thoughts she could not utter. She wrote for the press over various signatures, her contributions appearing in the "Water Bucket," "Temperance Star," "Free Soil Union," and other papers. On the first of January, 1849, a few months after the inauguration of the first woman's rights convention, she began the publication of the "Lily," a folio sheet devoted to temperance and the interests of woman.

That journal was a novelty in the newspaper world, being the first enterprise of the kind ever owned, edited and controlled by a woman and published in the interest of women. It was received with marked favor by the press and continued a successful career of six years in Mrs. Bloomer's hands. At the end of that time, on her removal to the West, she disposed of her paper to Mary B. Birdsall, of Richmond, Ind., who continued the publication for two years and then suffered it to go down. Mrs. Bloomer was indebted to Mrs. Stanton, Miss Anthony and others for contributions. In the third year of the publication of her journal her attention was called to the neat, convenient and comfortable costume afterwards called by her name. She was not the originator of the style, but adopted it after seeing it worn by others, and introduced it to the public through her paper. The press handed the matter about and commented on this new departure from fashion's sway, until the whole country was excited over it, and Mrs. Bloomer was overwhelmed with letters of inquiry from women concerning the dress. All felt the need of some reform that should lift the burden of clothes from their wearied bodies. Though many adopted the style for a time, yet under the rod of tyrant fashion and the ridicule of the press they soon laid it aside. Mrs. Bloomer herself finally abandoned it, after wearing it six or eight years, and long after those who preceded her in its use had doffed the costume they loved and returned to long skirts. In 1852 Mrs. Bloomer made her début on the platform as a lecturer, and in the winter of that year, in company with Susan B. Anthony and Rev Antoinette L. Brown, she visited and lectured in all the principal cities and towns of her native State, from New York to Buffalo. At the outset her subject, like that of her co-workers, was temperance, but temperance strongly spiced with the wrongs and rights of woman. In 1849 Mr. Bloomer was appointed postmaster of Seneca Falls. On the reception of the office he at once appointed Mrs. Bloomer his d puty. She soon made herself thoroughly acquainted with the details of the office and discharged its duties for the four years of the Taylor and Filmore administration. In the winter of 1853 she was chairman of a committee appointed to go before the legislature of New York with petitions for a prohibitory liquor law. She continued her work in her native State, writing and lecturing on both temperance and woman's rights, and attending to the duties of her house and office until the winter of 1853-54, when she removed with her husband to Mt. Vernon, Ohio. There she continued the publication of the "Lily," and was also associate editor of the "Western Home Visitor," a large literary weekly paper published in that place. In the columns of the "Visitor," as in all her writings, some phase of the woman question was the subject of her pen. About that time, and in the fall of 1853, she visited and lectured in all the principal cities and towns of the North and West, going often where no lecturer on woman's enfranchisement had preceded her. She everywhere received a kindly welcome and very flattering notices from the press. In January, 1854, she was one of a committee to memorialize the legislature of Ohio on a prohibitory liquor law. The rules were suspended and the committee received with marked respect and favor, and the same evening the legislature, almost in a body, attended a lecture given by her on woman's right of suffrage. In the spring of 1855 Mr and Mrs. Bloomer made their home in Council Bluffs, Iowa, where they have since resided. Owing to weariness of her charge, and the want of facilities for printing and carrying so large a mail as her four-thousand papers from that new land, at so early a day, Mrs. Bloomer disposed of the "Lily" before leaving Ohio, and intended henceforth to rest from her public labors. But that was not permitted to her. Calls for lectures were frequent, and to these she responded as far as possible, but was obliged to refuse to go long distances on account of there being at that day no public conveyance except the old stage coach. In the winter of 1856 Mrs. Bloomer, by invitation, addressed the legislature of Nebraska on the subject of woman's right to the ballot. The Territorial house of representatives shortly afterwards passed a bill giving women the right to vote, and in the council it passed to a second reading, but was finally lost for want of time. The limited session was drawing to a close, and the last hour expired before the bill could come up for final action. Mrs. Bloomer took part in organizing the Iowa State Suffrage Association and was at one time its president. Poor health has compelled her of late years to retire from active work in the cause.

BLYE, Miss Birdie, pianist, born in New York City, in 187–. Her parents are Americans of English descent. Miss Blye early manifested a love of music. Her talent was developed under able masters in London, Paris and Germany. When eleven years of age she made her début in orchestral concerts in London and on the Continent, with success. She played from memory concertos, sonatas and other compositions by Mendelssohn, Beethoven, Schumann, Rubinstein, Liszt, Schubert and Chopin, and could play the whole clavichord without notes and transpose in every key.

BIRDIE BLYE.

She received many certificates and medals, and was fêted and admired as the little "wonder child." Within the past three years she has played in more than two-hundred concerts and musicales in chief

American, English and European cities with gratifying success. She is an excellent violinist, a pupil of the Joachim School of Berlin. Miss Blye is highly educated, is a linguist of note, and paints like an artist in oil and water colors. She studied in the Grosvenor Art Gallery in London. Her first exibited picture, painted when she was fourteen years of age, was sold for seventy-five dollars.

BODLEY, Miss Rachel L., scientist and doctor of medicine, was born in Cincinnati, Ohio, 7th December, 1831. Her parents were Anthony

RACHEL L. BODLEY.

R. and Rebecca W. Talbot Bodley, who settled in Cincinnati in 1817. Her paternal ancestry was Scotch-Irish. The American head of the family, Thomas Bodley, came from the north of Ireland early in the eighteenth century. His wife was Eliza Knox, of Edinburgh, Scotland. Her maternal ancestry runs back to John Talbot, an English Friend, who settled in Virginia. Rachel was the oldest daughter and the third child in a family of five. Her mother taught a private school, in which Rachel studied until she was twelve years old. She entered the Wesleyan Female College in Cincinnati in 1844, only two years after the opening of that institution, which was the first chartered college for women in the world. She was graduated in 1849, and in 1860 she was made preceptress in the higher collegiate studies. Dissatisfied with her own attainments, she went to Philadelphia, Pa., and entered the Polytechnic College as a special student in physics and chemistry. After two years of study she returned to Cincinnati and was made professor of natural sciences in the Cincinnati Female Seminary, which chair she filled for three years. While there she distinguished herself by classifying the extensive collection of specimens in natural history bequeathed to the seminary by Joseph Clark. Her work on that collection is crystallized in a catalogue that was recognized by Asa Gray, the eminent botanist, as a valuable contribution to science. In 1867 and 1868 she gave a series of important lectures on cryptogamous plants of land and sea. In 1865 she was elected to the chair of chemistry and toxicology in the Woman's Medical College of Pennsylvania, being the first woman professor of chemistry on record. In 1874 she was elected dean of the faculty, and she held both of those positions until her death. She was called to the deanship while the college building was being erected. Among her many achievements was the collection of facts in reference to the success of the graduates of the Woman's Medical College of Pennsylvania in their professional work. That work was entitled "The College Story." The graduates were at that time practicing in Utah, Manitoba, India, China and European lands, and in every state in the Union. Their replies to the questions she sent them showed an unbroken line of success. Dr. Bodley received many honors in recognition of her contributions to science and literature. In 1864 she was made corresponding member of the State Historical Society of Wisconsin. In 1871 she was elected a member of the Academy of Natural Sciences of Philadelphia, and in that year the degree of A. M. was conferred upon her by her alma mater in Cincinnati. That college, up to that time, had never given a degree to any of its alumnæ subsequent to the degree of A. B. at graduation. Dr. Bodley was one of the first three to receive that honor. In 1873 she was elected a corresponding member of the Cincinnati Society of Natural History. In 1876 she was elected a corresponding member of the New York Academy of Sciences and a member of the American Chemical Society of New York. She was elected first vice-president of the meeting called in 1874 to celebrate the centennial of chemistry, the month of August in that year being the date chosen in honor of the discovery of oxygen by Dr. Joseph Priestly in 1774. At Dr. Bodley's suggestion the meeting was held in Northumberland, where Dr. Priestly is buried. In 1879 the Woman's Medical College of Pennsylvania conferred upon her the honorary degree of M. D. In 1880 she was made a member of the Franklin Institute of Philadelphia, and she delivered a course of lectures on "Household Chemistry" in the regular course of the Institute. In 1882 she was chosen a member of the Educational Society of Philadelphia, and in the same year was elected school director of the twenty-ninth school section, in which office she served until 1885. She was again elected to that position, and served until she died, 15th June, 1888.

BOHAN, Mrs. Elizabeth Baker, author and artist, born in Birmingham, England, 18th August, 1849. She is the daughter of Joseph and Martha Baker. They came to America in 1854 and have lived most of the time in Wisconsin. She received her education in the Milwaukee public schools and was for a time a teacher. She was married to M. Bohan, then editor of the Fond du Lac "Journal," in 1872. They now reside in Milwaukee, Wis., have a pleasant home and are surrounded by four bright children. Mrs. Bohan is the fortunate possessor of a combination of talents. She is a devoted and successful homekeeper, wife and mother. She is a painter of acknowledged ability and of far more than local celebrity. She is something of a musician, and there are many in Milwaukee and other portions of the State who take high rank as painters and musicians who received their first and only instruction from her. From her earliest youth she has practiced composition. As she grew to womanhood the taste for writing increased. She wrote great numbers of poems and a still greater number of prose sketches, but offered none for publication until within the last

five or six years. Since then large numbers of her poems and sketches have been published in the best papers and magazines throughout the country. She is a close student, seven days in a week, and

ELIZABETH BAKER BOHAN.

stores away everything she learns where it can be drawn upon on the instant. While she has done much literary work the past five or six years, it has always been a secondary consideration. Her daily duties have been as numerous and exacting as those of almost any mother, wife and homekeeper, and everything that she has done in a literary way has been accomplished in odd moments, and sometimes when duty to herself required that she be sleeping instead of thinking and writing.

BOLTON, Mrs. Sarah Knowles, author, born in Farmington, Conn., 15th September, 1841. She is a daughter of John Segar Knowles, descended from Henry Knowles, who moved to Portsmouth, R. I., from London, England, in 1635. Her grandmother, Mary Carpenter, was descended from Elizabeth Jenckes, sister of Joseph Jenckes, Governor of Rhode Island. Mrs. Bolton comes on her mother's side from Nathaniel Stanley, of Hartford, Conn., Lieutenant Colonel of First Regiment in 1739; Assistant Treasurer, 1725-49; Treasurer, 1749-55, and from Colonel William Pynchon, one of the twenty-six incorporators of Massachusetts Bay Colony, and the founder of Springfield, Mass. At the age of seventeen she became a member of the family of her uncle, Colonel H. L. Miller, a lawyer of Hartford, whose extensive library was a delight, and whose house was a center for those who loved scholarship and refinement. The aunt was a person of wide reading, exquisite taste and social prominence. There the young girl met Harriet Beecher Stowe, Lydia H. Sigourney, and others like them, whose lives to her were a constant inspiration. She became an excellent scholar and graduated from the seminary founded by Catherine Beecher. Her first published poem appeared in the "Waverly Magazine," when she was fifteen years old. Soon after her graduation she published a small volume, "Orlean Lamar and Other Poems" (New York, 1863), and a serial was

SARAH KNOWLES BOLTON.

accepted by a New England paper. Later she was married to Charles E. Bolton, a graduate of Amherst College, an able and cultivated man, and they removed to Cleveland, Ohio. She became the first secretary of the Woman's Christian Association of that city, using much of her time in visiting the poor. When, in 1874, the temperance crusade began in Hillsborough, Ohio, she was one of the first to take up the work and aid it with voice and pen. She was soon appointed assistant corresponding secretary of the National Woman's Christian Temperance Union, and as such, says Miss Willard, "She kept articles, paragraphs and enlightening excerpts before the public, which did more toward setting our new methods before the people than any single agency had ever compassed up to that time." At the request of the temperance women of the country, Mrs. Bolton prepared a history of the crusade for the Centennial temperance volume, and of the Cleveland work for Mrs. Wittenmyer's general history. At that time she published her temperance story entitled "The Present Problem" (New York, 1874). Invited to Boston to become one of the editors of the "Congregationalist," a most useful and responsible position, she proved herself an able journalist. She passed two years abroad, partly in travel and partly in study, that being her second visit to Europe. She made a special study of woman's higher education in the universities of Cambridge, Oxford, and elsewhere, preparing for magazines several articles on that subject, as well as on woman's philanthropic and intellectual work, and on what was being done for the mental and moral help of laboring people by their employers, reading a paper on that subject at

a meeting of the American Social Science Association held in Saratoga in 1883. Mrs. Bolton's additional published works are "How Success is Won" (Boston, 1884); "Lives of Poor Boys who Became Famous" (New York, 1885); "Girls who Became Famous" (New York, 1886); "Stories from Life" (New York, 1886); "Social Studies in England" (Boston, 1886); "From Heart and Nature, Poems" (New York, 1887); "Famous American Authors" (New York, 1887); "Famous American Statesmen" (New York, 1888); "Some Successful Women" (Boston, 1888); "Famous Men of Science" (New York, 1889); "Famous European Artists" (New York, 1890); "English Authors of the Nineteenth Century" (New York, 1890); English Statesmen of Queen Victoria's Reign" (New York, 1891); "Famous Types of Womanhood" (New York, 1892). Several of these books have been reprinted in England. Mrs. Bolton's home is an ideal one for the lover of art and literature. Her husband is a man of wide travel and reading, and has given thirteen-hundred lectures during the past nine seasons. They have but one child, a son, Charles Knowles Bolton, graduated from Harvard College in 1890, and an assistant now in the Harvard University Library.

BOLTON, Mrs. Sarah T., poet, born in Newport, Ky., 18th December, 1812. Her maiden name was Barritt. When she was only three years old, her parents removed to Jennings county, Ind. Thence they removed to Madison, where Sarah grew to womanhood. She was educated in North Madison. She became a thorough English scholar, and at subsequent periods of her life acquired a knowledge of German and French. When fourteen years of age, she wrote verses. When not

SARAH T. BOLTON.

more than sixteen years old, several of her poems were published in a Madison paper. The editor was Nathaniel P. Bolton, and her literary ventures led to an acquaintance with him which resulted in marriage. The early years of her married life were passed on a farm west of Indianapolis. Her time and energies were chiefly devoted to home cares, having been blessed with a son and daughter. In the year 1850 William D. Gallagher, William C. Larrabee and Robert Dale Owen each wrote a biographical notice of her, highly commendatory of her personal and intellectual charms. Mr. Bolton was appointed consul to Switzerland in 1855 by President Pierce. He was accompanied to Europe by his wife and children, the latter of whom spent considerable time in Germany, Italy and France. From all these countries Mrs. Bolton wrote poems, besides sending many valuable prose contributions to the "Home Journal" and Cincinnati "Commercial." Hitherto she had known no trouble but that caused by vicissitude of fortune and the hard cares of life, and in November, 1858, her first great sorrow came in the death of her husband. Mrs. Bolton's life has been full of effort. During the Civil War she wrote many stirring songs, among them "The Union Forever" and "Ralph Farnham's Dream." It is interesting to trace Mrs. Bolton's patriotic blood to its Revolutionary source. Her father was the youngest son of Col. Lemuel Barritt, who distinguished himself as an officer in the war of Independence. Her mother was a Pendleton of Virginia and closely related to James Madison. Mrs. Bolton has spent several years of her life abroad, and she now resides near Indianapolis. She has published "The Life and Poems of Sarah T. Bolton" (Indianapolis, 1880). Her last volume is entitled "The Songs of a Lifetime." This volume is edited by Professor Ridpath, of De Pauw University, with a preface by General Lew Wallace. Mrs. Bolton is in poor health, but her pen is not idle.

BONAPARTE, Mme. Elizabeth Patterson, wife of Jerome Bonaparte, king of Westphalia, born in Baltimore, Md., 6th February, 1785, and died there 4th April, 1879. She was the daughter of William Patterson, the son of a farmer in county Donegal, Ireland. Her father came to the United States while he was a boy and settled in Baltimore. He went to Philadelphia, Pa., and was there employed in the counting-house of Samuel Johnson. He developed remarkable financial ability and soon became the owner of a line of clipper ships. During the Revolution he traded to France and brought back cargoes of arms and gunpowder. He acquired a large fortune and was the wealthiest man in Maryland, with the exception of Charles Carroll, of Carrollton. Elizabeth Patterson was a young woman of remarkable beauty of person, of strong powers of intellect, and of great fascination of manners, when, in the autumn of 1803, at a ball in the house of Samuel Chase, in Baltimore, she met Jerome Bonaparte, then in command of a French frigate. As the brother of Napoleon I, he was hospitably received. On their first meeting Captain Bonaparte and Miss Patterson fell in love. Marriage was proposed, but her father, foreseeing the grave difficulties implied in such an alliance with the brother of the First Consul, forbade the lovers to meet. Miss Patterson was sent to Virginia. The lovers corresponded, and Jerome procured a marriage license. The wedding was postponed until 24th December, 1803, when Jerome should have passed his nineteenth birthday. On that date the marriage ceremony was performed by Archbishop Carroll. All the legal formalities had been carefully provided for. The contract was drawn by Alexander Dallas, and the wedding was attended by the mayor of Baltimore, the vice-consul of France and many distinguished persons. Napoleon I obstinately opposed the match from first to last. He notified Jerome that, if he would

leave "the young person" in the United States and return to France, his "indiscretion" would be forgiven, and that, if he took her with him to France, she should not be permitted to set foot on French territory. He actually gave orders that neither Jerome nor his wife should be permitted to land at any port controlled by France. In spite of that order, Jerome and his wife sailed in 1805, on one of Mr. Patterson's ships, for Europe. The ship was wrecked between Philadelphia and the Capes. Embarking on another vessel, they sailed for Lisbon. There the wife remained, while Captain Bonaparte went on to Paris, hoping to make peace with his brother. Napoleon I was obstinate and absolutely refused to recognize the marriage. Madame Bonaparte sailed from Lisbon for Amsterdam, but at the mouth of the Texel two French men-of-war met her, and refused to allow her to land. She then sailed for England. So great a throng of persons gathered to see her land at Dover, that Pitt sent a regiment to that port to preserve order. She went at once to Camberwell, where her only child, Jerome Napoleon Bonaparte, was born 7th July, 1805. Her husband continued to send her messages of love and fidelity. Napoleon asked Pope Pius VII to dissolve the marriage, but the pontiff refused to do so. The Imperial Council of State, at Napoleon's order, passed a decree of divorce. In September, 1805, Madame Bonaparte returned to the United States. Her family gave her an ungracious reception. Her father refused to pay the stipulated income, because Napoleon had annulled the union. Jerome soon afterward was married to Princess Frederica, of Würtemburg. He offered his discarded wife the principality of Smalcand, with an annual income of $40,000. Her reply was: "Westphalia, no doubt, is a considerable kingdom, but not large enough to hold two queens." The reply pleased Napoleon, who directed the French Minister in Washington to intimate his desire to serve her. She replied: "Tell the Emperor I am ambitious; I wish to be made a duchess of France." The Emperor promised to confer that rank upon her, and offered immediately a gross sum of $20,000, with a life annuity of $12,000. That she accepted, "proud to be indebted to the greatest man of modern times." She stipulated that the receipts for payment should be signed by her as "Elizabeth Bonaparte." To that the Emperor acceded, and until his dethronement the annuity was regularly paid. Her husband was angry because she refused aid from him and accepted it from his brother, but she retorted that she "preferred shelter beneath the wing of an eagle to suspension from the pinion of a goose." The submission of Jerome to the commands of his brother was rewarded. He received a high command in the Navy of France and showed himself a competent officer. In 1806 he was made a brigadier-general in the army, and in 1807 was created King of Westphalia. Mme. Bonaparte applied to the Maryland Legislature for a divorce, which was granted without difficulty. Her motive for taking this step is not easily comprehended. The Pope had refused to annul a marriage which had received the open sanction of the Church. The social position of Mme. Bonaparte had never been in the least compromised by her domestic misfortunes. After the fall of Napoleon Madame Bonaparte visited France, where she was honorably received. Only once after the separation did she ever see Jerome. In the gallery of the Pitti Palace, in Florence, they met. She simply said: "It is Jerome." He whispered to his wife: "That lady is my former wife." Madame Bonaparte was well received in Florence and in Rome. Returning to the United States, she made her home in Baltimore. She lived economically and amassed a fortune. Her son, Jerome Bonaparte, was graduated from Harvard College in 1826. He studied law, but never practiced. He was married in early life to Susan Mary Williams, a wealthy lady of Roxbury, Mass. He visited France and was on intimate terms with his father. He was never naturalized, and always called himself a citizen of France, although the French courts never recognized his legitimacy. He died in Baltimore 17th June, 1870. His two sons, Jerome Napoleon and Charles Joseph, survived him. Madame Bonaparte's later years were passed in quiet. Her proud spirit, her ambitious temper and her misfortunes alienated her from her father and her son, and her wit took a biting turn with old age. She put forward the claims of her grandson to the throne of France, but without hope of success. She left an estate valued at $1,500,000.

BOND, Mrs. Elizabeth Powell, Dean of Swarthmore College, Swarthmore, Pa., born in Clinton, N. Y., 25th January, 1841. Her parents, Townsend and Catherine Macy Powell, belonged to the Society of Friends. The mother was a

ELIZABETH POWELL BOND.

discendant of the "Goodman Macey" of whom Whittier writes in his poem "The Exiles," and who was, on account of his religious tolerance, driven in 1660 from his home on the mainland to the Island of Nantucket, where, ever since, Macy has been one of the leading and most honorable names. In 1845 Mr. and Mrs. Powell removed to Ghent, N. Y., and there on her parents' farm Elizabeth's childhood and youth were spent. A gentle, thoughtful child, endowed with perfect health and "a spirit equable, poised and free," labeled, as she expresses it, a ' teacher" almost from her birth, she began early to exercise her powers. At fifteen she was for one winter assistant teacher in a Friends' school in Dutchess county. Graduating at seventeen

from the State Normal School, Albany, N. Y., she taught for two years in public schools in Mamaroneck and Ghent, N. Y., and afterwards for three years carried on a home school in the house of her parents. Among her boarding pupils were colored and Catholic children. As a young girl she developed the spirit of a reformer and began active work in behalf of temperance, personally pleading with intemperate men, whose families she saw suffering, and instituting in the bar-room of the village tavern a series of readings and talks, hoping so to turn its frequenters away from their cups. At that time she was, with her older brother, Aaron M. Powell, identified with the Abolitionists. The anti-slavery leaders, Garrison, Phillips and Pillsbury, were her personal friends. With them she attended and occasionally spoke in anti-slavery and woman suffrage conventions. Public speaking has, however, generally been auxiliary to her other work, that of teaching. In the summer of 1863 she attended Dr. Lewis' normal class in gymnastics, in Boston, and was the valedictorian of the class at its graduating exhibition in Tremont Temple. The two following winters she conducted classes in gymnastics in Cambridge, Boston and Concord, Mass. In 1865, soon after its opening, she was appointed teacher of gymnastics in Vassar College, and continued in that position for five years. After a few months of rest at home Miss Powell was invited to Florence, Mass., as superintendent of the Free Congregational Sunday-school and as occasional speaker to the society, whose work was conducted by Charles C. Burleigh. After a year's work in that field Miss Powell was married to Henry H. Bond, a lawyer of Northampton, and resigned most of her public duties, though for a time editing, with her husband, the Northampton "Journal," and acting as one of the working trustees of the Florence kindergarten from its founding. Two sons were born to Mr. and Mrs. Bond, one of whom died in infancy. The years 1879-80 were spent in traveling and residence in the South, in search of health for her husband. After his death, in 1881, Mrs Bond returned to Florence and devoted herself to the education of her son, gathering about her a class of children, whom she taught with him. In 1885 she resumed her relations with the Free Congregational Society, becoming its resident minister, preparing written discourses for its Sunday meetings, and performing the social duties of a pastor. At the expiration of a year's service Mrs. Bond tendered her resignation to the society and took the position of matron in Swarthmore College. The title matron was, in 1891, changed to the more appropriate one of dean. That co-educational college, founded by and under the management of Friends, offered a field which Mrs. Bond's principles, experience and gifts eminently fitted her to occupy. Her office is that of director of the social life of the college and special adviser to the young women. The religious meetings of the college are conducted according to the order of Friends. Mrs. Bond's published writings are few. Several tracts on the subject of social purity, occasional addresses at educational meetings, and her messages to the Swarthmore students, which have appeared in the "Friends' Intelligencer," comprise the list.

BONES, Mrs. Marietta M., woman suffragist and social reformer, born upon a farm in Clarion county, Pa., 4th May, 1842. Her father, James A. Wilkins, was born in Clarion county, where he resided for forty-eight years, when he removed to Iowa, and died six months later. Mr. Wilkins was a noted Abolitionist, known to have maintained an "undergound railroad station." The mother's (Jane Trumbull) family, the

Trumbulis, were orginally from Connecticut, and were descendants of Jonathan Trumbull, better known by Washington's pet name, "Brother Jonathan." Her education was received in the Huide-

MARIETTA M. BONES.

kooper Seminary, Meadville, Pa., and in the Washington, Pa., female seminary. Mrs. Bones was elected vice-president of the National Woman Suffrage Association for Dakota Territory, in 1881, and was annually re-elected for nine years. She made her début as a public speaker in an oration at a Fourth of July celebration in Webster, Dak., in 1882. In September, 1883, she addressed Dakota's State Constitutional Convention on behalf of woman's enfranchisement. Failing to have her claim for woman's equality before the law recognized in the State Constitution there framed, she earnestly petitioned both houses of Congress to deny Dakota's admission to the Union as a State. Then she carried on several lively newspaper controversies against efforts to make the social question of temperance a political question. She is an active temperance worker and was secretary of the first Non-partisan National Woman's Christian Temperance Union convention in Chicago, in 1889, for which the local Woman's Temperance Union in Webster, over which she had presided the previous year, discharged her, returning her dues, paid nearly three months before, with an official notice "That the ladies of Webster union moved and carried that Mrs. Bones' dues be returned on acccount of her having joined the secession movement, and also on account of her antagonism to our State president." As a pioneer settler in her town, she secured for it a donation of a block of lots for a courthouse and county buildings, and through her influence Day county was divided and a part added thereto, in order that the county-seat should be centrally located. So interested was she that their State capital should be situated at the geographical center, that the board of trade in the city of Pierre

invited her to be the guest of their city. Through her intercession three infirm veterans of the war have been sent, at the expense of her county, to the Soldiers' Home in Hot Springs, S. Dak. Mrs. Bones was an able assistant of Mrs. Matilda Joslyn Gage in organizing the Woman's National Liberal Union. She addressed the convention in Washington, D. C., and is one of the executive council of that organization. The energy of Mrs. Bones knows no bounds when work is needed, and her perfect health helps her willing hand.

BONHAM, Mrs. Mildred A., traveler and journalist, born in Magnolia, Ill., in August, 1840. She is of southern blood from Virginia, South Carolina and Tennessee ancestry. Her parents removed to Oregon in 1847, settling in the Willamette valley. In 1858 she became the wife of Judge B. F. Bonham, of Salem, Ore. In 1885 Judge Bonham was appointed Consul-General to British India, and removed his family to Calcutta the same year. Mrs Bonham had always a liking for literary work, but the cares of a large family and social duties gave her scant leisure, and it was not until her residence abroad the opportunity came. During five years her letters over the name "Mizpah" attracted much attention and were widely copied by the Oregon and California press. Mrs. Bonham has a gift of observing closely, and her descriptions of foreign scenes make a valuable addition to our knowledge of Anglo-Indian life and customs. Her letters from the Himalayas, the island of Ceylon and other notable places are the best. Her deepest sympathy was aroused by the miserable condition and soul-starvation of the women of India, and she set about relieving, so far as lay in her power, their cheerless lot. By her personal appeal a Hindoo girl was

MILDRED A. BONHAM.

educated by a number of young ladies of Salem. The child became a home missionary. Through Mrs. Bonham's further efforts a fund of one-thousand dollars was raised to found a perpetual scholarship.

Since her return to the United States she has given several lectures embodying her experiences in the far East, life among the Zenanas, and kindred subjects.

BOOTH, Mrs. Agnes, actor, born of English parents, in Sydney, Australia, 4th October, 1843.

AGNES BOOTH.

Her maiden name was Marion Agnes Laud Rookes. Her father was a British army officer, and he died just before she was born. Her mother was married a second time, her second husband being a Church of England clergyman. Her dramatic tastes and talents were not inherited, for none of her family had ever been on the stage or shown any talents in the histrionic line. As a child she was fond of dancing, and she made her début in 1857 in Sydney as a dancer, under the stage-name Marion Agnes, with her sister Belle. She joined a minstrel company and played Miss Lucy Long with a "corked" face. In 1858 she went to San Francisco, Cal., where, in 1861, she was married to Harry A. Perry, who died in 1862. In Sacramento she joined the company of Mrs. John Wood, in which she played leading parts. She next joined Tom McGuire's company, in which she played various parts on a rough tour through the mountains. In 1867 she was married to J. B. Booth, jr., who died in 1883. She is now the wife of Manager John B. Schoeffel, and she retains her stage-name, Agnes Booth. In California she joined the Adah Isaacs Menken "Mazeppa" company. She worked hard and studied thoroughly, and her progress on the stage was rapid. From San Francisco she went to New York in 1865, where she made her début in the old Winter Garden with John S. Clarke, the comedian. She next supported Edwin Forrest in Niblo's Garden, where, on 13th November 1865, she appeared as Julie in "Richelieu." She then played successively as Desdemona, Virginia, Ophelia, Marianne in "Jack Cade," Cordelia, Colenthe in "Damon and Pythias," and Julia in "The

Gladiator." Her reception by press and public was favorable. She became absolute mistress of all the "business" of the stage, and her dash, spirit, vivacity and fine appearance combined to place her in the front rank of actors. After the Forrest engagement she played with Miss Bateman in "Leah." She made a success in Washington, Chicago and Boston. In Boston she joined the stock company of the Boston Theater, where she remained for five years. After her marriage to Junius Brutus Booth, she played Constance in "King John" in the theater of his brother, Edwin Booth, in New York. In 1876 she played Myrrha in Jarrett and Palmer's splendid production of "Sardanapalus" in Booth's Theater. In 1877 she played Cleopatra in the Niblo's Garden production of "Antony and Cleopatra." She next appeared in the Union Square Theater as Lady Fanny Wagstaffe in "Pink Dominoes." She then appeared in the "Celebrated Case," in "Engaged," in "Young Mrs. Winthrop," and in "Jim, the Penman," continually growing in art and winning ever new public favors. Notwithstanding her signal success as an actor, Mrs. Booth asserts that she does not like the stage. Her ambition is to own a theater and to be the guide of a stock company. Her home is now in New York City, and she possesses on the New England coast, in Manchester-by-the-sea, a beautiful country home, where, during the summer season, she entertains with most lavish and charming hospitality.

BOOTH, Mrs. Emma Scarr, author, born in Hull, England, 25th April, 1835. From her earliest childhood she had a passionate love of the beautiful in nature. This was fostered by her father, who often took her with him on long rambles

EMMA SCARR BOOTH.

through the flower-bedecked country lanes outside of the noisy town. When nine years old, her parents emigrated with their little family of three children, two daughters and a son, to America. The father, wishing to try farm life, purchased a farm in the township of North Royalton, near Cleveland, Ohio, being induced to settle there by an older brother, who had left England ten years before. At the age of twenty-two years Miss Scarr was married to a young Englishman residing in Twinsburgh, Ohio, and, shortly afterwards, began to contribute occasionally to some of the periodicals of the day under various pen-names. At a later period verses appeared under her own name. Upon the outbreak of the Civil War her brother enlisted in the Union Army, and soon after the battle of Shiloh, in which he fought, died of disease brought on by the hardships and exposure of a soldier's life. His death was succeeded by that of the older sister, a few months later. Emma's husband throughout all the dark years of war had been very outspoken in his denunciation of the secession project and all those favoring it, thus making enemies of certain secret sympathizers in the neighborhood. A few days preceding the date of Abraham Lincoln's assassination, while the family were on a visit to her parents, some twenty miles distant, a friend came post-haste on horseback from Twinsburgh to inform them that their house, together with all its contents, had been reduced to ashes during the night. Not an article was saved, since no one save the incendiary had witnessed the burning. Then came the news of the President's murder, and to her depressed mind all the world seemed going to "wreck and ruin," especially when, nine weeks later, her husband's mills with their entire contents were fired and totally destroyed. As none of the property had been insured, this misfortune reduced the formerly well-to-do pair to comparative poverty, and soon afterward they left the town, removing to Painesville, Ohio. There the wife obtained some needlework, while the husband went to the oil regions near Titusville, Pa., where he found employment. There, under the influence of lawless associates, he forgot his duties as a husband, and the result was a final separation a few years later. Meanwhile, Emma had removed to Cleveland, Ohio, and there supported herself by teaching music, not wishing to become dependent upon her parents, who had, however, kindly offered her a home with them. Some time later her parents sold their farm and went to reside in Cleveland, in order to be near their daughter. After the father's death, in 1872, Emma took up her abode with her mother, still continuing to give music lessons. In 1873 she was married again. Her second husband was an American. Her home since that time has been in Cleveland. Three years ago she went alone to Europe, among other places visiting the haunts of her childhood. Since her return she has become much intererested in all movements for the advancement of women. Mrs. Booth has published three volumes in book form, "Karan Kringle's Journal" (Philadelphia, 1885), "A Willful Heiress" (Buffalo, 1892), and "Poems" (Buffalo, 1892). She has composed songs and instrumental pieces, which have been published.

BOOTH, Miss Mary Louise, author, translator and editor, born in Millville, now Yaphank, N. Y., 19th April, 1831. On her father's side she is descended from John Booth, who came to the Colonies in 1649. Her mother was the granddaughter of a refugee of the French Revolution. Mary's talents were displayed in childhood, and she was yet only a girl when her first contributions were published. Her father was a teacher, and in 1845 and 1846 she taught in his school in Williamsburg, L. I. Her health failed and she was obliged to abandon teaching. She then turned to literature. She wrote many stories and sketches for newspapers

and magazines, and translated from the French "The Marble-Worker's Manual" (New York, 1856), and "The Clock and Watch Maker's Manual." For "Emerson's Magazine" she translated Mery's "André Chenier" and About's "King of the Mountains," and for that journal she wrote a number of stories. She translated Victor Cousin's "Secret History of the French Court; or, Life and Times of Madame de Chevreuse" (1859). The first edition of her "History of the City of New

MISS MARY L. BOOTH.

MARY LOUISE BOOTH.

York" appeared in 1859. It is a work embodying the results of much study and research. She next assisted in making a translation of the French classics, and she translated About's "Germaine" (Boston, 1860). During the Civil War she translated the writings of eminent Frenchmen who favored the cause of the Union. Among these were: Gasparin's "Uprising of a Great People" and "America before Europe" (New York, 1861), Edouard Laboulaye's "Paris in America" (New York, 1865), and Augustin Cochin's "Results of Emancipation" and "Results of Slavery" (Boston, 1862). Her work in that field won the commendation of President Lincoln, Senator Sumner and other statesmen. Among others of her translations at that time were the Countess de Gasparin's "Vesper," "Camille" and "Human Sorrows," and Count de Gasparin's "Happiness." Her translations of French documents were published in pamphlet form by the Union League Club, or printed in New York City newspapers. Her next translation was Henri Martin's "History of France." In 1864 she published two volumes treating of "The Age of Louis XIV." In 1866 she published two others, the last two of the seventeen volumes, under the title of "The Decline of the French Monarchy." In 1880 she published the translation of Martin's abridged "History of France." Her later translations from the French include Laboulaye's "Fairy Book" and Macé's "Fairy Tales."

In 1867 she published an enlarged edition of her "History of the City of New York," and in 1880 a second revision brought that valuable work down to date. Miss Booth was the editor of "Harper's Bazar" from its establishment in 1867, until the time of her death, 4th March, 1889.

BOTTA, Mrs. Anne Charlotte Lynch, author, born in Bennington, Vt., in 1820, died in New York City, 23rd March, 1891. Her father was a native of Dublin, Ireland, and at the age of sixteen he joined the rebel forces under Lord Edward Fitzgerald. He was captured, imprisoned four years, refused to take the oath of allegiance, and was banished. He came to the United States, where he died a few years after his marriage. Anne was educated in Albany, N. Y. She showed a literary bent in childhood, and, while still a girl, she published a number of productions. She removed to Providence, R. I., where she edited "The Rhode Island Book" (Providence, 1842), which contained productions from the pens of the authors of that State. She next moved to New York City, where she made her home until her death. In 1855 she was married to Professor Vincenzo Botta, the educator, who was filling the chair of Italian language and literature in the University of the City of New York. For years their home was a literary and artistic center, and they entertained many of the famous authors, painters and musicians of Europe and America. In 1870 and 1871, when funds for the suffering women and children of Paris were collected in New York, Mrs. Botta raised $5,000 by the sale of an album of photographs, autographs and sketches by famous artists. As the Franco-Prussian war closed before the collection was complete, the money was used to found a prize in the French Academy for the best essay on "The Condition of Women," to be awarded every fifth year, when the interest on the fund should reach $1,000. She excelled as a writer of sonnets. Her literary productions include a great number of stories, essays, poems and criticisms. In 1848 she published her first volume of poems, and in 1884 she brought out a new edition, illustrated by eminent artists. In 1845 she published "Leaves from the Diary of a Recluse" in "The Gift." Another important book from her pen is "A Hand-book of Universal Literature" (New York, 1860), which has run through several editions and has been adopted as a text-book in many educational institutions. Mrs. Botta's style in verse is finished, elegant and melodious. Her prose is clear and telling.

BOUGHTON, Mrs. Caroline Greenbank, educator and philanthropist, born in Philadelphia, Pa., 9th August, 1854. She is the second daughter of Judge Thomas Greenbank of that city, whose family was of English extraction, a family devout and scholarly, represented in each generation by divines and jurists of superior order. Through her mother she is related to a branch of the North of Ireland gentry, the Huestons of Belfast. Mrs. Boughton was graduated from the Philadelphia Normal School in 1874, fifth in a class of eighty. In the autumn of the same year she began her career as a teacher in Miss Steven's Seminary, Germantown. In 1878 she took charge of the department of history in the Philadelphia Normal School, which position she filled for four years, winning by her talents and enthusiasm an enviable reputation in her profession, and by her charming manners the affectionate regard of all who came under her influence. She was married 25th July, 1882, to J. W. Boughton, a prominent manufacturer and inventor of Philadelphia. Mrs. Boughton, in her connection with the Home

Missionary Society of the M. E. Church, became especially interested in Indian Missions and was early chosen a manager of the Woman's National Indian Association, a position she filled during five years. That office she exchanged later for that of auditor of the association, in which capacity she has done effective work for three years, and which office she now holds. She was an active member of the Woman's Christian Temperance Union until failing health obliged her to curb her

CAROLINE GREENBANK BOUGHTON.

energies in that direction. Mrs. Boughton has always been deeply interested in the advancement of women. She is a member of the New Century Club of Philadelphia, and is also a member of the Woman's Suffrage Association, and an earnest advocate of the principles which that body represents.

BOURNE, Mrs. Emma, religious and temperance worker, born in Newark, N. J., 5th September, 1846. Her father, John Hill, was of English parentage. Her mother, known among the temperance workers since the early days of the Woman's Christian Temperance Union as "Mother Hill," was of Scotch-Huguenot ancestry, a woman of great strength of character. Emma was educated in the Newark Wesleyan Institute and, after receiving her diploma, spent eight years as a successful teacher in the Newark schools. She was a vivacious and ambitious student. After her marriage she went abroad with her husband three times, spending several years beyond the Atlantic. During the last seventeen years she has resided in her native city, actively engaged in church work and prominently identified with the great temperance movement of the age. For ten years she served as State recording secretary of the Woman's Christian Temperance Union, and after the death of Mrs. Sarah J. C. Downs, State president, she was elected to fill the vacancy. For many years she was an efficient superintendent of the infant department of her church Sunday-school. Left to bear the burden and responsibility of training and caring for her four children when they were very young, she is realizing a rich reward for her faith-

EMMA BOURNE.

fulness as a mother. In her public duties she is gentle, firm and full of tact. With her "The Golden Age is not behind, but before us." In her public addresses she makes no attempt at oratory, but says what is in her heart to say in an unassuming, convincing manner.

BOUTON, Miss Emily St. John, journalist, born in New Canaan, Fairfield county, Conn. On her father's side she traces her ancestry to one of the partisans of William the Conqueror, who was knighted for saving the king when in danger. The family bore a prominent part in the Revolution among the Connecticut patriots. Her father moved to the West when she was yet a child. She was graduated in the public schools of Sandusky, Ohio, but had previously taught a primary school in that city when only fourteen years of age. After graduating, she became assistant high-school teacher in Milan, Ohio, then in Tiffin, and then, for several years she filled the same position in the Toledo high-school. She occupied the chair of English literature in the Chicago central high school for two years, but relinquished her work on account of failing health, going to California for rest and recuperation. In 1877 she returned to Toledo and became a member of the editorial staff of the Toledo "Blade," a position she has so well filled ever since. To many American households she is endeared as the "household editor" of the paper, but the work, original and editorial, of that one department of that journal by no means measures the extent of her labors. She is a literary critic of no mean order, and is a good "all round" newspaper worker. She has done much regular editorial writing in political campaigns in the colums of the paper with which she is connected.

Her leaders on political topics are marked by direct and close reasoning, her diction is clear, and her logic is convincing. Of late years she has not been called on so frequently to do that kind of writing, leaving her time free for the, to her, more congenial fields of purely literary work and the management of her own department of the paper. Her special field is in work for women. She is a believer in equal rights for her sex, and her labors are directed to the advancement of woman's sphere through the personal advancement of every individual of the sex. Her literary style is so clear and pleasing that it seems to convey an idea of her personality to her readers. She has written several successful books on topics pertaining to the home circle. Besides her work upon the Toledo "Blade," she has written stories, letters and essays for other papers and magazines. Mrs Bouton has a pleasant home in the beautiful residence portion of the city of Toledo, the family circle consisting of her mother, her widowed sister and two nephews. There is dispensed a refined hospitality, and there Miss Bouton, surrounded by her books, in the prime of her days, and with an almost unlimited

EMILY ST. JOHN BOUTON.

capacity for work, leads a busy life, devoted to what she believes to be the interests of humanity.

BOWERS, Mrs. D. P., actor, born in Stamford, Conn., 12th March, 1830. Her maiden name was Elizabeth Crocker McCollom. Her father was an Episcopal clergyman, who died while she was an infant. She was from early childhood fond of dramatic presentations. In 1846 she made her début in the Park Theater, in New York City, in the rôle of Amanthis. On 4th March, 1847, when only seventeen years old, she was married to David P. Bowers, an actor in the same company. They went to Philadelphia in the same month, and in the Walnut Street Theater she appeared as Donna Victoria in "A Bold Stroke for a Husband." She was successful from the beginning. She next filled a successful engagement in the Arch Street Theater, in Philadelphia, where she remained until the death of her husband, in June, 1857. In December, 1857, the leased the Walnut Street Theater, which she

ELIZABETH McCOLLOM BOWERS.

managed successfully until 1859. She then leased the Philadelphia Academy of Music for a season. In 1860 she was married to Dr. Brown, of Baltimore, Md., who died in 1867. Mrs. Bowers retained the name under which she had won her reputation. In 1861 she went to London, England, where she played Julia in "The Hunchback," in Sadler's Wells Theater. She was successful with the London public and played an engagement in the Lyceum Theater, appearing as Geraldine d' Arcy in "Woman." In 1863 she returned to the United States and played an engagement in the Winter Garden, in New York. She soon afterwards retired from the stage and lived quietly in a suburb of Philadelphia, until October, 1886, when she organized a strong company and made a successful tour of the United States. Her rôles cover the field of high comedy and tragedy.

BOWLES, Mrs. Ada Chastina, Universalist minister, born in Gloucester, Mass., 2nd August, 1836. On her father's side her ancestry runs through the Choates and on her mother's side through the Haskells, back into staunch old English families. Her youth was spent by the sea, and her outdoor sports laid the foundation for the vigor and health that have always characterized her. She was born with a sound mind in a sound body. Her early opportunities for acquiring education were limited. After easily and rapidly learning all that was taught in the public schools of Gloucester, she was wholly unsatisfied with her attainments and pushed forward with different studies by herself. At the age of fifteen she began to teach in the public schools. She continued in that vocation until she was twenty-two, employing, meanwhile, such leisure as she could command in writing for the

press. She was then married to a popular clergyman, Rev. B. F. Bowles, pastor of the Universalist Church in Melrose, Mass. Although by that marriage she became the stepmother of three children, and later the mother of three more, she still found time for a variety of church work, including teaching an adult Bible class. Her success with that class led her to deeper theological study, under the direction of her husband. Mr. Bowles desired that his wife should be in all things his companion, and, after giving her a thorough course in theology, he encouraged her to preach the gospel, which she had long felt called to declare. She began in 1869 by supplying vacant pulpits in New England. In 1872 she was licensed in Boston to preach and became the non-resident pastor of a church in Marlborough, Mass. Mr. Bowles, at that time settled in Cambridge, soon after accepted a call to the pastorate of the Church of the Restoration in Philadelphia, and Mrs. Bowles was called as non-resident pastor of the Universalist Church in Easton, Pa., a position she held for three very successful years, although the church had been for many years dormant. She closed her connection with that parish that she might lay the foundation of a new church in Trenton, N. J., which she accomplished in six weeks of energetic work. She was regularly ordained in 1874 and has preached and lectured since that time in most of the large cities of the United States. When without a church of her own, she has shared the parish work of her husband and has been constantly engaged in charitable and philanthropic work. In addition to all her ministerial work, she lectured in various parts of the country under the auspices of the Woman's Christian Temperance Union, in which organization she has been

ADA CHASTINA BOWLES.

state superintendent of various departments. She has been national lecturer of the American Suffrage Association and president of State, county and city suffrage organizations, as well as an active member of many other reforms. Notwithstanding all these duties and labors, she is famed among her acquaintances as a wise and affectionate mother and a model housekeeper. One of her most popular lectures is on "Strong-minded Housekeeping," which embodies her own experience in household cares and management. She is an expert swimmer, perfectly at home in or on the water, and can handle a saw, hammer or rolling-pin with equal dexterity. Her public life has never in any way been allowed to interfere with the exercise of a gracious private charity. She is a very popular and convincing speaker. In all that she undertakes Mrs. Bowles is prompt and incisive, and in private life is as constant in good works as she is able in public in inspiring others to all worthy endeavors. Her present home is in Abington, Mass.

BOYD, Mrs. Kate Parker, artist, born in New York, 23rd October, 1836. Her maiden name was Kate Parker Scott. She is a daughter of Andrew Scott, of Flushing, N. Y., who was a son of Andrew Scott, born in Paisley, Scotland. She inherited her talent for drawing from her father, who was a fine amateur artist from his boyhood to his nineteenth year, and whose portfolios of water-colors are a source of delight to artists of the present time. Miss Scott attended the Flushing Female College, then in the charge of Rev. William Gilder. After leaving that school and traveling awhile, she was married in 1862 to Rev. N. E. Boyd. They have lived in Portland, Me., and in Canastota, N. Y. Their family consisted of two sons, who died at an early age. When circumstances made it necessary, Mrs. Boyd was able to earn a good income with her pencil. Her pictures were exhibited and sold in

KATE PARKER BOYD.

New York and Brooklyn. She was an exhibitor in the Academies of Design in both of those cities. She won a number of medals and prizes in the Centennial Exposition in Philadelphia, in 1876, and

in various State and county exhibitions. They moved to San Francisco, Cal., in 1877, and in that city her work was highly successful. She now writes and draws for the "American Garden," New York, and for other periodicals, using the signature K. P. S. B. She is interested in reforms and humanitarian work in general, and is a member of the Society for the Prevention of Cruelty to Animals, of the Association for the Advancement of Women and of the Pacific Coast Women's Press Association. She works zealously for the sailors' branch of the Woman's Christian Temperance Union and for the Sailors' Lend-a-Hand Club.

BOYD, Mrs. Louise Esther Vickroy, author, born in Urbana, Ohio, 2nd January, 1827.

LOUISE ESTHER VICKROY BOYD.

When she was about four years of age, her parents removed to Ferndale, a picturesque valley among the mountains near Johnstown, Pa. Although good schools were scarce in those days, her education was not neglected, and for two years she was a pupil in the select school of Miss Esther R. Barton, in Lancaster, Pa. While a young woman she made frequent visits to Philadelphia, and she there became acquainted with many of the authors and literary people of that city. Her first poem was written in 1851. The next year she became a regular contributor to Grace Greenwood's "Little Pilgrim," and frequently, since that time, her poems as well as prose sketches have appeared in magazines and newspapers, among others the "Knickerbocker," "Graham's Magazine," "Appleton's Journal," the New York "Tribune," the Philadelphia "Saturday Evening Post," the Cincinnati "Gazette," "Woman's Journal," the Indianapolis "Journal," "Wide Awake," the "Century," and others. For several years she was engaged in teaching, until in September, 1865, she became the wife of Dr. S. S. Boyd, since which time her home has been in Dublin, Ind. Mrs. Boyd's married life was a most happy one. Her husband was a man of fine literary taste and an ardent worker in the cause of humanity, and she was strengthened and encouraged by him in the causes of temperance and woman suffrage. She is well known as an advocate of woman suffrage. Well acquainted with history, she has watched with unfailing interest all the movements of our eventful times, her sympathies ever on the side of the oppressed. She has frequently appeared on the platform, where she has a good presence, is natural, womanly, logical and sprightly. She is greatly interested in creating a State literature, and she has not only furnished much material for it, but has done a great deal toward creating a correct and pure literary taste in her own town and county. She was reared in the faith of the followers of Emanuel Swedenborg, but is now an earnest member of the Christian Church. She has been a widow since 1888.

BRACE, Miss Maria Porter, educator and elocutionist, born in Penn Yan, N. Y., in July, 1852. Her early life was spent in Leavenworth, Kans. Her father was one of the first settlers in Kansas,

MARIA PORTER BRACE.

and there the family home has always remained. Miss Brace was educated in Vassar College and was graduated in 1872. A special course in elocution followed under Prof. Robert R. Raymond, in the Boston School of Oratory. These studies, preceded by practice in teaching and reading in the West, were followed by an engagement as teacher of elocution in Vassar College. During several years of residence there, a certain time was reserved every winter for work outside of the college community. In teaching as well as in reading Miss Brace has always associated the art of elocution with the interpretation of the best literature. Her annotated readings from the English classics and from recent masterpieces of prose and poetry often formed a supplement to the course in English literature in schools. In 1883 Miss Brace made her first visit to Europe. Through the influence of

Monsieur Regnier, the French actor and teacher, she was admitted to the daily sessions of the dramatic classes in the Conservatoire National de Musique et de Declamation, in Paris. A close study of the French classics in the hands of the pupils and of their masters, the four leading actors of the Théatre Francais, proved a valuable lesson in dramatic reading and criticism. In addition to the daily rehearsals in the Conservatoire, there were talks with M. Regnier, who generously gave his criticism of her own work. The course in the Conservatoire was supplemented by frequent visits to the Théatre Francais, where the professors were often seen in their well-known rôles as actors. Miss Brace's interest in the art of acting received a great impulse from that winter in Paris. Upon her return to New York she read, in the Madison Square Theater, an account of the methods of the Théatre Francais as taught in the National Conservatoire. The lecture attracted the attention of actors and critics who were present and has been repeated many times in New York and elsewhere. During the spring of 1884 an effort was being made to establish in New York a school for actors. Miss Brace became actively interested in the undertaking and was at once engaged as a teacher of dramatic elocution and lecturer upon dramatic literature She has also taught elocution in the Brearley School for Girls since its opening in New York, in 1884. Her lectures and readings have become favorably known in Philadelphia and New York. The topics are "Francois Del Sarto in Paris," "Colloquial Elocution" and "Professional Elocution." Miss Brace has made occasional contributions to periodical literature upon various phases of her chosen subject, and she is constantly collecting material, both at home and abroad, for further essays and lectures, including a text-book of elocution. In addition to her active work in her profession, Miss Brace has been interested in the social life of her cotemporaries. She has been a frequent contributor to the monthly conversations of the Meridian Club. She has represented the alumnæ of her own college on the governing board of the College Settlement. That home in the slums of the East Side represents the first organized effort of college-bred women to improve the condition of life among the poor. She was one of the founders and the first president of the Women's University Club of New York.

BRADEN, Mrs. Anna Madge, author, born in Pennsylvania near historic Valley Forge. She is of English and German descent, and her ancestors have lived in or near Philadelphia, Pa., for over a century and a half. Her father was John Conver Rile. Her mother's maiden name was Frantz. She is fifth in direct line of descent from Gen. Joseph Reed, of Revolutionary fame, his daughter being her great-grandmother. In 1880 she was married to Findley Braden, of Ohio, and they now reside in Philadelphia. For six years before her marriage she wrote under her maiden name, Madge Rile, and several pen-names, but since her marriage she adopted her husband's name, signing her articles Mrs. Findley Brayden. She began writing for the newspapers and magazines when but a school-girl of fifteen. It is her life-work, and she thoroughly enjoys it. She has written over seven-hundred humorous and pathetic sketches, poems and serials, many of which have appeared in the secular journals of New York, Boston and Philadelphia. She has also written a number of songs that have found their way into public favor. She is equally at home in the five dialects, Scotch, Irish, Negro, Dutch and Quaker. She is a fine elocutionist and is a graduate of the National School of Elocution and Oratory, Philadelphia. Mrs. Braden is a member of the Presbyterian Church and an earnest worker. Her kindly Christian character can best be seen in her

ANNA MADGE BRADEN.

own home, which is a model of neatness and cheerfulness. Her life is spent, not for her own gratification, but for the comfort of those around her. She is an ardent student, painstaking and ambitious.

BRADFORD, Mrs. Mary Carroll Craig, correspondent, born in Brooklyn, N. Y., 10th August, 1856. She comes from a long line of mental aristocrats, being a direct descendant from Charles Carroll, one of the signers of the Declaration of Independence. She never attended school, but was educated privately by masters and governesses. She has traveled extensively both at home and abroad. She was in Geneva, Switzerland, during the year of the Arbitration, and while there met and enjoyed the society of some of the arbitrators. Her first appearance in print was at the age of twelve in a story, but she only began to write regularly and professionally at twenty-two. At the age of nineteen she was married to Lieut. Edward Taylor Bradford, of the United States Navy, a son of the Paymaster-General of the Navy, and grandson of the famous Boston preacher, familiarly called "Father Taylor." Her literary work has been diversified. She has been a regular contributor to the Brooklyn "Eagle," the New Orleans "Picayune," the "Esoteric," the "Commonwealth," "Christian Union," the "Rocky Mountain News," and other magazines and papers. Her lectures have been on glimpses of her travels and on theosophy. Her home is now in Colorado Springs, Col.

BRADLEY, Miss Amy Morris, educator, born in East Vassalboro, Maine, 12th September, 1823. She is a granddaughter of Asa Bradley, a soldier of the Revolution who gave his life for his

country. She was educated in her native town. In 1840 she began to teach in country schools, and four years later was appointed principal of one of the grammar schools in Gardiner, Me. In 1846 she became assistant teacher in the Winthrop grammar school of Charlestown, Mass., and taught until the autumn of 1849, when, prostrated by pneumonia, she was compelled to seek a milder climate. The winter of 1850-51 was passed in Charleston, S. C., but with little benefit, and, advised by her physician to seek a country entirely free from frost, in 1853 she went to San José, Costa Rica, whose climate proved a healing balm to her lungs. In three months after her arrival she opened a school. It was a success. She quickly mastered the Spanish language, and her pupils rapidly acquired the English. For nearly four years she continued her educational work in San José, and in the summer of 1857 she returned to New England to her early home in East Vassalboro, where her venerable father died in January, 1858. The thorough knowledge of Spanish acquired by Miss Bradley in Costa Rica led the New England Glass Company, of East Cambridge, Mass., to seek her services in translating letters. She was in Cambridge in 1861, when the first gun was fired at Fort Sumter, and immediately after the battle of Bull Run she offered her services as nurse to the sick and wounded soldiers. On the first of September, 1861, Miss Bradley entered the hospital of the Third Maine Regiment, encamped near Alexandria, Va., but was transferred to the Fifth Maine Regiment, and a few days later was appointed matron of the Seventeenth Brigade Hospital, General Slocum's Brigade, of which she had charge during the winter. In the spring of 1862, after the Army of the Potomac went

MARY CARROLL CRAIG BRADFORD.

to the Peninsula, Rev. F. N. Knapp, head of the relief department of the United States Sanitary Commission, telegraphed to Miss Bradley to report immediately to him at Fortress Monroe, and she went in the same boat with Miss Dorothea L. Dix. All through the Peninsular Campaign she was on transport boats, which brought the sick and wounded from the battlefields. After the Seven Days Battles

AMY MORRIS BRADLEY.

she returned to Washington and helped to organize a home for discharged soldiers. In December, 1862, she was sent to Convalescent Camp, Alexandria, and remained in charge of the Relief Department until the close of the war, when, her special work for country and humanity being ended, her heart and mind turned anew to her original calling. In 1866, at the request of the Soldiers' Memorial Society, of Boston, Mass., and under the auspices of the American Unitarian Association, she went to Wilmington, N. C., as a teacher of poor white children. Her position at first was a trying one, for she was a stranger and a northerner. Modestly and firmly she took her place and began her work. She opened her school 9th January, 1867, with three children, in a very humble building. Within a week sixty-seven pupils were enrolled, and soon two additional teachers were engaged by her, and, as the number of pupils rapidly increased, new schools were opened, the "Hemenway," the "Pioneer" and the "Normal," and the corps of teachers increased accordingly. Such was the character of the instruction given, such the tone, spirit and influence of the schools, that within a few months, instead of being regarded with suspicion and aversion, Miss Bradley and her co-workers had the confidence and the grateful affection of the community, and large-minded citizens co-operated with the trustees of the Peabody Fund and other benefactors in erecting the needed buildings and forwarding the work. On the thirtieth of November, 1871, the corner-stone of the Tileston Normal School was laid, and it was opened in October, 1872. This building was the gift of Mrs. Mary Hemenway, of Boston, Mass., who had been deeply interested in Miss Bradley's work from its

beginning, and whose appreciation of its importance and beneficence found expression in the annual contribution of $5,000 toward the support of the Tileston Normal School, from its opening in 1872 to its close in 1891. Failing health led Miss Bradley to resign her position in 1891.

BRADLEY, Mrs. Ann Weaver, educator and temperance worker, born in Hartland, Niagara county, N. Y., 19th May, 1834. Her parents, William and Mary Earl Weaver, removed from New York to Michigan during her infancy, and she was reared in that State. Her early philanthropic tendencies, fostered by home training, prepared her to espouse the anti-slavery cause and to engage heartily in all reformatory efforts. Loving study for its own sake and feeling that in brain culture one could exert an influence for good on humanity, her earliest ambition was to become a teacher. Attaining that position before her fourteenth birthday, she continued thus to labor with never-failing zest for over thirty years. With a power to impress her own personality upon others and to evoke their latent capabilities, her work in the class-room was especially happy, particularly in the department of literature. While attending Hillsdale College, she publicly gave herself to Christ. In 1858 she was married to George S. Bradley, a theologue from Oberlin, then tutor in Hillsdale. Thereafter her influence for good was felt in all his labors, whether as pastor's wife or lady principal in the seminaries under his charge in Maine, Wisconsin and Iowa. While in Wisconsin, her husband, as chaplain of the Twenty-second Wisconsin Regiment, went with Sherman to the sea. While he was in that service, the last one of their three children died. Mrs. Bradley returned to Hillsdale and

ANN WEAVER BRADLEY.

engaged in teaching. At the close of the war her husband resumed his old pastorate near Racine, Wis., and there for two years they worked. Then followed two years of seminary work in Rochester, and six in Evansville, Wis. There was born to them their last and only living child, Charles Clement. Wilton, Iowa, was for the next five years the scene of their labors. Then Mrs. Bradley began her public work for temperance. The Iowa agitation for prohibition roused her to action. Stepping into the ranks of the Woman's Christian Temperance Union, she organized and carried on a union, a temperance school, and lectured in her own town and vicinity. Later, in central and eastern Kansas, where her husband's labors led, her temperance efforts cost her a three-years' invalidism, from which she has never fully rallied. Her husband is at present pastor of the Congregational Church in Hudson, Mich., and she is State superintendent of narcotics for the Woman's Christian Temperance Union. Her inherited hatred of those destroying agents, her gift of persistence, her thoroughness of research and her love of humanity especially fit her for this work.

BRADWELL, Mrs. Myra, lawyer and editor, born in Manchester, Vt., 12th February, 1831. She is a daughter of Eben and Abigail Willey Colby. Her parents removed to New York State in her in-

MYRA BRADWELL.

fancy. When she was twelve years old, Chicago became her home. Her family were well represented in the War of the Revolution, two of her ancestors having been in the battle of Bunker Hill. Myra was educated in Kenosha, Wis., and at the seminary in Elgin, Ill., and afterwards taught school in Memphis, Tenn. In 1852 she was married to James B. Bradwell, whose father was one of the leading pioneers of Illinois. She studied law under the instruction of her husband, and passed a creditable examination. She was the first woman in America to ask for admission to the bar, and it was refused because she was a married woman. She immediately set to work, with the aid of her husband, to have this legal disability removed, and the success of their undertaking is a matter of

congratulation for all women. Mrs. Bradwell declared that she should never again apply for admission to the bar, but, to her surprise, she one day received a certificate upon the original application from the court that had refused her years before. Mrs. Bradwell was the first woman who was made a member of the Illinois Bar Association, and also of the Illinois Press Association. The first weekly legal paper published in the Western States was the Chicago "Legal News," established twenty-three years ago by Myra Bradwell, who has always been its manager and editor. The legislature gave her a special charter for the paper, and passed several acts making it evidence in the courts and a valid medium for the publication of legal notices. The law giving to married women their own earnings was drawn by Myra Bradwell, and its passage was secured through her efforts in 1869. Judge Bradwell retired from the bench in order to assist his wife in the large business to which the Legal News Company had grown. The Bradwells made place in their busy lives for much charitable and philanthropic work. During the Civil War they were active helpers among the sick and wounded soldiers, and did good service in the Sanitary Commission. Mrs. Bradwell has been for nearly thirty years a member of the Soldiers' Home Board. She was untiring in her efforts to secure the World's Fair for Chicago, and is one of the Board of Lady Managers and chairman of the committee on law reform of the World's Congress Auxiliary. She is a member of the Chicago Women's Club and of the Illinois Women's Press Association, and is treasurer of the South Evanston Industrial School, of which she was one of the organizers. Four children form her family. Of these, two died in infancy. Thomas and Bessie remain. They are both lawyers. Bessie's husband, Frank A. Helmer, is also an attorney. Notwithstanding her profession and her numerous activities, Mrs. Bradley is a favorite in the society of Chicago.

BRAEUNLICH, Mrs. Sophia, business manager, born in Bethpage, L. I., 2nd July, 1860. Her maiden name was Toepken. Her parents were Germans, both from old and aristocratic families. When she was twelve years old, she was sent to Europe, where she received a first-class education. She remained there until her sixteenth year, when she returned to her native country and made Brooklyn her home. Shortly afterwards she was married, and after a brief time she was left dependent upon her own resources. She then entered Packard's business college in New York, taking a full course there, and after graduating from the college, in 1879, she obtained a situation as private secretary to Richard P. Rothwell, the editor of the "Engineering and Mining Journal" and president of the Scientific Publishing Company. She has risen step by step from the bottom to the top rung of the business ladder in that office. Mrs. Braeunlich displayed such intelligence and energy that ere long Mr. Rothwell availed himself of her services as both secretary and assistant exchange editor. She mastered the technical details pertaining to the paper, attended the meetings of the American Institute of Mining Engineers, and frequently went down into mines on such occasions, thus gaining practical knowledge of various details that increased her usefulness in the office. When the secretary and treasurer of the publishing company resigned his position, Mrs. Braeunlich was elected to fill the vacancy. She displayed such remarkable executive ability, combined with energy and ambition, that at the first opportunity she was promoted to the office of business manager of the entire establishment. She has full charge of the general business and financial departments, and, in addition to the multiplicity of mental labor entailed by her position, she assisted in the government work connected with the collection of gold and

SOPHIA BRAEUNLICH.

silver statistics for the Eleventh Census. The room in which Mrs. Braeunlich spends most of her time, and which she has occupied for over twelve years, is the same one which Henry Ward Beecher used at the time of his editorial work on the "Christian Union." It is brightened with flowers, birds and pictures, and its neatness presents an agreeable contrast to the majority of journalistic business offices. She is described by one of the "Journal's" staff as "a modest, warm-hearted, accomplished and irreproachable woman, of strong character, with an instinctive clearness of vision that seems to be confined to women, and with the sound judgment of a man," and it is added that "she possesses the absolute esteem and good-will of all the gentlemen in the office, and is always a courteous lady, though a strict disciplinarian. The office, as well as the work, is the better for her influence." Mrs. Braeunlich has for years worked very hard, giving up almost all social and other pleasures, and devoting all her thoughts and time to business.

BRAINARD, Mrs. Kate J., musical educator, born in New York City, 18th February, 1835. Her father, Rev. D. E. Jones, compiler of the first hymn and tune book ever used and made popular in this country, was of Welsh descent. Her mother was a woman of great natural gifts, both of voice and mind, and a regular contributor to the literature of the day. The daughter inherited in a marked degree their musical talent. When but a very little girl, she studied the elements of music under her father and began piano lessons when seven years old. At an early age she surprised her friends by carrying the alto in part-singing, "making it up" with wonderful correctness. At fifteen she was

obliged to begin to earn her living by teaching piano. At the same time her musical studies were faithfully carried on under the best masters. Vocal lessons were begun at that time and she made rapid progress in florid singing. Her last year in the East was spent with the best vocal teachers in Boston. In 1855 she moved to Chicago and there became quite noted as a vocalist. In 1858 she was married, and in 1865 moved to St. Louis, where she was looked upon as one of the leading sopranos, receiving a large salary in one of the choirs. In 1866 Mrs. Brainard assumed charge of the music in Mary Institute, the female department of Washington University, numbering in recent years nearly four-hundred girls. Mrs. Brainard's class-work, as systematized and developed in that institute, is remarkable. During her career in Mary Institute she has frequently spent her vacations in the East with some prominent teacher, to obtain new ideas for her work. Among these was a trip to Europe, where she studied in Paris and London with Viardot, Garcia and Sainton Dolby. Many girls with promising voices have been started on their musical career by Mrs. Brainard. During the past twenty-five years her name has been associated with the progress of musical art in St. Louis, and many singers now prominent as professionals or amateurs refer to her as their conscientious guide during their struggles and studies. She has been deeply and actively interested in church work since she was thirteen years old, at which time she united with Dr. Hatfield's church in New York City. During forty-three years of teaching she has

KATE J. BRAINARD.

done an enormous amount of labor, having gained a reputation abroad as well as at home. Mrs. Brainard gives a portion of her time to private pupils.

BRAMAN, Mrs. Ella Frances, lawyer and business woman, born in Brighton, now a part of Boston, Mass., 23rd March, 1850. She comes of good Puritan stock. In 1867 she was married to

Joseph Balch Braman, of the same place, then a member of the Boston Bar. In 1872 they went to the city of Los Angeles, Cal., where her husband practiced law until the spring of 1874, when

ELLA FRANCES BRAMAN.

he resumed law practice in Boston. Soon after their return to Boston, Mr. Braman required some one to assist him in his Boston office as commissioner for the different States to which he had just been appointed, and Mrs. Braman volunteered to become his assistant. She proved so competent that it was decided to ask for her appointment also, so that she could act, especially when clients called for a commissioner during Mr. Braman's temporary absence from the office. Each State governor was written to. Governor Long adding his endorsement, but only ten governors could then be found who either believed in a woman's being appointed or thought they had the power to grant the commission to a woman. Soon Mr. and Mrs. Braman removed to New York City to practice, and then it was determined to continue asking for the appointments from the governors until she had them all. She lacks only about eight States, which will shortly fall into line and give her their commission, as President Harrison has recently done. Soon after settling in the metropolis she became a regular partner with her husband. They have a down-town day office in the Equitable Building, 120 Broadway, and an uptown office and residence at 1270 Broadway. Mrs. Braman is a thoroughbred lawyer and is enthusiastic in her liking for the law. The extent and variety of what she accomplishes in a field generally supposed to be the exclusive property of men may be seen in a mere mention of her titles. She is a lawyer, a notary public, a commissioner of deeds for the States, Territories and District of Columbia, the United States Court of Claims, a United States passport agent at New York, and a consular agent. She holds about fifty commissions

and appointments from the President of the United States and from governors of States. Mrs. Braman's uptown office is in her residence, and it is never closed. Her theory seems to be that a person who carries on business should always be ready to attend to business, and to that end her office is kept open, night and day, every day in the year, making no exception even for Sundays and holidays. Here she keeps the laws, blanks and forms for all the States. She is an energetic, intelligent, agreeable woman, and her advice and services are sought by women as well as by men having legal business to transact. She has made a good record for accuracy in the intricate work of her profession.

BRAUMULLER, Mrs. Luetta Elmina, artist, born in Monson, Mass., 4th December, 1856. Her family name, Bumstead, is still a familiar one in Boston, where it was among the foremost before and after the Revolutionary War. Bumstead Hall, which was built next after Faneuil Hall, and Bumstead Place are still old landmarks in that city. Her line of ancestry on the mother's side is Puritan, the family, Wood, having come to America in 1638 and with others founded the town of Rowley, near Boston. Mrs. Braumuller's earliest recollections are closely allied to the pencil and brush, and at the age of eight years she received her first instruction in art. Since that time until the present, with the exception of a few short intervals, she has applied herself to the study of drawing and painting in all its branches. In 1880 she made her first trip to Europe, and remained nearly one year in the best studios of Berlin. In 1882 she made a second visit to Paris and Sèvres, in which cities she studied porcelain painting exclusively under celebrated ceramic artists, and later in the same year she continued with a noted practical china and glass painter in Berlin. In 1889 she went to Dresden, where she acquired a knowledge of the methods of the Dresden artists. In 1890 she was again in Paris, where

LUETTA ELMINA BRAUMULLER.

she pursued the study of flesh-painting after the method of Hortense Richard. Mrs. Braumuller is distinctly a figure painter, although she has a complete knowledge of every branch of work connected with porcelain painting and firing. As a student and teacher it has been her greatest ambition to advance the art in America. She published a small work entitled "Lessons in China Painting," in 1882, but, believing that a periodical would have a wider circulation and give better results, she established in New York City, in 1887, a monthly magazine devoted exclusively to the interests of amateur decorators, and known as the "China Decorator." It was a success from the first issue and now enjoys a wide circulation both in this country and in Europe. Mrs. Braumuller has the reputation of being one of the best informed women in this country on the subject of modern porcelain and pottery. She is the wife of a well-known piano manufacturer of New York City and is the mother of two children, a son and daughter.

BREED, Mrs. Alice Ives, social-leader, born in Pavilion, Ill., 15th January, 1853. At the age of eighteen years she removed to Boston, Mass. In 1873 she was married to Francis W. Breed, who is connected with important business interests in Boston and Lynn, Mass. Mrs. Breed has traveled much, read much and thought much. She has shown an intelligent sympathy with every movement in the world of music, art and literature, and her home has been a center of attraction for men and women distinguished in all those fields of effort. She is an accomplished musician. Her family consists of five children. Their home is in Lynn, Mass. Mrs. Breed has for years served as chairman of the Lynn branch of the Emergency Association, as president of the Woman's Auxiliary of the Young Men's Christian Association, and as vice-president of the Lynn Woman's Club. She is now president of the North Shore Club, a social and literary organization

ALICE IVES BREED.

of the highest character, which has a membership of one-hundred-fifty-five and a waiting list of one-hundred. She is a member of the Massachusetts State committee for correspondence of the General

Federation of Women's Literary Clubs. She was appointed a member of the Women's Committee of the World's Congress Auxiliary on moral and social reform. She is a woman of marked executive ability, and her energies find expression in religious, philanthropic, literary and social channels. She is especially a social leader who aims to lift the community to a higher level.

BREWSTER, Miss Cora Belle, physician and surgeon, born in Almond, Allegany county, N.

CORA BELLE BREWSTER.

Y., 6th September, 1859. She was educated partly in Alfred University where she studied five years. She left school to take a position as teacher, and her work in the schoolroom covered several years. Her last work as a teacher was done in the high school in Smethport, Pa. In 1877 she went west and took a special course in the Northwestern University. While studying in that institution, she decided to abandon pedagogy, and on leaving the school she took a position as purchasing agent for a large millinery establishment in Chicago. The climate of Chicago proved too severe for her, and after three years of active service in that city she moved to Baltimore, Md. There her health was perfectly restored, and she began the study of medicine. She was graduated from the College of Physicians and Surgeons (Boston, Mass.) in May, 1886. During her course of study she spent eighteen months in Bellevue Hospital in New York, where she gained a great deal of valuable experience in treating the thousands of cases of every sort that are always to be found in that great institution. After graduating, she returned to Baltimore, where, in partnership with her sister, Flora A. Brewster, M. D., she began in 1889 the publication of the Baltimore "Family Health Journal," the name of which was in 1891 changed to the "Homeopathic Advocate and Health Journal," and made a hospital journal with a corps of ten editors. She was in 1890 elected gynæcological surgeon to the Homeopathic Hospital and Free Dispensary of Maryland, under the auspices of the Maryland Homeopathic Medical Society. She has achieved marked success as medical writer, surgeon, editor and practicing physician.

BREWSTER, Miss Flora A., physician and surgeon, born in Alfred, Allegany county, N.

FLORA A. BREWSTER.

Y., 26th February, 1852. Her family moved to northern Pennsylvania in 1863. In 1866 she was sent to Alfred University, where, after passing the examinations, she began the scientific course of study, showing great talent for mathematics. In 1868 her father died suddenly, and she was obliged to leave the university in order to attend to the finances of her family. She took a position as copyist in a tax-collector's office, which she soon left to begin work as a teacher. She hoarded her money with the purpose of returning to the university to complete her course of study, but two years of hard work, teaching school and at the same time carrying on her university studies, so seriously impaired her health that she was compelled to devote her time exclusively to teaching. In 1872 she was appointed teacher in the Mansfield Orphan School, in Mansfield, Pa., which was then the training school for the Mansfield State Normal School. In 1875 she took the degree of B.E. in Mansfield, and in 1877 the degree of Master in Elementary Didactics, while still teaching. In 1877 she was forced by failing health to give up teaching. She spent a year in travel in the West and Northwest, and her health was so greatly improved that in 1878 she went to Chicago and took the editorial and business management of the "Newsboys' Appeal," an illustrated journal published in the interest of the Newsboys' Home in that city. The following year she began to read medicine with Dr. Julia Holmes Smith, of Chicago, and conducted a night school on the kindergarten plan in the Newsboys' Home. In 1882 she

completed the course in the Chicago Homeopathic Medical College, after which she went to Baltimore, Md., where she spent six months in the office and private hospital of the late Prof. August F. Erich, the noted gynæcological surgeon. She opened an office and began to practice in Baltimore in 1882. At that time only one woman had succeeded in establishing a paying practice in Baltimore, and that one was Dr. Emma Stein Wanstall, who died in September, 1882. No female physician in the city had been entrusted with surgical cases, but Dr. Brewster believed that the field for women physicians in the South was open to sensible, energetic and educated women, and she persevered. For the next four years she worked arduously, acquiring a large practice and doing a good deal of charitable work. In 1886 she formed a partnership with her sister, Dr. Cora Belle Brewster. In 1890 the agitation caused by the application for the admission of women to the medical department of Johns Hopkins University enlightened the people of the entire South in regard to the status of women in the medical profession. Both the sisters were elected surgeons, and they gave clinics in the new homeopathic hospital in Baltimore. Besides their general practice, the doctors Brewster have a large practice in gynæcological surgery, extending over the entire South. They have opened the medical field to the women of the South, and many southern women have become physicians and trained nurses, and are successfully practicing their profession.

BRIDGMAN, Miss Laura Dewey, blind deaf-mute, born in Hanover, N. H., 21st December, 1829, died in South Boston, Mass., 24th May, 1889. Her parents were Daniel and Harmony

LAURA DEWEY BRIDGMAN.

Bridgman. Laura was a delicate infant and subject to severe convulsions. Her health improved until she was two years old, at which age she was a very active and intelligent child, able to talk and familiar with some letters of the alphabet. As she was entering her third year, the family were smitten by the scarlet fever. Two older daughters died of the fever, and Laura was attacked by it. For seven weeks she could not swallow solid food, and then both eyes and ears suppurated and her sight, hearing and sense of smell were totally destroyed. For a year she could not walk without support, and it was two years before she could sit up all day. When she was five years old, her health was once more perfect, and her mind, unaffected by her distressful affliction, began to crave food. She had forgotten the few words she knew when she was smitten. Her remaining sense, that of touch, grew very acute. Her mother taught her to sew, knit and braid. Communication with her was possible only by signs that could be given by touch. She was an affectionate, but self-willed, child. Dr. S. G. Howe, director of the Institution for the Blind in Boston, heard of her, and she was placed in his charge 12th October, 1837. Dr. Howe, assisted by Mrs. L. H. Morton, of Halifax, Mass., developed a special system of training that accomplished wonders. A manual alphabet was used, and Laura learned to read and write in sixteen months, having acquired a considerable vocabulary. Her intellect developed rapidly, and she learned mathematical operations to a limited extent. Her case attracted a great deal of attention, and the system of instruction developed by Dr. Howe in her case was applied successfully to other children similarly deprived of their senses. Laura had no conception of religion up to her twelfth year, as her instructors purposely refrained from giving her any ideas of God until she was old enough to take a correct idea. She could not, as has been asserted, distinguish color by feeling. Laura was visited by many prominent persons, among whom were Mrs. Lydia H. Sigourney and Charles Dickens. The "Notes on America" mention Mr. Dickens' visit. George Combe, of Scotland, visited Laura in 1842, and at his suggestion arrangements were made to keep a full record of everything connected with the remarkable girl. By dint of training she learned to speak many words. Her imagination developed more slowly than any other faculty, and her moral ideas were perceptibly different, in some phases, from those of ordinary persons. Her education is fully recorded in Mary Swift Lawson's "Life and Education of Laura Dewey Bridgman," published in 1881.

BRIGGS, Mrs. Mary Blatchley, born in Valparaiso, Ind., 1st January, 1846. She is of Scotch, English and Dutch descent. The father was a practicing physician and surgeon of prominence in the allopathic school. Mrs. Briggs' early school-days were spent in the public schools of Iowa. Later her education was continued in the young ladies' seminary in Council Bluffs, Iowa, receiving prizes for excellent scholarship. In the month of August, 1861, her family removed to Quincy, Ill., where she resumed her studies and there enjoyed the advantages of the best schools until she was nineteen years old. In religious belief Mrs. Briggs is strictly a Presbyterian, was born "in the faith," and has always lived the practical life of a consistent Christian. Rev. F. S. Blayney, LL.D., the first pastor of the Second Presbyterian Church of Omaha, writes of Mrs. Briggs's practical and valuable aid during the long and severe trials from 1880 to 1886 in the struggle to found and build his church, she being one of the foremost workers for the society's welfare. She has always taken a vivid interest in public characters and the local and foreign politics discussed in the newspapers. She was married to

John S. Briggs, 24th December, 1867, since which time they have resided in Omaha, Neb. Mr. Briggs was born in Ohio, but was reared in Iowa,

MARY BLATCHLEY BRIGGS.

removing to Nebraska in 1856. He is the son of the late Ansel Briggs, first governor of the State of Iowa. To Mr. and Mrs. Briggs three promising children have been born. Mrs. Briggs has filled many important public positions. During eleven years she served as assistant secretary, superintendent, reporter for the press, and manager of county, State and inter-state fairs. While on a visit to Idaho, she and her husband prepared a collection of minerals, stalactitic and calcareous deposits, which, at the suggestion of the officials of the Union Pacific Railroad, was sent to the Mechanics' Institute in Boston, Mass. Mrs. Briggs is interested in art and is secretary of the Western Art Association, which has three-hundred members. In literature she has won an assured position by her poems, one volume of which has been compiled and published. Mrs. Briggs was selected by Mrs. Potter Palmer as one of the six representative women of the West to serve on the executive committee of the Board of Lady Managers of the World's Columbian Commission for the Exposition in 1893. She was appointed a member of the by-laws judiciary committee and was elected an honorary and corresponding member of the woman's branch of the World's Congress Auxiliary, and served on several committees. She possesses an intimate knowledge of Nebraska, its history, its resources, its development and its people.

BRINKERHOFF, Mme. Clara M., singer and musical educator, born in London, England, 8th September, 1828. She is the daughter of Mr. and Mrs. John A. Rolph, cultured people, who came to the United States when Clara was an infant. Her father was an artist, whose specialty was steel engraving. Her mother was an artistic, literary and musical woman, with a fine voice that had been trained in the old Italian school by Maestro Corri. Mrs. Rolph trained Clara in singing from her fifth to her twelfth year. After the death of the mother, Clara's musical education was continued under the late Henry Derwort, who tried to persuade her to go on the stage in grand opera, but respect for her dead mother's wishes kept her from an operatic career. She next studied with Mr. Chadwick, a teacher of ballad and English song. Her next instructor was Mme. Arnault, a pupil of Bordogni, who prepared her for her début on the concert stage. She took lessons in oratorio music from George Loder, and also studied with Mrs. Edward Loder. In her first musical season she had the principal parts in "The Seven Sleepers," "Waldenses," "Judas Maccabæus," "Lobgesang" and Spohr's "Last Judgment"; afterwards in "Elijah," "Athalie" and "Stabat Mater," and in classical concerts from Gluck, Beethoven, Mozart, Haydn and Wagner, with a full repertoire of the best Italian composers. She gave in New York City and other places a remarkable series of vocal recitals, comprising portrayals of the best compositions, planned and executed by herself, with no assistance beyond piano-forte accompaniment. Mme. Brinkerhoff was the soprano of Grace Church at the time of her marriage, and sang the full Christmas service on the morning of her wedding day. She was married to C. E. L. Brinkerhoff on 25th December, 1848, and has one child, Charles Rolph. She has sung in concerts in many cities of the United States and abroad. In 1861 she visited Europe, where she received much flattering attention. Among the acquaintances she made there was that with Auber, who admitted her as an auditor to all vocal classes in the Paris Conservatoire, where she made a critical study of the different methods pursued in training. In Paris she was urged to sing in grand opera, but refused. As a singer she is master of the methods of the English, French, German and Italian schools. Her voice is a rich soprano with a range of nearly three octaves. She lives in New York City, where she gives much of her time to teaching. Besides her talents and accomplishments as a singer, she is a composer, and she is the author of a number of songs. She inherited the literary talent of her mother, which has found expression in her romance, "Alva Vine." She has lectured before the polytechnic section of the American Institute.

BRINKMAN, Mrs. Mary A., homeopathic physician, born in Hingham, Mass., 22nd February, 1845. She is of an old New England family, which has produced some of the ablest and best men and women that have given its high character to Massachusetts. She is a woman who seems predestined by training, education, acquired knowledge and natural endowments to exert a wide and beneficent influence upon our time by the application of the truths of physiology to the physical welfare of women. This is shown alike by her lectures, her medical writings and her contributions to current literature. She received only such educational advantages as were common to New England girls of forty years ago, but her quick intelligence and the enthusiasm with which she entered into her studies early marked her as one who would become an intellectual adornment to any society. On arriving at womanhood she visited Europe, where she devoted herself to study and travel. It was at that time her thoughts were first turned to the study of medicine. Believing that women physicians were demanded by the times, she determined to adopt the medical profession, not only as a means of livelihood, but also because it would enable her to do her part towards the physical

regeneration of society. Soon after returning to this country, in 1871, she entered as a student the New York Medical College and Hospital for Women. At her graduation, three years later, she was chosen the valedictorian of her class, and her medical thesis, which was a part of the final examination, was published in the "North American Journal of Homeopathy" and attracted considerable attention. After receiving her diploma, she continued to take instruction in the clinical department of the hospital, under private tuition, but was almost immediately chosen instructor in diseases of children. From that time she continuously occupied one or another of the college chairs, averaging for half the year two lectures a week. In 1876, while retaining her professional chair in the Women's Medical College, she was appointed physician to the New York Dispensary for Women and Children, and later, to the college dispensary, and in those positions she did active service for

MARY A. BRINKMAN.

several years. The work was without compensation, but in doing it Dr. Brinkman was ministering to the poor of her own sex and also, as she believed, contributing to form a public opinion which would open more avenues of usefulness to women. In 1881 she was chosen professor of diseases of women (gynæcology) in the New York Medical College and Hospital for Women. The trustees were slow to award the honors of the profession to women, even in a woman's college, and Dr. Brinkman was among the first to hold such a position. She filled it with success until forced by ill health to resign it, in 1889. Meanwhile she held other positions of honor and usefulness, being appointed, in 1886, visiting physician on the medical staff of the New York College for Women, and in 1889 consulting physician to the hospital. She has done a vast amount of gratuitous work for the needy, and in every possible way has labored to improve the condition and advance the cause of women, with a view to molding public sentiment to a broader outlook for her sex. Among these good works are the lectures she has given before women's clubs and societies. Another of her beneficent labors has been the course of lectures she has delivered on medical subjects to the young women of the Girl's Friendly Society of St. Thomas, St. James, and Calvary Churches, in New York City. In connection with this may be mentioned the Bible talks to workmen gathered from the streets, which from week to week, for one entire year, she gave under the auspices of the Galilee Mission of Calvary Church, which mission she helped to organize. These lectures were a decided aid in the progress of woman's work in the church, and as an object lesson to the uncultivated working men they undoubtedly led to their holding their wives in higher esteem and treating them with more consideration. Dr. Brinkman is an active member of many State and county societies, both medical and philanthropical, among which are the New York State and County Medical Societies, the Christian League for Promoting Social Purity, the New York Woman Suffrage Society, and the Society for Promoting the Welfare of the Insane. As associate member of the Girls' Friendly Society of the Episcopal Church she has done active work. This gratuitous labor for the public is the more noticeable from the fact that, during the greater part of the time in which it has been done, she has cared for a large and constantly increasing private practice. Dr. Brinkman has written articles for the medical journals which have extended her reputation among the profession. In her special line of work, the diseases of women, she is an authority, and no papers in medical journals give a more able, judicious and scientific treatment of their subject than do hers. Of late she has employed her leisure in literary work, for which she shows a brilliant aptitude. Her style is clear and marked by unusual terseness, euphony and impressiveness. On the subject in which she is most interested, the physicial education of our young women, she has written articles for the "North American Review" and other leading journals, which have attracted wide attention.

BRINTON, Mrs. Emma Southwick, army nurse and traveler, born in Peabody, Mass., 7th April, 1834. She was a daughter of Philip R. and Amelia D. Southwick, and the oldest of seven children. Her ancestors, (Lawrence and Cassandra,) were among the earliest colonists to this country from England. Lawrence received a gift of land for the first tanning establishment in the settlement, near Salem, Mass., on which he built the first house with glass windows. They were also the first in the Colonies to be persecuted for their belief, being Quakers, and for harboring a preacher. Miss Southwick entered, at an early age, into the activities of New England home life. She was educated in Bradford Academy, and, with the firing of rebel guns on Fort Sumter, she was on the alert to aid by needle and by the collection of supplies those who were marching to the relief of Washington. Communicating with Dr. S. G. Howe, of the Sanitary Commission, who was then in Washington, he soon sent for her to join the corps of nurses in Mansion House Hospital, Alexandria. A year was spent there; then, after a rest at home, nearly another year was spent in Armory Square Hospital, Washington. Then came service in the field at Fredericksburg, White House Landing and City Point. At the last place, while fighting was going on around Richmond, with thirty-five tents full of wounded, with a constant call for food and care, scant water supply and great heat, with no

shelter but a tent, where nearly all the food for her patients was provided, weeks passed into months, the overburdened nurse became a patient, and was sent to Washington and then home, broken down. Quiet and rest prepared her for some years of active service in the Freedmen's work in Petersburg and the Sea Islands. Her next move in public work was as foreign correspondent for the Boston press, and in that capacity she visited nearly all the countries of Europe, spending a summer in Scandinavia and Russia and a winter in Egypt and Palestine. In 1873 she spent several months in the Vienna Exhibition, where so much interest was shown by all other countries and so little by the United States, that she resolved to take some active part in our Centennial in 1876 in Philadelphia. Having been especially interested in the illustration of the home life of the peasantry of the various provinces of Austria, with their houses, gardens and costumes, she applied for permission to illus-

EMMA SOUTHWICK BRINTON.

trate the ancient life of New England by a log cabin and its accessories. At the same time she was invited by the State of Massachusetts to take partial charge of the office of the Centennial Commission in Boston, a position which she held a year. She then went to Philadelphia and spent six months in presenting to the multitude of visitors, inside her log house, a most interesting collection of furniture and domestic utensils, which ladies illustrated. In June, 1880, Miss Southwick was married to Dr. J. B. Brinton, of Philadelphia, and while there was an active member of the New Century Club, the Woman's Christian Association and the Woman's Hospital Staff. She has now a pleasant home with her mother in Washington, D. C., and is interested in the various activities of that city, and a member of the Woman's National Press Association. An enthusiastic traveler, she spends her summers, with various parties of ladies under her chaperonage, amid the highways and byways of the Old World.

BRISBANE, Mrs. Margaret Hunt, poet, born in Vicksburg, Miss., 11th February, 1858. She is the youngest daughter of the late Col. Harper P. Hunt, a southerner of the old régime,

MARGARET HUNT BRISBANE.

whose wife was Margaret Tompkins, a member of the well-known Kentucky family of that name. Her childhood was passed in the happy freedom of out-door sport, amid the trees that surrounded the "old house on the hill," as the Hunt mansion was called, and in companionship with bees and birds, flowers and pet horses and dogs, growing up with a naturally poetic temperament, fully developed by her surroundings. Early in life she began to express her musings in verse, and some of her earliest poems gave evidence of the poetical qualities she has revealed in her later and more important work. She has always possessed a sunshiny disposition and a fondness for society, and is a model mother, wife and housekeeper. She was married in 1883 to Dr. Howard Brisbane, of New York, a grandson of Albert Brisbane, of Brook Farm fame. Their family consists of three children. Mrs. Brisbane is a woman of great versatility, of strong womanly sympathies, and of marked refinement. She is a leader in the society of Vicksburg, and Mississippians are proud of her achievements in literature. She is artistic in temperament and aspiration, and in her life she is charitable.

BRISTOL, Mrs. Augusta Cooper, poet and lecturer, born in Croydon, N. H., 17th April, 1835. Her maiden name was Cooper, and she was the youngest of a family of ten children. She was a precocious child, and her poetical taste showed itself in her early infancy. Her first verses were written at the age of eight, and she had poems published when only fifteen. She was forward in mathematics and showed in her early life an aptitude for logical and philosophical reasoning. The greater part of her education was acquired in a public school, but she was also a student in

Canaan Union Academy and Kimball Union Academy. She began teaching at fifteen and was thus employed summer and winter for seven years. At twenty-two years of age she was married to G. H. Kimball, from whom she was divorced five years later. In 1866 she was married to Louis Bristol, a lawyer of New Haven, Conn., and they removed to southern Illinois. In 1869 she published a volume of poems, and in that year she gave her first public lecture, which circumstance seems to have changed the course of her intellectual career. In 1872 she moved to Vineland, N. J., her present residence, from which date she has been called more before the public as a platform speaker. For four years she was president of the Ladies' Social Science Class in Vineland, N. J., giving lessons from Spencer and Carey every month. In the winter of 1880 she gave a course of lectures before the New York Positivist Society on "The Evolution of Character," followed by another course under the auspices of the Woman's Social Science Club of that city. In the following June she was sent by friends in New York to study the equitable association of labor and capital at the Familistère, in Guise, in France, founded by M. Godin. She was also commissioned to represent the New York Positivist Society in an international convention of liberal thinkers in Brussels in September. Remaining in the Familistère for three months and giving a lecture on the "Scientific Basis of Morality" before the Brussels convention, she returned home and published the "Rules and Statutes" of the association in Guise. In 1881 she was chosen State lecturer of the Patrons of Husbandry in New Jersey, and in the autumn of the following year was employed on a national lecture bureau of that order.

AUGUSTA COOPER BRISTOL.

Since her husband's death, which occurred in December, 1882, Mrs. Bristol has appeared but seldom on the public platform. She is occupied with the care of an estate and in directing the educational interests of her youngest daughter. Some of her philosophic and scientific lectures have been translated and published in foreign countries.

BROOKS, Miss Ida Joe, educator, physician and surgeon, born in Muscatine, Iowa, 28th April, 1853. She is the daughter of Rev. Joseph Brooks. When she was very young, her parents moved to St. Louis, Mo., and she there entered the public schools, beginning in the primary department of the Clay school, when Dr. William T. Harris began his career as a teacher. Her father removed to the South after the war, and Miss Brooks went to Little Rock, Ark., in 1870. Two years afterwards, in conversation with a friend, she warmly argued that women should earn their own money, and he made a wager that she would not do it herself. As a joke, he found her a school in Fouche Bottom, where the gnats were so thick that a smudge had to be kept continually burning. She accepted the position and taught there

IDA JOE BROOKS.

faithfully and well. In 1873 Miss Brooks, with a liking for the work, began to teach in the public schools of Little Rock. The following year she was made principal of the grammar school, and in 1876 she was made principal of the Little Rock high school. In 1877 she was elected president of the State Teachers' Association. In the same year her father died, and the family came to shortened means, but were sustained by the independence and noble work of the daughter. In 1881 the Little Rock University was opened. Having become a Master of Arts, she was placed in charge of the mathematical department, where she taught until, in 1888, she entered the Boston University School of Medicine, a course which had for years been her desire. She was graduated there with high honors, and afterwards took a post-graduate course on nervous diseases in the Westborough Insane Hospital. She spent one year as house officer in the Massachusetts

Homeopathic Hospital, being assigned half the time on the surgical and half the time on the medical work. That was an unusual appointment. Returning to Little Rock in September, 1891, she began the practice of her profession and from the start won recognition and patronage. Dr. Brooks is an earnest woman suffragist and a thorough temperance advocate.

BROOKS, Mrs. M. Sears, poet and author, born in Springfield, Mass. She is of English ancestry, descended from the Tuttles, of Hertfordshire, England, who settled in New Haven, Conn., in 1635, upon the tract of land now occupied by Yale College, part of which tract remained the family homestead for more than a century. She is of Revolutionary stock, her grandfather being one of Mad Anthony Wayne's picked men at the storming of Stony Point. Her family has been remarkable for strong religious inclination, high regard for education and culture. Some of the most noted names in American letters are descended from this stock. Among them are Presidents Dwight and Woolsey, of Yale, Prescott, the historian, Goodrich (Peter Parley), and many others. Mrs. Brooks received her education in the public and private schools of her native city. After her marriage she removed to Missouri, in 1859, and subsequently to Madison, Ind., in 1863, where she now lives. Her earliest contributions to the press appeared in eastern publications under a pen-name. Latterly her poems, essays and short stories have appeared over her own name in newspapers and magazines in various cities. She has been engaged in regular newspaper work in southern Indiana, as editor and contributor. The advancement of women has been a subject claiming her attention, and for the past two years she has held the office of press superintendent for the State under the Indiana Woman Suffrage Association. Mrs. Brooks partakes in a large degree of the family characteristics, and in associations of prominence, in both State and Nation, her aid and influence have been felt. In her literary work she displays great force and beauty of diction, originality of thought and clearness of perception. She has published in holiday form "A Vision of the Mistletoe" (Buffalo, 1888).

BROTHERTON, Mrs. Alice Willams, author, born in Cambridge, Ind. Her family is of Welsh and English descent, with six generations on American soil. Her father resided in Cincinnati, Ohio, and afterward in St. Louis, Mo., then in Cambridge, Ind., and again settled in Cincinnati. She was educated mainly in the St. Louis and Cincinnati public schools, graduating in 1870 from Woodward high school, Cincinnati. In October, 1876, she was married to William Ernest Brotherton. Since then she has resided in Cincinnati. Two children, a boy and a girl, compose her family. Her oldest son, a bright boy of eleven, died in 1890. Living from her birth in an atmosphere of books, she was early trained by her mother in careful habits of composition. Her first appearance in print was in 1872. Her specialty is poetry, but she has written considerable prose in the form of essays, reviews and children's stories. From the first her success, in a pecuniary way, has been marked. Writing only when the spirit moves, in the spare moments of a busy home life, she has contributed at intervals to a variety of periodicals, the "Century," the "Atlantic," "Scribner's Monthly," the "Aldine," the "Independent," and various religious journals. Her booklet, "Beyond the Veil" (Chicago, 1886), was followed by "The Sailing of King Olaf and Other Poems" (Chicago, 1887), and by a volume of prose and verse for children, entitled "What the Wind Told the Tree-Tops" (New York, 1887). Her work shows a wide range of feeling and a deep insight into varying

ALICE WILLIAMS BROTHERTON.

phases of life. Many of her poems have been set to music in this country and in England.

BROWN, Mrs. Charlotte Emerson, president of the General Federation of Women's Literary Clubs, born in Andover, Mass., 21st April, 1838. She is the daughter of Professor Ralph Emerson, who was for twenty-five years professor of ecclesiastical history and pastoral theology in Andover Theological Seminary, in Massachusetts, and a relative of the philosopher, Ralph Waldo Emerson. Miss Emerson early showed a marked aptitude for linguistic learning. At the age of ten years she could read, write and speak French with facility. She was graduated while young from Abbott Seminary, and then began in earnest the acquirement of several other languages. For many years of her life she has devoted from ten to twelve hours daily to intense study. After mastering the Latin grammar and reading carefully the first book of Virgil's Æneid, she translated the remaining eleven books in eleven consecutive week-days. Horace, Cicero and other classical authors were read with similar rapidity. She spent one year in the study of modern languages and music, and as teacher of Latin, French and mathematics in Montreal, with Miss Hannah Lyman, afterward the first woman to serve as principal of Vassar College. Subsequently she spent several years in studying music and languages in Germany, Austria, France, Italy, Greece, Turkey, Egypt and Syria. On her return from foreign study and travel Miss Emerson was able to speak, read and write at least a half-dozen foreign tongues almost as readily as she did her native English. On reaching her home in Rockford, Ill., whither her parents had removed, she felt the need of a more thorough business education, and at once entered a commercial college

in Chicago, and was graduated after a term of six weeks. In order to complete her business knowledge and make it practical, she became for a time private secretary of her brother, Ralph Emerson, the well-known Rockford manufacturer. Subsequently she organized there two clubs that met regularly in her own house; one was a musical club, the Euterpe, and the other a French club, and both were extremely successful. She was at the same time teaching modern languages in Rockford Seminary. In 1879 she was married to Rev. William B. Brown, D.D., then of New York City. Soon after their marriage Dr. and Mrs. Brown went abroad for two or three years, and visited for study the chief art centers of Europe, passing in every country as natives. On their return to America they settled permanently in East Orange, N. J. Mrs. Brown was soon elected president of the Woman's Club of Orange, which greatly prospered under her leadership. She was also engaged in arranging plans of work for the Woman's Board of Missions and was active as a member of the advisory board for the organization and success of the General Federation of Women's Literary Clubs. At the organization convention, in the spring of 1890, Mrs. Brown was elected its first president. There were then fifty literary clubs in the federation. In less than two years that number had increased to over one-hundred-twenty, representing twenty-nine States and enrolling twenty-thousand of the intelligent, earnest women of the land. Mrs. Brown is greatly interested in the woman's club movement and gladly devotes her whole time to work for its advancement. She possesses unusual power of memory, mental concentration, energy and business ability,

CHARLOTTE EMERSON BROWN.

combined with such sweetness of disposition and deference for others as to make it easy for her to accomplish whatever she undertakes. She is enthusiastic and inspires others with her own magnetism. She combines the power of general plan with minute detail, and her motto is that what should be done at all should be done promptly and thoroughly. She is the author of many articles that have appeared in magazines and in other forms, mainly in the interests of whatever work she may at the time have had in hand. She is carrying on a very extensive correspondence and relies largely upon this agency for the full accomplishment of her well-considered plans for women's advancement.

BROWN, Mrs. Corinne Stubbs, socialist, born in what is now the very heart of Chicago, Ill., in 1849. Her mother, Jane McWilliams, was born in London, England, and when a child was keenly alive to the part taken by her elder brothers in the repeal of the Corn Laws of England. Coming to the United States when she was seventeen years old, she met and was married to Timothy R. Stubbs, the father of Corinne. He was from Maine, with

CORINNE STUBBS BROWN.

its hard, stony soil, a stair-builder by trade, and a man of strong and somewhat domineering character. His idea of parental duty led him to keep strict watch on his daughters. He forbade the reading of fiction and insisted on regular attendance at the Swedenborgian church. The latter command was obeyed, but the former was by Corinne considered unreasonable, and therefore disregarded. She read everything that came in her way, but her vigorous intellect refused to assimilate anything that could weaken it, and to-day fiction has little attraction for her, unless it be of marked excellence or originality. She acquired her education in the public schools of Chicago, continuing after her graduation to identify herself with them as a teacher. Good order and discipline were the rule in her department, and her governing ability led in time to her appointment as principal, a post which she relinquished to become the wife of Frank E. Brown, a gentleman well known in business circles, whose name may be

found on the list of officers of many benevolent enterprises. During the quiet of domestic life succeeding her marriage, Mrs. Brown's active mind prepared itself for new fields of thought and research, and she eagerly seized upon the social problems which began to thrust themselves upon the notice of all thinking people. She read, studied and talked with those who had investigated the causes of the glaring inequalities in social position, and of the increasing number of immense fortunes on the one hand and pauperism on the other. For a time she affiliated with the single-tax party, but its methods did not satisfy her as being adequate to effect the social revolution necessary to banish involuntary poverty. After much research she accepted socialism as the true remedy and Karl Marx as its apostle. Out of this naturally grew her desire to work for the helpless and oppressed, especially among women. She joined the Ladies' Federal Labor Union, identifying herself with working women and gaining an insight into their needs. In 1888 a meeting of that society was called to take action on an exposure of the wrongs of factory employées made in a daily paper. The result of the meeting was the organization of the Illinois Woman's Alliance, to obtain the enforcement and enactment of factory ordinances and of the compulsory education laws. As president of that society, which now includes delegates from twenty-eight organizations of women, Mrs. Brown has become widely known. In addition to her work in the Alliance, Mrs. Brown is connected with the Nationalists, the Queen Isabella Association and other societies, chiefly those having for their object the advancement of women.

BROWN, Miss Emma Elizabeth, author, born in Concord, N. H.. 18th October, 1847. Her

EMMA ELIZABETH BROWN.

girlhood memories are of that comely and prosperous inland city, historic in age and act. There she lived among her own people till the requirements of her work drew her to Boston, Mass. She now resides in Newton Highlands. The education of the schools, though good, was of less value than that of the home, where the father's greatest pleasure was in opening to his daughters the treasures of his choice library. If from her father she inherited a love of good reading, of pictures and preeminently of nature, she was no less indebted to her mother for a certain executive ability, indispensable to success, while from both parents she received constant help and encouragement in her early efforts. During her school-days she sent to the Concord "Monitor" a poem. That was the first of many contributions to various literary and religious newspapers, the "Atlantic Monthly," "Aldine," the "Living Age," and other magazines. Her only volume of poems is a brochure entitled "A Hundred Years Ago" (Boston, 1876), written with an insight and enthusiasm worthy the descendant of a Minute Man who gave his life at Lexington. Six volumes of the "Spare Minute Series" are of her compiling, and five of the "Biographical Series" are of her writing. Her Sunday-school books are "From Night to Light" (Boston, 1872), a story of the Babylonish Captivity, and "The Child Toilers of the Boston Streets" (Boston, 1874). One of Miss Brown's charms is the power of throwing herself into her subject

BROWN, Mrs. Harriet A., inventor, born in Augusta, Maine, 20th February, 1844. She is of Scotch parentage and early in life was thrown upon her own resources. By contact with working girls she learned of the long hours, hard work and small wages of which most of them complained, and her ardent desire was to alleviate their distress. Mrs. Brown conceived the idea of establishing a

HARRIET A. BROWN.

regular school of training for women who desired to make themselves self-supporting, and, on the solicitation of many prominent and philanthropic women of Boston, she opened the Dress-Cutting

College in that city on 17th October, 1886. In opening her college, she had the cooperation of those who induced her to establish such a school in Boston, but the underlying ideas, the scientific rules for dress-cutting, the patented system used, and all the methods of instruction, are her own. It is to her judicious wisdom and practical experience the college owes its success. The chief aim of the institution is to be one in which girls of ability and taste, who are now engaged in stores, workshops and kitchens, may find employment for which they are better adapted. Mrs. Brown's system of cutting is the result of years of study. All its points she has thoroughly mastered, and has succeeded in patenting rules for cutting, and also obtained the only patent for putting work together. She has received numerous medals and diplomas as testimonials of the superiority of her methods, and her system is being used in the leading industrial schools and colleges of the country. Delegates from the Pratt Institute, Brooklyn, N. Y., after investigating all the principal European methods, adopted Mrs. Brown's system, and it has been in use for two years in that institution. It is one of the regular features of the Moody Schools, Northfield, Mass., where young women are educated for missionary work. Mrs. Brown is an occasional contributor to the newspaper press.

BROWN, Mrs. Martha McClellan, born near Baltimore, Md., 16th April, 1838. On the father's side she is descended from the McClellans, Covenanters of Scotland, and on the mother's side from the old Maryland families of Manypenny and Hight. At the age of about two years she was taken by her parents to eastern Guernsey county, Ohio, where, before she reached her eighth year, both parents had died. The little girl and an only older sister were admitted to full family privileges in the home of neighbors, Thomas and Nancy Cummings Cranston, the husband a Protestant Irishman, and the wife of the old Quaker Cummings family, of Philadelphia, Pa. At the age of twenty years Martha made the acquaintance of Rev. W. K. Brown, of the Pittsburgh Methodist Episcopal Conference, and on 15th November, 1858, they were married. The young people were imbued with a strong purpose of educating and projecting woman personally along religious lines. In the fall of 1860 Mrs. M. McClellan Brown was a pupil in the Pittsburgh Female College, and in 1862 was graduated at the head of her class. In 1863 she became the mother of a son, who at nineteen was professor of sciences in Cincinnati Wesleyan College, and who in his twenty-second year founded and became president of Twin Valley College, Germantown, Ohio. In 1864 Mrs. Brown appeared in a public lecture in support of the Civil War in the court-house hall of the strong Democratic county of Westmoreland, Pa., where her husband was pastor. That movement was followed by public lectures in Philadelphia, Pittsburgh and many smaller places. In the summer of 1865 her oldest daughter was born, who became vice-president of the college with her brother before she had completed her twentieth year. In 1866 Mrs. Brown, owing to the unexpected death of the principal of the public schools in the county-seat of Columbiana county, Ohio, where her husband had been appointed pastor, was engaged as associate principal with her husband. She was elected superintendent of the Sunday-school, although the Methodist Church had not at that time arranged its law to admit women to such responsibility. She delivered temperance and literary lectures. In 1867 she was elected to a place in the executive committee of Ohio Good Templary, and immediately founded the temperance lecture system. That position she held from 1867, through the organization of the Prohibition party in 1869, the Ohio Woman's Crusade in 1873, and the founding of the National Woman's Christian Temperance Union in 1874, in each of which movements she was a leader. In 1868 she took editorial charge of the Republican newspaper of Alliance, Ohio. At that time the Republican party was known to weaken before the demands of the German Brewers' Beer Congress, and Mrs. Brown openly denounced the demands of the brewers as "un-American." She also sharply criticised the efforts of what she recognized as the rum oligarchy at political domination, and she reprimanded the truculent spirit and conduct of many politicians. Julius A. Spencer, of Cleveland, secretary of Ohio Good Templary in 1868, proposed to Mrs. Brown the formation of an independent political party, and she extended her hand to assist him. The question being further discussed, Mrs.

MARTHA McCLELLAN BROWN.

Brown's husband required that, before his wife should unite in the movement for a new party, there must be an agreement to place woman on an equal status with man. Mr. Spencer finally agreed that woman should have equal status in the new party, and that a plank asserting this fact should be inserted in the platform, provided they were not expected to discuss that issue before the people. The Prohibition party was organized in Ohio early in the following year, 1869. The present name of the party was suggested by Mrs. Brown's husband as more appropriate than "Anti-Dram-Shop," the name proposed by another friend of the cause. Mrs. Brown was present in Oswego, N. Y., in May, 1869, at the first caucus for a national organization of the new temperance party. In 1870 Mr. Brown purchased the political newspaper, of which his wife was editor, and for years that paper was made the vehicle of vigorous warfare against the liquor traffic. As a member of the executive committee

of Good Templars in Ohio, Mrs. Brown had almost constant opportunity, apart from her position as editor of a local city paper, for the circulation of her views. Her family had increased until the number of the children was four, two sons and two daughters. Mrs. Stanton desired to enlist Mrs. Brown in her efforts for the suffrage reform, but both Mr. and Mrs. Brown refused; and they steadily avoided, from policy, the discussion of the question or any identification with the woman suffrage workers. In 1872 Mrs. Brown was elected a delegate of Good Templary to Great Britain. Very shortly thereafter she was called to the headship of the order in the State of Ohio. When Mrs. Brown appeared upon the platform in Scotland and England in 1873, audiences of from 5,000 to 10,000 greeted the American temperance woman, and her title of Grand Chief Templar of Ohio was a passport to recognitions of royalty, even so far remote as Milan, Italy. Returning from the European tour, her services were in constant demand. She was elected at the State Grand Lodge of Ohio, held in Columbus in 1873, to succeed herself in the office she held. When Mrs. Brown heard of the work of the new revival, she hastened to examine and determine its spirit. Believing that it was a visitation from the Lord in answer to years of work and much prayer, she in her capacity of Chief Templar issued an order in January, 1874, for a day of fasting and prayer in the three-hundred lodges of Ohio under her jurisdiction, and encouraged that all ministers of religion favorable to the order and the cause of temperance be invited to unite with the Good Templars in a day of humiliation and worship for enlightenment and power for a dispensation of a much-needed temperance revival. During the year of the women's uprising 3,000 letters crowded her tables. Finding that the women who had become active in the out-door work of the crusade, were not satisfied to enter the Good Templar lodges, Mrs. Brown, at the suggestion of her husband, prepared a plan for the organization of crusaders in a national society without pass-words or symbols, under which plan open religious temperance meetings and work should be prosecuted, women being the chief instruments of such work. It was her purpose to project this effort of organization at a proposed visit to the first meeting of the Chautauqua Assembly, which purpose was fully carried out 12th August, 1874. She afterwards was chiefly instrumental in gathering the women in the first national convention in Cleveland, Ohio, where she largely assisted in developing her plan, which was made the basis of the permanent organization of the National Woman's Christian Temperance Union. Just after the founding of the Woman's Christian Temperance Union in August, 1874, Mrs. Brown was elected Right Grand Vice-Templar of the International Order of Good Templars, in Boston, Mass. That gave her a place in a board of five, which held supervision over upwards of 800,000 pledged temperance workers. When nominated for the president of their union by the women in Cleveland, Ohio, the ladies were sarcastically reminded that Mrs. Brown was an active official of the Prohibition Party, Chief Templar of Ohio, and a member of the International Executive of Good Templary, and ought not to be made president of the Woman's Union. She immediately arose and withdrew her name, and Mrs. Wittenmyer was elected to the place. In 1876 Mrs. Brown objected to the attitude of the majority of the Right Grand Lodge of Good Templars in rejecting lodges of colored people, and so withdrew and united with the English delegates in constituting a more liberal body. After ten years of separation the two bodies adjusted their issue by providing for regular lodges of colored people, and Mrs. Brown marched at the head of the English delegation on entering the hall for the re-union of the bodies of Good Templars, in 1886, in Saratoga, N. Y. In 1877, after repeated personal efforts with leading Republican officials, State and National, had failed to secure any actual, or even fairly promised political, antagonisms of the liquor interests, Mrs. Brown went to New York City and assumed the management of the newly organized National Prohibition Alliance. She had also a secondary aim, which was to make that organization a barrier and corrective against the growing defection of temperance workers from radical measures of reform. Hence she gave herself for five years to the projection of prohibition reform by means of the National Prohibition Alliance, which she caused to be operated chiefly in the churches and independent of party policy. Through those years she maintained an office in New York City without salary, while her husband continued in the ministry and, with their family of five children, remained at his work in Pittsburgh, Pa. In the winter of 1881–82, from a caucus of Republicans, directed by Simon Cameron, she received the tender of the highly remunerative position of Superintendent of Public Instruction in the State of Pennsylvania. To have accepted that offer, she would have been compelled to abandon her work with the Prohibition Alliance, without any one to take her place; hence she did not accept. In October, 1881, Mrs. Brown gathered through personal letters special circulars and press notices a large National Conference of leading Prohibitionists and reformers in the Central Methodist Episcopal Church, New York City. Before that Conference she made one of her most impassioned appeals for unity among temperance workers, whereby the National Prohibition Alliance was led to unite formally with the Prohibition Reform Party. The success of the New York conference led to a similar conference in Chicago the following year, August, 1882, which was arranged for by Mrs. Brown, and which was more successful than the one held in New York. Many of the old leaders of the Prohibition Reform Party were induced to attend the Chicago conference. At that conference Miss Frances E. Willard and her immediate following of Home Protectionists and the Woman's Christian Temperance Union were brought into the Prohibition Party, besides many local organizations of temperance workers. Mrs. Brown thereupon dropped the non-partisan National Prohibition Alliance, believing that it had served its purpose. In the summer of 1882 Dr. and Mrs. Brown were elected to the presidency and vice-presidency of the Cincinnati Wesleyan College. The entire management of the institution has since devolved upon them, Mrs. Dr. McClellan Brown holding a professorship as well as the vice-presidency of the college. During that time she has twice visited Europe and has been warmly received among reformers and scholars abroad. Her sixth child, a son, was born in January, 1886. She has lost nothing of the grace and power which marked her early platform work. Among others she has received the degrees of Ph. D. and LL. D.

BROWN, Miss M. Belle, physician and surgeon, born in Troy, Ohio, 1st March, 1850. She was educated in the high school of her native town, and in the Oxford Female College, Oxford, Ohio. Her father was born in Rhode Island and went west in 1828. The genealogy of that branch of the Brown family of which she is a member is notable. Chad Brown emigrated from England in the ship "Martin," which arrived in Boston, Mass., in July, 1638. He went to Providence, R. I.,

in the year of his arrival. He was one of a committee of four to prepare the first written form of government adopted and continued in force until 1644, when Roger Williams returned from

M. BELLE BROWN.

England with the charter and Chad Brown was the first one of the thirty-nine who signed that charter. In 1642 he was ordained the first settled pastor of the Baptist Church. His great grandsons, John and James, repurchased a part of the land that had originally belonged to him and presented it to the college of Rhode Island. In 1770 the corner-stone of University Hall was laid by John Brown. In 1804 the name of that institution was changed to Brown University. Dr. Brown's mother's name was Telford, and her ancestors were of the Jennings family from England. From her mother, who was the neighborhood doctor in an emergency and kept salves and liniments for everybody who desired them, she inherited her taste for medicine. Doctor Brown commenced the study of medicine in 1874. In 1876 she went to New York and entered the New York Medical College and Hospital for Women. She was graduated in 1879 and entered immediately upon a general practice in West 34th street, New York, where she still resides. She is one of the few women in medicine who practice surgery. She makes a specialty of diseases of women and is professor of diseases of women in the New York Medical College and Hospital for Women, and is also secretary of the faculty of that institution. She is a member of the American Institute of Homeopathy, of the New York County Medical Society, a member of the consulting staff of the Memorial Hospital in Brooklyn, and of the New York Homeopathic Sanitarium Association.

BROWN, Olympia, Universalist minister, born in Prairie Ronde, Kalamazoo county, Mich., 5th January, 1835. Though a Wolverine, and always claiming to be a representative Western woman, Olympia's ancestry belonged to what Oliver Wendell Holmes would call "The Brahmin Caste of New England," though both her parents were Vermont mountaineers. On her father's side she traces her lineage directly back to that sturdy old patriot, Gen. Putnam, of Revolutionary fame, and through her mother she belongs to a branch of the Parkers, of Massachusetts. Olympia's parents moved to Michigan, as pioneers, in what was then the remote West. Her birthplace was a log-house, and her memories of childhood are the narrow experiences common to a farmer's household in a new country, with only the exceptional stimulus to mental culture afforded by the self-denial of a mother determined that her daughters should enjoy every advantage of study she could possibly obtain for them. At the age of fifteen Olympia was promoted to the office of mistress of the district school and was familiarized with all the delights of "boarding around." She alternated teaching in a country school in summer with study in the village academy in winter, till, in the fall of 1854, she entered Mount Holyoke Female Seminary, in South Hadley, Mass. Though she remained only one year, reviewing branches already quite thoroughly mastered, she there first began to be interested in those theological investigations that have shaped her life. Questioning the doctrinal teaching made prominent in the seminary, she secured the strongest Universalist documents she could find and laid the foundations of a faith never since shaken. Attracted by the reputation of Horace Mann as an educator, she became a student in Antioch College, Ohio, and was graduated from that institution in 1860. The question confronted her then, "what use shall I make of my life?" To a careful paper, asking advice of the college faculty on that point, she received, as their best deliberate thought, direction to an indefinite course of reading and study, with the one aim of selfish intellectual enjoyment, varied by purely private acts of charity. Against the narrow limitations of such an existence all the activities of her soul rebelled, and, after much thought and in spite of determined opposition from every quarter, she chose the profession of the ministry, and was graduated from the Theological seminary, in Canton, N. Y., a branch of St. Lawrence University. She was ordained in Malone, N. Y., in June, 1863, by vote of the ordaining council of the Universalist Church, the first instance of the ordination of a woman by any regularly constituted ecclesiastical body. There had been woman preachers and exhorters in America ever since the days of Anne Hutchinson, but in no case had such preachers been ordained by ecclesiastical council or by the authority of the church of which she was a representative. This public recognition of a woman minister by a body of the church militant opened the pulpit to women so effectively that her ordination was followed by others of other denominations. Her first pastoral labors were as pulpit supply in Marshfield, Vt., in the absence of Rev. Eli Ballou, pastor, and preaching every alternate Sunday in East Montpelier. Desirous of better perfecting herself for efficient service, early in 1864 she moved to Boston and entered the Dio Lewis Gymnastic School, taking lessons in elocution of Prof. Leonard. There she received and accepted a call to the church in Weymouth, Mass., and was formally installed as pastor on 8th July, 1864, the Rev. Sylvanus Cobb preaching the installation sermon. Early in her pastorate the question was raised concerning the legality of the marriage rite solemnized by a woman. The subject was brought before the Massachusetts Legislature and referred

to the judiciary committee, who decided that, according to the definition of legislative statutes, the masculine and feminine pronouns are there used interchangeably, and the statutes, as then worded, legalized marriages by ministers of the gospel, whether men or women. In the spring of 1866 Olympia attended the Equal Rights convention, held in Dr. Cheever's Church in New York, and there met Susan B. Anthony, Parker Pillsbury and other prominent advocates of woman's enfranchisement. From her early girlhood she had taken a keen interest in every movement tending toward a wider scope for girls and women, but on that occasion she was first brought into personal relations with the active reformers of the day. In 1867 the Kansas Legislature submitted to popular vote a proposition to amend their constitution by striking out the word "male." That was the first time the men of any State were asked to vote upon a measure for woman suffrage. Lucy Stone im-

OLYMPIA BROWN.

mediately made arrangements with the Republican central committee to send one woman speaker to aid in the ensuing canvass. In response to urgent importunity that she should become the promised speaker, Olympia obtained the consent of her parish, and personally furnished a supply for her pulpit. She set forth on her arduous mission in July and labored unremittingly till after election. A tour through the wilds of Kansas at that time involved hardships, difficulties and even dangers. Arrangements for travel and fitting escort had been promised her, but nothing was provided. Nevertheless, overcoming obstacles that would have taxed the endurance of the strongest man, she completed the entire canvass of the settled portions of the State. Between 5th July and 5th November she made 205 speeches, traveling, not infrequently, fifty miles to reach an appointment. The Republican party, that submitted the proposition and induced her engagement in the field, so far stultified its own action as to send out circulars and speakers to defeat the measure, and yet, by her eloquent appeals, she had so educated public sentiment that the result showed more than one-third of the voting citizens in favor of the change. Olympia's pastoral connection with the church in Weymouth continued nearly six years. But, she said characteristically, the church was then on so admirable a footing she could safely trust it to a man's management and she desired for herself a larger field, involving harder toil. She accepted a call to the church in Bridgeport, Conn., then in a comatose condition. Immediately affairs assumed a new aspect, the church membership rapidly increased, the Sunday-school, which had had only a nominal existence, became one of the finest in the city, and the work of the church in all good causes was marked for its excellence and efficiency. She severed her connection with the church in April, 1876. She remained in New England, preaching in many States, as opportunity offered, till February, 1878, when she accepted a call to the pastorate of the Universalist Church in Racine, Wis. There she made for herself a home, which is the center of genial hospitality and the resort of the cultivated and intelligent. She faithfully continued her pastorate with the Racine church, toiling with brain and hand, with zeal unflagging, taxing her resources to the utmost to help the society meet its financial emergencies, till the time of her resignation, in February, 1887. Of her work there, a member of her parish writes: "When she came to Racine some of the parish were groping about in search of 'advanced thought;' some, for social and other causes, had become interested in other churches, and some were indifferent. Her sermons interested the indifferent, called many of the wanderers back and furnished food for thought to the most advanced thinkers. Her addresses were always in point." It is noticeable that all the churches with which Olympia has been connected have continued to be active, working parishes, dating a new life from the time of her union with them, thus showing that her quickening is not the transient development of an abnormal excitement, but healthy growth from central, vital truth planting. Since her resignation of her pulpit in Racine, while still keeping the interest of Universalism near her heart, and losing no opportunity to extend its borders and expound its doctrines, and continuing actively in the ministry, Olympia has given the larger part of her time to the Wisconsin Woman Suffrage Association, of which she has been for several years the president and central inspiration. As vice-president of the National Woman Suffrage Association she has been able to raise an eloquent voice in behalf of progress and has done much to recommend that organization to the people. In the course of her public career she has many times been called to address the legislatures of the several States, and her incisive arguments have contributed much to those changes in the laws which have so greatly ameliorated the condition of women. Olympia has not confined her sympathies to womans' rights or to Universalism. She has been and still is a persevering, faithful temperance agitator, working assiduously for almost a score of years in the orders of the Good Templars and the Sons of Temperance. In April, 1873, Olympia was married to John Henry Willis, a business man, entirely in sympathy with her ideas in regard to woman's position. It is by mutual agreement and with his full consent she retains the maiden name her toil has made historic, and continues her public work. Two children beautify the home, H. Parker Brown Willis and Gwendolen

Brown Willis. Perhaps one could hardly answer the sophistries of those who claim that the enlargement of woman's sphere of action will destroy the home-life better than by pointing to its practical illustration in her well-ordered home. Perhaps her most prominent characteristic, and one that has been sometimes mistaken for aggressiveness, is her absolute fearlessness in espousing and defending the right.

BROWNE, Mrs. Mary Frank, philanthropist, born in Warsaw, Wyoming county, N. Y., 9th September, 1835. She is the youngest daughter of Dr. Augustus Frank, who was born in Canaan,

MARY FRANK BROWNE.

Conn., and Jane Patterson, of Londonderry, N. H. Andrew Frank, father of Dr. Augustus and grandfather of Mrs. Browne, was a German, coming to America before the formation of the United States government. Professors and men of position in the schools and German universities were connected with the Frank families of the Old World. After the completion of Mrs. Browne's education she was engaged in teaching in Warsaw for a time, in the school established under the auspices of the Presbyterian Church. Her home remained in Warsaw until 1858, when she was married to Philo D. Browne, a banker of Montreal, Canada. Then began her life of regular, organized Christian activity. She was prominent in the organization of the Young Women's Christian Association of Montreal, and served as its president during its first years. She assisted in forming the Ladies' Canadian Foreign Missionary Society, and was one of its officers. Mrs. Browne aided in establishing and was one of the managers of the Infants' Home in Montreal, and was one of the founders and officers of the Canadian Board of Missions. She removed to California in 1876, where, with her husband and family, she made her home in San Francisco. There she found new fields of usefulness. She at once organized the San Francisco Young Women's

Christian Association, and for years was its president. When, later, she had her home in Oakland, Cal., she remained its vice-president and one of its most active workers. In 1877 she was elected president of the Woman's Occidental Board of Foreign Missions, an office which she now holds. Many perplexing social and political issues have come into the deliberation of the Occidental Board. The entrance into this country of Chinese women at first, and later the coming of Japanese women of the same class, the management of the home which is intended to be their asylum from slavery, the cases in courts where young Chinese girls are called to appear scores of times before they are finally awarded to the guardianship of the home, as in the famous case of the Chinese child, Woon Tsun, are some of the most perplexing questions for the society. In her broad, catholic spirit, Mrs. Browne was ready to help forward the Hyacinthe movement, under the patronage of Père and Madame Hyacinthe. She has been a constant writer for periodicals and is the author of the interesting temperance book, "Overcome" portraying the evils of fashionable wine-drinking and intemperance. She assisted in organizing the noble army of Christian temperance women of California into the State Woman's Christian Temperance Union, and served the union as president for several years. She was also editor for a considerable period of the organ of the society in California. In 1877 she organized the Young Women's Christian Association in Oakland, in the suburbs of which city is located her "Highland Park" home. Of that organization she is now president. A home for young women, a day nursery for poor laboring mothers, a kindergarten and station for gospel services are some of the plans provided for in the new building about to be erected by that association. For several years she was president of "The Ebell," an art and literary society in Oakland. The first free kindergarten in Oakland had its inception in Mrs. Browne's Bible class of young ladies. She is the mother of three children, two sons and one daughter.

BROWNELL, Mrs. Helen M. Davis, educator, born in Ossian, N.Y., 31st January, 1836. Her childhood was spent in a Christian home. At an early age she manifested an eager desire for knowledge, using with avidity the means within reach to fit herself for the position of teacher. She became a prominent educator in the public schools of Bloomfield, Lima and Geneseo, N. Y. Having attained success as an instructor in English branches, she entered the seminary in Lima, that she might fit herself for more advanced work in her profession. For some years she continued her studies in that school. There she met her future husband, W. A. Brownell, then a student in Genesee college. On the completion of his college course they were married, in July, 1865. In September, 1865, her husband became principal of Red Creek Seminary, N. Y. and she became preceptress. Later, her husband was called to the chair of Latin in Falley Seminary, N. Y., where she again took the position of preceptress and teacher of French. At that time Falley Seminary stood in the front rank of collegiate preparatory schools. Upon the call of her husband to the principalship of Fairfield Seminary, N. Y., she discontinued teaching, and during their three years' residence there her first son was born. In 1871, her husband having accepted a position in the high school in Syracuse, N. Y., they removed to that city, and there they still reside. Mrs. Brownell gave herself heartily to the making of a home, meanwhile carrying on with enthusiasm her studies in general literature and natural history, particularly in the

department of botany. Her home has been not only a safe retreat for her husband and children, but its doors have always been open to receive to its sheltering care young men and women who were

HELEN M. DAVIS BROWNELL.

struggling to prepare for life's duties. To these young people she has given advice, inspiring and inciting them to the highest aspirations, and aiding and directing them in their studies. She has enjoyed the advantages of travel, both in America and Europe. Within the last few years, since her household duties have been less imperative, she has given herself zealously to the work of the Woman's Home Missionary Society, speaking often in various conventions and conferences.

BROWNSCOMBE, Miss Jennie, artist, born near Honesdale, Pa., 10th December, 1850. Her father, a farmer, was a native of Devonshire, England. Her mother belonged to a family conspicuous among the Connecticut pioneers, who came to the Colonies in 1640 with Governor Winthrop. Miss Brownscombe was the only child. She was studious and precocious, and about equally inclined to art and literature. She early showed a talent for drawing, and when only seven years old she began drawing, using the juices of flowers and leaves with which to color her pictures. In school she illustrated every book that had a blank leaf or margin available. Her father died before she left school, and her mother in 1891. When Jennie was eighteen years old, she began to teach school, and at the age of twenty she became a student in the Cooper Institute School of Design for Women in New York, from which she won a medal at the end of a year, and for several succeeding years she studied in the National Academy, winning first medals in the life and antique schools. In the second year of her study she began to make drawings on wood for "Harper's Weekly" and other periodicals, and to teach drawing and painting. She devoted her study mainly to genre figure painting and has made a large number of portraits. Her first important picture was exhibited in 1876 in the Academy of Design in New York. She was one of the first members of the Art

JENNIE BROWNSCOMBE.

Students' League. In 1882 she went to Paris and studied under Harry Moster. On her return in 1883 she was incapacitated from work by an injury to her eyes, and for a year she did but little. Her pictures have been reproduced in photogravures, etchings and engravings for the past six years. Some of her most widely known pictures are "Grandmother's Treasures," "Love's Young Dream," "Blossom Time," "Halcyon Days," "The Gleaners," "Sunday Morning in Sleepy Hollow," "The Recessional" and "The Sirens." Miss Brownscombe now lives in Honesdale, Pa.

BRYAN, Mrs. Mary Edwards, author, born in Jefferson county, Fla., in 1846. Her father was Major John D. Edwards, one of the early settlers in Florida and a member of the State legislature. Mary was educated by her cultured mother until she was twelve years old. The family moved to Thomasville, Ga., where she enjoyed the advantages of good schooling and made rapid progress. When she was sixteen, she was married to Mr. Bryan, the son of a wealthy Louisiana planter, with whom she went to his plantation on the Red river. One year later, under the pressure of painful circumstances, she returned to her father's home. There she began to write for the press. She wrote regularly for the "Literary and Temperance Crusader," published in Penfield, Ga. She contributed many columns to that journal, in both prose and verse, and her productions attracted attention. In 1859 the "Crusader" was enlarged, improved and removed to Atlanta, and Mrs. Bryan was engaged as literary editor. She filled the position with brilliant success and brought the journal into prominence. At the end of 1859 she resigned her position on the "Crusader" and became a correspondent

of the "Southern Field and Fireside." After the Civil War she became the editor of the Natchitoches, La., "Semi-Weekly Times," writing political articles, sketches, stories and poems. Her next position was on the "Sunny South," published in Atlanta, Ga., which paper she edited for ten years. In 1885 she removed to New York City, where she served as assistant editor of "The Fashion Bazaar" and of "The Fireside Companion." Among her novels are: "Manch" (New York, 1879); "Wild Work," a story of the days of reconstruction in Louisiana (1881), and "The Bayou Bride" and "Kildee" (1886). Mrs. Bryan has a family of four children and several grandchildren. Her home is now in Atlanta, Ga., where she has editorial charge of "The Old Homestead," a monthly magazine."

BUCK, Mme. Henriette, educator, born in London, England, 8th January, 1864, during a casual sojourn of her parents, who are Parisians, in that city. Her maiden name was Berdot. Her father, Henri Berdot, is a descendant of a noble Spanish family. One of her aunts, the Baronne de Carbonnel and Marquise de Baudricourt, was a clever author of some reputation. Madame Buck was educated in the best schools in Paris, and after receiving various scholastic honors she obtained the highly prized diploma of the University of France, which entitles the receiver to hold the position of professor in any scholastic position in France. After teaching successfully for several years, she was married to W. Edgar Buck, an eminent bass vocalist and professor of singing, who was a former pupil of Signor Manuel Garcia. Madame Buck and her husband came to America and settled in Montreal, Canada, where they were successful in their respective professions. In June, 1890, Mr.

HENRIETTE BUCK.

Buck was called to Toronto, Canada, as conductor of the Toronto Vocal Society. Madame Buck formed French classes in that city, and has been very successful in private tuition. She is the leading teacher of French in Toronto. Her literary talent is shown in the comedies and plays which she writes for her classes to perform. She writes fluently in both English and French and is an accomplished musician.

BUCK, Mrs. Mary K., author, born in Ondreor, Bohemia, 1st April, 1849. Her parents came

MARY K. BUCK.

to America, when she was five years old, and for several years lived in New York City, where she went to school and acquired her knowledge of the English language. From New York they removed to Traverse City, Mich., which has since been her home. From a child she was fond of books, reading eagerly whatever came to hand. English books were rare in her Bohemian home, but the little town library, of which she was an unfailing patron, was well stocked with some of the best. Early in life she developed a talent for composition, especially of an imaginative kind, which was encouraged by her teachers and friends. She is happily married, and has three children. Always interested in the advancement of women, she has in her own career demonstrated the fact that a woman can at once be a good mother, an excellent housekeeper and a successful business woman. In an exceptionally busy life she has found time to write much for publication. During the summer of 1891 she published, together with Mrs. M. E. C. Bates, a book of short sketches entitled "Along Traverse Shores." She has contributed to the "Congregationalist," the "Advance," the Chicago "Inter-Ocean," the Portland "Transcript," "Good Housekeeping," "St. Nicholas" and many other periodicals.

BUCKNOR, Mrs. Helen Lewis, author, born in New York City, 10th October, 1838. She is of Revolutionary ancestry and New England parentage. Her maiden name was Lewis. Upon the father's side she is descended from the Lewises and Tomlinsons of Stratford, Conn. On the mother's

side she is descended from the Spragues and Ketchums, of Connecticut originally, but afterward of Long Island. Her grandfather Sprague settled in early times in New York City as a merchant. Her father died when she was a child, and, as she was very delicate, it was decided that she should be brought up in the South by an uncle, the brother of her mother, who had married and settled near Natchez, Miss. Her school life was passed there. In her early girlhood she went to the Northwest as a teacher, maintaining herself until the war broke out, when she returned to her southern home and to new and sad experiences. Soon after the close of the war she was married to W. F. Bucknor, of New York City. It was her husband's misfortune to have inherited a large tract of pine lands in Florida. In 1870 he with his wife removed to that State. They were unfitted to endure the privations and discouragements of a pioneer life in that devastated country at that period, and, holding, as they did, strong Republican principles, their experiences were sometimes thrilling in the extreme. Many able articles were published in the press from their ready pens. Mrs. Bucknor's articles of advice to Florida women, who, like herself, were making strenuous efforts to help their husbands to secure homes in that State, were marked by strength and good sense. The Toledo "Blade," the "Home Journal" and other periodicals published her articles. She is possessed of poetic talent, but excels in sharp, pithy, truthful sketches of human nature as she finds it. She is an earnest worker among the King's Daughters and is a member of the Woman's Christian Temperance Union. She

HELEN LEWIS BUCKNOR.

now lives in St. Augustine, Fla., and is a member of the Flagler Memorial Church in that city.

BUELL, Mrs. Caroline Brown, temperance worker and philanthropist, was born in Massachusetts. Her ancestry was New England and Puritan. She is a daughter of Rev. Thomas G. Brown, of the New England Conference of the Methodist Episcopal Church. Her early life was passed in the way common to the children of itinerant ministers. Hard work, earnest study and self-

CAROLINE BROWN BUELL.

reliance developed her character on rugged and noble lines. She had a thirst for learning that caused her to improve in study all the time that the only daughter of an itinerant minister could find for books. Arrived at womanhood, she became the wife of Frederick W. H. Buell, a noble and patriotic young Connecticut man, who had enlisted in the Union army at the beginning of the Civil War. During the war her father, husband and three brothers served the Union, three in the army and two brothers in the navy. Her father was the chaplain of her husband's regiment, and in war he earned the name of "The Fighting Chaplain." During those dreary years Mrs. Buell worked, watched and waited, and in the last year of the conflict her husband died, leaving her alone with her only son. She soon became identified with the temperance reform and in 1875 was chosen corresponding secretary of the Woman's Christian Temperance Union of Connecticut, which had been partially organized the previous winter. She entered heartily into the work, and her sound judgment, her powers of discrimination, her energy, her acquaintance with facts and persons, and her facile pen made her at once a power in the association. She came into office when much was new and experimental, and she gave positive direction to the work and originated many plans of procedure. She was the originator of the plan of quarterly returns in Connecticut, a system that has been quite generally adopted in other States. In 1880, in the Boston convention, Mrs. Buell was chosen corresponding secretary of the National Woman's Christian Temperance Union, and in that exalted and responsible position she has done good and effective work with pen, hand and tongue

for the association. She has been re-elected to that office regularly for twelve years. She is a dignified presiding officer and an accomplished parliamentarian, and in State conventions she has often filled the chair in emergencies. The war record of her family makes her a favorite with the veterans of the Civil War, and she has, on many occasions, addressed conventions of the G. A. R. Of singularly gentle nature and quiet manners, they are combined with exceptional force of character.

BULL, Mrs. Sarah C. Thorpe, wife of Ole Bull, the famous violinist, is the superintendent of the department of sanitary and economic cookery in the National Women's Christian Temperance Union. She has translated "The Pilot and His Wife" by Jonas Lie (Chicago, 1876), and "The Barque 'Future'" (Chicago, 1879), by the same author. She has also published a "Memoir of Ole Bull" (Boston, 1883.) She was largely instrumental in securing the monument to Ericsson on Commonwealth avenue, Boston. Her home is in Cambridge Mass.

BULLOCK, Mrs. Helen Louise, musical educator and temperance reformer, born in Norwich, N. Y., 29th April, 1836. She is the youngest daughter of Joseph and Phebe Wood Chapel, from of New England origin. While lacking no interest in other branches, she early possessed a great desire study to music, and at eighteen years of age began to teach piano and vocal music. Some years later she studied the piano with S. B. Mills, and the guitar with Count Lepicowshi, both of New York City. With the exception of two years, she taught music from 1854 to 1886, and was for many years a member of the National Music Teachers' Association. In 1881 she published two books of musical studies,

HELEN LOUISE BULLOCK.

"Scales and Chords" and "Improved Musical Catechism," both of which have had a large sale. When William A. Pond, who purchased the copyrights, was arranging for their publication, he requested the author's name to be given as H. L. Bullock, in order that the foreign teachers might not know they were written by a woman, and therefore be prejudiced against or undervalue them. At twenty years of age Miss Chapel was married to Daniel S. Bullock, son of Rev. Seymour Bullock, of Prospect, N. Y. Two children were born to them, a daughter who died at two years of age, and a son who died at the age of twenty-seven. Soon after the death of her son, in 1884, she adopted a little motherless girl five years of age, who has proved a very great comfort. Mrs. Bullock's religious training was in the Presbyterian Church and Sunday-school, but, when converted, her ideas on baptism led her to unite with the Baptist Church, of which she is still a member. She has always been actively interested in the Sunday-school and missionary work. From 1871 to 1885 her home was in Fulton, N. Y., but after a serious illness of pneumonia her physician recommended a milder climate, and the family moved to Elmira, N. Y. The following April, 1886, a Woman's Christian Temperance Union was re-organized in that city, and she was unanimously elected president. In September of that year Mrs. Mary T. Burt, president of the New York State Woman's Christian Temperance Union, organized Chemung county and urged Mrs. Bullock to go into the adjoining counties of Broome, Schuyler, Tioga and Yates and organize them, which she did. Taking up her public work with great timidity, she was pressed further and further into it, until she was forced to decide as to her future. It was very hard for her to give up her profession, but after much prayerful consideration she devoted the remainder of her life to the uplifting of humanity and the overthrow of the liquor traffic. In 1886 she was appointed State organizer of the New York Woman's Christian Temperance Union, in 1887 State superintendent of the department of narcotics, and in 1888 National lecturer on that subject. She was instrumental in securing the New York State law against selling cigarettes and tobacco to minors. In the interest of that department she wrote the leaflet "The Tobacco Toboggan." In 1889 she was appointed National organizer of the Woman's Christian Temperance Union, and in that work has gone from Maine to California, traveling thirteen-thousand miles in one year. In that department she has achieved marked success. During the first five years she held over twelve-hundred meetings, organizing one-hundred-eighty new unions, and securing over ten-thousand members, active and honorary. She is deeply interested in prison and police matron work, and has been president, since its organization, of the Anchorage of Elmira, a rescue home for young girls. In 1892 she was appointed superintendent of the school of methods of the New York State Woman's Christian Temperance Union.

BUMSTEAD, Mrs. Eudora Stone, poet, born in Bedford, Mich., 26th August, 1860. In 1862 her parents removed to Nebraska. Her earliest recollections are of the great West, with its prairie billows crested with pleasant homes, its balmy breezes and its sweeping gales. Her parents were highly cultured, and gave her every possible assistance and encouragement. She began to write rhymes in her childhood, and when ten years old a poem from her pen was published in "Our Young Folks," then edited by J. T. Trowbridge. Receiving a good common-school education, she was for a time a successful school-teacher. In 1878–79 she was a student in the Nebraska State University. There she met William T. Bumstead, to whom she was married in 1880. One of their

two children, a son, died in infancy, and the other, a daughter, brightens their pleasant home in Ontario, Cal. Mrs. Bumstead is of Quaker descent, and is like the Friends in her quiet tastes and sincere manners. Except to a congenial few, she is almost as much a stranger in her own town as abroad. Remarkably well informed and having an analytic mind, she is a keen, though kindly, disputant, accepting nothing as proved which does not stand the test of reason. She has had little time for

EUDORA STONE BUMSTEAD.

writing and has used her pen mostly to please the child-readers of "St. Nicholas" and the "Youth's Companion," having been a special contributor to the latter for several years. She thoroughly enjoys her work and asks nothing of fame but to win for her a circle of loving little friends.

BURLINGAME, Mrs. Emeline S., editor and evangelist, born in Smithfield, R. I., 22nd September, 1836. Her maiden name was Emeline Stanley Aldrich. Her father was a public speaker of ability, and her mother was a woman of much energy. After graduating in the Providence high school at the age of fifteen, she pursued a course of study in the Rhode Island Normal School, and then taught five years. In November, 1859, she was married to Luther R. Burlingame and subsequently lived in Wellsboro, Pa., and Whitesboro, N. Y., afterward removing to Dover, N. H., and then back to her home in Providence. She early became active in Christian work and, while living in Dover, became a regular contributor to the "Morning Star" and "Little Star," published by the Free Baptists. About the same time she became editor of the "Myrtle," a paper for children. On her removal to Providence she assisted her husband in editing "Town and Country," a temperance paper. In 1873 she was elected president of the Free Baptist Woman's Missionary Society, which position she held for thirteen years, resigning when elected editor of the "Missionary Helper," the organ of the society. She introduced into the magazine features which made it a helper to missionary workers. In 1879 she was elected corresponding secretary and organizer for the Rhode Island

EMELINE S. BURLINGAME.

Woman's Christian Temperance Union, and began at once to address audiences and to organize unions in different parts of the State. In 1884 she was elected president of the Union and devoted the next seven years to speaking and planning in its interest. In the securing of a prohibitory amendment to the constitution of Rhode Island, the Woman's Christian Temperance Union was the acknowledged leader, and to that work Mrs. Burlingame bent the energy of her life. In 1889 she was a delegate to the General Conference from the Rhode Island Free Baptist Association, that being the first year when women were sent as delegates to that body. In 1890 she was licensed to preach by the Rhode Island Free Baptist Ministers' Association. In 1891, being seriously worn by her prolonged labors for temperance, she resigned the presidency of the Rhode Island Woman's Christian Temperance Union, and was elected National Woman's Christian Temperance Union evangelist. She soon after accepted the position of general agent of the Free Baptist Woman's Missionary Society, and since that time has been traveling, visiting quarterly and yearly conferences and churches, and addressing them on the broadest phases of missionary work, including the important reforms of the day.

BURNETT, Miss Cynthia S., educator and temperance reformer, born in Hartford, Ohio, 1st May, 1840. She is the oldest daughter of a descendant of the early settlers of New Jersey. Her mother is a Virginian by birth and education. Her early life was divided between home duties and study till the age of seventeen, when she began her career as a teacher in the public schools near her home, a part of each year

being spent as a student in the neighboring academy. The Civil War changed the current of her life, and she resolved to obtain the best education possible and to devote her life to the profession of her choice. She studied four years in the Western Reserve Seminary, in her own county, from which she was graduated in the classical course in 1868. She at once accepted the position of preceptress and teacher of Latin in Orwell Normal Institute. Three years later she took the position of teacher of languages in Beaver College. Failing health made a change of climate necessary, and she went to the old home of her mother in Virginia, where for a time she had charge of a training-school for teachers. Two years were spent in the Methodist Episcopal College in Tullahoma, Tenn. There she became interested in the "New South," and many letters were written for the press in defense of the struggling people. At the first opportunity after the crusade she donned the white ribbon. Her first public work was done in 1879, in Illinois. Later she answered calls for help in Florida, Tennessee, Ohio and Pennsylvania. In 1885 she was made State organizer of Ohio. The first year she lectured one-hundred-sixty-five times, besides holding meetings in the day-time and organizing over forty unions. Her voice failing, she accepted a call to Utah, as teacher in the Methodist Episcopal College in Salt Lake City. She was made Territorial president of the Woman's Christian Temperance Union. Eight unions and fifteen loyal legions were organized by her. Each month one or more meetings were held by her in the penitentiary. She edited a temperance column in a Mormon paper. Tabernacles and school-houses were open to her, and through the assistance of

CYNTHIA S. BURNETT.

missionaries and Mormons alike the gospel of temperance was presented in many towns. Unable longer to work so hard, and believing that her real place was in the lecture field, she accepted a call to southern California as State organizer. She spent one year there and in Nevada, during which time one-hundred-fifty lectures were given by her. For efficient service in the West she was made National organizer in 1889, but was soon after called home by the serious illness of her mother, and she has remained near or with her parents ever since. She continued her work as State organizer until recently, when she accepted the position of preceptress in her Alma Mater now Farmington College.

BURNETT, Mrs. Frances Hodgson, novelist, born in Manchester, England, 24th November,

FRANCES HODGSON BURNETT.

1849. She lived in Manchester until 1864, acquiring that familiarity with the Lancashire character and dialect which is so noticeable in her works of later years. Her parents suffered financial reverses in 1865, her father died, and the family came to the United States. They settled in Knoxville, Tenn., and afterwards moved to Newmarket, Tenn. Mrs. Hodgson took a farm, where her two sons and three daughters could work and earn their bread. Frances began to write short stories, the first of which was published in a Philadelphia magazine in 1867. She persevered and soon had a market for her work, "Peterson's Magazine," and "Godey's Lady's Book," publishing many of her stories before she became famous. In 1872 she contributed to "Scribner's Magazine" a story in dialect, "Surly Tim's Trouble," which scored an immediate success. Miss Hodgson became the wife of Dr. Luan M. Burnett, of Knoxville, in 1873. They made a long tour in Europe and, returning in 1875, made their home in Washington, D. C., where they now reside. Her famous story, "That Lass o' Lowrie's," created a sensation as it was published serially in "Scribner's Magazine." It was issued in book form (New York, 1877), and it found a wide sale, both in the United States and in Europe, running through many editions. On the stage the dramatized story was received with equal favor. In 1878 and 1879

she republished some of her earlier stories, which had appeared in various magazines. Among those are "Kathleen Mavourneen," "Lindsay's Luck," "Miss Crespigny," "Pretty Polly Pemberton" and "Theo." These stories had appeared in a Philadelphia magazine, and had been published in book form, without her permission, by a house in that city, a proceeding which caused a controversy in public. Her plots were pilfered by dramatists, and all the evidences of popularity were showered upon her. Her later novels, "Haworth's" (New York, 1879), "Louisiana" (New York, 1881), "A Fair Barbarian" (New York, 1882), and "Through One Administration" (New York, 1883), have confirmed her reputation. But her greatest success, on the whole, has been won by her "Little Lord Fauntleroy," which first appeared as a serial in "St. Nicholas," in 1886. It was subsequently published in book form and was dramatized, appearing on the English and American stages with great success. Mrs. Burnett is very fond of society, but her health is too delicate to enable her to give time to both society and literary work. She has been a sufferer from nervous prostration, and since 1885, has not been a voluminous writer. She has published "Sara Crewe" (New York, 1888), "Editha's Burglar" (Boston, 1888), and "Little Saint Elizabeth" and other stories (New York, 1890). Mrs. Burnett is the mother of two sons, one of whom died at an early age. Despite her long residence abroad, she calls herself thoroughly American.

BURNHAM, Miss Bertha H., author and educator, born in Essex, Mass., 22nd April, 1865. She is a resident of Lynn, Mass. In her early childhood her love for reading and writing was

BERTHA H. BURNHAM.

manifested. It was not until her sixteenth year that any of her writings were published, and those possessed the many crudities common to immaturity. Since that time she has written short articles and poems, whenever school duties and health permitted, her themes generally being of a religious nature. Recently her mind has turned toward pedagogical writing, as she has been a successful teacher for the past four years. Her writings have appeared in the New York "Independent," "Wide Awake," Chicago "Advance," "Sunday-School Times," "Education" and other periodicals.

BURNHAM, Mrs. Clara Louise, novelist, born in Newton, Mass., 25th May, 1854. She is

CLARA LOUISE BURNHAM.

the oldest daughter of Dr. George F. Root, the eminent musical composer. Her father, becoming the senior partner of the Chicago firm of Root & Cady, removed with his family to that city when Mrs. Burnham was very young, and Chicago has been her home ever since. A return for several summers to the old homestead in North Reading, Mass., together with the memory of the first years of her life, gave the child an acquaintance with New England dialect and character of which she was to make use later. As a girl her time was given chiefly to music. Her marriage took place while she was still very young. Shortly after her marriage a brother, who enjoyed her letters, urged her to write a story. The idea was entirely novel and not agreeable to the young woman, but the brother persisted for many months, and at last, in a spirit of impatience and in order to show him his absurdity, the work was undertaken. To Mrs. Burnham's surprise her scornful attitude soon changed to one of keen interest. She wrote two novelettes and paid to have them criticised by the reader of a publishing house, her identity being unknown. The verdict was unfavorable, the reader going so far as to say that, if the author were of middle age, she would better abandon all hope of success as a writer. Mrs. Burnham was not "of middle age," and she was as reluctant to lay down her pen as she had been to take it up. Recalling her life-long

facility for rhyming, she wrote some poems for children, which were accepted and published by "Wide Awake," and that success fixed her determination. She wrote "No Gentlemen" (Chicago, 1881) and offered it to a Chicago publisher. He examined it, said it would be an unsafe first book, and advised her to go home and write another. The author's father, who until that time had not regarded her work seriously, liked "No Gentlemen" and believed in it. Through his interest the book immediately found a publisher, and its success was instantaneous. Other books followed, "A Sane Lunatic" (Chicago, 1882), "Dearly Bought" (Chicago, 1884), "Next Door" (Boston, 1886), "Young Maids and Old" (Boston, 1888), "The Mistress of Beech Knoll" (Boston, 1890), and "Miss Bagg's Secretary" (Boston, 1892). Besides her novels, Mrs. Burnham has written the text for several of Dr. Root's most successful cantatas, and contributed many poems and stories to "Youth's Companion," "St. Nicholas" and "Wide Awake." She resides with her father, and the windows of the room where she works command a wide view of Lake Michigan, whose breezy blue waters serve her for refreshment, not inspiration. She does not believe in the latter for herself. She has a strong love for the profession thrust upon her, and sits down at her desk as regularly as the carpenter goes to his bench. Mrs. Burnham is a cultured pianist. She has no family.

BURNS, Mrs. Nellie Marie, poet, born in Waltham, Mass., about 1850. She is a daughter of Dr. Newell Sherman, of Waltham, a descendant of Rev. John Sherman and Mary Launce, a granddaughter of Thomas Darcy, the Earl of Rivers. The family came to America from Dedham, England, in

NELLIE MARIE BURNS.

1642. Her mother's maiden name was Kimball, and she came from the English Brights and Bonds, of Bury St. Edmunds. She was twice married. By her first marriage she was the mother of George

C. Cooper, formerly editor of the Rochester, N.Y.,
"Union." By her second marriage she became the
mother of Mrs. Burns. Nellie became the wife of
Thomas H. Burns, the actor, in 1878. She had
been a member of the dramatic profession, and
she left the stage after marriage, in compliance with
the suggestion of her husband. They make their
summer home in Kittery Point, Maine. Mrs. Burns
has written much since 1886 and has prepared her
manuscript for publication in book form. She has
been a contributor to the Boston "Globe," the
Portsmouth "Times," the Waltham "Tribune"
and other journals.

BURNZ, Mrs. Eliza B., educator and spelling reformer, born in Rayne, County of Essex,
England, 31st October, 1823. From London she
came to this country at the age of thirteen, and
three years later took up, with her own hands,
the battle for bread, a battle she has since maintained unceasingly, and, for the most part, alone
and unaided. As an instructor in shorthand she
has been successful, and her career as a laborer in
her chosen field is a history to which none may
point save with pride and commendation. Through
the instrumentality of her classes in phonic shorthand in the Burnz School of Shorthand, and in
Cooper Institute and the Young Women's Christian Association, in New York City, at least one-
thousand young men and women have gone forth
to the world well equipped for the positions which
they are creditably filling. In addition to these,
through the large sales of her text-book, which for
many years has been extensively advertised and
sold for self-instruction, probably as many more
have entered the ranks of the shorthand army as
"Burnz" writers. Mrs. Burnz is a member of the

shown by her receiving, with the exception of Ed.
F. Underhill, the largest number of votes as one
of the committee to prepare the Isaac Pitman
medal. Aside from her success as a shorthand

MARY TOWNE BURT.

author and teacher, Mrs. Burnz has for many years
been prominently identified with the "spelling reform" movement, having been one of the organizers of the Spelling Reform Association in Philadelphia during the Centennial, in 1876, and for
several years a vice-president of that body. Aside
from the fact that she has probably published more
books and pamphlets in the interest of spelling
reform than any other publisher in this country,
she has, by her steadfast advocacy of the movement, both in private and public, and by her deep
interest at all times in its welfare and advancement,
proved herself to be one of the strongest pillars
the movement has known. Mrs. Burnz is not only
a theoretical, but a practical, spelling reformer, as
can be certified by her numerous correspondents.
She advocates what is known as the Anglo-
American alphabet, which was arranged during the
formation of the Spelling Reform Association in
Philadelphia, in 1876, by Mrs. Burnz and E. Jones
of Liverpool, England. Believing in the old adage,
"Never too old to learn," she is now devoting her
leisure to the study of Volapük. Although not a
strict vegetarian, she is a thorough hygienist. It is
to her method of living she attributes the fact
that, though puny when a child, she is in good
health now. In character she is high-minded, generous to the faults and shortcomings of those with
whom she is brought in contact, very strict in her
ideas of right and strong in her convictions, not the
least important in her eyes being a belief in woman
suffrage and equality before the law. She is a
stockholder in the Mount Olivet Crematory, located
in Freshpond, L. I., and thoroughly believes in that
method of disposing of the body after death. Still
a very hard worker, even at her advanced age, she

ELIZA B. BURNZ.

New York State Stenographers' Association, and
has been its librarian since that body began its collection of stenographic publications. Her popularity among shorthand writers of all schools was

attends to a large amount of teaching, as in years gone by. In her own school she superintends the instruction. She gives class lessons daily for two hours in the Young Women's Christian Association, and, until recently, when her text-book on shorthand was selected for use in the evening schools of the City of New York, she conducted the free evening class in shorthand in Cooper Union. Mrs. Burnz has been twice married, has had four children, and is the grandmother of eight.

BURT, Mrs. Mary Towne, temperance reformer, was born in Cincinnati, Ohio, of English-American parentage. Her father, Thomas Towne, was educated in England for the ministry. After the death of her father, which occurred in her early childhood, her mother removed with her three children to Auburn, N. Y., where Mrs. Burt received a liberal education, passing through the public schools and the Auburn Young Ladies' Institute. Four years after leaving school she became the wife of Edward Burt, of Auburn. When the crusade opened, in 1873, Mrs. Burt began her work for temperance, which has continued without intermission, with the exception of seven months spent in the sick room of her sister, Mrs. Pomeroy. So deeply was she stirred by the crusade that on 24th March, 1874, she addressed a great audience in the Auburn Opera House on temperance. Immediately after that, Mrs. Burt was elected president of the Auburn Woman's Christian Temperance Union, and served for two years. She was a delegate to the first national convention held in Cleveland, Ohio, in 1874, was one of the secretaries of that body, and in the next national convention, in Cincinnati, Ohio, was elected assistant recording secretary. In the year 1876, in the Newark, N. J., national convention, she was elected a member of the publishing committee of the "Woman's Temperance Union," the first official organ of the National union. She was afterwards made chairman of that committee and publisher of the paper. During the year 1877 she served as managing editor. At her suggestion the name "Our Union" was given to the paper, a name which it held until its consolidation with the "Signal," of Chicago, when it took the name of the "Union Signal." In Chicago, in 1877, she was elected corresponding secretary of the National Union, which office she held for three years, and during that term of office she opened the first headquarters of the National union in the Bible House, New York City. In 1882 she was elected president of the New York State Union, a position which she still holds. During the years of her presidency the State union has increased from five-thousand to twenty-one-thousand members and from 179 to 842 local unions, and in work, membership and organization stands at the head of the forty-four States of the National union. Mrs. Burt, with her husband and son, resides in New York. She is a member of the Protestant Episcopal Church.

BUSH, Mrs. Jennie Burchfield, author, born in Meadville, Pa., 28th of April, 1858. She is of Scotch, English and Irish descent. Her father was James Burchfield, a prominent journalist of Meadville and a brilliant writer. Her mother, Sarah M. Coburn, also a journalist, was a woman of poetic temperament. The daughter was placed in the State Normal School in Edinburgh, Pa., at the age of six years, and remained there until she was sixteen years old. In 1875 she went to Augusta, Kans., where her mother was living, and she has been since then a resident of that State. She became the wife, on the 21st October, 1877, of A. T. Bush, a well-known stockman, of Louisville, Ky. Her family consists of two sons. Mrs. Bush was unconscious of her poetical powers until a few years

ago. Since writing her first poem she has made a thorough study of the art of poetic expression. She has published extensively in newspapers and periodicals. Her literary work, while mainly poetic-

JENNIE BURCHFIELD BUSH.

al, includes a number of short stories and several serials. Her home in Wichita is an ideal one.

BUSHNELL, Miss Kate, physician and evangelist, born in Peru, Ill., 5th February, 1856. She is a descendant of a prominent family that traces its ancestors to John Rogers, the Smithfield martyr. She received a public-school education in her native State and attended the Northwestern University, in Evanston, Ill. Selecting the medical profession, she became a private pupil of Dr. James S. Jewell, the noted specialist in nerve diseases. Later she finished her medical education in the Chicago Woman's Medical College, was graduated M.D., and became a resident physician in the Hospital for Women and Children. She then went to China, and for nearly three years remained in that country as a medical missionary. Returning to America, she established herself as a physician in Denver, Col. In 1885, complying with earnest requests from the leaders, Dr. Bushnell gave up her practice and entered the field as an evangelist in the social-purity department of the Woman's Christian Temperance Union. It was she who laid the foundation of the Anchorage Mission in Chicago, Ill., an institution which has done great good for abandoned women, giving over five-thousand lodgings to women in one year. In 1888 Dr. Bushnell visited the dens and stockades in northern Wisconsin, where women were held in debasing slavery. That undertaking was heroic in its nature, for she took her life in her hand when she dared the opposition of those she encountered. Fearless and undaunted, she finished her investigations and her report made to the Woman's Christian Temperance Union startled the reading public by its revelations of the utter depravity she had witnessed. As a public speaker Dr. Bushnell is graceful, eloquent and earnest, and as a writer she is well known in her special field. This combination

KATE BUSHNELL.

of the woman and the physician, the orator and the author has made her the choice of the World's Woman's Christian Temperance Union for carrying the gospel of the white ribbon to foreign lands. In 1891 she left Chicago to circumnavigate the earth in the interests of humanity, representing over 500,000 women. Dr. Bushnell went as an evangelist to organize, instruct and encourage. She carried with her the "polyglot petition," a paper that was intended to be signed by at least two-million persons, representing a general protest against legalizing sale of alcoholics and of opium, and it is to be presented to every government on both hemispheres.

BUTIN, Mrs. Mary Ryerson, physician, born near Wilton, Iowa, 17th August, 1857. She lived on a farm until her eighteenth year, and then took up her residence in the village of Wilton Junction. There, with alternate schooling and teaching, she succeeded in nearly completing the course in the academy in that place, when its financial embarrassments necessitated the closing of its doors. Entering the high school, in one year she was graduated therefrom with the highest honors. At the age of twenty-one she felt the responsibility of choosing her life work. From her earliest remembrance she had heard her mother say that she was to be a doctor. The mother was farseeing and discerned that opening for woman and her fitness for her work. Though timid and sensitive as to the opinions of others, after deliberation she decided that her duty lay in that direction. She turned with keen perception of its responsibilities from the pleasures of a young girl's life and began the study of medicine, with the help and encouragement of the family physician and his

partners. She entered the medical college in Iowa, City, a co-educational institution, which at that time had enrolled a membership of ninety men and ten women. From that college she came forth a firm opponent of co-education in medical colleges. The following year she attended the Woman's Medical College in Chicago, Ill., from which she was graduated in the spring of 1881, afterwards entering the South Side Hospital as resident physician. Her duties were so arduous, the lack of nurses making it necessary for her to supply that position sometimes, that, after four months' service, she resigned and returned home for rest. While on a visit to her brother in Dorchester, Neb., her practice became so extensive as to cause her to settle there, where she gradually overcame all opposition among physicians and people to women practitioners. There she met and became the wife, in May, 1883, of Dr. J. L. Butin, a rising young physician. Before she had been in the State a year, she became a member of the Nebraska State Medical Society. She was the first woman to enter that society and was received in Hastings, in 1882. Placed upon the programme for a paper the next year, she has ever since been a contributor to some section of that society. She was elected first vice-president in 1889. She has been a contributor to the Omaha "Clinic" and other medical journals, and was State superintendent of hygiene and heredity for the Woman's Christian Temperance Union, county and local. Untiring in devotion to her profession, she has been ready to lend her aid to all progressive movements, and she has battled and

MARY RYERSON BUTIN.

conquered much of the prejudice against woman in the field of medical science.

BUTLER, Miss Clementina, evangelist, born in Bareilly, India, 7th January, 1862. Her father, Rev. William Butler, was commissioned in 1856 to open mission work for the Methodist Episcopal Church. After passing through great perils during the Sepoy rebellion, in 1857, Bareilly was settled as headquarters. The family moved their home seventeen times during the next eight years, according to the needs of the work. Returning to the United States, after a few years' rest, Dr. Butler was requested to organize mission work in Mexico. There the linguistic ability of the daughter was of great service. In 1884 Miss Butler went with her parents to revisit her native land, and her observations during an extended tour in that country have served as the theme of many of her addresses and articles. On account of the infirmities of age and the heavy responsibilities borne so long, Dr. and Mrs. Butler reside quietly in Newton Center, Mass., and from their home the daughter goes out to inspire others with her own belief in the glorious possibilities for women in every land, when aided by Christian civilization. Miss Butler is interested in missionary work of all kinds, medical missions for the women of the East being her favorite subject. As a King's Daughter she works in the slums of Boston, besides pleading in the churches and on public platforms for the needy in the uttermost parts of the earth. A short residence in Alaska gave her an insight into the condition of the people there, and she is an ardent champion of their rights in regard to suitable educational grants and the enforcement of the laws prohibiting the sale of liquor in that Territory. Miss Butler is her father's assistant in his literary labors, by which he still aids the cause

CLEMENTINA BUTLER.

he served so long. She uses her pen also for missionary publications.

BUTLER, Mrs. Frances Kemble, see KEMBLE, FRANCES ANNE.

BUTTERFIELD, Miss Mellona Moulton, china-painter, born in Racine, Wis., 15th May, 1853. She was educated in St. Louis, Mo., and Omaha, Neb., and is a graduate of Brownell Hall in Omaha. She was for twelve years engaged in teaching, which

vocation she followed with success in Plattsmouth, Grand Island and Hastings, cities of Nebraska. During those years she followed, as devotedly as circumstances would allow, the one art toward

MELLONA MOULTON BUTTERFIELD.

which her talents and inclinations tended. At last she gave up other work and applied herself exclusively to ceramic painting, establishing a studio in Omaha. She is one of the best artists in that line in the State. She received the first honorable mention for china-painting in the woman's department of the New Orleans World's Fair, and in 1889 the first gold medal for china-painting given by the Western Art Association in Omaha. She has received many favorable notices from art critics and the press.

BYINGTON, Mrs. Elia Goode, journalist, born in Thomaston, Ga., 24th March, 1858. Mrs. Byington is president of the Woman's Press Club of Georgia, and, with her husband, Edward Telfair Byington, joint proprietor, editor and manager of the Columbus "Evening Ledger," a successful southern daily. The flourishing condition of the Woman's Press Club bears testimony to the deep interest and zeal of its presiding officer. She declares that the work is made easier by the sympathy and approval of her husband. Mrs. Byington is deeply interested in the intellectual and industrial progress of woman, and that her interest is practical, rather than theoretical, is evinced in the fact that, with the exception of the carrier boys and four men for outdoor work, all of the employés of the "Ledger" office are women. A woman is employed as foreman, a woman artist makes the illustrations for the paper, a woman reads the proofs, a woman manipulates the type-writer, a woman is mailing clerk, and all the type is set by women, all of whom receive equal pay with men who are employed in similar capacities. Not content with the help extended to her sisters in her own profession, Mrs. Byington organized a Worker's Club as an aid to the many young girls who, while still burdened with the shrinking southern conservatism, have to go forth to battle with the world. Mrs. Byington comes of a distinguished Georgia family, being the

ELLA GOODE BYINGTON.

daughter of the late Col. Charles T. Goode, of Americus, and granddaughter of Gen. Eli Warren, of Perry. She is essentially a southern woman, having always lived in her native State, and having received her education in the Furlow Female College, in Americus, and in the Georgia Female College in Madison. She was married in 1877 and, becoming deeply interested in her husband's journalistic labors, began to assist him with her pen, and in that way cultivated a love for the work that has since brought her distinction. Her father was a man of brilliant attainments, while her mother is a perfect type of cultured Southern womanhood. From them Mrs. Byington inherits her intellectual gifts, which, together with her youth, personal beauty and charm of manner, make her a favorite with her friends. She is a constant worker, spending many hours daily at her desk and often working late into the night, but, notwithstanding her numerous duties, she finds time to give to society. She is secretary and treasurer of the Art Club, the leading social and literary organization of Columbus.

CABELL, Mrs. Mary Virginia Ellet, educator, born at the "Point of Honor," Lynchburg, Va., the home of her maternal grandfather, Judge Daniel, 24th January, 1839. Her father, the eminent civil engineer, Charles Ellet, jr., built the first suspension bridge in the United States, over the Schuylkill river at Philadelphia, presented the first plans for a bridge across the Mississippi river at St. Louis, and built the first bridge across the Niagara below the Falls. He first suggested and advocated a Pacific railroad, and his "temporary track" over the Blue Ridge, at Rock Fish Gap, was the most noted mountain railroad in the world. He was the author of the reservoir

plan for the improvement of the Mississippi and Ohio rivers. He invented the steam-ram and constructed and commanded the steam-ram fleet in the victorious battle of Memphis, where he was mortally wounded. Mrs. Cabell's education was directed by her father. At twelve years of age she had thoroughly read Gibbon, and at fifteen she had accomplished a remarkable course of reading, and was in fluent command of the French and German languages. She accompanied her parents to Cuba, remaining there some time. She spent nearly a year at Niagara, crossing the river repeatedly in the famous "iron basket" which first conveyed men and materials, and was the first female to view the Falls from the bridge before its completion. The years of 1854 and 1855 she spent in Europe, studying history and literature. She spent part of the winters of 1860 and 1861 in Richmond, Va., where, under the guardianship of her kinsman, Hon. A. H. H. Stuart and Hon. John B. Baldwin, the two Union leaders in the convention, she followed the proceedings and heard the views of the men who weighed the measure of secession. When the unhappy decision was reached which precipitated civil war, she returned to her family in Washington. After the battle of Memphis Mrs. Ellet and her daughter were permitted to join and nurse Col. Ellet, who sank rapidly from his wound. When the fleet moved to participate in the siege of Vicksburg, Charles Rivers Ellet, who had first hoisted the flag in Memphis, begged to accompany it. The decision was left to his sister, who sent the boy to his brief and glorious career. Col. Ellet died in Cairo, 21st June, 1862, his body was carried to Philadelphia, lay in state in Independence Hall, and was interred in Laurel Hill with military

MARY VIRGINIA ELLET CABELL.

honors. His wife survived him but one week. Charles Rivers Ellet died 29th October, 1862, from exposure and fatigue. The care of the two younger children and of their aged grandmother devolved upon the solitary young girl. After the war, Mary Ellet became the wife of William D. Cabell, of Virginia. In 1888 they removed with their family of six children to Washington, D. C., and opened a school for girls, which at once won great repute as Norwood Institute, and is now increasingly prosperous. In 1890 Mrs. Cabell aided in organizing a society of the descendants of Revolutionary patriots, the Daughters of the American Revolution. At the first meeting Mrs. Harrison was elected president-general and Mrs. Cabell vice-president-general presiding. At the first Continental Congress of the order, held in Washington 22nd to 24th February, 1892, Mrs. Harrison and Mrs. Cabell were unanimously reëlected.

CADWALLADER, Mrs. Allice A. W., philanthropist, born in St. Clairsville, Ohio, in 1832. Her father, George W. Moorehouse, was of English descent, and her mother, Elizabeth Linder, was of German descent. Alice was one of a family

ALICE A. W. CADWALLADER.

of twelve children. She was reared as a daughter of temperance. At an early age she became the wife of Mr. Cochran, a Virginian, who died, leaving her with a family of three small children. Six years after his death she was united in marriage to N. J. White, of a Quaker family in Belmont county, Ohio. He enlisted as one of the sixty-days soldiers at the beginning of the Civil War, and was killed in the battle of Antietam. Mrs. White went with her children to the house of her father, in Mount Pleasant, Iowa, where she gave her time to patriotic work. She first took charge of the sanitary supplies of Jefferson Barracks, Missouri. After one year's service there the Sanitary Commission placed her in charge of the supplies of the hospital steamer "R. C. Woods," and a year later she was removed to the control of the large Light-diet Kitchen in Jeffersonville, Ind. Putting that in complete running order, she next repaired to Nashville, Tenn., and under General Thomas took

charge of the work and supplies of the White Women Refugee's Hospital. In 1866 she returned to her father's home. Subsequently she spent a year and a half in temperance work in western New York. Her next movement was to turn pioneer. In company with one of her brothers she settled in Nebraska, preëmpting a homestead, on which she lived two years. During that period and for two years afterward she filled the office of Grand Vice-Templar in the order of Good Templars, and for the three years following she was the general superintendent of the juvenile work in the same organization. Then the crusade spirit fired the great West, and, laying down her Good Templar work, with other sisters, she joined in the crusade against the saloons in Lincoln, Neb. Since that period her heart and service have been with the Woman's Christian Temperance Union. In 1880, in Lincoln, Neb., she became the wife of Rev. Joseph Cadwallader, of the Congregational Church. On account of his failing health they removed to Jacksonville, Fla., where in 1886 she was made president of the State Woman's Christian Temperance Union. In that office she brought the work in that State from a condition of apathy and indifference to a healthy and steadily increasing growth in the principles of temperance and prohibition, and to a juster appreciation of the power of woman in the world's progress and philanthropies. In all her work she has been assisted by her husband, until Mr. Cadwallader is almost as well known in Woman's Christian Temperance Union circles as his wife. In addition to her temperance labors, Mrs. Cadwallader has entered into church service. She has been an active member of St. Luke's Hospital board of managers, composed entirely of women, and she has been on the board of the Orphanage and Home for the Friendless. These institutions are in Jacksonville. Mission and jail work have shared her labors. During 1890, when she was traveling with her husband, she everywhere found something to do, besides keeping a constant oversight of the work in her own State. Later she was in Asheville, N. C., attending the Woman's Christian Temperance Union Assembly and reporting the meetings to her State paper, the "Telephone." She resigned her position as State president and is now engaged in the crowning work of her life, the establishment of the Woman's Industrial Home, in Augusta, Ga. That institution has received from Mr. and Mrs. Cadwallader considerable sums of money, and it is now in successful operation. It is an institution designed for the reclamation of fallen women.

CADY, Mrs. Helena Maxwell, doctor of medicine, born in New Orleans, La., 26th April, 1849. She spent most of her youth in Cuba, where her father, Patric W. Maxwell, a civil engineer, was engaged in the erection of sugar engines and the building of bridges and railroads. Her grandfather, Dr. John Maxwell, of Dundee, Scotland, was a surgeon in the British army for many years. Her father never claimed his Scotch inheritance, which included a baronetcy. Helena did not enjoy the best of educational opportunities, as Cuba was not then a land of general education. She was married to Mr. Cady in 1870 and has a family of seven living children. While living in Arkansas, after the Civil War, she became interested in medicine, and in adversity she turned her attention to that profession. She took a course in the Homeopathic School of Physicians and Surgeons in St. Louis. After graduating M. D., she practiced for several years in Little Rock, Ark. Leaving that city, she settled in Louisville, Ky., where she is now engaged in successful practice. In addition to her professional and literary work, Dr. Cady has been active in philanthropic work. She is a member of the Episcopal Church, a King's Daughter, a worker and member of the Woman's Christian Temper-

HELENA MAXWELL CADY.

ance Union, a member of the Woman Suffrage Association of Louisville, and president of a circle of the women of the Grand Army of the Republic. She was for several years one of the staff of physicians of the Little Rock Free Dispensary. She is a member of the Southern Homeopathic Medical Association and of the Kentucky Homeopathic Medical Society. She is a busy and successful woman, and has written considerably, both in prose and verse.

CAMERON, Mrs. Elizabeth, editor, born in Niagara, Ont., Can., 8th March, 1851. Her maiden name was Millar. Her early years were passed in Montreal and Kingston, and afterwards in London, Canada, where she became the wife, 30th September, 1869, of John Cameron, founder and conductor of the London "Ontario Advertiser." In that city she now resides. Educated in private and public schools, Mrs. Cameron has always been an insatiable, but discriminating, reader. Her acquaintance with general literature is large, and she has established several reading clubs for women. She is strongly interested in temperance work, is superintendent of the franchise department of the London Woman's Christian Temperance Union, and is wholly of the opinion that the monster intemperance will never be overthrown permanently till women are allowed to vote. She conducts, with the coöperation of Miss Agnes Ethelwyn Wetherald, a monthly paper, "Wives and Daughters," which has a large circulation in the United States as well as in Canada. As presiding genius of that journal, her mission has been and is to stimulate women to become, not only housekeepers in the highest sense, but to be better furnished mentally by systematic good reading, more intelligent as mothers,

well informed concerning the chief wants of the day, and thoroughly equipped intellectually and spiritually for all the duties of womanhood.

CAMPBELL, Mrs. Eugenia Steele, temperance reformer, born in Springfield, Mich., 31st May, 1843. She is the daughter of the Rev. Salmon and Adelaide Ruth Steele. Her ancestors on her father's side were purely American, and were associated with the early settlement of the colonies of Connecticut and Massachusetts. On her mother's side she mingles both French and Scotch blood. Her mother's great-grandfather was in the French Revolution, and with his brother fled to America. They settled in Granby county, took up a section of land, married and raised families. Her grandfather Perrin was an American who fought in the Revolutionary War. At school Mrs. Campbell was proficient in her studies. At the age of eight years she attended a night-school, which was held for the benefit of the miners in the copper country. It was held next door, by a teacher whose home was with her family. At the age of thirteen years she entered Albion College, where her standing in scholarship was the highest. She spent her first vacation in teaching a district school. Her father being in the pastorate of the Methodist Episcopal Church for fifty years, and subject to frequent removals by the law of the church, she was brought into contact with all classes of people, and such a life developed in her a strong self-reliance. She was happily married to Robert A. Campbell, of New York State, 25th April, 1863. After spending eighteen months on the old homestead of the husband, they returned to Michigan. She has since devoted all her energies to the cause of temperance, in which she has been a prominent factor. She

ELIZABETH CAMERON.

was among the first to associate herself with the Woman's Christian Temperance Union, and she has spared neither time nor money to promote its interests. She has been called continuously to preside in its assemblies, as president of local, county and district unions. She has for the past eleven years been president of a district, and thus for that time a member of the State executive board of the Woman's Christian Temperance Union of Michigan. For nearly three years she acted as secretary for Henry A. Reynolds, of red-ribbon fame, making his dates and keeping him constantly in the field, winning at that time the name of "Never-say-die Campbell," which was given in a paper read at a State meeting by Mrs. C. H. Johnson. Modest and unassuming, she has by her faculty of perception and indomitable perseverance endeared herself to a large circle of the best workers in both church and temperance causes. She excels in parliamentary drills in her conventions, and in planning and sending through her district the best speakers. For twelve years previous to the Crusade, she conducted a large store in millinery and fancy goods. She is the mother of three sons, one of whom died in infancy. Her two remaining sons now grown to manhood, together with her husband, have given her much aid in carrying on her temperance work. Mr. and Mrs. Campbell have conducted a large hotel for four years past in Manistique, Mich.

CAMPBELL, Miss Evelyn, actor, born in Waterloo, England, in 1868. She is the daughter of Conrad and Helen Petrie. Coming to America when she was quite young, the family settled in New York City, where Evelyn entered the Lyceum School for Dramatic Expression, under the charge of L. D. Sargent. She remained there three months, after which she was with a traveling company for two years. She then became a member of Palmer's company in "Jim the Penman." She won a suc-

EVELYN CAMPBELL.

earned a fine reputation for a conscientious and natural portrayal of the characters she represents. She is interested in all that pertains to her profession and studies painting as a recreation. She has won the commendation of the fastidious Boston critics, and her career is one that promises future progress.

CAMPBELL, Miss Georgine, artist, born in New Orleans, La. She is a daughter of Dr. George W. Campbell, a descendant of the distinguished Scotch family of that name. Her father was one of the wealthiest and most influential men in the South, and the family have been prominent social leaders of New Orleans for many generations. Miss Campbell passed her early childhood in New Orleans, going thence to Paris. In that city the Louvre headed the list of attractions for her, and frequenters of the galleries were often surprised to see a little girl pulling her staid "bonne" by the hand to where some masterpiece was hanging, and standing in admiration before it. She spent several years of study in Paris. Loving her art as she does, she could but make it a success, and when, after the death of her father, the family suffered reverses, she used as a profession the art to which she had devoted herself as a pleasure. She made portraiture a specialty and her genius was soon recognized. Among her sitters have been many of the most prominent men and women of the country. She is now one of the successful artists of New York City, where her home and studio are. It is an indescribable touch of life in her pictures that has won for Miss Campbell her laurels. She has received favorable mention on several occasions when her pictures have been exhibited, and in the World's Fair in New Orleans in 1883 and 1884 she received the blue ribbon.

CAMPBELL, Mrs. Helen S., author and editor, born in Lockport, N. Y., 4th July, 1839. She is of Scotch ancestors on both sides of the

EUGENIA STEELE CAMPBELL.

cess in the character of the daughter and remained with that company two years. She then joined the Boston Museum Company and is always warmly received by its patrons. Although young, she has

house. Twelve months after her birth her father, Homer H. Stuart, removed to New York City, where he lived until his death, in 1890, and where as a lawyer and a citizen he filled with honor

GEORGINE CAMPBELL.

various responsible positions. Married at the age of twenty to an army surgeon, she thereafter lived in various portions of the United States, during which time she gained that broad experience which has reappeared in her literary work. Endowed with abundant vitality, great imagination, power of dramatic expression and a profoundly sympathetic nature, it was impossible for the young woman to live an idle life. At the age of twenty-three, under her married name, Helen C. Weeks, she began work for children, writing steadily for "Our Young Folks," the "Riverside Magazine" and other juvenile periodicals. Like all her subsequent work, these articles were vital, magnetic and infused with both humor and pathos. Soon her stories grew in length, and the "Ainslee Series" was issued in book form. This comprised "Ainslee," "Grandpa's House," "Four and What They Did" and "White and Red." They were exceedingly popular and still find a sale. All of them were reprinted in England. Her next works were "Six Sinners," "His Grandmothers" and "The American Girl's Hand-book of Work and Play." About 1882 she became literary and household editor of "Our Continent," and wrote for its pages the popular novel entitled "Under Green Apple Boughs," followed by the "What-to-do-Club." These latter books were preceded by several others, entitled "Unto the Third and Fourth Generation," "The Easiest Way in Housekeeping and Cooking" and the "Problem of the Poor." With the last mentioned book, which gave an impetus to much work along the same lines by other writers, began Mrs. Campbell's special interest in the poor. This appeared in 1880, and drew great attention toward plans

for alleviating the miseries of the ignorant and impoverished in New York City. Some of the conclusions reached by Mrs. Campbell appeared in her novel, "Mrs. Herndon's Income," which was printed first as a serial in the "Christian Union," and was afterward issued in book-form. This powerful book at once lifted Mrs. Campbell to an exalted place as a novelist, while her thrilling story won the attention of philanthropists and reformers the world over. Attracted by this volume, in 1886, the New York "Tribune" appointed her its commissioner to investigate the condition of women wage-earners in New York, and that work resulted in a series of papers under the title of "Prisoners of Poverty," which caused a profound and widespread sensation respecting the life of wage-women in the metropolis. It may be regarded as the seed from which has issued a vast amount of literature upon the topic, resulting in great amelioration in the condition of a large, and at that time nearly helpless, body of workers. Soon afterwards Mrs. Campbell went abroad to investigate the lives of wage-earners in London, Paris, Italy and Germany. There she remained eighteen months or more, the fruits of her work appearing, upon her return to this country, in "Prisoners of Poverty Abroad." Following that came "Miss Melinda's Opportunity" and "Roger Berkley's Probation," two short novels, and, later, "Anne Bradstreet and Her Time," a historical study of early colonial life, "A Sylvan City," having already done the same thing for Philadelphia. The latest published work of Mrs. Campbell, "Darkness and Daylight in New York," is a series of graphic portraitures of the salient features of the city. In 1890 Mrs. Campbell received a prize from the American

HELEN S. CAMPBELL.

Economical Association for a monograph upon "Women Wage-Earners." She has contributed many articles on economic subjects to reviews and magazines. Her home is in New York City.

CANFIELD, Mrs. Corresta T., physician, born in Chardon, Ohio, 6th March, 1833. The Canfields, for meritorious service, received from the king of England, in 1350, a grant of land on

CORRESTA T. CANFIELD.

the river Cam, in Yorkshire, and settled thereon. After occupying that grant for three-hundred years, they came to America, shortly after the arrival of the Plymouth Pilgrims, and were among the first settlers of New Haven, Conn. Dr. Canfield is descended from French Huguenots and New England Presbyterians. Her mother, reared at a time when it was thought a sin for a man to kiss his wife or babe on Sunday, did not neglect the moral training of her children. Intellectual, well-read, in advance of her time, the daughter has inherited energy, will power and executive ability. Corresta entered the seminary of Chardon at an early age, but she was soon married. Though a wife and mother, reading and study were kept up. From her childhood she was ambitious to be a physician. Left alone without resources, at the close of the Civil War, the ambitions of early youth revived. In 1869 she entered the Woman's Homeopathic College of Cleveland, Ohio. With the help of a half-year's scholarship Mrs. Canfield finished the first college year. In the second year she became an assistant of the president, Dr. Myra K. Merrick, and gained means to continue in college. She was graduated with first honors in 1871, having served for some time as demonstrator of anatomy. During the following summer she practiced in Fort Wayne, Ind., earning enough to enable her to enter the Men's Homeopathic College of Cleveland. While there, she was demonstrator of anatomy in the woman's department, and practiced enough, visiting patients mornings and evenings, to defray expenses. She attended all the lectures, passed through the whole curriculum and was graduated third in the men's course, the faculty acknowledging that she was entitled to a prize, but would not

establish a precedent by awarding it to a practicing physician. A full-fledged M. D., she settled in Titusville, Pa. Having but fifteen dollars capital, she borrowed enough to buy out a resident physician, and under great opposition so won public patronage as to pay all her debts the first year. There she remained nearly ten years and amassed a snug sum. She next spent a year in traveling. In 1882 she settled in Chicago, where she has built up a large practice and served in many public offices. She is at present a member of the board of censors of the American Institute of Homeopathy, having been elected for the second time. She was the first woman who served in that capacity. One was elected the previous year but was not allowed to serve on the board of censors. Three years before her admission women were not permitted to join that society, and much opprobrium was still attached to those "hybrids" who did. Even women shared in that feeling. After a time, seeing none of her sex actively represented in the society, she felt that, to enjoy its privileges, one should assume its duties. She therefore prepared a paper and read it before the institute. She has served as president, vice-president and secretary of the Woman's Medical Association of Chicago, vice-president of the Hahnemann Clinical for two years, and has been appointed on the woman's committee for a homeopathic congress to be held during the World's Columbian Exposition in 1893.

CAPPIANI, Mme. Luisa, operatic singer and musical educator, was born in Trieste, Austria. Her maiden name was Young. Her paternal grandfather was a noted Scotchman who was a professor in the University of Munich. Her father was a dramatic tenor, and her mother was a Ger-

LUISA CAPPIANI.

man woman of high social rank. At the age of six years Luisa was a musical prodigy, and she received a thorough musical education. At the age of seventeen she was married to Mr. Kapp, an

Austrian counselor. Her husband died three years after their marriage, leaving her with two children, a son and a daughter, and with only the usual small pension to support and educate her family. After a period of prostration Mme. Kapp aroused herself and began to make use of her talents and her training. She succeeded and earned ample means to educate her children. When Mme. Kapp began her musical career, she combined her names Kapp and Young, in the usual manner, Kapp-Young. Her teachers had been in Vienna Miss Fröhlich and the tenor Passadonna, and in Italy San Giovanni, Vanucini, Gamberini, the elder Romani and old Lamperti. Her aristocratic friends persuaded her to give two public concerts, which were so successful that Rubinstein and Piatti engaged her for their concerts in Vienna, where she lived with her mother. She was then called to court concerts in Vienna, Prague and Coburg-Gotha. In Munich her concerts brought an invitation to sing in opera. That decided her operatic career. She sang with her brother, Fred Young, in "La Juive," and under his guidance, while he sang Eleasar, her Rachelle was, on 13th May, 1860, a complete success. After that she appeared in London under the auspices and at the residence of Viscountess Palmerston, her crowning triumph being in a concert given by the Queen in the Golden Room of Buckingham Palace to the King of Belgium. Her teachers in dramatic action were her brother, the tenor Young, and his wife, and Lucille Grahn. After appearing in the Royal Theater, Hanover, she was called to Frankfort-on-the-Main, and thence to the Grand Duchy of Hesse-Cassel. At the request of the Intendant she made her début there as Lucrezia. Her Valentine in "The Huguenots," Fides in "The Prophet" and Leonore in "Fidelio" made an impression. Herman Levi, then leader of the Grand Opera in Rotterdam, engaged her after her rendering of Elizabeth in "Tannhäuser." Her appearance in Rotterdam as Ortrud in "Lohengrin" created a furore. After that she appeared in Pesth, Prague and Vienna. The sudden death of her mother caused a severe illness. A sojourn at Como restored her health so that she could sing in a festival in Bergamo. After that she sang in Italian her great rôle of Valentine in La Scala, in Milan, and then filled engagements for Italian opera in Bucharest and in the Imperial Theater, Nice. The great carnival of Parma followed, and there she created the rôle of Selika, singing it thirty-two times in one carnival. Vianesi, the leader of the Liceo in Barcelona, engaged her after that event. The Imperial Theater of Tiflis, Russia, was her next, though dearly bought, triumph. At the end of the season she contracted bronchitis. Permitted by a foolish physician and over-persuaded by the Intendant and the Prince, she sang, despite her illness. An enthusiastic torchlight procession in her honor closed the evening, but the voice which had entranced the populace was mute to acknowledge the ovation, and that night she was at the point of death by suffocation, in consequence of the ill-advised vocal exertion. September, 1868, the city of Arezzo bestowed upon her, for her singing in a festival, the gold medal of merit by King Victor Emanuel's decree. Six months after, imagining herself cured, she accepted an engagement from Max Maretzek for the Academy of Music, New York. The stormy passage brought on a relapse; still she appeared with remarkable success in "L'Africaine" at the Academy in 1868–69. At that time she discovered in her art fortunate secrets which enabled her to overcome the difficulties brought on her by bronchitis, and the knowledge of which has since made her

famous as a teacher. After one season in America she retired from the stage and went to Milan, and there soon and often was called upon to advise young singers. After teaching in Milan two years she accepted an invitation from Boston, and, when singing in a Harvard concert, fused her name into Cappiani, to satisfy an existing popular prejudice. In 1881 she was induced to settle in New York, and there she has been very successful as a trainer. Her essays on the voice are reproduced in many musical papers in this and foreign countries, notably in Germany. When the board of examiners of the American College of Musicians was organized in Cleveland, Ohio, she was the only woman elected among eighteen professors. At a subsequent meeting in New York she was reëlected.

CARDWILL, Miss Mary E., was born in Louisville, Ky. While she was yet a child, her parents moved to New Albany, Ind., where she has passed her life. In her early years her health was impaired by too close application to books, and she was forced to give up school work at fifteen years of age, just when it would have been most valuable to her. She began her literary career by working in the interests of reform. Almost every advance movement of the last ten years has re-

MARY E. CARDWILL.

ceived substantial aid from her pen. Some years ago she became very much interested in Shakespeare's dramas. After a course of careful training in that direction, she wrote a number of philosophical and discriminating essays upon the plays. Those articles attracted attention in high literary circles. In June, 1886, in the first convention of the Western Association of Writers, Miss Cardwill contributed a paper on "The Successful Study of Shakespeare." In June, 1888, she was chosen corresponding secretary of that association, and in the following year she was chosen as secretary. In her official capacity, as corresponding secretary, she was associated with Mrs. L. May Wheeler as editor of the "Western Association of Writers Souvenir for 1888," and in the following year she became the sole editor of the souvenir for that year.

CARHART, Mrs. Clara H. Sully, educator and reformer, born in Ottawa, Canada, 30th April,

CLARA H. SULLY CARHART.

1845. She is of English parentage. Her maternal grandfather, J. G. Playter, who was a government official from the first settlement of that city, was descended from an old family of English nobility of that name. In early life Mrs. Carhart showed an unusual aptitude for books. Her school duties were ever a source of enjoyment, and she decided to become a teacher. At ten years of age she was sent to a boarding-school in Ottawa, Canada, where she excelled in music. After two years she returned home, and studied in the Buffalo high school, until the removal of her parents to Darien Center, N. Y., where she attended the seminary. After graduating, she began to teach. In 1861, after the death of her father, the family removed to Davenport, Iowa. She immediately entered the city school there and for six years held high rank as a teacher. At the solicitation of the school-board she inaugurated a system of musical instruction, including every grade of all the city schools. On 5th October, 1871, she became the wife of Rev. Lewis H. Carhart, a young Methodist Episcopal minister, and with him went to live in Charles City, Iowa. Their family consists of two children. There she entered heartily into his work and seconded all his efforts to build up the church. Soon after the Civil War she went to Texas with her husband, who had been a captain in the Union army, and had volunteered in the work of reorganizing the Methodist Episcopal Church in the South. They had to work in the face of bitter opposition, but, largely owing to Mrs. Carhart's activity and popularity, large congregations were formed and churches were built in Dallas, Sherman and neighboring cities. In 1883 her husband

retired from the active ministry, and they went to make their home in Brooklyn, N. Y., to be near Mrs. Carhart's family. She became much interested in the work of the Woman's Christian Temperance Union, being secretary of one of the largest local unions, and afterward president of the young women's work in Suffolk county. While on a visit in Donley county, Texas, she organized a local union, which union so aroused public sentiment that within eight months afterward the saloons in that county were closed by popular vote. She became interested in the social condition of the working-girls of Brooklyn. Prominent women were called together from the churches of the city, and in 1885 they planted the Bedford Club in the heart of a district where shop-girls and factory operatives live. The aim was the bettering of the social condition of those girls, offering them innocent amusements and instruction in practical branches. The work has since grown incredibly. Of that society she was the first president. She was thus the pioneer in establishing girls' clubs, which become such an important factor in the lives of the working-girls of New York and Brooklyn. For six years Mrs. Carhart held the position of corresponding secretary of the Woman's Home Missionary Society of the Methodist Episcopal Church, in the New York East Conference, and she has been a great factor in its success. For six years she was sent as a representative to the national conventions, and in 1889 represented that society on the platform of the National Woman's Christian Temperance Union in Chicago. She is a member of the advisory council of the woman's branch of the World's Columbian Exposition in Chicago.

CARLISLE, Mrs. Mary Jane, social leader, born in Covington, Kenton county, Ky., 28th August,

MARY JANE CARLISLE.

1835. Her father, Major John Allen Goodson, fought through the war of 1812, and served several terms in the House of Representatives and the Senate, and was for four years mayor of Covington. He bore a strong resemblance to Gen. Jackson, both physically and mentally. He was a man of great will power and personal courage and exerted a strong influence in politics. He married, when forty years of age, Hetty Wasson, of Covington. His daughter possesses much of her father's strength of character. She was educated in the Covington schools and became the wife of John Griffin Carlisle, 25th January, 1857. She is the mother of five children, two of whom are living, William Kinkaed and Lilbon Logan, both lawyers. Mrs. Carlisle's strong personality has much to do with her husband's success in life. She is popular in Washington society, makes many friends and keeps them by being true in her friendships, gladly making sacrifices and suffering inconveniences for others. Her husband, Senator Carlisle, ex-speaker of the House, is known throughout the United States. The support of such women as Mrs. Carlisle is a powerful factor in the lives of all men, and to her more than any other does Mr. Carlisle owe all that is true to himself, that places him in the front rank of the great thinkers and of the great statesmen of the age.

CARPENTER, Mrs. Alice Dimmick, traveler, was born in Milford, Pa. She is descended from the English family of Dymokes. The founders of the American branch came to this country in 1635, and many members of the family have been conspicuous in the social, financial and political history of Pennsylvania and New York. Her father, Milton Dimmick, was a prominent lawyer of Milford, Pa. Her mother was Elizabeth Allen, a daughter of Rev. Edward Allen. The early death of Mr. Dimmick left the widow with three young children. Alice was delicate and passed the

ALICE DIMMICK CARPENTER.

years of her childhood as an invalid, but she possessed a bright and cheerful disposition that made her life a pleasure despite her weakness. The family lived in various cities. For seven years Mrs.

Carpenter lived in Chicago, where she was prominent in art, music and literature, and in club life. She has published one volume of verse, " Poems Original and Translated" (Chicago, 1882). One of her most important productions is a pamphlet entitled "The Man Material," which attempts to prove the doctrine of materialism. She has traveled extensively in this country, Canada and Europe. She passes her winters on the Pacific Coast.

CARPENTER, Miss Ellen M., artist, born in Killingly, Conn., 28th November, 1836. While

ELLEN M. CARPENTER.

noted in school for correct drawing, it was not until 1858 her attention was called to the study of art. She first studied with Thomas Edward, of Worcester, Mass., and afterwards drew in the Lowell Institute, Boston, for several years. In 1867 she went to Paris, where she gained a new impetus in study. From that time she has been a popular teacher, having, both in school and studio, numerous classes in drawing, water-color and oil painting. She accompanied some of her students on a European tour in 1873, traveling and sketching extensively. In her own country she has painted from nature numerous scenes in the South, in California and in many noted localities. In 1878 she began seriously to study face and figure, going to Europe for special work. She studied with the portrait painter, Gusson, in Berlin, for a while, and then went to Paris, where she attended Julien's and Carlo Rossi's schools. She copied portraits of several noted Masons for the Masonic Temple in Boston. Her commissions have been numerous. In 1890 she had commissions which took her to Paris, to copy "The Immaculate Conception" and "The Holy Family" by Murillo, and several of the noted modern paintings in the museum of the Luxembourg. In the same year she was in Algiers and Spain, sketching eastern life and manners, and painted several interiors from the Alhambra and Palace in Seville. Her home is in Boston.

CARROLL, Miss Anna Ella, political writer and military genius, born in Kingston Hall, the ancestral residence of her father, Governor Thomas King Carroll, Somerset county, Md., 29th August, 1815. Her mother was Juliana Stevenson, the daughter of Colonel Henry James Stevenson, who had come over in the British army as surgeon during the Revolutionary War. Dr. Stevenson, though a stanch Tory, was beloved for the care bestowed by him upon the wounded of both armies. He settled in Baltimore, became greatly distinguished in his profession and built a beautiful residence on Parnassus Hill. Thomas King Carroll married Miss Stevenson in his twentieth year, and Anna Ella was the oldest child of this youthful couple. She early showed a remarkable character, reading law with her father at a youthful age, and following with interest his political career. She soon began to write for the press. Her first published work was entitled "The Great American Battle, or Po-

ANNA ELLA CARROLL.

litical Romanism." This was followed by "The Star of the West," describing the origin of our claims to the western territories, their conditions and their needs, and urging the building of the Pacific railroad. Miss Carroll took an active part in the election of Governor Hicks of Maryland, in 1860, and when the Civil War broke out she used her influence to hold Governor Hicks to the Union, thus saving Maryland from secession and securing the safety of the National Capital. Seeing that slavery was at the root of the rebellion, she freed her own slaves at a great sacrifice and gave herself up enthusiastically to the support of the national cause, using her great social influence and her connection with the press to secure the loyalty of her State. Miss Carroll had become a communicant of the Presbyterian Church in Baltimore, of which Dr. Robert J. Breckenridge, a loyal unionist, was pastor. He was a man of great influence and distinction. His nephew, John C. Breckenridge, at one

time a warm friend of Miss Carroll, became a leading secessionist. Immediately after President Lincoln's accession he made a very clever and violent speech, charging Mr. Lincoln and the North with having made the war. This speech was especially designed to carry Maryland out of the Union. Miss Carroll, perceiving at once its baleful effect upon her own State, determined to answer it, and did so in a pamphlet of consummate ability. By the use of documents in her possession she showed that the Southern leaders from the time of Calhoun had been preparing for the war, and that for ten years previous the whole secession movement had been planned, even in its details. Mr. Lincoln and his cabinet were pleased with that vindication, and the Republican party decided that the pamphlet should be used as a campaign document and sent broadcast over Maryland. Thus encouraged, Miss Carroll herself, mainly at her own expense, printed and circulated 50,000 copies. James Tilghman, of the Union Committee of Baltimore, wrote her that he "set his son at the door of his house in Camden street, and that five-hundred men called for the pamphlet in a single day, and that these were the bone and sinew of the city, wanting to know in which army they ought to enlist." Mr. Lincoln and the war department, perceiving Miss Carroll's ability, engaged her to continue to write in support of the government. At their suggestion she prepared a pamphlet on the war powers of the government. Copies of two editions of this pamphlet may be seen side by side in the bound volumes of manuscript in the State department. That paper was followed by one on the "Power of the President to suspend the writ of habeas corpus," and later a paper on "Reconstruction," showing that emancipation could come only as a war measure, the State constitutions giving no opening for emancipation. The examination was made at President Lincoln's express desire. When Miss Carroll was preparing her war papers, it was suggested to her by Mr. Lincoln that she should go to St. Louis and endeavor to form an opinion of the probable success or failure of a most important expedition preparing to descend the Mississippi by means of gunboats. It was a critical time. The Union armies were costing the government two millions a day, and up to that time had met with little else than defeat. The country was deeply despondent, the failure of the Union cause was predicted and the European powers were in haste to grant recognition to the Confederacy. Mr. Lincoln and the administration were in the deepest anxiety, for they felt that defeat upon the Mississippi would be fatal. Miss Carroll repaired to St. Louis, visiting the encampments and examining carefully the topography of the country, conversing with pilots and others. She reported the Mississippi as frowning with fortifications and the tides as unfavorable. She became convinced that the proposed descent by the gunboats would be fatal, and, inquiring carefully concerning the Tennessee river, it occurred to her that that was the true strategic line. The rebel leaders not having perceived this, it had not been fortified. Miss Carroll called in her friend, Judge Evans, of Texas, who had a rare knowledge of the topography of that part of the country He was struck by the sagacity and wisdom of her plan and advised her to lose no time in laying it before the war department. He assisted her in drawing up a map to accompany her written plan of campaign, and she hastened to Washington, and on 30th November, 1861, taking both papers to the war department, she laid them before Thomas A. Scott, then assistant secretary of war, explaining her views. Mr. Scott, the great railroad magnate, recognized at once the immense importance of her plans and hastened with them to Lincoln, who evinced the greatest delight at the solution of the problem. He called in Benjamin F. Wade, president of the committee on the conduct of the war, telling him that he felt no doubt that this was the true move, but he feared to inaugurate a movement that was the work of a civilian and a woman. It was decided that the authorship of the plan must be kept secret so long as the war lasted, and urged by Mr. Wade, President Lincoln determined to take the initiative and change the plan of the campaign to the Tennessee. Mr. Stanton was put in office pledged to this measure, and the President was in favor of a plan that promised such fruitful results in the near future. Thomas A. Scott was sent to organize the Western troops, as he testified, to carry out her plans. In furtherance of this secret plan the western armies, to the amazement of the Confederacy, were suddenly transferred from the Mississippi up the Tennessee river. The most brillliant result followed. Fort Henry fell, Fort Donelson was taken, the Confederacy was divided and the rebel armies cut off from their source of supplies. The ultimate triumph of the Federal armies was assured. Great rejoicings took place. President Lincoln issued a proclamation of public thanksgiving, and discussions were held in the Senate and in the House to try to discover how this brilliant plan originated. Miss Carroll sat in the gallery, quietly listening, but made no sign, having been advised that it was absolutely necessary that the authorship of the plan should not be made known. She continued her work, suggesting new moves, by a series of letters to the war department, there placed on file. When repeated reverses were suffered in attempting to take Vicksburg by the river, Miss Carroll prepared another remarkable paper, accompanied by a map showing the fortifications, proving that they could not be taken from the water and advising an attack in the rear. She took those plans to the war office, and Mr. Wade has testified that they were at once sent out to the proper military authorities, and that the fall of Vicksburg and also of Island No. 10 was in consequence of her sagacious suggestions. On subjects connected with the war, and subsequently on reconstruction, Miss Carroll continued her contributions to the press, but, owing to Mr. Lincoln's untimely death, she was left unrecognized, and she presented in vain her very moderate bill to the government for her work in writing the pamphlets. Thomas A. Scott testified that the writings were authorized by the government, and that the bill was very moderate and ought to be paid, but the application met only neglect. After the war Miss Carroll was advised that she ought to make known her authorship of the plan of the Tennessee campaign, proved by a succession of letters in the keeping of the war department and by the direct testimony of Thomas A. Scott, assistant secretary of war, Hon. Benjamin F. Wade, president of the committee for the conduct of the war, Judge Evans, of Texas, and others. Accordingly, in 1871, a military commission under General Howard was appointed by Congress to inquire into the claim. Mr. Scott wrote to the committee, and Mr. Wade and Judge Evans gave their testimony in person. The evidence being incontrovertible, the committee through General Howard, reporting 2nd February, 1871, fully endorsed the claim, but when it came to public acknowledgment and award, political influence caused it to be ignored. Again it was brought up in 1872, and Mr. Wilson left it on record, that the claim was "uncontrovertible." Still it was neglected. In 1879 this claim was again examined by a congressional military committee, who reported through Mr. Cockrell, 18th February, 1879. Although this report was adverse to congressional recognition and award, it admitted the services, both literary and military, even conceding the proposition that "the transfer of the national armies from the banks of the Ohio up the Tennessee river to the decisive position in Mississippi was the greatest military event in the interest of the human race known to modern ages, and will ever rank among the very few strategic movements in the world's history that have decided the fate of empires and people"; and that "no true history can be written that does not assign to the memorialist (Miss Carroll) the credit of the conception." In 1881 a congressional military committee under General Bragg again reported after examining a great array of original letters and testimony. The report confirmed the admission of the claim in the strongest terms, and bills were brought in for the relief of Miss Carroll, now aged and infirm. But the report was reserved for the last day of Congress, and, like the preceding ones, was utterly neglected. Miss Carroll immediately after was stricken with paralysis. For three years her life was despaired of. Although she subsequently rallied, she has remained ever since a confirmed invalid, supported and cared for by her devoted sister, Miss Mary H. Carroll, now working as a clerk in the Treasury office, after a season of great privation and trial. In 1885 Miss Carroll's case was brought before the Court of Claims, but, owing to her illness, she could take no part in presenting the evidence. However, her papers were such that the Court of Claims gave its moral assent and retransmitted the case to Congress for action thereon, but nothing has yet been done. Each year a number of petitions are sent in from all over the land, praying Congress for Miss Carroll's recognition and award, and quietly the aged and noble authoress awaits the inevitable recognition of the future. A warm interest being taken in this case by prominent ladies, during the Woman's Council in Washington, in the spring of 1891, the case was brought up and a great desire expressed for an investigation and a biographical account of Miss Carroll. Subscriptions were secured, and a biography with the congressional documents was prepared by Miss Sarah Ellen Blackwell, and printed under the title, "A Military Genius; Life of Anna Ella Carroll, the Great Unrecognized Member of Lincoln's Cabinet."

CARRINGTON, Miss Abbie, operatic singer, born in Fond du Lac, Wis., 13th June, 1856. Her musical talents showed themselves at an early age. In September, 1875, she went to Boston, Mass., and studied under J. H. Wheeler. In 1887 she was graduated from the New England Conservatory. She then went to Italy, where she began the study of opera under Giuseppe Perini, and after one year of study she made her début in Milan, in "Traviata." In Cervia and Ravenna she won a triumph as Gilda, in "Rigoletto." She was next engaged for a season of two months in Turin and for one month in Brescia; then she went to Venice to sing during the Carnival season. She made her début in the United States on 7th October, 1879, in Boston, Mass., with the Strakosch Opera Company. She next appeared in New York City with Theodore Thomas and the Philharmonic Society. In January, 1879, she made a tour of the chief American cities, supported by the Mendelssohn Quintette Club of Boston. In 1880–81 she made her first operatic tour with the Strakosch-Hess Grand English Opera Company. In 1881–82 she was re-engaged by Mr. Strakosch to sing on alternate nights with Mme. Etelka Gerster. In 1883–84 Miss

Carrington visited Mexico and achieved so pronounced a success that in Vera Cruz, Orizaba, Pueblo, Monterey and the City of Mexico she received in writing the thanks of the municipality

ABBIE CARRINGTON.

for the great pleasure she had given their people during her stay among them, and as a declaration of their esteem and appreciation made and presented her subscriptions to the amount of $31,000, to re-visit them the following season with her own company. Miss Carrington returned to the United States early in April, and immediately sailed for Europe at the solicitation of Manager Ernest Gye, of Covent Garden Theater, London. While there she secured some of the excellent talent that supported her during the following season, commencing in Richmond, Va., going directly South and to Mexico. During 1884–85 the Abbie Carrington Grand Opera Company proved to be one of the most successful of the organizations on the road. During 1885–86 Miss Carrington reappeared in Italian opera with Her Majesty's Grand Opera Company. In 1887, after six consecutive seasons in grand opera, having sung the leading soprano rôles in twenty different operas, Miss Carrington took a much-needed rest, which resulted in opening a new sphere of work, and since that time she has traveled only with her own company in concert and oratorio. The season of 1890–91, the most successful and extended of her career, was a tour of the Pacific Coast and British Columbia. Miss Carrington's voice is a soprano. Her home is in Fond du Lac.

CARSE, Mrs. Matilda B., philanthropist, temperance worker and financier, is of Scotch-Irish origin. She has lived almost continually in Chicago, Ill., since 1858. Her husband, Thomas Carse, was a railroad manager in Louisville, Ky., during the Civil War. In 1869 they went abroad for the benefit of Mr. Carse's health. He died in Paris, France, in June, 1870, leaving Mrs. Carse

with three boys under seven years of age. The youngest of those while in Paris had a fall, which developed hip disease. He had almost recovered his health, when in 1874, in Chicago, he was run over by a wagon driven by a drunken man and instantly killed. His tragic death caused his mother to devote her life to the alleviation of the poor and suffering, especially among children. She registered a vow that, until the last hour of her life, she would devote every power of which she was possessed to annihilate the liquor traffic, and with a persistency never surpassed, has bravely kept her word. She early became prominent in temperance work, and has been president of the Chicago Central Woman's Temperance Union since 1878. That union is one of the most active in the country, and supports more charities than any other. To Mrs. Carse is due the credit of establishing, under the auspices of her union, the first creché, or day nursery in Chicago, known as the Bethesda Day Nursery. That was followed in a year or two by the establishment, through her efforts, of a second, known as the Talcott Day Nursery. Beside those nurseries the union supports two kindergartens among the very poorest class; two gospel temperance meetings that are nightly attended by crowds of intemperate men, seeking to be saved from themselves; two Sunday-schools; the Anchorage Mission, a home for erring girls who have only taken the first step in wrong doing, and desire to return to a pure life; a reading room for men; two dispensaries for the poor; two industrial schools, and three mother's meetings. Those charities are supported at a cost of over ten-thousand dollars yearly. Mrs. Carse personally raises almost the entire amount. She founded the Woman's Temperance Publishing Association, and in January, 1880, the first number of the "Signal" was published, a large sixteen-page weekly paper. Two years later "Our Union" was merged with it, and as the "Union Signal" it became the national organ of the society. Mrs. Carse also started the first stock company entirely composed of women, as no man can own stock in the Woman's Temperance Publishing Association. It was started with a capital stock of five-thousand dollars, which has been increased to one-hundred-twenty-five-thousand dollars; from having but one paid employee, it now has one-hundred-thirty-five persons on its pay-roll. Mrs. Carse has been the president and financial backer of the association since its first inception. In 1885 she began planning for the great building, the Woman's Temperance Temple in Chicago, the national headquarters of the Woman's Christian Temperance Union. The ground is valued at one-million dollars; the building cost one-million-two-hundred-thousand dollars; the rentals from the building will bring in an annual income of over two-hundred-thousand dollars; the capital stock is six-hundred-thousand dollars, one-half of which is now owned by the Woman's Christian Temperance Union, and it is expected all will be secured to that association. Mrs. Carse is founder and president of the Woman's Dormitory Association of the Columbian Exposition. That work was done in connection with the Board of Lady Managers of the World's Columbian Exposition, of which she is a member. She was the first woman in Cook county to be appointed on the school board where she served a term of years with great acceptability. Her name appears upon several charitable boards as a director. For years she was a member of the board of the Home for Discharged Prisoners. She is also on the free kindergarten boards, and is a member of the Woman's Club of Chicago. In all the wide range of charities to which she has given active help the one that probably lies nearest her heart, and to which she has given a stronger hand of aid than to any other, helping to raise for its buildings and maintenance tens of thousands of dollars, is the Chicago Foundling's Home, the Reverend Dr. George E. Shipman being its founder. She established its aid society, and has been its president since its inception. Mrs. Carse receives no compensation whatever for her services to the public.

CARSON, Mrs. Delia E., educator, born in Athens, N. Y., 25th January, 1833. Her father, Thomas Wilder, was one of eight brothers who migrated from Massachusetts when the eldest was yet a young man. Several were teachers of prominence, and all were closely identified with the development and progress of Genesee and Wyoming counties, New York, where they ultimately settled. Her mother's maiden name was Hannah Dow. Delia Wilder, afterwards Mrs. Carson, was educated in the Alexander Classical Academy. She spent one term in the Albany Normal School and received a diploma therefrom. During 1863 and 1864 she was a teacher in the Ladies' Seminary in Bloomington, Ill., from 1865 to 1871 in Beloit, Wis., and from 1871 to 1887 she was preceptress of Ladies' Hall, State University of Wisconsin, and teacher of mathematics. In the latter capacity she won high distinction, being possessed of liberal culture and having a remarkably healthful social influence upon the hundreds of young women surrounding her. In addition to other accomplishments, Mrs. Carson has devoted much time to the study of art. During recent years she has become identified with general art interests in Wisconsin, giving courses of lectures and leading classes of women in the study of the history of art. She has traveled extensively

DELIA E. CARSON.

in Europe, spending much time in Italy, Sicily, Morocco, Algiers, Egypt and Greece, in pursuit of practical knowledge in her favorite field. She resides in Madison, Wis.

CARTER, Mrs. Hannah Johnson, art educator, born in Portland, Maine. She is the only child of Jonathan True and Hannah True, his wife. Mrs. Carter's father was a wealthy im-

HANNAH JOHNSON CARTER.

porter and commission merchant. Her mother died young, leaving her infant daughter to the care of a devoted father who, early recognizing the artistic tastes of his child, gave her considerable training in that direction. In 1868 Miss True became the wife of Henry Theophilus Carter, a mechanical engineer and manufacturer. The marriage was happy and congenial, and with wealth and high social standing life seemed to hold out to the young couple only sunshine, but soon the shadows began to fall. Financial losses, the failing health of her husband, the death of a loved child and the terrible loneliness of widowhood all came in quick succession. Though nearly crushed by the weight of woe so suddenly forced upon her, Mrs. Carter, with noble independence and courage, began to look about for ways and means to support herself and child. Her mind naturally turned to art, and with the life insurance left her by her husband she entered the Massachusetts Normal Art School and was graduated with high standing. After a year's further study with private teachers in first-class studios, she went to Kingston, Canada, to direct an art school, which, if successful, would receive a government grant. Although laboring under great disadvantages, she succeeded in establishing the school on a permanent basis. At the close of the first year she was obliged to return to Boston, as the climate of Canada was too severe for her health. For two years she was associated with the Prang Educational Company, of that city, doing various work pertaining to its educational department, such as illustrating drawing-books and often acting as drawing supervisor where the Prang system of drawing was in use. In the fall of 1887 she was called to New York City to take the chair of professor of form and drawing in the College for the Training of Teachers, and in 1890 she was elected president of the art department of the National Educational Association. In 1891 she was made director of the art department in the Drexel Institute of Art, Science and Industry, in Philadelphia, Pa. Mrs. Carter has been appointed on many industrial, educational and art committees. She does not confine her energies to local work, but has an interest in general art education, believing enthusiastically in the necessity of educating and elevating public taste by beginning early with the training of children for a love of the aesthetic, through habits of close observation of the beautiful. Mrs. Carter stands among the leading educators, and is an ardent worker for art education.

CARTER, Miss Mary Adaline Edwarda, industrial art instructor and designer, born in Hinesburgh, Chittenden county, near Burlington, Vt. She is the oldest child of Edward H. and Mary

MARY ADALINE EDWARDA CARTER.

Adaline Kellogg Carter. Her parents were natives of Vermont, descended from the early New England settlers, of English and Scotch origin. Her early education was chiefly from nature and object study. After her eighth summer she attended private and public schools in Burlington, Vt., and in Vineland, N. J., where her family removed in 1866. The years of country life spent in southern New Jersey during youth were filled with formative influences that laid a broad and sound basis for her life-work. Circumstances and environments led to finding occupations for herself, or to having them given her, that promoted inventive and executive powers and stimulated love for science and art. Thirst for larger opportunities and higher education developed, but adversities came, over-work, intense mental strain, then long and severe illness. After health was restored, she was by degrees led to industrial art as her vocation. Though beset by obstacles that would have turned aside

one of less resoluteness, her course has been constantly progressive and largely successful. With simply the intention of becoming proficient as a teacher of drawing, she entered the Woman's Art School, Cooper Union, New York. After graduating with highest honors, in 1876, her services were immediately required as a designer for embroidery. While thus engaged, part of her time was still devoted to art study, and throughout her years of working she has been a constant student in art and other educational subjects. In the Centennial Exhibition, in 1876, she made a special study of the needlework, art embroideries and textiles of all countries. Not long after, her water-color studies from nature attracted the notice of John Bennett, the English painter of art-pottery, and she became his pupil and assistant. In 1879 a number of pieces of faïence decorated by her were sent by invitation to the exhibition of Howell, James & Co., London, England. One of her vases was presented to Sir Frederick Leighton, president of the Royal Academy, and others were sold to art museums in England, to be kept as examples of American art pottery. The same year some of her work in faïence was shown in New York, and won much praise. When the Associated Artists began their united enterprise which has done so much in revolutionizing and elevating household taste and interior decoration of American home and public buildings, Miss Carter's services were secured by Louis Tiffany, and she was connected with them several years. At first having to do with all the kinds of work undertaken, glass, mosaics, metals, wood, embroideries, hangings, wall and ceiling coverings, painting or anything else decoratively used in buildings, she was the first woman thus employed. Later, having developed marked ability in plastic art, she had special charge of their pottery and modeling department. Her ornamental relief-work, panels and friezes were often used with heads and figures by St. Gaudens, and combined with work by Colman, Armstrong and other well-known artists in the decoration of public and private buildings in New York and different parts of the country. Her designs for memorial and other windows, for decoration of interiors and for different purposes have been used in churches and homes, both east and west. Frequently artists, draughtsmen, teachers and others have sought instruction from her in special subjects. At different times she taught classes of children in drawing, and in the Woman's Art School one in porcelain painting. Since 1886 she has been instructor of the free classes in clay-modeling, applied design and normal training in form-study and drawing for the Young Woman's Christian Association of New York. The courses of study in those classes and all accessories have been planned by her and most effectively carried out. During the past seventeen years Miss Carter has resided with her family in the upper suburban part of New York City. She is a stanch member of the Woman's Christian Temperance Union and strongly interested in the leading questions and reforms of the day.

CARTWRIGHT, Mrs. Florence Byrne, poet, born in Galena, Ill., 27th December, 1863. She resided for many years in Grass Valley, Cal., where she had charge of the postoffice until May, 1890. In June 1890, she became the wife of Dr. Richard Cartwright, of Salem, Ore., who is a descendant of Edmund Cartwright, D.D., F.R.S., inventor of the power loom, and of Major Cartwright, of colonial fame. Mrs. Cartwright's sympathies are purely Californian, as her parents moved to that State when she was only four months old. Not being strong, she was unable to take a university course, but she had the best of teaching at home. She has traveled extensively. Her future will be devoted to literary work in the Northwest. She is one of the most earnest and enthusiastic devotees of metrical com-

FLORENCE BYRNE CARTWRIGHT.

position on the Pacific Coast, and she has a qualification which few other authors possess, that of taking infinite pains and observing the strictest rules of form, and at the same time producing a careless effect. Her talent runs particularly to old French forms, which appeal to her from their difficulty and novelty, but her favorite style is the sonnet, and her delight in that form never wearies. She has written everything from the simple triolet to the sestina and chant-royal. Her first rondeau was published in the "Californian" in 1882, and her first sestina in the "Overland" in November, 1883. A sestina appearing in "Harper's Magazine" in May, 1884, has been much copied.

CARY, Miss Alice, poet, born near Cincinnati, Ohio, in April, 1820, died in New York City, 12th February, 1871. The family to which she belonged claimed kindred with Sir Robert Cary, who was a doughty knight in the reign of Henry V of England, and with Walter Cary, who fled with the Huguenots from France to England after the revocation by Louis XIV of the Edict of Nantes. His son Walter, educated in Cambridge, came to the Colonies soon after the landing of the Mayflower and settled in Bridgewater. Mass., only sixteen miles from Plymouth Rock. He there opened a grammar school, probably the first one in America. He was the father of seven sons. One of the seven, John, settled in Windham, Conn., and of his five sons, the youngest, Samuel, was the great-grandfather of Alice and Phœbe Cary. Samuel was graduated from Yale College, studied medicine and practiced in Lyme. His son, Christopher, at the age of eighteen entered the Revolutionary army. After peace was declared, Christopher received a land grant, or warrant, and settled

in Hamilton county, Ohio. His son, Robert, was the father of the famous Cary Sisters, and of several other children, all of whom were persons of poetic temperament and fine intellectual powers. Alice Cary began to show her poetical talent at an early age. She wrote poetry when she was eighteen, much of which was published. Her mother, a woman of English descent, died in 1835, and her father married a second time and maintained a separate home near the cottage in which Alice, Phœbe and Elmira lived. In 1850 Alice and Phœbe decided to remove to New York City. They had won a literary reputation, and they had means to carry out their ambitious projects. Alice made her first literary venture in a volume of poems, the work of herself and her sister Phœbe, which was published in Philadelphia in 1850. Its favorable reception had much to do in causing the sisters to leave "Clovernook" and settle in New York. In 1851 Alice brought out the first series of her "Clovernook Papers," prose sketches of character, which won immediate success. Several large editions were sold in the United States and Great Britain. A second series, issued in 1853, was equally successful. In 1854 she published "The Clovernook Children," a juvenile work, which was very successful. Alice published her first volume of verse in 1853, entitled "Lyra and Other Poems." It met with ready sale, and a second and enlarged edition was published in 1855, which contained "The Maiden of Tlascala," a long narrative poem. Her first novel, "Hagar," published as a serial in the Cincinnati "Commercial," was issued in a volume in 1852. Another novel, "Married, not Mated," appeared in 1856, and her last novel, "The Bishop's Son," was published in 1867. Her

ALICE CARY.

"Pictures of Country Life" appeared in 1859. Alice Cary contributed many articles to "Harper's Magazine," to the "Atlantic Monthly," to the New York "Ledger" and the "Independent."

In those periodicals she published her earlier stories as serials. Her latest volumes were "Lyrics and Hymns" (1866), "The Lover's Diary" and "Snow Berries, a Book for Young Folks" (1867). Miss Cary and her sister entertained many prominent persons of their day in their New York home, among whom were Horace Greeley, John Greenleaf Whittier, Bayard Taylor and his wife, Mrs. Croly, Miss Anna E. Dickinson, Madame Le Vert, Elizabeth Cady Stanton, Mrs. Mary E. Dodge and others. Her home was a social and literary center. When Sorosis was formed, she became its first president. She was an invalid for several years before her death, and was tenderly cared for by her stronger sister. She is to-day more generally remembered by her poems than for her numerous and valuable prose works. The one romance of Alice Cary's life is told in the story of an engagement, in her early days of poverty and obscurity, to a young man who was forced by his family to break his plighted troth. Her poems reflect the sadness of her temperament that was supposed to have been influenced by that occurrence. She was a Universalist, and her religion was summed up in the simple creed of serving humanity, doing good and blessing the race.

CARY, Annie Louise, see RAYMOND, ANNIE LOUISE CARY.

CARY, Mrs. Mary Stockly, business woman and philanthropist, born in Allenburg, Canada, 18th August, 1834. Her father, John Galt Stockly, of Philadelphia, Pa., whose business interests in Canada led him to reside there for a few years, removed to Cleveland, Ohio, in 1837. He was a pioneer in the shipping and coal interests of northern Ohio. He built and owned the first docks in Cleveland

MARY STOCKLY CARY.

harbor. He was of an old Virginia family of Accomac county, and his wife, Catharine Duchatel, was of French descent. Mrs. Cary's paternal grandfather, Captain Ayres Stockly, was the owner

of an East Indiaman sailing from Philadelphia, and he was among the first to unfurl the American flag in the harbor of Canton. His vessel was at one time seized by the French government, and he was imprisoned in France, his heirs being among the claimants of the French spoliation funds recently ordered to be distributed by the United States Congress. Mrs. Cary's grandmother, Mary Stockly, was one of the remarkable women in Philadelphia before the Revolutionary War. As a school-girl, Mrs. Cary was quick to learn. Her marriage to John E. Cary, a prominent lawyer of Cleveland, occurred 1st September, 1852. Mr. Cary died in 1874, leaving her with three daughters and two sons. From the time of her husband's death Mrs. Cary, with the management of her property devolving upon herself, exhibited marked and practical business sagacity. Disposing of some of her property, she increased largely her interests in those investments of her husband which she regarded as most promising. She supplied largely the capital required for the development of the Brush electric light system, and, associated with her brother, George W. Stockly, was for many years a director in its board of control. Her wealth is wisely used. Public spirited and generous, she has always taken pride in her city. She is one of the founders of its School of Art and a liberal patron of its charitable and educational institutions. She inherited from her grandfather a love of the sea and of foreign travel, and she has made the circuit of the globe, and during recent years has spent much of her time with her children in European capitals. She is an especial admirer of Japan and its people, and her talk upon the "Houses and Homes of the Japanese," before the Cleveland Sorosis, was original and unique. She is one of the most conspicuous citizens of Cleveland.

CARY, Miss Phœbe, poet, born in Hamilton county, near Cincinnati, Ohio, 24th September, 1824, and died in Newport, R. I., 31st July, 1871. Her early educational advantages were superior to those of her sister Alice, whose constant companion she was through life, and from whom she differed radically in person, in mind and in temperament. Phœbe, like her sister, began to write verses at the age of seventeen. One of her earliest poems, "Nearer Home," written in 1842, has achieved a world-wide reputation. The story of her early life, the loss of her mother, the re-marriage of her father, the want of harmony with the step-mother, and the maintenance of a separate home, is told in the story of her sister's life. Her poems are her chief productions. Her genius did not take kindly to prose. Her verses were very different from those of her sister. Phœbe was a woman of cheerful and independent temper, and her verses were sparkling and hopeful, sunny and cheering, while those of Alice were more somber and redolent of the mournfulness of life. Some of her earlier productions were published in the "Ladies' Repository," in "Graham's Magazine," and in the Washington "National Era." Phœbe was in society a woman of wit and brilliancy, but always kind and genial. She and her sister, in their New York City home, after they had become famous and popular, did many kindly deeds to encourage and bring out obscure young authors of promise. Phœbe was the more robust of the sisters, and, after they had settled in New York City, she from choice assumed the greater share of the household duties, and thereby shortened her time for literary labor, while giving Alice, who was in delicate health for many years, greater opportunities for her literary musings. One of the most touching tributes to the dead ever written is the tribute to Alice, written by Phœbe only a few days before her own death. It was published in the "Ladies' Repository." Phœbe's robust health was not sufficient to carry her through the trial of her

PHŒBE CARY.

sister's death. Weakened by intense sorrow, she began to fail after Alice's death. Her prostration was intensified by a malarial attack, and she was taken to Newport, R. I., for a change of air and scenes. The change delayed, but could not avert, the blow. She grew gradually weaker and died there. Like her sister, Phœbe is mainly regarded as a poet. Her contributions to the "Poems of Alice and Phœbe Cary" (Philadelphia, 1850), number one-third of those contained in that volume. Her independent volumes are "Poems and Parodies" (Boston, 1854), "Poems of Faith, Hope and Love" (New York, 1867), and a large number of the poems in "Hymns for all Christians" (1869). Both of the sisters were women of great native refinement.

CASE, Mrs. Marietta Stanley, author and temperance advocate, born in Thompson, Conn., 22nd August, 1845. The Stanleys are of Norman descent. Matthew Stanley, the paternal ancestor of Mrs. Case, came to this country in 1646 and settled in Massachusetts. Her father, Rev. E. S. Stanley, is a retired Methodist clergyman of the New England Southern Conference. While yet a schoolgirl, Miss Stanley wrote short poems for various papers. She wrote the commencement poem upon her graduation in 1866 from the East Greenwich Academy, Rhode Island. She also read a poem at a reunion of the alumnæ of her alma mater in 1890. In June, 1868, she became the wife of A. Willard Case, a paper manufacturer of South Manchester, Conn., where they have since resided. She wrote little during the years intervening between her leaving school and the year 1884, for she believed that her domestic duties and the care and education of her children ought to occupy her whole time. She was graduated in Chautauqua in

the class of 1888. She has written poems for leading religious and temperance papers, and some of them have been issued in booklet form. Mrs. Case is interested in all work that has the uplifting of humanity for its object, and is especially interested in woman's temperance, home and foreign missionary work. She has three children, two daughters and a son, now in advanced schools. Her husband warmly approves her literary persuits.

CASSEDAY, Miss Jennie, philanthropist, born in Louisville, Ky., 9th June, 1840. An invalid for many years, and having burdens herself, she forgets them all in taking upon herself the burdens of others. Her father, Samuel Casseday, was a man of honor and a true Christian. His wife, Eliza McFarland, was the finest type of Christian womanhood, who with one other woman founded a Presbyterian Orphans' Home, which has been a shelter to many homeless little ones. When Miss Casseday was nine years of age, her mother died, and she was left to the care of her aunt, Miss McNutt. Miss Casseday's first work was the flower mission. When the National Woman's Christian Temperance Union met in Louisville, Ky., Miss Willard called upon Miss Casseday and inquired into the flower mission work. She was so impressed that she decided to have the flower mission in the Woman's Christian Temperance Union and to appoint Miss Casseday as the superintendent. Thus was formed the National Flower Mission, which carries to the poor, the neglected, the sick and the prisoners in the jails little bouquets with selected texts attached. Subsequently a World's Flower Mission was established, with Miss Casseday as its superintendent. That work is to embrace every country. Miss Casseday ap-

MARIETTA STANLEY CASE.

pointed 9th June, her birthday, to be observed as the National and Annual Flower Mission Prison Day. On that day the flower missionaries in every State visit all State and local prisons, reformatories and almshouses within their borders. In speak-ing of the training school for nurses, established in Louisville, Miss Casseday says: "It was born in my heart through the ministry of suffering and a longing to help others, as was my connection with the Shut-In Band." The district nurse work owes its birth to the same touch of pain that makes all the world kin and is an outgrowth of contact with the sick poor through the flower mission. The training school for nurses has been in success-ful operation for several years. The members of the Shut-In Band consist of men, women and chil-dren who are shut in by disease from the outside world, of invalids who seldom or never leave their rooms or beds. The name was selected from the sixteenth verse of the seventeenth chapter of Genesis: "And the Lord shut them in." These invalids write to one another and have an official organ, the "Open Window," which contains let-ters and news for invalid friends. This band has grown from three members to many thousands, living in all parts of the world. Miss Casseday has taken much interest in that work and has written many letters to her invalid friends. Another philan-throphy was the opening of Rest Cottage, as a country home for tired girls and women who have to support themseves. There they can obtain good comfortable board at a dollar a week and rest from their cares for a week or two, entertained by Miss Casseday herself. The King's Daughters have recently established a Jennie Casseday Free In-

JENNIE CASSEDAY.

firmary in Louisville, which is to benefit poor and sick women.

CASTLEMAN, Mrs. Alice Barbee, philan-thropist, born in Louisville, Ky., 5th December, 1843. She is the daughter of ex-mayor Barbee, of that city. Her father and mother were native Kentuckians and were numbered among the early pioneers. She was their oldest daughter. She became the wife of Gen. John B. Castleman on 24th

November, 1868. She is the mother of five chil-dren, three sons and two daughters. Mrs. Castle-man was educated in the East. Although she is a social leader, she finds much time for chari-

ALICE BARBEE CASTLEMAN.

table work and is a philanthropist in the broadest sense. Always on the alert to advance the cause of woman, she is progressive, cultured and liberal in her views. She is president of the board of the Louisville Training School for Nurses. She is a prominent member of the Woman's Club, a member of the Woman's Auxiliary of the Board of Missions, Foreign and Domestic, and a member of the National Board of Lady Managers of the Columbian Exposition. She is active in the affairs of the Filson Club of Louisville. In religion she is an Episcopalian and a member of Christ Church, of Louisville.

CATHERWOOD, Mrs. Mary Hartwell, author, born in Luray, Licking county, Ohio, 16th December, 1847. Mrs. Catherwood's father came from a line of Scotch-Irish baronets, the Scott family. He was a physician and took his young family to Illinois long before the prairies were drained and cultivated. He fell a victim to the arduous duties of his profession in that new and unsettled country Mary Hartwell was gradu-ated in the Female College, Granville, Ohio, in 1868, and on 27th December, 1887, became the wife of James S. Catherwood, with whom she resides in Hoopeston, Ill., a suburb of Chicago. They have one child. Among her works are "Craque-o'-Doom" (Philadelphia, 1881); "Rocky Fork" (Boston, 1882); "Old Caravan Days" (1884); "The Secrets at Roseladies" (1888); "The Ro-mance of Dollard" (1889), and "The Bells of Ste. Anne" (1889). Mary Hartwell Catherwood was always given to story-making, and she early formed the habit of putting her stories on paper. Her attention was attracted to Canadian subjects while on a visit to the American consul in

Sherbrooke. She has made the history of the old French régime a special study. She is best known through her "Romance of Dollard," published as a serial in the "Century." It attracted much attention all over the United States. Her later work, "The Story of Tonty," is the condensed result of much study. In January, 1891, Mrs. Catherwood became associated in an editorial capacity with the "Graphic," a weekly illustrated paper of Chicago. She is a member of the Universalist Church and identifies herself with its work, especially among children.

CATLIN, Mrs. Laura Wood, philanthropist, born in Rouse's Point, Clinton county, N. Y., 25th June, 1841. She comes from a family closely connected with the early history of New York State. Her grandfather, Dr. James W. Wood, was taken prisoner while carrying dispatches, during the war of 1812, to Commodore McDonalds' fleet, then stationed at Plattsburgh, N. Y. He was kept in Quebec a prisoner of war for six months and then exchanged. Mrs. Catlin's father was the oldest son of Dr. James W. Wood, and for many years held responsible town and county offices. Her

MARY HARTWELL CATHERWOOD.

CARRIE LANE CHAPMAN CATT.

mother, Mary B. Hammond, came from one of the old colonial families. Dying when Mrs. Catlin was a child, she left her to the care of two maiden aunts. Mrs. Catlin's writings, both prose and poetry, have been published in various newspapers in Chicago, New York and Milwaukee. Much of her leisure time is given to charitable objects. The Laura Catlin Kindergarten, Sewing School and Free Dispensary in Milwaukee, Wis., are supported entirely by her, and she personally visits and relieves the poor families brought to her notice through those channels. In 1872 she became the wife of Charles Catlin, a son of Julius Catlin, of Hartford, Conn., and since that time has made her home in Milwaukee. Besides her talent for writing, Mrs. Catlin is a thorough musician. She has all her life been active in church work, as Sunday-school teacher and organist.

LAURA WOOD CATLIN.

CATT, Mrs. Carrie Lane Chapman, journalist and lecturer, born in Ripon, Wis., 9th

January, 1859. Her maiden name was Lane. While yet a child, her parents moved to northern Iowa, where her youth was passed. In 1878 she entered as a student the scientific department of the Iowa Agricultural College and was graduated therefrom in 1880, with the degree of B. S. She was an earnest student and attained first rank in her class. For three years she devoted herself to teaching, first as principal of the high school in Mason City, Iowa, from which positions she was soon promoted to that of city superintendent of schools in the same place. In 1885 she became the wife of Leo Chapman and entered into partnership with him as joint proprietor and editor of the Mason City "Republican." Within a year Mr. Chapman died. Disposing of her paper, Mrs. Chapman went to California where for a year she was engaged in journalistic work in San Francisco. In 1888 she entered the lecture field and for some time spoke only in lecture courses. The cause of woman's enfranchisement soon enlisted her warmest sympathies, and she accepted a position as State lecturer for the Iowa Woman Suffrage Association. Since that time all her energies have been devoted to that cause and there her earnest, logical eloquence has won her many friends. Three times she has been called as a speaker to the annual convention of the National Association. In 1890 she became the wife of George W. Catt, civil engineer, of New York City. Her home is in Bensonhurst-by-the-Sea, on Long Island.

CAYVAN, Miss Georgia, actor, born in Maine, in 1858. Her childhood was passed in Boston, Mass., where she was educated mainly in the

GEORGIA CAYVAN.

public schools. She early showed fine musical and elocutionary talents, and her friends encouraged and assisted her in developing both. At an early age she began to make use of her elocutionary gifts. She gave readings and recitations in New England lyceums, and her ambition was to become

an elocutionist. After some experience she went to the Boston School of Oratory, from which institution she was graduated with honors. In 1879, on 14th April, she made her operatic début as Hebe in "Pinafore," with the Boston Ideal Opera Company, in the Boston Theater, and scored a success. She made her début in drama on 10th May, 1879, in the same theater, as Sally Scraggs in "Sketches in India." She was brought to the notice of Steele Mackaye in 1880, and he chose her a member of his Madison Square Theater model stock company. On 7th May, 1880, she made her début in New York as Dolly Dutton in "Hazel Kirke," and in 1881 she became the "Hazel" of that play, scoring an instant triumph, and then traveled with one of the Madison Square companies until 1882. Early in 1882 she appeared in the memorable production of the Greek tragedy "Antigone" and in the Greek play "Œdipus Tyrannus," in the Boston Globe Theater and in Booth's Theater in New York. On 3rd April, 1882, she appeared as the original Liza in "The White Slave," in Haverly's Fourteenth Street Theater in New York, and on 18th September, 1882, as the original Lura, in America, in "The Romany Rye," in Booth's Theater in New York, both special engagements. She played a successful season with the California Theater stock company, after several years with the Madison Square company. She then played with A. M. Palmer's company, and then returned to the Madison Square company. When Daniel Frohman organized, in New York, the Lyceum Theater stock company, in 1887, he selected Miss Cayvan as leading lady. She appeared in the Lyceum in "The Wife," in "Sweet Lavender," in "The Charity Ball," in "The Idler," in "Nerves," in "Old Heads and Young Hearts," and in "Squire Kate." She is still leading lady in the Lyceum company. Miss Cayvan is a hard worker and a thorough student. Her career has been one of steady growth in her art, and she now ranks among the foremost in her profession. Her home is in New York City with her mother and sister. In social life she is as charming as on the stage. She is now (1892) taking a long vacation and is traveling in Japan and other oriental lands.

CHACE, Mrs. Elizabeth Buffum, anti-slavery agitator and reformer, born in Providence, R. I., 9th December, 1806. She was the second child of Arnold and Rebecca Buffum, who were Quakers and were descended from some of the oldest Quaker families in the State. One of the mother's ancestors, Daniel Gould, the first of his name to settle in this country, was arrested on going into Boston in company with the two men who were afterwards hung with Mary Dyer, on Boston Common, for the crime of returning to Massachusetts after they had been banished thence because they were Quakers. Gould was sentenced to be whipped because of his religious opinions and the heretical company in which he was taken, and he received his punishment on the Common. Elizabeth Buffum was well educated for her times. During her childhood her family lived in Smithfield, R. I., the original home of her father. One of her teachers there was George D. Prentice. Later she attended the Friends' school in Providence. In her youth she was a very devoted Quaker. She became the wife of Samuel Buffington Chace and passed the first part of her married life in Fall River. In 1840 she removed with her husband to Valley Falls, R. I., and that place has been her home ever since. Her anti-slavery experiences have been given in her anti-slavery "Reminiscences" (1891, privately printed). That pamphlet has omitted to mention the important work she did in connection with Samuel May, jr., who was then agent for the Anti-Slavery Society, in getting up anti-slavery meetings and conventions all over the State of Rhode Island. She separated from the Society of Friends because she was dissatisfied

ELIZABETH BUFFUM CHACE.

with their course about slavery, and after that her religious opinions underwent much modification. In the latter part of her life she has engaged heartily in what was known as the "Free Religious Movement," and found herself in religious sympathy with such men as Theodore Parker, John Weiss, O. B. Frothingham, David Wasson, Samuel Longfellow, T. W. Higginson and Frederic A. Hinckley. Most of these men were personal friends and occasional guests in her house. After the Civil War Mrs. Chace's principal interests centered in prison reform and woman's rights. She was largely instrumental in establishing in Rhode Island a State school and home for dependent children, which should take them out of the pauper and criminal class. It was in great measure due to her efforts that twenty years ago a board of women visitors was appointed to penal institutions, and the recent appointment of women on the boards of actual management of some State institutions is in no small degree the result of her efforts. She was a delegate to the World's Prison Congress held in London, England, in 1872, and read there a paper on the importance of the appointment of women on the boards of control of penal and pauper institutions. Her husband died in 1870, and she had lost by death seven out of her ten children. She felt the need of change, and spent more than a year in travel in Europe with her daughters. Her work for woman suffrage has been unremitting, and she has been president of the Rhode Island Woman Suffrage Association for twenty years. She writes occasionally for the newspapers on such topics as interest her, and, while never a public speaker, she often reads papers at the meetings which she attends. She has always been a consistent believer

in total abstinence from the use of alcoholic beverages, and is a strong prohibitionist. She disapproves war under all circumstances. With all her public interests, Mrs. Chace has always been an unusually domestic woman, devoted to her family, solicitous for their education and moral nature, and zealous in her careful housekeeping.

CHAMPNEY, Mrs. Elizabeth W., author, born in Springfield, Ohio, 6th February, 1850. Her father was Judge S. B. Williams. She was educated in Vassar College and was graduated in 1869. During her girlhood she dreamed of literature as a profession, and she wrote many romances that were never printed. In 1876 she began to publish short stories, poems and romances in large numbers. She contributed to "Harper's Magazine" and the "Century" a series of observations on her travels in England, France, Spain, Portugal and Morocco, as well as other oriental lands. Among these papers was a striking one on Portugal, another on "A Neglected Corner of Europe," and a third, "In the Footsteps of Fortuny and Régnault." Since her return to the United States she has written about a score of volumes. Her novels are "Bourbon Lilies" and "Rosemary and Rue." Her stories for youth include "All Around a Palette" and "Howling Wolf and His Trick Pony." Among her historical stories for youth is "Great-Grandmother Girls in New France," suggested by the Indian massacre in Deerfield, Mass. One of her most successful works is "Three Vassar Girls Abroad," which consists of ten volumes. Mrs. Champney writes much on solicitation by publishers, and her time is thus too much taken up to permit her to indulge her bent and talent for poems and short stories. Her popularity has dated from

ELIZABETH W. CHAMPNEY.

the appearance of the Vassar series. She became the wife of J. Wells Champney, the artist, 15th May, 1875. Their union is a singularly happy one in every way. Mr. Champney has done some of his best work in illustrating his gifted wife's books. They have one son, Edward Frère. They make their winter home in New York City, and their summers are spent in "Elmstead," the old-fashioned house built in Deerfield, Mass., by Mrs. Champney's grandfather.

CHANDLER, Mrs. Lucinda Banister, social reformer and author, born in Potsdam, N. Y., 1st April, 1828. Her parents were Silas Banister and Eliza Smith, both of New England birth and ancestry. Mrs. Chandler suffered a spinal injury in early infancy from a fall, and that intensified the susceptibility of a highly nervous organization, and was the cause of a life of invalidism and extreme suffering. As a child she was fond of books and study, and when she entered St. Lawrence Academy, at nine years of age, her teacher registered her as two years older, because of her advancement in studies and seeming maturity of years. At the age of thirteen years her first great

LUCINDA BANISTER CHANDLER.

disappointment came, when her school course was suspended, never to be resumed, by the severe development of her spinal malady. For several years even reading was denied to her. In her twentieth year she became the wife of John H. Chandler, who was born and raised in Potsdam. The one child born to them was drowned in his third year. Mrs. Chandler's marriage was a happy one, and the tender, devoted care and provision for her relief and benefit by her husband were no doubt the providence that made it possible for her to enjoy a period of usefulness in later life. In the winter of 1870-71 she wrote "Motherhood, Its Power Over Human Destiny," while recuperating from a long illness, and it was so warmly received by a society of ladies in Vineland, N. J., that it was afterwards published in booklet form. That introduced her to many thinking women of Boston, where in 1871-72 she held parlor meetings and achieved the purpose of her heart, the organization

of a body of women who were pledged to work for the promotion of enlightened parenthood and an equal and high standard of purity for both sexes. The Moral Education Society of Boston has continued a vigorous existence to the present time. Societies were formed in New York, Philadelphia and Washington, D. C., by the efforts of Mrs. Chandler and with the coöperation of prominent women. That was the first work in this country in the line of educational standards for the elevation and purity of the relations of men and women, inside as well as outside of marriage. The publication of essays, "A Mother's Aid," "Children's Rights" and the "Divineness of Marriage," written by her, followed and furnished a literature for the agitation of questions that since that time have come to be widely discussed. During one of the long periods of prostration and confinement to her room, to which Mrs. Chandler was subject, she commenced study on the lines of political economy as a mental tonic and helpful agency to restoration. After her recovery she wrote extensively for reform publications upon finance reform, the land question and industrial problems. In Chicago, in 1880, the Margaret Fuller Society was founded, especially to interest women in those subjects and the principles of Americanism. A life-long advocate of the total abstinence principle, Mrs. Chandler served as vice-president of the Woman's Christian Temperance Alliance of Illinois. She was the first president of the Chicago Moral Educational Society, formed in 1882. She is an advocate of Christian socialism, and a firm believer in the final triumph of the Christian idea of the brotherhood of man as a practical and controlling principle in commercial and industrial systems.

CHANDLER, Mrs. Mary Alderson, educator, born near Le Raysville, Pa., 16th April, 1849. Her birth place was twenty miles from any town of importance, the only connection with which was the rumbling stage-coach. When other children of her age were profiting by the railroad, the telegraph, music, art, literature and other facilities for unconscious growth and education, she, benightedly, was looking through the little windows of the stone house, dreaming of another world beyond the hills. Her parents were plain English people, whose wealth, they used to say, lay chiefly in their children, of whom there were eight boys and three girls. Her education was begun in the district school, and afterwards she spent two years in the State Normal School, Mansfield, Pa., graduating with the honors of her class in the spring of 1868. She then began her work as a teacher. The first three years of public-school service were spent in western Pennsylvania, the following nine in California. She was everywhere successful. Being largely endowed with enthusiasm, she invariably left in her wake the spirit of progress. Deciding to become a specialist, she went to Philadelphia as a student. While there she met Willard M. Chandler, whose wife and co-worker she became, and whom she accompanied to Boston, her present home. Mr. Chandler was a gentleman of refinement, intelligence, breadth of thought and unusual power as an orator. Their lives were full of promise, but in a short time he died of consumption. Necessity, a strong commander, decided that stenography, which she had learned more as an aid to her husband than otherwise, should then become her vocation. Summoning courage, she threw herself into that educational work and turned out stenographers of so rare a quality as to attract general attention. That led to the publication of her "Graded Lessons" (Boston, 1889), for which her penetrating mind had discovered the greatest need. Foreseeing the time when shorthand would become a part of a common-school education, she devoted herself to the problem of preparing a work specially adapted to that end, and which she pub-

MARY ALDERSON CHANDLER.

lished, "Practical Shorthand for Schools and Collages" (Boston, 1891). By her strictly logical development she has brought that complicated subject within the ready comprehension of all.

CHANLER, Mrs. Amélie Rives, author, born in Richmond, Va., 23rd August, 1863. Her mother, Miss Macmurdo, was the granddaughter of Bishop Moore, of Virginia, and from her and the grandmother Mrs. Chanler inherits the beauty as marked as her mental gifts. Her father, Colonel Alfred L. Rives, is a distinguished engineer and the son of Hon. William C. Rives, three times minister to France, member of the United States Senate, and the author of a "Life of Madison." Miss Rives passed her childhood between Mobile, Ala., and William Rives' country place, Castle Hill, in Albemarle county, Va. When she was about sixteen years old, her father, on the death of his mother, fell heir to the estate, and from that time they made it their permanent home. From the time she was nine years old Miss Rives found her greatest delight in her pen, writing freely and without restraint whatever occupied her fancy for the time. Her writings were never criticised, and rarely read, and to that habit of freedom is perhaps due the strong individuality of style which has carried her so successfully through what has been, so far, a most daring as well as a most brilliant literary career. Her love of art only seconded that of literature, and her life has been spent in pursuit of both. In 1886 Miss Rives published anonymously, in the "Atlantic Monthly," "A Brother to Dragons," a story of the sixteenth century, so powerful that it attracted widespread attention both in this country and in England. The same year a sonnet of great strength appeared in the

"Century," signed by Amélie Rives, and she was soon identified as the author of "A Brother to Dragons." Many orders were received by her for stories and poems, but she preferred not to hurry into print, and published the following year, 1887, only two short stories, "The Farrier Lass o' Piping Pebworth" in "Lippincott's Magazine," and "Nurse Crumpet Tells the Story," in "Harper's Magazine." In 1889 appeared in "Lippincott's Magazine" "The Quick or the Dead." That story, or rather study, as Miss Rives called it, at once launched her on the sea of literature as a novelist of undoubted power. Criticism came from all sides. The story was translated into French, and appeared in the " Revue des Deux Mondes." It was impossible that so daring a venture should escape censure, but Miss Rives kept her balance through blame and praise alike, writing steadily and studying, filled with a purpose to perfect herself in the art she considers the greatest, determined to retain her individuality while constantly striving to throw aside the faults of youth and literary inexperience. In June, 1888, she became the wife of John Armstrong Chanler, a grandson of John Jacob Astor. Mr. Chanler, who has spent much of his life abroad, was imbued with the same love of art and literature that had formed the mainspring of Miss Rives' life, and was anxious that his wife should perfect her art studies. That summer she published her first drama, "Herod and Mariamne," written three years before, and in April, 1889, she sailed for Havre. After traveling for some months she settled in Paris for hard work, but was greatly interrupted by ill-health. Unable to paint, she continued to write and study, perfecting herself in French and reading widely in all branches of English literature. None of her European work

AMÉLIE RIVES CHANLER.

has been published, except a study of life in the Latin Quarter, entitled "According to St. John," which appeared in the "Cosmopolitan" as a serial, in 1891. In the month of August, 1891, she returned to America. She was followed shortly by Charles Lasar, an artist and teacher of prominence in Paris, under whom she will study at her home in Castle Hill during the fall and winter months for several years to come. A second drama, entitled "Athelwold," was published in "Harper's Magazine" of February, 1892, and has received high praise from the leading literary papers of the North. Mrs. Chanler has but just begun a career which promises to be enduring as well as brilliant. She is impressed by the feeling that what she has done is but a preparation, "studies," as she is fond of expressing it, for the message she feels she has to deliver, and every power of an intense and earnest nature is bent on putting to the best uses the talents which she looks upon with a deep sense of responsibility.

CHAPIN, Miss Augusta J., Universalist minister, born in Lakeville, near Rochester, N. Y., 16th July, 1836. She is a descendant, in the ninth

AUGUSTA J. CHAPIN.

generation, of Samuel Chapin, who came from Wales to Dorchester, Mass., in 1636, and settled in Springfield, Mass., in 1642. Her father, Almon M. Chapin, was a native of the latter place. Her family removed to Michigan while she was very young, and she was educated in that State. In her childhood she attended the common schools and made the most of her opportunities. Her father, who was a man of liberal culture, gave her much instruction at home. Books for children were few, but she possessed illustrated copies of the New Testament, Bunyan's Pilgrim's Progress and Robinson Crusoe. These she read with never-failing delight, until they were almost memorized, and that early familiarity with three great books became the foundation of her life-long love of all that is best in thought and literature. Of her studies, mathematics and language were her favorites, and so earnestly and successfully did she apply herself that, in the spring before her fourteenth

birthday, she received a certificate from the school inspectors of the county authorizing her to teach. She undertook the charge of a country school the following summer. Soon after, she became a student in Olivet College, where she remained several years. Some years later, Lombard University, Galesburg, Ill., acknowledged her high scholarship by conferring upon her an honorary degree. Miss Chapin is, at the present time, non-resident lecturer on English literature in that school. After the opening of the University of Michigan to women, she entered that institution and was graduated with the degree of M. A. While a student in Olivet, she became deeply interested in religion and resolved to enter the Christian ministry. She preached her first sermon in Portland, Mich., 1st May, 1859. From that time to the present she has been continuously in active ministerial work. She was regularly ordained by the Universalist denomination in Lansing, Mich., 3rd December, 1863. Her chief pastorates have been in Portland, Mich.; Iowa City, Iowa; Lansing, Mich.; Pittsburgh, Pa.; Aurora, Ill., and Oak Park, Chicago. The last place has been Miss Chapin's field of labor for the last six years, and her church there has enjoyed the most prosperous period of its history during her pastorate. During a continuous ministry covering the period of the coming and going of an entire generation of mankind, Miss Chapin has never once been absent from her pulpit on account of sickness. She has been in the active work of the Christian ministry longer than any other living woman. She has delivered more than four-thousand sermons and public addresses, has baptized and received many hundreds of persons into the church, has attended some two-hundred funerals, and has officiated at many marriages. Her vacations have usually been given to missionary work outside her parish, and on those occasions, in addition to many special trips, she has visited and preached in more than half the States and Territories of the Union, and from the Atlantic to the Pacific. She has written considerably for magazines and the denominational press, and has been much sought for in the lecture field. Her lectures are on humanitarian, literary and artistic themes, including lectures on "Temperance," "Woman's Work and Wages," "Shakespeare's Sonnets," "Wordsworth's Ethics" and courses on the "American Poets," "English Cathedrals," "Italian Cities" and other themes. Miss Chapin is an active member of the Art Institute, the Woman's Club and other important local organizations of Chicago, and also, among many others, of the National Society for the Extension of University Teaching. She is the chairman of the Woman's Committee on Religious Congresses in the World's Congress Auxiliary to the Columbian Exposition 1893. She has traveled extensively in the United States and has been twice to Europe. Miss Chapin has a fine voice, and excellent delivery, and her reading is beyond criticism.

CHAPIN, Mrs. Clara Christiana, woman suffragist and temperance worker, born in Gloucestershire, England, 26th December, 1852. Her maiden name was Morgan. Her father was of Welsh extraction, and her mother came of an old country family the Blagdons, proprietors of the manor of Boddington since the days of William the Conqueror. She was educated in Clifton Ladies' College and passed the Cambridge local examination the only form of university privilege open at that time to girls. She came to the United States with her parents and their five younger children in 1870. The family settled in Fillmore county, Neb., and Clara engaged in teaching. In September,

1872, she became the wife of Clarence C. Chapin, of Sheffield, Mass., and shortly after they removed to Franklin county, Neb., where both took a prominent part in the development of that new

CLARA CHRISTIANA CHAPIN.

State. Mr. Chapin served as a member of the State legislature, while his talented wife by the use of her pen and personal influence aided in securing the enactment of the famous Slocum license law, at that time supposed to be the panacea in temperance matters. They also aided materially in securing the temperance educational and scientific law for that State. She was particularly interested in all movements for the advancement of women and took an active part in the woman suffrage campaign of 1882. She was a prominent member of the Woman's Christian Temperance Union and wrote much for the press on the woman and temperance questions. Being a little body, Mrs. Chapin commonly went by the name "La Petite" among her co-workers in Nebraska, but, though small of stature, she is of that fine mental acumen which gives great individuality and force of character. Though of English birth, Mrs. Chapin's life-work has been and still is American. She now resides, with her husband, son and two daughters, in one of the pleasant suburban towns Chicago, Ill.

CHAPIN, Mrs. Sallie F., author and temperance worker, born in Charleston, S. C. Her maternal ancestors were Huguenots, who came to the Colonies in 1685. Her two great-grandfathers, Vigneron and Tousager, were killed in the Revolutionary War. Her maiden name was Moore, and on her father's side the strain is English. Her father was a Methodist minister. His home in Charleston was burned, and he moved to the northern part of the State. Miss Moore was reared and educated in Cokesburg, Abbeville county. From early childhood she showed a fondness and talent for authorship. Miss Moore became

Mrs Chapin while she was still a girl, and her married life has been singularly happy. Her husband was one of the founders of the Young Men's Christian Association of Charleston, and one of its chief officers for years. Mrs. Chapin's father died in the pulpit at a union camp-meeting, during the Civil War, after receiving a dispatch announcing the death of his son in a battle. Mrs. Chapin has written much, but she has published only one book, "Fitzhugh St. Clair, the Rebel Boy of South Carolina." During the war she was president of the Soldiers' Relief Society and worked day and night in the hospitals. The war broke their fortune, and her husband died after the conflict was ended. In the Woman's Christian Temperance Union she has been conspicuous for years, serving as State president, and she has done much to extend that order in the South, where conservatism hindered the work for a long time. In 1881 she attended the convention in Washington, D. C., where she made a brilliant reply to the address of welcome on behalf of the South, ending with a telling poem setting forth the intentions of the Woman's Christian Temperance Union. She believes in prohibition as the remedy for intemperance. She is a forcible and brilliant writer and conversationalist. In the Chicago Woman's Christian Temperance Union convention, in 1882, when the Prohibition Home Protection Party was formed, she was made a member of the executive committee, and by pen and voice she popularized that movement in the South. She was at one time president of the Woman's Press Association of the South.

CHAPMAN, Mrs. Carrie Lane, see CATT, MRS. CARRIE LANE.

CHAPMAN, Miss Millie Jane, doctor of medicine, born in Beaver, Crawford county, Pa.,

MILLIE JANE CHAPMAN.

23rd July, 1845. She is the daughter of Lewis K. and Robey Ormsbee Chapman. She had a happy early childhood, but reverses came to the family, and at the age of ten years she was not bound down by any weight or handicapped by wealth which might have prevented the development of the resources within herself. From that age she was self-supporting. The industrious spirit, perseverance, strong judgment, sympathy and kindness possessed by both parents were transmitted to her. Her education was obtained in the public schools and in the State Normal, supplemented by studies at night. She taught school twelve years and was recognized as an efficient instructor. Beginning when " boarding round " was the custom and five dollars per month was the salary, she gradually advanced to schools where higher attainments insured greater compensation. She studied medicine in the Homeopathic College of Cleveland, Ohio. She was graduated in February, 1874 and located at once in Pittsburgh, Pa., where she still resides. She found it a conservative city, unaccustomed to woman doctors and not realizing a demand for them. It required a great struggle to become established. The pioneer efforts and all influence connected therewith were borne as a necessary ordeal to one entering upon an unusual work. She labored with a firm determination to maintain true professional dignity and general courtesy to all deserving associates, cognizant of the fact that hard study and patient perseverance would be necessary to reach the goal. Her true womanly character in the profession has been endorsed by many exalted positions in local, district, State and national medical organizations. Her faith in God and in the brotherhood of mankind has induced her to make extensive efforts for humanity, for the relief of their physical distress and for their education and reformation.

CHARLES, Mrs. Emily Thornton, poet and journalist, born in Lafayette, Ind., 21st March, 1845. She comes of English ancestors, the Thorntons and Parkers. On the paternal side the Thorntons were noted as original thinkers. Her great-grandfather, Elisha Thornton, carried a sword in the War of the Revolution. Her grandfather, also Elisha Thornton, resident of Sodus, Wayne county, N. Y., served in the War of 1812. Her father, James M. Thornton, gave his life to the cause of the Union in 1864, and of her two brothers, Charles lost his life in the Civil War, and Gardner served in Harrison's regiment. The Parkers, her maternal ancestors, were among the primitive Puritans. Deacon Edmund Parker settled in Reading, Mass., about 1719, the family removing thence to Pepperell, Mass., which town they helped to found. For more than a century, from father to son, the Parkers were deacons and leaders of the choir in the Congregational Church. When Emily's grandfather married, the young couple took a wedding journey in a sleigh to find a new home in Lyons, Wayne county, N.Y., taking with them their household goods. Twenty years later their daughter, Harriet Parker, was married to James M. Thornton, a civil engineer, son of Elisha. The young couple moved to Lafayette, Ind., where Mr. Thornton established a large manufactory. Emily Thornton was educated in the free schools of Indianapolis, and at the age of sixteen she became a teacher. As a child in school she attracted attention by the excellence of her written exercises and her original manner of handling given subjects. She became the wife, while very young, of Daniel B. Charles, son of a business man long established in Indianapolis. At the age of twenty-four she was left a widow, in delicate health, with two little ones dependent upon her. Soon after the death of her husband, 1874, she began to write for a livelihood, doing reportorial and editorial work for

Indianapolis papers and correspondence for outside publications. She succeeded well. Having chosen journalism as a profession, she perfected herself in all its branches. She published her first volume of verse under the title "Hawthorn Blossoms" (Philadelphia, 1876). This little book was received with great favor and proved a literary and financial success. From the Centennial year to 1880 she continued to do newspaper work and biographical writing. She was associate editor of "Eminent Men of Indiana." In 1881 she accepted a position as managing editor of the Washington "World." Afterwards she established "The National Veteran" in Washington, D. C., of which she was sole proprietor and editor. In 1883 Mrs. Charles was prostrated through overwork and was confined to her bed for an entire year. While recovering slowly, she spent a year in revising and preparing for publication her later poems. The work appeared in "Lyrical Poems" (Philadelphia, 1886),

EMILY THORNTON CHARLES.

a volume of three-hundred pages. That volume fully established her reputation as a national poet. She has appeared upon the lecture platform with success. On the occasion of her departure from Indiana, when a complimentary farewell testimonial was tendered her by the leading citizens of Indianapolis, in 1880, she made a brilliant address. In 1882 she addressed an audience of 1,500 ex-prisoners of war in Cincinnati, Ohio. Her poetical address on "Woman's Sphere" was delivered before a National Woman's Suffrage Convention. She is a member of the executive committee of the National Woman's Press Association and chairman of the executive council of the Society of American Authors. She has been selected as one of the speakers at the World's Columbian Exposition in 1893. Mrs. Charles writes almost exclusively under the name of "Emily Thornton."

CHASE, Mrs. Louise L., born in Warren, Mass., 2nd September, 1840. She is a daughter of

Samuel and Mary Bond. Soon after her birth her parents moved to Brimfield, Mass., where she received her education, entering the Hitchcock free high school at the age of thirteen. Her attendance

LOUISE L. CHASE.

in that school was interrupted by a temporary residence in Columbia, Conn., where she attended a private school. She returned to Brimfield and finished her course at the age of sixteen. In 1857 she took up her residence in Lebanon, Conn., and there became the wife, in 1861, of Alfred W. Chase, a native of Bristol, R. I. Mr. and Mrs. Chase soon removed to Brooklyn, Conn., and in 1887 to Middletown, R. I., the home of Mr. Chase's family, where they still reside. In 1885 she was elected president of the Woman's Christian Temperance Union of Middletown, and in that way became prominent in the work. She was elected State vice-president of the Woman's Christian Temperance Union, and at about the same time State superintendent of the department of Sabbath observance. In 1886 she represented the State in the National Convention in Minneapolis, Minn. She was elected in 1891 State superintendent of scientific temperance instruction in schools.

CHEATHAM, Miss Kitty Smiley, actor, born in Nashville, Tenn., in 1869. She was educated in the public schools of that city and was graduated at fifteen years of age. While she was still a child, her father died, leaving his family in straitened circumstances. Realizing the necessity of personal exertion and prompted by her love for her mother, whose immunity from want she was anxious to secure, she cast about to see what her hands might find to do. The stage was her dream. She was even in childhood a lover of the theater. Home-made theatrical amusement was her favorite pastime. Mimicry came natural to her. As she grew older her desire to become an actor was made known. By that time she had already won approbation as an amateur of more than average

taste and still. Encouraged by critics and friends, she was enabled to overcome the opposition of her family and relatives to her adopting the stage as a profession, and in the spring of 1885 she removed to New York City to study singing under Errani, making such progress as justified her engagement when she was only sixteen years old, as leading lady in the J. O. Barrow "Professor" company. She met a flattering reception throughout the South. The following season she joined Col. McCall's traveling opera company and sang the prima-donna parts in the "Black Hussar," "Falka" and "Erminie." The next season she played second parts in the Casino, in New York. Her prospects on that famous stage were flattering, but she foresook them for Daly's company, with which she has since been identified. In the Daly company she has played in "The Midsummer-Night's Dream," "Love's Labor Lost," "The Inconstant," "The Foresters," and as "Kate," a part she created.

CHENEY, Mrs. Abbey Perkins, musical educator, born in Milwaukee, Wis., in 1853. She inherits her rare gifts through her mother, from a long line of singing ancestors, the Cheneys of Vermont, who for a hundred years have been famous for their fine and powerful voices and exceptional musical culture. Her mother, Mrs. Elizabeth Cheney Perkins, has a remarkably pure and strong mezzo-soprano voice, and was very successful before her marriage, as a church and concert singer in Buffalo, N. Y., and subsequently in Milwaukee, Wis., and in Leavenworth, Kans. She still enjoys, in her serene silver-haired old age, the musical and literary pleasures of her daughter's San Francisco home. Mrs. Cheney's father, one

KITTY SMILEY CHEATHAM.

of the enterprising young business men of Milwaukee in the 50's, was also a music lover. He died in 1861, and his last words to his little daughter were: "Lose no opportunity to cultivate your musical talent." The father's wish decided the child's future. Mrs. Perkins encouraged and aided her daughter in every way, and as her two other children early followed their young father,

ABBEY PERKINS CHENEY.

she was left sadly free from all hindrances to these efforts. The little girl soon achieved such successes that, when only fourteen years old, she was called with her mother to take charge of the music in Ingham University, LeRoy, N. Y. Two years later they resigned that position in order to go abroad for the prosecution of the daughter's musical studies. They went to Germany, where Miss Perkins entered the Conservatory of Leipsic, and also received private tuition from Louis Plaidy. During that year in Leipsic she was a pupil of Paul, of Coccius, of Reinecke and others on the piano, and of Richter in harmony. But the best teachers in Leipsic were unsatisfactory in point of technique, and through the counsel of honest Coccius, as well as by advice of the master, Liszt, she went to Stuttgart to study with Sigismund Lebert, whom Liszt pronounced the greatest living teacher of technique. The school year at Stuttgart had just closed, and the young American girl presented herself tremblingly to the master for examination, winning such favor that he offered to teach her, contrary to his custom, through vacation, going three times a week to his pupil's house and to the last refusing all compensation. When the school re-opened, the brilliant young musician was admitted to the artists' class, and there for four years she studied with Lebert and with Prückner, the friend of Von Bülow. Then, having received her diploma, she began in Germany her successful career as a musical educator. A term of study with Edward Neupert, the pupil of Kullak, closed her pupil life, but by no means ended her musical studies. She returned to America, thoroughly equipped for the profession and yet not so wedded to it as to prevent her being wooed and

won by the young musician, poet and littérateur, John Vance Cheney, with whom she went to California in 1876. First in Sacramento, and later in San Francisco, Mrs. Cheney has been the pioneer of a new school of musical technique, and the signal success achieved by her pupils is proof conclusive that in her treatment of piano-playing, primarily from the physiological standpoint, she has enlarged and improved the methods of her masters, Reinecke, Lebert and others. It is proper to state here that the physiological investigations, which have made Mrs. Cheney an originator in her field of work, were instigated by her own great suffering from partial paralysis of the right hand and arm, brought on by over-taxation when completing her studies abroad. It is without doubt, due to this fact that we have the sympathetic broad-minded, self-sacrificing educator in place of the brilliant concert pianist.

CHENEY, Mrs. Armilla Amanda, treasurer National Relief Corps, born in Windham, Ohio, 27th August, 1845, of Massachusetts and Vermont parentage. Her maiden name was Perkins. She is a lineal descendant of John Perkins, who, over two-hundred-fifty years ago, by strategy, saved the little Puritan colony of Ipswich, Mass., from the Indians. Left fatherless at an early age, without brothers or sisters, and with a mother in feeble health, more than ordinary cares and responsibilities came to her in her younger days. Her whole life has been characterized by the ability to do whatsoever her hands found to do. She received a liberal education and was thereby qualified for the useful and responsible positions she has held. She was in school when the war-cry rang out at the firing on Fort Sumter, and became

ARMILLA AMANDA CHENEY.

an earnest worker in the home labors that formed so large a part of the daily task of Northern women for alleviating the sufferings of the Boys in Blue. She became the wife of Capt. James W. Cheney, a native of Massachusetts, in May, 1868. Moving to Detroit, Mich., in the fall of 1870, where she still resides, she identified herself with one of the prominent churches, and engaged in its work and that of its Sabbath-school, having in charge the infant department for several years. She became a member of Fairbanks Woman's Relief Corps, of Detroit, early in its organization, was appointed department secretary of that order soon after, and in 1887 accepted the office of secretary of the national organization. So faithfully and conscientiously were her duties performed that she won the love and esteem of the order throughout the country, and in Milwaukee, Wis., in 1889, was elected national treasurer and was unanimously reëlected at the succeeding national conventions, held in Boston, Mass., in 1890, and in Detroit, Mich., in 1891.

CHENEY, Mrs. Edna Dow, author, born in Boston, Mass., 27th June, 1824. There in 1853 she became the wife of Seth W. Cheney, an artist of

EDNA DOW CHENEY.

local prominence, who died in 1856, leaving her with one daughter. The daughter died in 1882. Miss Cheney studied in the Institute of Technology, of which General Francis J. Walker is president, and her memory is preserved by the "Margaret Cheney Reading Room," devoted to the convenience of the women students. Mrs. Cheney's life has been devoted to philosophic and literary research and work. Her early womanhood was passed under the most stimulating influences. She was a member of one of those famous conversation classes which Margaret Fuller instituted in the decade of 1830-40. Emerson, Mr. and Mrs. Alcott, James Freeman Clarke and Theodore Parker were among those who strongly influenced her thought. Her parents, Sargent Smith Littlehale and Edna Parker Littlehale, gave her every educational advantage. In 1851 she aided in forming the School of Design for Women, in Boston, and served as secretary. In 1859 she aided in establishing a

hospital in connection with the Woman's Medical School. She took part in a woman's rights convention in 1860. In 1862 she was secretary of the New England Hospital. In 1868 she helped to found the New England Woman's Club and served as vice-president. In 1863 she was secretary of the teachers' committee of the Freedman's Aid Society and secretary of the committee to aid colored regiments. In 1865 she went to Readville and taught soldiers, and attended the convention of Freedmen's societies in New York City, and in the following year the one held in Baltimore, and for several years visited colored schools in various Southern States. In 1869 she assisted in founding a horticultural school for women. She lectured on horticulture for women before the Massachusetts State Agricultural Society in 1871. In 1879 she delivered a course of ten lectures on the history of art before the Concord School of Philosophy, and the same year was elected vice-president of the Massachusetts School Suffrage Association, of which she is now president. In 1887 she was elected president of the hospital she had helped to found. She was a delegate to the Woman's Council in Washington, D. C., in 1888. In 1890 she attended the Lake Mohawk Negro Conference. She has lectured and preached in many cities and has spoken at funerals occasionally. She is vice-president of the Free Religious Association. She has visited Europe three times and has traveled extensively in this country. Her works, all published in Boston, include: "Hand-Book for American Citizens" "Patience" (1870), "Social Games" (1871), "Faithful to the Light" (1872), "Child of the Tide" (1874), "Life of Susan Dimoch" (1875), "Memoir of S. W. Cheney" (1881), "Gleanings in Fields of Art" (1881), "Selected Poems of Michael Angelo" (1885), "Children's Friend," a sketch of Louisa M. Alcott (1888), "Biography of L. M. Alcott" (1889), "Memoir of John Cheney, Engraver" (1888), "Memoir of Margaret S. Cheney" (1888), "Nora's Return" (1890), "Stories of Olden Time" (1890), and a number of articles in books. She has contributed to the "North American Review," the "Christian Examiner," the "Radical," "Index," the "Woman's Journal" and other periodicals. She edited the poems of David A. Wasson (Boston, 1887), and of Harriet Winslow Sewall (Boston, 1889). Much of her work is devoted to religious and artistic subjects. Mrs. Cheney is now living in Jamaica Plain, Mass.

CHENOWETH, Mrs. Caroline Van Deusen, vice-consul and educator, born at the summer home of her parents, on the Ohio river, opposite Louisville, Ky., 29th December, 1846. She is the youngest daughter of Charles Van Deusen and Mary Huntington, his wife. The winters of her early life were passed in New Orleans, La., where was also the residence of her mother's family. Her academic training was had in the St. Charles Institute, New Orleans, and Moore's Hill College, near Cincinnati. She became the wife, while still in her girlhood, of Col. Bernard Peel Chenoweth, the son of Rev. Alfred Griffith Chenoweth, of Virginia. Mrs. Chenoweth has always held liberal views relative to woman's work, and the simple naturalness with which she has lived according to her faith is hardly less remarkable than the unusual and brilliant character of her achievements. For fourteen months following her marriage in 1863, she performed faithfully and with patriotic fervor the onerous duties of a military clerk to Col. Chenoweth, thereby returning to duty in the ranks, and as her substitute on the field, the soldier detailed for this clerical work. When Col. Chenoweth was made superintendent of schools in Worcester, Mass.,

Mrs. Chenoweth took the examination required for teachers, that she might be of service in the event of need. It was during her husband's term of office as United States Consul in Canton, China,

CAROLINE VAN DEUSEN CHENOWETH.

that she was able to render her most efficient aid. Upon one occasion she sat as vice-consul in an important land case between one of the largest American houses and a wealthy Chinese. She reserved her decision for several days, until it could be submitted to Col. Chenoweth, then some eighty miles distant, under medical care, who promptly returned it unchanged, with direction that she should officially promulgate it as his duly accredited representative. Thenceforth, until Col. Chenoweth's death, several months later, the affairs of the consulate were conducted by Mrs. Chenoweth. She is believed to be the only woman who has ever held diplomatic correspondence with a viceroy of China upon her own responsibility. She was officially recognized in her vice-consular capacity upon her return to Washington to settle her husband's affairs with the Department of State, and was cordially complimented by Hamilton Fish, Secretary of State, for the thoroughness and skill with which her mission was accomplished. The effort was made by influential friends in Massachusetts to return Mrs. Chenoweth to Canton as United States consul, a measure to which President Grant extended his warm approval and the promise of his support, provided his Secretary of State could be won over. The later life of Mrs. Chenoweth has been a most studious and laborious one, the more so that the support and education of her two sons fell to her unaided care. For some years she taught private classes in Boston, and was for a time professor of English literature in Smith College. Her interests are varied, and her literary work is graceful as well as full of energy. Her essays relating to experimental psychology are scholarly and abreast of the freshest thought. She

is a member of the London Society for Psychical Research, as well as of many other working societies, among which are the Brooklyn Institute, the New York Dante Society, and the Medico-Legal Society of New York. Her sketches of child-life in China are quaint and sweet. Her "Stories of the Saints" (Boston, 1882) is rich in an old-world charm. The book was written for some children of Dr. Phillips Brooks' parish in Boston, of which she was for twenty years a member. She now resides in New York City.

CHILD, Mrs. Lydia Maria, author, born in Medford, Mass., 11th February, 1802. Her father was David Francis. Lydia was assisted in her early studies by her brother, Convers Francis, who was afterwards professor of theology in Harvard College. Her first village teacher was an odd old woman, nicknamed "Marm Betty." She studied in the public schools and one year in a seminary. In 1814 she went to Norridgewock, Maine, to live with her married sister. She remained there several years and then returned to Watertown, Mass., to live with her brother. He encouraged her literary aspirations, and in his study she wrote her first story, "Hobomok," which was published in 1823. It proved successful, and she next published "Rebels," which ran quickly through several editions. She then brought out in rapid succession "The Mother's Book," which ran through eight American, twelve English and one German editions, "The Girl's Book," the "History of Women," and the "Frugal Housewife," which passed through thirty-five editions. In 1826 she commenced to publish her "Juvenile Miscellany." In 1828 she became the wife of David Lee Child, a lawyer, and they settled in Boston, Mass. In 1831 they became interested

LYDIA MARIA CHILD.

in the anti-slavery movememt, and both took an active part in the agitation that followed. Mr. Child was one of the leaders of the anti-slavery party. In 1833 Mrs. Child published her "Appeal in Behalf of that Class of Americans Called Africans." Its appearance served to cut her off from the friends and admirers of her youth. Social and literary circles shut their doors to her. The sales of her books and subscriptions to ner magazine fell off, and her life became one of battle. Through it all she bore herself with patience and courage, and she threw herself into the movement with all her powers. While engaged in that memorable battle, she found time to produce her lives of Madame Roland and Baroness de Staël, and her Greek romance, "Philothea." She, with her husband, supervised editorially the "Anti-Slavery Standard," in which she published her admirable "Letters from New York." During those troubled times she prepared her three-volume work on "The Progress of Religious Ideas." She lived in New York City with her husband from 1840 to 1844, when she removed to Wayland, Mass., where she died 20th October, 1880. Her anti-slavery writings aided powerfully in bringing about the overthrow of slavery, and she lived to see a reversal of the hostile opinions that greeted her first plea for the negroes. Her books are numerous. Besides those already mentioned the most important are "Flowers for Children" (3 volumes, 1844-46); "Fact and Fiction" (1846); "The Power of Kindness" (1851); "Isaac T. Hopper, a True Life" (1853); "Autumnal Leaves" (1856); "Looking Towards Sunset" (1864); "The Freedman's Book" (1865); "Miria" (1867), and "Aspirations of the World" (1878). Her reply to Governor Wise, of Virginia, and to the wife of Senator Mason, the author of the fugitive slave law, who wrote to her, threatening her with future damnation, was published with their letters in pamphlet form, and 300,000 copies were issued. A volume of her letters, with an introduction by John Greenleaf Whittier and an appendix by Wendell Phillips, was published in Boston, in 1882.

CHURCHILL, Mrs. Caroline M., editor and publisher, born in the township of Pickering, in the Upper Province of Canada, 23rd December, 1833. She lived with her parents in the township of Whitley until thirteen years of age, and was then sent to Lockport, N. Y., to attend school. How her father, Barber Nichols, came to settle in Canada is a matter not clearly understood by the family, as he was born in Providence, R. I., and served in the war of 1812, for which he drew a pension. He lived to be 100 years old. Her mother is now over ninety years old and drawing a widow's pension for the father's service in 1812. Her father was a prosperous tradesman and a leading man fifty years ago in what is now called Ontario. His mother was French, his father English. The mother was Holland Dutch and German, transplanted to the State of Pennsylvania. Mrs. Churchill became the wife of a Canadian, who died in 1862. One daughter, born in 1852, is her only child. In 1869 Mrs. Churchill was attacked with what appeared to be the dread disease, consumption. California was chosen as the best place at that time to overcome a difficulty of that nature. Thither she repaired and took to canvassing for the sake of life in the open air. The result was such that her cough ceased and her health was restored. Her constitution is a light one, however, and without very favorable conditions much development is hardly possible. Mrs. Churchill's most notable public work during six years of traveling life in California was the defeat of Holland's social evil bill by a burlesque. She drew up a bill for the regulation and control of immoral men similar to that introduced for the regulation of the same class of women. A member of the committee to whom the bill was submitted caused the

burlesque to be printed and extensively circulated, creating a great deal of amusement at the expense of the advocate of Holland's bill. The latter was never heard from again. An assembly and senate attempted to get the same bill passed in Denver, Col., within a year or two. That burlesque was reprinted and placed upon the tables in both houses, and the bill was defeated. Mrs. Churchill has written two books which have had a sale of over fifty-thousand copies, a little descriptive work called "Little Sheaves," and a book of travel entitled "Over the Purple Hills." While traveling in Texas, she introduced a bill in the legislature, the import of which was to keep the "Police Gazette" from being sold upon the news stands in the State. The bill passed, was signed by Governor Roberts, and has been in force for fifteen years. Feeling the need of preparation for age, Mrs. Churchill settled in Denver, and there established the "Colorado Antelope," a monthly. After publishing it for

CAROLINE M. CHURCHILL.

three years, the paper was changed to a weekly, the "Queen Bee," in 1879. She is a good speaker, but, from press of work in making a home for herself, she has had little opportunity to become known in the lecture field. Mrs. Churchill is by nature aggressively progressive.

CHURCHILL, Miss Lide A., born in Harrison, Maine, 9th April, 1859. She is the youngest child of Josiah and Catherine Churchill. From her father she inherited her literary tastes and refined nature, from her mother her strong will and decided traits of character. Three years after her birth Mr. Churchill removed to New Gloucester, Maine, where he resided with his family until his death. When quite young, Miss Churchill decided to learn telegraphy, and went to Saundersville, Mass., where she partially mastered the art. She took charge of a small office in Northbridge, Mass., and without assistance perfected herself in the science. From that office she was promoted to larger and larger ones, until she had charge of the most important station belonging to the road that employed her. She next mastered stenography without a teacher and practiced it for a time. In

LIDE A. CHURCHILL.

1889 Rev. Charles A. Dickinson, who is at the head of Berkeley Temple, Boston, desired a private secretary for stenographic and literary work, and offered the position to Miss Churchill, who accepted it. Its duties demand knowledge, skill, tact and literary ability. Miss Churchill has written and published continuously during all the years she has been engaged as telegrapher and literary secretary. Her first book, "My Girls" (Boston, 1882) has passed through several editions. She has also written "Interweaving" and "Raid on New England." She has done much good magazine work.

CHURCHILL, Lady Randolph, social leader and politician, wife of Lord Randolph Churchill, of England, is a native of the United States. She was born in Brooklyn, N. Y. Her maiden name was Jennie Jerome, daughter of Leonard Jerome, a prominent citizen of New York City. Miss Jerome and her two sisters were educated mainly in Paris, France, where they were thoroughly taught in all the accomplishments common to wealthy women of the time. While visiting the Isle of Wight, England, Miss Jerome met Lord Randolph Churchill, who was then known simply as the second son of the Duke of Marlborough. Their acquaintance ripened to love, engagement followed, and in January, 1874, they were married at the British Embassy in Paris. Lord Randolph's political career began immediately after his marriage, when he entered the House of Commons as a member from Woodstock. Lady Churchill entered into her husband's plans and aspirations with all her native energy and determination, and to her assistance and counsel is credited much of his success in Parliament. Lady Randolph was one

of the first members of the Primrose League, the organization of the Conservatives, and it is largely due to her efforts that in Great Britain the order can boast of nearly 2,000 habitations. Lady Churchill is an effective worker in political campaigns, and she has thoroughly mastered all the intricacies of British politics. Besides her activity in politics, Lady Churchill devotes much well-directed effort to art and charity, and in British society she is looked upon as a great force. Born in the Republic, she illustrates the self-adapting power of the genuine American in the ease with

LADY RANDOLPH CHURCHILL.

which she has taken up and mastered the difficult and delicate problems implied in her situation as a wife of a peer of the English realm.

CLAFLIN, Mrs. Adelaide Avery, woman suffragist, born in Boston, Mass., 28th July, 1846. She is a daughter of Alden Avery and Lucinda Miller Brown, both natives of Maine, and both of English extraction, although there is a little Scotch-Irish blood on the Miller side. Narcissa Adelaide was the second of four children. Her father, although an active business man, had much poetical and religious feeling. He is a prominent member of the Methodist Church, and, on account of his eloquence, was often in earlier life advised to become a minister. Her mother, of a practical, common-sense temperament, had much appreciation of nature and of scientific fact, and a gift for witty and concise expression of thought. So from both parents Mrs. Claflin has derived the ability to speak with clearness and epigrammatic force. Adelaide was sixteen when she was graduated from the Boston girls' high school, and a year or two later she became a teacher in the Winthrop school. Although in childhood attending the Methodist Church with their parents, both her sister and herself early adopted the so-called liberal faith, and joined the church of Rev. James Freeman Clarke. She became the wife of Frederic A. Claflin, of Boston, in 1870, a man of keen and thoughtful mind and generous and kindly spirit. They have for many years resided in Quincy, Mass., and have a son and three daughters. In 1883 Mrs.

ADELAIDE AVERY CLAFLIN.

Claflin began to speak in public as an advocate of woman suffrage. In 1884 she was elected a member of the Quincy school committee, and served three years in that position, being the only woman who ever held office in that conservative town. Although too much occupied with family cares to take a very active part in public life, her pen is busied in writing for the Boston papers, and she finds opportunity to give lectures, and has occasionally been on short lecturing tours outside of the limits of New England. Best known as a woman suffragist, she writes and speaks on various other topics, and her wide range of reading and thinking makes it probable that her future career as a lecturer will not be limited chiefly to the woman suffrage field.

CLARK, Mrs. Frances P., philanthropist, born in Syracuse, N. Y., 17th September, 1836. She was one of a family of seven children born to Dr. J. H. and Mary P. Parker, who were persons of fine character. Miss Parker was educated in Syracuse, and in November, 1858, became the wife of George W. Clark. In 1860 they moved to Cleveland, Ohio, remaining there until 1883, when they removed to Omaha, Neb., where they have since lived. Their family consists of a daughter and son. After recovering from an apparently incurable disease of long standing, Mrs. Clark, in a spirit of gratitude to God, devoted herself to charitable work, taking up the work most needed to be done and most neglected, as she felt, by Christians, that of care for the so-called outcasts of society. In 1884, in recognition of her ability and services, she was appointed State superintendent of the social purity department of the Woman's Christian Temperance Union of Nebraska. As a result of the agitation begun by Mrs. Clark and her colleagues,

the disgraceful statute making the age of consent twelve years was changed by the Legislature, in 1887, raising it to fifteen years. The women had prepared a bill making the limit eighteen years, and the result was a compromise. At the same time they petitioned the Legislature for a grant of $25,-000, to be used in establishing an industrial home in Milford, Neb. That institution accordingly was founded at once, and through the happy results since flowing therefrom has fully met the expectations of its founders. Mrs. Clark is a member of the board of management of the Milford home, and also of the Woman's Associate Charities of the State of Nebraska, under appointment by the Governor. Besides this, she is the superintendent of a local institution for the same purpose in Omaha, known as "The Open Door," under the auspices of the local Woman's Christian Temperance Union. That institution is supported by subscriptions from

FRANCES PARKER CLARK.

the citizens of Omaha. With all these calls upon her time, Mrs. Clark is busy constantly, and she stands in the foremost rank among the women philanthropists of Nebraska.

CLARK, Mrs. Helen Taggart, journalist, born in Northumberland, Pa., 24th April, 1849. She is the oldest of three children of the late Col. David Taggart and Annie Pleasants Taggart. She was educated in the Friends' central high school, in Philadelphia, Pa. In October, 1869, she made a six months' stay in Charleston, S. C., whither she went to make a visit to her father, then stationed in that city as paymaster in the United States army. Miss Taggart became the wife in 1870 of Rev. David H. Clark, a Unitarian minister settled over the church in Northumberland. Four years later they removed to New Milford, Pa., to take charge of a Free Religious Society there. In 1875 Mr. Clark was called to the Free Congregational Society in Florence, Mass. Attention was first drawn to "H. T. C.," by which some of her earlier work was signed, in 1880, by her occasional poems in the Boston "Index," of which her husband was for a time assistant editor, and in the Springfield "Republican." Her life, as she puts it, has been one

HELEN TAGGART CLARK.

of intellectual aspirations and clamorous dish-washing and bread-winning. Mrs. Clark left Florence in 1884, returning to her father's house in Northumberland with her youngest child, an only daughter, her two older children being boys. There for two years she was a teacher in the high school, varying her duties by teaching music and German outside of school hours, story and verse writing and leading a Shakespeare class. In August, 1887, she accepted a position in the "Good Cheer" office, Greenfield, Mass., whence she was recalled to Northumberland the following February by the illness of her father. His illness terminated fatally a little later, since which time Mrs. Clark has made her home in her native town. Mrs. Clark has a large circle of friends, and her social duties take up much of her time, but she contrives to furnish a weekly column for the Sunbury "News," to perform the duties pertaining to her office as secretary of the Woman's Relief Corps in her town, to lead a young people's literary society, and to contribute stories and poems to Frank Leslie's papers, the "Christian Union," the "Woman's Journal" and the Springfield "Republican."

CLARKE, Mrs. Lena Thompson, social leader, born in Americus, Ga., 10th January, 1857. Her ancestors were of that sterling Revolutionary stock whose strength of character can be traced through each generation following them. She is the daughter of James Egbert Thompson, and the granddaughter of Judge Amos Thompson, of Poultney, Vt. James Egbert Thompson went to St. Paul, Minn., and helped to found that city. He founded the First National Bank of St. Paul, which soon became the leading bank of the Northwest. He became influential in the development of the

State and was entrusted with numerous offices of importance, which his rare executive ability enabled him to fill with success. He died in the prime of life, with honors still awaiting him and beloved by all who knew him. His widow, a beautiful woman of southern blood, has lived for the most part in Europe since her husband's death. Mrs. Clarke was educated in Germany and thoroughly acquired a cosmopolitan polish of manner. She is an accomplished linguist, and in the midst of a busy life finds time to maintain her reputation as an excellent and sympathetic musician. For years she has been the president of a boarding-home for working women and has been its inspiration. She possesses great energy of character and the courage of her convictions, united with an amiable manner, rare tact and a thoughtful consideration for others. She was chosen commissioner from Minnesota to the World's Columbian Exposition and was appointed a member of the executive committee of the woman's department, chairman of the committee on music in the woman's building, and was elected president for Minnesota of the woman's committee of the World's Congress Auxiliary. Her tastes fitted her to become a valued member of the musical and literary clubs of her city, a feature which has become so helpful in the life of to-day. Above all, it is in her home that she finds her most attractive setting. She has a devoted husband, Francis B. Clarke, a prominent

LENA THOMPSON CLARKE.

and influential resident of St. Paul, and three children.

CLARKE, Mrs. Mary Bassett, born in Independence, N. Y., 18th November, 1831. She is the daughter of John C. Bassett, a well-to-do farmer of western New York, and Martha St. John Bassett, both persons of education and refinement. She was the seventh in a family of twelve children who lived to maturity. She was educated in Alfred University. Although ill-health limited her opportunities, she was graduated from the university in

1857. At the age of fifteen she commenced to write for publication, under the pen-name "Ida Fairfield," in the "Flag of Our Union." With some interruption by ill-health, she continued many

MARY BASSETT CLARKE.

years to be a contributor to that paper, to the "Rural New Yorker" and to local papers and periodicals. She became the wife of William L. Clarke on 8th September, 1859, and removed to Ashaway, R. I., which place has since been her home. For several years her writings, both prose and verse, have been principally given to periodicals issued by the Seventh-Day Baptists, of which sect she is a member.

CLARKE, Mrs. Mary H. Gray, correspondent, born in Bristol, R. I., 28th March, 1835. She is the daughter of the late Gideon Gray and Hannah Orne Metcalf Gray. Her father was of the sixth generation from Edward Gray, who came from Westminster, London, England, and settled in Plymouth, Mass., prior to 1643. Edward Gray was married to Dorothy Lettice and was known as the richest merchant of Plymouth. The oldest stone in the Plymouth burial ground is that of Edward Gray. Mrs. Clarke's great-grandfather, Thomas Gray, of the fourth generation, was during the war of the Revolution commissioned as colonel. Mrs. Clarke spent her early years on her father's homestead, a portion of the Mount Hope lands obtained from King Philip, the Indian chief. A farm on those famous lands is still in her possession. She attended the schools of her native town and later studied in the academy in East Greenwich. In 1861 she became the wife of Dr. Augustus P. Clarke, a graduate of Brown University, in the arts, and of Harvard, in medicine. During her husband's four years of service as surgeon and surgeon-in-chief of brigade and of division of cavalry in the war of the Rebellion, she took an active interest in work for the success of the Union cause. In the fall of 1865 her husband, continuing in the practice of his

profession, removed to Cambridge, Mass., where they have since resided. They have two daughters Mrs. Clarke has written quite extensively for magazines and for the press, principally stories for the young, poems and essays. In 1890, on the occasion of the meeting of the Tenth International Medical Congress in Berlin, Germany, she accompanied her husband and daughters to that place. She has traveled extensively through the British Isles and Europe. In the midst of her duties and responsibilities she has found time to paint many pictures, some in water-colors and some in oils. Much of the writing of Mrs. Clarke has been under the pen-names "Nina Gray" and "Nina Gray Clarke."

CLARKE, Miss Rebecca Sophia, author, born in Norridgewock, Maine, 22nd February, 1833. She has spent much of her life in her native town. Miss Clarke is widely known by her pen-name, "Sophia May," which she adopted in 1861 and attached to her first story, published in the Memphis "Appeal." When the story was finished, she signed her middle name, Sophia, and then said: "Well, I'll call it May, for I may write again and may not." Thus the surname was invented that has become so familiar to American boys and girls. Among her early productions were some stories for Grace Greenwood's "Little Pilgrim." She was asked by the editor of the "Congregationalist" to send to that journal all the stories she might write about "Little Prudy." She then had no thought of making a book of the stories. William T. Adams, known as "Oliver Optic," brought them to the attention of Mr. Lee, who published them and paid Miss Clarke fifty dollars for each of the six volumes. These charming stories of "Prudy" and her aunts,

MARY H. GRAY CLARKE.

sisters and cousins have been said to be portraits, but Miss Clarke disclaims any such delineation. The "Prudy" stories are sold in large numbers every year. In 1891 Miss Clarke published her last book, "In Old Quinnebasset." She resides with her sister, Miss Sarah Clarke, who, as "Penn Shirley," is also a successful author. Miss Clarke's publications, in book form, all issued in Boston, are:

REBECCA SOPHIA CLARKE.

"Little Prudy Stories" (1864-6), six volumes; "Dotty Dimple Stories" (1868-70), six volumes; "Little Prudy's Flyaway Series" (1871-74), six volumes; "The Doctor's Daughter" (1873), "Our Helen" (1875); "The Asbury Twins" (1876); "Flaxie Frizzle Stories" (1876-84), six volumes; "Quinnebasset Girls" (1877); "Janet, or a Poor Heiress," (1882); "Drones' Honey" (1887); "In Old Quinnebasset" (1891).

CLAXTON, Kate, actor, born in New York City, in 1848. Her father, Col. Spencer H. Cone, commanded the 61st New York regiment during the Civil War. Her grandfather, Rev. Spencer H. Cone, was a Baptist clergyman, who for a short period was an actor. Kate Claxton first appeared with Lotta in Chicago, soon afterwards joined Daly's Fifth Avenue Company, and then became a member of the Union Square Company. She attracted no special notice until she appeared as Mathilde in "Led Astray," in 1873, in which character she won considerable popularity. Her greatest success was Louise in "The Two Orphans" first brought out in the Union Square Theater, and afterwards produced throughout the United States. While acting the part in the Brooklyn Theater, the building was destroyed by fire, 5th December, 1876, with much loss of life. Miss Claxton's coolness on that occasion, and at the Southern Hotel fire in St. Louis, Mo., shortly afterwards, won for her much praise. She has more recently played in Charles Reade's "Double Marriage," in the "Sea of Ice" and in "Bootles' Baby." Miss Claxton was divorced from her first husband, Isidor Lyon, a merchant of New York. In 1876 she became the wife of Charles Stevenson, a member of her company.

CLAY, Mrs. Mary Barr, woman suffragist and farmer, born in Lexington, Ky., 13th October, 1839. She is a daughter of Cassius M. Clay and Mary J. Warfield. Her childhood and youth were passed in the country, and she was educated mainly by private tutors from Yale College. She became the wife of John Frank Herrick, of Cleveland, Ohio, 3rd October, 1860. She was divorced from him in 1872. The position of her father as an advocate of free speech and of the emancipation of the negro slave in a slave State, gave her, who sympathized with him, the independence of thought and action that was necessary to espouse the cause of woman's political and civil freedom in the same conservative community, and she met much opposition, ridicule and slights with equal fortitude. Her realization of the servile position of women under the laws was brought about by attending a convention held in Cleveland, Ohio, by Lucy Stone, in 1868 or 1869. She then and there subscribed for books and pamphlets and gave them to any one who would read them and wrote articles for the local papers, which the editors published with a protest, declaring that Mrs. Clay alone was responsible for them. She was the first native Kentuckian to take the public platform for woman suffrage. She went to St. Louis in 1879, and, presenting herself to Miss Susan B. Anthony, who was holding a convention there, asked to be admitted as a delegate from Kentucky. Miss Anthony warmly welcomed her and appointed her vice-president for Kentucky, which office she held in that association as long as it existed. In 1879 she organized in Lexington a suffrage club, the first in the State. In 1880 she and Mrs. James Bennett organized one in Richmond which has continued to this time. Mrs. Clay was a member

KATE CLAXTON.

and vice-president for Kentucky for many years of the American Suffrage Association, and was, in 1884, elected president of that association, when it held its convention in Chicago. She was the leading

Kentucky organizer of the first State association, formed in Louisville after the convention held there by Lucy Stone in 1881. Living in Ann Arbor, Mich., for some years, educating her two sons, she organized a suffrage club there and was invited by Mrs. Stebbins to help reorganize the State association. She was made president pro tem. of the convention in Flint, where the present Michigan State Association was reorganized. She edited a column in the Ann Arbor "Register" for some time on woman suffrage. By invitation of the Suffrage Association of Michigan, she spoke before the Legislative Committee, and was invited by the senior law class of the University of Michigan to address them on the "Constitutional Right of Women to Vote." She has petitioned Congress and addressed House and Senate committees for the rights of women. For years she has visited the State Legislature and laid the wrongs of women before that body, demanding as a right, not as a favor, the equality of women under the laws. Mrs. Clay was for years the only worker in the cause except her sisters, and she was the first to demand of the late constitutional convention that they emancipate the women of Kentucky, one-half the adult people of the State. Her letter was read before the convention, and she was the spokesman of the committee of women who were invited to the floor of the convention to hear the plea from the Equal Rights Association of Kentucky. To accomplish the civil and political freedom of women has for years been

MARY BARR CLAY.

her chief aim and labor. She is now vice-president of the Kentucky Equal Rights Association.

CLAYTON, Mrs. Florence Andrews, opera singer, born near Le Sueur, Minn., in 1862. She is the ninth child of Rev. Mr. Andrews, one of the pioneer Methodist ministers of Minnesota. At that time Le Sueur was well out on the western frontier, and most of the settlers of that region abandoned their homes and crowded into St. Peter

during the Indian outbreak. The Andrews family stuck to their farm near the little village Two of the older sons entered the army of defense against

FLORENCE ANDREWS CLAYTON.

the Indians and were in the battle of New Ulm. Both Mr. Andrews and his wife were natural, though untrained musicians, and all of their ten children, known as the Andrews Family, inherited musical ability. In 1876 Miss Andrews, then fourteen years of age, went upon the stage with her brothers and sisters for their first year with the "Swiss Bells." They played in Minnesota and adjoining States, making trips southward as far as the southern border of the Indian Territory. She has since then been continually before the public, except for longer or shorter vacations. She became the wife of Fred Clayton, of Cleveland, Ohio, in 1883, who is also with the present Andrews Opera Company. They have two sons. The musical culture of Mrs. Clayton has been received mostly by instruction from and association with some of the most competent vocal artists of the country, while she has been traveling and working with them. She has thus obtained that thorough and practical knowledge of her art which can be secured in no other way. Her repertoire consists of forty operas, tragic and comic. She is not only an excellent vocalist, but also a fine actor, with a natural adaptation to dramatic parts. Her voice is a contralto.

CLEARY, Mrs. Kate McPhelim, correspondent, born in Richibucto, Kent county, New Brunswick, 20th August, 1863. Her parents, James and Margaret McPhelim, were of Irish birth, the former, with his brothers, being distinguished for intellectual ability and business talents. They were extensively engaged in the timber business, and in 1856 her uncle, Hon. Francis McPhelim, was Postmaster-General of New Brunswick, and her father held the office of high sheriff of the county. Her father's death, in 1865, left his widow with three small children and limited means, which she devoted to their education. Kate was educated in the Sacred Heart Convent, St. John, N. B., and later attended other convent schools in

KATE McPHELIM CLEARY.

this country and in the old. Her pen, which had been a source of diversion and delight to her since she was a little girl, became, when necessity required, an easy means of support. Her first published poem appeared when she was fourteen years old, and from that time to the present she has written almost continuously poetry and fiction. On 26th February, 1884, she became the wife of Michael T. Cleary, a young lumber merchant of Hubbell, Neb. Mr. and Mrs. Cleary have kept a hospitable home, welcoming as guests many distinguished men and women. Mrs. Cleary's stories are largely those of adventure and incident, and are published in newspapers quite as much as magazines. She has contributed prose and verse chiefly to the New York "Ledger," "Belford's Magazine," the "Fireside Companion," "Saturday Night," "Puck," the "New York Weekly," the "Current," "Our Continent," the Chicago "Tribune," "St. Nicholas," "Wide-Awake," and the Detroit "Free Press."

CLEAVES, Miss Margaret Abagail, doctor of medicine, born in Columbus City, Iowa., 25th November, 1848. Her father was of Dutch and English and her mother of Scotch and Irish ancestry, but by birth they were both Americans. Her father, Dr. John Trow Cleaves, was born in Yarmouth, Maine, in 1813, and her mother, Elizabeth Stronach, in Baltimore, in 1820. In 1843 they were married in Columbus City, where Dr. Cleaves practiced medicine until his death, which occurred in October, 1863. He was a man who took a deep interest in public affairs, and twice he was elected a member of the Iowa Legislature, first in 1852, and again in 1861. Margaret was the third of seven children. She inherited her father's taste for medical

pursuits and as a child frequently accompanied him on his professional visits. Her education was obtained in the public schools and in the Iowa State University, but because of limited means she was unable to finish the collegiate course in the latter institution. After she was sixteen, she alternately attended and taught school for some years. In 1868 the family moved to Davenport, Iowa. There Margaret resolved to become a doctor instead of continuing a school teacher. Her choice of a profession was not regarded with favor by the various members of her family, who entertained the prevailing ideas concerning the limitations of woman's sphere, but her mind was made up, and in 1870 she began to read medicine and against their wishes entered the Medical Department of the Iowa State University. Their opposition did not continue long, for it was soon made manifest that her choice of a profession had been a wise one. In 1871 she entered the office of her preceptor, Dr. W. F. Peck, who was dean of the faculty and professor of surgery in the university. She was graduated 5th March, 1873, standing at the head of the class. Shortly after graduating, she was appointed second assistant physician in the State Hospital for the Insane, Mount Pleasant, Iowa. There she was a veritable pioneer, for up to that time only one other woman in the world had occupied the position of physician in a public insane asylum. She remained in the asylum for three years and then resigned her position to commence private practice in Davenport. She was subsequently appointed one of the trustees of the asylum. While practicing medicine in Davenport, she became a member of the Scott County Medical Society, being the second woman to gain admission

MARGARET ABAGAIL CLEAVES.

to that body. For several years she was the secretary of the society. She also joined the State Medical Society, where she was again the second woman to gain admission. She was the first woman to become a member of the Iowa and Illinois Central District Medical Association. During her residence in Davenport she was an active member of the Davenport Academy of Sciences. In 1879 the board of trustees of the State Asylum for the Insane chose her their delegate to the National Conference of Charities, which that year met in Chicago, Ill. In that conference she read a paper on "The Medical and Moral Care of Female Patients in Hospitals for the Insane." It attracted widespread attention, and was printed in a volume, "Lunacy in Many Lands," which was published by the Government of New South Wales. In June, 1880, she was appointed by the Governor of Iowa a State delegate to the National Conference of Charities in Cleveland, Ohio, and thus the distinction was conferred upon her of being the first female delegate from Iowa to that body. She reported for the State to the conference, and her report was subsequently incorporated in the Governor's annual message. That same year she was appointed physician-in-chief in the Female Department of the Pennsylvania State Lunatic Hospital in Harrisburg. After three years of hard work, rendered all the more arduous by her conscientious devotion to the minutest details of her duties, Dr. Cleaves was compelled by failing health to resign her position. She went abroad in 1883, remaining nearly two years, visiting insane hospitals in Scotland, England, France, Italy, Germany, Austria, Switzerland and Belgium, everywhere receiving flattering courtesies from men of recognized eminence in the treatment of insanity. She witnessed operations in general hospitals in England, France and Germany, and in Paris she was for several months a regular attendant at lectures and clinics. After returning to the United States, she opened a private home for the reception of patients in Des Moines, Iowa, conducting also an office practice in connection with her other work. In March, 1885, she was appointed one of the examining committee of the Medical Department of the Iowa State University. It was the first honor of that kind bestowed on a woman by any standard medical school in the United States. In July 1886, she was sent as a delegate to the yearly meeting of the National Conference of Charities, which was held in St. Paul, Minn. During her residence in Des Moines she was an active member of the Polk County Medical Society, of the Missouri Valley Medical Association and of the Iowa State Medical Association. Before all those bodies she read papers and she served the last-named body as chairman of obstetrics and gynæcology in the session of 1889. At that time she was the only woman who had received such an appointment. Her work was not confined to medicine alone. She took a deep interest in all that pertains to the welfare and advancement of women. She organized the Des Moines Woman's Club and was its first president. Some time prior to that she had become a member of the Association for the Advancement of Women. Becoming interested in the subject of electro-therapeutics, she went to New York in the winter of 1887 and to Paris in the following summer, to prosecute her inquiries and investigation. After her return she continued to practice for a while in Des Moines, but in 1890 she retired from that field and went to New York, where she opened an office. She there joined the Medical Society of the County of New York, the American Electro-Therapeutic Association and the New York Women's Press Club. In the Post-Graduate Medical School, New York, she is now clinical assistant to the chair of electro-therapeutics. Since she took up her residence in New York, she has read papers before the

Medical Society of Kings County, Brooklyn, the New York Medico-Legal Society, the American Electro-Therapeutic Association and the National Conference of Charities. Many of them have been published, and all of them are distinguished by painstaking research, clearness of statement and logical reasoning. Though a very busy woman, though her chosen fields of labor and study have taken her far away from the paths followed by most women, she has sacrificed none of those sweet, helpful and peculiarly womanly characteristics which endear her to her friends. She is a woman who combines in a most felicitous way gentleness of speech and manner with firmness of character. She has keen insight and quick sympathies, yet cool judgment.

CLEMENT, Mrs. Clara Erskine, see WATERS, CLARA ERSKINE CLEMENT.

CLERC, Mme. Henrietta Fannie Virginie, educator, born in Paris, France, 7th February, 1841. She is the daughter of Alexandre Louis Sulpice Clerc and Marie Josephine Virginie Grand-Fils. Her grandfather, Gen. Le Clerc, fought for the first Napoleon, and was knighted De Saint Clerc by him at the battle of Austerlitz. Sulpice Clerc was too strong a republican to bear any title. He was opposed to the Empire of Napoleon III and was

HENRIETTA FANNIE VIRGINIE CLERC.

one of the conspirators to take away his life. The plot was discovered, and those who escaped imprisonment were obliged to leave Paris, and all their property was confiscated. Sulpice Clerc and his wife lived in various parts of Europe until their children's education was finished. They had two sons and two daughters. Henrietta, the eldest daughter, was graduated from the Convent of the Dames Benedictines, where she had been since the age of five. The family then came to this country and settled in New York City. In April, 1861, Henrietta was married to her first cousin, Felix Clerc, who was killed the following July in the battle of Bull Run, having entered the Union army as a French Zouave at the outbreak of the Civil War. Since that time Mme. Clerc has supported herself by teaching, at first in a Quaker school in Bristol, then in the Packer Collegiate Institute, in Brooklyn, N. Y., and in St. Agnes' School, Albany, N.Y., in each of which schools she remained five years. In 1881 she established a school of her own in Philadelphia, Pa., where she is at present training a limited number of girls each year. For the use of her pupils she published several years ago a pamphlet entitled " First Steps in the Art of Speaking French." She is now editing a monthly paper, "L'Étude," for those wishing to perfect themselves in her native tongue.

CLEVELAND, Mrs. Frances Folsom, wife of Stephen Grover Cleveland, the twenty-second President of the United States, born in Buffalo, N. Y., 21st July, 1864. She is the only child of the late Oscar Folsom, who was killed in a carriage accident in 1875. Her mother is still living in Buffalo, the wife of Henry E. Perrine. Miss Folsom spent her early school days in Madame Brecker's French kindergarten. After Mr. Folsom's death the widow and daughter made their home in Medina, N. Y., with Mrs. Folsom's mother, Mrs. Harmon. Mr. Cleveland was appointed her guardian-at-law. In Medina Miss Folsom attended the high school. Returning to Buffalo, she became a student in the central high school, where she was noted for her brightness in study. She next went to Aurora, N. Y., where she entered Wells College, on her central high school certificate, which admitted her to the sophomore class without examination. She was a favorite in Wells College. She

FRANCES FOLSOM CLEVELAND.

was graduated in June, 1885, her graduating essay being cast in the form of a story. Her future husband was Governor of the State of New York while she was in college, and was elected President before her graduation, on which occasion a gift of

flowers was sent to her from the White House. After graduating from college she went abroad for a time for travel and study. She returned from Europe on 28th May, 1886, and was married to Mr. Cleveland, in the White House, 2nd June, 1886. The wedding was the occasion of many pleasant attentions to the President and his bride. Her reign as the first lady of the land, was a brilliant one, marked by tact and unfailing courtesy. She was the youngest of the many mistresses of the White House. When Mr. Cleveland's presidential term ended, in 1889, they made their home in New York City, where their daughter, Ruth, was born. In that city her life has been filled with social duties and charitable work in many directions. She is a member of the Presbyterian Church.

CLEVELAND, Miss Rose Elizabeth, author, born in Fayetteville, N. Y., in 1846, and

ROSE ELIZABETH CLEVELAND.

moved to Holland Patent, N. Y., in 1853. She is a sister of ex-President Cleveland and a daughter of Rev. Richard Falley Cleveland, a Presbyterian preacher, who was graduated from Yale College in 1824. Her mother's maiden name was Neal, and she was the daughter of a Baltimore merchant of Irish birth. The Clevelands are of English descent, in a direct line from Moses Cleveland, of the county of Suffolk, England, who came to the Colonies in 1635 and settled in Woburn, Mass., where he died in 1701. Miss Cleveland is in the seventh generation. Her father was settled as pastor of the Presbyterian Church in Holland Patent in 1853. Rose was one of a large family. Two of her brothers, Louis and Frederick, were lost at sea in 1872 on the return trip from Nassau. The father died in 1853 and the mother in 1882. One married sister, Mrs. Louise Bacon, lives in Toledo, Ohio. The parents were persons of marked force of character, morally and intellectually. Rose was educated in the seminary in Houghton. She taught in that school after graduation, and then was called to

Lafayette, Ind., where she took charge of the Collegiate Institute. She taught later in Pennsylvania in a private school. She then began to lecture on history before classes in Houghton Seminary. Her courses of lectures were well received, and after her mother's death, in 1882, she kept her home in Holland Patent and continued her school work. Her reputation as a lecturer grew, and her services were called for in other schools. When her brother was elected President, she accompanied him to Washington, D. C., and presided as mistress of the White House until his marriage, in June, 1886. Her best womanly qualities were displayed in that delicate and difficult position, and she took into the White House an atmosphere of culture, independence and originality that was exceedingly attractive. The brightest men of the time found in her a self-possessed, intellectual, thoroughly educated woman, acquainted with several modern languages and fully informed on all the questions of the day. After her brother's marriage she returned to Holland Patent. She afterwards taught history in a private school in New York City. She has not written much. Her published works are "George Eliot's Poetry and Other Studies" (New York, 1885), and "The Long Run," a novel, (Detroit, 1886). She accepted a position as editor of "Literary Life," a magazine published in Chicago, but, not satisfied with the management, she resigned. She has written some verse, but has published very little. She is now engaged in literary work.

CLYMER, Mrs. Ella Maria Dietz, poet, born in New York City. Even as a child she showed many signs of that varied genius which has made her remarkable among the women of her

ELLA MARIA DIETZ CLYMER.

time. Her father died while she was very young, and her mother at first objected to her selection of a theatrical career, but finally gave consent to her daughter's dramatic studies. Early in her teens she married the late Edward M. Clymer, of

Pennsylvania, brother of Heister Clymer, who was a member of Congress for several years. Mrs. Clymer made her professional début in New York, in 1872, as Pauline in the "Lady of Lyons." In the spring of 1874 she went to Paris, and in company of her brother and her sister, Miss Linda Dietz, so favorably known in America and in London, she spent some months in studying in the French school of dramatic art. She acted afterwards both in London and the provinces, and her performances of the principal Shakespearean parts were very highly commended. Her Juliet was spoken of as "a revelation, poetical and imaginative in the highest degree." In 1881 she brought out a version of "Faust," adapted by herself for the English stage, in which she played Margaret, and was called "the very living reality of Goethe's heroine." The fatigue of stage life proved too much for Mrs. Clymer's delicate constitution, and she was obliged to abandon the profession. She continued her public readings, however, a department of the dramatic art in which she probably has no peer, and Moncure D. Conway gave expression to the general opinion when he wrote: "As a dramatic reciter and interpreter of modern ballad poetry she is unequaled." Nor was her dramatic gift her only one. She has talent as an artist and has composed many songs full of dainty grace and melody. Her first poems were published in 1873, and since then she has written frequently for the English and American press. In 1877 she published "The Triumph of Love" (London), and seven years later "The Triumph of Time" (London, 1884), soon followed by "The Triumph of Life" (London, 1885). These are mystical poems, composed of songs, lyrics and sonnets, ranging over the whole gamut of human and divine love, and marked by the same high qualities that distinguished all her work. Notwithstanding all this self-culture, she has not neglected humanity. While in London she was an enthusiastic member of the Church and Stage Guild, and of the religious guild of St. Matthews; she lectured before workingmen's clubs and took part in many other philanthropic undertakings. She has been connected with Sorosis since its beginning, in 1868, and on her return to New York, in 1881, was immediately put upon many of its committees, and served for two years as its president. She has been a leading factor in the Federation of Women's Clubs, which is doing so much to forward the harmonious work of the best women for their own highest good and in the interest of the world.

COATES, Mrs. Florence Earle, poet, was born in Philadelphia, Pa. She is descended from Ralph Earle, of Rhode Island, who came from England to the Colonies in 1634, and was one of the petitioners to Charles II for permission to form Rhode Island into a corporate colony. Her grandfather, Thomas Earle, was a noted philanthropist, and the first nominee of the Liberty Party for vice-president of the United States. Her father, George H. Earle, is a lawyer of distinction. She was thoroughly educated, having studied in Europe for some time, is an accomplished musician, and possesses strong dramatic talent. The writings of Matthew Arnold have been a great inspiration to her, and have influenced her poetry. During his visits to Philadelphia, Mr. Arnold made his home with her and her husband, Edward H. Coates, who is president of the Pennsylvania Academy of the Fine Arts. He is a generous patron of art and of artists. Mrs. Coates' poems are finished productions. She is a regular contributor to the "Century" "Atlantic Monthly," "Harper's Magazine" and "Lippincott's Magazine," and to other periodicals, and her verses have been widely copied. Her home is in Philadelphia, where she is busied with the relations of a full social and domestic life. She has a summer home situated on the Upper St. Regis Lake in the Adirondacks.

COBB, Mrs. Mary Emilie, educator and philanthropist, born in Elmira, N. Y., 31st October, 1838. Her father, Dr. George Wells, a descendant of Thomas Wells, one of the earliest settlers of Hartford, Conn., and the first colonial governor, was early in life a physician and afterwards a preacher of the Disciples' Church. Leaving Connecticut when he was nineteen years old, his life was spent in central New York and northern Pennsylvania. Mrs. Cobb's maternal grandfather was Dr. Ebenezer Pratt, also of an old New England family. A graduate of Middlebury College, Vermont, after a few years spent in the practice of medicine, he became a teacher, in which profession he was for many years prominent in Chautauqua county and in Ovid, N. Y., and in Troy, Pa. Thus the passion for study and literature and the love for teaching, early shown by Mary E. Wells, were an inherited tendency fostered by early influence. At eight years of age she began to write verses, and about the same time to collect, wash, dress and teach the stray and forlorn children of the neighborhood. During her school years she was a contributor to Elmira and Troy papers and to the "Ladies' Christian Annual" and "Arthur's Home Magazine," of Philadelphia. At fifteen she began to teach as an assistant to Dr. Pratt, her grandfather, and under his influence became ambitious to excel in that profession, writing often on topics connected with it, besides her stories and poems for children. She became the wife in 1856 of S. N. Rockwell, of Troy,

tion " (Philadelphia, 1875), and had written much for religious and educational publications. "Facts and Thoughts About Reform Schools," in the "Educational Monthly," of New York, and many articles in the "Children's Hour," of Philadelphia, were illustrated by her brother, C. H. Wells, an artist, of Philadelphia. She has contributed some articles to "Scribner's Magazine," and one of her

MARY EMILIE COBB.

poems, "Acquainted with Grief," was widely copied. Mrs. Rockwell had become deeply interested in reformatory institutions for boys and girls, and she gave herself with enthusiasm to a work which seemed to open just the field for which her preferences and pursuits had prepared her. After some years spent as a teacher in schools of that kind in Philadelphia, New York and Providence, her work as assistant superintendent of the Connecticut Industrial School for Girls, in Middletown, attracted the attention of leading philanthropists and reformers, as seeming to give a practical solution of many questions in relation to reformatory and industrial training, which were then widely discussed. In 1876 the National Prison Congress met in New York. Mrs. Rockwell went upon a public platform for the first time and read a paper upon the topic assigned, "The Training and Disposal of Delinquent Children." Early in 1879, having been left alone with a little daughter of eight years, she accepted the position of superintendent of the Wisconsin Industrial School, in Milwaukee. There she remained seven years, during which time the school grew from thirty-eight pupils and three teachers, in one building, to two-hundred-twenty-five pupils and twenty assistants, and occupying three large and well appointed buildings, designed, erected and fitted up under her direction. In 1882 Mrs. Rockwell became the wife of Dewey A. Cobb, assistant superintendent of that school, and for four years they remained at its head, removing in 1886 to Philadelphia, where Mr. Cobb entered

FLORENCE EARLE COATES.

Pa., and resided in Iowa for several years, continuing to teach and write. Previous to 1870 she had published two juvenile books, "Tom Miller" (Philadelphia, 1872), and "Rose Thorpe's Ambi-

into business, desiring that Mrs. Cobb should retire from school work, to which she had given twenty-five years of continuous service. In Philadelphia she is an active member of the board of managers of the Woman's Christian Association, having been an editor of its organ, "Faith and Works," for three years, and she is one of the editors of the "National Baptist," Philadelphia. As secretary of Foulke and Long Institute and Industrial Training School, she is actively supervising the erection of its new building in Philadelphia. Mrs. Cobb has long been a member of the National Conference of Charities and Corrections and of the Association for the Advancement of Women, and she has several times read papers before those bodies. She is an advocate of institutional training, rather than of the "placing-out" system, for neglected and destitute children. She is earnest and practical in the promotion of manual training and technical education, and to her patient study and efforts much of the success of that movement in several States may be traced. Her more important recent papers have been "The Duty of the State to its Dependent Children," and "Training and Employments in Reformatories."

COBB, Mrs. Sara M. Maxson, art teacher and artist, born in Geneva, N. Y., 30th September, 1858. She traces her lineage on her father's side to the Maxtons, of Maxton-on-the-Tweed, in Scotland. Her father's family came to America in 1701, after having been settled in England for generations. Her father, E. R. Maxson, A.M., M.D., LL.D., a graduate of Jefferson Medical College, Philadelphia, Pa., had been a lecturer on medical subjects in the colleges of Philadelphia, Pa., and Geneva, N. Y. His "Practice of Medicine" and "Hospitals: British, French and American," are well-known books. Her mother, Lucy Potter Lanphere, was of French-English extraction. Mrs. Maxson-Cobb has lived in Geneva, Adams and Syracuse, N. Y., in Philadelphia, Pa., and Kent's Hill, Maine, and now resides in Boulder, Col. When very young she commenced to write for amateur papers. When about eight years of age, happening to read an article on drawing, she tried her pencil at reproducing the simple cuts given in it for copying, with a success so surprising to herself that she then and there resolved in her own mind to become an artist. Her parents had her taught in drawing from youth. In 1883 she was graduated from the Liberal Art College of Syracuse University, Syracuse, N. Y., and she has since received from it, on examination in a post-graduate course, the degree of Ph.D. She is a member of the Alpha chapter of the college society, Alpha Phi. In 1886 she was graduated from the Fine Art College of the same University with the degree Bachelor of Painting. Immediately after graduating she was induced to found and conduct an art school in connection with the college and seminary in Kent's Hill, Maine. Under her management the school soon became successful. In 1892 she was engaged by the regents of the State University of Colorado to introduce drawing there, and she still has it in charge. Her own artistic productions, though yet comparatively few in number, have been well received. She executes in all usual mediums. A strong literary taste and sympathy for active philanthropic and Christian enterprise have led her into many kinds of work. Her numerous poems, stories told in verse, translations from the German, travel-correspondence and articles on art subjects have found their way into prominent publications. She is a believer in united action, and in the many societies to which she belongs, missionary, temperance, art, literary and scientific, she

is recognized as a superior organizer and leader. Geology, microscopy and photography claim a share of her attention, and she has an interesting collection of specimens of her own finding, slides of

SARA M. MAXSON COBB.

her own mounting and photographs of her own taking. She delights in music and has a cultivated contralto voice. In March, 1890, she became the wife of Herbert Edgar Cobb, of Maine, a graduate of Wesleyan University, Middletown, Conn., and now one of the teachers of mathematics in the State University of Colorado.

COCHRANE, Miss Elizabeth, author, journalist and traveler, known the world over by her pen-name, "Nellie Bly," born in Cochrane Mills, Pa., 5th May, 1867, a place named after her father, who was a lawyer and for several terms filled the office of associate judge of Armstrong county, Pa. She is a descendant on her father's side of Lord Cochrane, the famous English admiral, who was noted for his deeds of daring, and who was never happy unless engaged in some exciting affair. Miss Cochrane's great-grandfather Cochrane was one of a number of men who wrote a declaration of independence in Maryland near the South Mountains a long time before the historic Declaration of Independence was delivered to the world. Her great-grandfather, on her mother's side, was a man of wealth, owning at one time almost all of Somerset county, Pa. His name was Kennedy, and his wife was a nobleman's daughter. They eloped and fled to America. He was an officer, as were his two sons, in the Revolutionary War. Afterward he was sheriff of Somerset county repeatedly until old age compelled him to decline the office. One of his sons, Thomas Kennedy, Miss Cochrane's grand-uncle, made a flying trip around the word, starting from and returning to New York City, where his wife awaited his arrival. It took him three years to make the trip, and he returned in shattered health. He at once set about to write the history of his trip, but his health became so bad that he had to give up his task. Her father died while Elizabeth was yet a child. She was educated at home until 1880, when she was sent to Indiana, Pa., where she remained in a boarding-school until 1881. Impaired health forced her to leave school, and she returned home. The family moved to Pittsburgh, and there she began her literary career. She saw an article in the Pittsburgh "Dispatch" entitled "What Girls are Good For." She wrote a reply to the article, and though the reply was not published, a paragraph appeared in the "Dispatch" the day after she sent the communication, asking for the writer's name. Miss Cochrane sent her name and received a letter from the editor, requesting her to write an article on the subject of girls and their spheres in life for the "Sunday Dispatch." This she did. The article was printed, and the same week she received a check for it and a request for something else.

ELIZABETH COCHRANE.

Her next subject was "Divorce," and at the end of the article appeared the now famous signature, "Nellie Bly." Miss Cochrane assumed it on the suggestion of George A. Madden, managing editor of the "Dispatch," who got it from Stephen Foster's popular song. The divorce article attracted attention. She was invited to the office and made arrangements to accept a salary and devote her time to the "Dispatch." Taking an artist with her, she went through the factories and workshops of Pittsburgh, and described and pictured the condition of the working girls. The articles made a hit. Miss Cochrane became society editor of the "Dispatch" and also looked after the dramatic and art department, all for a salary of ten dollars per week. She decided to go to Mexico to write about its people. At that time she was receiving fifteen dollars per week. She went, and her letters printed in the "Dispatch" were full of interest and were widely copied. She had never been out of

her State before, but she traveled everywhere in Mexico that a railroad could take her. Her mother was her companion on that trip. Returning to Pittsburgh, she became dissatisfied with that field, quit the "Dispatch," and went to New York City. She did syndicate work for a while. One day she lost her pocketbook and all the money she possessed. She was too proud to let her friends know, and she sat down and thought. Before that she had written to the "World," asking the privilege of going in the balloon the "World" was about sending up at St. Louis, but, as final arrangements had been completed, her suggestion was not favorably received. Now finding herself penniless, she made a list of a half-dozen original ideas and went to the "World" office, determined to see Mr. Pulitzer and offer them to him. Having no letter of introduction and being unknown, she found it almost an impossibility to gain an audience. For three hours she talked and expostulated with different employés, before she finally exhausted their denials and was ushered into the unwilling presence of Mr. Pulitzer and his editor, John A. Cockerill. Once there, they listened to her ideas and immediately offered her twenty-five dollars to give them three days in which to consider her suggestions. At the end of that time she was told that her idea to feign insanity and, as a patient, investigate the treatment of the insane in the Blackwell Island Asylum was accepted. Miss Bly did that with such marked success and originality of treatment, and attracted so much attention, that she secured a permanent place on the "World" staff. She originated a new field in journalism, which has since been copied all over the world by her many imitators. Her achievements since her asylum exposé have been many and brilliant. Scarcely a week passed that she had not some novel feature in the "World." Her fame grew and her tasks enlarged, until they culminated in the wonderful tour of the world in 72 days, 6 hours, 11 minutes and 14 seconds. That idea she proposed to Mr. Pulitzer one year before he approved and accepted it. Owing to delayed steamers, Miss Bly lost fifteen days on land, but she was the first to conceive and establish a record for a fast trip around the world. Since Miss Cochrane "girdled the globe," others have repeated the feat in less time. Her newspaper work resulted in many reforms. Her exposé of asylum abuses procured an appropriation of $3,000,000 for the benefit of the poor insane, in addition to beneficial changes in care and management. Her exposé of the "King of the Lobby" rid Albany of its greatest disgrace; her station-house exposé procured matrons for New York police-stations; her exposé of a noted "electric" doctor's secret rid Brooklyn of a notorious swindler. Miss Cochrane left journalism to do literary work for a weekly publication. She is now a resident of New York.

COE, Miss Emily M., educator, born near Norwalk, Ohio. She was graduated from Mt. Holyoke Seminary, in 1853, with the honors of her class. For a time she turned her attention to oil-painting and other art-work, for which she has a talent. She then taught with success in seminaries and colleges in New England and Pennsylvania, and afterward in the Spingler Institute, in New York City. Realizing more and more the futility of building upon the imperfect foundations of character usually laid in early childhood, she saw clearly that the hope of the world is in the right training of the little children. That led to the establishment of the American kindergarten, the first school of the kind in New York City. The American kindergarten system is the result of more than twenty years of practical work in the school-room. She erected a kindergarten building at her own expense, in the Centennial Exposition of 1876, where material, much of her own invention was exhibited and examined by educators from all parts of the world. In 1872 Miss Coe went to Europe for the purpose of studying educational methods. Her life is an exceedingly busy one. She has given courses of lectures and conducted training classes in Normal institutes in all parts of the country, besides single lectures in many places. At home she conducts the American Kindergarten and Normal Training School in New York City and East Orange, N. J. Miss Coe is editor and proprietor of the "American Kindergarten Magazine," established ten years. She is president of the American Kindergarten Society. She is a member of the Association for the Advancement of Science and a life member of the National Teachers' Association. She is a very earnest Christian.

COGHLAN, Rose, actor, born in London, Eng., in 1852. Her family was a religious one, and her mother desired Rose to become a cloistered nun. Her brother, Charles Coghlan, threw

ROSE COGHLAN.

aside wig and gown to marry a pretty actress. He went on the stage, and he advised Rose, who had shown talent in private theatricals, to adopt the profession of actor. Rose, whose only public appearance had been in the rôle of organist and singer in the village church choir, followed her brother's advice. The father, a well-known literary man, had died young, leaving his family poor, and Rose felt the need of earning her own living. Acting upon her brother's suggestion, she made her début as one of the witches in "Macbeth," in 1868, in Greenock, Scotland. She next appeared as Cupid in the burlesque, "Ixion." She next went to Cheltenham, Eng., where she played small soubrette parts in the Theater Royal. There the leading lady quarreled with the manager and

left, and Rose stepped into her place. She next went to London, and for four years she played in burlesque and comedy through the English provinces. In 1872 she came to the United States with the Lydia Thompson troupe. She made her début in New York on 2nd September, as Jupiter in "Ixion." The late E. A. Sothern engaged her to support him, and she left the "Ixion" company and played Mrs. Honeyton in "The Happy Pair." Lester Wallack next engaged her. Returning to England, Miss Coghlan played a number of important engagements with Wallack and made a tour of Ireland with Barry Sullivan. Returning to London, she received a cablegram from Wallack, offering her the position of leading lady in his New York theater. In 1880 she appeared in Wallack's Theater, in the rôles of Lady Teazle, Countess Leika, Lady Clare and Rosalind, winning a pronounced success in each. She played in Wallack's company until 1885. In 1887 she joined the Abbey-Wallack Company, but left it because displeased with a part assigned to her in "L'Abbé Constantin." She was recalled for a revival of old comedies, when Wallack's Theater ceased to be the home of a stock company. During the past few years Miss Coghlan has played in various new rôles, including two plays, "Jocelyn" and "Lady Barter," written by her brother. Miss Coghlan has been twice married. Her first husband was a Mr. Browne, from whom she got a divorce. She was married again in 1885, to C. J. Edgerly, who got a divorce from her in 1891. Miss Coghlan has won high rank as an actor.

COHEN, Miss Mary M., social economist, born in Philadelphia, Pa., 26th February, 1854. She is the daughter of Henry and Matilda Cohen, a prominent Jewish family. Henry Cohen was born in London, England, in 1810, came to the United States in 1844 and went into business in Philadelphia, where he died in 1879. He was identified with many Jewish and unsectarian philanthropic societies. Mrs. Cohen was born in Liverpool, England. She was a woman of fine musical and elocutionary talents and was prominent in charitable work. The daughter, Mary, studied in Miss Ann Dickson's private school in Philadelphia until she was fourteen years old, learning French, English, Latin and drawing. She then went to Miss Catherine Lyman's school, where she continued her studies. After leaving school she took a course in literature under Professor Chase, and studied German for three years. From the age of seven she was taught in music by her mother until prepared for instruction from masters. She began to write short stories when she was thirteen years old. Her first printed essay, "Religion Tends to Cheerfulness," appeared in the "Jewish Index," and she has since been a prominent contributor to religious periodicals, both Jewish and Christian, writing under the pen-name "Coralie." Her literary productions cover editing of letters of travel, biography, serial stories and religious articles and essays. She has prepared a number of important papers on Hebrew charities, on subjects of current interest and on social, literary and intellectual problems. She has visited Europe three times and has filled a number of responsible positions in various philanthropic societies. She is a woman of great versatility, a talented author, an artist, a wood-carver, a stenographer and typewriter, and a successful teacher. She has served as the president of the Browning Club of Philadelphia, of which she was the founder, as the corresponding secretary of the Jewish Publication Society of America, as a superintendent of the Southern Hebrew Sunday-school, as president of the society under whose direction the schools are conducted, as a member of some of the leading literary and art clubs of Philadelphia, such as the Contemporary Club, the Fairmount Park Association, and as a member of the board of directors of the Penn-

MARY M. COHEN.

sylvania Museum and School of Industrial Art. When the New Century Club was formed by the executive committee of the Women's Centennial Commission, after the Exposition of 1876 was closed, Miss Cohen became a member, and was subsequently elected to the executive board. For a year she had charge of the writing class organized by the New Century Guild, and for three years directed a Browning class. In November of 1888 that class developed into an independent society, which now has a membership of nearly six-hundred men and women, including some of the leading people of Philadelphia. In 1884 Miss Cohen was invited by Rev. Dr. H. L. Wayland, one of the directors of the American Social Science Association, to present to that organization a paper on Hebrew charities. The paper was read by its author before the convention held in Saratoga, N. Y., 12th September, 1884, was favorably received, discussed and published. Miss Cohen was elected a member of the association and placed in the social economy department. In the affairs of the Jewish community Miss Cohen has taken a strong interest and an active part. Receiving her religious inspiration from Rev. Dr. S. Morais, her love for the religion, the history, the achievements and progress of the Jewish people has been deep and abiding. She taught the Bible class in the Northern Hebrew Sunday-school for a number of years. Miss Cohen was chosen to serve on the Philadelphia committee of the Columbian Exposition, in the department of social economy.

COIT, Mrs. Elizabeth, humanitarian and temperance worker, born in Worthington, Ohio, 10th January, 1820. Her parents, Joseph and Nancy Agnes Greer, were natives of Belfast, Ireland.

Elizabeth was the fourth daughter of the family. She was educated in the female seminary in Worthington. After her graduation she was engaged as a teacher in that institution, and held her position until her marriage, 15th April, 1844, to Harvey Coit, of Columbus, Ohio. Her home has been in that city ever since her marriage. Mrs. Coit is an excellent housekeeper, but she has always found time for a good deal of philanthropic and charitable work outside of her home. She is the mother of eight children, three of whom are now living, the comfort of her declining years. During the Civil War she was one of the members of the committee of three appointed to draft the constitution of the Soldiers' Aid Society. To that organization she devoted much of her time for three years, and her work was invaluable to the society. She is interested actively in all the progressive and reform movements of the time. She was chosen president of the first Woman's Suffrage Association organized in Columbus. For many years she has served

ELIZABETH COIT.

as treasurer of the Ohio Woman Suffrage Association.

COIT, Miss Irene Williams, born in Norwich, Conn., in 1873. She is the only daughter of General and Mrs. James B. Coit. She won a reputation by success in passing the Yale College entrance examination in 1891, and is by no means insensible to the impetus her venture in knocking at the doors of Yale has been instrumental in giving to the cause of co-education in American colleges. Already that venture has been effective in modifying stringent college laws in various quarters. From her earliest school days she was proficient in her studies. She took the full classical course in the Norwich free academy and was graduated in June, 1891, with highest honors. Her determination to try the Yale examinations with the male classical students of her class, was born solely of her generous ambition.

Her instructor, Dr. Robert P. Keep, arranged to have Prof. Seymour, of Yale, give Miss Coit an examination with his class. Besides her aptitude as a student, Miss Coit has long manifested a

IRENE WILLIAMS COIT.

marked literary capacity. Her first essay in the field of letters some time ago was especially successful. Since the summer of 1891 she has contributed to various newspapers and publications a variety of articles. Miss Coit comes of old New England stock. Her father, General James B. Coit, was a distinguished soldier in the Civil War. In the administration of President Cleveland he was chief of a pension bureau in Washington. Her mother, a refined and charming lady, is a daughter of A. P. Willoughby, representing one of the oldest families in Norwich. Miss Coit lives with her parents in Norwich.

COLBY, Mrs. H. Maria George, author, born in Warner, N. H., 1st October, 1844. She is the daughter of Gilman C. and Nancy B. George and the wife of Frederick Myron Colby. She is of English descent on both sides of the family and inherits literary talents from ancestors connected with Daniel Webster of the present century, and on the George side from families whose coat-of-arms dates back to the days of ancient chivalry Her literary work was the writing of novelettes. Later she wrote considerably for juvenile publications, and she is an acknowledged authority upon domestic topics. Circumstances have rendered it impossible for Mrs. Colby to give her whole time to literary work, but her articles have appeared in the "Housewife," the "Housekeeper," the "Housekeeper's Weekly," the "Christian at Work," "Demorest's Monthly Magazine," "Arthur's Home Magazine," "Youth's Companion," the "Congregationalist," the Portland "Transcript," "Ladies' World," "Good Cheer," the Philadelphia "Press" the Chicago "Ledger," the "Golden Rule, "the "Household," "Good Housekeeping" and "St.

Nicholas." She was for five years fashion-editor of the "Household." Though naturally fond of society, delicate health and a desire to give her best energies and talents to her literary work have rendered her somewhat retiring. She has made use of various pen-names, but is best known to editors and the public by her maiden name, H. Maria George. A stanch advocate of temperance and equal rights for both sexes, she furthers these as well as every other good work by her pen. Her home is in Warner, N. H.

COLBY, Miss Sarah A., physician, born in Sanbornton, N. H., 31st May, 1824. She is one of eight children, of whom two survive, herself and a sister, Dr. Esther W. Taylor, of Boston, Mass. Dr. Colby was educated in the public schools of her native town and the academy in Sanbornton Square. After leaving school she taught for some time, but failing health compelled her to give up that work. She returned to her home and remained there until her health was improved. During her illness she realized the great need of women physicians, and she became much interested in studying to meet the exigencies of her own condition. After becoming much improved in health she went to Lowell, Mass., where she opened a variety and fancy goods store, continuing the study of medicine and prescribing for many who called upon her. Concluding to make the practice of medicine her life work, she sold out her store and, after preparing herself more fully, located for practice in Manchester, N. H., where she was received by the public and by some of the physicians with great cordiality. Dr. Colby gained a large and lucrative practice, which kept her there nine years, when, desiring a larger field, she removed to Boston,

H. MARIA GEORGE COLBY.

Mass. One object of her removal was to give her whole attention to gynæcology; that she accomplished to a great extent. Dr. Colby was one of the first women physicians in Boston, and she did a remarkable work there. She has been called to meet in consultation, in the large cities of New England, some of the most scientific men physicians of the age, from whom she received every

SARAH A. COLBY.

courtesy. In the first fifteen years of her professional experience she was eclectic in practice, but after her sister entered the Hahnemann Medical College of Chicago, she took up the study of medicine of that school, and for fifteen years that has been her mode of treatment, in which she has been very successful. She is still in practice, though her health does not permit her to give her entire time to professional duties.

COLE, Mrs. Cordelia Throop, temperance reformer, born in the town of Hamilton, N. Y., 17th November, 1833. Her mother, a young and beautiful woman, dowered with the fine instinct of the artist, died when her child Cordelia was but two years of age. In her early womanhood her father died, her nearest then of birth and kin being an only brother, two years younger than herself. She was received into the home of her grandparents and became a favorite among her numerous relatives. Her literary and religious impulses soon asserted themselves. One of the dreams of her early girlhood was a foreign mission. As education was the initial step toward future activities, she entered Hamilton Academy, and just before graduation an alluring offer of a home with an aunt and an uncle in Galesburg, Ill., and a position as a teacher in the West was accepted. Her life shaped itself to the vocation of a teacher. In Keokuk, Iowa, a private institute for young people was established under the management of R. M. Reynolds, with Miss Throop as associate. From that field of labor Mr. Reynolds and Miss Throop transferred their energies to the North Illinois Institute, in Henry, Ill. In December, 1856, Miss Throop became the wife of William Ramey Cole, an earnest student and active philanthropist, a graduate of the Theological Department

of Harvard and an ordained minister in the Unitarian Church. Seven children have been born to them, one dying in childhood and one in early manhood. Mrs. Cole served as secretary of the Iowa Unitarian Association, for seven years devoting the mature energies of her mind to that labor of love, preaching in various pulpits of the denomination, creating and carrying on a large correspondence in post-office mission work, attending conferences, forming religious clubs and lending a hand to any agency for the promotion of human welfare. She also, by special request, gave the charge at the ordination of Mary A. Safford in Humbolt, Iowa, in 1880, and a year later performed the same service at the ordination of Volney B. Cushing, in Iowa City. She took a conspicuous part in the temperance crusade, riding many miles to meet an appointment, with the mercury twenty degrees below zero, sometimes holding three or four meetings at different points in twenty-four hours. In 1885 she was made the Iowa superintendent of White Shield and White Cross work of the Woman's Christian Temperance Union. The new crusade against the subtle foe of impurity aroused the conscience, heart and brain of the wife and mother, and she gave herself unreservedly to that work, making hundreds of public addresses, handling the subject with rare delicacy and skill, and winning the sympathy and warm appreciation of all right-thinking people. Her earnest talks to women have been a marked feature of her work, and more recently her published leaflets, "Helps in Mother Work" and "A Manual for Social Purity Workers," are admirable. In 1889 she received the offer of the place of associate national superintendent, but, loyal to her feeling of duty to the

CORDELIA THROOP COLE.

non-partisan side of the dividing lines, she declined. The home of Mrs. Cole, in Mt. Pleasant, Iowa, is a center of generous hospitality to all humankind. There the outcast have been sheltered, the stricken comforted, the tempted strengthened, the sinful forgiven, the cultured and aspiring made glad.

COLE, Miss Elizabeth, author, born in Darien, Wis., 16th January, 1856. Her father's name

ELIZABETH COLE.

was Parker M. Cole, and her mother's maiden name was Amelia Y. Frey. The latter was a descendant of the Freys and Herkimers whom Harold Frederic describes so accurately in "In the Valley." She was also a descendant of one of the early settlers of Detroit, named St. Martin, who was a man of note in those days, and whose house, built in 1703, still stands and is known as the "Old Cass House." All that concerns Amelia Cole is of interest to western people, because, like her daughter, Elizabeth, she was a well-known writer. Cotemporaneously their sketches and stories appeared in such periodicals as "Good Cheer," "Outing" and the "Current." Both were frequent contributors to the "Weekly Wisconsin." Elizabeth Cole has also written acceptably for "St. Nicholas," "Good Housekeeping" and the "Housewife." She has done a great deal of excellent literary work, but her life has been exceedingly uneventful from the time she was born and brought up "in the edge of a little village, so small that the edge is very near the center," as she says, to the present time. Her mother died in 1889, and not long afterward she went to Pittsburgh, Pa., where she is at present living with a married sister. During her mother's lifetime the two made their home in Milwaukee. Their mutual gifts, their cheerful temperaments and the earnestness of their aims won for them many true friends in the best circles of that city.

COLLIER, Mrs. Ada Langworthy, poet, born in Dubuque, Iowa, 23rd December, 1843, in the first frame house ever built within the present bounds of the State of Iowa. Her father, a descendant of New England pioneers, was among the very first to explore the lead regions of Iowa, and he was one of the founders of the city

of Dubuque. Her mother was a member of an old Baltimore family. None of the hardships and privation that go with pioneer life were known to the little Ada. The lead mines were a source of wealth to her father and his brothers, and soon a group of spacious brick mansions arose on a beautiful bluff above the city, wherein dwelt the Langworthy households. In one of these Ada grew up, a strong, vigorous, attractive child. In early girlhood she was for a time a pupil in a girls' school taught by Miss Catherine Beecher in Dubuque. Afterward she went to Lasell Seminary, Auburndale, Mass. Having always found she could accomplish anything she chose to undertake, she there thought she could do the last two years' work in one year, and had nearly succeeded, when she was taken ill of brain fever. In spite of that she was graduated in 1861, at the early age of seventeen. In 1868 she became the wife of Robert Collier, and has since lived in Dubuque. She has one son. She began to write for periodicals in her girlhood. She is the author of many sketches, tales and short poems, of several novels, and of one long, narrative poem, "Lilith" (Boston, 1885). The last is her

ADA LANGWORTHY COLLIER.

greatest work, nor can there be any doubt that she should be accounted a poet rather than a novelist.

COLLINS, Mrs. Delia, educator, philanthropist and reformer, born in Franklinton, Schoharie county, N. Y., 25th November, 1830. Her mother died when she was a young woman, and her father soon afterward moved to Michigan. Miss Delia Krum at the age of fourteen years entered the State Normal School in Albany, N. Y., and was graduated after the usual course. In 1846 she accepted the assistant principalship of a school in Geneseo, N. Y., associated with Henry W. Collins as principal. He was a graduate of the State Normal School. They were married in Franklinton in 1849. They moved to Elmira, N. Y., and Mr. Collins was largely instrumental in the surveying and laying out of that city. In 1855 they moved to Janesville, Wis. Mr. Collins was elected superintendent of the city schools for several terms, and was connected with the founding and building up

DELIA COLLINS.

of the Institute for the Blind in Janesville. He was the first president and one of the founders of the Northwestern Mutual Life Insurance Company, of Milwaukee, Wis. In 1865 he became an invalid, and was confined to the house for eleven years. It was at that time the public life of Mrs. Collins began. Mr. Collins had founded a large business. His excessive labors brought on nervous paralysis, from which he never recovered. There were two sons and a daughter born to them in Janesville. Their daughter died, and business matters involved their property with great losses. Mrs. Collins, in the pressure of home matters, the continued and hopeless illness of her husband, opened a select school for young women, and taught French and German and English literature. Her influence among the literary societies of the city was extensive. In 1876 Mr. Collins died. In 1884 Mrs. Collins became interested in Bible study, Woman's Christian Temperance Union work, church and city charity, and did much in those lines. Her health became impaired, and, becoming acquainted with Miss Carrie Judd, of Buffalo, N. Y., known as the publisher of "Triumphs of Faith," she accepted the doctrine of "Divine Healing" and was healed of a long-standing spinal trouble, and has since been sustained in both health and the faith work. She is now established in Fort Worth, Texas, where she moved with her sons in 1888. In connection with Woman's Christian Temperance Union work, she, with Mrs. Belle Burchill, of Fort Worth, opened a bootblack's home, which finally resulted in the founding of an orphanage. A building was given for their work, and the home now contains nearly seventy children. She also assisted in opening the Union Bethel

Mission of Fort Worth. Its purpose is to reach the people on the street and the children. Mission Sunday-schools are founded and carried on, also nightly gospel meetings and tent gospel meetings. Her next work was the opening and founding, with other women, of a woman's home, a home for unfortunate women on the streets. A foundling home in connection with it has been started. She was engaged in the winter of 1891–1892 in delivering lectures throughout Texas in behalf of the home. She has had the State social purity department work of the Woman's Christian Temperance Union in charge, and is also the president of the Woman's Board of Foreign Missionary Work of the Cumberland Presbyterian Church of North Texas.

COLLINS, Mrs. Emily Parmely, woman suffragist, born in Bristol, Ontario county, N. Y., 11th August, 1814. She is of New England parents, who were early settlers of the "Genesee Country." Before the end of her first decade she became an industrious reader, especially of history and poetry. A large part of her second decade was spent in teaching country schools. As an evidence of her success, she received a salary equal to that given to male teachers, something as unusual in those days as in these. She always advocated equal freedom and justice to all. Quite possibly an early bias was given to her mind in that direction, while sitting on her father's knee, listening to his stories of the Revolutionary War in which he participated. The efforts of Greece to throw off the Turkish yoke enlisted her sympathy, which expressed itself in a poem, giving evidence of remarkable depth of mind in one but twelve years of age. Naturally she became an Abolitionist, even before the general anti-slavery agitation. With public affairs and po-

EMILY PARMELY COLLINS.

litical questions she was always familiar. The full development of woman's capacities she believed to be of supreme importance to the well-being of humanity and, chiefly through the press, has ever advocated woman's educational, industrial and political rights. According to the "History of Woman Suffrage," she organized the first woman suffrage society and sent the first petition for suffrage to the legislature. That was in 1848 in her native town. During the Civil War she went with her two sons, one a surgeon, to the battle-fields of Virginia and did efficient service as a volunteer nurse. In 1869 she with her family removed to Louisiana, where she buried her second husband. In 1879, as a new State constitution was being framed, a paper from Mrs. Collins, giving her ideas of what a just constitution should be, was read to the delegates and elicited praise from the New Orleans press. For the last twelve years she has resided in Hartford, Conn. In 1885 she, with Miss F. E. Burr, organized the Hartford Equal Rights Club, and she is its president. She wrote occasional stories, to illustrate some principle, for the "Pacific Rural" and other journals. Not ambitious to acquire a literary reputation, and shrinking from publicity, she seldom appended her name. For several years she wrote each week for the Hartford "Journal," under the pen-name "Justitia," a column or two in support of human rights, especially the rights of woman. She also urged the same before each legislature of Connecticut. As a solution of the liquor problem, some years since she advocated in the Hartford "Examiner" the exclusive manufacture and sale of liquor at cost by the government. She also urged a change from the present electoral system to that of proportional representation, and industrial coöperation in place of competition. Always abreast or in advance of the world's progressive thought, her pen is ever busy. Dignified and quiet, modest to a fault, she is justly noted among the intellectual inhabitants of Hartford.

COLLINS, Miss Laura Sedgwick, musician, dramatic reader and amateur actor, was born in Poughkeepsie, N. Y. At an early age she gave unmistakable evidence of marked ability, and even genius, both as a musician and an elocutionist. She studied under able masters and was graduated several years ago from the Lyceum School of Acting, New York City. She is a skilled pianist, a reader of established reputation, and, though not upon the professional dramatic stage, has appeared in many difficult rôles for the benefit of charities, in the theaters of New York, Brooklyn and other cities. She has studied vocal music and has a sympathetic voice of wide range. She has composed music, much of which is published, and has a large collection of songs, part-music and pianoforte selections and a volume of poems yet to be brought out. "The Two Republics," a march which she wrote, was played at the unveiling of the Statue of Liberty, and Monsieur Bartholdi expressed to her his compliments upon its merits. She composed a minuet for the first performances in English in this country of "Les Précieuses Ridicules," given at the Lyceum Theater, New York. She was also prominently identified with the performance of Sophocles' tragedy of "Electra," which was given in March, 1889, in the Lyceum Theater, New York, and subsequently in the Hollis Street Theater, Boston, Mass., and by the request of the Faculty in Harvard College, Cambridge, Mass. She composed all of the music for that play and taught it to the chorus, which contained only a few persons who could read music. On 10th December, 1889, at Proctor's Twenty-third Street Theater, New York, was the occasion of the first presentation of a character sketch in four acts, entitled "Sarah Tarbox, M.A.," which was written especially for Miss Collins by Charles Barnard. In that work she won

a brilliant success. She spoke with imaginary characters, rode in an imaginary railroad train, went to the theater, attended a reception; yet no one was before the audience but herself. She interpreted vividly all the different parts throughout the entire play; she held the audience during the phases of a scene on Broadway, New York, a scene in a boarding-house room, closing with a scene in St. Luke's Hospital, without the aid of any properties and with but two plain chairs on the stage. In the play she used her various gifts and figured as composer, pianist, singer, dancer and reciter. The

LAURA SEDGWICK COLLINS.

achievement was unique in the history of the stage. She has since brought out other successful monologues. Her versatility is coupled with high merit in each line of effort.

COLLINS, Mrs. Miriam O'Leary, actor, born in Boston, Mass., in 1864. Her father, William Curran O'Leary, of London, Eng., was an artist and designer by profession. Her mother's maiden name was Miriam Keating, and at the time of her marriage she was on a visit to Boston from Halifax, N. S., her native place. Their daughter Miriam was their first child. She received her education in the public schools of Boston, and attended the Franklin grammar school and the girls' high school, and was graduated from both with honors. Her aim throughout her years of preparation was to fit herself as a teacher. After her father's death, encouraged by her cousin, Joseph Haworth, and by other friends, she chose the stage as her profession and began at once her efforts in that direction. Her first success was as Rosalie in "Rosedale" during the engagement of Lester Wallack in the Boston Museum. She spent one season in the company of Edwin Booth and Lawrence Barrett, after which she returned to the Boston Museum, and is now (1892) a member of the stock company of that theater. She has appeared in many widely different rôles, ranging from

Smike in "Nicholas Nickleby," Topsy in "Uncle Tom's Cabin," and Sophia in "The Road to Ruin," to Jess in "Lady Jess." On 25th January, 1892, she

MIRIAM O'LEARY COLLINS.

became the wife of David A. Collins, a prominent physician of Boston.

COLMAN, Miss Julia, temperance educator and worker, born in the valley of the Sacandaga, Fulton county, N.Y. She is of Puritan and Huguenot ancestry. In 1840 the family removed to Wisconsin, her father, Rev. Henry R. Colman being sent as missionary to the Oneida Indians near Green Bay. In 1849 she entered the preparatory department of the Lawrence University, in Appleton, Wis. She was graduated in the collegiate course in Cazenovia, N. Y., in 1853, her specialties being natural history and languages. After teaching for a time, she entered the Sunday-school union and tract department of the Methodist Publishing House, in New York City, where she became known as "Aunt Julia" of "The Sunday-school Advocate," and by other literary work. While there, she started anti-tobacco leagues for boys, numbering over one-hundred in various parts of the country. In pursuing medical and hygienic studies she first learned the leading facts about the character of alcohol, and especially that it could be dispensed with in medicine. Always an abstainer, she then saw how she could work for total abstinence successfully, and she began in 1868 to write and lecture on the subject. She took partial courses in different medical colleges, that she might learn their teachings about alcohol and obtain a sound physiological basis for further studies. She spoke before local temperance societies, teachers' institutes and Methodist conferences, delivering upward of one-hundred lectures previous to the crusade. Other engagements prevented her from taking an active part in the uprising, but in 1875 she entered the local work and originated the first "temperance school." That marked a new

departure in the temperance work among the children, in that it was largely intellectual, the scholars being arranged in classes, reciting to teachers and reviewed by a superintendent, aided throughout by the systematized use of text-books, tracts, charts and experiments. Those educational methods commended themselves to the National Woman's Christian Temperance Union, and Miss Colman was elected editor of one page of the national organ for one year, to push that elementary work, which soon became the prevailing model throughout the woman's work and in other temperance organizations. In 1875 Miss Colman was appointed superintendent of literature in the Woman's National Christian Temperance Union, which position she held for fifteen years. During that time she wrote or edited and published upward of five-hundred books, tracts, pamphlets and lesson leaves. Among the books and pamphlets from her pen are: "The Catechisms on Alcohol and Tobacco" (1872), which has reached a circulation of 300,000; "The Juvenile Temperance Manual for Teachers"; "The Primary Temperance Catechism"; "The Catechism on Beer"; "The Sunday School Temperance Catechism;" "The Temperance School"; "Alcohol and Hygiene"; "The Temperance Hand-Book for Speakers and Workers"; "An Evening with Robinson Crusoe," and smaller pamphlets, tracts and leaflets for juveniles and adults. She edited during that time "The Young People's Comrade" and "The Temperance Teacher." She has issued many chromo cards with temperance mottoes for birthday, holiday, Easter, Valentine and everyday use. An effective testing apparatus, capable of showing a variety of helpful chemical experiments, has been

JULIA COLMAN.

put together by her, and with its aid she has delivered courses of illustrated lectures in Silver Springs, Ocean Grove, Toronto and other places, her main object being to simplify scientific teachings and make them attractive to persons of all ages. Her specialty in literary work for adults is the system of tract distribution by topics suited to the educational needs of communities, especially in the total abstinence line, laying a solid foundation for other wise and effective temperance work. She prepared a series of sketches of the State Woman's Christian Temperance Union presidents, published in "Demorest's Magazine." She has written much on health topics and the wholesome preparation of food for "Moore's Rural New Yorker," for the "Ladies' Repository," the "Phrenological Journal," "Good Health" and other periodicals. She is now superintendent of the health department of the National Woman's Christian Temperance Union, with her office in the Bible House, New York City, where it has been for years. From girlhood she has been a devout evangelical Christian, a member of the Methodist Episcopal Church, and her main object in all her philanthropic work is to aid others in attaining a physical development which shall enable them better to serve God, themselves and their fellowmen.

COLMAN, Mrs. Lucy Newhall, anti-slavery agitator and woman suffragist, born in Sturbridge, Worcester county, Mass., 26th July, 1817. Her maiden name was Danforth. Her mother was a

LUCY NEWHALL COLMAN.

Newhall and a direct descendant of John Alden and Priscilla. She was early a student of the puzzling problem of slavery in a land of freedom. In 1824 and up to 1830 a revival of religion swept over New England, and Lucy was again puzzled to understand the benefit of such a revival if human beings were elected to be saved from the beginning. She turned to the Bible and read, but her confusion became deeper. The result was that she became a Liberal in religion, a free thinker and a free speaker. She joined the Universalist Church while young, but afterwards became a Spiritualist.

At the age of eighteen years she was married and went to Boston, Mass. Her husband died of consumption in 1841. In 1843 she was married a second time. In 1846 she began to agitate for equal rights for woman and for the emancipation of the slaves. In 1852 her husband, who was an engineer on the Central Railroad, was killed in a railroad accident, leaving her alone with a seven-year old daughter. Mrs. Colman, left with a child and no resources, asked the railroad company for work, but they refused the favor. She applied for the position of clerk at the ladies' window in a post-office, for work in a printing office, and for other positions, but was in each case rejected because she was a woman. She then began to teach in Rochester, N. Y., doing for $350 a year the work that a man received $800 for doing. The "colored school" in Rochester was offered to her, and she took it, resolving that it should die. She advised the colored people to send their children to the schools in their own districts, until the school was dead. This was done in one year. Mrs. Colman was invited by Miss Susan B. Anthony to prepare a paper to read at a State convention of teachers. The paper caused a sensation. Mrs. Colman urged the abolition of corporal punishment in the schools of Rochester. Wearying of school work, she decided to begin her labor as an abolitionist. She delivered her first lecture in a Presbyterian church near Rochester, which had been secured by her friend, Mrs. Amy Post. She attented the annual convention of the Western Anti-Slavery Society in Michigan, and that meeting was turned into a spiritualistic gathering. She lectured in various towns in Michigan, Ohio, Indiana and Illinois. Her meetings were disturbed, and she and her co-workers were subjected to all kinds of annoyances and to malicious misrepresentation in the press on many occasions. She attempted some work in Iowa and Wisconsin, but the reformers were few in those sparsely settled States. In Pennsylvania and New York she did much in arousing public sentiment on slavery and woman's rights. In 1862 her daughter, Gertrude, entered the New England Woman's Medical College, and died within two weeks. The funeral was conducted by Frederick Douglass. Then Mrs. Colman went to Washington to serve as matron in the National Colored Orphan Asylum. She afterwards was appointed teacher of a colored school in Georgetown, D. C. She has held many other positions of the philanthropic kind. In late years she has been conspicuous among the Freethinkers. Her home is now in Syracuse, N. Y.

COMFORT, Mrs. Anna Manning, doctor of medicine, born in Trenton, N. J., 19th January, 1845. In her childhood Miss Manning's parents removed to Boston, Mass., where she received her academic education. An early liking for the studies of anatomy and physiology was discovered by her aunt, Mrs. Clemence Lozier, M. D., the founder and for twenty years the dean of the New York Medical College for Women. Miss Manning entered Dr. Lozier's office as a student. Dr. Lozier's large and generous hospitality brought to her house many of the leading reformers of the time, and from intercourse with them Miss Manning drew much of that sympathetic inspiration and breadth of view which marked her personality in later years. She was a member of the first class in the New York Medical College for Women. At the graduating exercises of that class speeches were made by Henry Ward Beecher, Horace Greeley, Henry J. Raymond and Hon. S. S. Cox in behalf of enlarging the sphere of woman's activities, and especially on her entering the domain of medicine. At that time the opposition to women students, which almost amounted to persecution, was manifested to the first class of lady students, among other things, by the rude treatment they received from the men

ANNA MANNING COMFORT.

students and even from some of the professors while attending the clinics in Bellevue Hospital. After graduation Miss Manning began the practice of her profession in Norwich, Conn., being the first woman graduate in medicine to practice in that State. By her strong personality and her professional success she soon won a large and important patronage in Norwich and eastern Connecticut. She there strongly espoused, in the press and otherwise, the cause of woman suffrage and of woman's equality with men in all moral, social and civil relations. In 1870 she removed to New York City, where she successfully practiced her profession, was appointed lecturer in the college from which she graduated, and was elected a member of the newly founded society of Sorosis. In New York Dr. Manning met the gentleman whom she married in 1871, Prof. G. F. Comfort, L.H.D., the distinguished scholar in linguistics and art criticism, who became the founder and dean of the College of Fine Arts of the Syracuse University. In 1872 they removed to Syracuse, where Dean Comfort entered upon his work in the newly established university in that city. Dr. Comfort relinquished her medical practice for some years, till her children had grown beyond the need of a mother's constant cares. On resuming practice she confined her work to gynæcology, which had before been her chief department, and in that field she has achieved success and distinction. In 1874 Dr. Comfort wrote "Woman's Education and Woman's Health," in reply to Dr. Clarke's "Sex in Education," in which he attacked the higher education of woman. In 1887 and 1891 she traveled extensively in Europe, where she visited many important hospitals and medical institutions. Her tastes and accomplishments are varied

and versatile; she has marked histrionic powers, and could have achieved distinguished success as an artist, musician or actor, or on the lecture platform.

CONANT, Mrs. Frances Augusta, journalist and business woman, born in West Burlington, N. Y., 23rd December, 1842. Her parents were Curtis and Martha R. Hemingway. She was educated in the western part of the State and in Brooklyn, where she became the wife, in 1864, of Claudius W. Conant, of New York. In early girlhood she became a contributor to New York publications. Since 1882 Mrs. Conant has been a resident of Chicago, Ill. She usually passes the winters in traveling through the South. She was for several years a special correspondent of the "Living Church" and a contributor to the "Advance" and other religious publications of Chicago, as well as to some class journals, and, occasionally, short stories of hers appeared in leading New York and Philadelphia publications. During the New Orleans Exposition of 1884-'85 she was the only special woman correspondent in that city for a mechanical and scientific journal, ably representing the "Industrial World," of Chicago. She often writes as a collaborator with her husband, who is connected with the "American Field," and they frequently do editorial work interchangeably. Mrs. Conant is an earnest advocate of the cause of industrial education, and she was editor and business manager of the "Journal of Industrial Education" in the early days of its publication. Her reputation as a writer of short sketches of travel led to an engagement as editor of the "American Traveler and Tourist," published in Chicago, which position she held for two years, until she became interested

FRANCES AUGUSTA CONANT.

in a commercial enterprise. Though rarely working in any associations, she has developed decided ability as a promoter and organizer. She was one of the founders of the Woman's National Press

Association, formed in New Orleans, in 1885, for the purpose of fostering State auxiliaries like the Woman's Christian Temperance Union. She was the principal promoter of the Illinois Woman's Press Association, the first independent State organization for the purpose of affording practical assistance to women in literary pursuits. She was secretary of that association for the first two years, and received an honorary life membership in recognition of her services. Mrs. Conant is noted for being most generous in giving time and thought to all appeals for help. It has been said by a long-time friend that if she had been half as zealous in forwarding her own interest as in advancing those of other people she would have made a great financial success in her career. Like all women in public work she has been the constant recipient of the most touching appeals from other women, usually those without technical training, for assistance to occupations by which they could earn their bread. She became oppressed by the problem: "What shall we do with this unskilled army?" When a plan for employing large numbers of these untrained applicants was presented to Mrs. Conant she withdrew from editorial work, in 1891, to engage in the promotion and organization of a corporation projected to give, eventually, remunerative employment to thousands of women in all parts of the country. She was secretary of the company during its first year and took an active part in the business management, then she resigned her trust to others, having made a record of phenomenal success. The year closed with the company well established.

CONANT, Miss Harriet Beecher, physician, born in Greensboro, Vt., 10th June, 1852. Her

HARRIET BEECHER CONANT.

father, E. Tolman Conant, was a life-long resident of that town. His immediate ancestors were natives of Hollis, N. H., and those more remote lived in Salem, Mass., and were of Puritan descent. Her

maternal ancestors were among the early inhabitants of Londonderry, N. H., which was settled by a colony of Scotch-Irish Presbyterians in 1719. Dr. Conant's childhood was spent on a farm. Being second in age in a large family, she early showed her natural gift as a leader and an organizer. Educational advantages in the rural districts of New England were somewhat limited, but she improved every opportunity to acquire knowledge. The death of her father, when she was quite young, changed the tenor of her life. The plan of an academical course of study was dropped, and in practice she accepted the principle of doing the work which came to her. She began to teach in the public schools of Vermont. After a good degree of success there, she went to Unionville, Conn., where she remained six years, the last three as teacher in the high school. From there she was called to be principal of the public schools in St. Johnsbury, Vt., which responsible position she held for three years, when she was obliged by ill health to resign. Going to Minnesota in search of strength and rest, she was enabled, after a time, to carry out her long-cherished wish, and she entered the medical department of the University of Minnesota in October, 1888, and was graduated in the class of 1891. Through the influence of the dean, she received the appointment of resident physician in the South Dakota Hospital for the Insane in Yankton, the duties of which office she assumed the day after receiving her diploma.

CONE, Miss Helen Gray, educator, born in New York City, 8th March, 1859. She was graduated from the New York City Normal College in 1876, in which institution she became instructor in English literature. At her graduation she gave evidence of her poetical gift by the composition of of the class song. Since that time she has contributed to the "Atlantic Monthly," the "Century," "Harper's Magazine," "St. Nicholas" and other periodicals. She was a helper in the preparation of the "Century Dictionary," and assisted Miss Jeannette L. Gilder in editing "Pen Portraits of Literary Women." She has published two volumes of poems, "Oberon and Puck, Verses Grave and Gay" (New York, 1885) and the "Ride of the Lady and other Poems" (Boston, 1891).

CONKLIN, Mrs. Jane Elizabeth Dexter, born in Utica, N. Y., 7th July, 1831. Her great-grandfather, George Grant, of Abernethy, Scotland, came to America in 1774. He joined the Continental Army and served during the Revolutionary War. Her mother was the daughter of William W. Williams, an architect of Albany, N. Y. An uncle of Mrs. Conklin, Asahel Dexter, was a captain in the War of 1812. Mrs. Conklin's father was born in Paris, N. Y., his parents having removed to that place from Mansfield, Conn., in the latter part of the last century. He was a cousin of John G. Saxe, the poet. Miss Dexter received her education in the Utica Female Academy and in Mrs. Brinkerhoff's school for young ladies, Albany, N. Y. Her first composition was written in verse. When she was fourteen years old, her poems were first published, and since that time she has been almost continuously writing. While none of her poems are strictly hymns, many of them are sung in religious meetings. She was, for many years, a contributor to the Utica "Gospel Messenger." She also wrote for a New York weekly, and for several local papers, prose articles as well as poetry. In December, 1865, she became the wife of Cramer H. Conklin, a veteran of the Civil War, and since that time she has lived in Binghamton, N. Y. Mrs. Conklin always took great interest in the War of the Rebellion and in the defenders of the Republic. When the Grand Army of the Republic post, to which her husband belongs, formed a Relief Corps of the wives and daughters of the members, her name was one of the first signed to a call for a charter. Shortly after the corps was

JANE ELIZABETH DEXTER CONKLIN.

organized, she was elected its president, and for three years held that office. In 1884 she published a book of poems, which was favorably received. She has in preparation a second volume of poems.

CONNELLY, Mrs. Celia Logan, see LOGAN, CELIA.

CONNELLY, Miss Emma M., author, born near Louisville, Ky., where she lived until 1880. Her father was a Virginian who went to Kentucky with his parents in his early youth. The family was connected with that of the English Governor of Virginia. One branch remained loyal to the king, but the immediate ancestors of the young Kentuckian had borne an active part in the struggle for freedom. Her mother's family were from Pennsylvania. Both her grandmothers were of a Quaker family, Douthett, of Welsh descent. Her mother died in the daughter's infancy, the father in her girlhood. Her first effort was a school-girl story, never thought of for publication till after her father's death, when it was sent to the Louisville "Courier-Journal." It was merely a story written because she liked to write, and so alarmed was she to see her thoughts in cold print, with her name attached, that she ran away to the country while it was being published. When Mr. Watterson afforded her the opportunity of the editorial incognito in a daily column on his paper, she gladly took the place, but, the unusual confinement of journalistic life proving too much for her, she gave it up at the close of the year. Of her father's estate sufficient remains to allow her careful study and deliberation in writing. Her taste has led her more and more from the story to the didactic, yet, with the highest aims, she has never given herself over wholly to moralizing. Her "Tilting at Windmills" (Boston, 1888) surprised

every one by its strength, its breadth of view, and the knowledge it evinced of human nature. Then followed her "Story of Kentucky" (Boston, 1891) for a historical series, "Stories of the States." Miss Connelly has but one near relative, a brother, John Allison Connelly, of Savannah, Ga. She makes her home mainly in New York City.

CONNER, Mrs. Eliza Archard, journalist and lecturer, was born on a farm near Cincinnati, Ohio. Her ancestors were among the pioneers of southern Ohio, and one of them founded the town of New Richmond. Her maiden name was Eliza Archard. She was educated in Antioch College, Yellow Springs, Ohio, taking the full course in classics and higher mathematics. In 1869 she became the wife of Dr. George Conner, of Cincinnati. In her early years she was a teacher, part of the time instructor in Latin and German in the Indianapolis high school. There her persistent refusal to accept less wages than had been previously paid to a man teacher for doing the same work resulted in the passing of a rule by the school board that teachers of both sexes in the high school should receive the same salary, a rule that remains in force to this day. Her first newspaper contribution was printed when she was thirteen years old. In 1865 she became a regular contributor to the "Saturday Evening Post," of Philadelphia, under the name of "Zig." Later she wrote for the Cincinnati "Commercial," signing the initials E. A. Her contributions attracted attention. In 1878 she became a member of the editorial staff of the "Commercial." She went to New York City in 1884 as literary editor of the "World." In 1885 she accepted a place on the editorial staff of the American Press Association syndicate in New York.

EMMA M. CONNELLY.

She is a member of Sorosis and of the New York Women's Press Club. Mrs. Conner has probably written as much newspaper matter as any other woman living. In editorial writing she furnishes regularly two columns daily of a thousand words each. She has done all kinds of newspaper work, from police-court reporting up. Her letters to the Cincinnati "Commercial" from Europe were published in a volume called "E. A. Abroad" (Cincinnati, 1883). She has also wrttten several serial stories. An important part of her work for the American Press Association has been the preparation of a series of newspaper pages of war history, descriptive of the battles of the Civil War. In her girlhood Mrs. Conner entered enthusiastically into the struggle for the emancipation and advancement of women. She originated classes in parliamentary usage and extempore speaking among women. Wherever occasion permitted, she has written and spoken in favor of equal pay for equal work, and of widening the industrial field for women. As a speaker she possesses the magnetic quality. She is deeply interested in psychological studies and in oriental philosophy, accepting the ancient doctrine of repeated incarnation for the same individual. She is an enthusiast on the subject of physical cul-

ELIZA ARCHARD CONNER.

ture for women, believing that mankind were meant to live out-doors and sleep in houses.

CONNER, Mrs. Elizabeth Marney, dramatic reader and educator, born in Rouse's Point, N. Y., 26th February, 1856. At the age of eighteen she became the wife of Marcus A. Conner, of Burlington, Vt., who died in 1881, leaving her with two young sons to care for and educate. It was then Mrs. Conner turned her attention to developing tastes and satisfying ambitions which heretofore had lain dormant. With decided abilities for music, literature and the drama, circumstances led her to choose some form of dramatic work, and she began the careful study of elocution. In January, 1884, the Buffalo School of Elocution was opened by Mrs. Conner, and since then she has rapidly won her way as teacher and artist in her profession, having gained for herself and school an enviable

local reputation, and being well-known in a far wider territory. She is a devotee to the art of which she is a true exponent, and every instinct of her being is absorbed in the success of her pupils.

ELIZABETH MARNEY CONNER.

and the advancement of that branch of education. Her lecture on "Expression" with illustrative readings has been in demand from school, pulpit and platform. She has published recitations in both prose and verse under the pen-name "Paul Veronique," and is the author of the popular operetta "Eulalie." Although her success as a teacher and reader is exceptional, it is considered by many that her true place is on the stage. For that profession she is gifted in a high degree with the essentials of success. She has a strong personality and magnetic presence, intense dramatic fervor, a fine voice and versatile powers of expression. She possesses in addition indomitable pluck, a cheerful, vivacious temperament, and is altogether one of the sunshiny people of the world.

CONVERSE, Mrs. Harriet Maxwell, author and philanthropist, born in Elmira, N. Y. She is Scotch by ancestry, American by birth and Indian by adoption. She is a daughter of Thomas Maxwell and Maria Purdy Maxwell. The history of the Maxwells, lineal descendants of the Earls of Nithsdale, is full of romance. The grandfather of Mrs. Converse was born on the shores of County Down, Ireland, his father and mother being cast there shipwrecked, having embarked for America in 1770. After the babe was some months old, they finally reached America and settled in Berkley, Va., in 1772. In 1792 the baby, Guy Maxwell, was a young man and removed to the spot now Elmira, N. Y. Of the children of Guy who became prominent, the father of Mrs. Converse, Thomas Maxwell, was remarkable. A man of ability, he was an influential factor in a region of country where it is yet said, "The word of a Maxwell was law." He served as a member of Congress and occupied various important positions. He was a graceful writer and a contributor to the "Knickerbocker Magazine." From him his daughter Harriet inherited her characteristics. Left motherless at a tender age, she was sent to Milan, Ohio, and there put to school under the care of an aunt. Early married, she became a widow while her former companions were yet girls, and in 1861 she was married to her second husband, Mr. Converse. For five years after her last marriage, she traveled in the United States and Europe, writing prose and verse under a pen-name. Not until 1881 did she begin to make use of her own name in print. She then set herself seriously to her work and published her first volume of poems, "Sheaves" (New York, 1883), which has passed through several editions. In 1884 Mrs. Converse was formally adopted by the Seneca Indians, as had been her father and grandfather before her. It was soon after the occasion of the re-interment by the Buffalo

HARRIET MAXWELL CONVERSE.

Historical Society of the remains of the famous Red Jacket, and her adoption made her the great-granddaughter of Red Jacket, with all the rights and honors pertaining to the relation. Mrs. Converse is an industrious writer of prose and a contributor to several magazines and newspapers. Among the works written by her are the historical volumes, "The Religious Festivals of the Iroquois Indians" and "Mythology and Folk Lore of the North American Indians." She has always defended the rights of the Indians of New York, and effectively aided the Indian delegation at Albany in 1891 to oppose a bill before the Assembly which would have deprived them of their lands. The bill was killed in committee. Before the hearing of the Indians by the committee, Mrs. Converse had been invited to sit in their Six-Nation Council held in Albany, an honor never before bestowed upon a white woman, save Mary Jemison. After the bill was killed, when the Seneca National Council, in

session at Carrollton, Cattaraugus county, N. Y., in the Allegany Reservation, was called, an application was laid before the body to the effect that, "by love and affection," it was the desire of the Indians that Mrs. Converse should be received into their nation as a legal member of it. Upon this appeal a vote was taken, and it was unanimously resolved that she be at once invited to appear before the Council and receive her Indian name. To this summons Mrs. Converse responded, and on her arrival at Carrollton was met by a delegation of Indians and escorted to the Council House, where she was received by the marshal of the nation and presented by him to the President and Board of Councillors. A runner was immediately sent out to notify the Indian people, and three-hundred of them gathered in the Council House, when Mrs. Converse was nominated by the Indian matrons to sit with them. Taking her place between two of the "mothers" at the head of the Council House, the ceremony proceeded, conducted by a head chief of the Snipe clan, of which Mrs. Converse had been made a family member in 1881. The resolution of the Council was then read in the Seneca language and interpreted to her. Then an eloquent address was made by the head chief of the Snipes, to which Mrs. Converse responded, recalling her inherited claim upon their friendship by reason of the adoption by their ancestors of her grandfather in 1794 and her father in 1804. After her address, she was presented by her "namer," the chief of the Snipe clan, to the president and members of the Council and the other Indian men and women who were present, with whom she shook hands individually. The name given Mrs. Converse is Yä-ih-wah-non, which signifies "ambassador," or the "watcher." This is a clan name, and the last bearer of it was the wife of the celebrated Gy-ant-wa-ka, or Cornplanter. In the fall of 1891, in a Six-Nation Condolence Council, held on the Tonawanda Reservation, N. Y., Mrs. Converse was nominated, elected and installed as a Six-Nation chief, thereby receiving a title never before bestowed upon a woman in all the history of the North American Indians. As a defender of the red man, Mrs. Converse is generally known among them as "our good friend," a distinction of which she is justly proud.

CONWAY, Miss Clara, educator, is a native and resident of Memphis, Tenn. She began her educational career as a public-school teacher. Her study of educational methods inspired her with the desire to establish a system of education for girls which should be based on absolute thoroughness. Her idea was and is that women should be so taught that, if conditions make self-support necessary, they can fill professional careers. She was the first woman in Tennessee to assist in the organization of teachers' institutes, and she was the first southern woman to attend the teachers' summer-school in the North. At the first session of the Martha's Vineyard Summer Institute she was the only representative of the South. At the meeting of the National Educational Association in Madison, Wis., 18th July, 1884, she read a paper on the needs of southern women. In 1886 she read a paper in the Saratoga convention, and in 1887 she was elected a member of the National Council during the San Francisco convention, although she was not present. She took a prominent part in the meeting of the Southern Association at Lookout Mountain in 1891, and in the meeting of the National Council in Toronto, Canada, in the same year. Her connection with the famous school that bears her name dates from 1878, when she originated the work with fifty pupils, one assistant and $300 of borrowed money. The growth of the school was remarkable. In 1884 Miss Conway's pupils numbered 250, and it became apparent that permanent accommodations must be provided. A few public-spirited citizens, impressed with the de-

CLARA CONWAY.

termination of the woman, who had fought such heavy odds, formed a stock company, incorporated the school and had a building erected. It was Miss Conway's proposition that it be called the Margaret Fuller school, but the trustees decided promptly that it should be named in honor of its founder, the Clara Conway Institute. The institute in 1891 had three-hundred pupils, a senior class of thirty, school property valued at $75,000, a strong faculty, nine of whom, former pupils, have been trained for special departments in the best schools of this country and of Europe, while its graduates are filling many useful positions in life.

CONWAY, Miss Katherine Eleanor, journalist, born in Rochester, N. Y., 6th September, 1853. She is the daughter of cultivated Celtic parents, who came to this country from the west of Ireland. Upon her mother's side are traditions of scholarship for many generations, several of her kindred having been prominent ecclesiastics in the Church of Rome. The name is of remote Welsh origin, and there is a slight trace of English blood in their veins, but the family pride is all in their Irish blood, and the Conways are "good rebels, every one." The name Conway has been notable in teaching and journalism. Katherine's sister, Miss Mary Conway, is the head of the Collegio Americano, in Buenos Ayres, Argentine Republic. Several of the same name and blood have been prominently associated with journalism in New York, and her kinsman, Rev. John Conway, edits a journal in St. Paul, Minn. The father of Katherine Conway, a successful railroad contractor and bridge-builder, was also active in politics. From the age of four to fifteen years Katherine was in school. The years from eleven to fifteen were spent in St.

Mary's Academy, Buffalo, N. Y., where her inclination to literature was strengthened by a gifted English teacher. At the age of fifteen, when her first poem appeared, Katherine was under the impression that ten dollars was the price usually paid to an editor for the honor of appearing in his columns in verse, and she supposed that, wishing to please her, some one of her family had been guilty of this blamable extravagance. Her busy mind was ever instinctively outreaching for wider fields of usefulness, and in her aspirations she was assisted by her sympathetic friend and adviser, Bishop McQuaid, of Rochester, N. Y. Her first work in journalism was done on the Rochester "Daily Union and Advertiser." She edited for five years the "West End Journal," a little religious monthly. She was assistant editor of the Buffalo "Catholic Union and Times" from 1880 to 1883. In that year Miss Conway was invited to visit Boston to recuperate her failing health. There she met for the first time the editor who had given her the earliest recognition for her poems by a check for their value, John Boyle O'Reilly. An opportune vacancy occurring upon the staff of the "Pilot," Mr. O'Reilly tendered it at the close of her visit to Miss Conway, who accepted and entered upon her new duties in the autumn of 1883. Besides a liberal salary, opportunities for outside literary work were often put in the young editor's way by her generous chief. Two years previous to that change, in 1881, Katherine Conway had gathered her vagrant poems into a volume, which was published with the appropriate title, "On the Sunrise Slope." Miss Conway's next venture through the hands of the publisher was in editing Mrs. Clara Erskine Clement Waters' collection, called "Christian Symbols

KATHERINE ELEANOR CONWAY.

and Stories of the Saints as Illustrated in Art." She has lately brought out a very successful little volume, "Watchwords from John Boyle O'Reilly," with an introductory chapter on O'Reilly as poet and literary writer.   Miss Conway is a woman with-out a grievance.   Her toil has been hard and long, but she has won recognition and made steady prog-ress.   Her influence is wide.   She organized the first Catholic reading circle in Boston, of which she is still president.   For years the chosen chairman of the literary entertainments of the New England Woman's Press Association, which office she has resigned, she has made an admirable presiding officer on occasions when any notable literary vis-itors to Boston were gathered about the board, and has done much to advance the dignity and preserve the harmony of that organization.   In the spring of 1891 Miss Conway was invited to give before the Woman's Council in Washington, D. C., her paper upon "The Literature of Moral Loveliness."   She was the first and is thus far the only Catholic who has appeared before the Educational and Industrial Union of Boston to speak upon a religious theme. In addition to that, during that year she read be-fore the Women's Press Club papers on "Some Ob-stacles to Women's Success in Journalism," "Per-sonal Journalism," and "On Magnifying Mine Office," a neat satire.   Besides all this, her poems have appeared in the Providence "Journal" and "Life," with thoughtful articles of literary trend in the Catholic and secular periodicals.   Miss Conway has lately been honored by being chosen president of the press department of the Isabella Associa-tion, in connection with the Columbian Exposition in Chicago.   She is still on the "Pilot," associate editor, with James Jeffrey Roche, chief editor. Miss Conway's life has been a full and generous one, overflowing with thought and help for others.

COOK, Miss Amelia Josephine, littérateur, born in Ballston Spa, N. Y.   She is the daughter of

AMELIA JOSEPHINE COOK.

Morton C. Cook, of French extraction, and the son of a Unitarian minister.   Her mother, Phebe A. Griffin Cook, was a Connecticut Quaker.   Amelia was one of a family of six children.   She was educated in the public schools in childhood, and subsequently studied in a select school, in a private seminary for young ladies, in an academy for both sexes, and finally in the State Normal School, where she studied with the object of becoming a teacher.   From her father she inherited a talent for poetry, which early revealed itself in connection with a remarkable facility for prose composition. Her specialty in literature is the short story.   Much of her work is designed for the boys and girls of the land.   Her recent work in various periodicals has appeared under several pen-names.   She has used her full name very seldom, preferring to re-main unknown to the public.   She is a member of the Women's National Press Association and of the Incorporated Society of Authors.

COOK, Miss May A., pianist, born in Paw Paw, Mich., 4th December, 1869.   Her father, Prof.

MAY A. COOK.

E. Cook, was born in Genesee county, N. Y.   During the Civil War he served in the Eighth New York Heavy Artillery as a member of the band, and saw the surrender of Lee's army at Appomattox Court House.   When the regiment was discharged, he re-turned to his native State and resumed his studies in the normal school in Brockport, N. Y.   After-ward his attention was devoted wholly to music. While teaching in Michigan, he became acquainted with Miss C. A. Tyler, and they were married in 1868.   Miss Cook showed an early predilection for music, and has always been an industrious student. At the age of sixteen years she was known as the finest pianist of the Pacific Northwest.   She was the first pianist to present to the musical public of that section the works of the great masters, and con-certos by Weber, Beethoven and Schumann, with full orchestra, were successively given, and in such an artistic manner as to make them popular.   A re-markably clear technic and great expression char-acterize her playing.   In the summer of 1891 Miss Cook, accompanied by her mother, went to

Germany, where she purposes to spend some years in musical study. Her home is in Portland, Ore.

COOKE, Mrs. Rose Terry, author, born on a farm near Hartford, Conn., 17th February, 1827.

ROSE TERRY COOKE.

Her father was Henry Wadsworth Terry, and her mother's maiden name was Anne Wright Hurlbut, and she was a daughter of John Hurlbut, of Wethersfield, Conn., who was the first New England shipmaster who sailed around the earth. When Rose Terry was six years old, her parents moved into Hartford. Her father educated her in out-door lore, and she was familiar with birds, bees, flowers and sunshine. She was carefully trained at home, and in school she was brilliant and noted for the ease with which she learned and for her skill in versification when only a child. She was graduated in 1843, and, although only sixteen years old, became a teacher in Hartford. She afterward taught in New Jersey. Family needs called her home, and she then began to study with the intention of becoming an author. She published poems in the New York "Tribune," and at once won a reputation. She published her first story in "Graham's Magazine," in 1845. Her reception was encouraging. Other productions followed, and in a short time she published a volume of verse. She contributed to "Putnam's Magazine," "Harper's Magazine" and the "Atlantic Monthly" poems and stories, and her productions were in general demand. In 1872 she became the wife of Rollin H. Cooke, a Connecticut manufacturer, and they lived in Winsted for some years. Her most important works are "Poems by Rose Terry" (Boston, 1860), "Happy Dodd" (Boston, 1879), "Somebody's Neighbors" (Boston, 1881), "Root-Bound" (Boston, 1885), and "The Sphinx's Children" (Boston, 1886). Her short stories, humorous and descriptive, of New England life would fill several volumes. She died in Pittsfield, Mass., 18th July, 1892.

COOKE, Mrs. Susan G., of Knoxville, Tenn., though for many years a resident of the South, was born in the State of New York. She is the daughter of George Spaulding Gale, one of the most prominent surgeons of Vermont, and a granddaughter of Gen. Summers Gale, of the same State, a hero of the War of 1812. Her mother, a woman of brilliant intellectual and social qualities, was a member of one of the oldest families in her section of the State of New York. From both her parents Mrs. Cooke inherits the energy and resolution which characterize all her undertakings. Graduating with high honors from a prominent school in New York City, Miss Gale shortly after became the wife of Sidney E. Cooke, a member of the New York Stock Exchange, who died in Knoxville in February, 1883. Mrs. Cooke has been identified with charitable work and for several years was one of the managers of the Brooklyn Orphan Asylum, and has held several positions of responsibility and honor. She is a member of the Board of Lady Managers of the World's Columbian Exposition from Tennessee, and was selected by Mrs. Potter Palmer to serve on the executive committee. She immediately assumed the duties of secretaryship of that committee, and on the retirement of Miss Phœbe Couzins as secretary to the full board, Mrs. Cooke was elected her successor. She is an indefatigable worker. Her excellent qualifications and amiability fit her for the heavy and numerous

SUSAN GALE COOKE.

responsibilities she assumed in connection with the great Exposition of 1893 in Chicago.

COOLBRITH, Mrs. Ina Donna, poet, was born in Illinois. Her parents were New Englanders. The family removed to Los Angeles, Cal., when she was a child, and there her youth was passed. She became a voluminous contributor to the "Overland Monthly," and she contributed also to the "Californian," the "Galaxy," "Harper's Magazine" and other important periodicals. Her recognition by the press, by the poets and by the critics was instantaneous. In 1874 circumstances forced her to accept the office of librarian in the free library of Oakland, Cal., where she has re-

INA DONNA COOLBRITH.

mained until the present time. In 1881 she published a small volume of poems, "A Perfect Day," most of which had been written before 1876. In 1876 her mother died, and since then her life has been one of self-sacrifice for those who depended upon her. Since the publication of her volume she has written very few poems.

COOLEY, Mrs. Emily M. J., religious and and temperance worker, born in Lima, N. Y., 1st November, 1831. Her maternal ancestry was of the French nobility who, for religion's sake, left title, fortune and home, and, casting their lot with the persecuted Huguenots, found in New Jersey, among the Quakers, a refuge and a home where they might worship according to their faith. Many of the descendants became distinguished soldiers during the national struggle. On her father's side she is descended from the Puritans of 1636. They settled in North Adams, Mass., and some of the eminent men of that State are of kindred blood. Till the age of sixteen she attended the public schools, and then was a student for a year each in Buffalo, in Rochester and in Aurora Academy, now Wells College. She was for five years a teacher in Buffalo, and then became the wife of Rev. R. Cooley, of the Methodist Episcopal Church, a graduate in Meadville, Pa. After that for one year she was preceptress of Cooperstown Seminary. They moved to Wisconsin in 1862, and she began her public work in the Woman's Foreign Missionary Society. She was for several years vice-president of the society in Wisconsin Conference and organized many auxiliaries. Her temperance work was begun in 1869. When once awakened to the extent of the liquor evil, she became one of its most determined foes. Though grown white-haired in

the service, she is still an indefatigable worker in the cause of prohibition. In 1880 her husband was transferred to the Nebraska Conference. She had resolved to enjoy home rest for a season after that change, but her fame preceded her in letters to the State officers from Miss Willard and others. She was made State organizer for the Woman's Christian Temperance Union of Nebraska, in her first year with that body. She served four years as State and three years as National organizer, speaking in every State of the Union. She has been for several years president of the second district Woman's Christian Temperance Union of Nebraska. Not alone in the temperance cause has Mrs. Cooley been known as a power for good. Though not an ordained minister of the M. E. Church, being a woman, she was known as an "exhorter," and she was twice appointed by the presiding elder to supply the pulpit of a church without a pastor. Each

EMILY M. J. COOLEY

time her labors were successful and the membership greatly increased.

COOLIDGE, Mrs. Harriet Abbot Lincoln, philanthropist, author and reformer, born in Boston, Mass. Her great-grandfather, Amos Lincoln, was a captain of artillery and one of the intrepid band who, in 1773, consigned the tea to the water in Boston harbor. He was in the battle of Bunker Hill, attached to Stark's brigade, in action at Bennington, Brandywine and Monmouth, and aided in the suppression of Shays's Rebellion, and was also one of Governor Hancock's aids. On 14th June, 1781, he was married to Deborah, a daughter of Paul Revere of revolutionary fame, which makes Mrs. Coolidge a great-great-granddaughter of that famous rider. Amos Lincoln's first ancestor in this country was Samuel Lincoln, of Hingham, Mass., one of whose sons was Mordecai, the ancestor of President Lincoln. The father of Mrs. Coolidge, Frederic W. Lincoln, was called the War Mayor of Boston, as he held that office all through the Civil

War and was reëlected and served seven years. Mrs. Coolidge was delicate in childhood, and her philanthropic spirit was early shown in flower-mission and hospital work in Boston. For several years she was instructed at home, and she was sent to the private boarding-school of Dr. Dio Lewis, of Lexington, Mass. In November, 1872, Harriet Abbott Lincoln became the wife of George A. Coolidge, a publishing agent of Boston. With maternal duties came the untiring devotion of conscientious motherhood. Mrs. Coolidge gave her children her best thoughts and studied closely the best methods of infant hygiene. She soon began a series of illustrated articles for the instruction of mothers in a New York magazine, and while residing in that city studied for three years and visited the hospitals for children. Ill health obliged her to return to Washington, D. C., where, before going to New York, she was interested in charities and hospitals for children. Meeting the mothers of both the rich and the poor, and seeing the great need of intelligent care in bringing up little children, she soon found a large correspondence on her hands. Her devotion to the waifs of the Foundling Hospital in Washington, and the great hygienic reformation she brought about, gave that institution a record of no deaths among its inmates during the six months she acted as a member of its executive board of officers. Frequent inquiries from mothers desiring information on hygienic subjects relating to children suggested the idea of a series of nursery talks to mothers and the fitting up of a model nursery in her residence, where every accessory of babyhood could be practically presented. "Nursery Talks" were inaugurated by a "Nursery Tea," and five-hundred women from official and leading circles were present. Classes were formed, and a paid course and a free one made those lectures available for all desiring information. Even into midsummer, at the urgent request of mothers, Mrs. Coolidge continued to give her mornings to answering questions. She remained in Washington during the summer, guiding those who did not know how to feed their infants proper food, and, as a consequence, her health was impaired, and she was obliged to give up her nursery lectures until her health was restored. She then commenced a scientific course of hygienic study, and was made president of the Woman's Clinic, where women and children are treated by women physicians, free of charge or for a mere trifle. Mrs. Coolidge is always busy. She is an active member of four of the leading charity organizations in Washington, a valued member of the Woman's National Press Association and devoted to every movement in which women's higher education is considered.

COOLIDGE, Susan, see WOOLSEY, MISS SARAH CHANNING.

COOPER, Mrs. Sarah Brown Ingersoll, educator, author and evangelist, born in Cazenovia, N. Y., 12th December, 1836. She was graduated from the Cazenovia Seminary in 1853. She subsequently attended the Troy Female Seminary. When but fourteen years of age she opened a Sunday-school class in a village adjoining Cazenovia, and that class was the germ which finally grew into a church congregation. When she started her school some of the committeemen came to her and told her that, while they believed her to be qualified in every way to teach, at the same time they would all like it better if she would go home and lengthen her skirts. When twelve years old, she appeared in print in the village paper, the "Madison County Whig," and from that time to the present she has been more or less engaged in literary work on papers and magazines. After her graduation from college she went to Augusta, Ga., as a governess in the family of Governor Schley. On the Governor's plantation there were five-hundred or more slaves, and Mrs. Cooper, then Miss Ingersoll, used to gather them about her to teach them the Scriptures. While in Augusta she became the wife of Halsey Fenimore Cooper, also a Cazenovia Seminary graduate, who had been appointed by President Pierce to the office of surveyor and inspector of the port of Chattanooga. Mr. and Mrs. Cooper were living in Chattanooga at the breaking out of the Civil War, but soon after removed to Memphis, where Mr. Cooper was appointed assessor of internal revenue. There Mrs. Cooper was elected president of the Society for the Aid of Refugees. She taught a large Bible class, which comprised from one to three hundred soldiers. In 1869 she removed with her husband to California. Her first Bible class in San Francisco was in the Howard Presbyterian Church, where Dr. Scudder was fill-

SARAH BROWN INGERSOLL COOPER.

ing the pulpit. From there she went to the Calvary Presbyterian Church, and still later opened the class in the First Congregational Church. That class numbered over three-hundred members and embraced persons representing every sect, including even those of the Jewish and the Roman Catholic faith. While the credit of establishing the first free kindergarten in San Francisco is due to Prof. Felix Adler and a few of his friends, yet the credit of the extraordinary growth of the work is almost entirely due to Mrs. Cooper, who paid a visit to the Silver street free kindergarten in November, 1878, and from that moment became the leader of the kindergarten work and the friend of the training school for kindergarten teachers. The rapid growth of the free kindergarten system in California had its first impulse in six articles written by Mrs. Cooper for the San Francisco "Bulletin" in 1879. The first of these was entitled "The Kindergarten, a Remedy for Hoodlumism," and was of vital interest to the public, for just at that time ruffianism was so terrific that a vigilance committee was organized to protect the citizens. The second article was "The History of the Silver Street Free Kindergarten." That aroused immediate interest among philanthropic people. In the early part of 1878 there was not a free kindergarten on the western side of the Rocky Mountains; to-day there are sixty-five in San Francisco, and several others in progress of organization. Outside of San Francisco they extend from the extreme northern part of Washington to Lower California and New Mexico, and they have been formed in Oregon, Nevada and Colorado, and in almost every large city and town in California. In a recent report issued by Mrs. Cooper she attributes the rapid strides in that work in San Francisco to the fact that persons of large wealth have been induced to study the work for themselves, and have become convinced of its permanent and essential value to the State. The second free kindergarten in San Francisco was opened under the auspices of Mrs. Cooper's Bible class, in October, 1879. In 1882 Mrs. Leland Stanford, who had been an active helper in the work from the very first, dedicated a large sum for the establishment of free kindergartens, in San Francisco and in adjacent towns, in memory of her son. Then other memorial kindergartens were endowed. There are now (1892) thirty-two kindergartens under the care of Mrs. Cooper and her daughter, Miss Harriet Cooper. Over $300,000 have been given to Mrs. Cooper to carry on this great work in San Francisco, and over 10,000 little children have been trained in these schools. Her notable and historical trial for heresy in 1881 made her famous as a religious teacher and did much to increase the wide interest in her kindergarten work. Mrs. Cooper is a philanthropist and devotes all her time to benevolent work. She is a director of the Associated Charities, vice-president of the Pacific Coast Women's Press Association, an active member of the Century Club and the leader of one of the largest Bible classes in the country. She possesses great heroism, but is quiet, magnetic and exceedingly sensitive and sympathetic. She is one of the best-known and best-loved women on the Pacific Coast. She was elected a member of the Pan-Republic Congress, one of five women of the world who had that distinguished honor.

COPP, Mrs. Helen Rankin, sculptor, born in Atlanta, Logan county, Ill., 4th August, 1853. She is descended from Scotch and German ancestors, who took a leading part in freeing America from the British yoke and from the curse of slavery. Her paternal grandfather, John Rankin, was one of the organizers of the Abolition movement. From her earliest childhood she dreamed of art. Stories and histories of artists were her favorite reading, and she tried to work out her dreams. It was weary labor, for the result was so far from her ideal. The few pictures the little country town afforded were but dreary disappointments. When she was five years old, her parents moved to Loda, Ill., where she passed her childhood and early womanhood. At the age of eighteen she attended the opening of the Chicago Exposition and for the first time saw a work of art. She returned home with renewed hope to the work of finding a way in the dark. In 1874 she became the wife of W. H. Copp, of Wolfboro, N. H., then engaged in the mercantile business in Loda. In 1884 they moved to Pullman, Ill., with one son, leaving four sons lying in the little prairie cemetery. The years of working in the dark were ended. In 1888 Mrs. Copp entered the Art Institute of Chicago. There she soon discovered that sculpture was her forte.

Abandoning all thoughts of painting, she plunged into the study of modeling and anatomy with a desperation born of the knowledge that half a lifetime was gone. Entering upon her work at an age when most artists begin to achieve success, she rapidly surmounted all difficulties, allowing herself no rest, even in vacation, and carrying off the honors of her class, until 1890, when she received the only medal ever given by the Art Institute for sculpture. Her instructor said that she had accomplished ten years' work in three. Mrs. Copp

HELEN RANKIN COPP.

then established a studio in Chicago. She has modeled portraits of a number of prominent citizens of that city, besides many ideal works.

CORNELIUS, Mrs. Mary A., temperance reformer, born in Pontiac, Mich., 25th September, 1829. Her maiden name was Mary A. Mann. In the veins of both her parents, who were of New England origin, flowed the blood of the Pilgrim Fathers. The child early developed the hereditary trait, a genius for leadership. Her first school composition, written when she was nine years of age, was a hit in the rural community where she lived, and was printed in the local newspaper. In 1850 she became the wife of Rev. S. Cornelius, D.D., of Alexandria, Va. Her husband encouraged her in writing short articles for the press on religious and philanthropic subjects, but when, with the cares of motherhood and the responsibilities of her position as a pastor's wife upon her, she brought to his notice a story of thirty-nine long chapters which she had written, he protested against this draft upon her vitality. Although a semi-invalid for many years, she struggled heroically against her weakness and was, as she still is, a moving spirit in Christian and philanthropic enterprises. She was president of the Woman's Christian Temperance Union of Arkansas, in 1885. While leading an effort for prohibition in that State, her course aroused the hostility of the liquor interest. Her life was threatened by the desperate element in the capital of Arkansas, and personal violence was attempted. In spite of all, she persevered in her work She edited a journal in the interest of the society about

MARY A. CORNELIUS.

the time of her husband's death, in 1886. Her pen has never been quite idle, except since her bereavement. She assisted her husband when he was engaged in editorial work. Her poems, numerous prose articles and voluminous newspaper correspondence testify to her industry. Perhaps the best known of her writings are "Little Wolf," which has had a wide sale, and the poem, "Sweet Marie." With lately renewed health she has resumed literary work. She is now living in Topeka, Kans.

CORNELL, Mrs. Ellen Frances, born in Middleboro, Mass., 20th July, 1835. She is the daughter of George and Marcia Thompson Atwood, and the youngest of a family of nine children. She is a descendant in the seventh generation from John Atwood, Gentleman, of London, Eng., who came to Plymouth soon after the landing of the Pilgrims. The first mention of him in the old Colonial Records is made in 1633. Her maternal ancestor, John Thompson, from the north of England, came to Plymouth in May, 1622, in the third embarkation from England. In the troubles with the Indians, the people in the vicinity of his home chose him as their commander, and the Governor and Council of Plymouth gave him a general commission as lieutenant-commandant of the field and garrison and all posts of danger. Ellen attended the district school near her home and public and private schools in New Bedford, and later the academy in Middleboro. She became a teacher, and to that work she gave six years of her life. She became the wife, in February, 1859, of Mark Hollingsworth Cornell, of Bridgewater, Mass. Since then they have resided in their pleasant home on the bank of the Taunton river, in one of the most beautiful spots in that region. For many

years Mrs. Cornell was an invalid, confined to her home, and for seven years of that time unable to leave her bed. Her interest in the world about her, from which she was isolated, never wearied. The influence of her patient life was felt far beyond the confines of her own room. Her poems have been printed in various papers and magazines. Mrs. Cornell is a member of the New Church. Her summers are now passed in Edgartown, Martha's Vineyard, where she employs many hours of her time in adding to her already large collection of marine shells, which she has carefully classified.

CORONEL, Señora Mariana W. de, Indian curio collector, born in San Antonio, Texas, in 1851. There she remained until eight years old, when her parents removed to Los Angeles, Cal., and have there resided ever since. Her father, Nelson Williamson, is a hardy New Englander from Maine, now ninety years old. Her mother is a woman of Spanish descent. Mrs. Coronel possesses the quiet disposition of her mother. She is the oldest of a family of six children. Having from infancy been familiar with the English and Spanish languages, she speaks them with equal fluency, and her knowledge of both has aided her materially while collecting her curios. She became the wife of Don Antonio F. Coronel, a native of Mexico and one of the most prominent participants in the early history of Los Angeles, in 1873. For many years, by travel in Mexico and California and by correspondence they have been collecting Indian and Mexican curiosities and have now one of the best private collections in Los Angeles. They are deeply interested in the mission Indians of California, having joined heart and hand with their friend, Helen Hunt Jackson, in aiding those unfor-

ELLEN FRANCES CORNELL.

tunates. Mrs. Coronel and her husband are active members of the Historical Society of California.

CORY, Mrs. Florence Elizabeth, industrial designer, born in Syracuse, N. Y., 4th June, 1851.

She is a daughter of Johnson L. Hall. She comes of Revolutionary stock and traces her descent back through those on her father's side, who won distinction worthy of historical mention in the War of

MARIANA W. DE CORONEL.

1812, and more notedly in the battles of Monmouth and Stony Point in the Revolution, to General Isaac Hall and to Col. Harry Hall. At the age of nineteen she became the wife of Hon. Henry W. Cory, of St. Paul, Minn., but in two years returned with her only child, a girl, to reside with her parents. Her education was of that sort so commonly sufficient for the average society girl, but wholly inadequate to meet her great desire of becoming independent. In spite of the fact that she had loving parents and a home replete with all the comforts and luxuries that money and refinement bring, her longing to do for herself could not be conquered, and she was continually casting about for some occupation in which to find support and, possibly, distinction. Noticing how inartistic were the designs on most of the carpets, curtains and tapestries which met her eye, the question arose "why can I not make them better?" Then began her life-work, which has placed her in the front rank of self-made women and won for her the enviable distinction of being the first practical woman designer in the United States, if not in the world. Mrs. Cory corresponded with leading carpet manufacturers, and they at once recognized the practicability of women designers, and from each she received encouragement and was advised to begin a course of instruction in Cooper Union, New York. That was in the spring, and she found she could not enter the institute till the following autumn. During the summer she employed her time constantly in studying the structure of fabrics by unraveling them and in making original designs, one of which was accepted by a prominent manufacturer, and she was the proud possessor of fifteen dollars, the first money she had earned. On entering Cooper Union in the fall, she

found, much to her amazement, that her instructors, while they knew the principles of design and could teach them well, could not at that time teach any practical method of applying those principles to an industrial purpose. She began a course in drawing, of which she felt a great need, and occupied her afternoons in the particular study of carpet designing in the factory of E. S. Higgins, where six weeks of instruction had been offered free. Her improvement was rapid She subsequently visited the representative factories of nearly every art industry in the United States and thoroughly familiarized herself with the technicalities of design and workings of machinery in each. She became an instructor in Cooper Union in the art she had herself come there to learn but a few months before. That position she was obliged to resign on account of ill health. After spending three years in the West, she returned to New York and established herself as a practical designer. In a short time she received more work than she could do. Much of her time was consumed by women who came to her for information and instruction, which she gave free. On account of the large number who applied to her for help, she set aside certain hours for receiving them, and finally was obliged to give whole afternoons to their service. That was the beginning of the institution now known as the School of Industrial Art and Technical Design for Women, to which for the last twelve years Mrs. Cory has devoted her entire time, attempting but little work not directly devoted to her pupils. By a system of home instruction Mrs. Cory has taught pupils in every State and Territory in the United States, and several foreign countries. Mrs. Cory is a member of the society of the Daughters of the

FLORENCE ELIZABETH CORY.

Revolution, of the Daughters of the American Revolution, and of the Daughters of 1812, and is president of the Society of Industrial Art for Women.

COTES, Mrs. Sara Jeannette Duncan, author and journalist, born in Brantford, Ontario, Canada, in 1862. She is most widely known by her maiden name, Sara Jeannette Duncan. Her

PHŒBE COUZINS.

father, Charles Duncan, is a merchant of Brantford and a man of wide information and keen intelligence. Her mother is a quick-witted Irish woman. As a child, Miss Duncan was an earnest reader. She received her education in the public schools and collegiate institute of her native town. She fitted herself for a public school-teacher and taught in the Brantford schools for a short time; the work was not congenial, however, and she soon relinquished it. She early began to write verse and prose, and after the usual discouragements she decided to make journalism a stepping-stone to literature. Her first newspaper work was in the year of the Cotton Centennial in New Orleans, whither she went to write descriptive letters for the Toronto "Globe," the Buffalo "Courier," the Memphis "Appeal" and other newspapers. After that she went to Washington, D. C., and became a member of the editorial staff of the Washington "Post." Her newspaper experience, especially that in Washington, was of great service to her. Her "copy" was freely and even severely criticised by the editor of the "Post," with the result of improving her manner of writing. Leaving Washington, she joined the staff of the Toronto "Globe," and later that of the Montreal "Star," passing one season in Ottawa as the special correspondent of the "Star." She made a hit with her unconventional book of travels, entitled "A Social Departure; or How Orthodocia and I went Round the World by Ourselves." Her companion on that journey, whom she calls "Orthodocia," was Miss Lily Lewis, a young woman engaged in literary and journalistic work, a contributor to "Galignani" and several London journals. Her next book was "An American Girl in London." On her trip

around the earth Miss Duncan met E. C. Cotes in Calcutta, India, and she became his wife within two years after their first meeting. Professor Cotes has a scientific appointment in connection with the Indian Museum, and has acquired considerable reputation in the field of his special research, Indian entomology. They make their home in Calcutta, India.

COUES, Mrs. Mary Emily Bennett, woman suffragist, born in New York City, 26th August, 1835. She was a daughter of Henry Silliman Bennett and Mary Emily Martin Bennett. On her father's side she is a collateral descendant of the famous Aaron Burr, cousin of Mr. Bennett, and is connected with the Silliman family of New Haven, Conn., which includes the two Benjamins, father and son, both distinguished scientists. The maternal ancestry includes the name of Foote, honored in New England annals, and of Martin, borne by several officers of high rank in the English navy. Sir Henry Byam Martin, K.C.B., the second son of Admiral Sir Thomas Byam Martin, G.C.B., admiral of the fleet and vice-admiral of the United Kingdom, for many years comptroller of the navy and member of Parliament for Plymouth, who died 21st October, 1854, was Mrs. Bennett's cousin. The Martin family resided in Antigua, where they owned large estates, and Sir William Byam, who died in 1869, was president of the council of Antigua and colonel of the Antigua dragoons. The grandaunts of Mrs. Coues were the Misses Martin, Catherine, Penelope and Eliza, long known in New England for their devotion to education, whose historical school in Portland, Me., attracted pupils from far and wide. A strong character might be expected in a descendant of ancestry which included such

MARY EMILY BENNETT COUES.

marked individualities and developed such diverse tendencies, so it is no wonder that Mrs. Coues has taken a recognized position among those women who represent the advance thought of the day on all the great questions which affect their sex. The child was reared in all the rigor of the Presbyterian creed, which her mind rejected early, and the revolt of her young heart was final. Her education was completed under private tuition in London and Paris, the first of the twenty-four times she has crossed the ocean having been in the vessel that carried to England the news of the firing on Fort Sumter in 1861. Many of her earlier years were passed amid the gaieties of various European capitals, in strong contrast with the severity of her early training, an experience which served to broaden and strengthen her intellectual grasp. She became an accomplished musician, an art critic, a linguist and a brilliant society woman. In Dresden, in Saxony, 28th March, 1866, she became the wife of Joseph W. Bates, a leading merchant of Philadelphia, Pa., who died in that city 27th March, 1886. She had no children. Mrs. Bates' twenty years of married life were divided between her homes in Yorkshire, England, and in Philadelphia. She was wealthy and could indulge her tastes for music and art. Her Philadelphia mansion was noted for the elegance and lavishness of its hospitality, its wonderful dinners and one of the finest private collections of paintings in this country. Since her marriage, in Boston, Mass., 25th October, 1887, to the well-known scientist and writer, Dr. Elliott Coues, of Washington, D. C., she has resided with her husband in their beautiful home on N street in that city, one of the most attractive literary, artistic and scientific centers of the national capital. She is in hearty sympathy with Dr. Coues' published views on the religious and social questions of the day, and her inspiration of one of his books is recognized in its dedication to his wife. Mrs. Coues is at present the secretary of the Woman's National Liberal Union and a prominent member of various other organizations for the promotion of enlightened and progressive thought among women, though she has thus far shrunk from taking the position of a public writer or speaker. Her attitude is that of the extreme wing of radical reform, now being agitated. Though at heart a deeply religious woman, Mrs. Coues has not found church communion necessary to her own spiritual aspirations. Among her dominant traits are a strong, intuitive sense of justice, a quick and tender sympathy for all who suffer wrongs and a never-failing indignation at all forms of conventional hypocrisy, intellectual repression and spiritual tyranny. No one appeals in vain to her sense of right and duty, and many are the recipients of her bounteous secret charities.

COUZINS, Miss Phœbe, lawyer, was born in St. Louis, Mo., in 184– and has passed most of her life in that city. On her father's side her ancestry is French Huguenot, and on her mother's side English. She inherits her broad views of justice from both parents. Her mother, Mrs. Adaline Couzins, was among the first to offer her services as volunteer aid to the Sanitary Commission in the Civil War, and Phœbe also was active in relieving the miseries of the wounded and sick soldiers. They served after many of the great battles of that conflict, and during those years the daughter was studying the question of prevention of war, and she came to the conclusion that woman, clothed with political powers, would be as powerful to prevent war, as, without such powers, she is to ameliorate its horrors and evils. In 1869 her ideas were crystallized in the Woman's Franchise Organization, which included some of the best and most intelligent women of St. Louis. Miss Couzins at that time began to think of entering some profession. Acting on the advice of Judge John M. Krum, she chose law and applied for admission to the Law

School of Washington University, in St. Louis, in 1869. She had been educated in the public schools and high school of St. Louis, and the board of directors and the law faculty of the university were familiar with her career. Her application for admission was granted without a dissenting voice, thus giving the St. Louis university the honor of first opening a law-school to the women of the United States. Miss Couzins was an earnest student in the law-school, and she was graduated in 1871, and a public dinner was given to signalize the event. She did not enter largely into the practice of law, but she was one of the few who presented their cases to General Butler, when he was chairman of the judiciary committee of Congress in Washington. In 1876 she entered the lecture field as an advocate of woman suffrage, and her record was a brilliant one. She has been admitted to practice in all the courts of Missouri, in the United States District Court, and in the courts of Kansas and Utah. She has held positions of trust and honor. She was at one time United States Marshal for the Eastern District of Missouri, the first woman in the United States appointed to a federal executive office, receiving her commission from Justice Miller. Two governors of Missouri have appointed her commissioner for that State on the National Board of Charities and Correction. Superintendent of the Eleventh Census Robert P. Porter appointed her manager of the division of mortgage indebtedness for the city of St. Louis. She was appointed in July, 1890, a lady commissioner for Missouri on the World's Fair Board of Directors.

COYRIÈRE, Mrs. E. Miriam, business woman, born in London, Eng., when her parents were traveling and visiting relatives there. She

E. MIRIAM COYRIÈRE.

comes of English ancestry, the Hopkins family on her father's side, who settled in New England and were prominent in the history of the Colonies, and on her mother's side the Archer family, at one time the owners of Fordham Manor, in Westchester county, N. Y. Lord John Archer received the letters patent on the estate in November, 1671. He was a descendant of Fulbert L' Archer, one of the companions of William the Conquerer. The manor was mortgaged in 1686 to Cornelius Van Steinwyck, a New York merchant, and he left it by will to the Dutch Church of New York. On her mother's side the families have been Episcopalians since the establishment of the Episcopal Church in England; on her father's side they have belonged to the same church for over one-hundred years. Mrs Coyrière's real name is Mrs. Carlos Pardo. She has been twice married. Her husband, Professor Carlos Pardo, is a writer on pedagogy. Both are members of the American Association of Science, and Mrs. Pardo, who has kept her business name, E. Miriam Coyrière, is interested in all the reform movements of the time. She is a member of the National Educational Association, of the Woman's Health Association and of other organizations. She inherits literary talent from her mother, who was both poet and artist. Her father, who was wealthy at the time of his marriage, was a talented and highly educated man, and he turned his attainments to account when his fortune was swept away. He was a fine linguist and an author. Mrs. Coyrière belongs to a family of six children. Her first marriage was unfortunate. Her husband failed, and her parents died and left three young sons to her and her sister's care. She soon set about the work of earning a livelihood for herself and her young charges. Aided by Peter Cooper, she became a teacher, after a course of study in Cooper Institute. To add to her labor, her first husband became an invalid from paralysis. Her only son died in infancy. After teaching for a time, she learned the school furniture business. In 1880 she opened a teachers' agency, that has earned a world-wide reputation. She worked diligently to build it up and has succeeded. She supplies teachers for every grade of educational institution, from colleges down to district schools, and her patrons are in every State of the Union and in Canada, in Central America, Mexico and South America, and she has supplied teachers for European institutions. Her school furniture business has been a part of her work ever since she started in business for herself. In 1884 she displayed furniture and school apparatus at the International Congress in Rio de Janeiro, Brazil, where she won a diploma. Mrs. Coyrière has no living children, but her home life is exceptionally happy. She became the wife of Prof. Carlos Pardo in 1884, and their home is a center of intellectual activity.

CRABTREE, Miss Lotta, actor, born in New York City, 7th November, 1847. Her father was a bookseller in Nassau street, New York, for many years. In 1851 he went to California, where he engaged in gold-mining. His wife and daughter followed him in 1854. They lived in a little log-house in the mining town, La Porte. Mr. Crabtree was only moderately successful in his search for gold. Lotta showed in childhood the talents which have made her famous. Her first appearance on the stage was in 1855, in an amateur performance in La Porte, in which she appeared as a singer. When she was seven years old, she took lessons in dancing, and she appeared as a singer and dancer in amateur entertainments, and she created a furore among the miners. At the end of one of the performances she was called before the curtain, and a shower of silver dollars and half-dollars greeted her. That event led her to become an actor, and shortly afterward she and her mother started on a tour of California. The bright little star every-

where won encouragement and reputation. She played the part of Gertrude, in the "Loan of a Lover," in Petaluma, in 1858. Her starring tour was made in 1860, and the troupe in which she and her mother played reaped a fortune. Lotta received countless presents, ranging from silver dollars and twenty-dollar gold-pieces up to sets of jewelry and diamond-studded watches. In her early tours she traveled in a suit of boy's clothes, for convenience in making horseback journeys among the mountains. In 1864 Lotta made her début in New York City, in a spectacular play in Niblo's Garden. She made her first great success in "Little Nell and the Marchioness." She at once took a distinct and high rank as a star in eccentric comedy, and her singing, dancing and drollery, in plays written especially for her, made her one of the leading theatrical stars for years. Her rôles include the "Marchioness," "Topsy," "Sam Willoughby," "Musette," "Bob," "Firefly," "Zip," "Nitouche" and

LOTTA CRABTREE.

"The Little Detective." Of the last-named play, Lotta says: "I have played it season after season and year after year, until I am really ashamed to show my face in it upon the stage again. That play has always been a great hit, and it has brought me no end of money. We paid just twenty-five cents for it, the cost of the book from which it was adapted to me, and we have made thousands upon thousands out of it." Lotta has played successful engagements in England. She has always been accompanied by her mother, who has successfully managed her financial affairs. Lotta's earnings have been large, and her investments represent about a million dollars. During 1891 and 1892 she did not play, but it is not her intention to retire from the stage yet. Besides her dramatic talent, she possesses a decided talent for art. She has been a student and hard worker, and her example has been powerful in winning public respect for the stage and for actors.

CRAIG, Mrs. Charity Rusk, national president of the Woman's Relief Corps, was born in Morgan county, Ohio, about 1851, and went with her parents to Wisconsin when about three years of age. Her father is Jeremiah M. Rusk, ex-governor of Wisconsin and a member of President Harrison's cabinet. Her mother's maiden name was Mary Martin, the present wife of the secretary of agriculture being her step-mother. At the age of thirteen years Charity Rusk entered a Catholic school, St. Clare Academy, where she remained for one year. She then entered a private school in Madison, Wis., and from that went to the University of Wisconsin, where she was graduated and afterward continued Latin and literature. She has had systematic studies every year since she left school, not neglecting them even during the four years spent in Washington, D. C., when her father was a member of Congress, and she had a brilliant social career. In 1875 she became the wife of a classical student of the Wisconsin University, Elmer H. Craig. They spent a year in Milwaukee, Wis., and a year in Boston, Mass. Mr. Craig was connected with the United States Pension Department. Resigning his position in order to connect himself with the banking firm of Lindeman & Rusk, he moved to Viroqua, Wis. where Mrs. Craig has since been the center of a coterie of distinguished people. In Viroqua is the Rusk homestead, which in summer is always sought by the Secretary of Agriculture and his family and more intimate friends. Mrs. Craig, after having long been quite prominently identified with various local charities and conspicuously interested in women's organizations, became a charter member of the Woman's Relief Corps, auxiliary to the Grand Army of the Republic. She was first president of

of awakening the interest of the Woman's Relief Corps and the G. A. R. in the Veterans' Home in Waupaca, Wis. As national president she consolidated the work and introduced a new system of accounts, which was more successful. She was instrumental in extending the work into the new States, and laid the foundations for a wide increase of membership. She is a model presiding officer, conducting the deliberations of a large convention with grace and dignity. She admits that she likes to talk to bodies of women.

CRANE, Mrs. Mary Helen Peck, church and temperance worker, born in Wilkes Barre, Pa.,

MARY HELEN PECK CRANE.

10th April, 1827. She was the only daughter of Rev. George Peck, D. D., of the Methodist Episcopal Church, the well-known author and editor. She became the wife of the late Rev. Jonathan Townsley Crane, D. D., when twenty years of age, and was the mother of fourteen children. She was a devoted wife and mother and was energetic in assisting her husband in his work in the church and among the poor. Mrs. Crane was an ardent temperance worker and, as her children grew up, she devoted much time to the work of the Woman's Christian Temperance Union. Mrs. Crane delivered addresses on several occasions before the members of the New Jersey Legislature, when temperance bills were pending, and she greatly aided the men who were fighting to secure good laws. As the pioneer of press-work by women at the Ocean Grove Camp Meeting, she did valuable work, and her reports for the New York "Tribune" and the New York Associated Press, during the last ten years of the great religious and temperance gatherings at the noted Mecca of the Methodists, are models of their kind. For about ten years she was the State superintendent of press for New Jersey of the Woman's Christian Temperance Union. She wrote several leaflets that were of great value to the press-workers of the local

CHARITY RUSK CRAIG.

the corps in Viroqua, then president of the State department, and was finally elected the national president. While serving as department president, she visited many places in the State for the purpose

unions. For over a half-century Mrs. Crane was an active member of the Methodist Episcopal Church. She led the life of a sincere Christian and died 7th December, 1891, after a short illness contracted at the National convention of the Woman's Christian Temperance Union in Boston. One daughter and six sons survive her.

CRANE, Mrs. Ogden, concert singer and musical educator, born in Brooklyn, N. Y., in 1850. She received her musical education in New York. She studied for six years under Antonio Barilli, and for five years under William Courtney. She adopted the pure Italian method and style of singing. Her voice is a dramatic soprano of wide range, and she is a successful singer. She has occupied many important positions as a member of the choirs in the South Congregational Church, Brooklyn, in St. Ann's Church, the Church of the Puritans and St. James's Methodist Episcopal Church, New York. She is well known on the concert stage, having traveled over nearly every state in the Union, and in 1890 made a tour through the South with her sisters, who are known as the Mundell Quartet. Her repertory of oratorios and standard concert pieces is very large, and during her career she has won for herself an enviable reputation. As an instructor she has been especially successful; she has a large number of pupils, both professional and amateur, from all parts of the

MRS. OGDEN CRANE.

country. In conscientious work lies the secret of her success.

CRANE, Mrs. Sibylla Bailey, composer, born in Boston, Mass., 30th July, 1851. She has always lived in that city with her parents. On the maternal side she is a descendant of Rev. Dr. Joseph Bellamy, the eminent theologian, and on the paternal side her ancestry runs back to the Mayflower Pilgrims. She became the wife of Rev. Oliver Crane, D.D., LLD., in September, 1891. Mrs. Crane is deeply interested in the work of the philanthropists

of Boston. She is an active member of the Women's Educational and Industrial Union, and an officer of the Beneficent Society whose members aid talented and needy students to pass the course

SIBYLLA BAILEY CRANE.

of study in the New England Conservatory of Music. She is a worker in the church and is a member of the committee of the General Theological Library. She has always been a student of music, language and literature. Among her works as a composer are music for some of the poems of Bryant, Whittier and Longfellow. Her musical compositions have been sung by her in the prisons and hospitals which she has visited in her philanthropic work. She has traveled extensively in America and in Europe, and her impressions of Europe are recorded in her book, "Glimpses of the Old World." One of her most valuable papers is her history of music, which she prepared to read before the Home Club of Boston. That lecture covers the whole field of music, in its historical phases, from the early Egyptians down to the present. Mrs. Crane uses her noble voice and fine musical training with good effect in illustrating the music of the various nations, while delivering this lecture. She has given this and other lectures before many of the principal educational institutions of Massachusetts.

CRANMER, Mrs. Emma A., temperance reformer and woman suffragist, born in Mt. Vernon, Wis., 2nd October, 1858. She is the daughter of Dr. J. L. Powers, was educated in Cornell College, and began to teach school when fifteen years old. In 1880 she became the wife of D. N. Goodell, who died in 1882. Three years later she was united in marriage to Hon. S. H. Cranmer, and their home is in Aberdeen, S. Dak. They have one child, a daughter, Frances Willard Cranmer. Mrs. Cranmer has been a member of the Methodist Episcopal Church since her early childhood, and is a class-leader in her church. She has written much for the press, both in prose and verse. She has lectured on literary subjects and on temperance in many of the cities and towns of the Northwest. As an orator she is eloquent and winning. She is

poetic temperament and bids fair to become as graceful a writer.

EMMA A. CRANMER.

ALICE ARNOLD CRAWFORD.

an earnest worker in the white-ribbon movement, with which she has been connected for years, and is president of the South Dakota Woman's Christian Temperance Union. In equal suffrage she is profoundly interested, and is president of the South Dakota Equal Suffrage Association. She is a woman of strong convictions, and a cause must appeal to her judgment and sense of right in order to enlist her sympathy.

CRAWFORD, Mrs. Alice Arnold, poet, born in Fond du Lac, Wis., 10th February, 1850. At an early age she gave promise of brilliancy of mind and facility of expression. Her youthful talent was carefully fostered and encouraged, both by a judicious mother and by her friends. Her father, a man of sterling qualities of mind and heart, died when she was but four years old. At sixteen she was graduated from the high school in Fond du Lac, with honors. For several years after her graduation she taught in the public school and gave lessons in music. At the same time she wrote for the papers of her city, in one of which she had a regular department, besides furnishing several continued stories. Her poems and short sketches were published by various periodicals. When the Grand Duke Alexis visited Milwaukee, Wis., she was called upon and furnished the poem of welcome. In September, 1872, she became the wife of C. A. Crawford, a banker of Traverse City, Mich., and that place was her happy home for two years before her death, which occurred in September, 1874. The year following an edition of her poems was issued in Chicago, and a second edition was published a few years later. Mrs. Crawford's whole life was in itself a poem. She left one child, a daughter, who inherits her mother's

MRS. JOHN CRAWFORD.

CRAWFORD, Mrs. John, newspaper correspondent, born near Syracuse, N.Y., 21st July, 1850.

She is of German descent, her maiden name being Quackenbush. At an early age her family removed to Canada, and for several years resided in Consecon, Ont., where Miss Quackenbush attended a grammar school. She lived in Michigan for some time, and while there she was engaged in teaching. It was at that time she .commenced to contribute to the literary press. In 1869 she returned to Canada, locating in Newtonville, Ont. Writing for various Canadian and American newspapers was there a pleasant pastime. In 1871 she became the wife of John Crawford, of Clarke, Ont. For a few years her literary efforts were rather desultory, owing to domestic cares. She has two children, a boy and girl. In 1887 an entire summer's illness afforded leisure for literary work, and since that time more or less writing for the press has occupied her time, and always under the assumed title, "Maude Moore." Her present residence is in Bowmanville, Ont.

CRAWFORD, Mrs. Mary J., church organizer and worker, born in Great Valley, Cattarau-

MARY J. CRAWFORD.

gus county, N. Y., 15th April, 1843. Her maiden name was Mary Mudgett. She became the wife of William L. Crawford, 11th June, 1866. His business called him to Florida in 1883, and they built a home on the St. John river, in South Jacksonville, a suburb of Jacksonville. Their family consists of one son. Mrs. Crawford's time and means have been given to further the work of the Episcopal Church, of which she is a devoted member. As soon as they were settled in their Florida home, the need of a church was forced upon her attention. Services were held in the ferry waiting-room, and later services were held regularly in her home for several months. Mrs. Crawford at once started a project to secure a church. She opened a Sunday-school with six or eight pupils and about as many teachers. In a short time the school grew, and it was necessary to rent a room for the work.

Increased attendance followed. Mrs. Crawford circulated a subscription list and personally secured the money needed to erect a new church building. The new building was dedicated as All Saints Episcopal Church on Whitsunday, in 1888, Bishop Weed, of Florida, officiating. In the new and handsome structure the church has prospered greatly, largely through Mrs. Crawford's work. At present her home is in St. Augustine, Fla., where she is an active member of Trinity Church, and the directress of the Ladies' Auxiliary Society of the parish.

CROLY, Mrs. Jennie Cunningham, pioneer woman journalist, was born in Market-Harborough, Leicestershire, England, 19th December, 1831. Her father was a Unitarian minister, descended from Scotch ancestors who left Scotland with James I and settled in England. Her mother belonged to an old country family. Her father, Rev. Joseph Howes Cunningham, brought his family to the United States when Jennie was about nine years old. He was a man of pronounced views, and he had made himself unpopular by preaching and lecturing on temperance in his native town. On account of his obnoxious temperance views his English neighbors once mobbed his house, and his children were assaulted on their way to school. He had visited the United States before settling here. Jennie inherited her father's traits of character. She was a precocious child and early showed her literary trend in little plays written in childhood. Her first production that was published appeared in the New York "Tribune." Her taste for journalism grew rapidly, and she at an early age took a position on the New York "Sunday Dispatch," at a salary of three dollars a week. Soon after she took a position on the New York "Sunday Times," at a salary of five dollars a week. That position she held for five years, doing general work in the line of items for women readers. She soon became a correspondent of the New Orleans "Delta" and the Richmond "Whig," an editorial writer on the "Democratic Review" and a regular contributor to the "Round Table." In 1856 she invented the duplicate system of correspondence and became one of the editors and the dramatic critic of the "Sunday Times." Her activity was remarkable. She became editor of the fashion department of "Frank Leslie's Magazine" and wrote the fashions for "Graham's Magazine." She aided in starting Madame Demorest's "Mirror of Fashions," a quarterly, which she wrote entirely for four years, and which was consolidated with the "Illustrated News" and became "Demorest's Illustrated Magazine." She edited it for twenty-seven years, and also started and controlled other minor publications for the same house. She introduced many novelties in New York journalism. Early in life she became the wife of David G. Croly, then city editor of the New York "Herald," on which paper she did much work. In 1860 her husband was chosen managing editor of the New York "World," just started, and Mrs. Croly took charge of the department relating to women, which she controlled until 1872, and during eight years of that time she did similar work for the New York "Times." When the "Daily Graphic" was started in New York, Mr. Croly became its editor, and Mrs. Croly transferred her services to that journal. During those busy years she corresponded for more than a score of prominent journals in different States, and she is still serving many of them in that capacity. Her work throughout has had the distinct aim of building up the intellectual status of women. Her ideas have taken form in the organization of women's clubs and societies. In March, 1868, Mrs. Croly,

"Fanny Fern," Alice and Phœbe Cary, Mrs. Char-
lotte B. Wilbour, Miss Kate Field, Mrs. Henry M.
Field, Mrs. Botta and other women met in Mrs.
Croly's home in New York and started Sorosis,
with twelve charter members. Alice Cary was
chosen president, Mrs. Croly vice-president, Kate
Field corresponding secretary, and Mrs. Wilbour
treasurer and recording secretary. The New York
Press Club invited Sorosis to a "Breakfast," at
which the ladies had nothing to do but sit and eat.
Sorosis, in return, invited the Press Club to a
"Tea," and there the men had to sit and listen
while the women did all the talking. The women
were soon recognized, and Sorosis grew in numbers and influence. Alice Cary resigned the presidency at the end of the first year, and Mrs. Croly
was unanimously elected in her place. She served
fourteen years. She was among those calling
woman's congress in New York, in 1856, and again
in 1869. In 1887 she bought a half interest in

JENNIE CUNNINGHAM CROLY.

"Godey's Lady's Book," and served as editor of
that journal. She resigned that position and started
a monthly publication, the "Cycle," in New York.
That journal was consolidated with the "Home
Magazine," and Mrs. Croly is at present the editor
of that periodical. She was chosen president of
the Women's Endowment Cattle Company, or
iginated by Mrs. Newby. That company, incorporated under the laws of New Jersey, had a capital
stock of $1,500,000 and controled 2,000,000 acres of
grazing land in New Mexico, with thousands of
head of cattle. Mrs. Croly has a pleasant home in
New York City. Her family consists of one son
and one daughter. She has contributed largely to
scientific journals. She is a member of the New
York Academy of Sciences, a member of the Goethe
Club and vice-president of the Association for the
Advancement of the Medical Education of Women.
Her home has for years been a center of attraction
for authors, artists, actors and cultured persons.

Her writings would fill many volumes. Her published books are "Talks on Women's Topics"
(1863), "For Better or Worse" (1875), "Three
Manuals of Work" (1885-89). In nearly all of Mrs.
Croly's literary correspondence she has used the
pen-name, "Jenny June."

CROSBY, Fanny J., blind song-writer, born
in 1823. For over a half-century she has been singing in her blindness, and her songs have gone
around the earth, been translated into many languages and been sung in every land. Miss Crosby
showed her talent for versification in childhood.
At the age of eight years she composed verses that
were remarkable in their way. She was educated
in a school for the blind, and she became a teacher
in the Institution for the Blind in New York City.
While engaged there, she wrote the words for many
of the songs composed by George F. Root, the
well-known musician. Among these were some
that became very widely known, including, "Hazel
Dell," "Rosalie, the Prairie Flower," "Proud
World, Good-bye, I'm Going Home," "Honey-
suckle Glen" and "There's Music in the Air."
She wrote the words for the successful cantatas,
"The Pilgrim Fathers" and "The Flower Queen."
Her most famous hymn, "Safe in the Arms of
Jesus," was written in 1868. That hymn is her favorite. In the same year she wrote that other famous hymn, "Pass Me Not, O Gentle Savior."
Every year she has added new songs of remarkable
power and taking qualities to her long list of productions. Her "Rescue the Perishing," "Jesus,
Keep Me Near the Cross," and "Keep Thou My
Way, O Lord," appeared in 1869. The last named
song was set to music and used for years as the
prayer-song in the Mayflower Mission connected
with Plymouth Church, Brooklyn, N. Y. In 1871
she wrote "The Bright Forever," in 1873 "Close
to Thee," in 1874 "O, Come to the Savior," "Like
the Sound of Many Waters" and "Savior, More
than Life to Me." In 1875 she wrote "I am Thine,
O Lord," "So Near to the Kingdom," and "O,
my Savior, Hear Me." She has always been known
as Fanny J. Crosby, but her name since her marriage has been Van Alstyne. She lives in New
York City. It is estimated that the hymns from
her pen number over 2,500, and in addition to that
wonderful total must be considered the many secular songs, cantatas and other lyrical productions
which have appeared under her name or anonymously. One house has published 1,900 of her
productions. No complete collection of her verses
has yet been made.

CROSS, Mrs. Kate Smeed, social leader,
born near Philadelphia, Pa., 18th November, 1859.
In 1869 she went with her parents to reside in Lawrence, Kans., where the next seven years were
spent in school and studying in the University of
Kansas. In 1876 she returned to Philadelphia and
devoted herself industriously to the study of music,
art and the great exhibition. In 1880 she returned
to her Kansas home and in that year became the
wife of Charles S. Cross, a banker and business
man of Emporia, Kans., where in their charming
home, "Elmwood," Mr. and Mrs. Cross, with their
little daughter live and dispense hospitality. Nature has endowed Mrs. Cross with large gifts, and
these gifts are ever made to administer generously
to the welfare of those about her and to the help of
every good cause. She is an efficient officer of
nearly every art, musical and literary circle of Emporia and is a staunch church woman, a member of
the Episcopal Church. Some of the finest classic musical entertainments given in Emporia have
been given under her direction, she herself taking
leading parts in such operas as the "Bohemian

Girl" and showing herself possessed of histrionic ability.

CRUGER, Miss Mary, novelist, born in Oscawana, N. Y., 9th May 1834. She belongs to

KATE SMEED CROSS.

the well-known Cruger family of English descent, whose members have always held distinguished positions in American society, since the days when Henry Cruger, who with Edmund Burke repre-sented the City of Bristol in the British Parliament, zealously and ably advocated the cause of Ameri-can independence. Miss Cruger is one of the children of the late Nicholas Cruger, of Westchester county, New York. Her father was educated in West Point and held the position of captain in the 4th Infantry of the regular army at the time of his marriage to Miss Eliza Kortright, daughter of Captain Kortright, of the British Army. He shortly afterwards left the army and built a house in Oscawana, on the Hudson. There most of the children were born and grew up, till the death of both parents broke up the family circle. Shortly afterwards Miss Cruger built a house near Mon-trose, N. Y., where she has since resided, and where most of her literary work has been accom-plished. At her home, called "Wood Rest," she lives a unique and poetical life. Miss Cruger's first published work was "Hyperæsthesia" (New York, 1885). Her next book was called "A Den of Thieves, or the Lay-Reader of St. Marks" (New York, 1886). She then published her third novel, "The Vanderheyde Manor-House" (New York, 1887), which was followed by "How She Did It" (New York, 1888). "How She Did It" was a great success, and gave Miss Cruger a personal as well as an extended literary fame. "Brotherhood" (Boston, 1891) is her latest publication. Humanity is her watchword and inspiration. Tragic as must always be the result of such short-sighted struggles as those that occur between labor and capital, that story goes far toward solving a great problem.

CRUGER, Mrs. S. Van Rensselaer, novel-ist and social leader, born in Paris, France. She is a daughter of Thomas Wentworth Storrow, who spent the greater part of his life in France. The Wentworths were of New England. Her mother was a daughter of Daniel Paris, a well-known law-yer of Albany, N. Y., and for many years a mem-ber of the New York legislature. Mrs. Storrow was the favorite niece of Washington Irving, and a diamond, which he gave her when she was mar-ried in his Sunnyside home, is now in Mrs. Cruger's possession. Mrs. Cruger is the wife of Colonel S. Van Rensselaer Cruger, a member of one of the old Knickerbocker families of New York, and they make their home in that city and in a pleasant place called "Idlesse Farm" on Long Island. Mrs. Cruger has long been known as a social leader, and during the last three or four years she has won a most remarkable success as a novelist. She is a master of French, having spoken only that language until she was nine years of age, and, with her liberal education, her long residence abroad, and her experience in many spheres of life, she unites a distinctly literary talent that has enabled her to cast her stories in artistic form, while preserving in them a most intense humanity. Her novels have been published under the pen-name "Julien Gordon," and the critics, without exception, sup-posed "Julien Gordon" to be a man. Her nov-els are "A Diplomat's Diary," "A Successful Man," "Mademoiselle Réséda" and "A Puritan Pagan," all of which appeared as serials first and then in volumes. All have passed through many

MARY CRUGER.

editions. She has written some poetry, but she has never published or even kept any of her verses.

CUINET, Miss Louise Adèle, doctor of dental surgery, born in Hoboken, N. J., 29th Novem-ber, 1855. She is of French parentage. On the maternal side she is a descendant of the Huguenot Humberts, a family of local eminence in Neuchâtel, where they sought refuge in the sixteenth century. Upon her decision to adopt dentistry as a profession, Dr. Cuinet realized that, in addition to the ordinary obstacles presented to youth and inexperience, she might also encounter the prejudice which confronts every woman who ventures upon an innovation and threatens to invade a field considered the exclusive province of men. She therefore determined to equip herself with great thoroughness. With that view, after completing the course in one of the best New York schools, she studied two years with a prominent dentist in that city, preparatory to entering, in 1881, the Pennsylvania College of Dental Surgery. That institution graduated one woman about twenty-six years ago and then closed its doors against women for eight years, until Dr. Truman became dean. Dr. Cuinet was graduated in 1883, in high standing, taking one of the first places in a class of fifty-nine. She is the one woman belonging to the Second District Dental Society of New York, and the only one practicing in Brooklyn. With very engaging personal qualities she unites great skill and conscientious devotion to her work. These have won for her a high place in the estimation of professional experts, and the confidence and esteem of a large and increasing clientage. Her success in a vocation generally repugnant to feminine sensibilities represents extraordinary natural qualifications and great industry. She is a master of her profession in all its branches. Dr. Cuinet has always been dis-

LOUISE ADÈLE CUINET.

tinguished by an ardent love of outdoor games and sports, in many of which she excels.

CULTON, Miss Jessie F., journalist, born in Henry, Ill., 14th February, 1860. Her grandfather on her father's side was a native of Tennessee. On her mother's side she is descended from the Blanchards of Massachusetts. Mr. and Mrs. Culton moved to Chicago when Jessie was but a few months old, and there she grew up. She removed to Richmond, Ind., in 1883, and took a position on the editorial staff of the "Register," in which capacity she served nearly a year, in the meantime doing reportorial work on the "Palladium" and

JESSIE F. CULTON.

"Item," daily papers of Richmond. In 1884 she went to California with her father, as Mr. Culton's health demanded a change of climate. They traveled extensively throughout the State, and settled in San Diego, where they built a pleasant home. She also has a home on a ranch in Garden Grove. Her duties as housekeeper prevent, to some extent, her journalistic work, but she contributes articles to St. Louis, Chicago and other eastern papers.

CUMINGS, Mrs. Elizabeth, see PIERCE, MRS. ELIZABETH CUMINGS.

CUMMINGS, Mrs. Alma Carrie, journalist, born in Columbia, N. H., 21st March, 1857. Her father, Abner L. Day, was a farmer in moderate circumstances, and she had only the advantages in childhood of a common-school education. On 27th January, 1875, she became the wife of Edwin S. Cummings, at that time a compositor in the office of the "Northern Sentinel." A little later that paper was consolidated with the Colebrook "Weekly News," the result being the "News and Sentinel." Mr. Cummings in 1885 purchased the plant and, until his death, two years later, Mrs. Cummings went daily to the office and materially aided her husband in advancing the prosperity of the new paper. His sudden death left the business in what Mrs. Cummings aptly termed the "usual unsettled condition of a country newspaper office." Instead of disposing of the property at a sacrifice, she determined to hold it and, if possible, improve it, and in that endeavor she has succeeded far beyond her expectations. As editor and proprietor she has enlarged the circulation, increased the volume of news, secured more advertising, and in short has made the "News and Sentinel" a valuable paper for northern New Hampshire.

Mrs. Cummings has two children, and to these and to her paper she devotes her life and energies.

CUMMINS, Mrs. Mary Stuart, educator, born in Jonesborough, Tenn., 31st May, 1854. Her maiden name was Mary Stuart Slemons. Her parents were strict Presbyterians of the old style, and the seven children were reared in that faith. Mary, the fourth child, was reared and educated to graduation at sixteen years of age in her native town. Ambitious to go beyond the academic course, she pushed her way, by her own efforts, to the attainment of a full diploma of the Augusta Female Seminary, Staunton, Va. Returning to Tennessee in 1874, she began to teach in the high school in Knoxville, where as teacher and principal she remained until 1886, meanwhile, in 1877, having become the wife of W. F. Cummins, a merchant of that city. Mrs. Cummins found her greatest pleasure in the school-room, yet finding time to enter other fields of labor, as well as to enjoy social pleasures. A very large mission Sunday-school was a part of her work. She was the president of the Synodical Missionary Society and a State member of the executive board of Home Missions of New York for the Presbyterian Church. An effort was made to place her in charge of school interests in Mexico, but that did not seem to be compatible with her other duties. In 1886, partly for her husband's health and partly from the energetic spirit of both, Mr. and Mrs. Cummins accepted business engagements in Helena, Mont., where they now reside. Mrs. Cummins was teacher and principal in the Helena high school for five years. Since going to Montana she has received every token of a high appreciation of her religious character in the public work to which she

MARY STUART CUMMINS.

part and is now filling her second year as president of the Montana Woman's Christian Temperance Union. In 1891 she was commissioned by Miss Willard as national organizer for the vacation months, to work in Montana, and she traveled over a large part of the State, organizing new unions. Partly as a result of that tour, the banner presented by Miss Willard for the largest percentage of gain in membership in the Western States was given to Montana in 1891. In September, 1891, Mrs. Cummins entered the Montana University, in Helena, as preceptress, in charge of the young ladies' department and professor of Latin and modern languages.

CUNNINGHAM, Mrs. Annie Sinclair, religious worker, born in the West Highlands, Scotland, 29th October, 1832. Her maiden name was Annie Campbell Fraser Sinclair. Her father, Rev. John C. Sinclair, a Presbyterian clergyman, was married in 1822 to Miss Mary Julia McLean, who was by close relationship allied to the noble houses of Duart and Lochbuy. There were nine children, of whom Annie was the fifth. Only five of the number lived to mature age. While the children were young, the parents emigrated to Nova Scotia, and removed a few years later to Prince Edward's Island, where ten happy years were spent by her father in home missionary work. To secure a more liberal education for their children, the family went to Newburyport, Mass., in 1852, where Annie was admitted to the girls' high school. Young as Annie was when the family left Scotland, she could read and speak two languages, Gaelic and English, though she had never been to school, except the home school in the manse. At the early age of eleven years she made a public profession of her faith and became a member of the church of which her father was the pastor. When her two brothers, the late Rev. James and Alexander Sinclair, were ready to study theology, choice was made of the Western Theological

ALMA CARRIE CUMMINGS.

has been called along that line. She was chosen by her co-laborers successively vice-president and president of the Montana State Teachers' Association. In temperance work she has taken a leading

Seminary, in Allegheny, and the family removed to Pittsburgh, Pa., in 1854. Four years later Annie became the wife of Rev. David Ayers Cunningham, who was at the time pastor of the Presbyterian Church, of Bridgewater, Pa. There their only child was born and buried. In 1864 Dr. Cunningham was called to Philadelphia, where he was for twelve years a successful pastor. During those twelve years there came a period of great activity among the women of the various denominations. When the Woman's Foreign Missionary Society of the Presbyterian Church was organized in 1870 she was one of its founders, and is still one of its officers. The Woman's Christian Association of Philadelphia came into existence about the same time. Mrs. Cunningham was the first chairman of its nominating committee, and was thus intimately associated with Christian women of every name in the city. She was for a time an officer in the organization of the women of Philadelphia for the Centennial Exhibition of 1876. From her young womanhood to later years she has been a faithful and successful Bible-class teacher. In 1876 Dr. Cunningham accepted a call to the First Presbyterian Church of Wheeling, W. Va. New work was found there with capable women ready to be organized for Christian labor, and for fifteen years she has been the president of a missionary society which includes all the women and children of the thirty-nine churches in the Presbytery of Washington. For nearly ten years she has been one of the secretaries of the Chautauqua Missionary Institute, in which women of all denominations meet annually. She is also an enthusiastic admirer of the Chautauqua Literary and Scientific Circle, and completed the course of reading in 1888. She was

come under the public eye, and Mrs. Cunningham invariably insists that much of the activity in which she has had the privilege of engaging could not have been successfully carried on, but for the co-operation of him who has been for more than thirty years her husband and pastor.

CUNNINGHAM, Miss Susan J., educator, born in Harford county, Maryland, 23rd March,

SUSAN J. CUNNINGHAM.

1842. On her mother's side she is of Quaker blood. Her mother died in 1845, and Susan was left to the care of her grandparents. She attended a Friends' school until she was fifteen years old, when it was decided that she should prepare for the work of teaching. She was sent to a Friends' boarding-school in Montgomery county, for a year, when family cares called her home, and she continued her studies in the school near by. At nineteen she became a teacher, and she has taught ever since, with the exception of two years, one of which she spent in the Friends' school in Leghorne, or Attleboro, and the other in Vassar College. She has spent her summer vacations in study. She studied in Harvard College observatory in the summers of 1874 and 1876, in Princeton observatory in 1881, in Williamstown in 1883 and 1884, under Prof. Safford, and in Cambridge, England, in 1877, in 1878, in 1879 and in 1882, under a private tutor. In 1887 she studied in the observatory in Cambridge, England, and in 1891 she spent the summer in the Greenwich, England, observatory. When Swarthmore College was established in Swarthmore, Pa., in 1869, she was selected teacher of mathematics, Professor Smith now of Harvard being nominally professor. Professor Smith was called to Harvard at the close of the first year, since which time she has had entire charge of the department of pure mathematics, having been made full professor in 1875. In late years she has had charge of the observatory, which was built with funds secured by her own exertions. She is a thoroughly

ANNIE SINCLAIR CUNNINGHAM.

chief officer of the Woman's Christian Association of Wheeling, and is the president of the West Virginia Home for Aged and Friendless Women. There is a great deal of work done which does not

successful educator, and her conduct of her departments shows that a woman can be quite as efficient as a man in the realm of mathematics and astronomy.

CUNNYNGHAM, Mrs. Elizabeth Litchfield, missionary and church worker, born in

ELIZABETH LITCHFIELD CUNNYNGHAM.

Abingdon, Va., 23rd February, 1831. Her maiden name was Elizabeth King Litchfield. Her parents were of old Virginia stock, true in all respects to the family history and traditions. Miss Litchfield received the best elementary training which the country could afford, and, when sufficiently advanced, was placed in Science Hill Academy, under the care of Mrs. Julia A. Tevis. While in that school she was converted and became an earnest and active Christian. After her return to Virginia she taught school, not from necessity, but of choice, her father having ample means. She felt it to be her duty to engage in some useful occupation, and she saw no position more promising than that of a teacher of young people. In March, 1851, she became the wife of Rev. W. G. E. Cunnyngham, a minister of the Methodist Episcopal Church, South, and in 1852 sailed from New York with her husband for Shanghai, China, as a missionary to the Chinese. She remained in the mission field nine years, when the failure of her health compelled her to return to her native land. During her stay in China she studied diligently, and with uncommon success, the Chinese language. She superintended native mission schools, instructed Chinese women and children orally, and translated into the local dialect tracts and small books, some of which have remained in use to the present time. A native woman, for years employed as a "Bible woman" by the mission in Shanghai, was brought to a knowledge of the gospel by Mrs. Cunnyngham's personal efforts. After she returned to America, she lost nothing of her missionary spirit, but labored as far as she had opportunity in

the home work, doing all she could to awaken a deeper interest among her own people in the cause of foreign missions. When the Woman's Board of Foreign Missions of the Methodist Episcopal Church, South, was organized, she was made one of the managers, a position she has held ever since. She was elected editor of leaflets by the board, and for six years discharged with acceptability the duties of that office. In addition to her labors in the missionary cause, she is an active Sunday-school teacher, an efficient helper in local church work, and a practical friend of the poor. She has traveled much. Her husband having been elected to one of the editorial chairs of the Methodist Episcopal Church, South, she removed to Nashville, Tenn., in 1875, and still resides in that city.

CURRAN, Mrs. Ida M., journalist and editor, was born in Waterbury, Vt. When a mere child, her family removed to Boston and afterwards to Woburn, Mass. She early showed a marked talent for literary work, and at school won her highest standing in rhetoric and literature. This proficiency in composition gained for her one of the four class honors in the Woburn high school when she graduated. She contributed largely to the Grattan "Echo," and afterwards became the wife of the publisher of the paper, F. P. Curran. Household duties compelled Mrs. Curran to withdraw for a time from literary labors, but in 1888 she once more became associated with newspaper work, her articles appearing in the Woburn "City Press," of which journal she assumed entire control in 1890. Mrs. Curran is a member of the New England Woman's Press Association. She is an accomplished violinist and an amateur actress. In addition to her newspaper duties, she presides over a

IDA M. CURRAN.

charming home, and personally directs the education of her three children.

CURTIS, Mrs. Martha E. Sewall, woman suffragist, born in Burlington, Mass., 18th May,

1858. She is descended from one of the oldest families of New England. Among her ancestors were Chief Justice Samuel Sewall, of witchcraft fame, and his son, Rev. Joseph Sewall, minister of

MARTHA E. SEWALL CURTIS.

the Old South Church, Boston. On her grandmother's side she is descended from Henry Dunster, first president of Harvard College. She was graduated from Cambridge high school in 1874, the youngest of her class. She subsequently pursued the study of various literary branches and accomplishments. For several years she was a teacher, and at one time was on the school committee of her native town. She became the wife of Thomas S. Curtis, 3rd July, 1879. They had two children, both of whom died in infancy. Her husband died 27th December, 1888. He fully sympathized with his wife in her literary and reformatory work. After her marriage she took a full course in elocution at the New England Conservatory and was graduated in 1883. She afterward spent a year in the study of oratory to fit herself for public speaking. A firm believer in the equality of the sexes, she began when quite young to work for the enfranchisement of women. Her first appearance as a public lecturer was in the meetings of the National Woman Suffrage Association in Boston and elsewhere. In 1889 she was appointed State lecturer of the Massachusetts Woman Suffrage Association, and in that capacity addressed many public meetings in different parts of the State. She has also done much work for the reform by contributing articles to the newspapers. She edits a weekly woman's column in the Woburn "News," and she is president of the Woburn Equal Suffrage League. She has been active in urging women to vote for the school committee, the only form of suffrage granted to them in Massachusetts. She is a thorough believer in temperance, but holds that the best way to obtain good laws is to put the ballot into the hands of women as well as men. From

her grandfather, Rev. Samuel Sewall, a famous antiquarian of the past generation, she has inherited a taste for historical research. She has recently written a history of her own town for the "History of Middlesex County."

CUSHMAN, Miss Charlotte Saunders, actor, born in Boston, Mass., 23rd July, 1816, died in Boston, 18th February, 1876. Miss Cushman was descended from two families of prominence in early New England. She was eighth in descent from Robert Cushman, the preacher who delivered the first sermon ever heard in New England. Her mother's ancestry ran back to the Puritan Babbits. The house in which Charlotte was born stood on the site of the present Cushman School, which was built in 1869. The school was named after her. Her early ambition was to become an operatic singer, and she made her début as a singer in Boston, in April, 1835, where she sang in a concert. After some experience as a singer in New Orleans, she decided to go on the dramatic stage. She at once began to study for the stage, and made her début as Lady Macbeth in New Orleans, in 1835. She made a good impression and played in a variety of characters, at first with no distinct preference for any particular line of drama, and finally settled on tragedy and Shakespearean rôles, in which she won her greatest fame. She was a charming comedian always, but her commanding talents drew her irresistibly to the higher walks of the profession. Her first appearance in New York City was in Lady Macbeth, 12th September, 1836, and she at once took a leading rank. After playing throughout the United States, always with growing power and reputation, she went to London, Eng., where she made her début in Bianca, 14th February,

CHARLOTTE SAUNDERS CUSHMAN.

1845. She returned to the United States in 1850, and played a second season in England in 1853. She played important engagements in the United States in 1857 and 1858, and again in 1860 and 1861.

In addition to her stage work she won fame as a reader. She gave her first public reading in October, 1870, in New York. Her last appearance in New York was 7th November, 1874, and in Boston, 15th May, 1875. Her last appearance as a public reader was in Easton, Pa., 2nd June, 1875. She was an ardent patriot, and during the Civil War she gave $8,267 to the Sanitary Commission. For over forty years her life was that of a great actor and a great-hearted woman of irreproachable character. She was buried in Mount Auburn, near Boston. She was a woman of intense emotional nature, an affectionate woman in private life, kind to a fault to the younger members of her profession, and generous in all ways to worthy causes. She had a voice of remarkable strength and flexibility, and her power over her audiences was sometimes appalling. Her famous female rôles included Lady Macbeth, Meg Merrilies, Nancy Sikes, Queen Katherine, Widow Melnotte, and many others, and she also played Romeo, Claude Melnotte, Hamlet, Cardinal Wolsey and other male rôles.

CUSTER, Mrs. Elizabeth Bacon, author, was born in Monroe, Mich. She was married 9th February, 1864, to Major George A. Custer, afterwards known as Major-General Custer. She accompanied her husband to the seat of war in 1864 and 1865, and after the close of the Civil War she accompanied him during his service in the West, going with him through all the perils of Indian warfare and all the discomforts of soldier life on the frontier. After her husband's death at the hands of the Indians, Mrs. Custer went to New York City, where she now makes her home. She has published two volumes on her life with her lamented husband in the West. The first of these was "Boots and Saddles, or Life in Dakota with Gen. Custer" (New York, 1885), and the second, "Tenting on the Plains, or Gen. Custer in Kansas and Texas" (New York, 1887). Both were successful volumes, and "Boots and Saddles" has gone well up towards its fiftieth thousand. Her style is racy, agreeable and different from that of any other author now before the public. She has written one novel. Besides her literary work, she has won a reputation as a lecturer on frontier life, in which rôle she has appeared in New York City and in the larger cities of the Eastern, Middle and Western States. Her lectures have been given principally before schools, and they have become very popular, so that her time is fully occupied.

DABBS, Mrs. Ellen Lawson, physician, born in her father's country home, five miles east from Mt. Enterprise, in Rusk county, Texas, 25th April, 1853. She was reared in the country. Her father, Col. Henry M. Lawson, was a typical southern planter and a Georgian by birth, who settled in Texas in 1844 with his young wife and her first child. The mother came of a wealthy Georgia family, and, reared as she had been in luxury, with her husband she braved the dangers and privations of a pioneer's life. Colonel Lawson took a prominent part in early Texas politics. He represented his county for several years in the legislature. Ellen was the only girl in a family of eight children, of whom she was the fourth She attended the country schools until she was fourteen years old, and then her father sent her to Gilmer, Tex. She attended school there for two years, and in that time made rapid progress in mathematics and the languages. She taught school as an assistant for six months, then went to Georgia, entered college and was graduated as valedictorian of her class from Furlow Masonic College, in Americus. After graduating, she returned to Texas and taught school and music for five years. In Galveston, Tex., she met J. W. Dabbs, a merchant of Sulphur Springs, Tex. In a year they were married. He was a widower with four children, all boys, and was struggling to get a foothold as a merchant. Mrs. Dabbs looked after his boys, did most of the housework, clerked in the store, bore five children in nine years, helped her husband to make a fortune, and, as his first wife's children came of age, she saw him deed over to them the property that she had made by work and economy. Feeling the need of some profession, she commenced the study of medicine. She read under the direction of Dr. E. P. Becton. She went north to Iowa and entered the College of Physicians and Surgeons in Keokuk, where she was graduated after two years of study. She then took a course in a school of midwifery in St. Louis, Mo. She returned to Sulphur Springs, her old home, in 1890, and practiced there eighteen months.

ELLEN LAWSON DABBS.

She owned an interest in a newspaper and did some editorial work. In 1891 she sold her interest in the paper and settled in Fort Worth, Tex., with her four surviving children. There she has done some writing for the reform press. She was sent as a delegate to the Industrial Union held in St. Louis, in February, 1892. She was put on the committee on platforms and resolutions, and was appointed by the Industrial Convention as one of the committee of thirty to confer with the executive committee of the People's Party. She was disappointed because the People's Party failed to recognize woman in their platform. Knowing injustice under existing laws, she is a firm believer in equality before the law, and constantly pleads for the right of suffrage. She is an advocate of temperance and was sent as a delegate to the State Woman's Christian Temperance convention held in Dallas in May, 1892. She is the State chairman of the Woman's Southern Council.

DAHLGREN, Mrs. Madeleine Vinton, author, born in Gallipolis, Ohio, about 1835. She is the only daughter of Samuel F. Vinton, who served for a quarter of a century with much dis-

MADELEINE VINTON DAHLGREN.

tinction as a Whig leader in Congress. Her maternal ancestors were French. At an early age she became the wife of Daniel Convers Goddard, who left her a widow with two children. On 2nd August, 1865, she became the wife of Admiral Dahlgren, and has three children of that marriage. Admiral Dahlgren died in 1870. As early as 1859 Mrs. Dahlgren contributed to the press, prose articles under the signature "Corinne," and, later, some fugitive poems. She also wrote under the pen-name "Cornelia." In 1859 her little volume, "Idealities" (Philadelphia), appeared, and this was her first work in book form. Since then she has found time to write upon a great variety of subjects. She has made several translations from the French, Spanish and Italian languages, notably Montalembert's brochure, "Pius IX.," the abstruse philosophical work of Donoso Cortes from the Spanish, and the monograph of the Marquis de Chambrun on "The Executive Power" (Lancaster, Pa., 1874). These translations brought her many complimentary recognitions, among others a flattering letter from the illustrious Montalembert, an autograph letter from Pope Pius IX., the thanks of the Queen of Spain, and a complimentary notice from President Garfield. She is the author of a voluminous "Biography of Admiral Dahlgren," and a number of novels including "South-Mountain Magic" (Boston, 1882), "A Washington Winter" (Boston, 1883), "The Lost Name" (Boston, 1886), "Lights and Shadows of a Life" (Boston 1887), "Divorced" (New York, 1887), "South Sea Sketches" (Boston), and a volume on "Etiquette of Social Life in Washington" (Philadelphia, 1881), "Thoughts on Female Suffrage (Washington, 1871), and also of a great number of essays,

articles, reviews and short stories written for papers and periodicals. Social questions and the live topics of the day have especially occupied her attention. Occasionally Mrs. Dahlgren has expressed herself in verse, and several of her efforts have found a place in anthologies of poets. Mrs. Dahlgren's estate is on South Mountain, Md., overlooking the battle-field. She is a woman of fine talents and a thorough scholar. Her writings show considerable versatility, and in the social circles of Washington, where her winters are spent, she is a literary authority. In 1870 and 1873 she actively opposed the movement for female suffrage, and drew up a petition to Congress, which was extensively signed, asking that the right to vote should not be extended to women. The Literary Society of Washington, of which she was one of the founders, held its meetings in her house for six years, and she was elected its vice-president. She was for some time president of the Ladies' Catholic Missionary Society of Washington, and has built the chapel of St. Joseph's of the Sacred Heart of Jesus, on South Mountain, Md.

DAILEY, Miss Charlotte Field, World's Columbian Exposition official, born in Providence, R. I., 19th December, 1842. She was graduated from Mme. C. Mears' boarding school in New York City. The name Dailey dates back four generations in Rhode Island, and is found as early as 1680 in Easton, Mass. Miss Dailey spent her first winter out of school with friends on the Island of Cuba, where her knowledge of the Spanish language added much to her enjoyment. In 1867 she went abroad with her parents to visit the Paris Exposition. She visited Italy, where her taste for art developed, and, after seeing Spain and the art-

CHARLOTTE FIELD DAILEY.

treasures of that country, she discovered her ability to appreciate and recognize the great masters. Austria, Germany, Russia, Denmark, Sweden and England were visited, and, wherever time permitted, her musical studies were pursued under famous masters, such as Allari, of Rome, and San Giovanni, of Milan. Miss Dailey in her life at home was active in philanthropic work and in associations of artistic, dramatic, musical and literary character. The sudden death of her father, and with it the loss of fortune, made it necessary for her to support herself. Lessons in vocal music and lectures upon art were successfully used as a means to that end. Of late years she has fortunately not found it necessary to overtax her strength. She has spent her winters for the last seven years in Washington, D. C. Her appointment to represent her State on the Board of Lady Managers of the World's Columbian Committee was followed by her appointment as secretary and treasurer of the Board of World's Fair Managers of Rhode Island. Mrs. Potter Palmer further assigned her to the chairmanship of fine arts, in oil-painting, water-colors and other departments.

DALL, Mrs. Caroline Wells, author, born in Boston, Mass., 22nd June, 1822. She was a daughter of the late Mark Healey. She was educated thoroughly in private schools and academies,

CAROLINE WELLS DALL.

and she became a teacher. In 1840 she entered Miss English's school for young ladies, in Georgetown, D. C., as vice-principal. In 1844 she became the wife of Rev. Charles Henry Appleton Dall. She kept up her studies and literary work uninterruptedly. Her earlier literary productions were principally on reform subjects and the opening of new spheres of occupation to women. Her later productions have been purely literary and critical. In 1877 she received the degree of LL. D. from the Alfred University, Alfred, N. Y. Much of her activity has been in the cause of woman's rights. Her books are numerous and important. They include: "Essays and Sketches" (1849); "Historical Pictures Retouched" (1859); "Woman's Right to Labor" (1860); "Life of Dr. Marie

Zakrewska" (1860); "Woman's Rights Under the Law" (1861); "Sunshine" (1864); "The College, the Market and the Court" (1867); "Egypt's Place in History (1868); "Patty Gray's Journey to the Cotton Islands" (3 vols., 1869 and 1870); "Romance of the Association" (1875); "My First Holiday" (1881); "What We Really Know About Shakespeare" (1885), and the "Life of Dr. Anandabai Joshee" (1888), all published in Boston. Mrs. Dall's works have found a wide sale and attracted the attention of critics everywhere. She has been an active member of the Social Science Association and has read many papers before that body. She was in 1854 associated with Paulina Wright Davis in the management of "Una," the woman's rights journal, in Boston. Her lectures were scholarly and profound. Her husband was a Unitarian clergyman and died 18th July, 1886, in Calcutta, British India, where he had been for many years a missionary.

DANA, Miss Olive Eliza, littérateur, born in Augusta, Me., 24th December, 1859. Her parents are James W. and Sarah Savage Dana. She is a direct descendant of Richard Dana, who came from England and settled in Cambridge, Mass., about the year 1640. From one of his sons descended Miss Dana's father; from another, Richard H. Dana, the poet. She is also a direct descendant of the Rev. John Campbell, a graduate of the University of Edinburgh, who came to New England in 1717 and was for forty years pastor in Oxford, Mass. Miss Dana was graduated from the Augusta high school in 1877, and has always lived in that city. Her first published article was a prose sketch, which was printed in 1877, and ever since its appearance she has been a prolific writer, sending out many poems, essays, stories and sketches. She has often been compelled by ill health to suspend literary work. Her poems have found a place in the "Magazine of Poetry" and other publications, and are always widely copied. Her prose work covers a wide range. Her short stories have appeared in the "Woman's Journal," "Union Signal," the "Morning Star," the "Christian Union," "Journal of Education," "New England Farmer," Portland "Transcript," "Golden Rule," the "Well Spring," "Zion's Advocate" and many other papers.

DANIELS, Mrs. Cora Linn, author, born in Lowell, Mass., 17th March, 1852. She is descended from the Morrisons, hereditary judges in the Hebrides Islands since 1613, on her father's side. The family motto being translated, reads: "Long-headedness is better than riches." She is descended from the Ponds, on her mother's side, upon whom a coat-of-arms with the motto, "Fide et Amore," was conferred by Henry VIII, in 1509. Her grandfather, General Lucas Pond, was for many years a member of the Massachusetts Senate. Her great-uncle, Enoch Pond, D.D., was president of the Theological College in Bangor, Me. She was educated in the grammar school of Malden, Mass. A private tutor took charge of her for two years. She was sent to Delacove Institute, near Philadelphia, and finished her studies in Dean Academy, Franklin Mass. At nineteen she became the wife of Joseph H. Daniels, of Franklin, a member of one of the historic families of the neighborhood. She has had no children. Her travels in her own country have been extensive. She has spent twenty winters in New York City, varied by trips to Washington, Bermuda and the West. Her literary life began with a poem published in the "Independent" in 1874. When William H. H. Murray conceived the idea of publishing the "Golden Rule," in Boston, he invited her to contribute a series of articles descriptive of prominent race-horses. That she did under the pen-name "Australia." The articles were attributed to Mr. Murray himself and were so successful that they immedi-

CORA LINN DANIELS.

ately led to an engagement, and she became literary editor, remaining on the staff three years. She contributed much poetry to the paper under the pen-name "Lucrece," but afterwards signed her own name, both to prose and poetry. Her poems were widely copied and sometimes translated into other languages, returning to this country by being retranslated for "Littell's Living Age." Becoming New York correspondent for the Hartford "Daily Times," her letters appeared regularly therein for ten years, touching upon every possible subject, but more particularly devoted to dramatic criticism, art and reviews of notable books. Among the reviews was a notice of Elihu Vedders' "Omar-Khayyám," which was reproduced in a pamphlet, which, being sent to Rome, was pronounced by Mr. Vedder the most comprehensive and excellent review that had been produced. Constantly contributing to a number of publications, her first novel, "Sardia" (Boston, 1891), was successful, and in future she will devote considerable time to fiction. The best work of her life, which she values beyond any possible novel, is a work treating of what might be designated "The Science of the Hereafter," or "The Philosophy of After Death," soon to be published. Despite travel and the life of cities, her existence has been one of mental solitude. She has never found companionship of thought and labor. She has collected a library of a thousand volumes during twenty years, but they have been packed in boxes for seventeen out of the twenty. What she has done has been done alone, without books at hand, and usual incentives to new thought gained through literary intercourse.

DANNELLY, Mrs. Elizabeth Otis, poet, born in Monticello, Ga., 13th June, 1838. Her father, Jackson Marshall, is a native of Augusta, Ga. On her mother's side she is descended from an old Huguenot family named Grinnell. Her grandfather, Peter Grinnell, was closely connected with Henry Grinnell, of Arctic Expedition fame, and was also a first cousin to Oliver Hazard Perry. Her grandmother was a daughter of Anthony Dyer, uncle of Elisha Dyer, Governor of Rhode Island. While quite young, her father moved to Oxford, Ga., the seat of Emory College, where her early education was begun. At the age of twelve years she was sent to school in Charleston, S. C., and from that city she entered the Madison Female College, Madison, Ga., from which institution she was graduated 26th July, 1855. Immediately after receiving her diploma, Miss Otis went to New York City, where one year was spent in studying painting. Her father in the meantime had moved from Savannah to Madison, where she became the wife, 4th September, 1862, of Dr. F. Olin Dannelly, the son of Rev. James Dannelly, of South Carolina, the celebrated preacher-wit of that time. Dr. Dannelly was at the time of his marriage a surgeon in the Confederate army, stationed in Richmond, Va. Shortly after, he was ordered to Columbia, S. C., where they continued to reside until the close of the war. About that time Mrs. Dannelly wrote her famous poem, "The Burning of Columbia," which was especially prized in the South and added to the popularity of her volume of poems, "Cactus, or Thorns and Blossoms" (New York, 1879). Soon after the close of the war Dr. Dannelly removed to Baltimore, Md., where he resumed the practice of medicine, in which profession he had attained distinction. During the years of her residence in Baltimore Mrs. Dannelly

ELIZABETH OTIS DANNELLY.

occupied a leading social position. She was a frequent contributor to many of the leading periodicals and magazines of that day. After living five years in that city, the family removed to Texas, where they settled in Waxahachie. After a few years in Texas, they returned to Baltimore, where Dr. Dannelly died. Mrs. Dannelly has had a life of varying fortune, from affluence to a moderate competence. In 1882 she returned to Texas with her six boys, again locating in Waxahachie, where she has since lived, the center of a large circle of friends. Although a busy mother, a painstaking and thrifty housekeeper, and giving much time to religious, charitable and temperance work, she has found time to add many graceful poems to her first volume, and to write a second volume, "Wayside Flowers" (Chicago, 1892). Within the past few years she has resumed her brush as a recreation.

DARE, Mrs. Ella, lecturer and journalist, born in West Batavia, Genesee county, N. Y., 1st

ELLA DARE.

May, 1842. Her maiden name was Ella Jones. Her father was born and reared in Point De Bute, New Brunswick, but came when a young man to the United States, and ever afterward gave to this country his unswerving allegiance. On her mother's side she is a direct descendant from William Cook, a distinguished soldier of the Revolution, who served faithfully upon the staff of both Washington and La Fayette. During the Civil War she was active in the line of sanitary service, and was associated with Mrs. Mary A. Livermore in that work. She has been an ardent advocate of all movements looking toward woman's advancement and has taken earnest part in philanthropic work. In the lecture field she has won success. For years she has been engaged in literary and journalistic pursuits in both prose and poetry. Mrs. Dare was married in 1872. She has no children, and therefore gives her life to her work, in which she is greatly aided by her husband's earnest sympathy. Her home is in Ridgeland, Ill., a suburb of Chicago.

DARLING, Miss Alice O., poet, was born near Hanover, N. H. She is the daughter of one

of the California pioneer gold-hunters of 1849. Her father was a farmer's son, and his youth was spent on a farm in Croydon, N. H., where he was born. His quest for gold in California was successful, and in 1855 he returned to New Hampshire and settled on a farm in the town of Lebanon. There he was married to Mary Ann Seavey. Several generations back his ancestry contained a drop of Indian blood, and to that fact Miss Darling attributes many of her mental and physical characteristics. She has an Indian's love for the fields and forests, a deep and lasting remembrance of a kindness or an injury, and a decided distaste for crowds and great cities. Unlike most New Englanders, she would rather go round than through Boston, whose architectural beauties are to her "only impressive and oppressive." Notwithstanding the regular and arduous toil of farm life, Miss Darling has found time to do considerable literary work of no mean order. She published her first poems when she was seventeen years old. When she was twenty-two years old, she wrote for the Newport, N. H., "Argus and Spectator," and later for the Boston "Traveller," the Boston "Record," the Boston "Globe," the

ALICE O. DARLING.

Boston "Transcript," the Buffalo "Express," the Hanover "Gazette," and "Good Housekeeping."

DARLING, Mrs. Flora Adams, novelist, born in Lancaster, N. H., in 1840. She is a member of the well-known Adams family, and inherits many traits of her ancestors. At an early age she became the wife of Col. Edward Irving Darling, a southerner, and they made their home in Louisiana. When the Civil War broke out, Colonel Darling went into the Confederate army. He was killed during the war, and Mrs. Darling was left a widow with one son, Edward Irving Darling, the musical composer. Mrs. Darling began to write industriously, and her works have brought her both fame and other rewards. She is the author of a number of books, the chief of which is "Mrs. Darling's Letters, or Memories of the Civil War" (1884). That book was written at the suggestion of Judge E. P. Norton, of New York City, who was her counsel in the "celebrated case" known as the Darling

FLORA ADAMS DARLING.

Claim, long pending in Congress and finally reaching the Court of Claims. That claim is founded on the fact that, while in custody of the New Orleans officials, her trunks were robbed of a casket of jewels and $25,000 worth of gold-bearing cotton bonds, that she never recovered, the authorities protesting that they were powerless to act upon the case. Mrs. Darling, after her return north, called on President Lincoln and stated her case, which he recognized as a just one, and manifested his intention to see it righted. His untimely death prevented, and for the past twenty years it has been in litigation, supported by eminent counsel, who have no doubt that she will ultimately succeed in recovering not only principal and interest, but compensation for the hardships to which she was subjected. Losing her means through unfortunate investments, she was for a long time seriously ill, and her illness resulted in deafness and impaired vision. After recovering, she resumed her literary work, contributing to magazines and periodicals Her books are "Mrs. Darling's Letters," "A Wayward Winning Woman" (1890), "The Bourbon Lily" (1890), "Was it a Just Verdict?" (1890), "A Social Diplomat" (1891), "From Two Points of View" (1892), and "The Senator's Daughter" (1892). Her short stories are numerous. During the Civil War she was an intimate friend of Jefferson Davis and his family, and the acquaintance deepened into lifelong friendship. She assisted Mrs. Davis in collecting materials for the "Life of Jefferson Davis." For that purpose Mrs. Darling made a thorough examination of the official records of the War Department in Washington, D. C. One of her most notable achievements is the organization of the society called

"The Daughters of the Revolution," which she served as historian. The aims and purposes of the society are purely patriotic, and it intends to perpetuate the memories of the men and women who achieved or helped to achieve American Independence in the Revolution of 1776, by the acquisition or protection of historic spots and their indication by means of permanent tablets or monuments; to encourage historical research in relation to the American Revolution, and to publish the results; to cherish, maintain and extend the institutions of American freedom, to foster true patriotism and love of country, and to aid in securing for mankind all the blessings of liberty; and to aid in the work of inducing the United States Government to gather, compile and publish the authentic records of every officer, soldier, sailor, statesman or civilian who contributed to the cause of American Independence in the War of 1776. Recently she has edited the "Adams Magazine," published by her nephew, Francis A. Adams, which is the organ of the society. Mrs. Darling has received the college degrees of A. M. and A. B. in recognition of her literary work.

DAUVRAY, Helen, actor, born in San Francisco, Cal., 14th February, 1859. Her family name is Gibson. Her childhood was spent in Virginia City, Nev., and she made her first appearance on the stage in San Francisco, in 1864, playing Eva in "Uncle Tom's Cabin." She attracted a good deal of attention and became known as "Little Nell, the California Diamond." Junius Brutus Booth, Frank Mayo and Charles Thorne were members of the Uncle Tom Company in which she made her début at the age of five. In 1865 she played the part of the Duke of York in "Richard

HELEN DAUVRAY.

III." Her next rôle was as the child in the "Scarlet Letter," with Matilda Heron as Hester Prynne. Helen afterwards played in "Fidelia," "No Name" and "Katy Did," and she was a remarkably bright and successful actor. She appeared in New York City in June, 1870, playing in Wood's Museum in "Andy Blake" and "Popsy Wopsey." Returning to California, she sailed to Australia, where she played successfully. A successful investment in the Comstock mine made her wealthy, and she disappeared for a time from the stage. She went to Europe to complete her education. She studied vocal and instrumental music in Milan and French in Paris. She decided to play in French, before a French audience, in Paris, but had great difficulty to find a manager brave enough to back her. Finally, M. Gautier, of the Folies Dramatiques, introduced her to Paul Ferrier, the dramatist, who wrote "Nan, the Good-for-Nothing" for her. She appeared in that play 1st September, 1884, and scored a success. She broke down from overwork and returned to the United States. She made her re-entrance upon the American stage 27th April, 1885, in the title rôle of "Mona," in the Star Theater, New York City. Her next play was "One of Our Girls," in which she made a triumphant hit as Kate Stupley, an American girl in Paris. That play was the work of Bronson Howard. He then wrote for her "Met by Chance," in which she appeared 11th January, 1887, but it was soon withdrawn. On 7th March, 1887, she played in "Walda Lamar," and in April, 1887, in "The Love Chase." On 2nd June, 1890, she appeared in New York City in "The Whirlwind." She was married 12th October, 1887, in Philadelphia, Pa., to John M. Ward.

DAVENPORT, Fanny Lily Gipsy, actor, born in London, England, 10th April, 1850. She is a daughter of the late Edward Loomis Davenport, the well-known actor, who was born in Bos-

FANNY LILY GIPSY DAVENPORT.

ton, Mass., 15th November, 1814, and died in Canton, Pa., 1st September, 1877. Her mother was a daughter of Frederick Vining, manager of the Haymarket Theater, London, England. Miss Vining became the wife of Mr. Davenport 8th January, 1849. Fanny was their first child. Mr. and Mrs. Davenport came to the United States, where both were for years favorite actors. Fanny was educated in the public schools in Boston, Mass., where she made her début as the child in "Metamora." At the age of twelve years she appeared in New York, in Niblo's, in "Faint Heart Never Won Fair Lady," making her début in that city 14th February, 1862. She afterwards played soubrette parts in Boston and Philadelphia, under Mrs. John Drew's management. Augustin Daly found her there, and he called her to New York, where she played Effie in "Saratoga," Lady Gay Spanker, Lady Teazle, Nancy Sykes, Leah, Fanny Ten Eyck and Mabel Renfrew. Encouraged by her evident success, she left Mr. Daly's company and formed a company of her own. She played "Olivia," in Philadelphia, and Miss Anna E. Dickinson's "An American Girl," both without success, when she conceived the idea of abandoning comedy and taking up tragedy. She induced Victorien Sardou, of Paris, to give her the American rights to "Fedora," "La Tosca" and "Cleopatra," and in those rôles she has won both fame and fortune in large degree. Her tours have been very successful, and the woman who was supposed to be merely a charming comedian has shown herself to be possessed of the very highest powers of tragedy. Miss Davenport, as she is known to the world, has been twice married. Her first husband was Edwin H. Price, an actor, to whom she was married 30th July, 1879. She secured a divorce from him in 1888. She was married in 1889 to Melbourne McDowell, the principal actor in her company. Recently Miss Davenport has given American theater-goers great pleasure in the magnificent staging and dressing of her plays. She has advanced to the extreme front rank in the most difficult of all histrionic fields, and comparison with the greatest actors can not fail to show that she is one of the most successful women who have ever lived before the footlights.

DAVIS, Mrs. Ida May, littérateur, born in Lafayette, Ind., 22nd February, 1857. Her maiden name was Ida May De Puy. Her father was of French descent, and from him Mrs. Davis inherits her humor and vivacity. She was thoroughly educated, and her poetic inclinations and talents showed themselves at an early age. She has always been a facile versifier, and her thoughts naturally flow in rhyme. When she was seventeen years old, she began to publish poems, all of which were extensively copied and commended. Her productions have appeared in newspapers and magazines of the Central and Rocky Mountain States. She is a member of the Western Association of Writers, founded in 1886, and she has been conspicuous in the annals of that society, which she now serves as secretary. She is an artist of much talent and paints well. Her poems are mainly lyrical in form. She became the wife of Henry Clay Davis, of southern birth, in 1876. Mrs. Davis resides in Terre Haute, Ind., where she is the center of a circle of literary and artistic persons. She is an ex-teacher and is a member of the board of education of Terre Haute, having been elected in 1891.

DAVIS, Mrs. Jessie Bartlett, prima donna contralto, born near Morris, Grundy county, Ill., in 1860. Her maiden name was Jessie Fremont Bartlett. Her father was a farmer and a country schoolmaster. He possessed a remarkably good bass voice and had a knowledge of music. The family was a large one, and a sister about a year older, named Belle, as well as Jessie, gave early evidence of superior vocal gifts. Their father was very proud of their talents and instructed them as well as he could. Before they were twelve years of age they were noted as vocalists throughout their neighborhood. They appeared frequently in Morris and surrounding villages and cities in concert work, and they soon attracted the attention of traveling managers, one of whom succeeded in securing them for a tour of the western cities to sing in character duets. The older sister was of delicate constitution and died soon after that engagement was made. Jessie Bartlett then went to Chicago in search of fame and fortune, and was engaged by Caroline Richings, with whom she traveled one season. She was ambitious to perfect herself in her profession, and she soon returned to Chicago and devoted herself to the study of music, and at the same time held a good position in a church choir. During the "Pinafore" craze Manager Haverly persuaded her to become a member of his original Chicago Church Choir Company, and she assumed the rôle of Buttercup. That was the beginning of her career as an opera singer. Since that time, through her perseverance and indefatigable efforts, aided by her attractive personality, she has steadily progressed in her art, until she is one of the leading contralto singers of the United States. Her histrionic powers are not in the least inferior to her vocal ability. She is one of the best actors among the singers now on the American stage. She made her début in grand opera in New York City with Adelina Patti and the Mapleson Opera Company. Adelina Patti sang Marguerite and Jessie Bartlett Davis sang Siebel. Other grand operas in which she has won distinction are "The Huguenots," "Martha," "The Merry Wives of Windsor," "Il Trovatore," "Dinorah" and others. In comic opera she has probably a

JESSIE BARTLETT DAVIS.

a Chicago theatrical manager, in 1880. Her home is in Chicago, with a summer residence in Crown Point, Ind. Mr. Davis owns an extensive stock farm at that place. Her home life is very pleasant, and she divides her time into eight months of singing and four months of enjoying life in her city home or on the farm in Indiana. She is the mother of one son, eight years of age. Besides her musical and histrionic talents, Mrs. Davis has decided literary gifts. She is the author of "Only a Chorus Girl" and other attractive stories and a number of poems. She has composed the music for several songs.

DAVIS, Miss Minnie S., author and mental scientist, born in Baltimore, Md., 25th March, 1835. Her parents, Rev. S. A. and Mary Partridge Davis, were natives of Vermont, but moved to Baltimore soon after their marriage. In that city Mr. Davis was one of the earlier Universalist ministers. When about six years of age, Minnie was thrown from a carriage and one of the wheels passed across her back. The shock of that accident was afterwards supposed to be the cause of frequent illness and great delicacy of health. These circumstances kept the child by the mother's side, and the close companionship had a marked influence upon her future life, for the gifted mother became her constant instructor until her death in 1848. When seventeen years of age, Minnie entered the Green Mountain Institute, Woodstock, Vt. When she was eighteen, she had completed a book, "Clinton Forest," which was afterwards well received by the public. Miss Davis spent a year as a teacher. Writing claimed her attention, and soon "Marion Lester," another book, and perhaps her strongest and best was ready for the press, and was published in 1856. Three years later "Clinton Forest" was published, and later "Rosalie." She had been a frequent contributor to the "Trumpet," "Christian Freeman" and local papers, and a regular contributor to the "Ladies' Repository."

IDA MAY DAVIS.

more complete repertoire than any other singer now before the public. For the last four years she has been the leading contralto of the Bostonians. Jessie Bartlett became the wife of William J. Davis,

Of the last, Miss Davis was for five years associ-ate editor with Mrs. Sawyer and Mrs. Soulé. In 1863 she removed with her father's family to Hart-ford, Conn. A few months after going into her new home she fell down stairs, and that was the begin-ning of long years of helplessness, suffering and partial blindness. All known means for her restora-tion had been tried, but with only partial and tempo-rary success. In 1885, when the wave of "Mental Healing" swept over the land and was accepted by those who were ready for the spiritual truth, Miss Davis was one of the first who recognized the reality of the philosophy. A friend visited her and offered to treat her according to the new method of healing. In four months the days of pain and the darkened room were but memories of the past. She then obtained the best teachers and studied with them the philosophy of healing, and went out in her turn to pass on the work, in which she has had unusual success. Teaching is evidently her forte, her lectures being clear, strong and logical. Miss Davis is interested in all the advanced move-

MINTA S. A. DAVIS.

woman. Her means were limited, but her brothers wished her to enter a profession, and she chose the study of medicine. At the request of two physicians, who had known the family for thirty years, her mother gave an unwilling consent. In 1887 she disposed of what property she had and put her all into a medical education. A few months later she entered the American Medical College in St. Louis, Mo. Shortly before her graduation came the terrible flood of Johnstown, Pa., and she has-tened there to find her people and friends home-less. That calamity made serious inroads on her slender capital. The two physicians who were to help her were dead, but she finished her lectures and answered a call for physicians from the North-west. She settled in Salem, Ore., in June, 1890. By patience and industry she has established a fine practice, and was elected vice-president of the Oregon State Eclectic Medical Society.

DAVIS, Mrs. Mollie Evelyn Moore, poet and author, was born in Talladega, Ala., in 1852. Her parents emigrating, she grew up on a Texas plantation. With her brother she learned not only to read, but to ride, shoot and swim, and received at home, under the supervision of a wise, book-loving mother and a highly intellectual father, her mental training. Very early she began to write. Her first volume of poems, entitled "Minding the Gap" (Houston, Texas, 1867), was published before she was sixteen, and enlarged and corrected it has passed through five editions. Her later work has attracted critics at home and abroad. "Keren Happuch and I" is a series of sketches contributed to the New Orleans "Picayune." "In War Times at La Rose Blanche" was a collection of delightful stories (Boston, 1888). That mys-tic and beautiful prose poem, "The Song of the Opal," the already classical "Père Dagobèrt," "Throwing the Wanga," "The Center Figger," and "The Elephant's Track," were written for the

MINNIE S. DAVIS.

ments of the day, in temperance, equal rights and everything that tends to the amelioration of the ills of humanity.

DAVIS, Miss Minta S. A., physician and surgeon, born in Johnstown, Pa., 31st October, 1864, of Welsh and English parents. Her father died in her twelfth year, leaving her mother, a younger sister and herself dependent upon the exertions of two brothers. When seventeen years old she began to teach school, but she broke down physically at the end of the first term. Then fol-lowed a weary apprenticeship at anything that promised support, sewing, proof-reading, type-setting by day, and earnest work with her studies and writing at night. Her ill health turned her thoughts to the study of medicine. Her mother, a conservative English woman, looked coldly upon any divergence from the stereotyped work of

Harpers, while many poems and sketches have been published in other periodicals. "Snaky Baked a Hoe-Cake," " Grief" and others, contributed to "Wide Awake" in 1876, were among

MOLLIE EVELYN MOORE DAVIS.

the first, if not the very first, negro dialect stories which appeared in print. Certainly they preceded the furore for southern negro stories. In 1874 Miss Moore became the wife of Major Thomas E. Davis, of an excellent Virginia family, and now editor-in-chief of the New Orleans "Picayune," a gentleman, genial, refined and scholarly, who develops and cherishes what is best in his gifted wife. In 1880 Major and Mrs. Davis made their home in New Orleans, and every year their historic house in Royal street receives all the clever people in town, both French and American residents, while strangers find their way to the cozy drawing-room where General Jackson once discussed his plans of battle. With all her social cares she finds time for much reading and study and much unostentatious hospitality. Her domestic life is as complete as if her fingers were innocent of ink stains and her desk of publishers' proposals. She is an accomplished French scholar and also a lover and student of Spanish literature. She is president of the " Geographics," a select literary circle, and is a vice-president of the "Quarante," a large and fashionable club, also literary. In both those organizations she is recognized as a mental guide, philosopher and friend. She is a successful author and a magnetic woman, who draws about her the best representatives of southern society.

DAVIS, Mrs. Rebecca Harding, author, born in Washington, Pa., 24th June, 1831. She was reared and educated in Wheeling, W. Va., where, in 1862, she became the wife of L. Clark Davis, at that time editorially connected with the Philadelphia "Inquirer," and a contributor to the prominent periodicals of the country. Mrs. Davis wrote from childhood, but her first successful bid

for public notice was in 1861, when her " Life in the Iron Mills " was published in the "Atlantic Monthly." That story was afterwards printed in book form and found a large sale. Her next work, " A Story of To-Day," appeared in the "Atlantic Monthly" and was republished as a book, under the title "Margaret Howth" (New York, 1861). After her marriage she went to Philadelphia, where she lived until 1869, when Mr. Davis became a member of the editorial staff of the New York "Tribune," and they took up their residence in that city. Mrs. Davis also contributed to the "Tribune." She was constantly writing, and short stories, sketches, essays and editorials without number flowed from her pen. Her other books are, "Waiting for the Verdict" (New York, 1867), "Dallas Galbraith" (Philadelphia, 1868), "The Captain's Story," "John Andross" (New York, 1874), "The Faded Leaf of History," and a number of novels, all of singular merit and attractiveness. Several years ago Mrs. Davis returned to Philadelphia, where her home now is. Her latest works include " Kitty's Chord " (Philadelphia, 1876), and "A Law Unto Herself" (Philadelphia, 1878), "Natasqua" (New York, 1886). Her son, Richard Harding Davis, one of the editors of "Harper's Weekly," has inherited her story-telling talent.

DAVIS, Mrs. Sarah Iliff, business woman and philanthropist, born in Oxford, Butler county, Ohio, 19th February, 1820. Her maiden name was Sarah A. Sausman. The family removed to Richmond, Ind., in 1832. At the age of fifteen she united with the Methodist Episcopal Church, and was a teacher in the first Sabbath-school which was organized in the church in her town. She

SARAH ILIFF DAVIS.

taught a private school for a time, and afterwards learned the millinery business. At the age of eighteen she went into business for herself. She became the wife of John K. Iliff, 23rd February,

1841. Mr. Iliff was an excellent man of good family, an old-time Methodist, earnest and devout. Seven children were born to them, five sons and two daughters. Two sons died in infancy. Mrs. Iliff never gave up her business, but carried it steadily forward, assisting in the education of the children and the acquisition of a competency. Mr. Iliff died in 1867, after a long illness. Mrs. Iliff became the wife in 1870 of B. W. Davis, editor of the "Palladium" and postmaster of Richmond. He died in 1884. Mrs. Iliff-Davis has marked executive ability. As early as 1844 she was a charter member and officer of the order of Daughters of Temperance. She was active in the Temple of Honor and the Good Templars. In 1861 the Woman's Aid Society of Union Chapel Methodist Episcopal Church, of which Mrs. Iliff was president from first to last, began sanitary work for the Union Army. It soon became auxiliary to the Indiana State Sanitary Commission. That society continued active work until the close of the war. Then her efforts were directed to giving entertainments to aid in establishing the State Soldiers' Orphans' Home. Later the Freedman's Aid Society claimed her attention. In 1868 she was appointed one of a committee of women by the Young Men's Christian Association of Richmond to organize a Home for Friendless Women. For twenty years she was in active work for the home, and for sixteen years she was president of its board of managers. In 1870 she was one of a committee of two women, appointed by the home management, to go before the county commissioners, asking that the home be legalized for the commitment of women prisoners. That request was granted. The same day these ladies attended the trial of a young woman, who received a sentence of imprisonment for two years, and who was committed to the home instead of the State penitentiary. They left the court-house in Centerville, taking the prisoner a distance of seven miles by railroad. That young woman served her time, working faithfully at domestic duties, and went out from the home to live an upright life. Afterwards the managers of the home petitioned the city council to give them the keeping of all women prisoners. That was granted, and an addition was built to the home for a city and county prison. The action of the Wayne county officials was an initial step towards separate prisons for men and women, and towards establishing the Indiana State Reformatory for Women. Mrs. Iliff-Davis is still actively engaged in business. As a writer her essays and reports show marked ability, and she has written poems and other contributions for the local press.

DAVIS, Miss Varina Anne, born in Richmond, Va., 27th June, 1864. She is more generally known as Winnie Davis, the second daughter of Jefferson Davis, President of the Southern Confederacy. She is endeared to the South as the "Daughter of the Confederacy." Shortly before the evacuation of Richmond, Mr. Davis sent his wife and daughter to Charlotte, N. C., where they remained until he instructed them to go to Chester, S. C. At Abbeville they heard the news of Lee's surrender, and Mrs. Davis and her children went on to Washington, Ga., where Mr. Davis joined them and accompanied them to Macon. After Mr. Davis had been taken to Fortress Monroe, Mrs. Davis took her children to Savannah. After Mr. Davis returned to his family, they visited Canada, Cuba, various parts of the South, and Europe, and then settled in Memphis, Tenn., where Winnie remained till 1877. In that year she went to Carlsruhe, Germany, where she remained until 1882. She next went to Paris, France, where she

attended a boarding-school and was joined by her parents. Miss Davis studied drawing and the drama, and her experience convinced her that it is folly to send American children to Europe to be educated. Leaving Paris with her parents, they returned to New Orleans, La., where in the following spring Miss Davis made her entrance into society at the Mardi Gras Ball. The family were invited to visit Alabama and were received with distinction. They extended their tour to Atlanta, Ga., and there Governor Gordon presented Miss Davis to the people as "The Daughter of the Confederacy." She went to Paris, on the advice of her physicians, and was ill there at the time of her father's death. She has made her home with her mother in Beauvoir, Miss., the family residence since 1879. Miss Davis has recently shown literary talent of a high order and has contributed to a number of periodicals. She is an accomplished musician, a skilled

VARINA ANNE DAVIS.

linguist, a ready writer, and a most attractive type of the southern woman of intelligence, culture and refinement.

DAVIS, Mrs. Varina Howell, widow of Jefferson Davis, was born in Natchez, Miss. She is a descendant of the famous Howell family, whose founder settled in New Jersey. Her grandfather, Gov. Richard Howell, was a Revolutionary officer, and her father, William Burr Howell, won high distinction under McDonough on Lake Champlain. Mrs. Davis's maternal grandfather, James Kempe, was an Irish gentleman, who came to Virginia after the Emmet rebellion. He was a man of large wealth and moved to Natchez, Miss., when her mother was an infant. Col. Kempe organized and drilled the "Natchez troope," a company that fought through the Revolution. Mrs. Davis's uncle, Franklin Howell, was killed on the "President." Mr. Davis's marriage with Miss Howell took place 26th February, 1845. While the public life of the Davis family in many respects was one

long storm, their private life was full of peace and
sunshine. Few men have been happier in their
domestic relations than Mr. Davis. Mrs. Davis has
recently published memoirs of her husband, a work
of great merit. She has the key of President
Davis's career. She has written with the pen of
truth and the ink of fact, for she, by loving ministrations and intellectual companionship, was his
confidante through the memorable years of his life
and greatly contributed to enable him more completely to achieve that career which has made his
name immortal. The war record of Mrs. Davis is
historical and cherished memory to those who
watched her unfaltering devotion in the dark days,
and when, overcome by misfortune, she met the
inevitable like a true daughter of noble sires. The
death of her husband ended a most remarkable chapter of national history and domestic
devotion. Only two of Mr. Davis's children are
now living, one the wife of Addison Hays, of
Colorado, a woman of sterling and womanly characteristics, and the other affectionately known as Miss
Winnie, "Daughter of the Confederacy." Mrs. Davis
was recently elected honorary president general of
the United States Daughters of 1812. She has her
pleasant home in Beauvoir, Miss.

DAVIS, Mrs. Virginia Meriwether, doctor of medicine, born in Memphis, Tenn, 18th
April, 1862. She deserves a place in the muster
roll of America's women as a representative of the
present generation. A daughter of Lide Meriwether, heredity and education made simple to her
the problem which had been complex to the generation before, and she took a personal independence naturally. This was without question due
to the environment to which she was born. Shortly

VIRGINIA MERIWETHER DAVIS.

after becoming a widow, she went to New York to
study medicine in the college of which Dr. Emily
Blackwell was founder and dean. She was graduated
in three years with the honors of her class, and she

has since remained in New York to practice. Her
medical work has been almost exclusively in connection with the New York Infant Asylum, where
she has served as resident physician for four years.
This city institution has the largest lying-in service
conducted by women in the United States, and, to
the credit of women be it said, the lowest mortality
and sick rates of any lying-in wards in the world.

DAWES, Miss Anna Laurens, author, born
in North Adams, Mass., 14th May, 1851. She is the

ANNA LAURENS DAWES.

daughter of Hon. Henry L. Dawes, United States
Senator from Massachusetts. She is of New England ancestry on both sides, her father having been
born in Cummington, Mass., and her mother, Electa
Sanderson, in Ashfield, in the same State. She
was educated in Maplewood Institute, Pittsfield,
Mass., and in Abbott Academy, Andover, Mass.
From her early years she has had the exceptional
advantage of a life in Washington, her father's
term of continuous service in Congress being almost
unprecedented. She has known personally most of
the noted men who have figured conspicuously in
public life. Such a large experience, combined
with a spirit of active inquiry, has caused her to be
interested in a variety of enterprises and subjects of
political and philanthropic character and to use her
pen in their behalf. Her literary life had at the
beginning a decided journalistic character. At
intervals during the years from 1871 to 1882 she was
the Washington correspondent of the "Congregationalist," the Springfield "Republican," the "Christian Union," and had charge of a department of the
"Berkshire Gazette," of Pittsfield, Mass., in 1883.
She has written book reviews for those papers as
well as for the "American Hebrew" and the "Sunday School Times." Since 1874 she has contributed articles to the "Christian Union," the "Congregationalist," the "Independent" and the
"Critic," and numerous articles to "Good Housekeeping," the "Andover Review," "America,"

"Lend a Hand," "Wide Awake," "Home Magazine," "Harper's Magazine," the "Century" and others. An article in "Wide Awake," "The Hammer of the Gentiles," was republished in the series of the Magna Charta stories. One on A United States Prison, had the honor of being twice read in Congress, and afterwards published in the "Congressional Record." An article on George Kennan in the "Century" has been translated into several languages. She has published a small volume, " The Modern Jew" (New York, 1884 and Boston, 1886), " How we are Governed " (Boston, 1885), and a " Biography of Charles Sumner, (New York, 1892). Miss Dawes is a trustee of Smith College, one of the Board of Managers for the World's Fair for the State of Massachusetts, and president of the Wednesday Morning Club, Pittsfield, Mass., since its organization, in 1880. She is a vice-president of the National McAll Association, a manager of " Home Work," a charity organization in Pittsfield, and holds various offices in connection with the American Missionary Association, the work for Indians, and the National Conference of Charities and Correction. She is interested in and connected with several missionary and charitable societies, a member of a Working-Girl's Club, the Prison and Social Science Association and several alumnæ associations and literary societies.

DAYTON, Mrs. Elizabeth, poet and author, born in Chertsey, Surry, England, 25th December, 1848. She is best known by her pen name, "Beth Day." When a child, she moved with her parents to Wisconsin, which has since been her home. Growing up in the intellectual atmosphere of a literary family, and endowed by nature with a peculiarly gifted and imaginative mind, she began

ELIZABETH DAYTON.

early to exercise the poetic faculty. Although Mrs. Dayton's lot has been cast among what would seem to be uncongenial associations, she has the happy faculty of idealizing common things, and some of

her best work has been wrought out of material that some might deem too coarse for a poet's uses. Although burdened with the cares and duties of a farmer's wife, she has found time to send out many stories, sketches and poems, and has written for a number of years for the "Youth's Companion," Chicago "Inter-Ocean," "Godey's Lady's Book," "Demorest's Magazine," the "Weekly Wisconsin," "Home Magazine" and many other prominent periodicals. During the brief but brilliant career of "Our Continent," edited by Judge Tourgée, she was one of its contributors. She writes for juvenile magazines, in addition to her other literary work. Her home was for some years in a pleasant spot on Fox river, near Wrightstown, Wis., but in the autumn of 1891 she removed to South Kaukauna, Wis. Up to that date Mrs. Dayton's literary work had been but the recreation of a busy woman, but now, relieved of the cares and almost endless labor of farm life, she is devoting more time to her pen.

DECCA, Marie, operatic singer, was born in Georgetown, Ohio. She is the only daughter of the

MARIE DECCA.

venerable Judge Sanders Johnston, of Washington, D. C., and a granddaughter of General Thomas Harney, of Mexican war fame. Of Scotch descent, she has the flexible qualities and the firmness of purpose which emphasize the character of that people, and, judging from her keen wit and remarkable gifts as a delineator of character, there is a vein of Irish in her lineage. Much of her early life was spent in Maysville, Mason county, Ky., and she enjoyed out-of-door pleasures with the intensity of healthy, happy girlhood. She was educated in the Sacred Heart Convent, New York, and later studied music in Philadelphia, Pa. During her school years Marie had a preference and great fondness for the stage, and she would have made it her profession, had not her friends strongly opposed her. While studying in Philadelphia, she had the pleasure of seeing and hearing Madame Gerster, and that distinguished artist heard the young student sing in "Daughter of the Regiment." Gerster was delighted and exclaimed: "An Italian voice and an American girl!" That eminent artist advised the American girl to go to Paris and take a thorough course, and, risking all and braving everything, she went and was under the tuition of Madame Marchesi for four years. Out of a class of sixteen, "John," as the pupils called her, was the only one who finished the course. Madame Marchesi often said to her: "You have a well-fed voice, and it is good care, plenty of sleep and beefsteak, Marie, that gives you the advantage of all these extra half-hours." Some of the very strongest traits in the character of this artist are her persistent painstaking as an artist, her fearless devotion to principle, her undaunted bravery and integrity to herself and to her friends. Her devotion to the flag of the Union made her a subject of ridicule sometimes in other countries. It is well known that Madame Marchesi has neither admiration nor fondness for our "Stars and Stripes," and the nearest approach to a rupture between her and Marie Decca was the former's taunting remarks concerning the Red, White and Blue. Mlle. Decca always carries the American flag wherever she goes, and she would fight to shield it from insult. Her voice is a soprano of the most flexible and remarkable range, reaching F natural, with exquisite tone and strength. She made her début in Covent Garden, England, under the management of Col. Mapleson, as the Queen of Night in Mozart's "Magic Flute," and made an instant success. She sang three seasons with Her Majesty's Italian Opera and one season with Carl Rosa's English Opera Company. Her répertoire has a wide range, Italian, French, English, and includes "Lucia," "Sonnambula," "Dinorah," "Lakme," "Hamlet," "Linda," "Rigoletto," "Faust," "Fra Diavolo," "Il Barbiere," "Don Pasquale," "Daughter of the Regiment," "Marriage of Figaro," "Mignon," "Masked Ball," "Magic Flute," "Bohemian Girl," "Nordisa" and many others. Since Mlle. Decca's début in America she has won a place few American singers have ever attained. Her first appearance in Boston was a triumph, and the entire press was unanimous in enthusiastic admiration of her wonderful execution.

DE FERE, Mrs. A. Litsner, musician and voice-trainer, was born in Hungary. She was educated in Germany, and from her earliest youth displayed wonderful aptitude and taste for music and singing. When she was fourteen years old, she appeared in public for the first time, having been chosen to sing a solo part in a festival in Mainz, Germany. The success she achieved on that occasion was such that it was determined that she should pursue a musical career. She presented herself at the customary examination of the National Conservatory of Music, of Paris, and was at once admitted. After four years of study she won two second prizes for singing and opera, and the next year she obtained two first prizes also for singing and opera, which were unanimously awarded to her. A gold medal, yearly awarded to the best singer by the Académie des Beaux-Arts, was also bestowed upon her. Having completed her studies, she was engaged as prima donna in the opera of Paris, Lyon, Marseilles and Bordeaux. She sang in Belgium and Germany, and, having returned to her native country, she was received with enthusiasm at the National Opera of Pesth. Later she sang with great success in the West Indies, and finally went to New York, where she resolved to devote herself to the instruction of singing. She made a study of classical music and constantly sought to improve her method, which seeks the perfection of the vocal instrument and of the quality of the sound. She settled in New York in 1876 and taught vocal music there until 1883, when she removed to Brooklyn and formed her conservatory of music. In New York she taught in the schools of Mrs. Sylvanus Reed, of the Misses Charbonnier, of the Charliers and of Dr. and Mrs. Van Norman. Her home is now in Brooklyn, where she is firmly established. Mrs. De Fere combines the French and Italian methods of singing in her system. Her husband, Eugene De Fere, a graduate of the University of Paris, assists her in the conduct and management of the De Fere Conservatory. Mrs. De Fere has won the palm of "Officier d' Académie" in Paris,

MRS. A. LITSNER DE FERE.

France, a distinction enjoyed by only one other woman in the United States, Madam Minnie Hauk.

DE JARNETTE, Mrs. Evelyn Magruder, author, born in Glenmore, Albemarle county, Va., 4th March, 1842. She is the third child of Benjamin Henry and Maria Minon Magruder. Her father was a prominent Virginia lawyer and legislator, and in 1864 was elected to the Confederate Congress. He was a great lover of good books and had a fine library. In the education of his ten children he took a lively interest and an active part. Her mother was from one of the leading families of Piedmont, Va. Evelyn May Magruder led in early childhood a free and happy country life, until boarding schools claimed her for several terms. Then she became an accomplished young lady of "before the war days in Virginia." She was frequently, during her father's connection with the General Assembly, a visitor to Richmond, where she enjoyed to the full the pleasant social gatherings of that city. In 1864 Miss Magruder became the wife of Captain Elliott H. De Jarnette, whose ancestral home, "Pine Forest," in Spottsylvania county, became her future abode. In the home of her childhood she had become impressed with a recognition of the heavy responsibilities of the ownership of slaves, and she had been the regular instructor of the young negroes on the plantation. Amid the cares attend-

EVELYN MAGRUDER DE JARNETTE.

ant upon the mother of a family of eight children, she began her literary career, in 1870. "Frank Leslie's Magazine," the "Century," the "Atlantic Monthly," "Youths' Companion" and various newspapers have accepted her contributions. In both prose and poetry she has given to future generations a glimpse of her country's old-time life and customs. Among these are her "Old Vote for Young Master" and "Out on A' Scurgeon."

DELAND, Mrs. Margaret, poet and novelist, born in Pittsburgh, Pa., 23rd February, 1857. Her maiden name was Margaret Campbell. She was reared in Pittsburgh, in the family of her uncle, Hon. Benjamin Campbell. When she was seventeen years of age, she went to Pelham Priory, a boarding school in New Rochelle, near New York, City. Afterwards she entered the Cooper Institute and took the course in industrial design. A little later and she taught drawing and design in the Normal College of New York for a short time. In 1880 she became the wife of Lorin F. Deland and with her husband removed to Boston, Mass., which city has since been her home. Mr. Deland is possessed of literary tastes and ability, and his critical interest is of much assistance to her in her work. Mrs. Deland began to write in 1884. Her introduction to the public was a curious incident. While walking one morning with Miss Lucy Derby in Boston, they stepped into a market to make some purchases. While they were waiting, Mrs Deland busied herself in writing several stanzas of rhyme on a piece of brown paper lying on the counter. Miss Derby read the verses with an exclamation of surprise and delight. The poem was the dainty and widely known "Succory." Miss Derby insisted on sending it to the editor of "Harper's Magazine."

The result was that she began to publish. Several of her poems were sent to the same magazine without her knowledge. Others followed in the "Century" and other magazines. These were received with such favor that she collected her poems and had them published under the title of "The Old Garden and Other Verses" (Boston, 1886). Not yet conscious of her power, she issued only a limited edition, which was exhausted within a few days. Since then that volume has gone through six editions. Her next and greatest work was the celebrated novel, "John Ward, Preacher" (Boston, 1888), which passed through six editions in five months. She has since written a descriptive work, "Florida Days" (Boston, 1889), a second novel entitled "Sidney" (Boston, 1890), and short stories for the "Atlantic Monthly" and "Longman's Magazine."

DELETOMBE, Miss Alice S., poet, born in Gallipolis, Ohio, 2nd April, 1854. She is descended from an old French family long identified with the history of her native town. In early childhood Miss Deletombe displayed a talent for music, inherited from her mother, but delicacy of health prevented full development of that rich faculty, and the musical bent was turned into poetical channels, the eager soul finding that outlet of expression a silent solace through many sad years. Her sensitiveness is averse to criticism and publicity, a peculiarity which has ever been at war with her best interests. It is a remarkable fact that but few of her friends knew of her as a poet until recently, and that for over twenty years she has written for the mere pleasure of expressing her poetical thoughts, and not for any ulterior ambition or reputation. The admixture of French and German blood, she

ALICE S. DELETOMBE.

might say, "puts glamour into all I see." She has the French vivacity subdued by German sentiment, subtlety and harmony. The result is music and poetry. Some of her best poems were published for the first time in the "Magazine of Poetry" for January, 1891.

DEVOE, Mrs. Emma Smith, woman suffragist, born in Roseville, Warren county, Ill., 22nd August, 1849. Her parents were strictly orthodox, her father having been a deacon in the Baptist Church for forty years. In early life Miss Smith moved with her parents to the village of Washington, Tazewell county, Ill., where she lived till her marriage. In youth she developed a remarkable talent for music, which her parents employed every means in their power to cultivate. At the age of nineteen years she was made a member of the faculty of Eureka College and placed in full charge of the department of music, which position she filled with honor to herself and credit to the institution. In 1879 Miss Smith became the wife of J. H. DeVoe, of Washington, Ill., and soon after they moved to Huron, Dak., where they lived till 1883, when they removed to Faulk county, Dak., and

EMMA SMITH DEVOE.

founded the village that bears their name. About a year thereafter they returned again to Huron, where Mr. DeVoe engaged in mercantile business. During the summer of 1889, while filling the office of assistant State superintendent of franchise for the Woman's Christian Temperance Union of South Dakota, Mrs. DeVoe first attracted public notice and began to develop as a public speaker. In a convention in St. Lawrence, S. Dak., in June of that year, she read an essay on "Constitutional Prohibition and How to Secure It," which was copied by various newspapers throughout the State and brought her before the reading public. During the following summer her fame spread over the entire State as a most forcible and logical public advocate of the equality of the sexes. A provision in the constitution under which South Dakota was admitted into the Union required a vote of the people to strike out the word male in the clause describing the qualifications of an elector, and in

consequence, at the first State election, a very spirited campaign was waged by the noble-minded women of the State, assisted by the officers of the National American Equal Suffrage Association, for the enfranchisement of their sex. Before the campaign had got fairly under way, Mrs. DeVoe's fitness for the work, coupled with her untiring energy, placed her in the front rank of the advocates of equal suffrage. Her house in Huron was the birthplace of the State organization, and all friends of the cause she cherished found warm welcome there. Her home was the headquarters of the noted workers within the State, and also of the committee having the campaign in charge. She was made State lecturer and a member of the executive board, and was constantly in the field from early spring till the close of the campaign. The State agricultural board placed her in charge of Woman's Day at the State fair, held in Aberdeen in September. That novel and entertaining feature of the fair originated with Mrs. DeVoe, and the success of the enterprise was abundantly manifest in the increased attendance, the gate receipts being more than double that of any other day during the fair. The suffrage songs, composed by her husband, with which she embellished her lectures, had a very pleasing effect. Although the cause of equal suffrage was unsuccessful in South Dakota, the courage of Mrs. DeVoe was in no wise daunted, for immediately after election she commenced planning for future work and was the first publicly to adjure her co-workers to renewed efforts. In the spring of 1891 Mr. and Mrs. DeVoe removed from Huron to Harvey, Ill., where they now reside. In their new home Mrs. DeVoe found many congenial spirits and immediately organized an equal suffrage society, which through her efforts has grown to be the largest local suffrage society in the State. She is president of the local and also of the first Congressional district societies. In 1892 she lectured throughout Iowa in the interest of the Iowa State Equal Suffrage Association.

DEYO, Rev. Amanda, Universalist minister and peace advocate, born in Clinton, N. Y., 24th October, 1838. Her maiden name was Amanda Halstead. She was reared in the Society of Quakers, and for many years she was an active participant in their meetings. At the age of fifteen she became a school-teacher. After teaching for some time she attended the Poughkeepsie, N. Y., Collegiate Institute, from which she was graduated in 1857. In that year she became the wife of Charles B. Deyo, a farmer and a cultivated man of Huguenot descent. He has always aided his wife in her labors for the elevation of humanity. Their family consists of two daughters. Mrs. Deyo was present at one of the early anniversaries of the Universal Peace Union in New York City, where she met Lucretia Mott, Alfred H. Love and others of the friends of peace. There she made her mark as an advocate of the doctrines of that organization, and she has ever since been an earnest supporter of the cause. She has attended all the peace anniversaries throughout the country, has traveled extensively, spoken often and organized numerous peace societies. In 1888 she was called to the pastorate of the Universalist Church in Oxford, N. Y., having previously served as pastor of the Universalist Church in Poughkeepsie, N. Y. She is now the pastor of All Souls Universalist Church in Scranton, Pa. She has always been so closely identified with the organizations devoted to the abolition of war that she is called the "Peacemaker." She was one of the delegates of the Universal Peace Union to the International Peace Congress and the Paris Exposition of 1889, and did some effective work in the peace cause. Her address to the congress was printed and distributed at the Exposition. She was also present and presented a paper in the Woman's Rights Congress in Paris. She represented the

AMANDA DEYO.

union in the Woman's Council held in Washington, D. C., in March, 1888, and signalized the occasion by calling a grand peace meeting in the Church of Our Father, where many prominent women made addresses. In addition to her arduous work in the ministry for the last six years, preaching three times each Sabbath day and attending funerals and weddings, she has been an active worker in the temperance and prohibition cause, and at one time traveled and lectured for that interest and organized its work. That labor she still continues as opportunity will permit; but her great work is her effort to substitute peace for war and harmonize the difficulties constantly arising in families, neighborhoods and churches. By the efforts of herself and her husband, the Dutchess County Peace Society, one of the large and flourishing branches of the Universal Peace Union, was organized in 1875 and kept by them in active life until her ministerial duties made it necessary to turn over the work to others.

DIAZ, Mrs. Abby Morton, industrial reformer, born in Plymouth, Mass., in 1821. She is descended from George Morton, one of the Plymouth Pilgrims. Her father, Ichabod Morton, was a prominent anti-slavery worker. Her early recollections are associated with anti-slavery meetings, and her first public work was as the secretary of a juvenile anti-slavery society, to whose funds each member aimed to contribute twenty-five cents weekly, a large s m in those days of scanty pence and simple living. To raise half her contribution she went without butter and knit garters to earn the other twelve. Educated in the public schools, she kept her influence at work, using for her home-made copy-books sheets of paper with the figure of a kneeling slave upon them. Among the men to

whose utterances Abby Morton listened were Garrison and Horace Mann. She early began to put her thoughts on paper. While aiding in the work of her home, she found time to write prose and verse. She was the only daughter, and her five brothers made plenty of work for her. When the "community" ideas were started, her father seized upon them as promising realization of his hope for the practical recognition of the brotherhood of the race, and joined the celebrated Brook Farm Community, building a house and moving there with his family. A few weeks convinced him of the failure of the scheme, and he returned to Plymouth and resumed his business. Mrs. Diaz' married life was very brief, and she was left with two little sons to care for. When the boys were small, she cut and made their garments, taught a juvenile singing school, private and public schools, and was for one summer housekeeper at a summer resort on an island near Plymouth, where she did all the bread and cake making, because her cook was unsatisfactory. At one time she "put out" work for a large clothing house and in visiting the "lofts" where this was done she received harsh proofs of the poorly paid work of skillful women, who had no other recourse. In 1861 Mrs. Diaz sent a story to the "Atlantic Monthly," under an assumed name, and was delighted with her success when it was accepted and she received a check for forty dollars for it. From that time she took up her life work, to reach and help her fellows through her pen. Her stories for children, originally published in "Young Folks" and other magazines, have a wide fame, and series after series, beginning with "William Henry's Letters to His Grandmother," "Pink and Blue," "The Little Country Girl," "Farmer

ABBY MORTON DIAZ.

Hill's Diary," "The Schoolmaster's Story" and "Some Account of the Early Life of a Bachelor," were full of the subtle yet simple humor that imbues all Mrs. Diaz's writings. When Rev. Edward

Eggleston became editor of "Hearth and Home," he was advised by William Dean Howells to write to Mrs. Diaz, and he did so, the correspondence resulting in the series of papers upon the household life of women which were feigned to have been found in "The Schoolmaster's Trunk." These and others are included in two volumes, "The Bybury Book" and "Domestic Problems." Her letters and articles on household and domestic difficulties caused her to be looked upon as one speaking with authority, and she was invited to lecture upon those questions. She read a paper in the Woman's Congress held in Philadelphia in 1876. The paper was entitled "The Development of Character in Schools," since published in the "Arena." She helped to organize the present Woman's Educational and Industrial Union of Boston. An important work of that association has been the impetus given to the legal protection of helpless women and girls from employers and advertisers who refuse to pay honestly earned wages, or by seductive printed promises wile from their victims money and hours of work, for which they elude payment by trickery. Mrs. Diaz is a profound believer in the "Science of the Higher Life," otherwise known as "Christian Science," and has tested its efficiency in healing and its power for spiritual good, and has written several pamphlets on the subject. Her latest work has been courses of talks on the questions of the day, including the ethics of nationalism, Christian socialism, progressive morality, life, or what is it to live? character work in homes and schools, human nature, competition, and another pamphlet of hers containing a series of papers on arbitration, first published in the "Independent." Mrs. Diaz now makes her home in Belmont, Mass., with her oldest son. She has been unanimously re-elected president of the educational and industrial association every year since its organization.

DICKINSON, Miss Anna Elizabeth, orator, author, playwright, actor, reformer and philanthropist, born 28th October, 1842, in Philadelphia, Pa. Her father, John Dickinson, died in 1844, leaving his family in straitened circumstances. Anna was sent to the Friends' free school, as her parents belonged to that society. Her early life was full of struggles against adverse conditions. She studied earnestly and read enthusiastically. Whenever she earned any money, she spent it for books. When she was only fourteen years old, she wrote an article on slavery for the "Liberator." She made her début as a public speaker in 1857, in a meeting for discussion held by the Progressive Friends, chiefly interested in the anti-slavery movement. One of the men delivered an insolent tirade against women, and Anna took up the cudgel in behalf of her sex and worsted her insulter. From that time she spoke frequently, generally on slavery and temperance. In 1859 and 1860 she taught school in Berks county, Pa., and in 1861, from April to December, she was employed in the United States Mint in Philadelphia. She was dismissed from the Mint because, in a speech in West Chester, she said that the battle of Ball's Bluff "was lost, not through ignorance and incompetence, but through the treason of the commanding general (McClellan)." After dismissal she made a profession of lecturing, adding political subjects to her former ones. William Lloyd Garrison, who heard one of her addresses in Kennett, Pa., named her "The Girl Orator," and invited her to speak in the Fraternity Course in Music Hall, Boston, Mass., in 1862. She spoke on "The National Crisis." She attracted attention and was engaged to speak in New Hampshire, in Connecticut, in New York City

and in Philadelphia. From that time till the end of the Civil War she spoke on war issues. In 1863 she was engaged to deliver a series of addresses, in the gubernatorial campaign, throughout the coal regions, as the male orators were afraid to enter those regions so soon after the draft riots. On 16th January, 1864, she spoke in Washington, D. C., and donated the proceeds, over $1,000, to the Freedmen's Relief Society. She delivered many addresses in camps and hospitals. After the war-echoes ceased, she spoke from the lyceum platform chiefly, her lectures being on "Reconstruction" and "Woman's Work and Wages." In 1869 she visited Utah, and afterward she lectured on "Whited Sepulchres," referring to Mormonism. Her subsequent lectures were "Demagogues and Workingmen," "Joan of Arc," and "Between Us Be Truth," the last-named devoted to Missouri and Pennsylvania, in 1873, where obnoxious social evil bills were up for discussion. In 1876 Miss Dickin-

ANNA ELIZABETH DICKINSON.

son decided to leave the lecture platform and go upon the stage. She made her début in "A Crown of Thorns," a play written by herself, and her reception was unfavorable. She next essayed Shakespearean tragic rôles, including Hamlet and others. She afterwards gave dramatic readings, but the stage and the dramatic platform were not suited to her, and she returned to the lecture platform. She gave a number of brilliant lectures, "Platform and Stage," "For Yourself," and others. In 1880 she wrote a play, "The American Girl," for Fanny Davenport, which was moderately successful. Among Miss Dickinson's published works are "What Answer?" a novel (Boston, 1868), "A Paying Investment" (Boston, 1876), and "A Ragged Register of People, Places and Opinions" (New York, 1879). Among the plays written by her are "Aurelian," written for John McCullough, but never produced, as his failing powers prevented "A Crown of Thorns" and "The Test of Honor." After leaving the stage, in 1883, Miss Dickinson made her home with her family in Pittston, Pa. In 1891 she again came before the public, through family difficulties and through a suit brought against the Republican managers of the Presidential campaign for services rendered by her in 1888. In 1892 she delivered a number of lectures. She has been under treatment for some time for failing health. Miss Dickinson in her younger days was a woman of singular powers of sarcasm, of judgment, of dissection of theories and motives, and of eloquence that can be understood only by those who have heard her on the platform. She has a strong, fine, intelligent face, self-possession, courage that enabled her to stand her ground when fired at by striking miners in Pennsylvania, and all the endowments of presence, voice, wit, pathos and intense dramatic fervor that go to make the great orator. Her work in each line was distinctly marked. In her school work, her novels, her sketches, her lectures, she was unique. Her plays contain passages of undisputed greatness, of poetic beauty and of sublime pathos. She acquired an ample fortune through her lectures, but she has given away the bulk of it in all kinds of charities.

DICKINSON, Miss Susan E., journalist, born near Reading Pa., was reared and educated in Philadelphia. Her mother's family were among the early settlers of Maryland. They were Quakers, who left England in 1660 and 1661 and settled on the eastern shore of the colony of Maryland. Her father's ancestors were of the same religious faith as her mother's, and were among the Maryland pioneers. About 1750 the Dickinsons moved into southern Pennsylvania. Miss Dickinson's father was a wholesale and retail dry-goods merchant

ADELAIDE LYNN DICKLOW.

and in the Westtown boarding-school in Chester county. Susan, at the age of seventeen, became a teacher in the public schools of Philadelphia. She began to write poetry at an early age. Her poems appeared first in the "Saturday Evening Post," the Boston "True Flag," and other journals, under the pen-names "Effie Evergreen," "Violet May" and "Ada Vernon." In 1872 she began to sign her own name to her productions. Her first book was a memoir of a young friend, written for the Presbyterian Board of Publication. Her first regular journalistic work was in the biographical or obituary department of the New York "Herald," to which she was a contributor from November, 1874, until 1881. From 1875 to 1878 she was a regular contributor to the New York "Daily Graphic." From 1875 to 1882 she was a correspondent from northeastern Pennsylvania to the Philadelphia "Press." She also wrote a good deal for the papers of Scranton and Wilkes-Barré, Pa., and for the Boston "Evening Traveller." Other duties seriously interrupted her literary work for years, but she has never wholly given it up. Since June, 1891, she has been a member of the editorial staff of the Scranton "Truth." She contributes occasionally to other journals. Miss Dickinson has been a member of the Protestant Episcopal Church ever since she left school. She writes herself down a journalist, although her inclinations have always been towards purely literary work, and she has accomplished enough to justify the name "author." Domestic cares have hindered her in her work, but the Quaker courage born in her has carried her over obstacles that seemed insurmountable.

DICKLOW, Miss Adelaide Lynn, educator, born of French Catholic parents, in Orwell, Vt., 6th March, 1859. At the age of fourteen she left the Catholic Church, and soon after united with the Baptist Church, of which she is now a member. As a girl she was bright and cheerful,

SUSAN E. DICKINSON.

in Philadelphia. He died and left a family of five young children, who were carefully reared by the mother. They were educated in the select schools of the Society of Friends in Philadelphia, fond of books and quick to learn. Her education was begun in the public schools of Orwell and Fair Haven, Vt., where her parents resided. In 1874 she entered the State Normal School in Albany, N. Y., and from there she went to the Syracuse University, where she was graduated with honors. Miss Dicklow's parents being in humble circumstances, she had to work her own way from begining to end. After graduating she taught for two years and then entered the Woman's Medical College of Philadelphia, with the intention of taking up the practice of medicine. At the end of one year she was called to Kansas, and soon after the position of professor of modern languages in Ottawa University was offered to her, which she accepted. Miss Dicklow did not give up her studies at graduation but continued a close student and will receive the degree of Ph.D. from her alma mater.

DIEHL, Miss Cora Victoria, register of deeds, born in Laurelton, Union county, Pa., 19th January, 1869. When eleven years old she moved with her parents to Great Bend, Kas., where the family lived on a farm for five years. Her father, H. C. Diehl, having no son, shaped his daughter's education with the view of bringing her forward as a reformer. At the age of sixteen years she appeared at many public meetings of the Greenback party and delivered recitations. Her parents moved to Montrose, Col., where they lived a short time and then returned to Kansas. The daughter accompanied them and soon accepted a position in the office of the register of deeds in Great Bend. Later she was appointed deputy register, which position she filled for two years, when she resigned 1st January, 1890, to go to her parents in Oklahoma.

CORA VICTORIA DIEHL.

Miss Diehl joined the Farmers' Alliance and, though but twenty-one years old, became a leader and speaker. She was unanimously nominated by the convention of the People's Party in session in Guthrie for register of deeds for Logan county and was afterward endorsed by the Democrats. She conducted an aggressive campaign and, accompanied by her father, stumped the county. Her speeches showed ability and earnestness, and she got the largest majority of any one on the ticket. She has the distinction of being the first woman to hold office in Oklahoma, and also is the youngest woman in the country to conduct a political campaign in her own behalf.

DIEUDONNÉ, Mrs. Florence Carpenter, littérateur, born in Stockbridge Falls, Madison

FLORENCE CARPENTER DIEUDONNÉ.

county, N. Y., 25th September, 1850. In early life her parents removed to Oshkosh, Wis., where her education was completed. In her writing as a school-girl was discerned exceptional excellence. After her marriage she resided for some years in Minnesota, and during that period published her first poems in the Oshkosh "Times" and "Peterson's Magazine." In 1878 she traveled extensively in Europe, and her descriptive letters, written for the papers of her own and other States, gained for her a reputation. "A Prehistoric Romanza" (Minneapolis, 1882), was the first poem she published in book form. She also wrote several cantatas, the most successful of which was "The Captive Butterfly," for which Prof. J. B. Carpenter composed the music. Her fondness for literary pursuits made her many social engagements burdensome, and her fondness for scientific and historical reading clashed with the attention which she felt it her first duty to give to her home, but by improving spare minutes during the last ten years she has written three prose works and many poems. Her descriptive style is vivid. She is a member of the Woman's National Press Association of Washington, D. C., vice-president of the Short Story Club and founder and president of the Parzelia Circle, a conversational and literary order. Mrs. Dieudonné now resides in Washington, D. C.

DIGGS, Mrs. Annie Le Porte, politician and journalist, born in London, Ontario, Can., 22nd Febuary, 1853. She became the wife of A. S. Diggs, of Lawrence, Kans., in 1873 Their family consists of two daughters and one son. Mrs. Diggs traces her ancestry in a direct line to General John Stark, of Revolutionary fame. She has certainly inherited his fighting qualities. After her marriage she began her career in public as a journalist. She entered the field to fight for political and personal independence and equality. She lectured before literary, reformatory and religious assemblages very successfully. In religion she is a radical Unitarian. When the Alliance movement among the western farmers began, she entered the field and soon found herself at the front among those who were engineering that great industrial movement. During the political campaigns in Kansas and neighboring States she made many speeches. She was chosen by the People's Party to reply to the platform utterances of John J. Ingalls, to whose overthrow she contributed largely. She was elected national secretary of the National Citizens' Industrial Alliance, at the annual meeting of that organization in St. Louis, Mo., 22nd Febuary, 1892. Mrs. Diggs is a clear, forcible writer, a strong, attractive orator, and a thinker and reasoner of unusual power. She has done considerable lecturing and preaching. In 1881 she addressed the annual convention of the Free Religious Association, in Boston, Mass., on "Liberalism in the West." She has for years been a member of the Woman's Christian Temperance Union. Much of her journalistic work was done on the "Advocate," the organ of the Alliance, on which journal she served as the leading editorial writer. She has spent much time in Washington,

MARY A. G. DIGHT.

DIGHT, Mrs. Mary A. G., physician, born in Portsmouth, Ohio, 7th November, 1860. She is the only daughter of Mary Y. Glidden and George Crawford. Her mother, who died 22nd April, 1891, was a woman of intelligence and refinement, inheriting from one of the cultured New England families the rare mental qualities which she transmitted to her daughter. Mrs. Crawford believed in the higher education of women and encouraged her daughter to pursue the profession of her choice, for which, by her natural abilities and her acquirements, she is qualified, and in which she is now actively engaged. Dr. Dight is a young woman of versatile talents. She is a fine musician, and a graduate of the New England Conservatory of Music, Boston. She speaks German fluently. She is a model housekeeper as well as mistress of the art of healing. She was graduated from the department of regular medicine and surgery of the University of Michigan, one of the youngest of the class of 1884. Returning to Ohio, she practiced a year and then went abroad and continued her studies in Paris and Vienna for two years. She returned to Portsmouth and was chosen president of the Hempstead Academy of Medicine. While a student in medicine, she made the acquaintance of Professor Charles F. Dight, M. D., at that time one of the medical faculty of the University of Michigan, who after a six year's professorship in the American Medical College in Beyrout, Syria, returned to America to marry her. As a lecturer Dr. Dight is pleasing and forcible. She is energetic in urging to efforts for social reforms and for the improvement of the race, by observing the laws of life, health and heredity. Her home is now in Faribault, Minn.

DILLAYE, Miss Blanche, artist, was born in Syracuse, N. Y. She is the daughter of the late Stephen Dillaye, of Syracuse, whose writings on paper money and the tariff won him an enviable reputation. From early childhood Miss Dillaye

ANNIE LE PORTE DIGGS.

D. C., since the upheaval caused by the Alliance, and has done notable work in correspondence for the western newspapers. She is president of the Woman's Alliance of the District of Columbia.

showed unusual talent from drawing and a genuine artistic appreciation of pictures. So marked was her ability and so strong her desire to be an artist, that she was allowed to devote a year to the study of

BLANCHE DILLAYE.

drawing. About that time an opportunity to teach drawing in a young ladies' school in Philadelphia was opened to her, and she was thus enabled to pursue her art studies for several years in the Philadelphia Academy of Fine Arts. Her preference for black and white was the source of much concern to her in her early art days. She took one lesson of Stephen Ferrier in the technique of etching. It seemed so simple that she unhesitatingly sent in her name as a contributor to an exhibition to be held in the Academy of Fine Arts, and went so far as to order her frame. She knew little of the vicissitudes of the etcher, but she was on the way to learn, for, when the exhibition opened, her labor was represented only by an underbitten plate, an empty frame, the name in the catalogue of a never-finished etching, and the knowledge that etching represents patient labor as well as inspiration. The same year Stephen Parrish came to her rescue, and by his counsel and assistance enabled her to work with insight and certainty. She has contributed to all of the leading exhibitions of this country. Her etchings have also been favorably received abroad. In the rage for etchings that has prevailed during the past few years Miss Dillaye has never condescended to degrade the art to popular uses, but has maintained that true painter-etcher's style which first brought her into notice. Her impressions are vivid and marked by a strong originality. Her ambition is not satisfied to travel in the single track of an etcher. Her studio on South Penn Square, Philadelphia, shows talent in various other directions. Her illustrations and manuscripts have found their way into several leading magazines.

DIX, Miss Dorothea L., philanthropist and army nurse, born in Hampden, Me., in 1802, and died in Trenton, N. J., 7th July, 1887. Her father, a Boston merchant, died in 1821, and Dorothea started a school for girls in that city. She became interested in the convicts in State prisons, visited them and worked to secure better treatment for them. Her school work and her philanthropic labors broke down her health in 1833, when she was prostrated by hemorrhages from the lungs. Having inherited a small fortune, she went to Europe for her health. The voyage benefited her, and in 1837 she returned to Boston and renewed her labors for the paupers, lunatics and prisoners, in which she was assisted by Rev. Dr. Channing. The condition of affairs in the East Cambridge almshouse aroused her indignation, and she set about to secure an improvement in the methods of caring for the insane paupers. She visited every State east of the Rocky Mountains, working with the legislatures to provide for the relief of the wretched inmates of the jails, prisons, almshouses and asylums. In Indiana, Illinois, North Carolina, New York and Pennsylvania she was especially successful in securing legislative action to establish State lunatic asylums. In January, 1843, she addressed to the Legislature of Massachusetts a memorial in behalf of the "insane persons confined within this Commonwealth, in cages, closets, cellars, stalls, pens; chained, naked, beaten with rods, and lashed into obedience!" The result was a great improvement. In twenty States she visited asylums, pointed out abuses and suggested reforms. She succeeded in founding thirty-two asylums in the United States, in Canada, Nova Scotia, Guernsey and Rome. She secured the changing of the lunacy laws of Scotland. She went to Europe, and there she visited Paris, Florence, Rome, Athens,

DOROTHEA L. DIX.

Constantinople, Vienna, Moscow and St. Petersburg in search of her wards. Sensitive and refined, she encountered all kinds of men, penetrated into the most loathsome places and faced cruel sights, that she might render effectual service to men and women in whom the loss of reason had not extinguished the human nature, in which her religious soul always saw the work of God. The years between her return from Europe and the outbreak of the Civil War Miss Dix spent in confirming the strength of the asylums that had sprung from her labors. On 19th April, 1861, she went to do duty as a nurse in the Union army. During the war she was chief of the woman nurses, and to her is due the soldiers' monument at Fortress Monroe. She established a life-saving station on Sable Island, and, after the war, took up again her asylums, seeking their enlargement, improvement and maintenance. At eighty years of age a retreat was offered her in the Trenton asylum, which she was wont to call her "first-born" child. There, after five years of suffering, she died. Besides being the author of countless memorials to legislatures on the subject of lunatic asylums, Miss Dix wrote and published anonymously "The Garland of Flora" (Boston, 1829), "Conversations About Common Things," "Alice and Ruth," "Evening Hours" and other books for children, "Prisons and Prison Discipline" (Boston, 1845), and a great number of tracts for prisoners.

DIXON, Mrs. Mary J. Scarlett, physician, born in Robeson township, Berks county, Pa., 23rd October, 1822. Her parents were members of the Society of Friends, and Mary was the youngest of

MARY J. SCARLETT DIXON.

seven children. Her father was a farmer. He died when she was about four years old, and a brother's death soon after left the mother with six children, on a farm not very productive, and with plenty of hard work, in which all the children did their full share. When the agitation against slavery loomed up in 1830, the family was the only one in the neighborhood that took an active part, and their house became the resort for anti-slavery lectures. When Mary was sixteen years old, her mother died. As soon as the estate was settled, she began to teach in country schools. After teaching a few years, she went to boarding-school for a year, and again taught for a time, and went again to boarding-school one term. Her thoughts were led towards medicine in early childhood. With the aim of becoming a physician, her teaching was to provide means. When in 1850 the Female Medical College of Pennsylvania, later changed to the Woman's Medical College of Pennsylvania, opened its doors to students, she received information from one of its professors that she was wanted. Duties to her oldest sister prevented her from entering until the autumn of 1855. She was graduated in 1857. Feeling that the time for study was too short, she took another course of lectures, better to fit her for general practice. During that course of lectures she took special pains to obtain practice among the poor, in order to build up the clinic at the college, not only for her own benefit, but for the general good of the college. During a part of 1858–59 she gave lectures on hygiene in country towns and villages. In the autumn of 1859 she was appointed demonstrator of anatomy in the Woman's Medical College and returned to Philadelphia to take the position. The hospitals in the city were not open to women physicians for instruction, and the college management felt it necessary to make some change for the better clinical instruction of the students. Larger buildings were purchased for a woman's hospital, in which rooms could be utilized temporarily for college purposes. In the hospital Emeline H. Cleveland, M.D., was appointed resident physician and Dr. Scarlett assistant physician. There they built up a good clinic and out-door practice, which, in addition to the hospital, afforded the students good opportunities for practical instruction. In 1862 she received the appointment of professor of anatomy in the college. After a few years, feeling she had undertaken too much, she resigned the position of demonstrator of anatomy. In 1865 she resigned the position of assistant physician in the hospital, to make a home for herself. In 1868 she returned to the hospital as resident physician, remaining there until 1871, when she returned to her home, at the same time being appointed visiting physician to the hospital. On 8th May, 1873, she became the wife of G. Washington Dixon, still retaining her professorship and engaged in active practice, along with her duties as professor of anatomy. In 1881 her connection with the college was discontinued. As glaucoma was troubling her, she placed herself under the care of a skilled ophthalmologist for the treatment of her eyes. She continued actively engaged until through diminished vision she was forced to hand over many patients to others. She still continues to treat some cases. She resides in Philadelphia.

DODD, Mrs. Anna Bowman, author, was born in Brooklyn, N. Y. She is a daughter of Stephen M. Blake. At the age of twelve years she began to write stories, and her subsequent education was supplemented by travel and study in Europe. One of her first efforts for the public was a translation of one of Théophile Gautier's works, which was published in the New York "Evening Post." She was engaged to contribute editorials and other articles to that journal. She wrote many short stories, essays and a series of articles on church music for "Harper's Magazine." She wrote a paper on the School of Philosophy in Concord. French and English journals copied it, and the author found her services and talents in growing demand. She was engaged by the Harpers to furnish an exhaustive article on the political leaders of France, to prepare which she went to

Europe, in order to be able to study her subject on the ground. She was cordially received by scholars, who had read her articles on the Concord School. Before returning, she went to Rome and prepared a description of the carnival for "Harper's Magazine." Her first book was "Cathedral Days" (Boston, 1887), and her second "The Republic of the Future" (New York, 1887), both of which were successful. She has published one novel, "Glorinda" (Boston, 1888), and a book on Normandy, "In and Out of Three Normandy Inns" (New York, 1892). She is busy with domestic duties, but she is working always in the literary field. She has a charming home in New York. In 1883 she became the wife of Edward Williams Dodd, of Boston, but whose residence has been for several years in New York.

DODDS, Mrs. Susanna Way, physician, born in a log cabin in Randolph county, near Richmond, Ind., 10th November, 1830. Her father was a lineal descendant of Henry Way, a Puritan, who

SUSANNA WAY DODDS.

emigrated from England to this country in 1630. Both father and mother were members of the Society of Friends. Their ancestors, who went west from Guilford, N. C., were originally from Nantucket. Susanna was the eldest of thirteen children. The father was in moderate circumstances and could give them only a common-school education. The eldest daughter was ambitious, and early set her heart on going to college. To her great grief, she soon found that, with the exception of Oberlin, there was not a college in the land that would admit women. There were only ladies' seminaries. She therefore decided to go to Oxford Female Institute, which was then conducted by Rev. J. W. Scott, the father-in-law of President Benjamin Harrison. To do this, Miss Way began teaching in the common schools at a salary of eight dollars a month, and boarded herself. She was then seventeen years of age. By

rigid economy she saved a small sum of money, and in her twenty-third year received her diploma from Dr. Scott's seminary. The much-coveted college course was not given up. The university in Ann Arbor was founded, and its doors were afterwards thrown open to women. Antioch, with Horace Mann at its head admitted women and in the spring of 1856 Miss Way entered the preparatory department of that college. Again her plans were frustrated. Sickness in her father's family called her home and also prevented her from earning money. The following year she became the wife of Andrew Dodds, a young Scotchman, whose liberal views were in harmony with her own. They made their home in Yellow Springs, Ohio, and Mrs. Dodds renewed her studies in Antioch, where she afterward graduated. She also completed a medical course, in 1864, in the New York Hygeio-Therapeutic College. Her husband at that time enlisted in the Federal army, and by exposure in the mountains of Virginia contracted a fatal disease. A short time before his death the family moved to St. Louis, Mo., and in 1870 Dr. Dodds began to practice in that city. She was joined by her husband's sister, Dr. Mary Dodds, with whom she is still associated. As physicians they have done much for the physical redemption of women. Dr. Susanna Way Dodds is dean of the St. Louis Hygienic College of Physicians and Surgeons, and also a member of its faculty. She has written and published a work on dietetics, entitled "Health in the Household," and has contributed to a number of health journals and other papers.

DODGE, Miss Grace Hoadley, philanthropist and educational reformer, born in New York City, in 1856. With large wealth and high social position, Miss Dodge has devoted much of her time to works of charity in her native city. In 1886 she was appointed a school commissioner on the New York school board, in company with Mrs. Agnew. Her work in that position fully justified the new movement that called for women members of that board. On entering her new field of labor she said: "I came into the board of education with three distinct objects in view, to remember my oath of office, which means to sustain the manual of the board of education; to consider for the 200,000 children in the public schools what is wisest and best for them; to be loyal to the 4,000 teachers, and to think of myself as the especial representative of 3,500 women teachers." Immediately after appointment Miss Dodge and Mrs. Agnew made a study of the manual, of methods in this country and in others, of books, buildings, school furniture and apparatus, discipline and all that pertains to schools and teaching, and Miss Dodge gave to these duties almost her entire time, and accomplished an unprecedented amount of work. She visited, with more or less frequency, every day school in the city, 132 in number, and the thirty-nine evening schools, became acquainted as far as possible with every teacher and principal, studied the conditions and necessities of each school, and made careful notes for reports. The committees on which she served were those on auditing, on school books and courses of study, on school furniture, on sites and new schools, and on evening schools, and the reports which were made while she was a member of those committees were peculiarly interesting and important, and several of them have deen the means of great and significant changes. When there are added to the duties already mentioned an attendance at school-board meetings twice a month, the sessions often lasting from four to eight o'clock, semi-weekly committee meetings, and a half day on Saturday, which Miss

Dodge devotes to the reception of teachers in her private office in her home on Madison Avenue, when she hears their grievances and gives them advice, it will be understood that not only were the regular duties of the position onerous, but the gratuitous and self-imposed ones were far from light. It was due conspicuously to Miss Dodge's influence that, in spite of opposition, manual training has been introduced into the schools in part. She secured relief for certain over-crowded primary and grammar schools. She succeeded in having the school board continue the evening schools for girls, and she aided in correcting the plan of apportioning the salaries of teachers and of holding examinations for certificates. In every way the presence and work of Miss Dodge and Mrs. Agnew were a benefit to the cause of education in New York. Besides her regular school work, Miss Dodge has done a good deal of philanthropic and educational work in New York. Her charitable

HANNAH P. DODGE.

labor has been based not on theory, but on practical knowledge of the conditions of the working people, gained by personal contact with them. Of this the proofs are the large number of working-girls' clubs, of which she is the founder, a movement of which she was the leader, and which has spread throughout the country, and the New York College for Training Teachers, of which she was the inaugurator. Observation convinced her that the needy should be helped to help themselves, and that was the origin of her interest in education, which dates back a considerable time before she was invited to serve on the board of education. She was an active member of the board of the State Charities Aid Association, and has been connected with hospitals, a training school for nurses, and is a trustee of the Medical College for Female Physicians.

DODGE, Miss Hannah P., educator, born on a farm in Littleton, Mass., 16th February, 1821,

where her girlhood was spent. She attended the public school and afterwards spent several terms in a select school for young ladies. When she was seventeen years old, she began to teach a district school in a neighboring town. She next taught successfully in her own town. After teaching for some terms, she went to the Lawrence Academy in Groton, Mass. She completed her education in the Townsend Female Seminary, in Townsend, Mass. After graduating from that school, she was chosen a teacher in the institution. One year later she was chosen principal of the school, a position which she held for seven years. She held the position of principal in the Oread Institute in Worcester, Mass., for several years, traveled in Europe for a year and there studied modern languages and art. She has traveled much in her own country. After her sojourn in Europe, she took a desirable position in Dorchester, Mass., where she successfully managed a young ladies' school for five years. Retiring from the school field, she purchased a pleasant home in Littleton, where her family had remained. In that town she was made a superintendent of schools, and served a number of years. She is president of the local Woman's Christian Temperance Union and one of the trustees of the public library, and is active in charitable work.

DODGE, Miss Mary Abigail, author, widely known by her pen-name, "Gail Hamilton," born in Hamilton, Mass., in 1830. She received a thorough education, and in 1851 became instructor in physical science in the high school in Hartford, Conn. She was next a governess in the family of Dr. Gamaliel Bailey, of Washington, D. C., and was a regular contributor to his journal, the 'National Era." In the years 1865 to 1867, inclusive, she was one of the editors of "Our Young Folks." Since 1876 she has lived principally in Washington. She has contributed much to prominent magazines and newspapers, and the name "Gail Hamilton" attached to an essay is a guarantee that it is full of wit and aggressiveness. Her published volumes include "Country Living and Country Thinking" (1862), "Gala-Days" (1863), "A New Atmosphere" and "Stumbling Blocks" (1864), "Skirmishes and Sketches" (1865), "Red-Letter Days in Applethorpe" and "Summer Rest" (1866), "Wool-Gathering" (1867), "Woman's Wrongs, a Counter-Irritant," (1868), "Battle of the Books" (1870), "Woman's Worth and Worthlessness" (1871), "Little Folk Life" (1872), "Child World" (2 vols., 1872 and 1873), "Twelve Miles from a Lemon" (1873), "Nursery Noonings" (1874), "Sermons to the Clergy" and "First Love is Best" (1875), "What Think Ye of Christ?" (1876), "Our Common-School System" (1880), "Divine Guidance, Memorial of Allen W. Dodge," (1881), "The Insuppressible Book" (1885), and "A Washington Bible Class" (1891). In 1877 she contributed to the New York "Tribune" a notable series of vigorous letters on civil service reform. Miss Dodge commands a terse, vigorous, direct style. She cuts through shams and deceits with an easy and convincing blow that leaves no room for doubt. Her essays are countless and cover almost every field of comment and criticism.

DODGE, Mrs. Mary Mapes, author and editor, born in New York City, 26th January, 1838. She is the daughter of Prof. James J. Mapes, the distinguished promoter of scientific farming in the United States. She was educated by private tutors, and early showed talents for drawing, modeling and musical and literary composition. At an early age she became the wife of William Dodge, a lawyer of New York City. He died in his prime, leaving Mrs. Dodge with two sons to care for. She turned to literature as a means to earn the money to educate her sons. She began to write short sketches for children, and soon brought out a volume of them, entitled "Irvington Stories," (New

MARY MAPES DODGE.

York, 1864), which was very successful. She next published "Hans Brinker, or the Silver Skates" (New York, 1865). With Donald G. Mitchell and Harriet Beecher Stowe, Mrs. Dodge was one of the earliest editors of "Hearth and Home," and for several years she conducted the household and childrens' department of that journal. In 1873, when "St. Nicholas" was started, she became its editor, which position she still holds. Her "Hans Brinker" has been translated into Dutch, French, German, Russian and Italian, and was awarded a prize of 1,500 francs by the French Academy. Her other published volumes are "A Few Friends, and How They Amused Themselves" (Philadelphia, 1869), "Rhymes and Jingles" (New York, 1874), "Theophilus and Others" (New York, 1876), "Along the Way," poems (New York, 1879), and "Donald and Dorothy" (New York, 1883). She is the author of "Miss Maloney on the Chinese Question," published in "Scribner's Monthly" in 1870. She has a pleasant home in New York, which is a literary center. One of her sons died in 1881, and the other, James Mapes Dodge is a successful inventor and manufacturer, residing in Philadelphia, Pa. Mrs. Dodge contributes to "Harper's Magazine," "Atlantic Monthly," the "Century" and other periodicals.

DODSON, Miss Caroline Matilda, physician, born near Keosauqua, Iowa, 17th December, 1845. Her father, Stiles Richard Dodson, was the son of Richard Dodson and Hannah Watson, being a descendant of Thomas and Mary Dodson, of whom the doctor's mother was also a descendant. Her mother, Mrs. Caroline Matilda Dodson, was the daughter of Stephen Harrison, and Mary Dodson. Miss Dodson's father and mother were

natives of Huntington Valley, Pa. On 28th July, 1836, they were united in marriage. The mother, Mrs. C. Matilda Dodson, was a woman of strong character and advanced thought. About six weeks after marriage they left Pennsylvania for the West and settled in Van Buren county, Iowa. Stiles R. Dodson died 28th October, 1847, leaving his widow with four daughters, the youngest not two years of age. That winter the mother taught school in her own house. In the spring of 1848 she returned with her family to her father's house in Pennsylvania. Caroline was baptized in November, 1857, and she was henceforth a laborer by the side of her mother, in the Baptist Church. Study at home under private teachers and at the district school supplemented the early lessons from the mother. At about twelve she was sent to an academy and normal institute. She began to teach in the winter of 1861. Returning at intervals to school, she followed the profession of teaching until the fall of 1871 when she matriculated at the Woman's Medical College of Pennsylvania, and entered upon the three year course just inaugurated. Dr. Ann Preston was then Dean. The summer of 1872 she spent in the Nurses' Training School of the Woman's Hospital of Philadelphia. The course required was completed and a certificate of the Training School for Nurses was given her. The summer of 1873 she spent in the same hospital as student in the wards and out practice. She received her diploma in March, 1874, and went to Ypsilanti, Mich., for further study with Dr. Ruth A. Gerry, one of the first women to practice medicine. After a year spent in hospital and private practice with that worthy medical pioneer, she went to Rochester, N. Y., and there in connection with practice opened

CAROLINE MATILDA DODSON.

a drug store. In 1877, her mother having gone West again, she started for Iowa, going by the Hudson and Great Lakes. She lost a car load of valuables in the riot at Pittsburgh, Pa. After her trip West she returned to Philadelphia and worked at whatever promised a shadow of support. For a time five dollars per week was depended upon to meet the living expenses of three, but offers came, and among them, unsolicited, one from the Philadelphia Society for Organizing Charity to act as superintendent of one of its districts. The position was accepted, and for eight years was filled in connection with her practice of medicine. As a teacher she has written and spoken boldly for the better methods of education, and advocated broadening the opportunities for study. She has read widely on subjects concerning the movements of women, and her voice and pen have been used with earnestness in their interest. She saw that a general movement might help to educate the masses and to spread a knowledge of self-care. To this end, after much deliberation, a call was issued for a public meeting to be held in Association Hall, Philadelphia, 23rd July, 1890, and an organization was effected under the name of the National Woman's Health Association of America. The association was chartered 1st November, 1890, and Dr. Dodson was elected first president. The plan of the association is broad and provides for extensive branch work.

DOE, Mrs. Mary L., woman suffragist, temperance reformer and business woman, born in Conneaut, Ohio, 27th July, 1836. She is of Puritan ancestry of Scotch-Irish blood, who came over the

MARY L. DOE.

seas in the third ship after the Mayflower. Her maiden name was Thompson. Her immediate ancestors, the Thompsons and Harpers, emigrated from Vermont and settled in that portion of Ohio known as the Western Reserve. The men of her family have been brave and patriotic, taking part in all the country's wars. The women, left at home, in addition to their family cares often took up the business that their war-going husbands laid down. It is not strange, therefore, that Mrs. Doe should be a self-reliant business woman, strong in her

disbelief of the "clinging-vine" theory. Mrs. Doe's early instruction was received from a private tutor and in select schools. At nine years of age she was sent to the Conneaut Academy, then just completed. At fifteen she began to teach a country school for one dollar a week and "boarded around." Later she attended the State Normal School in Edinboro, Pa. When she was eight years old, she attended a temperance meeting addressed by one of the original Washingtonians, and she then and there signed the pledge. In 1853 she joined the Good Templars, which was then a new organization and one of the first to embody the principles of equal rights for women and the prohibition of the liquor traffic by the State. In 1878 she became a member of the Michigan Grand Lodge of Good Templars, and she has attended every session since. She has held the office of grand vice-templar for two years and of grand assistant secretary for nine years. She has further shown her interest in temperance by joining the Woman's Christian Temperance Union and the various other temperance organizations in the towns where she has lived. In 1877 Mrs. Doe went to Saginaw, Mich., led there by her husband's business interests. There she at once made friends with the advocates of equal suffrage, a movement that has always been dear to her heart. In 1884, in a meeting called in Flint by equal suffragists of national prominence to organize a State suffrage association, Mrs. Doe was chosen president of the association. That office she held for six years. She has been active in securing many of the privileges granted to women by the Legislature of Michigan, and has spent much of her time with other equal suffragists in the State capital. She is at present chairman of the legislative committee, and also a member of the advisory committee of the Michigan Equal Suffrage Association. Mrs. Doe changed her residence from Saginaw to Bay City in 1886, and opened a store for fancy goods. That business she still continues. In Bay City she is a member of the board of education, doing important committee work in connection with that body. Most of her church work has been done in the Methodist Church. Her father was a preacher of that denomination.

DOLE, Mrs. Phebe Cobb Larry, poet, born in Gorham, Maine, 28th November, 1835. Her great-grandfather, Dennis Larry, came from Ireland to this country with the British army during the French and Indian war, and afterwards settled on land granted him in Gorham for services rendered during the war. Her mother was the great-granddaughter of Ezra Brown, one of the early settlers of Windham, Maine, who was killed by the Indian chief, Poland, during the last battle between the inhabitants of Windham and the Indians, 14th May, 1756. Her father, Joseph C. Larry, was a blacksmith and farmer, and resided in Windham. Her early life was quiet and simple. She was educated in the common schools of her own town and in Gorham Seminary. Some of her early poetical productions fell into the hands of a well-known critic and scholar, who secured their publication in several Maine papers, much to the surprise of their youthful author. In 1853 she became the wife of Samuel T. Dole, of Windham, a man of fine literary taste and good business capacity. In 1860 Mrs. Dole began to write for the Portland "Transcript," the Kennebec "Journal," Hallowell "Gazette" and other Maine papers. The late John Neal and Edward H. Elwell gave her much encouragement. Mrs. Dole has written for many of the leading magazines and has acquired a wide reputation outside of her own State. As an artist she claims to be but an amateur, but her paintings show the taste and fine feeling of the poet. She is a woman of strong character and well cultivated mind.

DONLEVY, Miss Alice, artist and writer on art, was born in Manchester, Eng. She is devoted

ALICE DONLEVY.

to the work of bringing about the establishment of free art industrial education for the youth of this country. In this line of effort she has been conspicuous for years. Miss Donlevy came to the United States in her infancy. She early showed a talent for drawing, and at ten years of age she exhibited water-color copies at the American Institute. At thirteen she was admitted to the School of Design through the influence of Horace Greeley and Mary Morris Hamilton. For seven years she devoted her attention to wood engraving for books and magazines, being one of the first workers in this art to introduce that original feature of American wood-engraving, the use of dots instead of lines for shades and shadows. Later her talent for form asserted itself so strongly that engraving was given up for designing for decoration. Since childhood she has drawn with pen and ink for reproduction, her father, John J. Donlevy, having invented certain valuable reproductive processes, which naturally aroused her interest, drawing her to work beside him. Original work once entered upon, she exhibited, while still very young, in the Academy of Design, and won prizes for general attainments. She received a second prize awarded by the Philadelphia Sketch Club for illumination. Simultaneously with the development of her artistic talents grew her love for and knowledge of letters. At the age of fourteen she wrote for the press. In 1867 she published a book on "Illumination," making all the designs of its illustrations. Since that time she has written for the "Art Review" of Boston, the "Art Amateur," the "Art Interchange," "St. Nicholas," "Harper's Young People," the "Ladies' World," "Demorest's Magazine" and the "Chautauquan,"

and is now the art editor of "Demorest's Magazine." In 1867 she was one of the nine professional women artists who founded the Ladies' Art Association of New York. The work of that association has been the art training of teachers for schools and seminaries and the opening of new avenues of art industrial employment of women. Among new professions for women established by the association was that of painting on porcelain. In 1887 she was one of the committee of three to go to Albany and lay before the legislature plans of free art industrial instruction for talented boys, girls and women, to be given during vacation seasons and on Saturday afternoons. The bill passed both houses. It was defeated later by eight votes when called up for reconsideration by Ray Hamilton, then one of the representatives from New York. She was prominent as an organizer of the meeting of American women in Cooper Institute, in the autumn of 1890, to call upon the Czar of Russia for clemency in the case of Sophie Gunzberg, condemmed to die in December, 1890. The meeting resulted in a commutation of the death sentence to banishment to Siberia. Probably the best work of Miss Donlevy has been the aid that she has given personally to promote the interests of struggling associations and individual artists by means of free lectures and free lessons, also by giving the latter introduction by means of public receptions at which their works were exhibited.

DONNELLY, Miss Eleanor Cecilia, poet, born in Philadelphia, Pa., 6th September, 1848. Her father was Dr. Philip Carroll Donnelly. Her mother possessed a fine intellect and great force of character. She died in June, 1887. Besides her poetic talent, Miss Donnelly possesses a fine con-

ELEANOR CECILIA DONNELLY.

tralto voice, which has been carefully cultivated. She and her sisters, the Misses Eliza and Philipanna Donnelly, who are also gifted with literary ability, have attained high positions as singers in musical circles in Philadelphia, and have always graciously responded to the numerous calls made upon them to give their services at entertainments in aid of charitable enterprises. Her brother is the well-known Hon. Ignatius Donnelly, of Minnesota. Miss Donnelly has been called "The morning star of Catholic song" in our land, for her poetic utterances, which form so valuable a contribution to the Catholic literature of the day, are of a lofty tone and great volume. Her devotional spirit, the exuberance of her poetic fancy, her ease of expression and her versatility have been acknowledged. Her lyrics have not only commemorated the joys of first communions, religious professions and ordinations, but have added a charm to numerous festivals of congratulation and welcome. When the Centennial of the Adoption of the Constitution was celebrated in Philadelphia, in 1887, an ode from her pen was read before the American Catholic Historical Society of that city. The first of Miss Donnelly's publications was a hymn to the Blessed Virgin, written at the age of nine. It appeared in a child's paper. Though best known as a writer of poems, she has, besides producing many tales for secular magazines, made a number of meritorious contributions to Catholic fiction. In the spring of 1885 the Augustinian Fathers showed their appreciation of Miss Donnelly's gifts by procuring for her from Rome a golden reliquary ornamented with filagree work, which contains relics of the four illustrious members of their order: St. Nicholas Tolentine, St. Thomas of Villa-Nova, St. Clare of Montefalco and the Blessed Rita of Cascia. On 1st February, 1885, Pope Leo XIII manifested his approval of her zeal and his admiration for her powers by sending her (notably in recognition of her "Jubilee Hymn," written to commemorate his golden jubilee) his apostolic benediction. He also accepted on that occasion a copy of her work, "The Birthday Bouquet." The "Jubilee Hymn" was translated into Italian and German. It was also set to music composed expressly for the words. The following is a list of Miss Donnelly's published works, in the order in which they appeared: "Out of Sweet Solitude," a collection of poems (Philadelphia, 1874); "Domus Dei," a collection of religious and memorial poems (Philadelphia, 1875); "The Legend of the Best Beloved" (New York, 1880); "Crowned with Stars, Legends and Lyrics for the Children of Mary, and other Poems" (Notre Dame, Ind., 1881); "Hymns of the Sacred Heart, with Music" (Philadelphia, 1882); "Children of the Golden Sheaf and Other Poems" (Philadelphia, 1884); "The Birthday Bouquet, Culled from the Shrines of the Saints and the Garden of the Poets" (New York, 1884); "Garland of Festival Songs" (New York, 1885); "Little Compliments of the Season, Original, Selected and Translated Verses" (New York, 1886); "A Memoir of Father Felix Joseph Barbelin, S. J." (Philadelphia, 1886); "The Conversion of St. Augustine, and Other Poems" (Philadelphia, 1887); "Liguori Leaflets" (Philadelphia, 1887), and "Poems" (Philadelphia, 1892). Miss Donnelly received an offer of an appointment as auxiliary to the committee on woman's work of the Pennsylvania Board of World's Fair Managers.

DOOLITTLE, Mrs. Lucy Salisbury, philanthropist, born in Farmersville, Cattaraugus county, N. Y., 7th October, 1832. On both sides she came of plain New England stock, both families having moved to western New York in the early days of settlement. Not long after her birth her parents moved to Castile, N. Y., where, with the exception of a few months, her early life was spent. She was but eight years old when her mother died, and after that event she lived with her grandmother's

sister. She had a good home, but was obliged to work hard and had but little time for recreation. In Castile she received a common school education. Not being satisfied, at the age of twenty she went to Yellow Springs, Ohio, where she entered the preparatory department of Antioch College. There she received the greater part of her education, having completed the work of the preparatory department and taken special collegiate studies. In Antioch she became the wife of Myrick H. Doolittle, a graduate of the college and for a while professor there. In 1863 she went to Washington, D. C., her husband following a few months later. She at once entered into the work in the hospitals and was thus engaged until the fall of 1865, a part of the time as volunteer nurse, and during the remainder as agent for the Sanitary Commission. Immediately after the war she became interested in the prisons and jails. It was her labor in them which brought to her a realization of the terrible condition.

LUCY SALISBURY DOOLITTLE.

of female convicts and convinced her of the need of suffrage for women, that they might have the power effectually to aid their suffering sisters of the lower classes. She was also at the same time conducting a sewing-school for women and girls of the colored race, who had flocked to Washington at the close of the war. It gave those poor women their first start in life. In that work, and also in that of the Freedmen's Bureau with which she was connected as agent, she saw so many homeless and friendless children that her sympathies were aroused for them. She and her husband helped to organize the Industrial Home School for poor white children of the District of Columbia, now a flourishing institution supported by appropriations from Congress. In 1875 her energies were enlisted in work for poor colored children, and she became a member of the National Association for the Relief of Destitute Colored Women and Children, with which she has been connected ever since, being its efficient treasurer for nine years and working at other times on various committees. A comparatively new branch of that institution is a Home for Colored Foundlings, in which she at present takes an especial interest. In the associated charities and in the charitable work of the Unitarian Church she has done good service. In all of her work for the poor of Washington she has shown practical ability and a marked talent for business.

DORR, Mrs. Julia C. R., poet, born in Charleston, S. C., 13th February, 1825. Her mother, Zulma De Lacy Thomas, was the daughter of French refugees who fled from San Domingo during the insurrection of the slaves near the close of the last century. The mother died during Mrs. Dorr's infancy, and her father, William Young Ripley, who was a merchant in Charleston, returned in 1830 to Vermont, his native state. There he engaged in business again, and devoted himself chiefly to the development of the Rutland marble

JULIA C. R. DORR.

quarries. There his daughter grew to womanhood, in a home of culture and refinement. When the poet was a little child, she began to write, but none of her poems were printed until she became a woman grown. In 1847 she became the wife of Hon. Seneca M. Dorr, of New York. Himself a man of wide culture, he gave to Mrs. Dorr the encouragement and stimulus which directed her to a literary life. In 1847 he sent one of Mrs. Dorr's poems, without her knowledge, to the "Union Magazine," and this was her first published poem. In 1848 her first published story, "Isabel Leslie," gained a one-hundred dollar prize offered by "Sartain's Magazine." In 1857 Mr. Dorr took up his residence in Rutland, Vt., and since that date the author's pen has rarely been idle. Her work has constantly appeared in the best publications, and her books have followed each other at intervals until 1885, when her latest volume, "Afternoon Songs," appeared. Her books are: "Farmingdale"

(New York, 1854), "Lanmere" (New York, 1855), "Sybil Huntington" (New York, 1869), "Poems" (Philadelphia, 1871), "Expiation" (Philadelphia, 1873), "Friar Anselmo and Other Poems" (New York, 1879), "The Legend of the Babouhka" (New York, 1881), "Daybreak" (New York, 1882), "Bermuda" (New York, 1884), "Afternoon Songs" (New York, 1885). In Mrs. Dorr's poems are found strength and melody, sweetness and sympathy, a thorough knowledge of poetic technique, and through all a high purpose which renders such work of lasting value. Her stories are particularly skillful in detail and plot, in the interpretation of the New England character. Her essays on practical themes of life and living have had a wide circulation and a large influence. A series of essays and letters published some years ago in a New England magazine and addressed to husbands and wives were collected and published without her consent by a Cincinnati publishing house. Mrs. Dorr's social influence in her own town is wide and strong, and from one who knows her well come these apppreciative words: "When summer days were long, and she was bearing the burden and heat of the day as a young wife and mother, Mrs. Dorr's life was eminently quiet and secluded, her pen being almost her only link with the outside world. But with the autumn rest have come to her wider fields and broader activities. In and around her beautiful home, enriched with treasures from many lands, there has grown up a far-reaching intellectual life, of which she is the soul and center. She is loved and honored in her own town, and there hundreds of women, of all ranks, turn to her for help and inspiration. The year of Mr. Dorr's death, she became the leader of a band of women who founded the Rutland Free Library, the success of which has been so remarkable. Mrs. Dorr is still president of the association, and has given to the library, in memory of her husband, what is said to be the finest and most complete collection of books on political science to be found in New England, outside of Cambridge University." The character of Mrs. Dorr's personal influence is such as to leave a lasting impression upon the men and women of her time, and the quality of her work assures for her books a permanent place among the best achievements of literary workers in America.

DORSEY, Mrs. Anna Hanson, author, born in Georgetown, D. C., 16th December, 1816. She is descended on her mother's side from the De Rastricks of Yorkshire, England, from the noble house of Vasa of Sweden, from the MacAlpine MacGregors and the Lingans. On her father's side she descends from the McKenneys. John Hanson became a distinguished colonist in Maryland, rose to the rank of colonel, and founded a race which stands second to none in the annals of the country. His grandsons, Samuel of Samuel and John Hanson, were two of the most earnest supporters of the cause of independence, the latter being one of the signers of the Articles of Federation. His great-grandson, Daniel of St. Thomas Jenifer, signed the Constitution. His great-great-grandsons, Thomas Stone and John H. Stone, were respectively a signer of the Declaration of Independence and governor of Maryland. The Lingans were among the early colonists from Wales, and held positions of trust in Maryland as early as the reign of William and Mary. Their noblest representative, Gen. James Lingan, the brother of her grandfather, after brilliant Revolutionary services, was murdered by the same mob in Baltimore, in 1812, that wreaked its savagery on Light Horse Harry Lee and Musgrove, his comrades in arms. Mrs. Dorsey's grandfather,

Nicholas Lingan, was educated in St. Omers, France, where his kinsman, barrister Charles Carroll, had been sent in his youth, and he was the first man in the District of Columbia to issue manumission papers. His objection to slavery extended down his line to his latest descendants. Mrs. Dorsey declined to answer "Uncle Tom's Cabin," because, as she said in response to the demand made on her by public and publishers, "with the exception of the burning of the slaves hinted at" (of which she had never heard an instance), "everything represented as the inevitable result of the system of slavery is true, however kind and considerate of the slaves the masters might be." She was brought up under the influence of the old emancipation party of the border States, who were conscientiously opposed to slavery, but never made themselves offensive to those who were not. Her father, Rev. William McKenney, belonged to an old Eastern Shore family, which has been represented in the Legislature, the courts and on the bench for generations. In politics her race were all Federalists and old-line Whigs, and she was an ardent Unionist during the Civil War. Her oldest brother was one of the last men in the Senate of Virginia to make a speech against secession. Her only son served in the Union Army and got his death-wound while planting the Stars and Stripes on the ramparts at Fort Hell. In 1837 she became the wife of Lorenzo Dorsey, of Baltimore, a son of Judge Owen Dorsey. She and her husband are converts to the Catholic faith. She has devoted herself exclusively to Catholic light literature, of which she is the pioneer in this country, with the exception of two ringing war lyrics, "Men of the Land" and "They're Coming, Grandad," the latter dedicated to the loyal people of East Tennessee, who suffered such martyrdom for their fidelity to the old flag. She began her literary career by a touching little story called "The Student of Blenheim Forest," and this was followed rapidly by "Oriental Pearl," "Nora Brady's Vow," "Mona the Vestal," "Heiress of Carrigmona," "Tears on the Diadem," "Woodreve Manor," "The Young Countess," "Dummy," "Coaina, the Rose of the Algonquins," "Beth's Promise," "Warp and Woof," "Zoe's Daughter," "Old House at Glenaran," "Fate of the Dane," "Mad Penitent of Todi," "A Brave Girl," "Story of Manuel," "The Old Grey Rosary," "Ada's Trust," "Adrift," "Palms," and others. Her books have brought her the friendship of whole religious communities, prelates and authors, and across the seas the venerable Catholic Earl of Shrewsbury and Lady George Fullerton were among her warm admirers. "May Brooke" was the first Catholic book published in Edinburgh since the Reformation, and "Coaina" has been twice dramatized and translated into German and Hindustani. Pope Leo has twice sent her his special blessing, first by the Cardinal Archbishop James Gibbons, and the second time by her granddaughter, Miss Mohun, at a recent special audience. She has also received the gift of the Lætare medal from the University of Notre Dame for distinguished services rendered to literature, education and religion. Mrs. Dorsey is now an invalid, and is living with her children in Washington, D. C.

DORSEY, Miss Ella Loraine, author, born in Washington, D. C., in 185-. She is the youngest child of Mrs. Anna Hanson Dorsey, the pioneer of Catholic light literature in America. Born a few years before the breaking out of the Civil War, her early childhood was spent amid the stirring scenes of border life. The entire kin on both sides were in the Confederacy, with the exception of her father

and her only brother, who received his death wound on the ramparts of "Fort Hell," where he had dashed up with the colors, caught from the color-bearer, and stood cheering his comrades to the charge. Miss Dorsey represents old and illustrious families of Maryland, counting among her kinsfolk and connections two signers of the Declaration of Independence, eight signers of the Act of the Maryland Convention of 26th July, 1776, two Presidents, seven Governors, thirty-six commissioned officers in the Continental Army, and a number of the young heroes of the famous old Maryland Line, who died on the field of honor at Long Island, Harlem Heights and Fort Washington. She began her literary career as a journalist and was for several years the "Vanity Fair" of the Washington "Critic," leaving that paper to take a special correspondence on the Chicago "Tribune." John Boyle O'Reilly and the Rev. D. E. Hudson, editor of the "Ave Maria," urged her into magazine

ELLA LORAINE DORSEY.

work. Her first three stories appeared almost simultaneously, "The Knickerbocker Ghost" and "The Tsar's Horses," in the "Catholic World," and "Back from the Frozen Pole," in "Harper's Magazine." "The Tsar's Horses" traveled round the world, its last reproduction being in New Zealand. It was attributed at first, because of its accuracy of detail, to Archibald Forbes, the war correspondent. Miss Dorsey's specialty is boys' stories. "Midshipman Bob" went through two editions in this country and England in its first year, and has been since translated into Italian. Scarcely second to it in popularity are "Saxty's Angel" and "The Two Tramps," while two poems printed in the "Cosmopolitan" have been received with marked favor. Miss Dorsey is the Russian translator in the Scientific Library of the Interior Department, Washington, D. C. She is an enthusiastic member and officer of the Daughters of the American Revolution, and her latest work is "Three Months with Smallwood's Immortals," a sketch written for and read before the Washington branch of that society. Last year four sketches, "Women in the Patent Office," "Women in the Pension Office," and "Women in the Land Office," were prepared by her for the "Chautauquan." They attracted much attention and secured wide recognition for the brave ladies who toil at their department desks. Her home is on Washington Heights.

DORTCH, Miss Ellen J., newspaper editor and publisher, was born in Georgia, 25th January, 1868. She is descended from Virginia families on both sides, and her ancestors have figured conspicuously in affairs of state. Her father, James S. Dortch, who died in August, 1891, was for a quarter of a century a prominent lawyer. Miss Dortch received a thorough education, which, with her progressive and enterprising spirit, has enabled her to take high rank as a journalist. She became the owner and editor of the Carnesville, Ga., "Tribune" in 1888, when the establishment consisted of one-hundred-fifty pounds of long primer type, mostly in "pi," a few cases of worn advertising type and a subscription book whose credit column had been conscientiously neglected. Now the old presses and worn type are replaced by new and improved ones, and the circulation of the paper has increased to thousands, and the energetic, spirited woman who has been typo, editor and business manager, who has solicited and canvassed the district for subscribers, because she wasn't able to hire any one to do it for her, has the satisfaction of seeing her efforts crowned with a full measure of success. Beginning the work when only seventeen years old, she has fought the boycotters and Alliance opponents and overcome the southern prejudice against women who use their brain in making their way in the world. After working for two years, she went to Baltimore, Md., where she studied for two years in the Notre Dame school. She resumed her work on the "Tribune" in June, 1890.

DOUGHTY, Mrs. Eva Craig Graves, journalist, born in Warsaw, Ky., 1st December, 1852. Her father, Judge Lorenzo Graves, was a politician and an able lawyer. Her mother was Virginia Hampton-Graves. Mrs. Doughty was educated in Oxford Female College, Oxford, Ohio, leaving her Kentucky home during the war years from 1860 to 1864, which years she passed in the college with her two other sisters. Prior to that she had been taught by private tutors. After a four-year course in Oxford, she entered the Academy of the Most Holy Rosary, in Louisville, Ky., conducted by sisters of the Dominican order, where she studied nearly three years, and left just two months before she would have been graduated, to accompany a sister, whose husband was in the regular army, to a frontier post. On 24th May, 1874, she became the wife of John R. Doughty, then editor and proprietor of the Mt. Pleasant, Mich., "Enterprise." She was at once installed as associate editor with her husband. Mrs. Doughty did regular newspaper work on that paper for fourteen years, keeping the office hours and doing anything connected with the office work, from proof-reading and type-setting to writing for any department of the paper where "copy" was called for. Subsequently Mr. Doughty sold the "Enterprise" and for three years engaged in business in Grand Rapids, Mich., where the family removed. There Mrs. Doughty engaged in public work. She was elected president of the Grand Rapids Equal Suffrage Association, which position she resigned when the family removed to Gladwin, Mich. While in Grand Rapids Mrs. Doughty, Mrs. Etta S. Wilson, of the "Telegram-Herald," and Miss Fleming, connected with the "Leader," held

the first meeting and planned the organization of the Michigan Women's Press Association, of which Mrs. Doughty has remained an active member. In 1890 Mr. Doughty commenced the publication of the "Leader" in Gladwin, being the founder and owner of the plant. She was regularly engaged on that paper. Besides this she has ever been an active member of the Woman's Christian Temperance Union, having been secretary of the Eighth Congressional District for four years. She also belongs to the Good Templars and the Royal Templars. She has always engaged actively in Sunday-school work and is a member of the Presbyterian Church. She is a member of Golden Rod Lodge, Daughters of Rebecca. In addition to general newspaper work, Mrs. Doughty has been the special correspondent of several city daily papers and was for some time a contributor to the "Sunny South," writing short stories, sketches and an occasional poem. For several years she was the

EVA CRAIG GRAVES DOUGHTY.

secretary of the Mt. Pleasant Library, Literary and Musical Association, an organization of which she was one of the founders. Having sold the Gladwin "Leader" in January, 1892, Mr. and Mrs. Doughty bought the "Post," of Port Austin, Mich., in May of the same year, and Mrs. Doughty is now engaged daily as assistant editor of that paper. She has three children, two sons and a daughter.

DOUGLAS, Miss Alice May, poet and author, born in Bath, Me., 28th June, 1865. She still resides in her native city. She began her career as an author at the age of eleven years, when her first published article appeared among the children's productions of "St. Nicholas." The reading of "Little Women" at the age of thirteen marked an epoch in her life. She determined to be an author like Jo, and, like her, send for publication a composition from her pen to test her chances of authorship. Consequently she sent a poem pertaining to a little sister, who shortly before death was seen throwing kisses to God. The "Zion's Herald," to which the poem was sent, published it, and from that time Miss Douglas has been a constant contributor to the press. She is also engaged

ALICE MAY DOUGLAS.

in editorial work on two monthly papers, the "Pacific Banner" and the "Acorn." Her first volume of poems was "Phlox" (Bath, Me., 1888). This was followed during the same year by a second volume, "May Flowers" (Bath, Me., 1888). Then she published "Gems Without Polish" (New York, 1890). She next wrote two juvenile books, one for boys and the other for girls, in the interest of the lend-a-hand clubs. Most of her books have first appeared as serials. Among them are "Jewel Gatherers," "Quaker John in the Civil War," "How the Little Cousins Formed a Museum," "The Peace-Makers" and "Self-exiled from Russia," a story of the Mennonites. Miss Douglas is State superintendent of the department of peace and arbitration of the Woman's Christian Temperance Union. She has also assisted the national peace department of that organization, by preparing much of its necessary literature and by founding a peace band for children, which has branches in Palestine and Australia.

DOUGLAS, Miss Amanda Minnie, author, born in New York City, 14th July, 1838. She was educated in the City Institute in New York. In 1853 she removed to Newark, N. J., where she took a course in reading with a private tutor. In childhood she was noted for her powers of story-telling, when she would tell her friends long tales, regular serials, that would continue for weeks. Much of her girlhood was taken up by sickness and family occupations. She was inventive, and one of her inventions, patented by herself, was a folding frame for a mosquito-net. She had no early dreams of becoming a great author. She knew Edgar Allen Poe and other conspicuous literary persons. After she had reached maturity, she began to write

stories for publication, and she was immediately successful. Among her published books are "In Trust" (1866), "Claudia" (1867), "Stephan Dane" (1867), "Sydnie Adriance" (1868), "With Fate Against Him" (1870), "Kathie's Stories for Young People" (6 vols., 1870, and 1871), "Lucia, Her Problem" (1871), "Santa Claus Land" (1873), "Home Nook" (1873), "The Old Woman Who Lived in a Shoe" and "Seven Daughters" (1874), "Drifted Asunder" (1875), "Nelly Kinnaird's Kingdom" (1876), "From Hand to Mouth" (1877), "Hope Mills" (1879), "Lost in a Creat City" (1880), "Whom Kathie Married" (1883), "Floyd Grandon's Honor" (1883), "Out of the Wreck" (1884), "A Woman's Inheritance" (1885), "Foes of Her Household" (1886), "The Fortunes of the Faradays (1887), "Modern Adam and Eve" (1888), "Osborne of the Arrochar" (1889), and "Heroes of the Crusade (1889). Miss Douglas has suffered much from long illness, but she keeps up courage and refuses to be borne down by fate. She is a fluent talker and well informed on current events. She has done but little work for magazines and newspapers. Her works have beer. very popular. Her first book, "In Trust," sold 20,000 copies in a short time, but she had sold the copyright, and others reaped the benefit. She holds the copyrights of all her other books.

DOUGLAS, Mrs. Lavantia Densmore, temperance worker, born in Rochester, N. Y., 1st March, 1827. She was one of seven children. Her parents, Joel and Sophia Densmore, were very poor in all the externals of life, but they were very rich in honor and integrity, in industry, in energy and in aspiration. When Lavantia was about nine years old, her parents removed to Crawford county,

LAVANTIA DENSMORE DOUGLAS.

Pennsylvania, upon a farm. The father was unique in character, eccentric in person, in speech and in manners. The mother was of a bright, joyous, laughter-loving nature. Appreciating keenly their own lack of education, both parents strove to give their children the best educational opportunities possible. The sole luxury of their home was literature. They took the "Democratic Review," almost the only magazine then published in the United States, and such papers as the "National Era" and the "Boston Investigator." In 1853, when she was twenty-six years of age, she became the wife of Joshua Douglas, then just entering the profession of the law, and removed to Meadville, Pa., where they have resided ever since. There her life was devoted to caring for her household, rearing her children and mingling somewhat in the social life of the place. In 1872 she made a visit to Europe. She arrived home from Europe on the 23rd of December, 1873, the day of the great Woman's Temperance Crusade. Meadville was aroused by the great spiritual outpouring, and the following March a mass meeting was called and a temperance organization effected which, under one form or another, still exists. Mrs. Douglas very early identified herself with the movement, and has always been a most active and enthusiastic worker in the cause. She early became a member of the Woman's Christian Temperance Union, and for many years was president of the Meadville Union. Her ardent enthusiasm and untiring zeal have made her name in her own community a synonym for temperance. For a few years Mrs. Douglas has been obliged to retire from active efforts in the cause. owing to failing eye-sight. Cataracts formed on both her eyes, and during these later years she has walked in gathering darkness. The cataracts have been removed, but with only partial success.

DOW, Miss Cornelia M., philanthropist and temperance reformer, born in Portland, Me., 10th

CORNELIA M. DOW.

November, 1842. She is the youngest daughter of Neal Dow, of Portland, Me. Her mother, who died in 1883, was Maria Cornelia Durant Maynard, who was born in Boston, Mass. Her daughter,

Cornelia, was born in the house where she now lives with her father, who is in the eighty-eighth year of his age. Miss Dow possesses many of the characteristics of both mother and father. She excels as a careful homekeeper, and yet is able to find a great deal of time for the world's work. For many years she was secretary of the Woman's Christian Association of Portland. She is the treasurer of the Home for Aged Women of Portland and also treasurer of the Temporary Home for Women and Children, a State institution situated in Deering, near Portland. The larger part of her time is given to works of temperance, which would seem the most natural thing for her to do. For years she has been officially connected with the Woman's Christian Temperance Union of Portland. She is president of the union in Cumberland county, one of the superintendents of the State union, as well as one of its most efficient vice-presidents. She is a member and a constant attendant of State Street Congregational Church in Portland.

DOW, Mrs. Mary E. H. G., financier, born in Dover, N. H., 15th December, 1848. Her maiden name was Mary Edna Hill. She is a daughter of Nathaniel Rogers Hill. She was educated partly in Dover. While she was yet a child, her parents removed to Boston, Mass., and it was there she got the larger part of her schooling. When seventeen years of age, she was graduated with high honors from the Charlestown high school. For some years she was a successful assistant principal of the Rochester, N. H., high school, and later went to St. Louis, Mo., where for three years she was instructor in French and German in a female academy. When twenty-five years old, she was wooed and won by a wealthy resident of Dover, George F. Gray, part owner and editor of the Dover "Press," a Democratic weekly paper published there. They spent two years in Europe. Three children were born to them, and after a few years Mr. Gray died. Before her marriage she was correspondent for several newspapers, among them the Boston "Journal" and "Traveller," "New Hampshire Statesman," the Dover "Enquirer," and some southern papers. Five years after the death of her first husband she became the wife of Dr. Henry Dow, of Dover. They spent some time in England. Returning to Dover, Mrs. Dow began to attract attention as a financier. In January, 1888, she was elected president of the Dover Horse Railway, an event that caused much commotion in railway circles. She was perfectly familiar with the affairs of the road and had secured a majority of its stock. The story of this occurrence is interesting. The road had been a failing enterprise. The patrons found fault with the accommodations and the excessiveness of fares, and the stockholders growled at the excessiveness of expenses and the small receipts. For years it had paid but a small dividend. A Boston syndicate made overtures for possession of the whole stock, and with such success that the board of directors reached the point of voting to sell. Mrs. Dow was out of town during these negotiations, but returned as the sale was about to be consummated. She held a small amount of the stock, and was approached with an offer for it at something like one-third the price at which it had been bought. With characteristic promptness she at once decided that, if the stock was so low, and yet the Boston syndicate expected to make the road pay, any other able financier might reasonably indulge the same hope; that, if there were any profits to be obtained, they ought to be saved to Dover, and that she would try her own capabilities in the matter. Her attitude interrupted the syndicate's scheme, and for some weeks there was a contest of wits to see who would get control of the most blocks. When the next meeting was called, it was supposed that the property would be transferred to the Boston party, but it transpired to every one's astonishment that Mrs. Dow was master of the situation; she had acquired more than half the stock. Her election to the presidency was certain. As her own votes would elect the directorate, that body would be necessarily of her own choice. Several among the Dover gentlemen, who desired to be on the board, said that they would not vote for a woman for president. It was simply preposterous and meant bankruptcy. But the matter presented itself to the ambitious gentlemen in this form: Agree to vote for Mrs. Dow, and you can hold office; otherwise you can not. They succumbed, but with chagrin and trepidation. Mrs. Dow at once demonstrated her ability to manage the road so as to make it a paying property. She did that to perfection, showing herself the equal of any male manager in the country.

DOWD, Miss Mary Alice, poet and educator, born in Frankford, Greenbrier county, W. Va., 16th December, 1855. Her parents were school-teachers of Puritan descent, their ancestors having landed in New England about the year 1630. In both families were found officers and privates of the Revolutionary army. On her father's side she is related to the well-known family of Field and the old English family of Dudley. She was the youngest of four children. Her early home was among the Berkshire Hills, whence her parents removed to Westfield, Mass., a town noted for its schools. Alice was a delicate child, and her parents scarcely dared to hope that she would be spared to

MARY ALICE DOWD.

years of maturity. Shy and reserved, she early showed a great love of nature and a deep appreciation of all natural beauty. She was educated at home and in the public schools of Westfield. She

was graduated from the English and classical departments of the high school, taking the two courses simultaneously. In the normal school she studied optionals with the prescribed branches and composed a class hymn sung at her graduation. Since that time she has been constantly employed as a teacher. During the past eleven years she has held her present position of first assistant in the high school of Stamford, Conn. Of scholarly attainments, she has helped many young men to prepare for college. She has taken several courses in the Sauveur Summer School of Languages and has especially fitted herself to give instruction in German. In 1886 the greatest sorrow of her life came to her in the sudden death of her mother. She has published one volume of verse, "Vacation Verses" (Buffalo, 1891).

DOWNS, Mrs. Sallie Ward, social leader, is descended on the paternal side from Lord Ward.

SALLIE WARD DOWNS.

of England. Her maiden name was Ward. On her mother's side she is descended from the Fleurnoys, Huguenots, a prominent family. She is a resident of Louisville, Ky., and has been a social leader in the society of the South and Southwest for many years. She is distinguished for her beauty of person, her charm of manners and her cultured intellect. Mrs. Downs has been married four times. She has traveled extensively in Europe, and was presented at various courts, and everywhere was admired for her graces of mind and person. She is a thoroughly educated woman, speaks French fluently and is a fine musician. In religion she is a Roman Catholic, a convert to that faith. She has one child, a son, John Hunt, of New York, who has won a reputation as a journalist. She is noted as a letter writer, and she has contributed to eastern journals. She is, despite her social prestige, a woman of democratic instincts. Her charities are numerous, large and entirely unostentatious. She has a fine and valuable collection of treasures, historical and religious, gathered from all parts of the world. Her husband, Major G. F. Downs, is a man of wealth, intellect and culture. They make their home in the Galt House, in Louisville, Ky.

DRAKE, Mrs. Mary Eveline, minister of the gospel and church worker, born in Trenton, Oneida county, N. Y., 8th June, 1833. Her maiden name was Mary E. McArthur. Her father was of Scotch parentage, and her mother was English, a relative of Lady Gurney, better known as the celebrated Elizabeth Fry. From her parents she inherited that strong religious bent of character that has distinguished her life. When about six years of age, she removed with her parents to southern Michigan, where she received most of her common school and academic education. From there the family removed to the town of Geneseo, Ill., where she spent her early married life, residing there most of the time for over twenty years. She joined her mother's church, the Congregational, and began that course of earnest personal effort for the con-

MARY EVELINE DRAKE.

version of others for which her nature peculiarly fitted her and in which she has been so successful. In addition to her work in prayer-meeting, Sunday-school and young people's Bible-classes, she was frequently called to assist evangelists by visiting and in revival meetings. During all that time she was active in all the various reforms and benevolences of the time. In war time she was especially active in the Women's Soldiers' Aid Society, going south as far as Memphis, and looking to the right distribution of the provisions sent to the hospitals there, and she was one of the leaders in the women's temperance crusade. She had the added care of her family, which she supported most of the time by the labor of her own hands. The natural result of such constant labors came in a severe attack of nervous prostration, which totally ended her work for a season. To secure full restoration, she went to reside for a time with her only

living son, Gen. M. M. Marshall, then a railroad official in western Iowa. There she became the wife of Rev. A. J. Drake, of Dakota. A very few weeks of the bracing air of Dakota sufficed to restore her to perfect health and strength. She entered with her husband into the home missionary work, for which, by her zeal and his long experience, they were so well adapted. Mr. Drake was then laboring in Iroquois, a village at the junction of two railroads, where he had a small church of eight members worshiping in a schoolhouse. Though living for the first two years at DeSmet, sixteen miles away, they soon had other preaching stations and Sunday-schools in hand and preparations made for building a church in Iroquois. Mrs. Drake went east as far as Chicago and raised sufficient means to buy the lumber and push forward the work. Encouraged by her success, she was readily urged by her husband to take part in the public services, addressing Sunday-schools, till she came very naturally to choose a subject or text and practically to preach the gospel. The wide extent of their field and the constant need of dividing their labors tended strongly to this. A very much needed rest and the kindness of an eastern friend enabled them to attend the anniversary of the American Home Missionary Society in Saratoga. On the way, by special invitation, she addressed the Woman's Home Missionary Union of Illinois in Moline. Being heard in that meeting by Dr. Clark, of the American Home Missionary Society, on arrival at Saratoga she was called to address the great congregation assembled there. She has since spoken in many of the large cities and churches of New England and other States. The result of these visits has been the raising of means sufficient, with what people on the ground could give, to build two other large churches in Esmond and Osceola, S. Dak. She and her husband are caring for a field forty-five miles in length and fifteen miles in breadth, with five churches and Sunday-schools. They also publish a monthly paper, entitled the "Dakota Prairie Pioneer." At the earnest request of the leading ministers in the State she consented to ordination and the largest Congregational council ever assembled in South Dakota ordained her to the work of the ministry in December, 1890. That was one of the first ordinations of a woman to the ministry west of the Mississippi.

DRAKE, Mrs. Priscilla Holmes, woman suffragist, born in Ithaca, N. Y., 18th June, 1812. She is the youngest child of Judge Samuel Buell and Joanna Sturdevant, both of Cayuga county, N. Y. Judge Buell was a man of much intellectual vigor and marked attainments. He held several important offices in his State, and as senator served more than one term with De Witt Clinton, Martin Van Buren and others of distinction. Judge Buell removed with his family from New York to Marietta, Ohio, where he was held in great esteem. In the year 1831 his daughter became the wife of James P. Drake, a native of North Carolina, at Lawrenceburg, Ind. He had held office under President Monroe and was then receiver of public moneys in Indianapolis, Ind., appointed by President Jackson. While a resident of Posey county, he had been brought into intimate business and social relations with the New Harmony Community, under the Rapps, father and son, and when their possessions were transferred to the Scotch philanthropist, Robert Owen, he naturally held the same relations with the Owen association. Those two communities, although striving in different ways to benefit humanity, had much to do with broadening his views and making his after-life tolerant and charitable, and probably had an influence in developing his young wife's interest in the laws relating to women. Their home was the center of happiness and progress, and it was only widening the circle of early associations to find therein a hearty welcome for David, Richard and Robert Dale Owen, the distinguished sons of Robert Owen. Colonel and Mrs. Drake worked with Robert Dale Owen during the Indiana Constitutional Convention of 1850 and 1851 to remove the legal disabilities of women. Before the sections were presented, which worked such benefit to women, they were discussed, line by line, in Mrs. Drake's parlor. She had an acute legal mind, and Mr. Owen was not slow to recognize her valuable aid in the construction of the important clauses. It was she who suggested a memorial to Robert Dale Owen from the many noble mothers who comprehended the scope of his work for women. When Lucy Stone delivered her first lecture in Indianapolis, Mrs. Drake was the only woman in attendance. She was also present at a notable meeting, shortly afterward, where Lucretia Mott presided. The acquaintance thus formed led to an interesting correspondence. Mrs. Drake was in possession of many valuable letters from distinguished men and women, addressed to herself and husband. In 1861 they removed to Alabama, near Huntsville, where they continued their interest and work in the cause of woman's suffrage. Mrs. Drake was left a widow in 1876 and died at her residence, 11th February, 1892. She was the mother of seven children, four of whom

CHRISTINE NIELSON DREIER.

PRISCILLA HOLMES DRAKE.

survive her and by inheritance and education are earnest supporters of the woman suffrage cause.

DREIER, Mrs. Christine Nielson, concert and oratorio singer, born in Madison, Wis., 10th June, 1866. Her father's name is Andrew Nielson, and both parents were among the early Scandinavian immigrants to this country and settled in Chicago in 1851, afterward removing to Madison. Christine Nielson still retains her maiden name on the stage, although she became the wife, 4th June, 1891, of Otto Albert Dreier, since 1886 the Danish Vice-Consul in Chicago, where they make their home. The career of Christine Nielson thus far is a striking example of what energy and perseverance can do for a young woman of genius. Her first teacher, and the one to discover her capabilities, was Prof. T. A. Brand. She then studied with Mrs. Earl De Moe, herself a successful concert singer. Christine began to sing in public at the age of thirteen, attracting, at an orphan's home concert in Madison, the attention of those whose foresight discovered future fame for the young vocalist. She chose Chicago for her more advanced studies, and became the pupil of Mrs. Sara Hershey Eddy. She accompanied Mr. and Mrs. Eddy to Europe in 1889, and after singing with great success in London, Paris and Copenhagen, she spent a year or more in London as a pupil of George Henschel. Her voice is a contralto of wide range, and the comments of the American and foreign press have been highly complimentary, showing her to be possessed of unusual musical accomplishments.

DREW, Mrs. John, actor, born in London, England, 10th January, 1820. Her maiden name was Lane. Her father was an actor, and he placed the child on the stage in juvenile parts when she was eight years old In 1828 she came to the United States with her mother and played in New York and Philadelphia. She made a tour of the West Indies and returned to the United States in 1832. In 1833 she played in a number of rôles in New York theaters. In 1834 she played the part of Julia in "The Hunchback" in the Boston Theater. In 1835, when fifteen years old, she played Lady Teazle in "The School for Scandal" in New Orleans. She won success from the beginning and was soon "leading lady" at a salary of twenty dollars a week. She became the wife of Henry Hunt, a veteran English opera singer, and from 1842 to 1846 she played at intervals in stock companies in New York theaters, in burlesques, light comedies and domestic dramas. In 1847 she went to Chicago, Milwaukee, St. Louis, Mobile

MRS. JOHN DREW.

and New Orleans, playing always to good houses and increasing her reputation as a comedian. In 1848 she separated from Mr. Hunt and became the wife of George Mossop, a young Irish comedian of fine powers. He died in 1849, and in 1850 she became the wife of John Drew. In 1857 Mr. and Mrs. Drew made a successful tour of the United States. In 1861 Mrs. Drew assumed the sole management of the Arch-street Theater in Philadelphia, Pa , which has since remained under her control. Mrs. Drew makes her home in Philadelphia. During the past few years she has played with Joseph Jefferson and William J. Florence. She has a large family of children, most of whom are connected with the stage. Although seventy-two years of age, Mrs. Drew retains the cheerful vivacity of her earlier years, and she is very popular with theater-goers. She excels in high-comedy parts.

DU BOSE, Mrs. Miriam Howard, woman suffragist, born in Russell county, Ala., 28th November, 1862. She is a daughter of Ann Lindsay and Augustus Howard. Though born in Alabama, her life has been spent in and near Columbus, Ga. At an early age she showed marked musical talent, playing simple melodies before she was tall enough to mount the piano stool unassisted. At fourteen years of age she began the study of music under a teacher in Columbus, and studied there about two years, which was the only instruction she received. At seventeen she applied for the organist's place in the First Presbyterian Church of Columbus, and held the position until her marriage. She was at that time the youngest organist in the State. She has composed several pieces of instrumental music. Her first piece " Rural Polka," was composed at

the age of fifteen. She performs on the piano with brilliancy. Gifted in sketching, she has done some life-like work in that line. For the last three years, having been aroused to the work of woman's enfranchisement, she has worked for woman suffrage with heart, pen and purse. Her articles in its interest are earnest and convincing. She is vice-president of the Georgia Woman Suffrage Association, and her busy brain and fingers have originated many schemes to fill the treasury of that organization. It was her generosity which made it possible for Georgia to send her first delegates to the twenty-fourth convention of the National American Woman Suffrage Association, held in Washington in January, 1892. The money donated was earned by her own hands. She has one son. Her home is in Greenville, Ga.

DUDLEY, Mrs. Sarah Marie, business woman, born in Carlton, Barry county, Mich. She is the youngest daughter of James T. and Catherine Lawhead, who went to Michigan, in the first years of their married life, from the State of New York, and settled in Carlton. She is of Scotch ancestry on her father's side, and pure American on that of her mother, back to and beyond the war for independence. At the early age of four years she was left an orphan and was adopted into the family of her uncle, Judge William McCauley, of Brighton, Mich., who was at the time State Senator from that district. She received her education in the private and public schools of Brighton. At the age of fifteen she became the wife of Thomas Robert Dudley, from county of Kent, England, and moved to Detroit, Mich., where, in 1876, her husband entered the mercantile business, in which he prospered so well that he retired from

MIRIAM HOWARD DU BOSE.

business, in 1889, with a competence. Mrs. Dudley has been successful in many ways. She proved herself a most excellent business woman. It was she who saw the business opening where her husband's fortune was made, and she has by judicious investments made another for herself. She works in pastel with the taste of a born artist. She is also an inventor, and the United States Patent Office

SARAH MARIE DUDLEY.

holds proof of her ingenuity. But it is as an architect, designer and builder she has won her greatest success. Buying land in what proved one of the best locations in Detroit, she designed and built a graceful group of residences, among which is one of the most palatial stone mansions in the city. She took all the responsibility of planning, building and furnishing the money, and is the proud possessor of a handsome income from the rentals. She does much charitable work in an unostentatious way.

DUFOUR, Mrs. Amanda Louise Ruter, poet, born in Jeffersonville, Ind., 26th February, 1822. She is the oldest daughter of Rev. Calvin W. Ruter, a pioneer Indiana preacher, and his wife, Harriet De Haas Ruter. Mr. Ruter was of Vermont and Puritan ancestry, and Mrs. Ruter of Virginia and Huguenot ancestry. Both were persons of marked character. Mr. Ruter was stationed in Jeffersonville when Louise was born. In her childhood school privileges were limited, and with her naturally delicate organization and the burden of household duties which devolved upon her as the oldest of five children, her attendance at school was often irregular. She was fond of books and had free access to her father's limited library. In 1842 she became the wife of Oliver Dufour, a descendant of an illustrious Swiss family, who immigrated to the United States early in the century. Mr. Dufour was elected to the Indiana Legislature in 1853, and in the same year received an appointment to a government position in Washington, to which place he removed with his family. He was a prominent member of the Independent Order of Odd Fellows, having been Grand Master of the State of Indiana, Grand Representative from that

State and also from the District of Columbia for eight consecutive years. He died in November, 1891. Mrs. Dufour composed verses when too young to wield a pen, or even to read. Her peculiarly sensitive temperament long kept her talents from being appreciated. Having no confidence in her own abilities, she shrank from criticism. She is fond of writing for children, and has published many poems adapted to their comprehension. In 1848 Hon. Joseph A. Wright, then governor of the State, sent from Indiana, for the Washington monument, a block of marble, on which was inscribed the motto: "No North, No South, Nothing but the Union." This incident suggested to Mrs. Dufour her poem entitled "The Ark of the Union." It was first published in the Washington "Union," and was afterward, without her knowledge, set to music. Some months before the death of the scientist, Baron Von Humboldt, Mrs. Dufour wrote a a poem on his distinction as "King of Science." An American in Berlin read the poem to the great man, who was then upon his death-bed, and it so pleased the Baron that he sent Mrs. Dufour the following message: "Tell that talented American lady, Mrs. Dufour, that I deem that poem the highest compliment that was ever paid to me by any person or from any clime." She has contributed to the "Ladies' Repository," the "Masonic Review," the "School Day Visitor," the "Republican," of Springfield, Ohio, the Louisville "Journal," whose editor was the talented author and

AMANDA LOUISE RUTER DUFOUR.

poet, George D. Prentice, and the Louisville "Democrat."

DUNHAM, Mrs. Emma Bedelia, poet, born in Minot, now Auburn, Me., 31st August, 1826. She was the fourth child in the family of Capt. Joseph Smith Sargent and Ann Hoyt Sargent. She attended the district school, but it may be questioned whether she gained as much education within its walls as without. She moved with her parents to the city of Portland, Me., at the age of nine years. There she attended public and private schools and had the benefit of private teachers, and grew into the mature poet, story-writer and teacher.

EMMA BEDELIA DUNHAM.

Her school education was finished in Westbrook Seminary. She now has a beautiful home in Deering, Me. Her library and collection of natural curiosities, the latter begun when she was about eleven years old, are used, like all her possessions, for doing good. She became the wife of Rufus Dunham, of Westbrook, now Deering, 25th August, 1845. She is the mother of three sons and two daughters. Four other children died young. She is still an enthusiastic writer and teacher. Children go to her school for the pleasure as well as instruction to be had there. Mrs. Dunham has had much influence, as a Christian, in the community in which she lives. At her suggestion, the Universalist Church, All Souls, was organized in 1881, she becoming one of the original members. She began to write when very young, and she fled from the shelter of one pen-name to that of another, dreading to have the public know her as an author, until, after years of success, she gained courage to use her own name. Her writings consist largely of poetry, but include also sketches on natural history, essays, letters of travel and stories for children. Some of her songs have been set to music. "Margaret, a Home Opera in Six Acts," is one of the best of her poetic productions. It was brought out in 1875. Mrs. Dunham is a typical New England woman, who, in spite of her more than three-score years, is still young, enthusiastic and hopeful.

DUNHAM, Mrs. Marion Howard, born in Geauga county, Ohio, 6th December, 1842, passed the first part of her life upon a farm. She early decided to be a teacher, beginning her first district school at the age of fifteen, and taught in the public schools of Chicago, Ill., from 1866 to 1873. In July, 1873, she became the wife of C. A. Dunham,

an architect, of Burlington, Iowa, where they now live. In 1877 she entered upon temperance work with the inauguration of the red-ribbon movement, but, believing in more permanent methods, she was the prime mover in the organization of the local Woman's Christian Temperance Union, and has ever since been an active worker in that society. In 1883 she was elected State superintendent of the department of scientific temperance, and held the office four years, lecturing to institutes and general audiences on that subject much of the time. She procured the Iowa State law on that subject in February, 1886. When the Iowa State Temperance Union began to display its opposition to the National Union, she was rather slow to declare her position, which was always fully with the National, but she was soon forced to declare herself, and came to be considered rather a leader on the side of the minority. When the majority in the State Union seceded from the National Union, 16th October, 1890, she was elected president of those who remained auxiliary to that body. At the State convention in 1891 she was re-elected. She has spent a large part of her time in the field. She has always been a radical equal suffragist, and has spoken and written much on that subject. She is a Christian socialist, deeply interested in all reforms that promise to better the

MARION HOWARD DUNHAM.

social system and the conditions of life for the multitudes.

DUNIWAY, Mrs. Abigail Scott, editor, born in Pleasant Grove, Tazewell county, Ill., 22nd October, 1834. There she grew to girlhood. Her father removed to Oregon in 1852. Of a family noted for sturdy independence in word and deed, it is not strange that these inherent qualities, united with keen mental powers, have made her one of the most widely known women on the Pacific slope. She began her public career many years ago through necessity, an invalid husband and a large family leaving her no alternative. Nobly has she fulfilled the double trust of wife and mother. While Mrs. Duniway has been engaged in every sort of reputable literary toil, her life-work has been in the

ABIGAIL SCOTT DUNIWAY.

direction of the enfranchisement of women. While advocating woman suffrage she has undoubtedly traveled more miles by stage, rail, river and wagon, made more public speeches, endured more hardships, persecution and ridicule, and scored more victories than any of her distinguished cotemporaries of the East and middle West. The enfranchisement of the women of Washington Territory was the result of her efforts, and, had they listened to her counsel and kept aloof from the Prohibition fight of 1886, they would not have lost afterwards, when the Territory became a State, the heritage of the ballot which she had secured for them at the cost of the best years of her life. As an extemporaneous speaker she is logical, sarcastic, witty, poetic and often eloquent. As a writer she is forceful and argumentative. Mrs. Duniway now fills the editorial chair of the "Pacific Empire," a new literary and progressive monthly magazine published in Portland, Ore., where she resides in a spacious home, the product of her own genius and industry.

DUNLAP, Miss Mary J., physician, born in Philadelphia, Pa., in 1853. Dr. Dunlap is superintendent and physician in charge of the New Jersey State Institution for Feeble Minded Women. When a mature young woman, of practical education, with sound and healthy views of life, she made choice of the profession of medicine, not through any romantic aspirations after "a vocation in life," but as a vocation to which she proposed to devote all her energies. One year of preparatory reading preceded the regular college course of three years. Having been regularly graduated from the Woman's Medical College of Pennsylvania in 1886, an office was secured in Philadelphia, and it was not long before the young doctor found her hands full. In

a few months she was induced to make arrangements with Dr. Joseph Parrish, which made her his assistant in the treatment of nervous invalids in Burlington, N. J. This special training prepared her for her present responsible position. Dr. Dunlap's position in New Jersey is similar to that of Dr. Alice Bennett in Pennsylvania, being superintendent and physician in charge, with all the duties that the term implies. These two women furnish the only instances, at the present date, where women have full control of the medical department of institution work in connection with the superintendency.

DURGIN, Miss Harriet Thayer, artist, born in the town of Wilmington, Mass., in 1848. She is the daughter of Rev. J. M. Durgin. Sprung from families who, leaving their homes for conscience's sake, sought New England's shores, and whose lives were freely given when they were needed in their country's defense, her father was a man of dauntless courage and remarkable intellectual power. He was of the Baptist faith and a man of broad and liberal sentiments. An enthusiast in the anti-slavery movement, he entered the army in the late war and left behind him a brilliant military record. The mother, a woman of exalted character, fine intellect and lovely disposition, united two good New England names, as she was of the Braintree-Thayer family. One of a family of five children, Miss Durgin's youth was surrounded by those gentle and refining influences which are the lot of those born into the environment of a clergyman's household. She pursued her preparatory studies of life, not only in the training schools of those towns where her father's profession called him, but in a home where every influence was

HARRIET THAYER DURGIN.

directed toward the upbuilding of a rich and well rounded character. She passed the concluding years of study in the New Hampton Institute, in New Hampshire. When it became necessary for

Miss Durgin to assume the duties and responsibilities of life on her own account, she chose teaching as a stepping-stone to the realization of her dream, an art education. Finally the way opened to enter upon her favorite field of study, and in 1880 she joined her sister Lyle in Paris, France, where she entered the studio of Mme. de Cool, and later that of Francois Rivoire, where daily lessons were taken. Having in company with her sister established a little home, she found many famous artists who were glad to visit the cosy salon and give careful and valuable criticism. After seven years of study Miss Durgin returned to Boston, where she had many friends, and in company with her sister opened a studio in the most fashionable quarter of the city. Their rooms were soon frequented on reception days by admirers and lovers of art, and commissions have never been wanting to keep their brushes constantly employed. As a flower painter she stands among the foremost of American artists. A panel of tea-roses received special notice in the salon of 1886, and a group combining flowers and landscape in 1890 won much notice.

DURGIN, Miss Lyle, artist, was born in Wilmington, Mass., in 1850. A sister of Harriet Thayer Durgin, she grew up as one with her, so far

LYLE DURGIN,

as environment and teaching were concerned. They drew the same life and inspiration from their home surroundings and studied in the same schools, and when their education was completed found themselves with the same inclination toward art. Lyle went to Paris in 1879 and became a pupil of Bonnat and Bastien Lepage. Later she entered the Julien Academy for more serious study in drawing, working enthusiastically, early and late, both in the school and in her own studio, supplementing her studio work by anatomical studies at the École de Médicine under M. Chicotôt. In summer time the sisters sketched in England, Switzerland and

France, drawing fresh inspiration from nature and travel and taking home collections of sketches for their winter's work. Lyle chose figure painting in oil and portraiture as her special department of art. So earnestly did she study from 1879 to 1884 that the Salon received her paintings in the latter-named year, and again two years later, when she offered a painting of beauty, which won for her recognition as an artist of power. In 1886 the Misses Durgin returned to America and opened a studio in Boston. Welcomed to the best society, in which they naturally found a home, the sisters began work, each in her own field of art. The first picture exhibited by Lyle in Boston was a portrait of a lady. Then followed in rapid succession one of Henry Sandham, a celebrated artist of Boston, and many others of persons of more or less distinction in the social and literary world. Receiving a commission for mural paintings for a church in Detroit, Mich., she started early in 1890 for a prolonged course of travel in Italy, finally settling in Paris for the execution of those great original works, which were completed and placed in the church in December, 1891. They represent the four Evangelists and are of heroic size, filling the four compartments of the dome-shaped interior. They are painted after the manner of the middle time of the Venetian school, corresponding to the Byzantine character of the edifice. Although the ecclesiastical traditions of saints and church fathers allow of but little variation, her works are characterized by freshness, originality and strength unusual to find at the present day, and are worthy of more interest from the fact that this is a branch of painting which hitherto has been almost exclusively in the hands of men.

DURLEY, Mrs. Ella Hamilton, educator and journalist, was born in Butler county, Pa. She is the oldest daughter of Mr. and Mrs. William Hamilton. In the spring of 1866 the family removed to Davis county, Iowa, where, in the most unpromising backwoods region, they made their home for a few years. It was in the rude log schoolhouse of that locality that the young girl acquired sufficient knowledge of the rudimentary branches to permit her to begin to teach at the age of sixteen. The loss of her father, whose ambition for his children was limitless, led her to make the attempt to carry out his oft-expressed wish that she should take a college course. To do so meant hard work and strenuous application, for every penny of the necessary expense had to be earned by herself. In the spring of 1878 she took the degree of B.A. in the State University of Iowa, and four years later she received the degree of M.A. After graduation Miss Hamilton accepted the principalship of the high school in Waterloo, Iowa, which she held for two years. She then went abroad to continue her studies, more especially in the German language and literature. She spent a year in European travel and study, features of which were the attendance upon a course of lectures in the Victoria Lyceum of Berlin, and an inspection of the school system of Germany and Italy. Upon her return the result of her observation was given to the public in the form of a lecture, which was widely delivered and well received. After a year spent in the Iowa State Library, Miss Hamilton decided to turn her attention to newspaper work. She became associate editor of the Des Moines "Mail and Times," which position she held over a year, when a tempting offer caused her to become editor-in-chief of the "Northwestern Journal of Education," where her success was very gratifying. Her later journalistic work has been in connection with the Des Moines "Daily News," upon which she served as reporter and editorial and special writer for several years. In 1884 Miss Hamilton was appointed a member of the State Education Board of Examiners for Iowa, which position she held until 1888, serving during the most of her time as secretary. In October, 1886, she became the wife of Preston B. Durley, business manager of the Des Moines "Daily News." Mrs. Durley's newspaper work was kept up uninterruptedly until the summer of 1890, when their home was gladdened by the birth of a son. At the present time she is president of the Des Moines Woman's Club, a large and prosperous literary society.

DURRELL, Mrs. Irene Clark, educator, born in Plymouth, N. H., 17th May, 1852. Her father, Hiram Clark, is a man of steadfast evangelical faith. Her mother was an exemplary Christian. Until twelve years of age, her advantages were limited to ungraded country schools. She was a pupil for a time in the village grammar-school and in the Plymouth Academy. Taking private lessons of her pastor in Latin and sciences, and studying by herself, she prepared to enter the State Normal School in Plymouth, where she completed the first course in 1872 and the second in 1873, teaching during summer vacations. In 1873 and 1874 she taught the grammar-school in West Lebanon, N. H. In the fall of 1874 she became the teacher of the normal department in the New Hampshire Conference Seminary, and a student in the junior year in the classical course. She was graduated in 1876. She then taught in the State Normal School in Castleton, Vt. On 23rd July, 1878 she became the wife of Rev. J. M. Durrell, D.D. As a Methodist minister's wife, in New Hampshire Conference, for thirteen years Mrs. Dur-

IRENE CLARK DURRELL.

organizer. For four years she was district secretary and was a delegate from the New England branch to the Evanston general executive committee meeting. With her husband, in 1882, she took an extended tour abroad. In the spring of 1891 her husband became president of the New Hampshire Conference Seminary and Female College, Tilton, N. H., and Mrs. Durrell became the preceptress of that institution.

DUSSUCHAL, Miss Eugenie, musical educator, born in St. Louis, Mo., 29th October, 1860. She

EUGENIE DUSSUCHAL.

is of French parents, and, with the exception of a short course of study in New York, received her school and musical education in her native city. Her father died when she was but four years of age, leaving herself and an older sister to be brought up by her mother, who was left in moderate circumstances. Eugenie showed her musical talent at an early age. The French citizens of St. Louis honored her by presenting her a gold medal after she sang the anthem "La Marseillaise," at the French Fête of 1890. She has a rich contralto voice, which has kept her in church positions and before the public since her fourteenth year. For a short time she traveled with an opera company and was most successful, but her family objected to her adopting the stage as a profession, and she returned to St. Louis. She was appointed public school music supervisor in the fall of 1890, a position that until then had been filled by men only.

DWYER, Miss Bessie Agnes, journalist, was born in Texas. She is the daughter of the late Judge Thomas A. and Annie C. Dwyer, of English descent. Miss Dwyer comes of a family renowned at home and abroad for uncommon gifts. Judge Dwyer left his native heath in youth, and his life became part and parcel of the early history of Texas and the Rio Bravo. Six children blessed his home, and upon the youngest daughter, Bessie, alone fell the mantle of his literary powers and

rell has had marked success in leading young ladies into an active Christian life and interesting them in behalf of others. As an officer in the Woman's Foreign Missionary Society she has been an efficient

histrionic ability. As a child she dominated amateur circles in Texas as an acknowledged star, and she played a wide range of characters. Death abruptly removed Judge Dwyer, and his daughter

BESSIE AGNES DWYER.

found herself alone on the threshold of womanhood, minus a practical education and heir to naught but her father's mental gifts. The War of of the Rebellion and other reverses dissipated a once generous fortune, and actual necessity faced the bereaved family. Casting to the winds the prejudices existing in the South against female occupation beyond the portals of home, Miss Dwyer accepted a position in the post-office department and held it six years. During that time vagrant poems and sketches from her pen were published. Waning strength necessitated change and rest, and in 1868 she resigned her position and visited her married sister at a remote army post in Arizona and later in New Mexico. Three years of rest restored her health, and she returned to civilization and entered journalism. Her sketches of army life and vivid word painting of scenes in two Territories and Old Mexico won notice at once. Her most remarkable works are two stories published in the Galveston "News," "Mr. Moore of Albuquerque" and "A Daughter of Eve." Miss Dwyer at present fills a position on the staff of the "National Economist," Washington, D. C. She is a correspondent for some of the prominent southern journals. Her home is in San Antonio, Tex.

DYE, Mrs. Mary Irene Clark, reformer, born in North Hadley, Mass., 22nd March, 1837. Her parents were Philo Clark and Irene Hibbard. Her father moved his family to Wisconsin in Mary's infancy. When she was ten years of age, the family removed to Waukegan, Ill. After removal to Illinois, she was under private tutors for two years, when she entered an academy. When she was sixteen years old, there came severe financial reverses, forcing her to abandon a plan for a full course in

Mount Holyoke, Mass. At that time, persuaded by a brother in charge of the village telegraph office, Mary learned telegraphy and assumed his place, having full care of the office for two years. There were but few women operators at that early day. Mrs. Dye is the only woman member of the Old Time Telegraphers' Association. She became the wife of Byron E. Dye in 1855. Of three children born to them, two survive, a daughter, and a son recently admitted to the bar. Mrs. Dye has been a widow many years and has lived in Chicago, Ill., entering into the various lines of work which the conditions of a large city present to a benevolent and public-spirited woman. Since her children have outgrown her immediate care and concern, she has devoted her time almost exclusively to philanthropic and reformatory work. She was among the first to perceive the need of the Protective Agency for Women and Children, assisting in its establishment in 1886 and serving as secretary for the first three years, and is still an active member of its board of managers. As a charter member of the Illinois Woman's Press Association, she has great satisfaction in the work accomplished for penwomen through its efforts. She is a member of the Chicago Women's Club. With the Margaret Fuller Society, established for the study of political problems, Mrs. Dye did good work. Since the formation of the Moral Educational Society, in 1882, she has been its secretary. She was among the first of the Woman's Christian Temperance Union women to see and teach that the ballot power is an essential factor in the furtherance of temperance work. When the free kindergarten system was inaugurated, Mrs. Dye's pen did good service in the interest of that charity. The placing of matrons in

MARY IRENE CLARK DYE.

police stations enlisted her sympathy, and her efforts contributed much to the granting of the demand. Her persistent work toward the establishment of the summer Saturday half-holiday is known to only two or three persons, and the same is true of that labor of love, extending over many months, creating a public sentiment that demanded seats for the shop-girls when not busy with customers. Mrs. Dye believes in individual work so far as practicable. In impromptu speeches she is fluent and forcible, and on topics connected with social purity, the obligations of marriage and parenthood she is impressively eloquent. As a speaker and writer on reform subjects she is dauntless in demanding a settlement of all questions on the platform of right and justice, manifesting the "no surrender" spirit of her ancestral relative, Ethan Allen. Religious as she is reformatory in her nature, Mrs. Dye seeks the highest estimate given to spiritual things.

DYER, Mrs. Clara L. Brown, artist, born in Cape Elizabeth, Maine, 13th March, 1849. Her father was a popular sea captain. On many of his voyages he was accompanied by his daughter, then only a child. From her mother's family she inherited artistic talent. Several of her uncles were wood-carvers and excelled in decorative work. In December, 1870, she became the wife of Charles A. Dyer, then a successful business man of Portland, Maine, now engaged in gold-mining in California. Her family consisted of a son and a daughter. The son survives, but the daughter died in childhood. Mrs. Dyer turned her attention to art and became very much interested, and her talent, so many years hidden, came to light. She soon became the most enthusiastic and persevering of students. She took a thorough course in an art school, under able instructors, drawing from the antique and from life. She has paid considerable attention to portrait painting. In landscape painting she is seen at her best. She has made many fine sketches of the

and have been highly spoken of by critics, as well as the general public.

DYER, Mrs. Julia Knowlton, philanthropist, born in Deerfield, N. H., in 1829. Her father

JULIA KNOWLTON DYER.

was Joseph Knowlton, and her mother Susan Dearborn. Upon Bunker Hill Monument are inscribed the names of her mother's grandfather, Nathaniel Dearborn, and of her own grandfather, Thomas Knowlton. Julia Knowlton was one of six children. Her father served in the war of 1812, and his namesake, her brother, Joseph H. Knowlton, was a member of the secret expedition against Fort Beaufort, in the Civil War. After graduation in her eighteenth year, Miss Knowlton taught a year in the high school in Manchester, N. H., where she was a successful instructor in French and English literature and higher mathematics. She became the wife, in her twenty-first year, of Micah Dyer, jr., now a lawyer of Boston. Three children were born to them, two sons and a daughter, the latter dying in infancy. The two sons still live, Dr. William K. Dyer, of Boston, and Walter Dyer. Mrs. Dyer is connected prominently with twenty-four associations, only one of which, the Castilian Club, is purely literary. She is president of the Soldiers' Home in Massachusetts, president and founder of the Charity Club, a member of the executive boards of the Home for Intemperate Women, the Helping Hand Association, and president of the local branch of the Woman's Christian Temperance Union. For twenty-six years she has been a manager for the Home for Female Prisoners in Dedham, Mass., and is a life member of the Bostonian Society. The association appoints a board of twenty-four women, two of whom visit the Soldiers's Home each month to look after the needs of the inmates. She is a member of the Methodist Church, but she attends regularly the services of her husband's choice, in the Church of the Unity, Boston, without comment, but without

CLARA L. BROWN DYER.

scenery about Casco Bay, and she has added to her collection some excellent sketches of mountain and inland scenery. Some of her studies have been exhibited in Boston, Portland and other cities,

affecting her own faith in the slightest. Mrs. Dyer is so engaged in philanthropic work that she hardly thinks of herself as being a leader.

EAGLE, Mrs. Mary Kavanaugh, church worker and social leader, born in Madison county,

MARY KAVANAUGH EAGLE.

Ky., 4th February, 1854. She is the daughter of William K. Oldham and J. Kate Brown. Her father is the son of Kie Oldham and Polly Kavanaugh and a native and resident of Madison county. He is of English descent on his paternal and Irish on his maternal side. Both his father's and mother's families were early settlers of central Kentucky, and were among the most successful farmers and stock-dealers in that section. That vocation he also followed with marked success for many years. Her mother, who died 11th July, 1880, was the daughter of Ira Brown and Frances Mullens, of Albemarle county, Va., and of Scotch-English extraction. Mrs. Eagle's early education was conducted mainly at home, under the watchful care of her mother, who selected the best of tutors and governesses for her three daughters. She was graduated in June, 1872, from Mrs. Julia A. Tevis's famous school, Science Hill, Shelbyville, Ky. She united with the Viny Fork Missionary Baptist Church of Madison county, Ky., in August, 1874, and has been a zealous church worker ever since. She became the wife of Governor Eagle 3rd January, 1882, and moved to his large cotton plantation in Lonoke county, Ark., where he was engaged in farming. Governor Eagle being a devoted church man and a member of the same denomination, they soon united their efforts in upbuilding the interests of their church for home and foreign missions and for Christian and charitable work of various kinds, contributing liberally of their ample means to support those objects. Governor Eagle has stood at the head of his church work for many years, and Mrs. Eagle has been the leader of the woman's work of her denomination in her State for

more than eight years. She has been president of the Woman's Central Committee on Missions since its organization in November, 1882, and is president of the Woman's Mission Union of Arkansas. Mrs. Eagle is her husband's most congenial companion and valued counselor, whether he is employing his time as a farmer, a churchman or a statesman. Their interests have ever been identical. In his political aspirations she has rendered him great assistance. She accompanied him in his canvass for the nomination for the office of governor in 1888. She accompanied him in his canvass with the representative of the Republican Union Labor Party, which immediately followed, and also in his canvasss for re-election in 1890. Governor Eagle has entered upon his second term as governor, and since his inauguration the mansion has been famous for true southern hospitality. Governor Eagle has for many years been president of the Baptist State Convention and was speaker of the House of Representatives in 1885. This caused Mrs. Eagle to take an interest in parliamentary practice and to take up that study. She is now one of the best parliamentarians in the State and takes great interest in the proceedings of all deliberative bodies. As a member of the Board of Lady Managers of the Columbian Exposition she was appointed a member of many important committees.

EAMES, Emma Hayden, operatic singer, known in private life as Mrs. Julian Story, born in 1867, in China, where her father held a diplomatic post. Her parents were natives of Maine and residents of Boston, Mass., where her father practiced law before going into the service of the government in Shanghai, China, where Emma was born. After the family returned to Boston, Emma began

EMMA HAYDEN EAMES.

to study music under the tuition of her mother, who was a cultivated singer. After a thorough grounding in the preliminaries, Emma went to Paris, France, to study with Madame Marchesi. In 1888 she made her début in the Grand Opéra in Paris, after waiting in vain for a chance to appear under a contract for one year made with the Opéra Comique. She secured a cancellation of the contract with the Comique and prepared to sing in "Romeo et Juliette" in the Grand Opéra. Madame Patti sang in the title rôle twelve times, and then Emma Eames succeeded her. Following directly after the most famous singer of the age, Miss Eames won a brilliant triumph on her début, and at once was ranked by the French critics as one of the greatest singers and actors of the day. Her répertoire includes Juliette, Marguerite, Desdemona, Santuzza, Elsa, and other famous rôles, and in each of them her success has been marked. After her father's death her talents enabled her to maintain the fortunes of her family. She was married, 29th July, 1891, to Julian Story, in London, England. She is regard in Paris and London as one of the greatest singers of the age. Her latest triumph was won in the opera "Ascanio."

EAST, Mrs. Edward H., philanthropist, born in Bethesda, Williamson county, Tenn., 15th March,

MRS. EDWARD H. EAST.

1849. Her father, Rev. H. C. Horton, was a Virginian, her mother, Elizabeth Elliotte Kennedy, was a South Carolinian. Her grand parents came from England and Ireland and could boast a coat-of-arms on both sides of the house, but strong republican sentiments forbade a display of them. She came of Revolutionary stock. Lieutenant Kennedy fought under Gen. Francis Marion and was rewarded for bravery, having on one occasion, with only himself and one other, put to rout twelve Tories. Her father moved to Mississippi, where her girlhood was spent. She was educated in the Marshall Female Institue, under the management of Pres. Joseph E. Douglas. As a young lady she was popular with old and young. When the Mississippi & Tennessee R. R. was being built through Mississippi, the work had to stop for want

of means when the road had been extended only fifty or sixty miles. A plan was suggested to get the men of the county together to raise a fund. A May Queen feast and a barbecue in the woods were chosen. The dark-eyed, rosy-cheeked little maiden, Tennie Horton, as she was called, only fourteen years old, was chosen queen, and she on that occasion made a railroad speech that brought thousands of dollars out of the pockets of that then wealthy people. She became the wife, when very young, of D. C. Ward, a merchant, who was killed in the war. During the war she was the only protection of her old parents, with the exception of a few faithful servants who remained with them. Her life has been one of great activity. In 1868 she became the wife of Judge East, a distingushed jurist, who sympathizes with and aids her in all her work. She is now and has been for several years in the Woman's Christian Temperance Union work. She is local president of the central union in Nashville, where she has for many years resided, and is also corresponding secretary of the State. She was appointed State chairman of the Southern Woman's Council. She has spent much time and money for the cause of temperance. In every reform movement she takes great interest. When the Prohibition amendment was before the people of Tennessee, she was active in the work to create a sentiment in its favor. A large tent, that had been provided in the city in which to conduct gospel services, she had moved to every part of the city for a month, and procured for each night able Prohibition speeches. She has been a delegate to every national convention since 1887. The poor of the city know her, for she never turns a deaf ear to their appeals nor sends them away empty-handed. She taught a night school for young men and boys for two years. She has written for several periodicals and been correspondent for newspapers. She has now a book ready for the publisher. Being an active, busy woman, she finds but little time to write. She is the mother of five children, all living.

EASTMAN, Mrs. Elaine Goodale, poet, born in a country home called "Sky Farm," near South Egremont, Mass., 9th October, 1863. Her mother, Mrs. D. H. R. Goodale, educated her and her sister Dora at home. Elaine at twelve years of age was a good Greek and Latin scholar, reading most of the classics with ease, and she was also familiar with French and German. She was a precocious child and never went to school, and in her isolated mountain home she grew to maturity, after astonishing the world with her poetical productions, written in the short-frock and mud-pie years of her youth. In 1878 Elaine published in conjunction with her eleven-year-old sister, Dora, a book of poems entitled "Apple Blossoms." A second volume, entitled "In Berkshire with the Wild Flowers," soon followed, and the fame of the Goodale sisters spread throughout the English-speaking world. Their father, Henry Sterling Goodale, an experimental farmer, was devoted to poetry and literature, a good mathematician, a clever poet and a failure as a farmer. Financial reverses came to the family, and Elaine and her sister made an attempt to save the homestead by their literary work. In 1881 Elaine was attracted to the cause of the Indians, through some of the Indian students from the Carlisle and Hampton Institutes in Pennsylvania, who were spending the summer in the study of farming in the Berkshire Hills. She took a position as teacher in the Carlisle school, where she taught successfully. In 1885 she went with Senator Dawes on a trip through the Indian reservations, where she made a close study of the condition of the Indians. She then became a government teacher in White Pine Camp, on the Lower Brulé Indian Agency, in Dakota. In 1890 she was appointed superintendent of all the Indian

ELAINE GOODALE EASTMAN.

schools in South Dakota, having her station in the Pine Ridge Agency. In that year she became acquainted with Dr. Charles A. Eastman, a full-blood Sioux Indian, known among the Indians as "Tawa Kanhdiota," or "Many Thunders," and became his wife, 18th June, 1891, in New York City. Dr. Eastman is a graduate of Dartmouth College. He is a man of marked intellectual power, and is engaged in the practice of medicine among his people. Mrs. Eastman is now living in the government house on the Pine Ridge Agency, devoting herself to her family and to the welfare of the wards of the nation. During several years past she has published little or nothing of importance.

EDDY, Mrs. Sara Hershey, musical educator, born in Lancaster county, Pa. She is a daughter of the late Benjamin and Elizabeth Hershey. She received her education and early musical training in Philadelphia, where she sang in a church choir for several years. Bad training resulted in the ruin of her voice, and she turned her attention to the piano. In 1867 she went to Berlin, Germany, where she studied harmony, counterpoint, score-reading and piano-playing with Professor Stern, singing with Miss Jenny Mayer, declamation with Professor Schwartz, elocution and stage deportment with Berndahl, and, afterward, piano with Kullak and singing with Gustav Engel and Gotfried Weiss. She became familiar with the German language and literature, and after three years in Berlin she went to Milan, Italy, where for eighteen months she took vocal lessons with Gerli and the older Lamperti. There she learned the Italian language. She then went to London, England, where she studied oratorio and English singing with Madame Sainton-Dolby. She returned to the United States

in October, 1871, and remained eighteen months in New York City, teaching private pupils and singing in concerts and churches. She was called to Pittsburgh, Pa., as a teacher in the vocal department of the Female College. In 1873 she was placed in control of that department. In 1875 she went to Chicago and founded the Hershey School of Musical Art with W. S. B. Mathews. Clarence Eddy afterwards became the general musical director of the school, which was very successful. In July, 1879, Miss Hershey and Mr. Eddy were married. In 1885 the duties of the school became too exacting, and Mr. and Mrs. Eddy withdrew from it and became the instructors of private classes. Mrs. Eddy has been a prominent member of the Music Teachers' National Association. In 1887 she was elected to the board of examiners in the vocal department of the American College of Musicians.

SARA HERSHEY EDDY.

She has contributed a number of valuable articles to musical journals.

EDDY, Mrs. Sarah Stoddard, reformer, born in Hudson, N. Y., 24th February, 1831. Her grandfather, Ashbel Stoddard, was among the first settlers of Hudson, who went from Nantucket and Providence, R. I., and were mostly of Quaker descent. He came of a severely orthodox family. Congregational ministers were numerous on both his father's and on his mother's side, but he had become more liberal. He established a printing office, book-store and bindery in the central part of the new city and, on 7th April, 1785, issued the first number of the Hudson "Weekly Gazette." That was the pioneer newspaper of the Hudson valley and the oldest in the State. In 1824 he sold that political newspaper and published the "Rural Repository," a literary weekly which had a wide circulation. To the editing of that paper and to the printing establishment the father of Mrs. Eddy, William Bowles Stoddard, an only son, succeeded. Familiarity bred a reverence for books with a great love for them and a desire for their constant companionship. The mother of Mrs. Eddy was of a Holland Dutch family. She had literary taste and skill. Mrs. Eddy was educated in private schools

SARAH STODDARD EDDY.

in Hudson and in Clinton, N. Y. Her preference was for literary studies, the languages and composition. In March, 1852, she became the wife of Rev. Richard Eddy, a Universalist clergyman of Rome, N. Y. After living in Rome two years, she removed to Buffalo, N. Y., then to Philadelphia, Pa., and then to Canton, N. Y., where she lived until the beginning of the Civil War. Mr. Eddy was appointed chaplain of the 60th New York State Volunteers and, having gone to the front with his regiment, Mrs. Eddy with her children went to live in Baltimore, Md., early in January, 1862, that her husband might more frequently see his family, and that she might find some way to be of service. She assisted in forming the aid associations in Baltimore and spent her days in the camps and the hospitals near the city. At the close of the war her husband became pastor of the First Universalist Church in Philadelphia, and, after living in that city for five years, she lived in Franklin, Gloucester, College Hill, Brookline and Melrose, Mass., and is now a resident of Boston. Mrs. Eddy is a member of the New England Women's Club, of the Women's Educational and Industrial Union, of the Woman Suffrage Association and of several purely literary clubs. She has organized several clubs in towns where she has lived, and presided over them for a time, and encourages women everywhere to band themselves together for study and mutual help. In literary matters she has done only fugitive work. She has three sons and two daughters, who have been educated to occupy honorable positions in life.

EDGAR, Mrs. Elizabeth, educator, born near the famous old Donegal Presbyterian Church of Lancaster county, Pa., in 1842. She is the daughter of Rev. Thomas Marshall Boggs, of Washington, Pa., and Amelia Jane Cunningham Boggs, of New London, Pa. At the time of her birth, her father was a pastor, and continued pastor for fourteen years, up to the time of his death, of the Donegal Church, being also pastor of the Presbyterian Church in the neighboring town of Mount Joy, Pa. She was educated in the Mount Joy Seminary, Rev. Nehemiah Dodge, principal, and on 7th July, 1870, became the wife of Rev. John Edgar, who had been pastor of the Mount Joy Presbyterian Church, but who, at the time of his marriage, had occupied a pastorate in New Bloomfield, Pa. There Mr. and Mrs. Edgar remained thirteen years, having two sons born to them, James Marshall Edgar, in 1872, and John Boggs Edgar, in 1878. In 1883, Dr. and Mrs. Edgar removed to Chambersburg, Pa., having been appointed respectively to the positions of president and lady principal of Wilson College for women, under the care of the Presbyterian Church.

ELIZABETH EDGAR.

The work of Mrs. Edgar in that college is highly successful.

EDHOLM, Mrs. Mary G. Charlton, journalist, is official reporter of the World's Woman's Christian Temperance Union, secretary of the International Federation Woman's Press League, and has for years been pushing the temperance reform with a lead pencil. Her journalistic gift is the inheritance from her father, James B. Charlton, and her mother, Lucy Gow Charlton, who were both fine writers along reformatory lines, especially the abolition of slavery, the prohibition of the saloon and the ballot for women. During her sophomore year in college in Monmouth, Ill., she wrote her exhibition essay on the subject, "Shall our Women Vote?" As a test she sent it for publication to the "Woman's Journal" of Boston, and it was published. Her marriage with E. O. L. Edholm, a journalist, developed still more her love for editorial and reportorial work, and for several years they traveled together extensively, and she thereby gained the knowledge and information which comes alone of travel. During those years her descriptive articles appeared in the New York "World," the

MARY G. CHARLTON EDHOLM.

Chicago "Tribune," St. Louis "Post-Dispatch," "Republican" and Chicago "Inter-Ocean." Both before and after the birth of her children she kept her pen busy. For years she was official reporter and superintendent of railroad rates of the California Woman's Christian Temperance Union, and annually wrote about two-hundred-fifty columns of original temperance matter for over two-hundred papers, including the San Francisco, Oakland, Portland, New Orleans, Boston and New York dailies, and the "Union Signal" and the New York "Voice." She conducted three Woman's Christian Temperance Union excursions across the Continent. Her promotion came through Frances E. Willard and Lady Henry Somerset, and she was unanimously elected official reporter of the World's Woman's Christian Temperance Union. Mrs. Edholm has for years been interested in the rescue of erring girls and has written hundreds of articles in defense of outraged womanhood, in such papers as the "Woman's Journal," the "Woman's Tribune," and the "California Illustrated Magazine," where her pen depicted the horrors of the slave traffic in Chinese women for immoral purposes. In evangelistic meetings in Oakland, Cal., she met the millionaire evangelist, Charles N. Crittenton, the founder of Florence Missions for the rescue of erring girls, and at once entered into descriptive articles of Florence Mission work with such enthusiasm that Mr. Crittenton made her reporter of Florence Missions, thus honoring her as a champion of her sex and widening her field of journalism. The horrors of this traffic in girls and their redemption through Florence Missions Mrs. Edholm is now bringing out in book form. She is compiling a book of the life of Mrs. Emily Pitt

Stevens, the Woman's Christian Temperance Union Demosthenes and national organizer. For years, Mrs. Edholm has resided in Oakland, Cal., and has been active in Rev. Dr. Chapman's Church of that city.

EDWARDS, Miss Anna Cheney, educator, born in Northampton, Mass., 31st July, 1835. Her father, Charles, was sixth in descent from Alexander Edwards, one of the early settlers of the town. Her mother, Ruth White, of Spencer, Mass., was also of Puritan ancestry. Anna early showed a fondness for books and a predilection for teaching. She remembers making up her mind, on her first day of her attending school, at the age of four years, that she was to be a teacher. This was an inherited fondness, as her father and grandfather had successively taught the district school near the old Edwards homestead. Her great-grandfather, Nathaniel Edwards, is worthy of mention in these days of higher education for women, for his labors in the instruction of the girls of his neighborhood in vacations, because in his time they were not allowed to attend school with the boys during the regular terms. Miss Edwards' career as a teacher began at the age of sixteen, after she had passed through the public schools of Northampton, in an outer district of the town. After two years of experience she entered Mt. Holyoke Seminary, South Hadley, Mass., in September, 1853. At the end of one year her studies were interrupted by three years more of teaching, after which she returned to the seminary and was graduated in July, 1859. She was recalled as assistant teacher the following year and has been a member of the Holyoke faculty most of the time since. She was absent at one period for about two years, her health being some-

ANNA CHENEY EDWARDS.

what impaired, and from 1866 to 1868 she was principal of Lake Erie Seminary, Painesville, Ohio. She has spent eighteen months in travel in Europe, and in vacations she has taken separate trips to

New Orleans, California, Alaska and various parts of the United States and Canada. She was appointed second associate principal of Mt. Holyoke Seminary in 1872, and first associate in 1883. A college charter having been obtained for that institution in 1888, she was made professor of theism and Christian evidences, and instructor of ancient literature. In scientific studies she shared the enthusiasm and the wide reading of Lydia W. Shattuck, the botanist, and became herself an earnest student and teacher of geology. She is identified with her alma mater in its religious character and work. For the use of her classes she printed in 1877 a volume of "Notes on Ancient Literature." She has given lectures to classes and to ladies' literary societies on a variety of topics. Her more public activities have been in the way of papers and addresses before the different associations of Holyoke alumnæ and in connection with women's missionary meetings. Since 1876 she has been vice-president of the Hampshire County Branch of the Woman's Board of Missions. In 1888 the degree of Master of Arts was conferred upon her by Burlington University, Vermont.

EDWARDS, Mrs. Emma Atwood, educator, born in East Pittston, Maine, 6th November, 1838. Her father, Rev. Charles Baker, a Methodist itinerant, was the chief promoter of education in the Maine Conference in that time, and fully alive to the importance of mental and moral training. Mrs. Edwards was graduated from the academy in Newbury, Vt., in 1860. She engaged at once in teaching, and, while preceptress in Amenia Seminary, she became acquainted with her future husband, Rev. James T. Edwards, D.D., LL.D., who was at that time one of the professors in the semi-

EMMA ATWOOD EDWARDS.

nary. Immediately after their marriage, in 1862, she became associated with him in teaching in East Greenwich Academy, Rhode Island, over which for six years he presided as principal. In 1870

Professor Edwards became principal of Chamberlain Institute, Randolph, N. Y., and Mrs. Edwards has been since that time associated with him as preceptress. Holding herself to the highest ideals of attainment possible, she is able to hold those under her charge to similar ideals, and thus confer upon them the greatest of benefits. Several thousand students have felt the molding influence of her elevated character.

EGGLESTON, Miss Allegra, artist, born in Stillwater, Minn., 19th November, 1860. She is the

ALLEGRA EGGLESTON.

second daughter of Edward Eggleston, the author, who came of a well-known Virginia family, with strains of Irish and Scotch in his descent. She inherited superior mental gifts from her father, combined with artistic qualities in her mother's family, which was of English origin. A delicate and high-strung child, she early showed a talent for drawing and modeling. One of her first works of art was an idol carved out of a piece of semi-decayed wood, when she was only six years of age. She drew constantly and modeled occasionally in clay, but she had no teaching until she was received into classes in Cooper Institute in October, 1875. She was under age, being not yet fifteen, but was accepted on account of remarkable promise. She did creditable work there for two years, after which she entered the studio of Wyatt Eaton, where she made rapid progress in painting from life. In 1879 she went to Europe in company with her father and family. While abroad she took two weeks' lessons under a Swiss wood-carver and astonished him by successfully carving the most difficult pieces as soon as she had learned the use of her tools. After her return home she occupied herself with wood-carving, painting also some portraits, which were exhibited in the annual exhibitions of the Society of American Artists. In 1882 she carved panels for a memorial mantel-piece in the editorial rooms of the "Century Magazine," on one of which was cut a portrait in bas-relief of Dr. J. G. Holland. That piece of work was destroyed by fire in 1888, and Miss Eggleston was called upon to replace it. Of late she has occupied herself much with book illus-

MAUD HOWE ELLIOTT.

trations. Her father's novel, "The Graysons," is illustrated by her, while many of the pictures in his popular school histories, as well as in other school books, bear her signature. She has illustrated a life of Columbus, written by her sister, Mrs. Elizabeth Eggleston Seelye, and edited by their father. Miss Eggleston is versatile. She does many kinds of artistic decorative work for amusement. Among other things she models in leather, having executed the cover for the album containing autographs of distinguished American authors, which was presented to Mrs. Grover Cleveland as an acknowledgment of her interest in the copyright bill, by Edward Eggleston. Miss Eggleston spends the winter in New York and makes her home during the rest of the year at Lake George, where she has a studio in her father's picturesque stone library.

ELLIOTT, Mrs. Maud Howe, novelist, born in Boston, Mass., 9th November, 1855. She is the youngest daughter of Julia Ward Howe, the poet, and of Dr. Samuel G. Howe, famous for his work in the Institute for the Blind in South Boston, Mass. She was carefully educated under the supervision of her mother and drawn into literary activity by her intellectual environments. She traveled abroad and early saw much of the world in Rome, Paris and other European centers of art and literature. In her earlier years she wrote a good deal, but only for her own amusement. Her fear of ridicule and criticism kept her from publishing her first poems and novels. Her first published story appeared in "Frank Leslie's Weekly." She then began to write for newspapers in New York, and letters from Newport to the Boston "Evening Transcript." She became the wife, in 1887, of John Elliott, the English artist, and they made their home in Chicago, Ill. Soon after her marriage her first book, "A Newport Aquarelle," was published anonymously. It was an instant success. Her next serious work was "The San Rosario Ranche," which appeared under her own name. After a visit to New Orleans she wrote her "Atalanta in the South," which scored a success. Her next book was "Mammon," which appeared in "Lippincott's Magazine." Her latest novel is "Phyllida." Among her miscellaneous works are a sketch of her mother in "Famous Women," "The Strike," a story published in the "Century," and a dramatic sketch entitled "Golden Meshes." Recently Mrs. Elliott has delivered lectures on "Cotemporaneous Literature," and has published a serial in the "Ladies' Home Journal." Among her productions is a play, "The Man Without a Shadow." Since her marriage, the greater part of her time has been passed in Chicago. Her summers she passes near Newport, R. I., where her summer home, "Oak Glen," is situated. In Boston she spends her time with her mother. Her life is full of literary, artistic and social activities.

ELLSLER, Miss Effie, actor, born in Philadelphia, Pa. She is a daughter of John A. Ellsler, the well-known actor and manager. Her mother also was an actor of merit. Effie's strongly marked talents are therefore an inheritance. She was early upon the stage. At the age of three years she made her début as the Genius of the Ring in "Aladdin." At the age of four years she played Eva in "Uncle Tom's Cabin," and she made a hit in that rôle. Soon after Effie's birth her parents settled in Cleveland, Ohio, where her father took the management of a theater. The child was called upon from time to time to play child parts. Her

EFFIE ELLSLER.

parents at first intended to train her for dancing, and Effie soon acquired remarkable agility in the preliminary training. She was sent for a number of years to the Ursuline Convent in Cleveland, where she received a very thorough education. She remained in that school until she was sixteen years old, at times leaving for a short space to assume child rôles in her father's theater. On one of those occasions she was cast as one of the witches in "Macbeth." The red-fire flash caused her to forget her lines, when she deliberately drew the book from her dress and read her words. At sixteen years of age she began the regular work of the stage, playing all sorts of parts from Juliet and Rosalind to a howler in a Roman mob. She made her first great success as Hazel in "Hazel Kirke," in the Madison Square Theater in New York City. She played in that rôle for three years, until her physician ordered her to discontinue it on account of the strain on her powers. During the past ten years she has traveled with her own company, presenting a variety of plays, most of them with great success. Her most successful play, aside from "Hazel Kirke," has been "Woman Against Woman." In 1891-92, in answer to countless requests, Miss Ellsler revived "Hazel Kirke," in which she again showed her great powers. She ranks among the foremost emotional actors of the United States.

ELMORE, Mrs. Lucie Ann Morrison, temperance reformer, born in Brandonville, Preston county, W. Va., 29th March, 1829. Her father was a Methodist clergyman, and she is an Episcopalian and a radical Woman's Christian Temperance Union woman. She is a pronounced friend of all oppressed people, and especially of the colored race in the United States. She is patriotic in the extreme. Her husband, who served as an officer in the Union Army through the Civil War, died in 1868, and her only child died in infancy.

LUCIE ANN MORRISON ELMORE.

Mrs. Elmore is widely known as a philanthropist. She is an eloquent and convincing speaker on temperance, social purity and the evils of the tobacco habit. She has suffered financial reverses,

but she has never given up her charitable work. Her home is in Englewood, N. J. Her chief literary works are her poems, one volume of which has passed through a large edition, and the popular story "Billy's Mother." She has held several important editorial positions, and her poems have been published in the leading magazines. A story now ready for the press is thought to bear in it promise of a great success, as it is the product of a ripe experience and close study of neighborhood influences for good and evil.

EMERSON, Mrs. Ellen Russell, author, born in New Sharon, Maine, 16th January, 1837

ELLEN RUSSELL EMERSON.

Her father, Dr. Leonard White Russell, was a man of character and ability. He was a descendant of the Russells of Charlestown, Mass. Dr. Russell had six children, the youngest of whom, Ellen, was born in the later years of his life. She early gave evidence of peculiarities of temperament, shy, dreamy and meditative, with an exceeding love for nature. At seventeen she was sent to Boston, where she entered the Mt. Vernon Seminary, in charge of Rev. Dr. Robert W. Cushman, under whose severe and stimulating guidance the student made rapid progress. There her literary work began to appear in fugitive poems and short essays. Her stay in the seminary was brought to an end by a severe attack of brain fever, caused by over study. In 1862 she became the wife of Edwin R. Emerson, then in the government service in Augusta, Maine. Social duties demanded her attention, but gradually she returned to her study, and then began her interest in Indian history. A foundation was laid in systematic research for her book, "Indian Myths, or Legends and Traditions of the American Aborigines, Compared with Other Countries." In all her work she has the cordial interest and sympathy of her husband. Trips to the West, to Colorado and California, brought her in sympathy with the red race, whose history and genius she had studied so earnestly. In 1884 she sailed for Europe, where she worked among the records and monuments in the libraries and museums, using not only the note-book, but the sketch-book and brush of the painter as well. Wherever she went, the scholars of Europe recognized her ability and conscientious work, giving her unusual privileges in the pursuit of her researches and showing cordial interest in her labor. In Paris she was elected a member of the Société Americaine de France, the first woman to receive that honor. There she completed the object of her European visit, and returned to America to prepare for the publication of her recent work, "Masks, Heads and Faces, with Some Considerations Respecting the Rise and Development of Art." Mrs. Emerson usually spends her winters in Boston, and lives a quiet, studious life with her one daughter.

ENGLE, Mrs. Addie C. Strong, author, born in the town of Manchester, Conn., 11th August, 1845. She traces her ancestry back to 1630, when John Strong, of some historic fame, came to

ADDIE C. STRONG ENGLE.

this country from Taunton, England. Her girlhood years were spent in the picturesque town of South Manchester, and her later life, until 1882 in Meriden, Conn. As a child she found her pen a recreation. Her talent for literary composition was inherited from her mother, who was Mary B. Keeney, whose ancestors were among the earlier settlers of South Manchester. When a girl of sixteen, she sent an article upon one of the terrible war years then just ended to "Zion's Herald," of Boston, in which it was printed as a leader, and she was engaged by its publisher to write a series of sketches for children. She spent several years in teaching in South Manchester. In 1866 she became the wife of J. H. Bario, of Meriden. Two daughters of that marriage survive and share her home. For years she gave her best labors to the Order of the Eastern Star, in which she was

honored by being called three years to fill the highest office in her native State. In the discharge of the duties pertaining to that position her executive ability and knowledge of jurisprudence won commendation as being "wonderful for a woman," a compliment she rather resented, as her pride and faith in the abilities of her sex are large. Her stories and poems have appeared for years in children's papers, the "Voice of Masonry," the "Churchman" and other periodicals. She has published many stories and poems. The odes used in the secret work of the Order of the Eastern Star and its beautiful memorial service were her contributions. In 1882 she became the wife of Rev. Willis D. Engle, of Indianapolis, an Episcopal clergyman, and removed to the Hoosier State. There she at once became identified, outside of church work, with local organizations of the Eastern Star, the Woman's Relief Corps, the McAll Mission and the King's Daughters, all of which received the hearty labors of her brain and pen. With her husband she commenced in 1889 the publication of a monthly illustrated magazine, the "Compass, Star and Vidette," in the interest of the Masonic, Eastern Star and Relief Corps Orders. The entire charge of the literary and children's departments fell upon her. In December, 1890, she ceased active participation in the work of the various societies to which she belonged, and joined the sadly increasing order of "Shut Ins." A fall the winter before had produced serious results. Nobly battling against heavy odds for nearly a year, nature finally succumbed, and congestion of the spine resulted. Still she keeps up her brain efforts, though in a lesser degree, and the incidents which came to her as she made in a hammock a short lake trip in the summer of 1891 were woven into a romance in the form of a serial, which was published. The injury to her eyes has impaired their appearance as well as their vision, and she wears glasses. Her Puritan ancestry shows plainly in some of her opinions, yet she is very liberal in her views and absorbed heart and soul in every great step toward progress and reform. She is a rapid talker, and when able to speak from the rostrum was an eloquent one.

ESMOND, Mrs. Rhoda Anna, philanthropist, born in Sempronius, N. Y., 22nd November, 1819. Her parents were Zadok Titus and Anna Hinkley Greenfield Titus, who were married in 1801. Zadok Titus was born in Stillwater, N. Y., and moved in 1795 to Sempronius, where he took up one-hundred-seventy-seven acres of wild land, which he converted into a beautiful farm, upon which he lived until his death, in 1836. Miss Titus' school-days, after leaving the district school, were spent for two years in Groton Academy and nearly a year in "Nine Partners Boarding School," Washington, N. Y. Here she met Joseph Esmond, a young Hicksite Friend, from Saratoga, N. Y., and became his wife 5th May, 1840. They resided in Saratoga two years and then went to Milan, Cayuga county, N. Y. In 1846 they moved to Fulton, and Mr. Esmond took up the study of law. What he read through the day was reviewed with Mrs. Esmond at night. That gave her much valuable legal knowledge and some acquaintance with the general rules of legal proceedings. In 1848 Mr. Esmond was admitted to the bar and practiced law in Fulton for twenty years. During those years Mrs. Esmond's health was very poor, but she was actively engaged in church work and often contributed articles to newspapers under the pen-name "Ruth." In 1872 Mr. Esmond moved with his family, consisting of his wife and three sons, to Syracuse, N. Y. When the influence of the Woman's Temperance Crusade of the West reached

Syracuse, she helped to organize a woman's temperance society of four-hundred members. She was made a delegate to the first State Woman's Christian Temperance Union conven-

RHODA ANNA ESMOND.

tion, held in Brooklyn, in February, 1875, with instructions to visit all of the coffee-houses and friendly inns in Brooklyn, New York and Pough-keepsie, to gather all the information possible for the purpose of formulating a plan for opening an inn in Syracuse. The inn was formally opened in July, 1875. As chairman of the inn committee she managed its affairs for nearly two years with re-markable success. Jealousies arose in the union, and Mrs. Esmond and thirty-two others resigned and formed a new union, called Syracuse Woman's Christian Temperance Union No. 2. Mrs. Esmond was elected president, but positively refused to act. In the first State Woman's Christian Temperance Union convention held in Brooklyn, in February, 1875, Mrs. Esmond was made chairman of the com-mittee on resolutions and appointed one of a commit-tee on "Memorial to the State Legislature." In the State's first annual convention held in Ilion, in October, 1875, she was made a member of the executive board. In its second annual convention in Syracuse, in 1876, she gave the address of welcome, was made chairman of the executive board, chosen a delegate to the National conven-tion and made a member of the State committee on visitations. In 1877, in the State annual con-vention, she was made chairman of the finance committee and a member of the committee to revise the State constitution. In 1881 she was elected State superintendent of the department of unfermented wine. In 1887 she was elected a delegate to the National convention held in Nash-ville, but resigned. She was there appointed national superintendent of the department of un-fermented wine. In 1888 she was delegate to the national convention, held in New York City. In

1889 she resigned the presidency of the local union, having held that office nearly six years. For the past four years her most earnest efforts and best thoughts have been given to the interest of her department work.

ESTY, Miss Alice May, operatic singer, born in Lowell, Mass., 12th April, 1866. She is of purely American descent. Her great-great-grand-father on the maternal side fought under Wash-ington. Her ancestors for generations have lived in New England. Early in life Miss Esty gave promise of great musical ability. As a child she possessed a wonderful soprano voice. At the early age of twelve she announced her intention to become a professional singer. Although from the outset she encountered difficulties that would have discouraged many of maturer years, she never wavered. She was fortunate in securing for her teacher Madame Millar, then Miss Clara Smart, with whom she studied for three years. Miss Esty's first engagement of importance in her native country was an extended tour through the United States with Madame Camilla Urso. That was followed by a very successful season in Boston. The hard work of years began to tell, and Miss Esty after a severe attack of typhoid fever went to England for a change and rest. One of her numerous letters of introduction was to the head of the leading musical house in London. That gentleman expressed a wish to hear the latest singer from what has become recognized in England as the land of song, America. An appointment was made, and, as Miss Esty was singing, several gentlemen dropped in to listen. Among them were Edward Lloyd and Mr. N. Vert. These gentlemen were struck with her beautiful voice and excellent singing. Although

ALICE MAY ESTY.

only in search of health, Miss Esty received so many flattering offers from managers that she de-termined to settle in England for a few years. After a flying trip to Boston she returned to London, in

March, 1891, and was in much demand for concerts during the season. She achieved a great success with Madame Adelina Patti in the Royal Albert Hall, and an equally successful appearance in a subsequent concert. She was well received in the best musical circles in England. An engagement with the Carl Rosa Grand Opera Company was entered upon in August, 1891. In seven months she learned the leading rôles in ten operas, singing to crowded houses on every occasion and never meeting an adverse criticism. During the winter of 1891–92 she filled concert engagements in Birmingham, Nottingham and other important musical centers in England. She has received flattering offers from Sir Charles Halle and other leading conductors. Miss Esty's voice is a pure soprano, of extended compass, powerful and sweet, she sings with warmth of expression as well as finished method, and her articulation is nearly perfection.

EVANS, Mrs. Lizzie P. E., novelist, born in Arlington, Mass., 27th August, 1846. She is the youngest daughter of the late Captain Endor and Lydia Adams Estabrook, and a granddaughter of Deacon John Adams, who owned and occupied the Adams house, which was riddled with bullets when war swept through the quiet streets of West Cambridge, now Arlington, as the British soldiers, on their retreat from Concord and Lexington, erroneously supposed that the patriot, Samuel Adams, a cousin of Deacon John Adams, was secreted within its walls. Lizzie Phelps Estabrook became the wife of Andrew Allison Evans of Boston, Mass. He died in May, 1888. Mrs. Evans resides in Somerville, Mass. Among her published works is the quaintly humorous book "Aunt Nabby," an enter-

LIZZIE P. E. EVANS.

taining picture of country life, customs, dialects and ideas. The book is a successful essay in laughing down the overdone conventionalities of fashionable life. Another of her successful books is "From Summer to Summer," an entertaining home story.

Many short stories and sketches from her pen have been published under the pen-name "Esta Brooks"

EVE, Miss Maria Louise, poet, was born near Augusta, Ga., about 1848. She is of old Eng-

MARIA LOUISE EVE.

lish ancestry. Her first literary success was a prize for the best essay awarded by "Scott's Magazine." She has since contributed, from time to time, articles on literary and other subjects to some of the prominent magazines and papers. In 1879 her poem "Conquered at Last" won the prize offered by the Mobile "News" for the best poem expressing the gratitude of the South to the North for aid in the yellow fever scourge of the preceding year. That poem was reproduced in nearly all of the papers and many of the magazines of the North, and also in some periodicals abroad. Its great popularity throughout the North, attested by the large number of letters received by her from soldiers and civilians, cultured and uncultured, was a complete surprise as well as a great gratification to her. In June, 1889, a short poem by her, entitled "A Briar Rose," won the prize offered by the Augusta "Chronicle." At the request of the secretary of the American Peace and Arbitration Society, in Boston, as a message of welcome to the English Peace Deputation to America in October, 1887, she wrote a poem, "The Lion and the Eagle." The underlying thought of the "Universal Peace," as found in one of her published poems, led the secretary to communicate with her in regard to it, and she has since written a number of poems bearing on the subject, which is perhaps the most practical work that she has done on any of the great lines of advancement and progress. Possessing that order of mind which crystallizes in thought rather than in action, she feels that anything she may hope to achieve must be chiefly through the channels of literary effort. Her writings are comparatively small in bulk, her endeavor being always toward force and directness, rather than expansiveness of thought.

EVERHARD, Mrs. Caroline McCullough, woman suffragist, born in Massillon, Ohio, 14th

CAROLINE McCULLOUGH EVERHARD.

September, 1843, where she now resides. She received her early education in the public schools. Subsequently she spent a year in a private school for young women in Media, Pa. Shortly after the close of her school days she became the wife of Captain Henry H. Everhard, who had returned from the war after three years of honorable service. The cares of home and family demanded her attention for several years, but, when her children were old enough for her to entrust their education to other hands, she resumed her literary pursuits. At an early age she began to investigate and reason for herself, and Goethe's words, " Open the Windows and Let in More Light," were the subject of her essay when she finished her course of study in the public schools. A natural consequence of her original and independent way of thinking was an unusual interest in woman's position in state and church, and she has done much to influence public sentiment in that respect in the community in which she has resided. Mrs. Everhard has been appointed to several positions of trust not usually filled by women, in all of which she has discharged her duties acceptably. In 1886 she was appointed by the Judge of the Court of Common Pleas to fill a vacancy caused by the death of her father, one of the trustees of the Charity Rotch School, an institution founded fifty years ago by the benevolent Quaker woman whose name it bears. That was the first instance in Ohio of the appointment of a woman to a place of trust that required a bond. She has been for several years a member of a board appointed by the court to visit the public institutions of the county, including the various jails, the county infirmary and the Children's Home. She has been a director of the Union

National Bank of Massillon for a number of years. She entered actively into the suffrage ranks in 1888 and became more and more deeply engaged until May, 1891, when she was elected to fill the office of president of the Ohio Woman's Suffrage Association. She organized the Equal Rights Association of Canton, Ohio, and the one in her own city, and to her influence are due their prosperity and power for good in that portion of the State. From childhood she has been an ardent friend of dumb animals and has promoted the work of the Massillon Humane Society, of which she has been an efficient officer from its organization. Mrs. Everhard is an indefatigable worker. Her office necessarily imposes a large correspondence, to which she must give personal attention, and for many years she has made her influence felt through the medium of the press. Three children have blessed her married life.

EWING, Mrs. Catherine A. Fay, educator and philanthropist, born in Westboro, Mass., 18th July, 1822. Her parents were in comfortable circumstances and, desiring a more liberal education for their children removed to Marietta, Ohio, in 1836, where they could have the advantage of both college and female seminary. On her father's side Mrs. Ewing is descended from Huguenot ancestry. His mother was a woman of rare piety, and through her influence her twelve children became Christians in early life. Mrs. Ewing's mother was of Scotch descent, and in the long line of Christian ancestors there were many ministers and missionaries. All of her eleven children were devoted Christians. Two became ministers and two are deacons. Mrs. Ewing, from her eighteenth to her twentieth year, taught school in Ohio and then went as a

CATHERINE A. FAY EWING.

missionary among the Choctaw Indians for ten years. Upon her return to Ohio, in 1857, she founded a home for destitute children, of which she had control for nine years. Through her efforts the

Ohio Legislature passed a bill in Columbus, which entitled every county to establish a Children's Home. In 1866 she became the wife of A. S. D. Ewing. She has since devoted much time and labor to the children about her, teaching a large infant class in the Sabbath-school and also establishing a sewing-school. She is the author of a comprehensive historical report on the origin and growth of the children's home movement in Washington county, Ohio.

EWING, Mrs. Emma P., apostle of good cooking, born on a farm in Broome county, N. Y. in July, 1838. Since her marriage she has lived in Washington, D. C., New York City, Chicago, Ill., and other cities. In 1866 she became impressed with the belief that good food is an important factor in the development of the individual, morally, mentally and physically, and since then the leading aim of her life has been to improve the character of the every-day diet of the people by the introduction of

EMMA P. EWING.

better and more economical methods of cooking. Most of her culinary studies and experiments have been in that direction. In 1880 Mrs. Ewing organized a school of cookery in Chicago and conducted it in a highly satisfactory manner for three years, when she was appointed professor of domestic economy in the Iowa Agricultural College. That position she held until 1887, and then resigned to accept a similar one, at a largely-increased salary, in Purdue University, Indiana. In the fall of 1889 she resigned her professorship in Purdue University and went to Kansas City, Mo., to organize and take charge of a school of household science; but before she had been there a year the calls upon her from all sections of the country for lectures and lessons upon culinary topics became so incessant and urgent that she resolved to leave the school. Placing it in other hands, she devoted her entire time and energies to itinerary work, preaching the gospel of good cookery to larger and more

appreciative audiences than she could possibly reach in schools and colleges. Some idea of the amount of missionary work that is being done by her may be gathered from the fact that during 1891 she gave nearly two-hundred-fifty lectures and lessons on the preparation of food. For several summers Mrs. Ewing has been in charge of the School of Cookery at the Chautauqua Assembly, and every season she delivers a series of lectures there on household topics. Her popularity as a lecturer and teacher is such that her services are in constant demand, many of her engagements being made a year in advance. On all subjects pertaining to household science Mrs. Ewing is a leading authority. In addition to her other labors Mrs. Ewing has written two books, "Cooking and Castle Building" (1880) and "Cookery Manuals" (1886), and is now devoting her leisure time to the preparation of a text-book on cookery for schools and homes, to be entitled "The A B C of Cookery." Her home is in Rochester, N. Y.

EYSTER, Mrs. Nellie Blessing, author, was born in Frederick, Md. She is of good ancestry, with a commingling of Huguenot and Anglo-Saxon blood. On the maternal side she is a granddaughter of Captain George W. Ent, a commander at Fort McHenry in the war of 1812 and an intimate friend of Francis Scott Key. On the same side she is a kinswoman of famous old Barbara Frietchie. Abraham Blessing, Mrs. Eyster's father, who died in his early prime, when she was but ten years old, was a man of noble character, the youngest brother of George Blessing of Maryland, whose loyalty and patriotism, as displayed during the late Civil War, has won for him in history the title, "The Hero of the Highlands." The mother was a woman of unusual refinement and poetic taste, leaving as an inheritance to her five children the memory of a life of Christian rectitude and usefulness. The eldest of these five, Nellie, baptized Penelope, early gave promise of literary ability. When sixteen years old, she was wooed and won by her private tutor, David A. S. Eyster, a young lawyer of Harrisburg, Pa. From the beginning of their acquaintance to Mr. Eyster's death, in 1886, he was her teacher, best friend and critic. Her family consists of one daughter, Mary, born a year after her marriage, and one son, Charles, several years later, who died at the age of ten, in 1872. Mrs. Eyster's first public work was in aid of the purchase of Mt. Vernon and she put forth earnest activity in the Sanitary Commission during the Civil War. Her first literary venture of any note was a series of children's books called the "Sunny Hour Library" (Philadelphia, four volumes, 1865-69). The success of these books gave fresh impetus to Mrs. Eyster's pen. She has written for many leading periodicals, "California Illustrated Magazine," the New York "Tribune," "Lutheran Observer," Harrisburg "Telegraph," "Our Young Folks," "St. Nicholas," "Wide Awake," "Harper's Magazine," the "Riverside Magazine," and others. She worked for a year with Gail Hamilton on "Wood's Household Magazine," editing the juvenile department. Mr. Eyster held a useful and remunerative post as financial clerk of the Pennsylvania State Board of Education. In 1872 and 1873 the death of her son and her mother caused her health to give way, and in 1876 the family removed to California, where, in San José, a delightful new home was made, and Mrs. Eyster rallied from her depression to take hold of religious and benevolent work once more. In Pennsylvania the family had been members of the English Lutheran Church, but in San José they became connected with the Presbyterian denomination, and Mrs. Eyster was linked with all its Christian and benevolent enterprises. Mrs.

Eyster was made president of the San José Ladies' Benevolent Society, president of the Woman's Christian Temperance Union and secretary of the Woman's Missionary Society of the Presbyterian

NELLIE BLESSING EYSTER.

Church. Pecuniary reverses made her more than ever her husband's helper, and she taught literature and music in schools and homes with success. During those years her pen was never idle, and another book for children was written, "A Colonial Boy" (Boston, 1890). Ten years went by, and the sudden death of Mr. Eyster broke up the new home. Mrs. Eyster then went to San Francisco to live with her daughter, now Mrs. Scott Elder. Mrs. Eyster is state superintendent of juvenile work in the Woman's Christian Temperance Union, president of the California Women's Indian Association, and president of the Woman's Press Association of the Pacific Coast. None of these positions are sinecures, and all receive her supervision.

FAIRBANKS, Miss Constance, journalist, born in Dartmouth, Nova Scotia, 10th May, 1866. She belongs to an old provincial family nearly all of whose representatives have possessed more or less literary ability, and several of whom were long associated with the history of Nova Scotia. She is the second child and oldest daughter of L. P. Fairbanks, and is one of a family of nine children. Owing to delicate health when a child, Miss Fairbanks was able to attend school only in an irregular manner, but, being precocious and fond of the society of those older than herself, she gained much knowledge outside of the school-room. At the age of thirteen years she ceased to have systematic instruction, and with patient determination she proceeded to carry on her education by means of careful reading. Finding it necessary to obtain employment, she became, in 1887, secretary to C. F. Fraser, the clever blind editor of the Halifax "Critic," and in that position gained a practical

knowledge of the work which now occupies her attention. Gradually, as her ability to write became known, and as she developed a keen recognition of what was required by the public, Miss Fairbanks was placed in charge of various departments of the paper, until in June, 1890, the management of the editorial and certain other departments was virtually transferred to her and has since remained in her charge.

FAIRBANKS, Mrs. Elizabeth B., philanthropist, born in Elbridge, Onondaga county., N.Y., 17th October, 1831. Her father was Dr. Jared W. Wheeler, a physician of considerable prominence. Her mother's maiden name was Electa Brown, a Quakeress by birth and education, having received her school instruction at the "Hive," under the supervision of the Motts. From such parentage she naturally inherited clear perceptions, generous impulses and a sympathetic heart, combined with pure aims and unusual practical ability. Her maiden name was Wheeler. She was educated in the Monroe Collegiate Institute, founded by her uncle, Nathan Monroe, and in the Auburn Female Seminary. In 1857 she became the wife of John I. Fairbanks, of the firm of Ford & Fairbanks, booksellers in Milwaukee, Wis., in which city they have ever since resided. Her benevolent work in that city commenced the first Sabbath after her arrival, and as her husband was a young deacon in the First Presbyterian Church, mission-school work claimed her early attention. She was one of the prime movers in various local charities, which have enlarged and broadened as time has advanced. She took to the State of Wisconsin the first plans for the organization of the present associated charities, and to her efforts is due in large measure the securing of

CONSTANCE FAIRBANKS

the Wisconsin State Public School for Dependent Children. In 1880 she was appointed by the governor a member of the State Board of Charities and Reform, on which she served for a period of eleven years, being the only woman member. During that time the board became noted for its advanced views and methods of treating and caring for the chronic insane in the county asylums, a

ELIZABETH B. FAIRBANKS.

system pronounced by all who have investigated it superior to any other ever devised. By virtue of her official position and attention to its duties she soon became familiar with the condition and management of every institution in the State, winning friends wherever she went and becoming a welcome visitor and valued adviser both to officials and inmates, irrespective of nationality, religion or creed.

FAIRCHILD, Miss Maria Augusta, doctor of medicine, born in Newark, N. J., 7th June, 1834. Orphaned at the age of six years, she was left to the guardianship and care of her uncle, Dr. Stephen Fairchild, widely known as a philanthropist and temperance and medical reformer. He was surgeon in the army during the war of 1812, practiced allopathy a number of years and later adopted homeopathy, being foremost in its introduction into New Jersey. Augusta very early showed a strong preference for the study of anatomy, physiology, materia medica and even pathology. Both her uncle and his son, Dr. Van Wyck Fairchild, were amused and not a little pleased to observe the strong likings of the child, and they gave much encouragement in the directions so welcome to her. She unfolded rapidly under their instruction. She was often permitted to visit both their hospital and private patients, and there she learned to diagnose and prescribe with accuracy and skill. When she was sent to school, she found the work and surroundings distasteful, but she persevered in her studies and left school fitted to teach. For three years she forced herself to faithfulness in a work for which she had no liking beyond that of filling her position in the best possible way. Longing to become a physician, she read the names of a small band of women, medical pioneers, and encouragement

came to her. At length the way was opened. Her health failed, and she was ill for months. In the very early stage of convalescence she felt the uprising of her unconquerable desire. With restored health she resolved to carry out her long-cherished plan, and soon she found herself in the New York Hygeio-Therapeutic College, New York City, from which in 1860, three years later, she was graduated. To be a woman doctor meant a great deal in those days. Immediately upon leaving college, Dr. Fairchild became associated with the late Dr. Trall, of New York, in both infirmary and outside practice. From the first she has given much attention to measures which elevate the standard of health among women. She was one of the earliest practitioners of the hygienic medical school, and probably there is no physician of that school now living who bears such unwavering testimony to the truths of its principles. During her thirty-two years of practice, in both acute and chronic ailments, she has never administered either alcohol or drugs. She is enthusiastic in whatever goes to make humanity better. In religion she is New Church, or Swedenborgian. As an author she has published "How to be Well" (New York, 1879), and her later work, entitled "Woman and Health" (1890). She contributes to various health journals and magazines, and has during all the years of her professional life occupied the lecture field as a champion for women, claiming that emancipation lies in the direction of obedience to the laws of health and total extinction of disease. She has lived in the West about twenty years, and is known as a leading physician, and proprietor of her own Health Institution in Quincy, Ill. She is a careful hygienist, eats no meat,

MARIA AUGUSTA FAIRCHILD.

drinks only water, eats but one meal a day and wears neither corsets nor weighty clothing.

FALL, Mrs. Anna Christy, lawyer, born in Chelsea, Mass., 23rd April, 1855. She acquired her early education in the public schools of that city, graduating from the high school in 1873. Six years later she entered the College of Liberal Arts of Boston University. There she was graduated in

ANNA CHRISTY FALL.

1883 with the degree of Bachelor of Arts. She at once commenced a post-graduate course of study, and in 1884 received the degree of Master of Arts. The following September she became the wife of one of her class-mates, George Howard Fall, of Malden, Mass., who was then teaching, but who immediately after marriage commenced the study of law. Five years later she began the study of law, having become deeply interested in it as a result of going into court and taking notes for her husband, who had meanwhile entered upon the practice of his profession in Boston, Mass. In March, 1889, she entered the Boston University Law School. In December, 1890, while still a student in the school, she took the examination for admission to the Boston bar, being the only woman among forty applicants. Twenty-eight of these, including Mrs. Fall, succeeded in passing and were sworn in before the Supreme Court of Massachusetts the following January. In June, 1891, Mrs. Fall graduated from the law school, taking the honor of magna cum laude. During the following autumn and winter she lectured in various parts of the State on the "Position of Women under the Massachusetts Law," and kindred subjects. She is now, although the mother of two children, engaged with her husband in the practice of law, and in November, 1891, won her first case before a jury, one of the ablest and most noted lawyers of Massachusetts being the principal counsel on the opposite side. That case was the first jury case in Massachusetts tried by a woman. Mrs. Fall is at present a member of the Malden School Board.

FARMER, Mrs. Lydia Hoyt, author, was born in Cleveland, Ohio. Her family and ancestry include names prominent in the professions of law, theology

and literature. Her father is the Hon. J. M. Hoyt, of Cleveland, Ohio. Her mother was Mary Ella Beebe, daughter of Alexander M. Beebe, LL. D. of New York. Her husband is the Hon. E. J. Farmer, of Cleveland, who is the author of several works on politics and finance, and is engaged in large mining enterprises in Colorado. Mrs. Farmer was thoroughly educated in music, art and literature. For the past ten years she has contributed to the leading newspapers and popular magazines. Her writings have been various, consisting of poems, essays, juvenile stories, historical sketches and novels. She is the author of "A Story Book of Science" (Boston, 1886), "Boys' Book of Famous Rulers" (New York, 1886), "Girls' Book of Famous Queens' (New York, 1887), "The Prince of the Flaming Star" (Boston, 1887), "The Life of La Fayette" (New York, 1888), "A Short History of the French Revolution" (New York, 1889), "A Knight of Faith" (New York, 1889), "A Moral Inheritance" (New York, 1890), and other works. Mrs. Farmer's books have received high commendation from the press, have had wide circulation throughout the country, and her "Knight of Faith," which is a strong religious novel, received flattering recognition from the Hon. William E. Gladstone, from whom Mrs. Farmer was the recipient of a personal note regarding her religious books. Her "Prince of the Flaming Star" is an operetta, and the words, music and illustrations are all of her production. Her "Moral Inheritance," is founded upon "Soul Heredity" and enters into rather novel fields in the realms of fiction. In her "Life of La Fayette" she had access to original files of newspapers, unique copies of works now out of

LYDIA HOYT FARMER.

print, and the private papers of the La Fayette family, and therefore has been able to incorporate in the book much that had been inaccessible to previous biographers. She has completed a historical novel, "The Doom of the Holy City: Christ and

Cæsar," founded on the destruction of Jerusalem, and the scenes are laid in that city and in Rome as they appeared in the first century. She is an indefatigable student, pursuing metaphysical and philosophical research with intense avidity. Her novels are always written for a high purpose, and their whole tendency and teaching are healthful and elevating. Mrs. Farmer has for years instructed Bible classes of young ladies, having devoted a large portion of her time to Biblical study. She has passed most of her life in Cleveland, having resided in that city from childhood, with the exception of five years spent in the City of New York.

FAWCETT, Mrs. Mary S., temperance reformer, born near Burlington, Ontario, Canada, 22nd February, 1829. In 1852 she became the wife of an older brother of Rev. D. V. Lucas, of the Montreal Methodist Conference. She was a worthy helpmate to her husband. Together they labored in church and Sabbath-school work and were equally useful in the neighborhood in which they resided. At the end of six years her husband lost his health. His death in 1862 left her alone and childless. For the next six years she devoted herself to the welfare of others, using her means as well as giving her time. She labored in the Sabbath-school and was most successful as a Bible-class teacher. In 1868 she became the wife of Rev. M. Fawcett, an honored minister of the Toronto Methodist Conference, and for years shared with him the life of an itinerant. Four years of that time, from 1872 to 1876, he labored as a missionary in Manitoba, and, as the country was then comparatively new, there were hardships and privations to endure which are unknown in older countries. There, as elsewhere, Mrs. Fawcett

was organized, and in a short time organizations sprang up in many of the towns and villages. She became interested, and from that time has been connected with it, first as corresponding secretary of the Ontario Woman's Christian Temperance Union, which office she filled for eight years, but, her husband being at the time in poor health, she refused office for a year. When his health was restored, she again took up the work and since then has filled the position of provincial and dominion president of the Canadian Woman's Christian Temperance Union. She is at present vice-president of the Provincial, but can not work as in former years. Her health began to fail in 1890 from overwork, and she is now obliged to rest.

FAY, Miss Amy, musician and author, born on a plantation on the Mississippi river, eighty

AMY FAY.

miles from New Orleans, La., 21st May, 1844. She is the daughter of Rev. Charles Fay, of Cambridge, Mass., and Charlotte Emily Fay, a daughter of the late Bishop John Henry Hopkins, of the Protestant Episcopal Church of Vermont. Both families were musical, and Mrs. Fay was a pianist of remarkable gifts. The family consisted of six daughters and one son, and Amy was the third of the children, all of whom were singers and players. Amy showed remarkable musical talents at an early age. At the age of four years she played airs by ear and composed little airs, which she rendered on the piano. At five years of age she began to study regularly under her mother's tuition. The family removed to St. Albans, Vt., in 1848. Amy studied Latin, Greek, French and German with her father, and music, drawing and composition with her mother. Her education was liberal and careful. Her mother died in 1856, and Amy went to live with her married sister in Cambridge, Mass. There she began the study of Bach with Prof. J. K. Paine, and piano with Otto Dressel, in the New England Conservatory

MARY S. FAWCETT.

found a field of labor. While in that distant province, she first read of the woman's Crusade, and her heart went out for the women engaged in it. About the time of their return, the first union in Canada

of Music. She next studied piano technique with Prof. Pychowski, of New York. In 1869 she went to Europe. In Berlin she studied with Carl Tausig one year and with Prof. Kullak three years. In 1873 she went to Weimar and studied in Liszt's school. She studied again with Kullak and Deppe, and finished with a second course under Liszt. In 1875 she returned to the United States. She made her début in New York with the Mendelssohn Glee Club. She settled in Boston, where she gave a number of concerts, and was the first to add piano concerts to the programmes in the Worcester festivals. In 1878 she settled in Chicago, Ill., where she now lives. Her concerts, styled "Piano Conversations," are very popular. Her principal literary work is her book, "Music Study in Germany," published on the suggestion of Henry Wadsworth Longfellow, and translated into German on the request of Liszt. It is a standard book in the United States, Germany and England. Miss Fay has been a successful piano teacher as well as concertist. She is the founder of the Artists' Concert Club, of Chicago, a club composed of musicians. She is one of the students whose names appear in Liszt's own roll of his best pupils.

FEARING, Miss Lillian Blanche, lawyer and poet, born in Davenport, Iowa, 27th November, 1863. She was educated partly in the Iowa College in Vinton, Iowa, and was graduated in 1884. In 1888 she removed to Chicago, Ill., and entered as a student in the Union College of Law. She was graduated in the spring of 1890, the only woman in her class, and one of four students whose records were so nearly equal that the faculty of the college could not decide to whom the scholarship prize should be awarded. The difficulty was solved by the division of the prize between the four. Miss Fearing is thus far the only woman who has received a scholarship prize from that college. She is now practicing law in Chicago and achieving success in that arduous field of labor. She is the author of two volums of verse, entitled "The Sleeping World, and other Poems" (Chicago, 1887), and "In the City by the Lake" (Chicago, 1892). Her literary work shows merit of high order. Miss Fearing's success in life is nothing short of remarkable, when it is remembered that she is blind.

FELTON, Mrs. Rebecca Latimer, orator, born seventeen miles south of Atlanta, Ga., 10th June, 1835. Her father was a native of Maryland, and her ancestry is a blending of English, Scotch and Irish. Governor Talbot of Georgia was a maternal relative. Mrs. Felton looks back upon her childhood as a time of surpassing freedom and happiness. She lived in the country, rode, romped, fished and was as free as air to come and go. Music has always been a passion with her, and as she developed it became an accomplishment and an art. She shared the first honor when she was graduated and was the youngest girl in her class. In her early education and through her college life she had the best and most thorough instruction to be had in the State. She became the wife of William H. Felton early in life, and after the war assisted her husband in a large school of nearly a hundred pupils. In 1874 her husband became a candidate for Congress, as an independent Democrat, removed from the sectionalism and ostracism of the regular organization, which dominated southern politics at that era. The wife became the helper of her husband and at once stepped to the front. Her pen was as ready as her brain, and the State gazed in wonder at the heroic work and indomitable perseverance of this remarkable woman. During the six years that her husband remained in Congress, she was

his private secretary and general counselor. She intuitively comprehended his duties to his constituents and became so prompt and skillful in her work that it was hard to tell where her work ended and his began. His fame as a debater and student of public questions became national, and yet every printed speech passed through her hands, and his super-excellence as an orator and collector of statistical facts perhaps was largely due to her discriminating mind and thorough revision, as well as her inspiring sympathy and enthusiastic loyalty to his interests. During six years of Congressional life and six years in the State legislature her hand was on the helm of his political barque, and he took no important step without her aid and counsel. She traveled with him during campaigns and talked to the people in private, while he addressed them in public. Yet with all these efforts Mrs. Felton is an enthusiastic farmer and a regular contributor to farm journals. She keeps up the duties of a house-

REBECCA LATIMER FELTON.

keeper as well as the duties of a wife and mother. Of her five children only one survives, and perhaps her distinguished domestic trait is her devotion to her only child and to her family. She makes frequent temperance addresses, her temperance work being as illustrious as her political life. She is the first southern woman who has been selected to deliver commencement addresses to female colleges. Her vindication by speech and in print of the maligned factory people of the South has endeared her to all fair-minded persons. She is treasured in the hearts of the laboring people. When she visits the factory towns, she is met by welcoming crowds. Two years ago, during a visit to the State capital, she was invited by the House of Representatives to occupy a seat beside the Speaker "as a woman in whom the State takes pride." As she was escorted down the aisle, the body stood to do her honor, and the speaker welcomed her "as the first woman ever so honored by the State." She is one of Georgia's lady managers of the World's Fair. When the board met to organize, Mrs. Felton was selected as their temporary president, and under her ruling, the permanent president, Mrs. Potter Palmer, was elected. Her later life has been one of continual triumph, and her struggle for truth, justice and reform is bearing sweet fruit in the reverence and love of her people. Of her early life she writes: "With a snow-white head and the sun declining to the West, I believe I can honestly say that a free, happy life in childhood is the best solace of old age." In appearance Mrs. Felton is distinguished and impressive, in speaking she is eloquent, and her ringing, sympathetic voice goes to the hearts of her hearers.

FENNER, Mrs. Mary Galentine, author, born in Rush, Monroe county, N. Y., 17th May, 1839. Her grandparents were among the first settlers of the Genesee Valley and traced their lineage back to sturdy Hollanders. From the time of reaching his majority, her father, John Galentine, occupied a prominent place in his native town. At a very early age Mrs. Fenner wrote for the "Rural New Yorker." She was educated in Genesee Wesleyan Seminary, Lima, N. Y., where she was graduated in 1861, one month before her marriage to Rev. F. D. Fenner, a graduate of Rochester University. Among her school essays are several written in blank verse, but she never gave the full expression of her thought in a satisfactory manner to herself until the revelation of her power of poesy came to her at a time of weakness and suffering. Her first published poem, "In Memoriam," dedicated to her mother on the anniversary of her father's death, in 1873, was written while she could not raise her head from her pillow

MARY GALENTINE FENNER.

She then became a prolific versifier. Her home is now in North Manlius, N. Y., where, among people of her husband's parish, she finds her most delightful work. She has published one volume of poems.

FERREE, Mrs. Susan Frances Nelson, journalist and reformer, born in Mount Pleasant, Ia., 14th January, 1844. She is a daughter of John S. Nelson, who was a lineal descendant of Thomas

SUSAN FRANCES NELSON FERREE.

Nelson, the founder of Old York, Va., where his mansion still stands. His oldest son, William, was at one time president of the king's council. William's oldest son, Gen. Thomas Nelson, was the most illustrious of his race one of the signers of the Declaration of Independence, the war governor of Virginia, and a very brilliant member of that body of great men who distinguished the country's early history. Mrs. Ferree is a fitting representative of her noble line of ancestors. Educated and refined, her influence is always on the side of kindness and right. At the age of one year she, with her parents removed to Keokuk, which was her home for many years. Her home at present is in Ottumwa, Ia., where she is the center of a large and interesting family of children. Her husband is a successful business man of that city. Mrs. Ferree is a great lover of poetry, of which she has written much, but she excels in journalism. Some of her newspaper correspondence from Washington, D. C., is exceptionally fine. She is an untiring worker for temperance and for the advancement of woman. She is a member of the Order of the Eastern Star, Woman's Relief Corps, the Iowa Woman's Suffrage Association, and the local Woman's Christian Temperance Union, and a communicant of St. Mary's Episcopal Church, of Ottumwa.

FICKLEN, Mrs. Bessie Alexander, born near Fredericksburg, Va., 10th November, 1861. Her maiden name was Bessie Mason Alexander. Her mother's maiden name was Mason. On her father's side she is of Scotch descent. Her great-grandfather, a graduate of Edinburgh, emigrated from Scotland to America in Colonial days. He settled in Georgia and served as a surgeon in the

War of the Revolution. Her father, Gen. E. P. Alexander, was educated at West Point, and, after completing the course of study there, entered the engineer corps of the United States army. On the

BESSIE ALEXANDER FICKLEN.

breaking out of the Civil War he enlisted in the Confederate army and served with distinction as Longstreet's chief of artillery. Miss Alexander was graduated from the Columbia Female Institute, Columbia, Tenn. In 1886 she became the wife of John R. Ficklen, professor of history in the Tulane University, New Orleans, La. On the opening of the art school in Sophie Newcomb College, in New Orleans, Mrs. Ficklen became a student there, showing special excellence in the direction of drawing and modeling. In the latter department she has done some good work, notably the head of a child, shown at the autumnal exhibition in 1891. In 1889 was published "Catterel, Ratterel, Doggerel," a set of satirical verses composed by General Alexander. The very clever illustrations which accompany these humorous verses are the work of Mrs. Ficklen. An essay of Mrs. Ficklen's, entitled "Dream-Poetry," appeared in "Scribner's Magazine" in 1891.

FIELD, Miss Kate, journalist, lecturer and author, born in St. Louis, Mo., in 1840. She is a daughter of the late Joseph M. Field, the well-known actor and dramatist. She was educated in seminaries in Massachusetts, and her education was broad and liberal, including thorough culture in music. After finishing her studies in the Massachusetts schools, she went to Florence, Italy, where she studied music and the modern languages. While living in Europe she corresponded for the New York "Tribune," the Philadelphia "Press" and the Chicago "Tribune," and contributed sketches for various periodicals. She studied music with Garcia and William Shakespeare. She became known in Europe as a woman of great powers of intellect and remarkable versatility.

Among her acquaintances was George Eliot, who took a strong fancy to the sparkling American girl. Returning to the United States, Miss Field, in 1874, made her début as an actor in Booth's Theater, New York City, where she won a fair success. Afterward she gave a variety song, dance and recitation. In 1882 and 1883 she was at the head of the Coöperative Dress Association in New York, which was abandoned for want of success. During the following years she lectured on Mormonism and Prohibition, as well as other current topics. In 1890 she went to Washington, D. C., where she founded her successful journal, "Kate Field's Washington." Her published works are "Planchette's Diary" (New York, 1868), "Adelaide Ristori" (1868), "Mad On Purpose," a comedy (1868), "Pen Photographs from Charles Dicken's Readings" (Boston, 1868), "Haphazard" (1873), "Ten Days in Spain" (1875), and a "History of Bell's Telephone" (London, 1878). She is the author of an analysis of George Eliot's character and works, of dramatic criticisms without number, of a life of Fechter, and of numerous political and economical essays. She is an enthusiast in art, and she has spent much time and effort to secure an art congress in Washington, for the advancement of free art, with a governmental commission of art

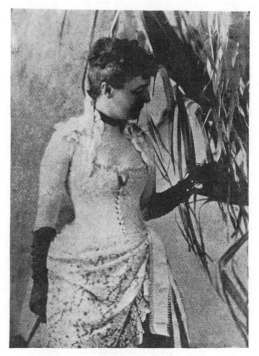

KATE FIELD.

and architecture, and a national loan exhibition of paintings by American artists exclusively.

FIELD, Mrs. Martha R., journalist, widely known by her pen-name, "Catherine Cole," born in New Orleans, La., in 1856, where she passed her youth and received her education. She early showed her literary bent in rhymes, some of which were published in the New Orleans "Picayune," when she was only a child. She was a leader among the students in school, and soon after leaving the school-room she went into service on the "Picayune," of which journal her father was an editor. She did various work in New Orleans, covering the entire field of city journalism. She afterwards worked on the San Francisco "Post." She became a wife, mother and widow all in a short space of time, and then turned her attention regu-

MARTHA R. FIELD

larly to journalistic work, and became a member of the staff of the New Orleans "Times." She was the first woman newspaper reporter to draw a salary in that city. She served for ten years as a leader-writer on the New Orleans "Picayune." Failing health compelled her to take a rest, and in 1890 she visited Great Britain. She has done a vast amount of work in the newspaper line, and she has won and holds a most enviable position in the South. Mrs. Field founded the first circulating library in New Orleans, and her pen has always been ready to aid the cause of literature and education.

FIFIELD, Mrs. Stella A. Gaines, journalist, born in Paw Paw, Mich., 1st June, 1845. Her family removed to Taylor Falls, Minn., in 1861. She was liberally educated and was graduated from the Chicago Seminary, Minnesota, in 1862. She taught school in Osceola, Wis. In 1863 she became the wife of Hon. Samuel S. Fifield, ex-Lieutenant-Governor of Wisconsin, who was then editing the "Polk County Press," the pioneer newspaper of the upper St. Croix valley. Mrs. Fifield at once associated herself with her husband in journalism. She has written much for newspapers, and she is a member of the Wisconsin Press Association. In 1872 she and her husband settled in Ashland, Wis., which was then a wilderness border hamlet, and they have been identified with that city up to the present time. Besides her literary work, she does much religious and charitable work. She was chosen a member of the Wisconsin Board of Lady Managers of the Columbian Exposition, and in that position her executive capacity enables her to accomplish a great deal of valuable work.

FILLEY, Mrs. Mary A. Powers, woman suffragist and stock-farmer, born in the town of Bristol, N. H., 12th December, 1821. Her great-grandfather, William Powers, an old Revolutionary soldier, was one of the early settlers of the neighboring town of Groton, and lived on what is known as Powers' Hill, where her grandfather and father, Jonathan Powers, were born. Her mother, Anne Kendall, whose grandparents were early settlers of the town of Hebron in 1771, became the wife of Jonathan Powers, and, dying early, left a family of six children, of whom Mary was the oldest daughter. At eleven years of age she was left with the cares and responsibilities of a woman, filling the place of the mother and making the bread, when she was obliged to stand on a chair to reach the table. The cares so early thrust upon her developed strong traits of self-reliance and capabilities that were afterward shown in her maturer life work. About 1840 she went to reside with her aunt, Mrs. Deborah Powers, of Lansingburg, N. Y., a woman of remarkable individuality of character, in business for many years, who died in 1891 at the advanced age of 101 years. In 1851 Mary Powers became the wife of Edward A. Filley, of Lansingburg, and went to St. Louis, Mo., to live. There her three children, a son and two daughters, were born. Mrs. Filley, though always feeling the justice and need of equal political rights for all, lived a quiet domestic life, till the passage of the law legalizing prostitution in St. Louis roused all the mother indignation in her, and she felt the time had come to act. Mrs. Filley with other prominent ladies felt that they must do what lay in their power to secure the repeal of such a law. She worked vigorously with pen and petition, though against great odds, sparing no effort, from vigorous articles written for the papers to personal appeals for influence from mem-

STELLA A. GAINES FIFIELD.

bers of the legislature. Anything that could be done to save the youth of St. Louis from the degradation of such a law was done. The effort was crowned with success, and the law was repealed.

Soon after Mrs. Filley removed to her country home in North Haverhill, N. H. Upon her uncle's death, in 1880, she bought his large stock farm, which she has since conducted. It was a dairy farm, and

MARY A. POWERS FILLEY.

though entirely new work to her, she learned the process of butter-making, found a market in Boston for her butter and made one year as much as 4,000 pounds. In connection with the dairy work she continued to raise a fine grade of Jersey stock. Finding the work too great a tax upon her strength, she sold the greater portion of her stock and turned the farm into a hay farm. While raising stock, her attention was called to the fact that the average man is cruel to animals, and it has been one of her special points to teach by precept and example the good effects of kindness to dumb animals. Her interest in all reforms has been active. From her small community she has sent long petitions to Congress for equal suffrage. She has drawn lecturers into the village, and in many ways made the moral atmosphere of those around her better for her having lived among them.

FILLMORE, Mrs. Abigail Powers, wife of President Fillmore, born in Stillwater, Saratoga county, N. Y., in March, 1798. Her father was Rev. Lemuel Powers, a well-known Baptist clergyman, a man of Massachusetts ancestry. He died in 1799, and the widow was left in straitened circumstances. In 1809 she removed to Central New York, where she made her home with her brother in Cayuga county. Abigail was a brilliant girl, and soon gained enough education to enable her to teach school. She taught and studied diligently, and acquired a remarkably wide and deep education. While living in Cayuga county she became acquainted with Millard Fillmore, then a youth "bound out" to learn the trade of a clothier and fuller, but who was devoting every spare moment to books. He abandoned the trade to study law, and removed to Erie county to practice.

In February, 1826, they were married in Moravia, N. Y. Mrs. Fillmore took an active interest in her husband's political and professional career. In 1828 he was elected to the State Legislature, and his success was largely due to the assistance of his wife. They were poor, but they made poverty respectable by their dignity and honesty. After serving three years in the State Legislature, Mr. Fillmore was elected to Congress. In 1830 they settled in Buffalo, N. Y., where prosperity smiled upon them. When her husband became President of the United States, she presided over the White House, but she had only recently been bereaved by the death of her sister, and she shrank from the social duties involved. Her daughter, Miss Mary Abigail Fillmore, relieved the mother of the onerous duties attached to her position. Under their régime the White House became a center of literary, artistic, musical and social attractions somewhat unusual. Mrs. Fillmore died in Washington, 30th March, 1853.

FINLEY, Miss Martha, author, born in Chillicothe, Ohio, 26th April, 1828. She has lived many years in Maryland. Her father, Dr. James B. Finley, was the oldest son of General Samuel Finley, a Revolutionary officer, major in the Virginia line of cavalry, afterward general of militia in Ohio, and of Mary Brown, daughter of one of Pennsylvania's early legislators. Her maternal grandmother was the daughter of Thomas Butler, who was a great-grandson of that Duke of Ormond who was influential in making the treaty of Utrecht. The Finleys and Browns are of Scotch-Irish descent and have martyr blood in their veins. The name of their clan was Farquharson, the Gaelic of Finley, and for many years Miss Finley used that name as her pen-name. The Butlers were

MARTHA FINLEY.

military men. Five of Miss Finley's great-uncles of that name were in the war of the Revolution, two of them on Washington's staff. One of her great-uncles, Dr. Finley, was one of the early presents of Princeton College. Her grandfathers, both on her father's and mother's side, were wealthy. Her grandfather Finley received large tracts of land from the Government in acknowledgment of his services to his country during the Revolution. He laid out and owned the town of Newville, Pa. Some of his land was in Ohio, and he finally removed to that State. In the winter of 1853 Miss Finley began her literary career by writing a newspaper story and a little book published by the Baptist Board of Publication. Between 1856 and 1870 she wrote more than twenty Sunday-school books and several series of juveniles, one series containing twelve books. These were followed by "Casella" (Philadelphia, 1869), "Peddler of LaGrave," "Old Fashioned Boy" (Philadelphia, 1871), and "Our Fred" (New York, 1874). It is through her "Elsie" and "Mildred" series that she has become popular as a writer for the young. Of the "Elsie" series there have been seventeen published, and she is at work upon another. The "Mildred" series is also very popular, six of that series having been published. Miss Finley's pen has not been employed in writing exclusively for the young. She has written three novels, "Wanted—A Pedigree" (Philadelphia, 1879), "Signing the Contract" (New York, 1879), and "Thorn in the Nest" (New York, 1886). Miss Finley resides in Elkton, Cecil county, Md., in a cottage which she has built in a pleasant section of that town.

FISHER, Miss Anna A., educator, born in Cambridge, N. Y., in 1858. She comes of New England parentage and inherited from her father a taste for literature and history, and her early reading and education were well and wisely directed. From

ANNA A. FISHER.

her mother she inherited many charms of person, and a poise of character marked by decision, excellence of judgment, great force and a heart full of tenderness and thoughtfulness for others. As

principal of Wyoming Seminary, Kingston, Pa., she passed nine years of eminent usefulness, giving an amount of mentality and strength that left a marked impression upon that institution. She is a graduate of Antioch College, from which institution she received her degree of A. M. In connection with teaching she has found great delight in continuing her studies in certain lines of work, especially literature and history. An associate member of the committee on education in the World's Congress, she has had various positions of honor offered her. She was a candidate for consideration as president of Barnard College. In the autumn of 1891 she was elected to the chair of literature in Denver University, Col., and is now lady principal. She is filling that position successfully.

FISHER, Mrs. Rebecca Jane Gilleland, philanthropist, born in Philadelphia, Pa., in 183-.

REBECCA JANE GILLELAND FISHER.

Her maiden name was Gilleland. On both her father's and mother's side she is of distinguished ancestry, and belongs to the Johnstone, Barber and Chase families. Her parents were highly cultured and devout members of the Old School Presbyterian Church. Mrs. Fisher's father moved to Texas with his family in an early day, believing it to be a good place for investment, but utterly ignorant of frontier life. Never having been inured to hardships, they were ill-prepared for the trials which awaited them. Her father joined the Texas army in 1838, and soon after both parents were killed by the Indians. In a few hours after their death, loving ones took charge of the daughter and did all that was possible for her comfort and happiness. Mrs. Fisher's fondness for literature was shown at an early age. For many years she has contributed articles for the press, which have received high encomiums. She was educated in Rutersville College, and in May, 1848, she became the wife of Rev. Orceneth Fisher, D.D. California, Oregon and Texas have been their especial fields of labor. For forty-five years she has been actively engaged in church and charitable work. She has been president of various societies and associations, and always presided with dignity, grace and tact. She has resided in Austin, Texas for nearly a score of years, and there she is held in the highest esteem and admired for her intellectual and Christian worth. She is a strong advocate and worker in the temperance and missionary causes. She has been a widow eleven years and will soon celebrate her sixtieth birthday.

FISKE, Miss Fidelia, missionary, born in Shelburne, Mass., 1st May, 1816. She was the fourth daughter of Rufus and Hannah Woodward Fiske, and could look back through an unbroken line of godly ancestors' to William Fiske, who came from Suffolk county, England, in 1637. Her great-grand-father, Ebenezer Fiske, jr., moved from the eastern part of the State to Shelburne, where Fidelia was born. Among her earliest memories was the departure of her missionary uncle, Rev. Pliny Fiske, for the Holy Land, in 1819. The thoughtful and observing child had a strong will, but the early subjection to authority required by her parents prepared the way for a submissiveness of Christian character. Soon after her conversion she joined the Congregational Church in Shelburne, 12th July, 1831. Her school-days were marked by a desire for thoroughness and a spirit of self-reliance. Most of the time from 1833 to 1839, except for brief periods of study, she taught in the schools of her native town. In 1839 she entered Mt. Holyoke Seminary. A severe illness in the summer of 1840 prevented her return to the seminary till the next year, when she entered the senior class and was graduated in 1842. Miss Lyon at once engaged her as a teacher. The next January a call came to the seminary for one to go to Persia with Dr. and Mrs. Perkins, to take charge of a school for Nestorian girls in Oroomiah. Miss Lyon laid the call before the school. Of the forty notes written in response, one of the shortest read: "If counted worthy, I should be willing to go. Fidelia Fiske." Already her services to the seminary seemed too valuable to be spared, but that point was soon yielded. Her widowed mother could not consent so readily. The same reason kept others from going, and a month later the question came back to Miss Fiske. "Then we will go and see your mother," said Miss Lyon, and within an hour they were on their way for a drive of thirty miles through the snowdrifts. It was ten days before Dr. Perkins was to sail. Roused from sleep by the midnight arrival, the mother knew at once their errand. Her consent was obtained. Miss Lyon returned to the seminary, and Miss Fiske followed, to find that the teachers and students had prepared a very good outfit for her. The next morning she was on the way to Boston. She sailed on Wednesday, 1st March, for Smyrna, and arrived in Oroomiah 14th June, 1843. When the mission to the Nestorians began, nine years before, only one woman among them, the sister of the Patriarch, could read. Men opposed the education of women, and the women were content to be menials and ignorant. A few girls had been gathered as day scholars, but little could be done for them till separated from their degrading surroundings and brought into a Christian home for continuous training, a course repugnant to their ideas of social propriety. At that time an unmarried girl of fourteen was scarcely to be found. Miss Fiske made arrangements for six boarding pupils, not knowing one whom she might expect besides day scholars. On the 16th October, the day appointed for the school to open, Mar Yohanan, a Nestorian bishop who had visited America with Dr. Perkins, brought her two girls, one seven and the other ten years old, saying:

"These are your daughters. Now you begin Mount Holyoke in Persia." By spring she had six girls, wild and untutored. Ragged and filthy when they entered, a lesson in cleanliness was the first thing in their training for a work as teachers, wives and mothers. The course of study fixed upon was in their native Syriac and was largely Biblical. Notwithstanding interruptions, now from papal or Mohammedan persecutions, now from ravages of fever or cholera, the school made steady progress. In its fourth year it numbered over forty. Its first public examination in 1850 marked an era in the history of that oriental nation and in the lives of its three graduates. The ten graduates of 1853 were between the ages of seventeen and nineteen. Lying, stealing and other vices, general at first, were put away, and scores of pupils went forth transformed in character to labor for similar changes in their own homes and villages. Miss Fiske's cares as mother, housekeeper and teacher so increased that

ALICE C. FLETCHER.

Miss Rice went from Mt. Holyoke Seminary, in 1847, to be her assistant and to give her more time for work among the women of the city and of the mountains around. Her faithful labors won mothers as well as daughters to the cross. When failing health forced her to leave for America, after fifteen fruitful years, there were ninety-three native women in the company that sat down with her at the table of the Lord. Her influence in the mission and on Nestorian character is well set forth in the book entitled "Woman and her Savior in Persia." The home voyage seemed to give a new lease of life, and her last five years were as useful as any that had preceded. Besides responding, as strength allowed, to the many urgent calls from the ladies' meetings for the story of her work in Persia, she spent many months in Mt. Holyoke Seminary, where her labors in the remarkable revivals of 1862–64 were a fitting close to her life's work. She died 26th July, 1864, in the home of her aged mother, in

Shelburne. Her finely balanced mind, deep and delicate sensibilities, intuitive knowledge of human nature, and her discretion, all controlled by ardent Christian love, made her a power for good. Her career is described in the title chosen by her biographer: "Faith working by Love."

FLETCHER, Miss Alice Cunningham, ethnologist, born in Boston, Mass., in 1845. She received a thorough and liberal education. After studying the archæological remains in the Ohio and Mississippi valleys she went, in 1881, to live among the Omaha Indians, in Nebraska, to make an investigation of their customs and traditions, under the auspices of the Peabody Museum of American Archæology, of Harvard University. She became interested in the affairs of the Omahas and secured the passage of a law allotting lands to them. She was chosen to make the allotment in 1883 and 1884. She caused a number of the children of the Omahas to be sent to the Indian schools in Carlisle, Pa., and Hampton, Va., and she raised large sums of money to defray the expenses of the education of other ambitious Indians. Under the auspices of the Woman's National Indian Association she established a system of loaning money to Indians who wished to buy land and build homes of their own. Her scientific researches have been of great value, covering Indian traditions, customs, religions, moneys, music and ceremonies, and many ethnographic and archæological subjects. In 1884 and 1885 she sent an exhibit of the industries of civilized Indians to the New Orleans Exhibition, prepared on request by the Indian Bureau. Her labors and lectures on that occasion won her a diploma of honor. In answer to a Senate resolution of 23rd February, 1885, she prepared her valuable book, "Indian Civilization and Education." In 1886 she was sent by the Commissioner of Education to visit Alaska and the Aleutian Islands, where she made a study of the conditions of the natives. In 1888 her reports were published in full. Acting for the government, she has allotted lands in severalty to the Winnebagoes, of Nebraska, and the Nez Percés, of Idaho. Her work in behalf of the Indians has been incessant and varied. She brought out the first Indian woman physician, Susan La Flesche, and induced other Indians to study law and other professions. Her work has been of the highest order, both scientific and philanthropic.

FLETCHER, Mrs. Lisa Anne, poet, born in Ashby, Mass., 27th December, 1844. Her maiden name was Stewart. When she was two years old, her father died, and when she was sixteen, her mother died. There were no other children in the family. In 1864 she became the wife of Edwin S. Fletcher, of Manchester, N. H., since which time her home has been in that city. From earliest childhood she has shown an almost equal fondness for music, painting and poetry. In 1865 she was stricken with diphtheria in its most malignant form, and since that time her life has been full of suffering, and these later years she has been an invalid. She is an example of what can be accomplished under great difficulties by firmness of spirit, force of will and a brave perseverance. All her work is done in a reclining position. She has a large correspondence, partly through the Shut-In Society. Thousands of letters have gone forth from her corner and fulfilled their mission of cheer and comfort. It is as an artist she excels. She is now painting a collection of wild flowers that grow about Manchester, and has already about one-hundred-thirty kinds. With firm health she would doubtless have made a great name for herself, especially in painting wild flowers. In June, 1888, she

allowed herself for the first time to write verse in earnest. Her poems have appeared in a large number of the best magazines and periodicals. Her love for birds amounts to a passion, and much that is interesting might be said of her studies of the wild birds from her window. A local secretary of the Audubon Society, she has done noble work in their behalf. A constant sufferer both physically and mentally, she yet accomplishes more work than many who are strong and well. Possessed of an intense love of beauty in every form, she deeply feels the fetters under which her spirit

LISA ANNE FLETCHER.

struggles, and longs for the freedom of larger opportunities.

FOLEY, Miss Margaret E., sculptor, born in New Hampshire, and died in Menan, in Austrian Tyrol, in 1887. Miss Foley was an entirely self-taught artist. She began her career in a small way, modeling in chalk and carving in wood. In youth she moved to Boston, Mass., where she worked hard and suffered much privation, making a bare living at first by carving portraits and ideal heads in cameo. After working seven years in Boston, she went to Rome, Italy, where she passed the rest of her professional life in the company of Harriet Hosmer, Gibson, Story, Mrs. Jameson and William and Mary Howitt. In 1877 her health failed, and she accompanied Mr. and Mrs. Howitt to their home in Austrian Tyrol, where she died. Among the works she left are portrait busts of S. C. Hall, Charles Sumner and Theodore Parker, and medallions of William and Mary Howitt, Longfellow, Bryant and S. C. Hall. Her artistic work includes "The Albanese," a medallion, "Cleopatra," a bust, and statues of "Excelsior," "Jeremiah" and many others.

FOLTZ, Mrs. Clara Shortridge, orator and lawyer, born in New Lisbon, Henry county, Ind., 16th July, 1849. Her father was the eloquent Christian preacher, Elias W. Shortridge. When seven years old, she removed with her parents to Mt. Pleasant, Iowa, where she attended, at intervals, Howe's Female Seminary for nearly three years. Leaving there she went to Mercer county, Ill., and

CLARA SHORTRIDGE FOLTZ.

taught school six months, completing the term on her birthday. The same year she was married. Household cares occupied her time for several years. In 1872, having removed to the Pacific coast, she began to write for the press and showed flashes of genius as a correspondent. Four years later she began the study of law, supporting herself and five children by her pen and occasional lectures. But women were not then allowed to practice law in the Golden State. In the winter of 1877–78 she went to Sacramento, the State capital, and secured the passage of an act opening the doors of the legal profession to women, and was the first to avail herself of the privileges of the new law, which she did in September, 1879, by being admitted to practice in the district court, and in December of the same year by admission to the supreme court of the State. During the year 1879 she applied for admission to the Hastings College of Law, which was refused. Acting on the theory that the law college was a part of the State University, to which men and women were alike entitled to admission under the law, she sued out a writ of mandate against the regents to compel them to admit her. Against the ablest counsel in the State she won her case, both in the district and in the supreme court. When the decision came at last, she was unable to avail herself of its benefits, having passed the student period and already acquired a promising practice. In the winter of 1880 she was made clerk of the judiciary committee of the assembly, and upon the adjournment of the legislature began the practice of law in San Francisco. The political campaign of 1882 gave opportunity for the first real display of her oratorical powers. She made a dozen or more speeches, and at once took rank

among the leading orators of the coast, speaking in the campaigns of 1884, 1886 and 1888. In 1885 and again in 1887, as a respite from a laborious practice, she lectured a short time in the Eastern States under the auspices of the Slayton Lyceum Bureau. Upon her return from the East, Governor Bartlett appointed her trustee of the State Normal School, which place she filled for the full term. She settled in San Diego in 1887 and started the "Daily Bee," an eight-page paper, which she edited and managed with success until its consolidation with the "Union." Upon the sale of her paper she resumed practice in San Diego, and continued there until the fall of 1890, when she returned to San Francisco, where she now commands a large and growing practice. Her sunny temper, genial disposition, broad views, liberal sentiments, never failing charity and ready repartee make her a brilliant conversationalist. As a lawyer she stands prominent among the lawyers of the country. Her success has brought her into general favor and won for her the complimentary title, "The Portia of the Pacific."

FONDA, Mrs. Mary Alice, musician, linguist, and author, born 21st October, 1837. She is known by her pen-name, "Octavia Hensel." Her maiden name was Mary Alice Ives. She is descended from General Michael Jackson, of Newton, Mass., who commanded a regiment of minute-men in the battle of Lexington. His son, Amasa Jackson, was the first president of the Union Bank of New York, in 1812. He was married to Mary Phelps, the only daughter and heiress of Oliver Phelps, of Boston, who with Nathaniel Gorham purchased in the interior of New York State from the Indians the tract of land now known as the Phelps and Gorham purchase. Mary Charlotte Jackson,

MARY ALICE FONDA.

the grandmother of Mrs. Fonda, was married to Ralph Olmstead, of New York. Their only child, the mother of Mrs. Fonda, Mary Phelps Olmstead, was married to George Russell Ives, of New York.

Mrs. Fonda's childhood was most fortunate. Her parents were surrounded by literary people. Mrs. Fonda's early taste tended toward literature. In 1865 she became the wife of Rev. William Wood Seymour, at one time connected with Trinity Parish, New York. In 1886 her books on the festivals of the church, known as the "Cedar Grove Series," were published in New York, and have become standard. After Mr. Seymour's death his widow returned to her father's house, but his loss of property during the Civil War and his feeble health led her to go to Europe for study to become a vocal teacher. She never appeared on the stage, except for charitable objects, as her relatives were opposed to a professional life. Before she went to Europe, her "Life of Gottschalk (Boston, 1870) was published. During her residence in Europe she corresponded for several journals, the "Home Journal" of New York, the San Francisco "Chronicle" and the St. Paul "Pioneer Press" of Minnesota. She held the position of musical instructor and English companion to the Archdukes and Archduchesses, children of the Archduke of Austria, Carl Salvator of Tuscany, and his wife, Princess Marie Immaculate of Naples. After the death of her father she returned to her home in the United States and taught music in New York and Philadelphia. In 1884 she brought out her papers on "The Rhinegold Trilogy" (Boston), which had been written in Vienna under the supervision of Liszt and Richard Wagner. After the death of her grandmother, in 1885, she opened a school of vocal music in Nashville, Tenn. She removed to Louisville, Ky., in 1887, where she now resides. In the summer of 1888 she became the wife of Abraham G. Fonda, a descendant of the New York Fonda family, whose ancestor, Major Jelles Fonda, had purchased the Mohawk Valley land from the Phelps and Gorham estate, where the town of Fonda now stands. Mrs. Fonda is one of the most cultivated women in America. She speaks seven languages fluently, German, French, Spanish, Italian, Portuguese, Roumanian and Magyar dialects, while her musical abilities are marked. She plays the piano, harp, guitar and organ, and is the possessor of a fine voice. She has studied under the best European teachers. Her rare musical accomplishments have won the commendation of Liszt, Rubenstein and other masters. As a critic Mrs. Fonda has won renown. Her musical nature, her superior education, her thorough knowledge of the laws of theory and familiarity with the works of the great composers of the classic, romantic and Wagnerian schools, and the newer schools of harmony, give her a point of vantage above the ordinary. She is prominent among the Daughters of the American Revolution and has in her possession many rare Revolutionary relics. Her novel, "Imperia" (Buffalo, 1892), is a success.

FOOTE, Mrs. Mary Hallock, author and artist, born in Milton, N. Y., 19th November, 1847. Her maiden name was Hallock. She became the wife of Arthur D. Foote, a mining engineer, in 1876, and lived some years in the mining districts of Colorado and California, and afterwards in Boisé City, Idaho. She studied art in the Cooper Institute, New York City, working there four winters under the instruction of Dr. Rimmer. She afterward studied with Frost Johnson and William J. Linton. Her artistic training ended with block-work with Linton. She has illustrated many books in black and white, and done much work for magazines. She has been particularly successful in her drawings of western and Mexican life and scenery. Many of her best detached illustrations have appeared in the "Century," "Scribner's Magazine," "St. Nicholas" and other periodicals. She is the author of "The Led Horse Claim" (Boston, 1883), "John Bodewin's Testimony" (Boston, 1886), and "The Last Assembly Ball" (1888). Her home is now in New York City.

FORD, Mrs. Miriam Chase, musician and journalist, born in Boston, Mass., 20th September, 1866. Her parents are S. Warren Chase and Sarah Virginia Hulst. When she was three years old, her parents moved to Omaha, Neb. Until her eleventh year she received instruction from her mother and private teachers. On the removal of her parents to Milwaukee, Wis., she entered the Milwaukee College, where the artistic element in her soon found expression in some admirable crayons and free-hand sketches. French was one of the studies in which she excelled. When fourteen years of age, she accompanied her grandmother, of Omaha, Neb., to Europe. With eighteen months of travel

MIRIAM CHASE FORD.

and study on the Continent, with six months divided between Egypt, Palestine, Turkey and Greece, she gained knowledge and experience, perfected her French and learned some Italian, German and Spanish. The next two years she spent in Milwaukee College, during which time she began her vocal training under a German master. The family then returned to Omaha, and the next two winters she spent in New York City, studying under Errani. At that time she entered the literary field as special correspondent of the Omaha "World." The year 1886 found her again in Europe. She studied a year in Milan, under San Giovanni and Giovannini, and was a student for some time in the Paris Conservatory. Afterwards she went to London to become a pupil of Randegger. There she remained but a short time. Having suffered in Milan from an attack of Roman fever, a severe illness necessitated her return home for rest. On leaving England she became engaged to Percival Boys Ford, of London, who traveled with her family to Omaha, where they were married in 1890. During her last long sojourn in Europe she was special correspondent of the Omaha "Bee." She has since written a good deal in the way of critiques, reminiscences and special articles. Mrs. Ford uses her voice in a public way only for the benefit of charity or some public enterprise.

FORNEY, Miss Tillie May, author and journalist, born in Washington, D. C., in 1861. She is the youngest child of the eminent journalist, John W. Forney, founder and editor of the Philadelphia "Press," a man who wielded an acknowledged great political and social influence. This daughter, having inherited many of her distinguished father's tastes and ambitions, became his almost constant companion after leaving Miss Carr's celebrated academy on the Old-York-Road, Pa. She had written for publication from early girlhood, and she then took up the task systematically and wrote regularly for prominent journals, besides acting frequently as her father's amanuensis, both in this country and in Europe. Under his experienced eye she received careful training for the work she preferred above all others. No accomplishment suitable to her sex was neglected in her education. She possesses a voice of unusual range and sweetness, and at that period it was her teacher's wish that all her interest should be centered on her musical talent, but it seemed impossible for her to drop her pen. She grows fonder of her literary duties every year, and is a constant contributor to New York, Philadelphia and western dailies, besides writing regularly for several well-known magazines. She resides with

TILLIE MAY FORNEY.

her widowed mother in the old family residence, on South Washington Square, Philadelphia. She has been reared in a home of luxury, and the Forney library is one of the finest in Philadelphia.

Mrs. John W. Forney is an accomplished lady of the old school, and she and her daughter are both social favorites, although each has aims and tasks that are preferred to those of fashionable life. Miss Forney's progress in literature, though rapid, is evidently but the promise of what she is yet to accomplish.

FOSTER, Mrs. J. Ellen Horton, temperance worker and lawyer, born in Lowell, Mass.,

J. ELLEN FOSTER.

3rd November, 1840. She is a daughter of Rev. Jotham Horton, a Methodist preacher. She was educated in Lima, N. Y., and removed to Clinton, Ia., where, in 1869, she became the wife of E. C. Foster, a lawyer. Mrs. Foster studied law and was admitted to the bar of the Supreme Court of Iowa in 1872. She was the first woman to practice before that court. At first she practiced alone, but she afterwards formed a partnership with her husband. She followed the legal profession for a number of years. She is widely known as "The Iowa Lawyer." In religion she is a Methodist. She joined the temperance workers when the crusade opened, and soon became prominent as a worker. Her home in Clinton was burned, presumably by the enemies of temperance. As a member of the Woman's Christian Temperance Union she was able to give most valuable service as superintendent of the legislative department. Her knowledge of law enabled her to direct wisely all the movement for the adoption of constitutional amendments in the various States, aimed to secure the prohibition of the sale and manufacture of alcoholic liquors. She has written a pamphlet on the legal bearings of the question. She has been exceedingly popular and successful as a lecturer. She is a pronounced suffragist, and she maintains that no organization has the right to pledge the influence of its members to any other organization for any purpose. Her views naturally led her to affiliate with the Non-Partisan League, and she served that body for several years as corresponding secretary, having her office in Boston, Mass. She served her own State union as corresponding secretary and president for years. In 1887 she visited Europe, where she rested and studied the temperance question. In England she addressed great audiences. Returning to the United States, she took part in the International Council of Women in Washington. She has published a number of pamphlets and magazine articles on temperance. Her two daughters died in youth. Two sons make up her family. A part of each year she spends in Washington, D. C.

FOSTER, Mrs. Susie E., author and philanthropist, born in Torbrook, Nova Scotia, Canada,

SUSIE E. FOSTER.

18th May, 1846. Her maiden name was Holland, and she was born and grew up on a farm. When she was twelve years old, she was sent away from home for better educational advantages. Two years later her mother's failing health made her presence at home necessary, and the routine of the school-room was never resumed. Her studies were continued at home, and her tastes were formed and her mind developed by a close perusal of the best authors. Both parents were of more than ordinary intellectual ability. Her grandfather Henderson was well known in educational circles. In his academy were trained men who became prominent in the religious and political history of Nova Scotia. Her father's father had been a member of the Provincial Parliament. The Hollands possessed literary and poetic ability, which was handed down to her. She became the wife of Mr. Foster when she was nineteen years of age. Brought up in the same faith, they pledged their allegiance in early years to God and Methodism. Three years after their marriage they joined the tide of migration westward, first to Illinois, and then to northwest Iowa. In the prairie homestead and later among a cultivated circle in town she

contributed articles to the press. There the Woman's Christian Temperance Union won her to its great work. She served as corresponding secretary of the eleventh Congressional district during the stormy year that gave a prohibitory amendment to Iowa. She spent four years in Walla Walla, Wash., and her work continued along the lines of reform in local, county and State organizations. Going to Oregon for better educational advantages for their children, she was soon elected State corresponding secretary. Her pen is busy in the interests of the work, and while she sometimes is called upon to address an audience, she is not a ready speaker, and her thoughts find best expression through the medium of pen and paper. She has found, like other busy women, that her temperance work does not set her free from the claims of church and missionary effort, to which she gives much attention. Their home is in a suburb of Portland, near the university, where their daughter and son are students.

FOXWORTHY, Miss Alice S., educator, born in Mount Carmel, Fleming county, Ky., 22nd December, 1852. Through her paternal grandmother, Mary Calvert Foxworthy, she is a lineal descendant of Cecil Calvert, Lord Baltimore, of Maryland. Her early education was received in the Stanford Academy, Stanford, Ky., and there she began her career of teaching immediately after her graduation. In her native State she taught successfully in the Stanford Academy, the Catlettsburg High School and the East Kentucky Normal School. From the last mentioned position she was called to the responsible post of presiding teacher in the Tennessee Female College of Franklin, Tenn. She next received a call to the position of lady principal

ALICE S. FOXWORTHY.

in the Nashville College for Young Ladies. Since 1884 Miss Foxworthy has occupied that position. Dr. G. W. F. Price, the president of that college, early invested her with full authority, leaving her to work out her ideas in the practical organization and management of the school. Miss Foxworthy's attainments are by no means insignificant. Her school training has been continued and extended

SUSAN STUART FRACKLETON.

by reading and study during the whole of her professional life. In 1890 the University of Nashville, Nashville, Tenn., conferred upon her the degree of M.A. Though the duties of principal have gradually withdrawn Miss Foxworthy from class-room work, her intimate acquaintance with each pupil under her care is not lessened. The Sabbath-school class of over one-hundred pupils and the flourishing missionary society which she has built up give her an opportunity for a strong influence in forming the characters under her charge. She is an original and impressive teacher of the Bible. Her religion is a religion of justice and unselfishness, her energy is inexhaustible, her perseverance indomitable. Her close observation, her keen and accurate judgment of men and things, and her long experience as a practical educator place her easily in the first rank in her profession.

FRACKLETON, Mrs. Susan Stuart, artist and inventor, born in Milwaukee, Wis., in 1851. Her father's name was Goodrich. Her mother's maiden name was Mary Robinson, of Penn Yan, N.Y. Before her marriage to Richard G. Frackleton, this gifted young woman was a fellow-student with Carl Marr in the studio of Henry Vianden, in Milwaukee. Later she studied in New York City under the Harts, Mrs. Beers and Greatorex. She commenced china-painting in 1874, and in that field she has achieved great distinction in America and Europe. Mrs. Frackleton was the only woman in the country who exhibited in Philadelphia among the men, and her medals are numerous. She received the diploma awarded by the United States Potters' Association in 1889. Seeing the need of a portable gas-kiln for firing her artistic work, she invented and patented one. For her technical book,

personal artistic work, colors and invention she has been honored by a special letter from the Queen of Italy. She has also been most flatteringly recognized and honored by the Academy of San Carlos, in the Mexican Republic. As an artist her admirable work has had court presentation in Rome at the request of the Queen. Mrs. Frackleton has written a very successful book on china painting. It is entitled "Tried by Fire" (New York, 1886). It has been accepted as a text-book in the library of the South Kensington Art Museum, and the thanks of the Lords of the Committee of Council on Education were tendered to the author. The volume and its results won the author four international medals. Over five-hundred women in America have been made self-supporting by means of Mrs. Frackleton's skill in all that pertains to the ceramic art. She stands at the head of one of the most eminently successful china color and decorating works in the United States. In April, 1892, she was elected president of the National League of Mineral Painters. Her success in life she owes entirely to her own temperament and the full use of all the opportunities for developing her own genius.

FRAME, Mrs. Esther Gordon, minister and evangelist, born in Washington, Ind., 10th July, 1840. Her maiden name was Gordon. Her father was born in Hamilton county, Ohio, and his ancestors came from the Scottish Highlands and were Scotch-Irish. In early life he resided in Centerville, Ind., and there studied law. From Centerville he removed to Thorntown, Ind., and in 1854 represented Boone county in the Indiana Legislature. In 1856 he went to Salem, Iowa, and was there admitted to the bar as a lawyer. Deborah

ESTHER GORDON FRAME.

Mendenhall, Mrs. Frame's mother, was born in New Garden, Guilford county, N. C. She was of English stock, and her people were inclined to the learned professions. Mrs. Frame was educated mostly among the Friends. In her school-days she often called her companions around her and preached to them with such effect that her juvenile audiences were brought to tears. She wove beauti-

LOUISE E. FRANCIS.

ful stories, to which her auditors listened with delight. In March, 1857, she became the wife of Nathan T. Frame, of Salem, Iowa. She has had three children, one of whom, a boy, died in infancy, and two daughters, Itasca M., and Hettie C. She was formerly a member of the Methodist Episcopal Church, but, feeling that she was called to preach and that the Methodists would not ordain her, she joined the Society of Friends and was ordained a minister by them. She began her ministry in New Garden Friends Meeting, in Indiana, 1869. Her home is now in Jamestown, Ohio, where she has lived since 1880. Her ministry has not been confined to her own denomination. For more than twenty years, with her husband, who is a minister, she has preached as an evangelist among all the principal churches of the United States.

FRANCIS, Miss Louise E., journalist, born in St. Helena, Cal., 23rd April, 1869. Her teacher, noticing the marked love for books manifested by his pupil, "Still Water," as she was called, took pains to see that her thirst for reading was quenched only by good books and the master-spirits. She was educated in the public schools of her native town, graduating at the age of fourteen, the salutatorian of her class. She afterwards attended a private academy for eighteen months, and subsequently finished her education in the State Normal School. Her forte was writing compositions, and her part in the school exercises was always to furnish one of her own articles. Her talent for writing grew, and when at the age of seventeen she went out in the world to make a living for herself, she naturally turned to an editor's office. She remained in the office of the "Santa Clara Valley," a monthly magazine, for three

years, taking full charge of the household and young folks' departments, and adding an occasional literary note. She then rested for a year. Next she acted as correspondent for the San José "Daily Mercury" during the summer meetings of the Chautauqua Literary and Scientific Circle. Through that engagement she formed the acquaintance of T. A. Peckham, and with him went into partnership and started a newspaper in Monterey, called the "Enterprise." The project did not prove a financial success, and after six months was discontinued. On 3rd April, 1891, a new "Enterprise" was started, this time in Castroville, of which Miss Francis was sole editor and proprietor. The new venture was successful, and Miss Francis is making her paper one of the brightest in the State. It is the official organ of the Pacific Coast Women's Press Association, and thus has a wider influence than the ordinary newspapers. Miss Francis was elected one of the delegates to the National Editorial Association, that met in California in May, 1892.

FRANK, Miss Rachel, author, born in San Francisco, Cal., 10th April, 1866. She is more generally known as Ray Frank. She is of Jewish blood. Self-reliant from an early age, she entered upon the career of a school teacher when but fifteen years old, and, considering that her first field of labor was in the rough mining regions of Nevada, her success as an educator was remarkable. From childhood she gave evidence of literary and oratorical ability. Having a family of younger brothers and sisters dependent upon her, she patiently labored in a profession for which she had no real liking, and even gratuitously conducted evening classes for the benefit of young miners who were unable to

RACHEL FRANK.

attend the day school. In addition to her school work she contributed to various local and other papers and taught private classes in elocution with success. Her dramatic ability is undoubted, and she has had numerous inducements to adopt a stage career, but in this, as in all else, she has original ideas which have prevented her from accepting many good offers. Deciding that journalism is a preparatory school for those wishing to engage in higher literary work, she became a regular and conscientious contributor to various periodicals on diverse subjects. In 1890 she accepted an offer of several journals to write up the great Northwest, and one of the features of the consequent trip was the organization of permanent congregations of her people. Her fame as a young woman of rare good sense and eloquence had preceded her, and her co-religionists conferred upon her the great honor of inviting her to address them on the eve of the Day of Atonement, the most sacred of all Hebrew festivals. She is probably the first woman in the history of the world who has ever preached to the Jews upon that day. The Jews, as a people, have ever been opposed to women occupying the pulpit, but in Miss Frank's case they have made an exception, believing that her sincere earnestness, natural eloquence and intense zeal peculiarly fit her for preaching. She is extremely liberal in her religious views, but possesses an intense interest in her people and their welfare. She has recently accepted the editorship of the " Pacific Coast Home Monthly," a journal of excellent standing. She has contributed to the New York " Messenger," " American Hebrew," Oakland "Times," " Jewish Times and Observer," " The Young California " and other periodicals in Tacoma, Seattle and San Francisco. One of her stories, " An Experience Extraordinary," has proved very popular. Miss Frank's home is in Oakland, Cal., and her time is given up to teaching, preaching, housekeeping and journalism.

FRANKLIN, Miss Gertrude [Virginia H. Beatty], singer and musical educator, born in Baltimore, Md., of a wealthy and aristocratic family. She is a granddaughter of the late James Beatty, the millionaire, of Baltimore, and is also closely related to some of the oldest Maryland families. Miss Franklin early manifested musical gifts of an uncommon order, and while still young her education in music was begun. She soon gave promise of becoming a pianist of the first rank, but her tastes ran rather in a vocal than an instrumental direction, and, at the age of thirteen, prompted by her natural impulses and by the possession of a voice of sweetness and purity, she devoted her attention to singing. After pursuing her studies for a time in this country, she was at length induced by Signor Agramonte, with whom she had been studying, to go to Europe to complete her musical education. She went to London and became a pupil of Shakespeare, and then to Paris for two years, where she became a pupil of Madame Lagrange. She also studied with Professor Barbot, of the Conservatoire. Before leaving Paris, Miss Franklin appeared in a concert in the Salle Erard and achieved a flattering success, which was emphasized by immediate offers of concert engagements, and an offer from the Italian Opera management for a season of opera. Miss Franklin was in haste to reach London, where she made arrangements to study oratorio and English ballad music under Randegger, who was so pleased with her voice and method that he besought her to remain and make a career in England. Eager to return home after her prolonged absence, she declined that, and also an offer from Carl Rosa to join his English Opera Company. After her return to America she took an extended course of study under Madame Rudersdorff for oratorio and the more serious range of classical concert music.

Miss Franklin has appeared in New York, Boston and Brooklyn in symphony concerts, and in classical and other concerts in most of the leading cities in America with success. She has also sung with marked favor in London and Paris, where her artistic worth is perhaps still more appreciated than it is in her own country. Miss Franklin is in constant receipt of offers for opera and concert tours in Europe and America, but she objects to the fatigue and excitement of travel and does not appear before the public as often as she otherwise would. Being financially independent, she prefers the quiet of home and occasional appearances.

GERTRUDE FRANKLIN.

in important concerts. Miss Franklin is fully as successful as a teacher, as she has been as a singer.

FRAY, Mrs. Ellen Sulley, reformer, born in the parish of Calverton, Nottinghamshire, England, 2nd December, 1832. She is descended from both Huguenot and Danish ancestors. Her mother was a near relative of Lord Denman, Chief Justice of England, and from both sides of the house she inherited intellectual qualities. Her father was Richard Sulley, who married Elizabeth Denman in 1827, and of their six children Ellen was the third daughter. When she was but a child, Mr. Sulley moved with his family to the United States, and after some years located in Rochester, N. Y. During those early years of her life, while they were traveling from place to place, opportunities for education were limited so far as books were concerned. Her father thought that it mattered little, as all that girls needed was to write and read, with a little knowledge of arithmetic added. Ellen became a reader and a student of history. Her father was a well-known writer upon social and economical questions, and had distinguished himself at the time of the repeal of the Corn Laws in England. As a young girl Ellen heard such subjects discussed constantly and became deeply interested in all reforms of the day. In 1848 she first became roused upon the question of woman suffrage, through attendance upon a convention held in Rochester and presided over by Abigail Bush, with Lucretia Mott, Mrs. Stanton and others of the earlier agitators as speakers. That marked an epoch in her life. She had learned of woman's inferiority through the religious instruction which she had received, but henceforth she felt that something in it was wrong. She was advised by her Sunday-school teacher carefully to study and compare passages in the Old and New Testaments. That she did thoroughly, and became satisfied that Christ nowhere made any difference between the sexes. Henceforth her work lay in the direction thus given, and she has labored faithfully to promote political equality for woman and to advance her rights in the industrial fields. In 1853 she became the wife of F. M. Fray, and made her home in Toledo, Ohio, where she now lives. It was a happy union, lasting for twenty years, until the death of Mr. Fray. Her two children died in childhood, leaving her alone and free to devote herself to those things which she felt were of a character to help humanity. She has formed suffrage clubs in several different States and in Canada, and has been repeatedly a delegate to National councils, giving her time and money without stint. She has been foremost in testing woman's eligibility for various positions. In 1886 Mrs. Fray entered into a political canvass in Rochester to put a woman upon the board of managers of the State Industrial School. With Miss Mary Anthony, the sister of Susan, she worked for three weeks and gained the victory. Mrs. Fray is still full of vigor and energy in the cause to which she has given the best of herself for so many years. At present she is one of

ELLEN SULLEY FRAY.

the district presidents of the Ohio Woman's Suffrage Association and a prominent member of several of the leading clubs, literary, social and economic, in Toledo.

FRAZIER, Mrs. Martha M., educator and temperance worker, born near Springfield, Mass., 12th December, 1826. Her father's name was Albert Chaffee, and her mother's maiden name was

MARTHA M. FRAZIER.

Chloe Melinda Hyde. Her only memory of her mother was of being held to look at her as she lay in her coffin. Her father, being poor, took his young family west. They stopped in Washtenaw county, Mich., and he was taken ill, as were the children also, of whom one died. Being discouraged, he gave his children to kind-hearted neighbors and disappeared. Martha was adopted into the family of John and Lois Thompson, and was always known by that name. When in her eighth year, the family moved to Illinois, twenty-five miles west of Chicago, a country then nearly a wilderness. She had the same privileges as the rest of the family, but a few terms in a select school in Warrenville rounded out her educational career, and that was gained on promising the good man of the house that she would wear her home manufactured woolen dress, which promise she kept. Afterward, in teaching district school, she received in compensation one dollar per week and boarded around, then one dollar and fifty cents, and later two dollars and board herself, for which extravagance the board were censured. When nineteen years of age, while visiting a sister residing in Waukesha county, Wis., she became acquainted with a young farmer, W. M. Frazier, whose wife she afterward became. She is an ardent lover of the church of her choice, and is an active sympathizer and helper in all modern reforms. She is an uncompromising advocate of prohibition, total abstinence and equal privilege and equal purity for men and women. She is a member of the school board and superintendent of scientific temperance instruction, and is president of the local Woman's Christian Temperance Union, and also president of the home library association in Mukwonago, Wis.

FREEMAN, Mrs. Mattie A., freethinker and lecturer, born in Sturgis, St. Joseph county, Mich., 9th August, 1839. Her ancestors were French and German, Americanized by generations

MATTIE A. FREEMAN.

of residence in the State of New York. Her father was a freethinker, her mother a close-communion Baptist. The mother tried to keep the children from what she considered the contamination of infidelity. They attended revivals and passed through all the usual experiences, but the daughter became an infidel in her early youth. Mrs. Freeman as a child learned rapidly. Her first public discussion was at the age of fourteen. An associate editor of a weekly newspaper had written an article on the inferiority of woman. Over a pen-name the school-girl replied to it. The controversy was kept up through several papers, the German student wondering, in the meantime, who it was that was making so effective an argument against him. He was thoroughly disgusted when he discovered that his opponent was a girl. At fifteen she taught her first school. It was a failure. She was yet in short dresses, and the "big" pupils refused to obey her. She endured it for six weeks, and then, disheartened and defeated, sent word to her father to take her home. About that time she heard Abby Kelly Foster speak on abolition, and the young girl's heart became filled with a burning hatred of slavery. Being invited soon after to take part in a public entertainment, she astonished all and offended some by giving a most radical anti-slavery speech. Her father was an old-time Whig and retained an intense admiration for Henry Clay. Even he was horrified to hear his young daughter, of whom he had been so proud, attack his dead pro-slavery idol. If her first attempt at teaching was a failure, the subsequent ones were crowned with success. She was hired to take charge of a winter school, receiving only one-third the pay that had been given to the male teachers, and had the credit of

having had the best school ever taught in the district. Soon after the war, in a city in Illinois, whither she had gone from the East, a prominent so-called liberal minister preached a scathing sermon against women. Highly indignant, a committee of the suffrage association went to Mrs. Freeman and requested her to reply. At first she hesitated, but finally consented, and her lecture was a success. She has delivered many public lectures. After the Chicago fire Mrs. Freeman devoted herself to literary work, writing four years for a Chicago paper. She is the author of many serials, short stories and sketches. "Somebody's Ned," a story of prison reform, was published in 1880, and received many favorable notices. At that time Mrs. Freeman began her work in the Chicago Secular Union. To this for ten years she has devoted herself almost exclusively. She gave the first lecture on Henry George's "Progress and Poverty" ever delivered in Chicago. She is interested in the reform movement, and especially in woman's emancipation, which she is convinced underlies all other questions. Her last venture is the publication of the "Chicago Liberal." Her home is now in Chicago, and she is corresponding secretary of the American Secular Union.

FRÉMONT, Mrs. Jessie Benton, born in Virginia, in 1824. She is a daughter of the late Hon. Thomas Hart Benton, of Missouri, who was conspicuous as editor, soldier and statesman, and famous for thirty years in the United States Senate, from 1820 to 1851. During the long period of Col. Benton's public life Jessie Benton was an acknowledged belle of the old régime. She possessed all the qualities of her long and illustrious ancestry, illuminated by her father's record, and was the

JESSIE BENTON FRÉMONT.

center of a circle of famous men and women. She became the wife of John Charles Frémont, the traveler and explorer, who was born in Savannah, Ga., in 1813. Gen. Frémont is known to the world as the " Great Path Finder," and a " Grateful Republic" recognized his services. In 1849 he settled in California and was elected senator for that State. He received in 1856 the first nomination ever made by the Republican party for president. His wife was a prominent factor in that campaign. A major-general's commission was conferred in 1862, but General Frémont was more famous as explorer than as statesman or general. In 1878 he was appointed Governor of Arizona, where both he and Mrs. Frémont were very popular. Then closed the long and honorable public life of the Pioneer of the Pacific. In all these public positions Mrs. Frémont won renown in her own right. As a writer she is brilliant, concise and at all times interesting. Her extensive acquaintance with the brightest intellects of the world enabled her to enter the field of literature fully equipped, and since the death of Gen. Frémont she finds pleasure in her pen. The memoirs of Mrs. Frémont will find a large circle of readers. She is now a resident of Los Angeles, Cal., and lives with her daughter. Congress has recognized the services of "The Great Explorer" and given his widow a pension of two-thousand dollars per annum. Her published books are " Story of the Guard, a Chronicle of the War," with a German translation (Boston, 1863), a sketch of her father, Thomas H. Benton, prefixed to her husband's memoirs (1886), and "Souvenirs of my Time" (Boston, 1887). She is passing her days in quiet retirement.

FRENCH, Miss Alice, novelist, born in Andover, Mass., 19th March, 1850. She is widely known by her pen-name, "Octave Thanet." She has lived in the West and South for many years.

ALICE FRENCH.

On both sides she is a descendant of the Puritans. She has Mayflower people and Revolutionary heroes, witch-hangers and modern rulers of Massachusetts among her ancestors, as well as godly ministers not a few, so that, as she has two centuries of unadulterated New England behind her, as she was educated there and goes there every summer, while she lives in the West and spends her winters in the South, she is so much of a composite that she says she hesitates to place herself. Two of her brothers were educated abroad, and one of them married one of the Irish Hamiltons. Her father was a manufacturer of agricultural implements. He was a loyal westerner, but he never lost his fondness for the East, going there regularly every summer. He was much more than a business man, being an enthusiastic lover of books and a connoisseur in the fine arts. Miss French began to write shortly after she was graduated from Abbot Academy, Andover, Mass. The editors gave her the good advice to wait, and she waited several years, when she sent "A Communist's Wife" to the the Harpers, who declined it, and she sent it to the Lippincotts, who accepted it. Since that time she has always found a place for her works. The criticisms that editors offer she has found very valuable. Among her published works are " Knitters in the Sun" (Boston, 1887); "Otto the Knight" (Boston); "Expiation" (New York, 1890), and " We All " (New York). She has also edited "The Best Letters of Lady Mary Montagu " (Chicago). She is very fond of the Gallic models of style. She is interested in historical studies and the German philosophers. She likes all out-of-door sports and declares that she is a great deal better cook than a writer. It is a delight to her to arrange a dinner. She has a fad for collecting china. In politics she is a Democrat, a moderate free-trader and a firm believer in honest money. Miss French has a deep interest in English history and a great affection for England. She pursued her studies assiduously, going to original sources for her pictures of by-gone times, and finding the most inspiration in the period which saw the rise of our present industrial system, the reign of Henry VIII and his children. Her pen-name was the result of chance. "Octave" was the name of her room-mate at school, and had the advantage of being suited to either sex. The word "Thanet" she saw written or printed on a passing freight-car. She prefers the Scotch to the French pronunciation of the word, although she regrets ever having used a pen-name.

FRISBY, Miss Almah J., physician, born in West Bend, Wis., 8th July, 1857. Her father was Hon. Leander F. Frisby, a lawyer and at one time Attorney-General of the State of Wisconsin. Her mother's maiden name was Frances E. Rooker. They were originally from Ohio and New York. Almah Frisby was graduated from the University of Wisconsin in 1878, receiving the degree of B.S., and from the Boston University School of Medicine, in 1883, with the degree of M. D. She then located in Milwaukee, Wis., and took up active practice, in which she was very successful. In the winter of 1886–87 she was resident physician in charge of the Women's Homeopathic Hospital, Philadelphia, Pa. In the summer of 1887 she was homeopathic resident physician of the Hotel Kaaterskill in the Catskill mountains, after which she returned to Milwaukee and resumed local practice. Possessing keen insight, medical skill and deep womanly sympathy, she won in that city a large circle of friends in all walks of life. More especially did she interest herself in the dependent classes generally, who missed a valued benefactor when she was called to a chair in the University of Wisconsin and changed her field of labor. She is now preceptress of Ladies' Hall and professor of hygiene and sanitary science. Hundreds of young women yearly under her influence are enriched by her cultured mind and eminently noble and practical character.

FRISSELL, Miss Seraph, physician, born in Peru, Mass., 20th August, 1840. She is a daughter of Augustus C. and Laura Mack Emmons Frissell. Her father and grandfather were captains of the State militia. Her great-grandfather, William Frissell, was a commissioned officer in the Revolutionary War and a pioneer settler in western Massachusetts. Her mother's father, Major Ichabod Emmons, was a relative of Dr. Nathaniel Emmons, and was one of the first settlers of Hinsdale, Mass. Her grandfather, Col. David Mack, was the second white man to make a clearing in the town of Middlefield, Mass., then a wilderness. The first eleven years of her life were spent within sight of Saddleback Mountain, the highest point of land in the State. As a child she was quiet and diffident, not mingling freely with her schoolmates, and with a deep reverence for religious things. After her father's death,

SERAPH FRISSELL.

which occurred when she was eleven years of age, the problem which confronted her mother was to gain a livelihood for herself and six children, Seraph being the third. Her twelfth year was spent with an aunt in western New York, during which time she decided she would rather earn her own living, if possible, than be dependent on relatives. Returning home, the next year and a half was devoted to school life and helping a neighbor in household work, thereby earning necessary clothing. When she was fifteen, her oldest sister decided to seek employment in a woolen mill, and Seraph accompanied her. The next six years were divided between a factory girl's life and school life. During those years she earned her living and, besides contributing a certain amount for benevolent and missionary purposes, saved enough for one year's expenses in Mt. Holyoke Seminary. The week she made her application for admittance, the proposition was made to her to take up the study of medicine,

but the goal towards which her eyes had been directed, even in childhood, and for which she had worked all those years, was within reach, and she was not to be dissuaded from carrying out her long cherished plan of obtaining an education. Hence she was found, in the fall of 1861, commencing her student life in that "Modern School of Prophets for Women," remaining one year. Then followed one year of teaching, and a second year in the seminary. After four years more of teaching, in the fall of 1868 she resumed her studies and was graduated in July, 1869. The following three years were spent in teaching, during which time the question of taking up the study of medicine was often considered. It was in the fall of 1872 she left home to take her first course in the medical department of the University of Michigan. She received her medical diploma 24th March, 1875. The same spring found her attending clinics in New York City. In June, 1875, she went to Boston for hospital and dispensary work, remaining one year. In September, 1876, she opened her office in Pittsfield, Mass., where for eight years she did pioneer work as a woman physician, gaining a good practice. In 1884 she removed to Springfield, Mass., where she now resides. During the school years of 1890 and 1891 she was the physician in Mt. Holyoke College, keeping her office practice in Springfield. She was the first woman admitted to the Hampden Medical Society, which was in 1885, the law to admit women having been passed in 1884. A part of her professional success she attributes to not prescribing alcoholic stimulants. Dr. Frissell has held the office of president, secretary and treasurer of the local Woman's Christian Temperance Union, and is now county superintendent of the department of heredity and health. For years she has been identified with home and foreign missions, seven years having served as president of auxiliary to the Woman's Board of Missions.

FRY, Mrs. Elizabeth Turner, philanthropist, born in Trenton, Tenn., 22nd December, 1842, where she resided with her parents until the death of her father, James M. Turner. In 1852 her widowed mother, with five children, among them Elizabeth, moved to Texas, settling in Bastrop. During the succeeding years of her life she attended school in different places, making one trip back to Tennessee, where she entered an academy for a term. Upon returning to Texas, she taught for a time in Bastrop, the remuneration going towards paying her tuition in special branches. In 1861, while on a visit to her sister, Mrs. O'Connor, who resided in Corpus Christi, she met, and one year later became the wife of, Lieut. A. J. Fry. The young couple moved to Seguin, where Mr. Fry engaged in general business on a large scale. Having accumulated a fortune, he moved with his family of three sons and one daughter to San Antonio. Mrs. Fry from her earliest youth possessed much religious reverence. She professed faith when but fifteen years old and joined the Methodist Church. For three years she faithfully followed its teachings, but, as she grew older and read more, she analyzed her feelings to find that the Christian Church opened the path. Accordingly she was baptized in that faith. She is a woman full of energy of spirit and mental endurance, which has been the secret of her success, both as a philanthropist and a Christian. She has taken an active and aggressive part in all temperance projects. In the Prohibition campaign in Texas, in 1889, she followed every line of defense and gained admiration for her pluck and willingness to express publicly her strongest views. Several years ago a bull-fight on Sunday was a public sport in San Antonio. The public and officers did not seem to suppress it, and finally Mrs. Fry decided to take the matter in hand. On a Sunday, when the fight had been announced and flyers were floating into every door, she determined

ELIZABETH TURNER FRY.

to do what she could to prevent it from taking place, and accordingly circulated a flyer addressed "To All Mothers," setting forth the wickedness and degeneracy of such a sport, and the necessity of its suppression for the sake of husbands, sons and humanity. The bull-fight did not take place, and there has never been one on Sunday since that time in San Antonio. Being blessed with a goodly share of wealth, charity has flowed from her hands unrestrained. She is a prominent member of ten beneficent societies, and keeps up her voluminous correspondence without aid, besides distributing quantities of temperance and Christian literature. She is a woman suffragist from the foundation principle. Her sympathies were always with the Union and against slavery. She now holds a commission as a lady manager from Texas to the World's Fair, besides being vice-president of the Queen Isabella Association. She was selected as a delegate to the national convention of the Women's Christian Temperance Union, in Boston, in 1891. With all these responsibilities, she attends to her many household duties.

FRY, Mrs. Emma V. Sheridan, actor and playwright, born in Painesville, Ohio, 1st October, 1864. Her mother was a niece of the well-known New England clergyman, Rev. Joseph W. Parker. Her father, General George A. Sheridan, made a fine record in the Army of the Cumberland during the late Civil war, and he has since won a national reputation as an orator. Emma has always been his friend, confidant and counselor, sharing his hopes, his disappointments and the joy of his successes. She is a graduate of Mrs. Hay's preparatory academy, Boston, Mass., and of the Normal College in New York City. Choosing the stage as

the field of her work, she went through a thorough course of study and training in the New York Lyceum School of Acting. She began at the bottom and in six seasons she rose to the front rank among American actors. She has filled many important rôles. In 1887 she played a notable engagement with Richard Mansfield in the Lyceum Theater, London, England. Returning to America, she played a round of leading Shakespearean parts through the country with Thomas Keene. In 1889 she became leading lady in the Boston Museum. At the close of her second and most successful season there her stage career was cut short by her marriage. She became the wife of Alfred Brooks Fry, Chief Engineer of the United States Treasury service, a member of the Loyal Legion and of the Order of the Cincinnati by heredity. During her stage experience Miss Sheridan had plied a busy pen and was well known as " Polly " in the " Dramatic Mirror," and by many articles, stories and verses published in the daily press, in magazines and in dramatic papers over her signature. Since her retirement from the stage Miss Sheridan, for she retains her signature, E. V. Sheridan, is devoting all her time to her pen, and she is in this second profession rapidly repeating the progress and notable success of her stage career. Miss Sheridan is quoted in her own country as an actor and a woman widely known, whose name has never been connected with scandal or notoriety. She is a member of the New England Woman's Press Association, and is president of the Alumni Association of the Lyceum School of Acting. On 23rd February, 1892, Richard Mansfield produced at the Garden Theatre, New York, a play by Miss Sheridan entitled, "£10,000 a Year," founded on Dr. War-

EMMA V. SHERIDAN FRY.

ren's famous book of the same name, and it won a flattering success.

FRY, Miss Laura Ann, artist, born in White county, Ind., January 22nd, 1857. She is of

English descent. Her father and grandfather are artistic designers and wood-carvers in Cincinnati, Ohio. Miss Fry, when still a child, was sent to the Art School in Cincinnati, to develop the

LAURA ANN FRY.

talents for drawing and modeling which she had already displayed. She remained in the institution for twelve years, studying drawing under Professor Noble and modeling under Professor Rebisso. She then went to the Art Students' League in New York City. She learned the art of carving from her father and grandfather. One of her productions, a panel showing a bunch of lilies and dedicated to Mendelssohn, took the first prize, a hundred dollars in gold, when the Cincinnati women had offers of prizes for designs to decorate the organ screen of Music Hall. Miss Fry has made good use of her talents and training. She has had charge of the wood-carving school at Chautauqua Assembly for three years. The work done by her pupils there is quite equal to work done in the same line by the pupils of the best school in London. Miss Fry has worked much in china and pottery. She was one of the original members of the Cincinnati Ladies' Pottery Club, organized in April, 1878, to make original experiments and researches in the work of underglaze coloring and decorations. That club existed for ten years, and to it is due the credit of having set many good styles and methods, which have been meritorious enough to be adopted by the regular profession, and without credit acknowledged to the originators. Miss Fry's present home is on a farm in Ohio, but most of her work has been done in Cincinnati. She has been connected with Purdue University, Lafayette, Ind. Although she is the daughter of an Englishman, she is proud to call herself an American. She glories in being a Hoosier and in living in a land where she enjoys the privilege of doing the work for which her inclinations and talents best fit her.

FRYATT, Miss Frances Elizabeth, author and specialist in art as applied to the house, was born in New York City, but spent her girlhood in the country. In her childhood she wrote for pleasure and chiefly in verse, taking up literature as a life-work on the death of her father, Horatio N. Fryatt, who had written able articles on science, law and finance during the intervals of his busy life as a New York merchant. After the death of her father, the family removed to the city. She commenced to write for New York newspapers, the "Evening Post," the "Commercial Advertiser," the "Tribune" and the "Daily Graphic," a line of work soon relinquished for the more congenial field of magazine literature. An article entitled "Lunar Lore and Portraiture," written for the "Popular Science Monthly" and published in August, 1881, involved extended reading and research. About 1879 she became a contributor to "Harper's Magazine," the "Independent," the "Churchman," the "Illustrated Christian Weekly," the "Art Age" and later to "Harper's Young People" and "Wide Awake." In 1881 she commenced the work which, carried up to the present day, has made her a specialist, writing articles for the "Art Interchange" on art applied to the house, including monographs on embroidery, glass painting and staining, wood-carving, painting on china, designing for carpets and wallpaper, schemes of exterior and interior coloring and decoration from architects' plans and sketches. She wrote all the answers to queries on house-furnishing and decoration published by the "Art Interchange" during the last ten years, as well as the answers to numberless queries on a great variety of subjects. In 1886 Miss Fryatt became editor-in-chief of the "Ladies' World," a monthly devoted

FRANCES ELIZABETH FRYATT.

to the home, conducting eight of its departments, and writing all the editorials and most of the technical articles up to the present day. Miss Fryatt had previously occupied the positions of assistant editor and art-editor of the "Manhattan Magazine" of New York. Among other work not mentioned may be included Miss Fryatt's articles on art-industry and notes on the fine arts. A few years ago she retired to a suburb of Brooklyn, on account of failing health, and built "Fairhope," the cottage in which she now resides. There she has her private editorial office and library. She keeps up her interest in various humanitarian movements. A lover of children, old people and animals, she delights in their companionship, their helplessness and responsiveness appealing strongly to her emotional nature, and her pen is active in the humanitarian movements in their behalf. In 1891 Miss Fryatt was elected president of the Ladies' Art Association of New York, and she was re-elected in May, 1892.

FURBER, Miss Aurilla, poet, born in Cottage Grove, Minn., 19th October, 1847. She is a daughter of Warren Furber, who was well-known

AURILLA FURBER.

among the pioneers and founders of that State. He served as a member of the legislature of Minnesota Territory, also of several of the early State legislatures. On her mother's side Miss Furber is descended from the Minklers and Showermans of eastern New York, who were of unmixed Holland Dutch blood, although the families had lived in the United States for several generations. The Furber strain in her blood is English. Her great-grandfather, General Richard Furber, of New Hampshire, served in the Revolutionary War, and her grandfather, Major Pierce P. Furber, in the war of 1812. Nearly all her life has been passed in a farming community. She received her education in a log school-house, and after leaving school she engaged in teaching. Severe illness incapacitated her for school-room work, and she has been forced to play the part of a looker-on in the world's battles. Her seclusion developed the strongly poetical bent of her mind, and for years she has written much in

verse. Her poems reflect her life. Although forced from the common highway, she has found a way of her own, and her verse shows that she has not lost spirit, or courage, or thought in her enforced inactivity. Her work is finished in a technical sense, and telling in a poetical sense. None of her school-day poems are in print. It is even doubtful that she wrote much in her youth, so that her present work comes to her readers in a finished dress, as the result of matured thought. Miss Furber is not, in a broad sense of the term, a scholar. Her limited opportunities for schooling in youth and her continued ill-health in late years made it impossible for her to become a liberally educated woman, but she is a thinker, and her life has not been without its rich compensation. Since 1885 she has made her home in St. Paul, Minn. Selections from her poems have been made for the "Magazine of Poetry" and "Women in Sacred Song." Her poem "Together" has been set to music by Richard Stahl. She has also written prose articles for the "Pioneer Press," "Church Work" and other papers, and was one of the contributing editors of the "Woman's Record," at one time the organ of the Woman's Educational and Industrial Union of St. Paul. She has been identified with Woman's Christian Temperance Work for years as an officer in local, county and district organizations.

FURMAN, Miss Myrtie E., professor of elocution, born in Mehoopany, Pa., 8th November, 1860. Losing her sight in her fourteenth year, she went to Philadelphia and entered upon the seven-year course of study in the Educational Institution for the Blind. So rapid was her progress that in a little more than four years she had finished the studies in that institution. Manifesting a decided inclination and talent for dramatic recitation, the faculty gave her the privilege of taking private lessons in elocution. Her advancement was marked. She entered the National School of Elocution and Oratory in Philadelphia, from which she was graduated in two years with high honor, receiving a diploma, a silver medal and the degree of Bachelor of Oratory. A few days afterward, in June, 1884, she received a diploma and the highest honors awarded for scholarship from the Institution for the Blind, having finished the curriculum of studies in both educational institutions in less than the seven years usually given to the latter. Miss Furman enjoys the peculiar distinction of being the only blind graduate from the School of Elocution and Oratory, and it is believed that she is the only blind person in this country, or in the world, who ever accomplished a similar course of study and physical training. For two years after her graduation she gave many successful elocutionary entertainments in various cities and towns of Pennsylvania and New York. In 1886 she accepted the position of professor of elocution in a young ladies' school in Ogontz, near Philadelphia. She remained there two years. For the past four years she has filled the chair of elocution in Swarthmore College. Miss Furman has been successful as an instructor. Her methods are abreast with those of the best educators, and her work is thoroughly and conscientiously done. Although entirely sightless, Miss Furman enjoys travel and has a more enthusiastic appreciation of the beauties of nature than many who, having eyes, see not.

FUSSELL, Miss Susan, educator, army nurse and philanthropist, born in Kennett Square, Pa., 7th April, 1832, and died in Spiceland, Ind., in 1889. Her parents were Dr. Bartholomew and Lydia Morris Fussell, both of old Quaker families, and both in advance of their time in intelligence and ideas. The daughter Susan was the woman of the house in her early years, as her mother died when she was only a child. The death of the mother broke up the home circle. Susan, when fifteen years old, began to teach school, and from that time she was her own supporter. In 1861 her oldest brother, then living in Fall Creek, Ind., entered the Union Army as a volunteer, and she offered her companionship in his home so long as her brother should be absent. She was thus introduced to western life, resuming her occupation as a teacher and continuing until 1862. By that time the Civil War had grown to vast proportions. A call came for more nurses for the army hospitals in the South, and Susan Fussell at once volunteered. She started south in April, 1862, and under the auspices of the Indiana Sanitary Committee she went to their station in Memphis. The nature of her work there may be judged from the fact that one-hundred-twenty sick were under her personal care; that for sixty of these she was to see that a special diet was

MYRTIE E. FURMAN.

prepared; that in addition she had the giving out of the food to be prepared for all, with a personal supervision of all the medicines and stimulants administered. In Memphis eight hospitals had been fitted up preparatory to the siege of Vicksburg. Her brother, under General Grant, had charge of the engineering operations of that siege, and until Vicksburg had fallen Susan Fussell remained at her post in Memphis, a period of eight months. A much needed rest of five weeks followed, and then she was sent to Louisville, Ky. She labored in other hospitals in Tennessee and in Jeffersonville, Ind. She became sick, and her brother removed her to Fall Creek, Ind. Restored to health, she again entered the service and remained until the war ended. She then devoted her attention to soldiers' orphans' homes. George Merritt, of Indianapolis, Ind., hoping that the State would adopt the "Family Plan," if it saw the experiment, resolved to establish such a home at

his own expense, and he requested Susan Fussell to take charge of it. She entered upon the work in December, 1865, and continued until the children were grown and settled in life, a period of eleven years. Miss Fussell was teacher, seamstress, florist and horticulturist for the family. After a time the Soldiers' Home Association purchased the Knightstown, Ind., Home, and the Family Home of Mr. Merritt was invited to use a cottage on the grounds. The Government, while not adopting Mr. Merritt's plan, assumed the support of the children, but Mr. Merritt still continued to employ Miss Fussell. He further manifested his appreciation by bestowing upon her the remainder of the sum he had set apart for the maintenance of his family home. In 1877, to secure additional school advantages, Miss Fussell removed her family to Spiceland, Ind. With that change of residence government support ceased, but the children's pensions, hitherto untouched, were made available for their education. Four of the children were married from their home in Spiceland. A legacy bequeathed to Miss Fussell by a relative of her mother greatly widened her opportunities for doing good. She secured a sufficient number of acres of land to supply a bounteous home. During the first year of her residence in Spiceland, Miss Fussell, impressed with the importance of good, pure home influences in rearing children to be honest, useful men and women, applied to the county commissioners for the pauper children of Henry county. Her request was for a long time held under consideration. Pending the decision, she determined to secure the establishment of a school in which feeble-minded children might be taught. To gain that end, she promised to secure the needed statistics, if the representative in the Indiana State legislature would present the bill. She fulfilled her promise, and under the care of Charles Hubbard the bill was secured, and the Knightstown Home for the Feeble-Minded is the monument of her work. After two years the county commissioners of Henry county agreed to permit Miss Fussell to take the children from the almshouse, provided she would furnish a home and board, clothe, nurse and educate them for twenty-three cents each per day. So earnest was she to secure for the experiment a fair trial, that she consented to the unjust and ungenerous terms. The manliness of the county would not long endure this, and the sum was speedily raised to twenty-five cents, and finally to thirty. Thus was begun the home for the unfortunate children in Spiceland. Its success is now assured, and other homes of a similar character throughout the State are largely due to the influence of Miss Fussell. She died in Spiceland, mourned by thousands. She had been elected an honorary member of one of the Posts of the Grand Army of the Republic, and six of the members were chosen as her pall-bearers. She was interred in the Friends' Burial Ground, in Fall Creek, Ind. She was a member of the Friends' Society and always valued her right of membership, but she belonged to mankind and knew no bounds of sect in doing good.

GAGE, Mrs. Frances Dana, woman suffragist and author, born in Marietta, Washington county, Ohio, 12th October, 1808. Her father was Joseph Barker, a native of New Hampshire, and her mother was Elizabeth Dana, allied to the Dana and Bancroft families of Massachusetts. Frances Dana Barker, as she was named, was educated at home, in a frontier log cabin. She was studious and thoughtful, and she became a clear reasoner, a good writer and an effective orator. Her father was a farmer and a cooper, and her early days were filled with work. She could make a good barrel and till a farm in her girlhood. Her sympathies early went out for the fugitive slaves, of whom she saw many. In 1829 she became the wife of Mr. Gage, a lawyer practicing in McConnellsville, Ohio. They reared a family of eight children, and, in spite of all her domestic distractions, Mrs. Gage continued to read, write, think and speak on woman's rights, temperance and slavery. In 1851 she attended the woman's rights convention in Akron, Ohio, and was chosen president of the meeting. From that time she has been conspicuous in the councils of the woman suffragists. In 1853 she moved to St. Louis, Mo., with her family. There her views caused her to be branded as an abolitionist and ostracised by "good society." The resources of the family were reduced by three disastrous fires, doubtless the work of incendiaries. Her husband's health failed, and she took a position as assistant editor of an agricultural paper, published in Columbus, Ohio. The war destroyed the circulation of the paper. Her four sons enlisted in the Union army, and she went, in 1862, to Port Royal, to care for the sick and wounded soldiers. She spent thirteen months in Beaufort, Paris and Fernandina, ministering to soldiers and freedmen alike. In her work she was aided by her daughter, Mary. She lectured throughout the North to soldiers' aid societies in advocacy of the Sanitary Commission. She went without commission or salary to Memphis, Vicksburg and Natchez. She aroused great interest in the work for the soldiers. After the war she lectured successfully on temperance. In 1867 she was made helpless by paralysis, which shut her from the world, being able only to talk, read and write. Her mental faculties were unimpaired. She was for years prominent in national woman's rights conventions. Under the pen-name "Aunt Fanny" she has written many juvenile stories, poems and social sketches. She has been a contributor to the "Saturday Visitor" and the New York "Independent." Her latest published works are a volume of poems and a temperance story, "Elsie Magoon."

GAGE, Mrs. Matilda Joslyn, woman suffragist, born in Cicero, N. Y., 24th March, 1826. She was an only child, very positive in nature, yet very sympathetic and eager to discover the meaning of life. Her father, Dr. H. Joslyn, was a physician of large practice, varied and extensive information, strong feelings, decided principles, an investigator of all new questions, hospitable and generous to a fault. His house was ever the home of men and women eminent in religion, science and philosophy. Thus from her earliest years Matilda was accustomed to hear the most abstruse political and religious questions discussed. She was early trained to think for herself, to investigate all questions, and to accept nothing upon authority unaccompanied by proof. It was a law of the household that her childish questions should receive full answers. Her mother was an accomplished woman of an old Scotch family, the youngest daughter of Sir George Leslie, and through him related to the celebrated Gregory family, whose members as mathematicians, astronomers and physicians gave much impetus to those sciences in the seventeenth and eighteenth centuries. While inheriting her fearlessness, her decided principles and her love of examining everything new from her father, from her mother came her historical tastes, sterling honesty of purpose, intense love of justice, regard for truth and love of the refined and beautiful. Although Mrs. Joslyn was in sympathy with her husband upon reform questions, yet her early training, habits and hereditary tendencies gave a

conservative bias to her social views, which was not without its effect upon her daughter. While the grandfather of Matilda upon her mother's side was of conservative political views, her grandfather upon her father's side, a New England patriot of the Revolutionary War, had not alone defended his fireside against the stealthy Indian foes, but had served his country both on sea and land. Under such opposite hereditary tendencies the struggle between conservatism and liberalism in the young girl's heart was long and severe, but, endowed with an intense love of liberty, she developed into a radical reformer. With no college open for girls at that day, she was largely educated at home. It was the pride and delight of Dr. Joslyn that his daughter should pursue branches of learning rarely studied by girls, he himself teaching her Greek and mathematics, giving her practical instruction in physiology, and even considering the idea of a full medical education for her in

MATILDA JOSLYN GAGE.

Geneva College, of which his own old preceptor, Dr. Spencer, was then president. Although that plan was not consummated, her father's medical library helped to mold her thoughts. At a later date she was sent to the Clinton, N. Y., Liberal Institute. She early stood upon the platform, giving her first lecture at the age of seventeen, before a literary society of her native village. Her subject was astronomy. When eighteen, Matilda Joslyn became the wife of Henry H. Gage, a young merchant of her own town. The young couple lived first in Syracuse, N. Y., afterward in Manlius, in the same county, and thence removing to Fayetteville, N. Y., where Mrs. Gage now resides, having lived in the same house thirty-eight years. There her family of one son and three daughters have been reared. One son died in infancy. Although her husband's business and a rapidly increasing family demanded much of her time, Mrs. Gage never lost her interest in scientific and reform questions. She early became interested in the subject of extended opportunities for woman, publicly taking part in the Syracuse convention of 1852, the youngest speaker present. Chosen during the Civil War by the women of Fayetteville to present a flag to the 122nd Regiment New York Volunteers, whose color company was recruited in that village, Mrs. Gage was one of the earliest to declare in her speech of presentation that no permanent peace could be secured without the overthrow of slavery. When under Governor Cornell the right for women of the Empire State to vote upon school questions was accorded, she conducted an energetic campaign, which removed incompetent male officials, placing in office a woman trustee, woman clerk and woman librarian. The work of Mrs. Gage in the National Woman's Suffrage Association is well known. From her pen have appeared many of the most able state papers of that body and addresses to the various political parties. As delegate from the National Woman Suffrage Association in 1880, she was in attendance upon the Republican and Greenback nominating conventions in Chicago, and the Democratic convention in Cincinnati, preparing the address presented to each of those bodies and taking part in hearings before their committees. The widely circulated protest of the National Woman's Suffrage Association to the Men of the United States, previous to the celebration of the national centennial birthday, 4th July, 1876, was from her pen, as were also important portions of the Woman's Declaration of Rights presented by the National Woman's Suffrage Association in that celebration, Independence Hall, 4th July, 1876. From 1878 to 1881 Mrs. Gage published the "National Citizen," a paper devoted to woman's enfranchisement, in Syracuse, N. Y. Urged for many years by her colleagues to prepare a history of woman suffrage, Mrs. Gage, comprehending the vastness of the undertaking and the length of time and investigation required, refused, unless aided by others. During the summer of 1876 the plan of the work was formulated between herself and Miss Anthony and Mrs. Stanton, comprising three large octavo volumes, of one-thousand pages each, containing engravings of the most noted workers for woman's enfranchisement. "The History of Woman Suffrage" (1881-87) is now to be found in the most prominent libraries of both Europe and America. In the closing chapter of volume one Mrs. Gage included a slight resumé of "Woman, Church and State," a work she has still in hand. Several minor works have appeared from her pen. Among them are "Woman as Inventor" (1870), "Woman Rights Catechism" (1868), "Who Planned the Tennessee Campaign?" (1880), as well as occasional contributions to the magazines of the day. Among her most important speeches are "Centralization," "United States Voters," "Woman in the Early Christian Church" and "The Dangers of the Hour." Usually holding responsible positions on the resolution committees of both State and national conventions, Mrs. Gage has been enabled to present her views in a succinct manner. Her resolutions in 1878 on the relations of woman and the church were too radical for the great body of woman suffragists, creating a vast amount of discussion and opposition within the National Woman's Suffrage Association, ultimately compelling her to what she deems her most important work, the formation of the Woman's National Liberal Union, of which she is president.

GAINES, Mrs. Myra Clark, heiress, born in New Orleans, La., in 1805, and died in that city, 9th January, 1885. She was the daughter of Daniel Clark, a native of Sligo. Ireland. He emigrated from Ireland and settled in New Orleans. In 1796 he inherited a large property from an uncle. He died in New Orleans, 16th August, 1813, and his estate was disposed of under his will dated 20th May, 1811, giving the property to his mother, Mary Clark, then living in Germantown, Pa. Then began the singular case which made Mrs. Gaines famous. Daniel Clark was reputed a bachelor, but he had a liaison with Zulime des Granges, a beautiful French woman, during the absence of her supposed husband in Europe. She bore two daughters, one in Philadelphia, Pa., in 1802, and the second in New Orleans, La., in 1805. The second was Myra. She was taken to the home of Colonel Davis, one of Mr. Clark's friends, where she was nursed by Mrs. Harper. In 1812 the girl was taken to Philadelphia with the Davis family, and there she was known as Myra Davis. In 1830 Myra discovered letters that revealed the secret of her birth. In 1832 she became the wife of W. W. Whitney, of New York City. Her husband received from Colonel Davis a letter containing an account of a will made by Daniel Clark in 1813, shortly before he died, acknowledging Myra as his legitimate daughter and giving her all his estate. Mr. and Mrs. Whitney at once set about to regain the estate, then grown to great proportions. Evidence was produced to prove that such a will had been made, and on 18th February, 1856, the supreme court of Louisiana received the evidence as sufficient, but the lost or stolen will itself was never seen in all the years of the famous case. Then came a difficulty. The Louisiana law forbade a testator to devise to his illegitimate child. Then it was shown that her father had been married to her mother in 1803, in Philadelphia, by a Roman Catholic priest, at a private ceremony. Mrs. Des Granges had learned that her supposed husband was not legally her husband, as he had a living wife. She was therefore free to marry Mr. Clark. After he had made arrangements to acknowledge the marriage, he became suspicious of her fidelity. She was deserted by him, and she afterward was married again. The United States supreme court decided the fact of the marriage to Clark, and thus Myra's legitimacy was established. Her husband died, and Mrs. Whitney, in 1839, was married to Gen. Edmund Pendleton Gaines, who died in 1849. In 1856 Mrs. Gaines filed a bill in equity to recover valuable property held by the city of New Orleans, and in December, 1867, she received a favorable decision. In 1861 the estate was valued at thirty-five-million dollars. Up to 1874 Mrs. Gaines had got possession of six-million dollars. The bulk of the great estate was consumed in litigation. In April, 1877, the probate of Daniel Clark's will was recognized by the United States circuit court, and the city of New Orleans and other defendants were ordered to give account to a master in chancery for all the income derived by them from the property, and their titles were taken from them. An appeal was made, and was unsettled when she died. She showed great magnanimity in refusing to dispossess four-hundred families occupying her lands. She preferred to obtain judgments against the city, and she refused to sell her claims to those who offered her large sums of money. Her whole life was a battle to free her own and her mother's name from stain, and she had the supreme satisfaction of knowing that she had succeeded.

GALE, Mrs. Ada Iddings, author and educator, was born in Dayton, Ohio. A long line of Quaker ancestry accounts perhaps for one of her most prominent characteristics, an extreme conciliatoriness of nature. Her education was received in Albion College. In her early childhood her literary inclining was apparent and received careful fostering from her father, Rev. Joseph T. Iddings, who was also largely her teacher. There yet remain fragments of her early fancy scrawled in a

ADA IDDINGS GALE.

round childish hand. Her home is in Albion, Mich. A woman of family, with numerous social demands upon her time, she yet sets apart certain hours of the day for research. As a student of English history and literature she has been painstaking and has gained a remarkable proficiency in these favorite branches of study. As a dramatic reader she is far above the ordinary, and as a teacher of dramatic art she excels. She has lectured on the "Attributes of Beauty" and has ready for publication two manuscripts, one a volume of verse, the other a seventeenth century romance. Owing to the care and education of her three children, it is with difficulty she has achieved work of any great length, but her endeavor is marked by eagerness and whole heartedness.

GALPIN, Mrs. Kate Tupper, educator, born in Brighton, Iowa, 3rd August, 1855. She is a sister of Mrs. Wilkes and Miss Tupper, whose lives are found elsewhere in this book. She lived during her girlhood on a farm near Brighton. As a child she was very frail, but the free and active life of her country home gave her robust health. Her first teacher was her mother, who taught school while her father was in the war. Her mother would go to school on horseback, with Kate behind her and a baby sister in her lap. Later she attended the village school until she was fifteen, when she was sent to the Iowa Agricultural College in Ames, where she was graduated in 1874. The vacations of the college were in the winter, and in the vacation following her sophomore year she had her first experience in teaching, in a district school three miles out of Des Moines, Iowa, where the family was then living. The next winter, when seventeen years of age, she was an assistant in a Baptist

college in Des Moines, her earnings enabling her to pay most of her college expenses. As a student her especial delight was in oratory. In an oratorical contest, during her senior year, she was successful over a number of young men who have since become well-known lawyers of the State, and in the intercollegiate contest which followed she received second honor among the representatives of all the colleges of the State. She has very marked dramatic ability, but this has been chiefly used by her in drilling students for the presentation of dramas. Her first schools after graduating were in Iowa. From 1875 to 1879 she taught in the Marshalltown, Iowa, high school, having held responsible positions in summer institutes in many parts of the State. In 1878 she taught an ungraded school in the little village of Beloit, Iowa, in order to be near her parents, who were living on a homestead in Dakota, and to have with her in the school her younger brother and sister. Later she taught for four years as principal of the academic department of the Wisconsin Normal School in Whitewater. During the following three years she held positions in the high school of Portland, Ore. Next she was called to the professorship of pedagogics in the State University of Nevada, with salary and authority the same as the men of the faculty. In 1890 she resigned her professorship in the university and received a call to the presidency of a prominent normal school, which she refused. That summer she became the wife of Cromwell Galpin, of Los Angeles, Cal., consummating a somewhat romantic attachment of her college life. Since then she has rested from her profession, but has taught special classes in oratory in the University of Los Angeles. All the ambition, energy and ingenuity that made her so distinguished

KATE TUPPER GALPIN.

as a teacher are now expended with equal success in the management of her housekeeping and the care of her husband's children. She has one child, a daughter.

GANNETT, Mrs. Abbie M., author, born in North Brookfield, Mass., 8th July, 1845. Her girlhood was passed in that town. Her love for the country and her early associations is shown

ABBIE M. GANNETT.

in her dainty volume of poems, "The Old Farm Home" (Boston, 1888). She taught school a few years in Massachusetts, Michigan and St. Louis, Mo. She became the wife of Captain Wyllys Gannett, of the latter place, a nephew of the distinguished Unitarian clergyman of Boston, and himself a writer of sketches of travel and sea stories. Captain Gannett served through the Civil War in the 24th Massachusetts and the 55th Massachusetts colored regiment. After living a few years in St. Louis, the Gannetts went to Boston, where they made their home for a short time. For many years they lived in Malden, Mass. They have three children. Mrs. Gannett, while devoted to her home interests, has yet found time to do able outside work. She is well known in the womens' clubs as a reader of thoughtful essays on current themes. She has filled the Unitarian pulpit on a few occasions and has served on the Malden school board. Her essays, poems, sketches and stories have had a wide publication, many of them appearing in the leading magazines and periodicals. She is deeply interested in the welfare of women and their higher education. Her paper on "The Intellectuality of Women," printed in the "International Review" a few years ago, excited wide comment. Mrs. Gannett is philanthropical in her labors. She espoused the cause of the neglected Anna Ella Carroll with enthusiasm. By a series of articles in the Boston "Transcript" and other papers she has done as much as any one woman to bring her case to public notice. She joined the Woman's Relief Corps and attended the Grand Army of the Republic encampment in Minneapolis to advocate that lady's cause. She won recognition for her and was appointed chairman of a national relief

committee to raise funds for Miss Carroll. The effort was successful. Not content with that, Mrs. Gannett visited Washington and argued Miss Carroll's case before the military committees of both Senate and House.

GARDNER, Miss Anna, anti-slavery agitator, born on the Island of Nantucket, 25th January, 1816. Her father, Oliver C. Gardner, was related to most of the prominent families in Nantucket, among whom were the Cartwrights, and through them Miss Gardner is descended from Peter Folger, the grandfather of Benjamin Franklin, and she is thus related to Lucretia Mott, Maria Mitchell and other distinguished men and women. Through her mother, Hannah Mackerel Gardner, she can claim descent from Tristram Coffin, the first magistrate of Nantucket. Seven generations of her ancestors lived in Nantucket. Miss Gardner's literary tastes and talents were inherited from her mother, who was known for her love of classical poetry. On her father's side, also, she received a literary strain, as the Cartwright family has produced poets in each generation. Slavery and its horrors were early forced upon Miss Gardner's attention. She became a student, a teacher, a lecturer and a worker in the cause of human liberty and equal rights. She was a regular reader of the "Liberator" when she was eighteen years old. In 1841 she was instrumental in calling an anti-slavery convention upon her native isle, which was largely attended. In that meeting Frederick Douglass made his first appearance as a public speaker. He had been exhorting in the Methodist Church and was unprepared for the call made upon him. Nevertheless, he responded and electrified his audience. Miss Gardner spent many years in

ANNA GARDNER.

teaching the freedmen in the South. Her work was done in North Carolina, South Carolina and Virginia. She returned to the North in 1878, and in Brooklyn, N. Y., she was injured by a carriage accident. The result was long weeks of suffering, a partial recovery, crutches and a return to her Nantucket home, where she is passing her days in serenity. She is still engaged in teaching those around her, and her pen is still active in the interests of truth and philanthropy. Besides her anti-slavery work, Miss Gardner has worked faithfully and potently in the cause of woman's rights. She lectured several times before the Nantucket Athenæum. In 1881 she published a volume of prose and verse, entitled "Harvest Gleanings." The work shows Miss Gardner's talents at their best.

GARDENER, Mrs. Helen H., scientist and author, born near Winchester, Va., 21st January, 1853. Her father, the late Rev. A. G. Chenoweth, freed his inherited slaves and moved north with his family before the war. He saw the evils of slavery and determined that his children should not be educated where the atmosphere of race subjugation might taint them. Helen, the youngest of her

HELEN H. GARDENER.

father's family, was then less than one year old. She grew into young girlhood, little differing from other children of her surroundings and condition, and her school and college career did not vary much from that of girls whose environment and education were of a similar character. She was not remarkable, either as being the brightest or the dullest pupil of her classes. Her talent is not a result of scholastic training. Although books, from her babyhood, have been her friends, and she has eagerly absorbed from them all the information they could give, she has been and is a greedy student in a broader and deeper school than the colleges afford. She is a believer in the subtle law of heredity, and her own life is corroborative of that belief. She traces her paternal lineage back to Oliver Cromwell and her maternal to the Peels of England and Virginia. The first representative of her father's family in America was John Chenoweth of Baltimore county, Md., whose wife was Hannah

Cromwell, whose mother was a daughter of Lord Baltimore. Her paternal grandmother was the daughter of Judge John Davenport, of Virginia, to whose family belongs the well-known southern writer, Richard M. Johnston, and she is a cousin of Gen. Strother (Porte Crayon). Her oldest brother, Col. Bernard Chenoweth, served with distinction during the war of the rebellion and was sent by President Grant as consul to Canton, China, where he died at the early age of thirty years. She did not choose literature or authorship as a profession, nor did a desire for fame induce her to write for the public. With her habit of close observation, rapid mental analysis and logical conclusion, she soon saw and appreciated the world-wide difference between the man and the woman as to advantages accorded by society to each in the struggle for existence and advancement. It seemed to her that the strong were made stronger by every aid society could give, and the weak were made weaker by almost every conceivable hindrance of custom and law. Her sense of right was shocked and she sought for the cause or causes for this manifest injustice. So she began to write because she had something to say to her fellow-creatures. For three or four years she simply wrote as she communed with herself. She was too diffident to let the public or even her friends, except one or two of the nearest, know what she wrote or that she wrote, and her first published article was sent by one of her most intimate friends to the press, against her desire. At length, when she was induced to send some of her writings for publication, she was so timid and distrustful of her own work that she used pseudonyms, generally masculine, and she rarely used the same name to more than one article. She was twenty-seven years old when the name of Helen H. Gardener was first given to her readers. She has devoted her life to the disenthrallment of women and thereby of humanity. Everything she has written has been done for the good of her sex and of humanity. She is a pronounced agnostic, not an atheist. She has generous hospitality for all honest opinions and principles. Her first book published, "Men, Women and Gods" (New York, 1885), was composed of a series of agnostic lectures, in which she called attention to the attitude of the Old and the New Testaments toward women, as interpreted by the adherents of the religions based upon those so-called sacred writings. She wrote other lectures in that direction, which were given to the public through the press and on the platform. She undertook the study of anthropology in order that she might satisfy herself as to the correctness of the dictum of the doctors, generally accepted as indisputable, that woman is by nature man's inferior, having smaller brain and of inferior quality and less weight, and consequently having less mentality and less physical strength. Her investigations, in which she was aided by the leading alienists and anthropologists of America and Europe, caused her to discover the utter fallacy of the theory upon which this dictum, as to sex difference in brain, is based. Her work in that direction is the first scientific, basic work and the most thorough that has ever been done, and she settled beyond question the error of the assertion that there is any difference known to science, in brains, because of sex. She gave an epitome of her conclusions on that subject, a part of which was published in the "Popular Science Monthly," to the Woman's International Congress held in Washington, in 1888, in the form of a lecture on "Sex in Brain" (New York, 1888), and her paper was a revelation to all who heard it. It was favorably noticed and commented on by medical journals in this country and in Europe. Knowing that the general public does not read and would not understand essays and scientific articles, she concluded to incorporate some of her scientific and sociologic ideas and theories in stories. These stories appeared first in magazines. Their reception by the general public was immediately so cordial that a publisher brought out a number of them in a book entitled, "A Thoughtless Yes" (New York, 1890). They were read as interesting stories by the general reader, while the leading alienist in America wrote of them: "I have put the book in my scientific library, where I believe more works by the same able pen will appear later. I had believed there were but three persons in America able to do such work, and these are professional alienists." Her first novel, "Is This Your Son, My Lord?" (Boston, 1890), won extraordinary favor. Twenty-five-thousand copies were sold in the first five months, a success equaled by few other novels. All her vigor of thought and expression, her delicacy of wit, fine sense of humor and clever dramatic powers, so manifest in "A Thoughtless Yes," are equally marked in her volume of short stories, "Pushed by Unseen Hands" (New York, 1892). She has recently published a novel, "Pray You, Sir, Whose Daughter?" (Boston, 1892).

GARFIELD, Mrs. Lucretia Rudolph, wife of James A. Garfield, twentieth President of the United States, born in Hiram, Portage county, Ohio, 19th April, 1832. She was the daughter of Zebulon Rudolph, a farmer. She received a classical education in Hiram, in a school in which her future husband was a teacher. She became the wife of James A. Garfield, 11th November, 1858, in Hiram, Ohio, where he was president of the college. Their family consisted of several children,

ELIZA A. GARNER.

officiating in the churches of the sect of Disciples. His career is a matter of familiarity. When he was elected to the Presidency, Mrs. Garfield's public career began. Her occupancy of the White House was suddenly ended by the murder of her husband. During her reign in Washington she showed a great deal of force of character. She was in the most difficult position that any woman can hold in the United States, and she acquitted herself with tact and dignity. She was averse to publicity, discreet, retiring and reticent. The duties of her position broke her health, and she was taken to Long Branch to recover strength. While she was there, President Garfield, just starting from Washington to join her, was shot. Her devotion to him during the agonizing weeks that ended in his death, is historical. After his death Mrs. Garfield received a large amount of money presented to her by citizens of the country, and she made her home in Cleveland, Ohio. She visited Europe and lived for a time in Bournemouth, England. Returning to the United States, she settled in the Garfield homestead in Mentor, Ohio. Mrs. Garfield is passing her days in quiet retirement, doing good work for those about her in the unostentatious manner that distinguished her when she held the position of mistress of the White House. One of her philanthropic deeds was the donation of $10,-000 to a university in Kansas, which took the name of her martyred husband. Her life has throughout been an illustration of American womanhood, wifehood and motherhood of the loftiest character.

GARNER, Miss Eliza A., educator, born in Union, S. C., 23rd April, 1845. She is the daughter of G. W. Garner, sr., the oldest child of a family of seven. She received her early education from her mother, and she subsequently attended a select school, two boarding schools and a State Normal School. Miss Garner, after finishing her studies, began to teach in the public school

LUCRETIA RUDOLPH GARFIELD.

one of whom, a daughter, died in infancy. The living children are four sons and one daughter. Her husband, after their marriage, was both college professor and a Campbellite preacher, often

of her neighborhood. She taught successfully for twelve years. She was the first woman candidate for political office in South Carolina or in the South. In 1888 she announced herself a candidate for county school commissioner, with the proposition to the people that, if elected, she would use the salary of the office to lengthen the school term from three to six months and to supply the schools with books. A few conservatives and her own family prevented her election. The Democratic committee refused to print her ticktes or to allow them to be printed. She engaged the editor of the county paper to print her tickets, paying him in advance, and he printed them on inferior paper and in an unlawful shape, saying afterward that he had done so under the direction of the committee. When the votes were counted, her tickets were thrown out because of their unlawful shape. She was thus defeated. In 1890 she renewed her candidacy and her offer. She attended campaign meetings and read an address to the voters, but was again defeated in a similar way. Her opponent in 1890 was a former schoolmate. She returned to the work of teaching, only to receive a notification from him that the public money of the school district in which she was teaching had been appropriated to other schools. He requested her to close the school. She refused. She taught the school a full term and claimed her salary by law. Miss Garner's experience illustrates the disagreeable nature of the obstacles in the way of women in the South, who venture out of the beaten path.

GAUSE, Mrs. Nora Trueblood, humanitarian, born on a farm fifty-five miles north of Indianapolis, Ind., 9th February, 1851. She is a

NORA TRUEBLOOD GAUSE.

daughter of Thomas E. and Sarah J. Trueblood. Her parents being members of the Society of Friends, well educated and of a progressive spirit, the daughter naturally championed the cause of the downtrodden. She early manifested a love for declamation and composition, and her first writings are remarkable for their emphatic denunciation of wrong and earnest pleadings for right.

ELMINA M. ROYS GAVITT.

From 1868 to 1888 she served in the public schools of Indiana as a teacher. The succeeding five years, as far as lay in her power, were given to home and family, but, so successful was she in reaching the public that she was often called to the platform as a lecturer and organizer. In October, 1886, just one year from the date of her husband's death, she joined the humane workers of Chicago and spent the four succeeding months in writing for the "Humane Journal." In March, 1887, she began to organize societies for the prevention of cruelty, holding public meetings and doing whatever she could to awaken thought on the humane question. To say that her efforts have been attended with enthusiasm and success would be a mild statement, for thousands have been made to see the error of their ways by her convincing arguments and earnest appeals for better protection for all helpless life. She publishes occasional letters descriptive of her travels and work accomplished, and other articles in the "Humane Journal."

GAVITT, Mrs. Elmina M. Roys, physician, born in Fletcher, Vt., 8th September, 1828. She is the second of eight children. She came of old Puritan stock, developing in her life that intense conscientiousness with regard to what she believes to be right, and that stern, uncompromising devotion to duty that characterized her New England ancestors. Her parents were to a great extent the instructors of their flock, both in religious and secular matters, for there were public schools but half of the year, and church privileges were few and far between. When Elmina was fourteen years old, business interests caused a removal of the family to Woonsocket, R. I. For the next twelve years the shadow of ill-health stretched across her pathway, and the possibilities of life lay dormant. At last the door opened for her to begin what has proved a most successful occupation. Hoping to benefit herself by striving for what seemed then almost unattainable, and seeing no avenue open to American women which promised more usefulness than the profession of medicine, she entered the Woman's Medical College of Philadelphia, in 1862. In 1865 she was called to Clifton Springs, N. Y., as house physician in an institution there. Two years later she went to Rochester, Minn., and commenced a general practice, winning from the first signal success, which has always since followed her. In 1869 she removed to Toledo, Ohio, where she has since lived. During that year she showed one of her most marked characteristics, self-sacrifice, by adopting a blind sister's six children, the youngest but two days old and the oldest but twelve years old. She bravely bore her burden and now has the satisfaction of seeing all those children prosperous and happy. In 1876 she became the wife of Rev. Elnathan Gavitt, an elder of the Methodist Episcopal Church, but her marriage did not cause her to give up her profession, in which she had come to stand among the first in the State. Mrs. Gavitt is a woman of strong individuality of character. She has absolute belief in the brotherhood of humanity, and for that reason her skill has been exercised for the poor and the rich alike. For her work she has a peculiar fitness, and it has brought her into the closest contact with suffering and sorrow, for which her sympathies never fail.

GEORGE, Mrs. Lydia A., army nurse and philanthropist, born in New Limerick, Me., 1st April, 1839. Her maiden name was Philpot, and

LYDIA A. GEORGE.

she traces her ancestry back to English sources upon her father's side. In May, 1854, the family removed to Elk River, Minn., where, in 1857, she became the wife of Charles H. Hancock, of that

place. Two years after her marriage, having no children of her own, she took to her home an orphan girl, who remained with them until she was married. Later, she took a motherless boy, who remained with them five years. A devout Christian of non-sectarian spirit, she was earnest in the work of various missions carried on by different denominations. The fateful signal gun which boomed out over Fort Sumter found her superintending a Sabbath-school in Elk River. In August, 1862, her husband enlisted in Company A, Eighth Regiment, Minnesota Volunteer Infantry. She sought an interview with General Pope, then stationed in St. Paul, and obtained permission to go with the regiment. The Indian outbreaks along the frontier at that time made it necessary for Minnesota troops to remain in the Northwest, and after the necessary drilling they were assigned by companies to their respective stations in the Sioux and Chippewa countries. Company A was ordered to the Chippewa Agency in September, and thither Mrs. Hancock soon followed. Arriving at the agency, she was assigned to a room in the agency building, which was the headquarters and also served as a hospital for the company. Work was awaiting her, for thirteen of the company were prostrated with measles, which rapidly spread until it attacked every man who had not previously had the disease. In April, 1863, the company were ordered to Fort Ripley, and remained there two months. From Fort Ripley they went to the Sauk Valley. The winter following they were ordered to Fort Abercrombie, Dak., in the Sioux country, where she remained until spring, having shared in all the vicissitudes of camp life on the frontier. Then her health demanded a rest. In Anoka, Minn., in the fall of 1865, her husband was brought to her in the arms of his comrades, that she might once more look upon his face and minister to his last wants. Her interest in the soldier, his widow and his orphans did not cease with the close of the war. In June, 1885, she joined the Woman's Relief Corps, at the institution of Dudley P. Chase Corps, of Minneapolis, Minn., of which organization she was chosen president. She served in that capacity for two years. On 11th January, 1887, she became the wife of Capt. J. W. George, Company G, Thirty-third Massachusetts Volunteers, one of the most prominent Grand Army men in Minnesota. Captain and Mrs. George worked hand in hand, and their voices were heard at many camp-fires and patriotic gatherings throughout the districts of the State, and pecuniary assistance was given by them to many enterprises for the assistance of needy comrades. Captain George organized William Downs Post, No. 68, in Minneapolis, and she was interested in the organization of an auxiliary corps, and in January, 1888, at the institution of William Downs Corps, she was elected president. She served in that capacity until she was called to serve the State as its department president. Her husband died in May, 1891. Mrs. George has served the Woman's Relief Corps in many capacities, both in the State councils and in national conventions. She is now actively engaged in temperance work.

GIBBONS, Mrs. Abby Hopper, philanthropist, born in Philadelphia, Pa., 7th December, 1801. She is a daughter of Isaac T. Hopper, the Quaker philanthropist. She received a liberal education and taught in Philadelphia and New York City. In 1833 she became the wife of James Sloane Gibbons. In 1834 they settled in New York City. Mrs. Gibbons became at once prominent in charitable work. In 1845 she aided her father in organizing the Women's Prison Association, and the father and daughter coöperated in founding a home for discharged prisoners. Both were frequent visitors to the prisons in and around New York. The home was called the Isaac T. Hopper Home. For twelve years she was president of a German industrial school for street children. During the Civil War she worked in camp and hospital. In 1863, during the draft riots in New York, her house was one of the first to be sacked by the mob, as she had been conspicuous in anti-slavery agitation. After the war she founded a labor and aid association for soldiers' widows and orphans. In 1871 she aided in founding the New York Infant Asylum. In 1873 she founded the New York Diet Kitchen. She has for years been active in the management of these and other institutions. Her life has been one of singular purity and exaltation. With all her charity for the criminals, she believes in the prevention of crime by reasonable methods. All the prominent philanthropies of New York bear the impress of her spirit and hand.

GIBBS, Miss Eleanor Churchill, educator, was born in the plantation home of her parents, "Oak Shade," near Livingston, Ala. Being descended from families pre-eminent for many generations for culture, refinement and talent, Miss Gibbs possesses these in a marked degree. The Revolutionary hero, Capt. Churchill Gibbs, of Virginia, was her grandfather. Through her mother she claims as her ancestor Rev. John Thomas, of Culpepper, Va. Her education was given to her principally by her mother, a very brilliant woman. She pursued her studies also in Livingston College. Later she continued her studies in higher mathematics and science under Dr. Henry Tutwiler. In 1865 she accepted the position of assistant teacher in Livingston Academy, and in

ELEANOR CHURCHILL GIBBS.

1870 she was elected principal of the institution. In 1875 she resigned that position in order to take charge of high-school work in Selma, Ala. In 1887 she resigned to accept the position which she

now fills as professor of English literature and history in Shorter College, Rome, Ga. Miss Gibbs is an able, earnest, enthusiastic and successful teacher, and stands in the front rank in her chosen profession. She wields a strong and graceful pen and is a paid contributor to leading journals in Boston, Philadelphia, Chicago and elsewhere.

GIBSON, Mrs. Eva Katherine Clapp, author, born in Bradford, Ill., 10th August, 1857.

EVA KATHERINE CLAPP GIBSON.

Her father removed from western Massachusetts and pre-empted a section of the best farming land in the State. There he built a log house of the frontier type, and in this his children were born. Miss Clapp's paternal grandmother was Lucy Lee, who was a direct descendant, on her father's side, from the famous Indian princess, Pocahontas. Her mother was Ann Ely, from Litchfield, Conn., a direct descendant from Lady Alice Fenwick, a romantic figure in Colonial times, of Old Lyme, Conn. Miss Clapp passed the first eleven years of her life under her mother's watchful care, on her father's farm. After her mother's death she lived with a married sister. She attended school in Amboy, in the Dover Academy, and subsequently in the Milwaukee Female College. While her studies were pursued in a desultory manner and at irregular intervals, she learned very rapidly and easily. When about sixteen years old, she visited for a time in the large eastern cities, and subsequently taught school in western Massachusetts. She commenced to write at an early age. Her first story, written when she was twenty years old, was a novel, entitled "Her Bright Future," drawn largely from life. Some thirty-thousand copies were sold. That was followed by "A Lucky Mishap" and "Mismated," which reached a sale of about ten-thousand copies, "A Woman's Triumph," and a serial first published in one of the Chicago dailies as "Tragedies of Prairie Life," and subsequently published in book form as "A Dark Secret." She has written many short stories and sketches, and has done considerable editorial work. Her poems have had a wide circulation. They are to be published in book form, under the title, "Songs of Red Rose Land." She became the wife of Dr. C. B. Gibson, of Chicago, in 1892, and spent a year in Europe, where Mrs. Gibson made a special study of the literature of Germany and France.

GILBERT, Miss Linda, philanthropist, born in Rochester, N. Y., 13th May, 1847. She removed to Chicago, Ill., with her parents when she was fifteen months old, and was educated in St. Mary's Convent, in that city. From an early period she has regarded criminals with profound interest. At the age of eleven years she gave books from her grandfather's library to the prisoners in the jail of Cook county, Ill. Her home was directly opposite. The first county jail library ever established she placed in that prison when she was seventeen years old. At the age of fifteen years she inherited a handsome fortune. After spending one-hundred-thousand dollars in philanthropy, the remainder was lost in a bank failure. After that her benevolent work was a continuous struggle. She entered into several business speculations to keep it alive, hoping that some rich man would leave it a legacy to place it on a permanent foundation. In all, she has established twenty-two libraries in six different States, each containing from two-thousand-five-hundred to three-thousand volumes. In Lincoln, Neb., her library has been the means of educating eighteen or twenty native Indians, who were sentenced for long terms. She has procured employment for six-thousand ex-convicts, over five-hundred of whom she started as pedlars, furnishing them with an outfit worth from three to five dollars. Less than ten

LINDA GILBERT.

per cent. of that number have turned out unsatisfactorily. For the last ten years she has constantly agitated the question of building an industrial and educational home to meet the wants of this class,

who find it so impossible to secure employment after their release from prison. Miss Gilbert feels that society more than the criminal is to-day responsible for crime. She is known as "The Prisoners' Friend." Miss Gilbert has patented several devices, including a noiseless rail for railroads and a wire clothespin, and has used these for the purpose of gaining money to carry on her philanthropic work.

GILBERT, Miss Ruby I., business woman, born in Junius, N. Y., 1st December, 1851. She

RUBY I. GILBERT.

has been for many years recording secretary of the Woman's Christian Temperance Union of Illinois and book-keeper of the Woman's Temperance Publication Association, and is a most interesting and fit survival in the growing group of business women which this modern time has developed. Miss Gilbert handles from two to three hundred thousand dollars a year, and has completely gained the confidence of all associated with her. She has the remarkable combination of a delicately poised conscience and a perfectly level head. Many persons might intend to be accurate as she is, but their intellectual make-up would render it impossible. Mathematical and ethical qualities must balance each other to produce such a result. Miss Gilbert was engaged in clerical work in Freeport, Ill., when Miss Willard lectured there early in the crusade movement, and then first became especially interested in temperance work. The education of Miss Gilbert has been wholly in the public-schools, and in various relations that she has sustained she has received a diversified and thorough business training. In 1882 she came into association with Mrs. Mary B. Willard, who was at that time editor of the "Union Signal." She has since then sustained an intimate relation with Mrs. Willard, serving also as her legal business representative in this country after the American School for Girls was established in Berlin, Germany, in 1885. Miss

Gilbert has escorted parties of young ladies to Mrs. Willard's school, and has in every way contributed to the utmost to insure the success of that excellent and growing enterprise. Her parents are of old New England stock. Her father, like his father before him, is a Baptist minister and was educated in the public schools and academies of western New York. He did pioneer work in Illinois and endured the privations incident to such a dedication of his life and energies. Her mother is a woman of superior mental vigor, always a leader in religious and temperance circles. The sacrifice and devotion demanded by the difficult life of itinerants have impressed themselves deeply on the character of their daughter. She went to Illinois with her parents in 1855, and was reared in the town of Mendota. The record of her life-work is closely and successfully identified with the white-ribbon movement.

GILCHRIST, Mrs. Rosetta Luce, physician, author and poet, born in Ashtabula, Ohio. In youth she was a student in the Kingsville, or Rexville, Academy, and later in Oberlin College. She is thoroughly versed in many lines of work. She has been a successful teacher in the Cleveland public schools, and has recently, after graduating from the Cleveland Homeopathic College, gained a lucrative practice in the medical profession. Though she has given little attention to literature, her chief talent lies in that direction. It seems evident to those who have read her "Apples of Sodom," "Margaret's Sacrifice," "Thistledew Papers," and numerous poems, which were written during the press of business or housekeeping affairs, that she would have attained a high place among American authors. She possesses talent as

ROSETTA LUCE GILCHRIST.

an artist, having done some excellent work in oils, wholly without instruction. Mrs. Gilchrist has a family of three bright children. She is an honored member of the Woman's National Press Association

and the Cleveland Woman's Press Association, and president of the Ashtabula Equal Rights Club.

GILDER, Miss Jeannette Leonard, journalist, born in Philadelphia, Pa., in 185-. She showed her literary bent at an early age. Her father was a contributor to the journals in Philadelphia, and at one time he edited a literary monthly of his own. Jeannette published her first story, "Katie's Escapade," in the New York "Dispatch," when she was fourteen years old. At the age of seventeen she contributed to the Newark "Daily Advertiser," of which her brother was editor. He started a morning paper in Newark, and Jeannette contributed a column a day on "Breakfast-Table Talk." She soon advanced to dramatic and musical criticism. Since that year, 1869, she has been regularly and actively engaged in journalism. When her brother became assistant editor of "Scribner's Magazine," in New York City, he disposed of the Newark "Morning Register," but Miss Gilder continued for a time to serve it in every conceivable capacity. She became a correspondent of the New York "Tribune" and for a time served in a clerical position on "Scribner's Magazine." In 1875 she joined the staff of the New York "Herald" as a book-reviewer. She also reported for that paper. In December, 1880, in conjunction with her brother, she started "The Critic." In addition to her work on her own paper, Miss Gilder has corresponded for a number of journals outside of New York. In 1876 she wrote a play, "Quits," which was brought out in the Chestnut Street Theater, Philadelphia, by F. F. Mackey. It had a short run and was favorably received. She dramatized "A Wonderful Woman" for Rose Eytinge. She dramatized Dr. Holland's "Sevenoaks" for John T. Raymond. She wrote a comedy for Harry Becket, who died while preparing to produce it in England. Miss Gilder claims to be a journalist, and she holds very modest views of her own talents.

GILES, Miss Anne H., philanthropist, born in Prairie du Chien, Wis , 1st August, 1860. She removed to Chicago in early life. Her father is William Alexander Giles, in pioneer days of Wisconsin a representative of the press. Later he was the head of the firm of Giles Brothers, jewelers, and is to-day one of Chicago's most prominent citizens. Her mother's maiden name was Elizabeth Harper. In the public schools of Chicago Anne Giles was conspicuous for her superior scholarship. During her course in Smith College she excelled in Greek, Latin and other studies. She was graduated from that institution in 1882, taking the degree of A. B. From her childhood she was imbued with the missionary spirit, always attempting to help the poor and the suffering, seeking them out rather than waiting for circumstances to appeal to her. As a teacher of the Chinese she was a special leader among church-workers for a number of years. As foreign corresponding secretary of the Woman's Presbyterian Board of Missions she has become widely known. Practically interested in the education of the freedmen, associated with various societies of Christian Endeavor, devoting all her time to benevolent work, and being a general financial contributor to home and foreign missions, she is recognized as one of the most earnest and useful daughters of philanthropy in Chicago. The story of the "Poacher's Daughter," which has gone through numerous editions, was translated by her for Sunday-school libraries.

GILES, Miss Ella A., author, was born in Dunkirk, near Madison, Wis., 2nd February, 1851. She is the daughter of Hon. H. H. Giles, for twenty years a member of the Wisconsin State

Board of Charities. He was once president of the National Conference of Charities. From him Miss Giles has inherited a philanthropic spirit, which is visible in her writings. She has published a large number of essays on social science topics. Her mother's maiden name was Rebecca S. Watson. From the maternal side Miss Giles inherited a love of art and literature. She early showed musical talent. Her fine voice was carefully cultivated by Hans Balatka. She was quite distinguished as an oratorio and church singer when her health failed, and she was compelled to abandon what promised to be a successful career in music. During the isolation illness rendered necessary she wrote her first romance, "Bachelor Ben" (Chicago, 1875). It had a very wide sale, reaching the third edition in a few months and making its young author exceedingly popular throughout the Northwest. Her stories "Out From the Shadows" (1876), and "Maiden Rachel" (1879) followed with the same publishers. Meanwhile Miss Giles received many calls for lectures and achieved success in that field. In 1879 she became librarian of the public library in Madison and held the position for five years, doing at the same time much literary work. She resigned after her mother's death, in 1884, so as to devote herself to the care of her father's home. Her first verses then began to appear and won an immediate favor. She has published one volume of poems entitled "Flowers of the Spirit" (Chicago, 1891). Her winters are always passed in the South, and she has written many newspaper letters from the Gulf coast of Mississippi and various parts of the South. She has made a study of Scandinavian literature and is known for her scholarly sketches of Swedish and Norwegian

Woman's Congress committee on journalism. Her letters, poems and sketches have appeared in the New York "Nation," the "Evening Post," the Chicago "Times," the "Home Journal," the

ELLA A. GILES.

"Magazine of Poetry," and many other northern and southern papers. Being deeply interested in liberal religious thought, she attended a course of lectures in the Meadville Theological School. She was on the staff of the Chicago "Times" for three years, still keeping her home on Lake Monona in Madison. She was the first woman to read a paper before the Wisconsin Academy of Science, Arts and Letters.

GILLESPIE, Miss Eliza Maria, religious devotee, known in the Roman Catholic Church as Mother Mary of Saint Angela, born in Brownsville, Pa., 21st February, 1824, in the Gillespie homestead, in which was reared a whole family of this name. When a son or a daughter was married, a wing was added to the homestead, in which to establish a new colony. In one of these wings was born James Gillespie Blaine. Eliza Maria was the oldest daughter of John P. and Mary Myers Gillespie. The father died while the children were still young, and their mother removed to Lancaster, Ohio. Eliza Maria was placed in school with the Dominican Sisters in Somerset, Perry county, Ohio, and afterward with the Sisters of the Visitation, in Georgetown, D. C., where she became a favorite for her talents and engaging qualities. She was graduated from that institution with the highest honors. The few years she spent in the world were marked by the most earnest work for the sick and distressed, especially the victims of the cholera in 1849 In 1853 she entered the Congregation of the Holy Cross, taking the name of Saint Angela

ANNE H. GILES.

writers. These sketches were translated into Swedish and Norwegian by different authors. She has written many valuable articles on prison reform and ethical subjects, and now belongs to the

to be known as "Mother Angela." Almost immediately she sailed for Europe. She made her novitiate in France and took the vows of her religious profession at the hands of Rev. Father

Moreau, the founder of the Congregation of the Holy Cross. In 1855 she returned to the United States and was made Superior of the Academy of St. Mary's, then in Bertrand, Mich., to be removed

ELIZA MARIA GILLESPIE.

the following summer to its present site, one mile from Notre Dame, South Bend, Ind. The academy was chartered, the foundation of the present conservatory of music was laid, the art department was fairly started, and the future of St. Mary's was established as an educational center. From that time there stood forth from the ranks of the Sisters of the Holy Cross in the United States a personage so remarkable that even the leveling rule of religious profession could not lessen the charm of her individuality, one who, whether as Mother Superior or Mistress of Novius, or director of studies, or simply Sister Mary of Saint Angela, carried into her obedience the same exaltation of purpose, the same swiftness of execution, the same grace, the same self-denial, the same oblivion of her brilliant place in the world, excepting as the ties of a noble connection could aid her in the work to which she had set her hand, the service of God in the perfection of the religious state according to the rule and the spirit of her order. When the beat of drum, calling on the nation to arm her sons for the defence of the "Stars and Stripes," broke the stillness of seclusion in St. Mary's as well as Notre Dame, that peaceful barge, with its graceful figurehead, was changed into a swift companion of mighty ironclads, not freighted with guns, but with Sisters, taking possession, in the name of charity, of empty warehouses and unfinished barracks, to which they gave the name of hospitals, and which became hospitals in very truth under their transforming hands. Floods were braved, and short rations were made shorter by care for the suffering soldiers. The war over, Mother Angela and her Sisters returned to St. Mary's to take up the old obedience, whatever it had been. The only thing

to indicate their part in the national crisis was the spiked cannon, sent a few months after to Mother Angela and her community, as a recognition of their services, by the commander of the division in which they labored. From their return from the war, a new energy pervaded the ranks of the Sisters of the Holy Cross. Called for from the Atlantic to the Pacific, from the Northwest to Texas, asylums, hospitals, schools from parochial to academy and normal, were opened by the vigilant and enthusiastic Mother Angela, and their departments were overlooked with an eye to perfection. She was generous to the sick, outside her own wards, to the needy of all sorts. She died 4th March, 1887. A woman of genius, who would have had a brilliant career in the world, "she was," as her cousin, Mrs. Ellen Ewing Sherman, wrote, "one, of whose noble and exalted qualities, loving heart and life of labor for her God, in whose bosom she is at rest, only poets could speak worthily." She was not to be distinguished by one line in her habit or one crimp in her cap from the least in her community, yet standing forth, in the radiance of a life devoted to God and humanity, as a typical American woman as well as a devoted religious one.

GILLETTE, Mrs. L. Fidelia Woolley, Universalist minister, born in Nelson, Madison county, N. Y., in 1827. She is the daughter of Rev. Edward Mott and Laura Smith Woolley, and the oldest of a family of seven children. Her ancestry was English and French. She was an extremely timid and sensitive child, but an enthusiast about her studies. Her father expected her, when she was a mere girl, to read books upon abstruse subjects and to be able to talk about them with himself and his friends, but the distinguishing

L. FIDELIA WOOLLEY GILLETTE.

characteristic of her childhood was spontaneous sympathy for every living thing, and all her life it has made her the helper of the helpless and the friend "of such as are in bonds." In 1847 her father removed to Michigan, where she was married, and where she has lived many years. Mrs. Gillette's literary work has continued since her sixteenth year under the pen-names "Lyra" and "Carrie Russell," and her own name. Her poems and prose articles have appeared in various papers and magazines. Her published works are her poems, entitled "Pebbles From the Shore" (1879), "Editorials and Other Waifs" (New York, 1889), and a memoir of her father (Boston, 1855), who was a popular minister in the Universalist Church. There is a faint suggestion of the dramatic in Mrs. Gillette's style of speaking that gives it charm ; the elegance of her language, the richness of her imagery, the striking and original character of her illustrations are as refreshing as they are entertaining. Her missionary and pastoral work has been of several years duration. Her lectures have received high praise.

GLEASON, Mrs. Rachel Brooks, physician, born in the village of Winhall, Vt., 27th November,

RACHEL BROOKS GLEASON.

1820. She was a teacher from choice, not from necessity, much of the time up to her marriage on 3rd July, 1844. No colleges were open for women during her girlhood, but she gave herself a fair collegiate education from college text-books studied at home. Her husband, Dr. Silas O. Gleason, when he became professor of hygiene in the Central Medical College in Rochester, succeeded in persuading the faculty and trustees to open the college doors to women. Mrs. Gleason studied with her husband and was graduated in medicine in 1851. She then practiced three years in a sanitarium in Glen Haven, N. Y., and one year in Ithaca, N. Y. She has been at the head of the Gleason Sanitarium in Elmira, N. Y., for forty years, and still is at its head. She has had a large consulting practice, extending to most of the towns in the State. Her book on home treatment for invalids, "Talks to my Patients" (New York,

1870), has run into its eighth edition. After her graduation in medicine she gave lectures on physiology and hygiene to women, assisted by the best models and charts to be had at the time. She continues to give these lectures in schools for women and as parlor talks. She held Bible and prayer classes every Saturday for twenty-five years. She was an advocate of dress reform and women's freedom from early girlhood. She has assisted eighteen women students through medical colleges, all of whom were dependent upon her for financial support, and most of them rescued from invalidism. Many of these students have become prominent, and all are competent physicians. Mrs. Gleason was a strong anti-slavery worker before the Civil War, and has rendered constant assistance to Freedmen's schools ever since.

GOFF, Mrs. Harriet Newell Kneeland, temperance reformer and author, born in Watertown, N. Y., 10th October, 1828, of New England parentage. Her father, Mr. Kneeland, was a mechanic, but possessed strong literary inclinations and was a frequent contributor to the press of his day. He died while still young. His daughter was a quiet, thoughtful, old-fashioned child, with quaint speech, odd and original ideas, delicate health and extreme sensibility to criticism. When eleven years of age, she was received into the Presbyterian Church, and has retained that connection. A year previously her mother had removed to Pennsylvania and again married. In the step-father's house she often met itinerant lecturers upon temperance and anti-slavery, and she read with avidity the publications upon those subjects, and Sunday-school and other religious books. At sixteen she began to teach a public school in a country district, boarding among her pupils. During several years, teaching alternated with study, mainly in Grand River Institute, Ohio. At twenty-two she relinquished her cherished purpose of becoming a missionary, and became the wife of Azro Goff, a young merchant and postmaster in the town of her residence, but continued her studies. A few years later they were passengers upon the steamer Northern Indiana when it was burned upon Lake Erie, with the loss of over thirty lives; and while clinging to a floating plank new views of human relations and enforced isolations opened before her, and she there resolved henceforth to follow the leadings of her own conscience. She has devoted much time and effort to the unfortunate, preferring those least heeded by others. For many years she was a contributor to the public press, her first article being published in the "Knickerbocker." She entered the temperance lecture field in 1870, and has traveled throughout the United States, in Canada, New Brunswick, Nova Scotia, Newfoundland, England, Ireland, Scotland and Wales, speaking more or less extensively in all, and under various auspices. In 1872 she was delegated by three societies of Philadelphia, where she then resided, to attend the prohibition convention in Columbus, Ohio, and there she became the first woman ever placed upon a nominating committee to name candidates for the presidency and vice-presidency of the United States. To her presence and influence was due the incorporation of woman's suffrage into the platform of that party at that time. She published her first book, "Was it an Inheritance?" (Philadelphia, 1876) and early the next year she became traveling correspondent of the New York "Witness," besides contributing to "Arthur's Home Magazine," the "Sunday-school Times," the "Independent" and other journals. In 1880 she published her second book, issuing the sixth edition that year. Her third volume was, "Who Cares" (Philadelphia,

1887). Adhering to the British branch in the rupture of the Order of Good Templars, Mrs. Goff was in 1878 elected Right Worthy Grand Vice-Templar, and the following year was re-elected in

HARRIET NEWELL KNEELAND GOFF.

Liverpool, England, over so popular a candidate as Mrs. Margaret Bright Lucas, on account of her acceptable and still desired services in the supervision and secretaryship of the order in America. She joined and lectured for the Woman's Temperance Crusade early in 1874 in several States, was a leader in the organization and work of the Woman's Temperance Association of Philadelphia, afterwards rechristened the Woman's Christian Temperance Union. She was a delegate therefrom to the first national convention of the Woman's Christian Temperance Union in Cleveland, Ohio, and again from the New York State Union to the convention in Nashville, Tenn., in 1887. Her especial work from 1886 to 1892 was for the employment of police matrons in Brooklyn, N. Y., her place of residence for the past fourteen years, whence she removed to Washington, D. C. in 1892. As committee of the New York State Union she endeavored to procure such amendments of an ineffective law as would place every arrested woman in the State in care of an officer of her own sex For this she has labored with her usual diligence, drafting and circulating petitions, originating bills, interviewing mayors, commissioners, councilmen, committees of senate and assembly, and individual members of those bodies, and governors on behalf of the measure, and by personal observations in station-house cells and lodging-rooms, jails and courts, originated or substantiated her every argument. She is a believer in the cause of woman suffrage.

GOLDTHWAITE, Mrs. Lucy Virginia, author, born in Florence, Ala. She is the youngest of her family. Her maiden name was Lucy Virginia Harmon. Her ancestors for generations were born and bred in Petersburg, Va., where her parents and their children, with the exception of Mrs. Goldthwaite, were reared. Her sister, called "Lizzie of Woodlawn," for years was a writer for the Louisville "Journal." Woodlawn, the beautiful home where Mrs. Goldthwaite passed her childhood, may still be seen in Florence. Several little poems, written at five and six years of age by Miss Harmon, are still retained by relatives. Verses written at eight were published, with many sketches and poems at intervals in later years. Her most popular poem was on the death of Gen. Pat. Cleburn. For fifteen years the public have read nothing from the pen of Mrs. Goldthwaite, except at long intervals. During that time she was not idle, however, as she has numerous sketches and songs and several novels in manuscript. Her first novel, "Veta, a Story of the Blue and Gray," was published in "Sunny South," in 1890. Mrs. Goldthwaite has written many songs that have received public approval, and a tragedy for Lillian Lewis, which that actor pronounces exceptionally fine, and several other plays for leading actors. Mrs. Goldthwaite is a thorough scholar, a fine artist, a proficient linguist, and reads, writes and speaks fluently several languages. She has a high soprano voice of great sweetness and power. She was a pupil of the German composer, August Newmayer. She is happily married, and is the wife of George Goldthwaite, a prominent judge, an able lawyer, a nephew of ex-United States Supreme Court Judge, John A. Campbell, and son of ex-United States

LUCY VIRGINIA GOLDTHWAITE.

Senator, George Goldthwaite. Mrs. Goldthwaite resides at present in Leadville, Col.

GOOCH, Mrs. Fanny Chambers, author, is a native of Texas, where the greater part of her life has been spent. Through her book, "Face to Face with the Mexicans" (New York, 1888), she has become known to fame. The story of the inception, growth, publication and success of this book gives a luminous insight into the character of its author, and is at the same time an interesting illustration of the changed conditions of the modern American woman's life. Several years ago Mrs. Gooch removed with her family to the city of Saltillo, Mexico. She, who in her American home was famous as a housewife, went to Mexico almost entirely ignorant of the domestic manners of those most unyielding devotees of ancient custom, and set up her home among them, expecting to order her household affairs after the same comfortable fashion which made her home in Austin, Texas, a place of ease and plenty. The story of the disillusionment told in the opening chapters of her book is exquisitely ludicrous. To a woman less keenly alive to the humor of the situation it would have been less profitable as a lesson than it proved to the author. After a determined effort to force the immovable Mexican customs, she found herself compelled to yield to the inevitable. She

FANNY CHAMBERS GOOCH.

might be compelled to do without a cooking-stove and to forego the delights of attending to her own marketing and shopping, but her genial soul demanded that, if foiled in her domestic plans, she would at least refuse to be shut out from social intercourse with the people among whom she found herself. That was hardly less difficult than to keep house in the American fashion with the help of Mexican servants and furniture. Her neighbors looked with small favor on Americans in general, having learned much to prejudice them against their brethren across the Rio Grande, and little in their favor. But here was an anomaly in the shape of an American, a woman full of the independent spirit of her people, but as full of sympathy and ready appreciation as the most courteous Latin. The result was that Mrs. Gooch obtained an insight into the innermost life and less superficial characteristics of our neighbors, which she afterward used in her book on Mexico so successfully as to give the

work a peculiar value. Returning after some years to her former home in Austin, her descriptions of her Mexican experiences so entertained her friends that she was asked to prepare a series of articles on the subject for a Texas newspaper. Mrs. Gooch at once set to work. She soon found, however, an embarrassment of riches in the abundant material her memory supplied, and, abandoning her first intention, she decided to publish her work in book form. Her first intention had been to limit her book to her experiences in Saltillo, but the greatness of her overmastering idea soon proved that intention too narrow, and, putting aside her pen, she returned to Mexico, where she spent some time in its principal cities, mingling with its people in every station. She was fortunate in carrying on her new venture to have letters to the leading men and women of the Mexican capitol. When the literary portion of her work was complete, she went to New York and superintended the publication of the work. The book at once attracted the notice of the leading reviewers and became very successful. The year following the publication of "Face to Face with the Mexicans" Mrs. Gooch was married to Dr. D. T. Inglehart, of Austin, and has since devoted herself almost entirely to her extensive domestic and social duties. At present she has in contemplation another literary venture, the subject of which is to be Texas.

GOODALE, Miss Dora Read, poet, born in Mount Washington, Berkshire county, Mass., 29th October, 1866. Her life and literary career have been intimately associated with those of her older sister, Elaine Goodale, now Mrs. Charles A. Eastman. The story of the childhood and remarkable literary achievements of Dora is similar to the story of Elaine's early life. At the age of six years Dora composed verses that are simply remarkable, in certain qualities of rhythm and insight, for so youthful an author. She was an earnest student, and she enthusiastically coöperated with her sister in publishing a monthly paper for the entertainment of the family. In conjunction with her sister she published "Apple Blossoms: Verses of Two Children," selected from their earliest work, (New York, 1878); "In Berkshire with the Wild Flowers" (1879), and "Verses from Sky Farm," an enlarged edition of the preceding volume (1880). Dora's verses are no less praiseworthy than those of her sister, and the achievements of these two remarkable girls, when the older was fifteen and the younger twelve years of age, set the critics of the world to work, and stirred them as critics had not been stirred by the work of virtual children since the time of Chatterton.

GOODRICH, Mrs. Mary Hopkins, originator of village improvement associations, born in Stockbridge, Mass., in 1814. Her maiden name was Hopkins. She inherited the same intellectual qualities which marked her cousin, President Mark Hopkins, of Williamstown, with others of the name hardly less distinguished. She was born with a love of nature and a humanitarian spirit. She was left an orphan when barely two years old, and was brought up by older sisters. From the planting of a tree, when she was five years old, dates practically the beginning of the Village Improvement Association which has made of Stockbridge, Mass., the most perfectly kept village in the United States. After an absence of many years in the South, she returned to find the village cemetery in a neglected state, and she resolved to attempt to remedy that and other unnecessary evils, and, as far as possible, by the aid of children. To interest them she had a tree planted for every child in town, to care for themselves, and that secured their interest in what was projected and begun for the rest of the village. A wretched street known as Poverty Lane, where some of them were then living, was thus gradually transformed

MARY HOPKINS GOODRICH.

into one of the prettiest streets in the village. Her health was always extremely delicate, but the out-of-door life necessitated by her interest in the work of the association, which soon became incorporated, and enlisted all Stockbridge, was of great benefit. A constitution was adopted on 5th September, 1853, and amended and enlarged in scope in 1878. Miss Hopkins became the wife of Hon. T. Z. Goodrich, whose interest in the work had been hardly less than her own, and who till his death never lost it. Mrs. Goodrich is not only the mother of every village improvement society in the United States, but the unwearying helper of every one who seeks to kindle this love in children, or to rouse interest in their elders. Though owing much to wealth, she has always contended that much the same results are possible for the poor, and even in her advanced age, she is in constant correspondence with innumerable inquirers who are interested in her methods.

GOODWIN, Mrs. H. B., novelist, was born in Chesterville, Me., but she has been a resident of Boston, Mass., for many years. She is the daughter of the late Benjamin B. and Elizabeth Lowell Bradbury. Her school-life was spent mainly in Farmington Academy, under the tuition of Alexander H. Abbott. Before her marriage she had written many short stories and sketches, which were published in magazines and papers over her initials, H. E. B. She was a successful teacher of girls in Bangor, Me., and afterward she was principal of the Charlestown Female Seminary, at that time a popular and widely-known school. The judicious criticism and commendation of her teacher, Prof. Abbott, first stimulated her ambition to be known as an author, but her pen was mainly inspired by

her desire to assist in educating young women. For the last fifteen years Mrs. Goodwin has been intimately associated with the educational work of Wellesley College. She is an active member of its board of trustees and of its executive committee, and has also written and read to the students of Wellesley many essays on art, the studies for which were made in the great art centers of Europe, where she traveled in England, France, Germany, Italy and Spain. Her first novel was "Madge" (New York, 1864), and was favorably received. Mrs. Goodwin regards it as the least worthy of her books, though it was written with as high an aim and as serious a purpose as any of its successors. Her second book, "Sherbrooke" (New York, 1866), is a story of New England life. The success of that story was instantaneous. Her third book, "Dr. Howell's Family" (Boston, 1869), was written during months of great physical pain, and many readers regard it as the author's strongest work. After the publication of that book Mrs. Goodwin was for several years an invalid and employed her pen only in writing short stories and sketches and letters from Europe to religious newspapers. "One Among Many" (Boston, 1884), added to the well earned success of its author and gave new evidence of her ability to represent real life. Another of her well-known stories is "Christine's Fortune" (Boston), a picture of German life. "Our Party of Four" (Boston, 1887), describes a tour in Spain. Perhaps to "Dorothy Gray" the highest praise is awarded by critics and literary friends. Mrs. Goodwin's extensive reading, her knowledge of art and her acquaintance with foreign cities have given her pen a rare facility. Culture, refinement

MRS. H. B. GOODWIN.

and morality characterize all her work. She has compiled a volume of essays on art and history.

GOODWIN, Mrs. Lavina Stella, author and educator, born in St. Johnsbury, Vt., 4th February, 1833. Her maiden name was Tyler.

In King's Chapel, cemetery, Boston, is the grave of an ancestor marked by a stone from a foreign quarry, dating back to the Colonial period and bearing the coat-of-arms of the English Tyler family. From childhood she was an earnest reader and an ambitious student, yet no less a lover of nature and replete with physical activity. While very young her habit of whispering "made-up" stories to herself on her nightly pillow furnished amusement to older listeners. From sensitiveness on the point, her earliest writings were either destroyed or sedulously concealed, until finally some pieces of verse that accidentally fell under a friendly eye were forwarded to a city newspaper and published without her knowledge. When between fourteen and fifteen years old she taught a district school, and for a few years until her marriage was alternately teacher and pupil. Circumstances have developed Mrs. Goodwin's literary talent in the direction of versatility rather than specialty. After having conducted departments for women and children, and become favorably known as a writer of stories, at the beginning of 1869 she was made associate editor of the "Watchman," in especial charge of its family page, and the connection exists still, after an interval of service on the "Journal of Education." A season in California and Mexico tested her ability as a correspondent, and she was employed in that capacity in the Philadelphia Centennial and in the Paris Exposition of 1878, her published letters winning general admiration. She has produced a number of serials, one for a leading London journal. Two juvenile volumes from her pen have appeared, "Little Folks' Own" and "The Little Helper." The former, a collection of stories and verses, had a large sale. Besides contributing much to various popular publications for young people, she has gained recognition in art and general literature. As a writer of poetry she is represented in many anthologies.

GORDON, Miss Anna A., author and temperance worker, born in Boston, Mass., 21st July, 1853. Miss Gordon studied for years in the Newton high school and in Mount Holyoke Seminary. She went to Europe in 1875 and spent a year with her sister, Mrs. Alice Gordon Gulick, the founder of the College for Girls in San Sebastian, Spain. Miss Anna has fine musical talents. She was studying the organ in Boston, in 1877, when she was introduced to Miss Willard, who was holding meetings, on D. L. Moody's invitation, in connection with his Boston tabernacle. Miss Gordon was a member of the Congregational Church, and she became organist in Miss Willard's daily gospel meeting. Miss Willard promptly recognized her abilities, and for years these two zealous women have worked in the same field. Miss Gordon has served as Miss Willard's private secretary, as superintendent of juvenile work for the World's Woman's Christian Temperance Union, and as associate national superintendent of the same department. As a speaker to children she excels, having a winsome presence, graceful bearing, great earnestness, sincere consecration and something to say. She has put her methods to the proof by conducting juvenile organizations for years in Evanston, Ill., where she lives with Miss Willard and her mother in their "Rest Cottage" home. Miss Gordon is an excellent writer and has a charming gift of verse-writing, both humorous and pathetic. She also composes music that is in large request among white-ribboners. She has furnished to the children her "Marching Songs," of which 300,000 copies have been sold, and a second series, with the same title, reached an edition of 50,000 in a few months. She

has prepared the "Songs of the Young Women's Christian Temperance Union" for the "Y's," and on invitation of the National Woman's Christian Temperance Union now has in hand a hymnal for that great society. Her book of "Questions Answered" is a complete manual of juvenile temperance work, and her "Prohibition Programme" is a delightful evening entertainment, by means of which the Band of Hope "puts money in its purse," while her droll "collection speech," in rhyme, has been used a thousand times. All of these have been given to the Women's Temperance Publishing House, Chicago. She has published a "White Ribbon Birth-day Book." Miss Gordon has traveled with Miss Willard an average of 10,000 miles a year, and in 1883 went with her to every State and Territory, making a trip of about 30,000 miles and assisting in twenty State and Territorial conventions. Public-schools, Sunday-schools, summer Chautauquas, conventions, all have heard her

ANNA A. GORDON.

plans and pleas for the temperance cause. Miss Gordon is a notable housekeeper, after the choicest New England pattern; a famous financier, so that her chief never carries a purse or looks after a bill; and as a mere item in her daily duties she turns off an amount of correspondence that would be occupation enough for the average private secretary.

GORDON, Miss Elizabeth P., temperance advocate, was born in Boston, Mass., and is the third daughter of James M. Gordon, who was for eleven years treasurer of the American Board of Foreign Missions, for twenty years cashier of the Columbia National Bank and one of the most typical and beloved honorary members of the white-ribboned army. Three of his daughters are prominent in the councils of that society. Miss Bessie was for seven years corresponding secretary of the Woman's Christian Temperance Union of Massachusetts, and is now one of its speakers and organizers. Reared in the most conservative manner in a Congregational church, Miss Gordon has made her experience in the thick of the fight and has become one of the acceptable speakers, writers, organizers and managers of the white-ribbon work. She has especial generalistic qualities which will be likely to carry her into that field ultimately, and a hopefulness of spirit that is a benediction to every one she meets.

GORDON, Mrs. Laura De Force, lawyer and journalist, was born in 1840. Her first ambition was in the line of journalism, and in that she soon succeeded, becoming, in 1873, the editor and publisher of the "Daily Leader" of Stockton, Cal., which she afterward continued as the "Daily Democrat" in Oakland, Cal. While attending the session of the California legislature, in 1877, for the purpose of reporting its proceedings for her paper, Mrs. Gordon, together with Mrs. Knox Goodrich, Laura Watkins and Mrs. Wallis, assisted in the preparation of a bill asking the legislature to allow the admission of women to the bar. That bill was known as "The Woman Lawyer's Bill." When it was presented to the legislature, a long and acrimonious debate took place, in which Mrs. Gordon bore a spirited and brilliant part, and the bill was finally passed. At the same session the legislature founded the Hastings College of Law. Mrs. Gordon decided to become a lawyer, and, when that institution was opened, she applied for admission, but was excluded. Together with Mrs. Foltz, another law student, she brought a writ of mandamus, which was successful, and a year later both women were admitted. Mrs. Gordon was a diligent student and, in 1879, was admitted to the bar. She immediately began the practice of her profession in San Francisco, where she remained for five years.

S. ANNA GORDON.

GORDON, Mrs. S. Anna, physician and author, born in Charlemont, Mass., 9th January, 1832. On her father's side she is a descendant of John Steele, who founded the colony of Connecticut and established the town, now city, of Hartford. Among the distinguished persons in her family lineage was Noah Webster. On her mother's side she is a descendant of William Ward, of Sudbury, many of whose descendants won historic distinction as military men and statesmen. She early removed with her parents to New York, where she was reared and took the first year of a college course of study, which was afterwards completed in Illinois. She was married in Wisconsin, in 1858, to W. A. Gordon, M. D., of Wausau. Some years previous she had charge of the ladies' department in Rock River Seminary, and subsequently the same position was twice tendered her in Ripon College. The principalship of the State Normal School of Wisconsin, which was soon to be opened, had been tendered her through the governor of the State, and was awaiting her acceptance. She attended teachers' institutes, wherever held throughout the State, for the purpose of agitating the subject of a normal school, until the desire became an object accomplished. After her marriage she immediately commenced the study of medicine with her husband, attended a partial course of lectures, and was called upon by the people to assist him in an overburdening practice. In 1859 and 1860 they were connected with the Smithsonian Institution, taking meteorological notes and making collections for the same. She filled an engagement of one year as associate editor on the "Central Wisconsin," and then joined her husband in Louisville, Ky., where he was stationed most of the time during the Civil War. There she gave considerable time to the study of art, the remaining time being devoted to the relief of the suffering soldiers around her. Situated near her husband's headquarters at

LAURA DE FORCE GORDON.

She was admittted to the bar of the United States Supreme Court, 3rd February, 1887, being the second woman allowed to plead before that high court. She is now located in Stockton, Cal.

one time was a camp of homeless southern refugees, overtaken by the smallpox. They could find no physician to serve them. Dr. Gordon was prohibited both by want of time and the exposures it would bring to the soldiery. She learned of their pitiful condition and at once went to their relief and fought the scourge until it vanished. She served her husband as hospital officer in different capacities as unavoidable circumstances created vacancies not readily supplied. She was a weekly contributor to the literary columns of the Louisville "Sunday Journal" during the war. She has been a member of the Dante Society since its organization, and in 1882 and 1883 was State editor for the Missouri Woman's Christian Temperance Union on the Chicago "Signal." During a residence in Denver, Col., she was the first person to suggest the demand for the newsboys' home there, which she had the opportunity of aiding in establishing. She was also assistant superintendent of Chinese work in that city for some time. She is author of a book entitled "Camping in Colorado," and several papers and poems that have entered into other collections. In medicine she is a homœopathist. She was graduated in 1889 with honors from the Hahnemann Medical College of Chicago. Her home is now in Hannibal, Mo.

GORTON, Mrs. Cynthia M. R., poet and author, born in Great Barrington, Berkshire county, Mass., 27th February 1826. Her father, Samuel Roberts, died when she was but one year old. She was the youngest of a family of five children, and the young mother, feeble, burdened with sorrow, care and toil, felt obliged in her widowed condition to yield to the solicitations of relatives, and place her little flock among friends, whose tender care they shared for several years. At fourteen years of age she was left an orphan, and soon after began the supreme struggle of her life, to relieve the darkness that subsequently folded its sable wings about her. When her sight began to fail, she was a pupil in Mrs. Willard's Seminary, Troy, N. Y., where she lived with her widowed mother. Not until the death of her mother, and she began to realize the stern fact that she was alone in the world, did she yield herself to that grief which, combined with arduous application to study, produced severe inflammation in her eyes, aggravated by shedding tears. She was thereafter unable to resume her studies, her fondest hope, and the anxious desire of her sympathizing friend and teacher, Mrs. Willard. At twenty-one years of age Miss Roberts became the wife of Fred Gorton, a prosperous paper manufacturer. Six years after, during a most painful and lingering illness, the pall of darkness encompassed her, and she was blind. With the return of physical strength the natural powers of her mind became active and prolific. One of her first efforts was the successful rehearsal of an original poem, entitled "Adolphus and Olivia, or a Tale of Kansas." That she performed with great acceptance to her audience. Her oratorical powers were unusual, and her remarkable memory enabled her to recite for one-and-a-half hours a poem of historical and tragic interest. Of this Gov. Fenton said, at its second rehearsal, "One must conclude, after listening to 'The Blind Bard of Michigan,' that if we would find the best and deepest poetical thoughts, we must look for them in the emanations from the imprisoned soul." For the last twenty years Mrs. Gorton has lectured many times before large and enthusiastic audiences. She has written many serials, stories and poems for the Detroit "Christian Herald" and other papers and periodicals. She has published two books, her domestic cares and public duties having prevented her

from preparing the manuscripts of her other productions for publication. Of late she has relinquished all demands of the platform, as the slight, feeble body rebels against the exhausting ordeal. Ever active, industrious and hopeful, she has not permitted the shadow of darkness to withdraw her from the duties of life. For the last fifteen years she has proved herself an expert with the type-writer. Being a member of the Shut-in Band, this accomplishment has enabled her to extend her efforts in blessing the lives of others, by sending loving words and sympathy to many lonely hearts. Her home is in Fenton, Mich. During her long literary career she has become widely known as "Ida Glenwood," this being her chosen pen-name. She has also been

CYNTHIA M. R. GORTON.

called "The Sweet Singer" and "The Blind Bard of Michigan."

GOUGAR, Mrs. Helen M., orator and woman suffragist, born in Litchfield, Mich., 18th July, 1843. From her earliest years Mrs. Gougar has been an intense and unflinching enthusiast for the right. Originality, energy, keenness of intellect, self-reliance and concentration of force enlivened by a ready wit and buoyant impulses have characterized her every purpose from girlhood to the present. Never to compromise a principle to present expediency is a resolution often upon her lips in answer to the suggestions of the more conservative; and the intriguing, the cowardly, or the weak, whether in the chair of state, divinity or discussion, have frequent opportunities to see themselves as she sees them, and to mend their methods, inspired by her pertinent words. At forty years of age her hair was prematurely whitened by a bitter and hard-fought attempt to weaken her power, in political circles, by defamation, but, the battle over and her enemies completely vanquished, she goes on unflinchingly and contests heroically for what she believes to be the right and patriotic course to a higher civilization. In this battle she decided forever the right of women to take an active part in political warfare without being compelled to endure defamation. As a speaker she is earnest, easy, dignified and at times impassionedly eloquent,

HELEN M. GOUGAR.

wholly without affectation or oratorical display. She speaks without manuscript or notes, rapidly and convincingly. Her special work in reforms is in legal and political lines, and constitutional law and statistics she quotes with marvelous familiarity, when speaking in public. She has been repeatedly called upon to address special committees in Congress, also the legislatures of Indiana, Illinois, Nebraska, Iowa, New York, Wisconsin and Kansas. She recognizes the historical fact that popular governments are overthrown by corrupt municipalities. She believes that the "home vote" is the only power that can control the proletariat mob of large cities, and this causes her to espouse woman suffrage on the platform and with a forcible pen. Mrs. Gougar is the author of the law granting municipal suffrage to the women of Kansas, and the adoption of the measure was largely due to her efforts. She proved the correctness of her theory by redeeming Leavenworth, the largest city in the State at that time, from slum rule by the votes of women. The success which has attended that law, in the interest of political honor and the exaltation of public service, is well known. As a writer she is concise, direct and fluent. She was for many years a contributor to the "Inter-Ocean" and is still held in high esteem by the management of that Republican organ, notwithstanding her radical Prohibition party affiliation. As a business woman she is thorough, prompt and systematic; as a companion, cheerful, witty, voluble. In her domestic life she is happy and fortunate, the wife of a man of wealth, education and refinement, a successful lawyer, respected and beloved by all who know him, and whose affectionate sympathy, self-poise and financial independence have sustained her in

the aggressive methods peculiar to her public work. Their home in Lafayette, Ind., is one of unusual elegance and comfort. Although childless, both she and her husband are fond of children and young people, and they are seldom without a youthful guest in the house, the children of her five sisters, or other relatives or friends, and sometimes a waif of charity, who share the cheery hospitality of their elegant surroundings.

GOULD, Miss Elizabeth Porter, critic and author, born in Manchester-by-the-sea, Mass., 8th June, 1848. She is the daughter of John A. and Elizabeth C. Gould, and is descended from generations of worthy Essex county people, including the famous schoolmaster, Ezekiel Cheever. Had she never given to the public any other work than her "Gems from Walt Whitman" (Philadelphia, 1889), she would be entitled to a lasting place in the literary world. No word said of the poet has brought a deeper expression of thanks from him than the essay in the book on his life among the soldiers. Her essays on education during the past ten years have been valuable additions to the educational thought of the day. One, "John Adams as a Schoolmaster," published in pamphlet form, attracted the notice of the leading educators of the country. Through the courtesy of Charles Francis Adams, who called it a most thorough piece of historical work, it has been placed in the leading libraries of the land. Another, "Daniel Webster as a Schoolmaster," with other articles on that great statesman, gave her an honorary membership in the Webster Historical Society. Those on "Robert College" and "Bulgaria under Alexander," the former the only full account of that American institution on the Bosphorus ever written,

ELIZABETH PORTER GOULD.

brought her most complimentary words from the ex-Prince himself. Others, such as, "Friedrich Froebel," "School Life in China," "The Steele Orphanage in Chattanooga" and "The Woman

Problem," have become authority on those subjects. The versatility of Miss Gould's mind, as well as her conscientious research, are seen in articles published in the Chicago "Law Times," the New York "Critic," "Literary World," "Independent," "Christian Union," "New England Magazine," "Woman's Journal," and other periodicals. Her article in the "Century," in 1889, on Pundita Ramabai, was but an outline of the lecture which, with those on Abigail Adams, Hannah Adams, Mary Somerville and Caroline Herschel, has brought her as an interesting lecturer before the chief woman's clubs in Boston and vicinity. Besides having inspired clubs in the city of her long residence, Chelsea, Mass., she has been, and still is, an intellectual power among the society women of Boston, Brookline, Newton and other places, by her "Talks on Current Events." Besides her unique work in private circles, Miss Gould, as an officer in philanthropic organizations in Boston and Chelsea, has struck important chords for more efficient work, especially in the line of reform. Her brochure, "How I became a Woman Suffragist," is a book of personal experience. She has written poetry, a volume of her verse, "Stray Pebbles from the Shores of Thought" (Boston, 1892), having been recently published. She has a novel ready for the press.

GOULD, Miss Ellen M., philanthropist, born at The Hope, near Providence, R. I., 7th January, 1848. Her father, Daniel Gould, was born in Middletown, R. I., where his ancestors settled in 1637. Her mother, an Earle, descended from the Chases, who were the earliest settlers of Nantucket, was born in Providence. Both parents are of unmixed English lineage, and both are by birth and education Quakers. The father of Ellen is the eighth in the direct line of descent who has borne the name of Daniel Gould. In 1852 the family removed to Providence, where they remained till 1857, when they made a final remove to Davenport, Iowa. During the stormy decades in the middle of the century, Mr. and Mrs. Gould took an active part in the progressive movements of the time, especially the abolition of slavery. Their three daughters have inherited a like interest in the philanthropic efforts of the present. This has been especially the case with Ellen. Although naturally of a strong literary bent, a systematic training in that direction was rendered impossible by delicate health in early youth and by the imperative nature of home duties. Yet, so eager has been her thirst for knowledge and so persistent her efforts in making the most of every opportunity for self improvment offered, that no one but herself can discover any deficiency. She has contributed short stories to children's magazines, and has also contributed able papers to the various societies of which she is a member. Her sympathies were enlisted during the Civil War in a Soldier's Aid Society. She was the only young girl member, and she was sent as a delegate to one of the large sanitary fairs. She has been a member of the Unitarian Church of Davenport from its first organization and at a critical period in its history did much to restore its prosperity. Always an advocate of woman suffrage, she has done all in her power to promote its interests. With the help of a friend she organized the first and only suffrage association in Davenport. She has been for many years a member of the Library Association and also of the Academy of Science, but circumstances have hindered her from taking an active part in the work of either. She organized a literary club for young women, which had a very successful course for six years. It was called the Bric-a-Brac Society, and it aided in a

very substantial way several important enterprises. She has been a most energetic member of the Ladies' Benevolent Society, and also of the Association for the Advancement of Women, and of the Ramabai Association. For six years she was directress of an industrial school for poor children, having worked as a teacher for two years. After a careful personal examination of the working of such schools in the East, she was able, with the aid of others, to systematize and give to the school such plans that few changes have since been necessary. In 1887, with the aid of a generous friend, she organized a cooking school, which proved so successful that in the following year it was incorporated into the public school system. To the two last mentioned enterprises she has given much time and strength gratuitously. Circumstances in her home have obliged her of late to give up all public work with the exception of that connected with the

ELLEN M. GOULD.

church, called the Post-Office Mission, the duties of which can be performed quietly at home. In this mission she has been a pioneer worker.

GOWER, Mrs. Lillian Norton, opera singer, widely known by her stage-name, "Lillian Nordica," born in Farmington, Maine, in 18—. When she was five years old, her parents removed to Boston, Mass., where she studied in the New England Conservatory of Music. After graduating she made an extensive concert tour of the United States, singing with the Händel and Haydn Society and with Theodore Thomas's Orchestra. She visited Europe with Gilmore's Band, and there won distinction as a singer. She decided to remain in Europe and to prepare for an operatic career. She studied in Milan with San Giovanni. In six weeks she learned ten operas completely. She sang in opera in Brescia, Aquila and Genoa. In St. Petersburg, Russia, she won her first great triumph as Filina in "Mignon." In 1881 she went to Paris. She made her début in that city as Marguerite in

Gounod's "Faust," where she scored one of the most brilliant triumphs on record. Mrs. Gower is not only a great singer, but a great actor as well. She sang in Her Majesty's Theater, in London,

LILLIAN NORTON GOWER.

England, for three years. She returned to the United States with the reputation of one of the great queens of the lyric stage. She has a repertory of forty grand operas at her command. She became the wife, in London, of Mr. Gower, a man of wealth. Her husband disappeared in a tragic manner. He made a balloon ascension from Paris, and balloon and men were never heard from afterward. Mrs. Norton's latest triumphs have been won in Covent Garden, London.

GOZA, Miss Anne, humorist, born in Hatchett Creek, Ala., 4th July, 1872. Her home has always been in her native town, excepting the time spent in school. Although one of the very youngest of the rising writers of the South, Miss Goza has already acquired a wide reputation as a writer of humorous and dialect stories. She has chosen the dialect of the people of the Alabama mountains, and she has made skillful use of that peculiarly interesting jargon. She is a regular contributor to the Burlington "Hawkeye," the Atlanta "Sunny South," the Cleveland "Plain Dealer," the New Orleans "Times Democrat," and many other prominent journals. Her success has been marked and remarkable. She is a prolific writer, and in the quaint people around her she has abundant material for her future work. She is distinctly original, and her sketches record much that will be of interest to the future students of American folk-lore. She has published one volume, "The Fall of Queen Prudence."

GRANBERY, Miss Virginia, artist, born in Norfolk, Va. When she was a child, her parents moved to New York, where they have resided ever since. She early showed a fondness for drawing, but, as there was no drawing

taught in the schools, she did not have the benefit of instruction. She learned to copy engravings and made several drawings from casts, without a teacher. After she was grown, she went to the Cooper Institute for a short time, spending a part of each day under the instruction of A. F. Bellows in his studio, where she worked in colors. She studied in the Academy of Design school in the antique, portrait and life classes, and received honorable mention for a drawing. She began to paint fruits and flowers from nature, many of which have been chromoed by Prang, of Boston. From 1871 to 1882 she was teacher of the art department of the Packer Institute, Brooklyn, N. Y. On entering the Packer Institute she received the same salary as her predecessor, but at the end of the first year her method had doubled the number of pupils, and she had offers from other large schools that wished to secure her services. The board of trustees decided to increase her salary fifty per cent. and also gave her a further substantial recognition of their appreciation of her services in a check for a handsome amount, accompanied by a very complimentary letter. The department increased so that an assistant was necessary. After eleven years of work she broke down under the constant demand on her strength, and was obliged to send in her resignation. She and her sisters were among the very few women artists whose work was accepted with that of the men to be exhibited in the Centennial of 1876, in Philadelphia. Recently she has devoted herself principally to portraits. She is very successful in painting small pictures of children. She

ANNE GOZA.

has shown pictures in all the principal exhibitions thoughout the United States.

GRANGER, Miss Lottie E., educator and school officer, born near Granville, Ohio, 28th January, 1858. Her father, Sylvester Granger, was of New England descent, and her mother, Elizabeth Walrath, of German origin. Village and country schools afforded sufficient tuition to Miss Granger to enable her to begin teaching at the age of sixteen years. For three consecutive summers she followed teaching, when her desire to add to her education had become so great that she made for herself a way to gratify this ambition. Through the coöperation of the president of Shepardson College, then Young Ladies' Institute, she was enabled to complete a classical course of study in that excellent institution, deserving a medal for her brave and sterling character as well as a diploma for her mental proficiency. She was graduated in 1880, and spent the following year in Kansas, and the next five years in Shenandoah, Ia., occupied with the duties of the school-room. In 1886, having been elected to the office of county superintendent of the public schools of Page county, she held the position for six years, and by the excellence of her work made for herself a name that is State-wide among educators. At the annual meeting of the Iowa State Teachers' Association, held in Des Moines in 1888, she was unanimously elected president, being the second woman ever chosen to fill that honorable place during the thirty-five years of the organization. She has also been a member of the Educational Council, which is the senate of the teachers' association. From its organization she has served on the board of managers of the Iowa State Teachers' Reading Circle. She is an active Sunday-school and temperance worker, is a Chautauqua graduate, a ready speaker, a forcible writer and of magnetic presence on the platform. Declining a fourth term of service as county superintendent, Miss Granger, never being satisfied with present attainments, will pursue a post-graduate course of study in the Chicago University. Since

synonymous in Page county as an ardent friendship has taken them together into every township where political canvass, school visitation and temperance work have made their interests common.

LOTTIE E. GRANGER.

Being of an unassuming disposition, Miss Granger seldom passes, on chance acquaintance, at her true worth. A close observer, however, will discover beneath her unpretentiousness an equipoise of character, a cool decisive judgment, a penetrating eye and an activity of thought.

GRANT, Mrs. Julia Dent, wife of General Ulysses S. Grant, the eighteenth President of the United States, born in St. Louis, Mo., 26th January, 1826. She is a daughter of Frederick and Ellen Wrenshall Dent. Her grandfather, Capt. George Dent, led the forlorn hope in Fort Montgomery, when it was stormed by Mad Anthony Wayne. On her mother's side she is descended from John Wrenshall, an English Puritan who settled in Philadelphia, Pa. She began to attend Miss Moreau's boarding-school in 1836, and she remained in that school until 1844. Returning home in that year, she met Lieutenant U. S. Grant, then stationed in Jefferson Barracks, in St. Louis. She became his wife 22nd August, 1848. They lived in Detroit, Mich., until 1852, and then went to Sackett's Harbor, N. Y., where Captain Grant was stationed. When Captain Grant was ordered to California, Mrs. Grant returned to St. Louis, her health not being strong enough to endure so great a change of climate. During the Civil War she remained much of the time near her husband. She was with him in City Point in the winter of 1864 and 1865, and she accompanied him to Washington when he returned with his victorious army. She for eight years filled the arduous position of mistress of the White House in a most charming manner. Her régime was marked by dignity, simplicity and home-like ways that endeared her to all who came into contact with her. She accompanied her

VIRGINIA GRANBERY.

her election to office, her home has been in Clarinda, Ia., where she is a member of the household of Mr. and Mrs. Edwin Henshaw. The names of Mrs. Henshaw and Miss Granger are almost

husband around the earth. After General Grant's death, Congress voted her a pension of $5,000 a year. Her family consists of three children, Frederick Dent Grant, Ulysses S. Grant, jr., and Mrs.

JULIA DENT GRANT.

Nellie Sartoris. She now lives in New York City, occupied much of the time with literary labors.

GRASER, Miss Hulda Regina, customhouse broker, born in Montreal, Canada, 23rd June, 1869. In 1870 the family removed to Chicago, Ill., where, in the great fire of 1871, they lost all their property and nearly lost their lives. Her father, Ernst G. Graser, was a native of St. Gallen, Switzerland, where he was born in 1842. He came to America in 1867 and settled in Montreal. Her mother was a resident of Zurich, Switzerland. After the loss of their home and property in Chicago, the family went to Cincinnati, Ohio, where they began life anew. Mr. Graser, who was a thoroughly educated man and could speak several languages well, secured employment with the government. He also gave private instruction in foreign languages. He remained in the customhouse ten years, after which time, in 1882, he opened what is called a customs brokerage business, and one year prior to his death, which occurred in 1884, he took into partnership with him his older daughter, styling the firm E. & M. Graser. After his death the daughter continued the business until her marriage, in 1885, to Dr. E. H. Rothe, when she sold it. Hulda, the younger daughter, was educated in the Cincinnati free schools, and in 1885 she was employed as clerk and then as cashier in a wholesale and retail notion house. She afterward studied stenography, did some reporting and helped on the senatorial investigation, in the above capacity, and in the fall of 1886, when seventeen years old, opened a new office as customs broker and forwarder, her sister's successor having sold out to her present competitor. In 1887, about five months after she commenced,

there was a decision by the department, on the strength of false representations made to the department, prohibiting brokers or their clerks from getting any information from customs officials without an order from the different importers, thus making her beginning doubly hard. That necessitated her calling upon every importer in the city, securing his signature to a petition asking for any and all information regarding each firm's importations. In 1890, in connection with brokerage, she took up an agency for tin-plates, and she handles large quantities of that article. The greater amount of tin-plates arriving at Cincinnati between January and July, 1891, went through her office, and her undertaking has proved very successful. She occupies a unique position, and her success in that arduous line of work is another demonstration of the truth that women can conduct business that

HULDA REGINA GRASER.

exacts great care, sound judgment, originality and untiring industry.

GRAVES, Mrs. Adelia C., educator and author, born in Kingsville, Ohio, 17th March, 1821. She is the wife of Dr. Z. C. Graves, a noted educator both north and south, founder and for forty years president of Mary Sharp College, in Winchester, Tenn. She is the daughter of Dr. Daniel M. Spencer and Marian T. Cook, and a niece of P. R. Spencer, the originator of the Spencerian system of penmanship. The mother of Mrs. Graves was a woman of fine intellect. Her people were wealthy and cultured, all the men having for generations had the benefit of collegiate education. Her father especially excelled in the Greek and Latin languages. Perhaps one of the most critical linguists of the time was his youthful granddaughter. For years she taught classes of young men in languages in the Kingsville Academy, who desired her instructions in preference to all others. Many of them have since attained positions as lawyers, ministers, physicians, presidents and

professors of colleges. The present president of
Beyrout College, in Syria, Asia Minor, was for some
time a student with her, especially in the Latin language. Mrs. Graves may be said to have inherited
the poetic temperament from both sides of the
house. The Mary Sharp College under Dr. Graves'
presidency acquired a national reputation, and he
avers that its success was owing quite as much to
her wise counsels and management as to his own
efforts. There were few positions in the college
she did not, at some time, occupy, save that of
mathematics. For thirty-two years she was matron
and professor of rhetoric, belles-lettres, elocution
and English composition, at different times, as
need be, teaching French, ancient history and
ancient geography, English literature, or whatever
else was required. The published works of Mrs.
Graves are "Seclusaval, or the Arts of Romanism" (Memphis, Tenn., 1870), a work written to
deter Protestants from sending children to Catholic
schools, and "Jephtha's Daughter," a drama,
(Memphis, 1867). Besides these are two prize
stories. Twelve or thirteen small volumes were
also compiled from the Southern Child's Book, at
the request of the Southern Baptist Sabbath School
Union, for the use of Sabbath-schools. Mrs.
Graves for years edited and wrote for that
publication. She wrote the "Old Testament Catechism in Rhyme" (Nashville, Tenn., 1859), on request of the same society, for the use of the colored
people while still slaves, for which she received
twenty cents a line, they, her employers, saying,
they knew of no one else that could do it. Her
unpublished poems are numerous. Mrs. Graves
has found a place in "Woman in Sacred Song,"
and "Southland Poets," and she is mentioned in the

GRAVES, Miss Mary H., Unitarian minister,
born in North Reading, Mass., 12th September,
1839. Her parents were Eben Graves and Hannah
M. Campbell Graves. Her maternal ancestors, the

MARY H. GRAVES.

Campbells and Moores, were descendants of the
Scotch-Irish settlers of Londonderry, N. H. Mary
was graduated from the State Normal School,
Salem, Mass., in February, 1860. She taught in
the public schools of her native town and of South
Danvers, now Peabody, Mass. She was inclined
to literature and wrote for the "Ladies' Repository"
and other journals. She took a theological course
of study under Rev. Olympia Brown in Weymouth,
Mass., and in Bridgeport, Conn., preaching occasionally in the neighboring towns. In the summer
of 1869 she supplied the pulpit of the Universalist
Church in North Reading, Mass. In the summer
of 1870 she preached in Earlville, Ill. On December, 14th, 1871, she was regularly ordained as pastor
of the Unitarian Church in Mansfield, Mass., having
already preached one year for that society. In
1882 she had pastoral charge of the Unitarian
Society in Baraboo, Wis. She has done some
missionary work in the West, mainly in Illinois and
adjoining States. In 1885 and 1886, while living in
Chicago, she assisted in the conduct of "Manford's
Magazine," acting as literary editor. For one year
she was secretary of the Women's Western Unitarian Conference. At present her strength is not
sufficient to allow her to do the full work of the
ministry, and she is devoting herself to literary
work. She contributes occasionally to the "Christian Register," the "Commonwealth," the Boston
"Transcript," the "Leader" and other journals.

GRAY, Mrs. Jennie T., temperance worker,
born in Pilot Grove, Iowa, 16th September, 1857.
Her father, Stephen Townsend, was of English
descent. Her mother was of Welsh and English
descent. She was reared in the faith of the Quaker
Church. From her father she inherited literary

ADELIA C. GRAVES.

"Successful Men of Tennessee" for her extraordinary financial ability, having managed a business
of fifteen-thousand to twenty-thousand dollars per
year for years at a time, most successfully.

taste and ability, and from her mother a fearless firmness for the right. She always showed an intense love for books and at an early age made herself acquainted with a large number of the best

JENNIE T. GRAY.

authors. From Iowa her father removed with his family in the spring of 1865 to Fountain City, Ind., near the place of his nativity, where the remainder of her childhood was spent. She and her older sisters identified themselves early in life with the temperance cause, and they are still active, enthusiastic workers in the Woman's Christian Temperance Union. She became the wife of Dr. C. F. Gray, of Winchester, Ind., 18th December, 1878. Her husband not only encourages her in every good word and work, but supplies with lavish hand all the financial assistance which she may feel called upon to bestow in any good cause. She consecrated herself wholly to Christian work in the spring of 1889, and since then she has been led into more active service in the line of temperance. At present she is president of the Woman's Christian Temperance Union of Randolph county, Ind. In all her travels from ocean to ocean and gulf to lakes she has tried to carry the strongest possible influence for temperance, often finding suitable occasions for advocating her theme in a modest but convincing way.

GRAY, Mrs. Mary Tenney, editorial writer and philanthropist, born in Brookdale, Liberty township, Susquehanna county, Pa., 19th June, 1833, and became a citizen of Kansas by adoption. Her fitness as a leader in the struggles and labors of the new State was the result of a thorough training in her father's theological library, supplemented by a course of study in the Ingalls Seminary, Binghamton, N.Y., and continued in a Pennsylvania seminary. After she was graduated, she was for several years preceptress in Binghamton Academy. On the editorial staff of the New York "Teacher" for two years her influence was felt among the teachers of the State. After she became the wife of Judge

Barzillai Gray in 1859, and her removal to Wyandotte, Kansas Territory, and afterwards to Leavenworth, she entered upon many enterprises in the line of charities, church extension, the upbuilding of State and county expositions, and was a prominent mover in the Centennial exhibit for Kansas in Philadelphia in 1876. She was a contributor or correspondent to the leading magazines and papers of Kansas and to the eastern press. The orphan asylum in Leavenworth was debtor to the appeals of her pen for recognition and assistance. The "Home Record," of the same city, was an outgrowth and exponent of her deep and abiding interest in the welfare and elevation of women. The compilation of the Kansas "Home Cook Book," for the benefit of the Home for the Friendless, was and is still a source of financial strength to the institution, more than ten-thousand copies having been sold. She has been for twenty years one of the officers of the board of control for the Home. As editor of the home department of the "Kansas Farmer" for some years she showed both sympathy and interest in a class who by force of circumstances are largely debarred from intellectual pursuits. As one of the original founders and first president of the Social Science Club of Kansas and Western Missouri, she has given an impetus to intellectual culture in those localities, and through skill, tact and personal influence has seen the organization grow from a small number to a membership of five-hundred of the brightest women of the two States. To these labors have been added

MARY TENNEY GRAY.

scientific attainments unusual among women, and artistic work of much merit.

GREATOREX, Mrs. Eliza, artist, born in Manor Hamilton, Ireland, 25th December, 1819. She was the daughter of Rev. James Calcott Pratt, who removed to New York in 1840. Eliza became the wife, in 1849, of Henry Wellington Greatorex, the musician. After marriage she studied art with

William H. Witherspoon and James Hart, in New York, with Emile Lambinet, in Paris, and with the instructors in the Pinakothek, in Munich. In 1879 she studied etching with C. H. Toussaint. She visited Europe in 1861 and 1870, spending several years, studying in Italy and Germany. In 1868 she was made a member of the National Academy of Design, in New York City. She was the first woman member of that organization, and she was the first woman to belong to the Artists' Fund Society, of New York. Her reputation as an artist rests largely on her pen-and-ink sketches, many of which have appeared in book form, filling four large volumes. She has painted many notable pictures in oil. Her work is of a singularly great quality. Her home is in New York City. Her two daughters have inherited her artistic talents.

GREEN, Anna Katharine, SEE ROHLFS, ANNA KATHARINE GREEN.

GREEN, Mrs. Julia Boynton, poet, born in South Byron, Genesee county, N. Y., 25th May, 1861. When she was fifteen years old, she and her older sister entered Ingham University, in LeRoy, N. Y., where they remained a year as students. Another year was spent by both in preparation for Wellesley College. After entering that institution, they were called home on account of domestic bereavement. Their interrupted course of study was continued for several years, chiefly in Nyack-on-the-Hudson, and Miss Boynton afterwards passed two winters in New York in the study of art, for which she has marked talent. She spent a season in London, England, and in 1888 she was preparing for an extended tour in Europe, when she was called home by the illness of her mother. Since then both her parents have died. In June,

disturbed by so many changes and diversions, but Mrs. Green has found time to write some strikingly excellent poetry. Most of her work has appeared in local journals and in the Boston "Transcript." She has published one volume of poems, "Lines and Interlines" (New York, 1887).

GREEN, Mrs. Mary E., physician, born in Machias, N.Y., 6th August, 1844. Both her parents

MARY E. GREEN.

were of New England stock. They moved to Michigan, when she was very young, and with limited means they were obliged to endure all the hardships of pioneer life. As there were no brothers in the family, little Mary worked both indoors and outdoors, preferring the latter, until, the little house being built and a few acres about it cleared, she was allowed to think about education. She went to a neighbor's, several miles distant, where she worked for her board and began to attend school At fourteen years of age she passed the required examination and began to teach, her salary being two dollars a week, with the privilege of boarding round. She was soon able to enter Olivet College. There she earned her own way, chiefly by doing housework, and partially so in Oberlin College, which she attended later. While yet in her teens, she realized the necessity of choosing some life work for herself, and as she desired to pursue the study of medicine, she quietly determined to do so. Undaunted by the criticism of her friends, in 1865, after one year's study with a physician, Miss Green entered the New York Medical College. She was soon chosen assistant in the chemical laboratory, and besides that work, every evening found her, knife in hand, making the dissections to be used on the following day by the demonstrator of anatomy. She entered Bellevue Hospital and remained there, in spite of the hisses and insults which the students felt in duty bound to offer any of the "weaker" sex who presumed to cross their pathway. Miss Green's thorough

JULIA BOYNTON GREEN.

1890, Miss Boynton became the wife of Levi Worthington Green, and after a six-months' tour in Europe they made their home in Rochester, N. Y. Necessarily, her literary work has been seriously

womanliness, as much as her stronger qualities, won her cause. On account of its hospital advantages, the next year she entered the Woman's Medical College in Philadelphia, and for two years was an interne of the hospital. In 1868 she was graduated from that college with honor, her thesis being entitled "Medical Jurisprudence." Two years before graduation Dr. Green became the wife of her cousin, Alonzo Green, then a practicing lawyer in New York, whither she went in 1868 and engaged in active practice. Outside of office hours Dr. Green's time was occupied with charitable work, as she was visiting physician to the Midnight Mission, the Five Points Mission, Dr. Blackwell's Infirmary and the Prison Home for Women. By personal effort she organized and built up a large dispensary for women and children in a neglected quarter of the city, which was so successful that, after the first year in which over two-thousand patients were cared for, it received State and city support. Dr. Green's consulting physicians and surgeons were the most eminent in the city. In 1870 she delivered part of a course of lectures on medical subjects in connection with Dr. Elizabeth Blackwell, Dr. Willard Parker and others. The year after her graduation Dr. Green's name was presented for membership to the New York Medical Society, and after a stormy discussion she was admitted, being the first woman in America to win that opportunity for broader work. Soon after, she became a member of the Medico-Legal Society. Wishing to pursue a higher course in the study of chemistry, she applied for admission to Columbia College, but her request was not granted. She entered upon a course of evening lectures given by Professor Chandler in the College of Pharmacy, and, although she could not graduate, as she was a woman, the coveted knowledge was gained. During those years of constant mental and physical work Dr. Green became the mother of two children. She removed in 1873 to Charlotte, Mich., where she now resides. There three more little ones came into her family. Several years ago she took up wood-carving in Cincinnati. While in New York, she attended the Cooper Institute lectures regularly, and was otherwise interested in both literary and art work. Dr. Green has been twice elected health officer of the city in which she lives, and has three times been elected delegate to the American Medical Association by the State Medical Society.

GREENE, Mrs. Belle C., author, born in Pittsfield, Vt., 17th March, 1844. Her maiden name was Colton, and her descent is a mixture of American, English and Indian. One of her ancestors on her father's side married an Indian princess belonging to a Massachusetts tribe, and settled in that State. Her mother, Lucy Baker, came from Puritan stock. She died at the age of forty-seven, leaving her husband and a family of six girls. Isabel, who was next to the youngest, was but four years old at the time. She was taken into the family of a distant relative living in a New Hampshire country town, where she was reared and educated in strictest orthodox ways. In 1868 she became the wife of M. B. V. Greene, of Nashua, N. H., where she has since made her home. It was not till the year 1881 that Mrs. Greene began her literary work in earnest. She sent a short story and a humorous sketch to her friend, Mrs. Phelps-Ward, then Miss Phelps, asking for advice and encouragement. Miss Phelps replied with characteristic honesty and kindness that Mrs. Greene's voice was doubtless her one great gift, and, as mortals were seldom blest with two, she advised her to stick to music, but added, since she must give an opinion, that she considered the humorous sketch better than the story. Upon this

scanty encouragement Mrs. Greene offered the humorous sketch to "Godey's Lady's Book," and it was accepted. She continued to furnish sketches for a year or more, and concluded her work for the magazine by writing her first story proper, a novelette, afterward published in book form under the title "A New England Idyl." "Adventures of an Old Maid," a second book, was a collection of humorous sketches published first in the magazines, and has had a sale of over seventy-five-thousand copies. Her religious novel, "A New England Conscience," attracted wide comment. Though severely denounced by some of the critics, it was regarded by others as a masterpiece of condensed thought and realistic character drawing. In 1887–88 Mrs. Greene made an extended tour of southern California and the Pacific Coast, and during her stay of several months in Los Angeles and San Diego she contributed to the newspapers a series of humorous sketches founded

BELLE C. GREENE.

upon the phases of the boom, which added greatly to her reputation as a humorous writer. These last-mentioned articles constitute her only newspaper work, with the exception of the "Mill Papers," regarding the operatives in the cotton-mills, written for the Boston "Transcript" in 1883 and 1884. Mrs. Greene's success thus far has been largely as a short-story writer. Her family consists of her husband and one son.

GREENE, Miss Frances Nimmo, educator, born in Tuscaloosa, Ala., in the late sixties. She is known to the public as "Dixie." She is descended through her father from an old South Carolina family, and through her mother from the best Virginia stock. Her mother's family have been literary in taste for several generations. Miss Greene received her education in Tuscaloosa Female College, where she made an excellent record for earnestness and intelligence. Since leaving school she has made teaching her profession.

While teaching in a mining town in north Alabama, she first conceived the idea of writing sketches for publication. Her first attempt, "Yankees in Dixie," was promptly accepted by the

FRANCES NIMMO GREENE.

Philadelphia "Times." Since that time she has contributed to that paper many letters on southern affairs. She also writes for the Birmingham "Age-Herald" and other southern papers. She has directed her efforts as a writer toward bringing about a better state of feeling between the sections by giving the people of the North a correct understanding of the negro and his condition, and also of the temper of the southern whites. Besides writing in prose, she sometimes writes verse, but has published only one poem.

GREENE, Mrs. Louisa Morton, reformer and author, born in Ashburnham, Mass., 23rd May, 1819. She is a descendant from sturdy New England ancestors. Her father, Henry Willard, blacksmith and farmer, removed from Vermont and settled in Ashburnham in the early years of the present century. Bereft of both parents in early childhood, she was deprived of schooling and thrown upon her own resources at the age of thirteen years. She obtained employment in a woolen factory in Dedham, Mass., and worked for several years for the pittance of one to two dollars per week and board, working fourteen hours a day. There, upon the heads of bobbins, she learned to write. Notwithstanding her long hours of labor, she found time for constant improvement by reading and study. Her habits of strict economy enabled her to save a portion of her wages, and at the age of seventeen she had one-hundred-fifty dollars in the bank. Then came her first revolt against the injustice shown to women in industrial pursuits. Gross discrimination in the matter of wages was made, simply on the ground of sex. Called upon at one time to take a man's place at a spindle, she performed her duties with greater dispatch and to

the acknowledged satisfaction of her employer. When pay-day came around and she demanded the same compensation that the man had been securing, her request was received with amazement. The plucky young girl stood her ground and refused to return to the spindle unless paid at the same rate as the man whose place she was filling. She was promptly dismissed from the factory, to be recalled a few weeks later at increased wages. In 1840 she taught school near Portsmouth, N. H. There she formed the acquaintance of Jonas Greene, of Maine, becoming his wife in 1841. Mr. Greene subsequently became a prominent politician, representing his district in each branch of the State legislature for several successive terms. His success in life he ascribed largely to the coöperation and support of his prudent, intelligent and broadminded wife. Removing with her husband to the then somewhat sparsely settled Oxford county, Maine, a new and active life opened for her. While performing faithfully her duties, she found time to enter vigorously into the philanthropic and reform work of the times. Early becoming a convert to the "Water Cure" system of treating the sick, she familiarized herself with it and soon developed a remarkable ability for the care and treatment of the sick. Physicians and medicines were unknown in her household, and her skill was in demand in the community. In 1850 Mrs. Greene began to espouse the anti-slavery cause. She, with a few kindred spirits, gathered the country women together and organized anti-slavery societies. Literature was distributed, "Uncle Tom's Cabin" was read far and near, and many stirring articles from her pen appeared in the local papers, and sentiment against the system was rapidly created. During

LOUISA MORTON GREENE.

the Civil War Mrs. Greene's patriotic labors were untiring. When hospital supplies were called for, she spent much time in collecting, preparing and forwarding them. Mrs. Greene's newspaper contributions for years covered a wide range of subjects. The temperance and suffrage causes were early championed by her and have ever commanded her best service of pen and voice. In 1869 she removed with her family to Manassas, Va., where her husband died in 1873. With advancing years, Mrs. Greene has withdrawn largely from active philanthropic work.

GREENE, Miss Mary A., lawyer, born in Warwick, R. I., 14th June, 1857. She is a lineal descendant of Roger Williams, and also of John Greene, the founder of the famous Greene family of Rhode Island, prominent in the military and civic affairs of the State and the nation. Her Revolutionary ancestor, Colonel Christopher Greene, the gallant defender of Red Bank on the Delaware, was a cousin of General Nathaniel Greene. Miss Greene began the study of law in 1885, in order to be able to manage her own business affairs and to assist other women to do the same. She took the full

MARY A. GREENE.

course of three years in the Boston University Law School, graduating in 1888 with the degree of Bachelor of Laws, *magna cum laude*, being the third woman to graduate from the school. She was at once admitted to the Suffolk bar, in Boston, becoming thus the second woman member of the Massachusetts bar. After practicing eighteen months in Boston, she returned to her native State. She now resides in Providence, where she is engaged in the work of writing and lecturing upon legal topics. Always frail in constitution, Miss Greene found herself unable to endure the strain of court practice, although she was successful in that line of work. For that reason she has never applied for admission to the Rhode Island bar, her standing at the Boston bar being sufficient for the kind of work she is at present doing. She is a regular lecturer upon business law for women in Lasell Seminary, Auburndale, Mass., the first girls' school to give systematic instruction in principles of law. Among her literary

productions are a translation from the French of Dr. Louis Frank's essay, "The Woman Lawyer," which appeared in the Chicago "Law Times," and the original articles: "Privileged Communications in the Suits between Husband and Wife," in the "American Law Review"; "The Right of American Women to Vote and Hold Public Office," in the Boston "Evening Traveller"; "A Woman Lawyer," and a series of articles upon "Practical Points of Every-Day Law," in the "Chautauquan." Miss Greene is firmly impressed with the importance to all women of a practical knowledge of the principals of business law, and in all her professional work she endeavors to educate her hearers and readers in those most necessary matters. As a public speaker she is very successful. She always speaks without notes and with great fluency and felicity. At the fortieth anniversary of the first woman's rights convention, celebrated in Boston in January, 1891, Miss Greene was invited to speak for "Women in Law" as the representative of that profession. She is not, however, identified in any way with the woman suffrage movement, possessing, as she does, that spirit of conservatism mingled with independence which has always characterized the people of Rhode Island. She believes that her mission is to educate women to an intelligent use of the rights they possess, and that to others may be left the work of demanding further rights for her sex.

GREENLEAF, Mrs. Jean Brooks, woman suffragist, born in Bernardston, Franklin county, Mass., 1st October, 1830. She is the daughter of John Brooks, M.D., and Mary Bascom Brooks. Dr. Brooks was a man of decided opinions, a liberal in both religion and politics, and had the courage of his convictions. His ideas were advanced, for his time, with regard to the training of his daughters for lives of usefulness and independence, and the cultivation of a habit of independent thought on matters of vital interest. Mrs. Brooks, a devoted mother, was very domestic in her taste, caring well for her household, and, although an invalid, actively alive in alleviating the wants of those less fortunate in life than herself. Jean was the youngest of the six children of Dr. Brooks who lived to advanced years. Her school life was limited to a few years in the public schools and academy of her native village, supplemented by two terms in Melrose Seminary, in West Brattleboro, Vt. At the age of seventeen years the confirmed invalidism of her mother necessitated the ending of school life, and from that time until her marriage, three years later, she assumed largely the cares and duties of her father's household. Her interests in the rights and wrongs of woman was early awakened while listening to the spirited remonstrance of a widowed aunt, Mrs. Willard, against paying taxes upon property that she had acquired by her own exertions, when she had no representation at the polls, while a miserable drunkard in the neighborhood, who was supported by his wife and daughters, and who owned no property, was allowed to vote in opposition to what both she and the wife and daughters of the drunkard believed to be for the best interests of the community. Since 1862, the year of Mrs. Greenleaf's marriage to Halbert S. Greenleaf, her life has been passed quietly at home. Her husband has given both military and civil service to his country, having commanded the 52nd Massachusetts Volunteers in the late war for the Union, and is now serving his second term as member of Congress. He is in full sympathy with his wife in her views respecting the enfranchisement of women. The changes brought about by the war made a residence in Louisiana necessary for a few years, but for the last twenty-four years, Rochester, N. Y., has been the home of their adoption. The cause of woman suffrage is most dear to Mrs. Greenleaf. For its sake she is ready

JEAN BROOKS GREENLEAF.

and happy to make all needful sacrifice. For the past three years she has been president of the Woman's Political Club of Rochester, and in December, 1890, was elected to succeed Mrs. Lillie Devereux Blake as the president of the New York State Woman's Suffrage Association.

GREENWOOD, Miss Elizabeth W., temperance reformer, born in Brooklyn, N. Y., in 1849. Her father was a lawyer. She was converted at the age of fourteen and turned from a fashionable life to her books and to philanthropic work. She was educated in Brooklyn Heights Seminary and was graduated in 1869. She took a post-graduate course and spent some time as a teacher in that school, giving instruction in the higher branches and weekly lectures to the junior and senior classes. When the Woman's Temperance Crusade opened, she enlisted at once. Her peculiar talents fitted her for good work for temperance, and she has been conspicuous in the white-ribbon movement throughout the State and the nation. When scientific temperance instruction in the New York schools was being provided for, Miss Greenwood did important work with the legislature, as State superintendent of that department. She served as national superintendent of juvenile work. She has for years served as president of the Woman's Christian Temperance Union on the Hill in Brooklyn, as superintendent of its juvenile work, and as lecturer and evangelist. She spends her summers in the Berkshire Hills, Mass., where she preaches on Sundays to large audiences. In 1888 she was made superintendent of the evangelistic department of the National Woman's Christian Temperance Union. In 1889 she visited Europe, and there she continued her reform efforts.

GREENWOOD, Grace, SEE LIPPINCOTT, MRS. SARA JANE.

GREGORY, Mrs. Elizabeth Goadby, author, born in London, England, 25th April, 1834. She came to the United States when young. She is the only daughter of the late Dr. Henry Goadby, F. L. S., author of "Animal and Vegetable Physiology," and well known in the scientific world thirty years ago through his valuable original work in the field of microscopical investigation. Elizabeth Goadby became the wife, in 1855, of John Gregory, a civil engineer and author in Milwaukee, Wis. She has since resided in that city, and was for eleven years a teacher in the Milwaukee public schools. Her name has been familiar in newspaper literature of the Northwest since 1861, when she first began to write for the press. She has written on industrial and social topics. As a translator of French and German, in the department of fiction and biography, she has done some excellent work. She

ELIZABETH GOADBY GREGORY.

has raised to manhood a family of three sons, two of whom are still living.

GREGORY, Mrs. Mary Rogers, artist, born in Apalachicola, Fla., 6th May, 1846. Her maiden name was Mary Bland Rogers. Her father, Charles Rogers, was a prominent cotton merchant of Columbus, Ga. Her paternal ancestors were distinguished Revolutionary heroes. Among them were the celebrated Platt family of Dutchess county, New York. One of them, Zephadiah Platt, was the first Senator elected by the State of New York to the first Congress of the United States. Another, Richard Platt, was aid-de-camp to General Montgomery at the fall of Quebec. On her mother's side she belongs to the Virginia families of Bland and Spottswood, and she is closely connected with the family of the artist Rembrandt Peele. She became the wife, at an early age, of Dr. John R. Gregory, of a well known Tallahassee, Fla., family. Mrs. Gregory is one of the most distinguished artists of

the South.   She has painted many portraits of
prominent men and women.   Among her best-
known works are portraits of Hon. Ben. H. Hill,
Judge James Jackson, Henry Grady and Mary E.

MARY ROGERS GREGORY.

Bryan.   The legislature of Georgia paid her the
high honor of appointing her to paint the full-length
portraits of Hon. Alex. Stephens and Hon. Herschel V. Johnson.   These pictures adorn the walls
of the new capitol in Atlanta.   She holds a life
membership in the Academy of Fine Arts in Philadelphia, where she studied for several years.   She
also worked in Cooper Institute and has had training under several noted European artists.

GREW, Miss Mary, anti-slavery agitator and
preacher, born in Hartford, Conn., 1st September,
1813.   Her childhood and early youth were spent
there.   In 1834 she removed to Boston, Mass., and
afterwards to Philadelphia, Pa., where she still resides.   The principal work of her life has been
performed in the interest of our colored population.
By inheritance and training she was a radical Abolitionist.   When the Boston Female Anti-Slavery
Society was organized, she became a member of it.
On her removal to Philadelphia she joined the Female Anti-Slavery Society of that city, became its
corresponding secretary, and wrote its annual reports until 1870, when the society disbanded.   She
was a member of the Woman's Anti-Slavery Convention in 1838, which held its sessions in Pennsylvania Hall, surrounded by a furious mob, which
destroyed the building by fire a few hours after the
convention adjourned.   Her public speaking was
for many years confined to anti-slavery platforms
almost exclusively.   That cause demanded much
of its advocates during the years when their number was few and the name of Abolitionist was
counted odious in church and state.   After slavery
was abolished and the fifteenth amendment of the
United States Constitution was ratified, she devoted
her energies and time to other reforms, especially

to the enfranchisement of women.   She became a
member of a Unitarian Church, in which there were
no distinctions based upon sex.   There she commenced the work of occasional preaching.   She
found the pulpits of Unitarian churches freely opened
to her, and in northern New England also the pulpits of Free-will Baptists, Methodists and Congregational churches.   She was one of the founders
of the New Century Club, of Philadelphia.   She
was also one of the founders of the Pennsylvania
Woman Suffrage Association, and is still its president.

GRIFFITH, Mrs. Eva Kinney, journalist
and temperance worker, born in Whitewater,
Wis., 8th November, 1852.   She is a daughter of
Francis Kinney and Sophronia Goodrich Kinney.
She was educated in the Whitewater State Normal
School and   as graduated in the class of 1871.
She entered journalism and wrote for the Detroit
"Free Press," "Pomeroy's Democrat," the Educational Weekly," the Cincinnati "Saturday
Night" and many other journals.   Overwork
broke her health in 1878, and she was not able to
resume her pen to any great extent until 1883.   In
1879 she went to Kansas for her health.   In 1880
she became the wife of Charles E. Griffith, and
they moved to St. Louis, Mo.   The marriage
proved a mistake.   They separated, and Mrs.
Griffith returned to Whitewater and entered the
temperance field.   She was made lecturer and
organizer of the Wisconsin Woman's Christian
Temperance Union for seven years.   Her illustrated
lectures won her the name of "Wisconsin Chalk
Talker."   She wrote temperance lessons and poems
for the "Temperance Banner" and the "Union
Signal."   She has published a temperance novel,

MARY GREW.

"A Woman's Evangel" (Chicago, 1892), and a
volume named "Chalk Talk Hand-Book" (1887).
In 1889 she published the "True Ideal," a journal
devoted to social purity and faith studies.   In 1891

she removed to Chicago, Ill., where she became a special writer for the "Daily News-Record" and afterward society editor of the Chicago "Times." She is a regular contributor to the "Union Signal,"

EVA KINNEY GRIFFITH.

writing the semi-monthly "Queen's Garden" for that journal.

GRIFFITH, Mrs. Mary Lillian, philanthropist and author, born in Germantown, Philadelphia, Pa., 5th October, 1854, and died in Tamaqua, Pa., in March, 1884. She was the only daughter of Thomas and Mary Thurlby. As a child she was devoted and conscientious. She attended the grammar-schools, and was graduated from the Normal School of Philadelphia. She accepted a position as teacher, and for herself and pupils pursued her ideals of highest culture. On 12th October, 1875, she became the wife of Rev. T. M. Griffith, pastor of the Cumberland Street Methodist Episcopal Church, of Philadelphia. She entered with zeal into work that appealed on every side to her sympathetic heart. In 1877 she was appointed secretary of the Ladies' and Pastors' Christian Union, a benevolent organization designed to call out the women of the churches to work among the people. She became deeply interested in moral educational work. Her tract, "Wifehood," which she printed and circulated privately, was so highly appreciated that, to meet the demand for it, another edition of a thousand copies was printed. The Moral Educational Society published a third edition, and the organ of that society, the "Alpha," gave it to the world with her name appended. She organized a local Woman's Christian Temperance Union, speaking and writing in behalf of that organization and other reform movements. Her articles attracted the attention of Miss Frances E. Willard, who urged her to take the national superintendency of the branch of work now known as "Heredity" in that society, which was then in the process of development. She accepted the arduous task and wrote a series of twelve papers, some in tract form, doing all that work in addition to her labors as a pastor's wife. Early in life she was led to adopt advanced opinions in relation to the position and rights of women. She was often impelled to speak and write in behalf of her sex. That, together with her moral educational work, brought out antagonism. A pamphlet entitled "An Open Letter," a most pathetic and powerful plea for unselfishness and purity in the marriage relation, excited hostility and criticism. She was interested in the woman's branch of the Society for Prevention of Cruelty to Animals. Her religious life was remarkable for fervor, activity and consecration. She was often called upon to address public assemblies on Christian themes. A series of six religious tracts she wrote at the request of Rev. Dr. John H. Vincent, which were published by the Tract Society of the Methodist Episcopal Church. When the General Conference of that church met, she wrote, published and sent to each member of that body an eight-page pamphlet entitled, "The Position of Women in the Methodist Episcopal Church." Another on "License and Ordination of Women," which she had prepared for the next meeting of that chief legislative body, was sent when the hand that had written and the head that had planned were at rest.

GRIMKÉ, Miss Sarah Moore, reformer, born in Charleston, S. C., 6th November, 1792, died in Hyde Park, N. Y., 23rd December, 1873. She was a daughter of the famous jurist, John Faucheraud Grimké. After her father's death, in 1819, Sarah and her sister, Angelina, freed their slaves and left their home. They could not endure the scenes connected with slavery, and they sought more congenial surroundings. Sarah went to Philadelphia, Pa., in 1821. She became a prominent anti-slavery and woman's rights advocate. She lectured in New England, and then made her home with her sister, who had become the wife of Theodore D. Weld and was living in Belleville, N. J. Sarah taught in Mr. Weld's school. Among her published works are "An Epistle to the Clergy of the Southern States," an anti-slavery document, in 1828; "Letters on the Condition of Woman and the Equality of the Sexes" (Boston, 1838), and a translation of Lamartine's "Joan of Arc" (1867). She was a woman of great force and directness of character.

GRINNELL, Mrs. Katherine Van Allen, (**Adasha**) religious worker, born in Pillar Point, Jefferson county, N. Y., 20th April, 1839. Her maiden name was Katherine Van Allen, and her father was the owner of a fine estate near Sackett's Harbor. About the time of her birth a great religious revival swept over the country. Her parents came under its influence and joined the Methodist Episcopal Church. Their home thereafter was the home of the Methodist preacher and a center of active work for building up the interests of the town. At the age of fourteen years she became a member of the church. At fifteen she was sent to Falley Seminary. Her preceptress was Miss Rachel C. Newman, and the young student owed much to the influence of that noble woman. In 1864 she became the wife of Graham G. Grinnell, a deacon in the Presbyterian Church in Adams, N. Y., and united with that church, frankly asserting her inability to accept its doctrines as she understood them, engaging to acquaint herself with them and to come into harmony with them if possible. As the years passed, her spiritual life deepened and her sympathy with dogmatic teachings grew less. In 1871, just before the great fire, the family removed to Chicago, Ill. Soon after she took up seriously spiritualistic study and has written much

KATHERINE VAN ALLEN GRINNELL.

SADIE PARK GRISHAM.

upon that subject. Whatever success she may have achieved has been the result of the sincerity

and spirit of absolute self-renunciation with which she strove to find the truth of things. Mrs. Grinnell is now living in Mayfair, Cook county, Ill., devoting her time to the propagation of her exalted theories.

GRISHAM, Mrs. Sadie Park, educator and office-holder, born in Litchfield Township, near Athens, Bradford county, Pa., 22d July, 1859. Mrs. Grisham is a direct descendant of Josiah and Thomas Park, and is the daughter of J. P. and Jane A. Park. She spent the first ten years of her life in her native place. In 1870 her father removed with his family to Kansas and settled on Middle creek, in Chase county, where he still resides. Sadie spent the greater part of her time in the common schools until 1876, at which time she went to the State Normal School in Emporia, Kan., graduating in 1882. She then engaged in school teaching, until December, 1882, when she became the wife of Thomas H. Grisham, a lawyer of Cottonwood Falls, Kan., who was at that time the prosecuting attorney of Chase county. In 1886 Mrs. Grisham accepted and still retains a position in the public schools of Cottonwood Falls. In 1890 she was employed as principal, with a corps of seven teachers. In the spring of 1889 she was elected a member of the common council of Cottonwood Falls. She was made president of the council and chairman of the committee on streets and alleys. Mrs. Grisham is an industrious worker in all educational matters.

GRISWOLD, Mrs. Frances Irene Burge, author, born in Wickford, R. I., 28th April, 1826. She is a daughter of Rev. L. Burge and Elizabeth Frances Shaw. Mrs. Griswold inherited from her father, many of those traits of character most

FRANCES IRENE BURGE GRISWOLD.

clearly manifest in her writings. He was a man of lofty purposes, broad sympathies and tender Christian piety. The child grew to womanhood beneath the historic shades of St. Paul's Narragansett

Church, of which her father was for twenty years the rector. Mrs. Griswold began to publish her literary work in 1853, and, though thirty-two volumes have already been published, besides innumerable

HATTIE TYNG GRISWOLD.

fugitive articles for newspapers and other periodicals, her fruitful pen is not yet idle. Perhaps the most widely known of her books are the "Bishop and Nanette" series, which, as a carefully prepared exposition of the Book of Common Prayer, have long been in use in advanced classes of Episcopal Sunday-schools; "Sister Eleanor's Brood," a story of the lights and shadows of a country clergyman's family life, in which the gentle, optimistic nature of the author works in its best vein, and which is understood to figure, under a thin veil of fiction, the actual experience of her mother, and the third book, "Asleep," to whose pages so many have turned for comfort in bereavement. Mrs. Griswold is an ardent Episcopalian, and the church has been from her earliest youth a spur to her glowing imagination and the outlet of her abundant energy. Her Christmas and Easter poems represent her most finished poetic work. She has been twice married. After the death of her first husband, Allen N. Smith, of Stockbridge, Mass., she became the wife of her distant kinsman, Judge Elias Griswold, of Maryland. Judge Griswold passed the latter days of his life in Brooklyn, N. Y., the home through many years of Mrs. Griswold's family, where she still resides. Mrs. Griswold descended, on her father's side, from the Mucklestons of Muckleston Manor, Oswestry, and on her mother's side, from the Brentons of Hammersmith, England. Most of her books were written under the name of F. Burge Smith.

GRISWOLD, Mrs. Hattie Tyng, author and poet, born in Boston, Mass., 26th January, 1842. Her father was Rev. Dudley Tyng, a Universalist minister. Her mother's maiden name was Sarah Haines. Both parents were typical New Englanders.

They were Universalists, converted by Hosea Ballou, in Boston, in early life, and abolitionists, even at that period of the great national conflict. Mrs. Griswold's unusual inheritance of the poetic gift and intense practicality combined may be traced as a cross between her father's ideality and her mother's Puritanical attention to actual details. The childhood days of Hattie Tyng were spent in Maine and Michigan until she was eleven years of age, when she went to Wisconsin, which State has been her home ever since. In 1863 she became the wife of Eugene Sherwood Griswold and in Columbus, Wis., their three daughters have been reared. When the "Home Journal" of New York was under the control of N. P. Willis, and the "Knickerbocker" the leading magazine of the country, Hattie Tyng, a mere girl, was a contributor to both. In 1874 she published her first volume of poems, "Apple Blossoms" (Chicago). Her other books are "Home Life of Great Authors" (Chicago, 1877), "Waiting on Destiny" (Boston, 1889), and "Lucille and Her Friends" (Chicago, 1890). None of the women poets of America have written anything more widely known or popular of its class than Mrs. Griswold's short poem, ' Under the Daisies.' Much of the work of her later years has been in the field of practical philanthropy as well as literature. She has been actively interested in associated charities, temperance and all efforts looking toward the amelioration of suffering and reform of evils. She was a delegate from Wisconsin to the National Conference of Charities in St. Paul, and has read papers that attracted much attention in various Unitarian conferences and in State associations.

GROENEVELT, Mrs. Sara, littérateur, was

SARA GROENEVELT.

born on the "Bon Dieu," a cotton plantation of her uncle, F. G. Bartlett, which was romantically situated on a bend of the Red river called Bon Dieu, near Natchitoches, La. She is a daughter of Dr.

Sylvanus Bartlett, of Maine, and Julia Finch Gresham, of Kentucky. Mrs. Groenevelt is a cousin of the late Washington journalist, Ben. Perley Poore. At the age of fifteen she was graduated from the girl's high school of New Orleans. A few years later she became the wife of Eduard Groenevelt, a descendant of the old Dutch noble, Baron Arnold de Groenevelt, of Netherland fame. Shortly after her marriage she accompanied her husband to Europe, where she spent several years, completing her musical education under the careful guidance of Moscheles, Reinecke and other masters. She was the only lady solo-player at the Haupt-Prüfung of the Leipzig Conservatory of Music, held in the Gewandhaus, 2nd May, 1867, where she played with success Moscheles' Concerto for piano, accompanied by the famous Gewandhaus Orchestra, Moscheles himself leading. Mrs. Groenevelt has written under various pen-names, and her poems have received recognition from the "Times-Democrat," of her own State, and also from the Chicago "Current," for which latter she wrote under the pen-name "Stanley M. Bartlett." Her home is now in New Orleans, La.

GRUBB, Mrs. Sophronia Farrington Naylor, temperance worker, born in Woodsfield,

SOPHRONIA FARRINGTON NAYLOR GRUBB.

Ohio, 28th November, 1834. Her father and mother were persons of force, character and intellect. Her educational training was directly under the care of her father. When seventeen years old, she was graduated from the Illinois Conference College, in Jacksonville, and at nineteen she was put in charge of the woman's department of Chaddock College, Quincy, Ill. In 1856 she became the wife of Armstead Otey Grubb, of St. Louis, Mo. In the home they made she was engrossed until 1861, the beginning of the Civil War, when she and her family returned to Quincy. In the emergencies of war-time began to be manifest the ability, energy and enthusiasm that have distinguished her through life.

Devoted to her country and humanity, she served them for four years, as those who, without compensation, gave time and strength in loving help in hospital, camp and field. At times she helped bring up the sick and wounded from southern swamps and fields. Again, surgeons and nurses being scarce, she was one of the women of nerve in requisition for surgical operations. Meanwhile the needs of the colored people were forced on her attention. Many of them, as refugees, went to Mr. Grubb's office, asking assistance, and were sent by him on to his home, with directions that their wants were to be supplied. The work became so heavy a drain on time, strength and sympathy, that Mrs. Grubb called a public meeting, and with her sister, Mrs. Shields, and with others, organized a Freedman's Aid Society. In the three years following they cared and provided for over three-thousand destitute negroes. At the close of the war Mr. and Mrs. Grubb returned to St. Louis. When her sons grew to manhood, the dangers surrounding them growing out of the liquor traffic led Mrs. Grubb to a deep interest in the struggle of the home against the saloon. She saw there a conflict as great, and needs as pressing as in the Civil War, and she gradually concentrated upon it all her powers. In 1882 she was elected national superintendent of the work among foreigners, one of the most onerous of the forty departments of the national organization of the Woman's Christian Temperance Union. By her effort and interest she has brought that department up to be thoroughly organized, wide-reaching and flourishing. She publishes leaflets and tracts on all the phases, economic, moral, social and evangelistic, of the temperance question in seventeen languages, at the rate of fifty editions of ten-thousand each per year. These are distributed all over the United States. She established a missionary department in Castle Garden, New York City, through which instructions in the duties and obligations of American citizenship are afforded to immigrants in their own tongues as they land. She has also recently been made president of the Kansas Woman's Christian Temperance Union. Her home is now in Lawrence, Kan.

GUINEY, Miss Louise Imogen, poet and essayist, born in Boston, Mass., 17th January, 1861. She is of Irish descent, with a blending of French blood. From her father, Gen. P. R. Guiney, a brave soldier of the Union, who was also an excellent lawyer, his only child inherits her dauntless spirit and her critical faculty. Her education, both in private and public schools, and later in the Convent of the Sacred Heart, in Providence, R. I., was supplemented by constant affectionate study of English literature, which developed into fuller expression her inborn talent for writing. Beginning with fugitive essays and verse, which at once attracted attention, and were received from the first by such periodicals as "Harpers' Magazine" and the "Atlantic Monthly," she had made for herself an early and honorable place among literary people at the appearance of her first volume. That was a book of poems, entitled "Songs at the Start" (Boston, 1884), and was followed by "Goose-Quill Papers" (Boston, 1885), a collection of prose sketches, "The White Sail and Other Poems" (Boston, 1887), and "Brownies and Bogies," a book of fairy lore, compiled from "Wide Awake" (Boston, 1888). She has also published "Monsieur Henri, A Foot Note to French History" (New York, 1892), a concise and romantic memoir of Henri de la Rochejaquelein, the brilliant young hero of La Vendée. The quality of Miss Guiney's work is of such subtle

and delicate beauty as to be difficult of classifica-
tion.   Her original thought has felicity of form
and is brightened by a wit which reminds one of
her favorite authors in the golden age of 17th

LOUISE IMOGEN GUINEY.

Century English.   Her poetry, always interesting,
is dominated, sometimes over-strongly, by peculiarities of phrasing, but ranges at its best from tender
and pure sentiment to a splendid concentration of
dramatic force. Both forms bear mark of conscientious and studious revision. Miss Guiney is a lover
of nature, fond of all out-door sports, an adept
with canoe and bicycle, and able to walk any distance without fatigue.   Her poetic gift is in the
heroic vein.   She is an excellent scholar and has
so much of the classic spirit that she has won the
sobriquet of the "Sunny Young Greek."

GULICK, Mrs. Alice Gordon, missionary,
was born in Boston, Mass., and graduated in Mt.
Holyoke College, where she afterwards taught. After
becoming the wife of Rev. William Gulick, of the
famous missionary Gulick family, she went to Spain,
twenty years ago, where she has wrought efficiently
with her husband, not only in the regular work of
the mission, but has been the chief force in establishing a college for young women in San Sebastian,
the chief watering place of the kingdom.   Mrs.
Gulick is now raising funds to erect a first-class
college building, to be called the Isabella College,
where American ideas will be set forth.   She is an
unusually fine writer and speaker.   She has four
children, who are being educated in this country.
She is the president of the Woman's Christian
Temperance Union of Spain.

GUSTAFSON, Mrs. Zadel Barnes, author
and poet, born in Middletown, Conn., 9th March,
1841.   Her maiden name was Zadel Barnes. She
wrote a good deal in her youth, but not till 1871
did she win general notice through "The Voice
of Christmas Past," a tribute to Dickens, published
in "Harper's Magazine."   In 1873, "Where is

the Child?" published in the same magazine, increased her reputation.   She has contributed much
to "Harper's Magazine," the Springfield "Republican," the "Home Journal" and the "Independent."   She has also been a contributor to "The
Magazine of Poetry."   In 1878 she published a
volume of verse, entitled "Meg, a Pastoral," which
drew the attention of Whittier, Whipple and Longfellow.   Besides her exquisite poems, Mrs. Gustafson has written many short stories of high merit.
Among these are "Karin," "Laquelle" and others.
In 1880 Mr. and Mrs. Gustafson went to London,
England, where they remained until 1889.   There
she formed many literary acquaintances and saw
much of life.   They saw in London sights that
stirred in their hearts the impulse to a crusade
against drink.   The result was "The Foundation
of Death, a Study of the Drink Question," written
jointly, and pronounced by thinkers in all countries
to be one of the most effective and the best considered work ever published on the subject.   Its
sales in England and South Africa, India, the far
East and Australia have been very large.   Her

ZADEL BARNES GUSTAFSON.

home in the United States is in New York City,
but she spends much time in London, England.

GUTELIUS, Mrs. Jean Harrower, artist
and business woman, born in Perthshire, Scotland,
24th March, 1846.   Her maiden name was Jean
Harrower Reid, and her parents were honorable
and Christian persons, whose lives were models of
inspiration for their daughter.   The Reid family
came to the United States just before the Civil War
broke out, and Jean saw her brother, Tom Chal-
mers Reid, and other relatives enter the Union
army.   Her brother died in the army at the early
age of seventeen years.   Connellsville, Pa., her
home, was the center of great business activity and
pleasant social life between the years 1865 and 1875,
and Miss Reid was fitted by nature to enjoy the
animated life that came to her in those years.   In

1874 she became the wife of N. P. Gutelius, a son of the Rev. Samuel Gutelius, a well known clergyman of the German Reformed Church. During two years she traveled with her husband over the United States. In 1878 she found herself alone in the world, with her infant daughter to care for. For several years she managed her father's home and attended her delicate mother, and in 1884 she began to study painting with S. Kilpatrick, who had a summer class in Connellsville. She was encouraged by the praise and advice of Frank Millet, to whom she submitted specimens of her work for criticism, and who introduced her to prominent and influential New York friends. She worked and painted industriously, and in 1886, at the suggestion of her teacher, Frank Fowler, she entered into the competition for the Cassel's prize in landscape painting, and received the first prize. Her mother died in that year, and Mrs. Gutelius took her head for a model, sending a photograph of the

JEAN HARROWER GUTELIUS.

drawing to a magazine for illustration. The picture was seen by Marion Harland and Mrs. M. C. Hungerford, who at once wrote to secure it for an article on "Beautiful Old Age," which was published in the "Home Maker" of September, 1890. Her paintings found a ready sale in Pittsburgh, and her brush was seldom idle. She assisted her aged father in the management of his book-store, soon mastering all the details of the business. The father died on 9th April, 1891, at the age of seventy-six years, leaving Mrs. Gutelius alone in the management of the concern. She is now dividing her time between the care of her daughter, the details of her business and the delight of the successful artist at her easel.

GUZMAN, Madame Marie Ester, social leader, born in Baltimore, Md. She is the wife of Señor Don Horacio Guzman, minister from Nicaragua to the United States. Her grandfather, Hon. Samuel Ewing, belonged to the old Maryland family of that name. He was a member of the bar and a life-long resident of Philadelphia, Pa. Her father, Rev. Charles Henry Ewing, was a theologian. He married a Miss Page, of Virginia, and was also a resident of Philadelphia. Although Madame Guzman was born in Baltimore, while her parents were temporarily residing there, her early life was spent in Philadelphia, except the time she spent in Boston, studying the languages and music. The death of her mother occurred in her girlhood, and much responsibility rested on her in presiding over her father's household. While Señor Guzman was in this country, in 1878, attending the Jefferson College in Philadelphia, as a medical student, Miss Ewing met him. Señor Guzman was graduated, and after two years of acquaintance their marriage took place, and Dr. Guzman took his bride to Granada. His father, one of the former presidents of Granada, was an active politican, but Dr. Guzman, always devoted to medical science, built up a large and extensive practice in Granada and became a recognized leader in literature as well as medical science. Madame Guzman is a good musician, sings well, and is devoted to her home. She has studied every phase of life and character in Granada. Dr. Guzman was a delegate to the International Congress, and is one of the directors in the Nicaragua Ship Canal project. Madame Guzman is very found of company and entertains a good deal. She has no children.

HAENSLER, Mrs. Arminta Victoria Scott, physician, born in Kinsman, Ohio, 27th July, 1842. Her maiden name was Scott, and her parents were of Scotch-American extraction. Her father, a teacher, married one of his pupils. Of this union Mrs. Haensler is the third child. She had more trials during her childhood than at any time since, owing to her parents' belief in and practice of "good wholesome restraint" and her own intense dislike of being curbed or controlled. She became converted in her eleventh year, and then earnestly began to control herself. At that early age she showed a quick mind, an excellent memory and fine mathematical powers. She entered Kinsman Academy at fourteen years of age, doing domestic service in the family of a Presbyterian minister for her board. She made rapid progress in study and began to teach when she was eighteen years old. Her attention was turned to medicine by reading a newspaper article concerning Elizabeth Blackwell and her trials in securing a medical education. Miss Scott then determined to be a physician in some large city, and thenceforth all her energies were spent in earning the money and preparing herself for the medical profession. She taught for six years. At the age of twenty-four she entered Farmington Seminary, and a year later she went to Oberlin College. There she helped in household work as an equivalent for her board. After some months she went to the Ladies' Hall, where, during the rest of the course, she taught both private pupils and college classes. As soon as she had earned the degree of A.B., she received the offer of an excellent position, not only as teacher, but as reviewer, editor and reporter. She was true to her aim and entered the Woman's Medical College of Pennsylvania, from which, in 1875, she received the degree of M.D. Since then Dr. Scott has practiced in Philadelphia and at different times has held the positions of resident physician of the Mission Hospital, gynæcologist to the Stockton Sanitarium, consulting gynæcologist to the Pennsylvania Asylum for the Insane, consulting physician to the Woman's Christian Association, lecturer to the Woman's Christian Association, lecturer to the

Working Women's Club, member of the Phila-
delphia Clinical Society, member of the Philadelphia
Electro-Therapeutic Society, member of the Alumni
Association of the Woman's Medical College of

ARMINTA VICTORIA SCOTT HAENSLER.

Pennsylvania, resident physician to the Franklin
Reformatory Home for Women, physician to the
Hospital and Dispensary for Women and Children,
and lecturer before the National Woman's Health
Association of America. Dr. Scott is the author of
a lecture on Alaska, which country is among the
many she has visited, and is the author of several
articles on medical topics. On 13th November,
1890, she became the wife of Franz Joseph Haensler,
M.D., of Philadelphia.

HAGER, Mrs. Lucie Caroline, author, born
in Littleton, Mass., 29th December, 1853. Her
parents were Robert Dunn Gilson and Lydia Gilson. There were nine children in the family, of
whom Mrs. Hager was the youngest. Heavy and
peculiar trials attended her childhood, yet these
circumstances deepened and intensified her poetical
nature, while the more practical side of her character was strongly developed. She had a thirst for
knowledge and used all available means to satisfy
it. Her education was acquired in adverse circumstances. Having entered the normal school in
Framingham, Mass., in 1875, she was recalled to
her home during the first weeks of the school year,
and her studies were exchanged for days of patient
watching with the sick, or such employment as she
could obtain near her home. Her first poems appeared at that time. She met the daily ills of life
with courage and lifted herself above them, seeking
out what good she could find. With such private
instruction as her country home afforded, she took
up her studies with earnest purpose. She became
a successful teacher of country schools and a book-
keeper. In October, 1882, she became the wife of
Simon B. Hager. She has one child, a boy. Most
of her poems have appeared over the name Lucie

C. Gilson. She has written a number of short
prose stories. Her estimate of her own work is
modest. She has recently written and published
a very interesting history of the town in which she
resides, entitled "Boxborough: A New England
Town and its People."

HAHR, Miss Emma, pianist, composer and
musical educator, was born in Fayetteville, N. C.
She is of Swedish parentage on the paternal side,
and on the maternal of French Huguenot extraction. Her father, Franz Josef Hahr, was a Swedish general whose ancestors had for generations
held prominent places at court. He was both
musical composer and artist. He gave Emma the
choice of music or painting. She turned to music.
The groundwork of her musical education was laid
by her father. After his death she was sent to
Germany, where she had the peculiar good fortune
to be received into the home of Karl Klinworth as
a private pupil. That led to another privilege, the
happiest that could have fallen to the ambitious
young genius, that of becoming a pupil of Liszt.
She studied under the great master at Weimar the
summer before he died. In him she found her
ideal guide. One of the highest of the many honors conferred upon her on her return to America
was an invitation to appear in concert in the Music
Teachers' National Association in Philadelphia.
Then followed a series of triumphs throughout the
South. There was but one verdict, from the press,
from critical audiences, from rival artists: A musical genius of rarest type. Though Miss Hahr has
made Atlanta, Ga., her home for several years,
where she has been perhaps a more potent factor
than any other in awakening and developing
musical interest throughout the South, being a

LUCIE CAROLINE HAGER.

teacher of teachers, it is, however, her intention to
accept one of the many calls she has received to go
on a concert tour through America. In all her
labors, as teacher and on the concert stage, she has

never ceased to be a student, and she has found time for much earnest composition. Her "Lullaby" and "Good-Night Song" are perhaps her best known contributions to the music of America. She

EMMA HAHR.

has also composed the music for two ballads, a "Song" from Browning's "Pippa Passes," and Orelia Key Bell's "Lady in the Moon." Besides these, there are yet many studies which have met the enthusiastic endorsement of the judges, but which the composer modestly withholds until she shall have more fully tested her strength with less ambitious efforts.

HALL, Miss Lucy M., physician, was born among the rugged hills of northern Vermont. She carries in her veins some of the best blood of New England, certain strains of which can be traced back to a titled ancestry in the Old World. Her education was begun in her native State, continued in Milton College, Wisconsin, and in the Dearborn Seminary, Chicago, Ill., from which she was graduated. She taught successfully for a few years, but soon after the death of her mother and father she was persuaded by the family physician to begin the study of medicine. In the spring of 1878 Dr. Hall was graduated with distinction from the medical department of the University of Michigan, Ann Arbor. She continued her medical observations in the hospitals and clinics of New York City, and later in those of London, England, where in St. Thomas Hospital she was the first woman ever received at its bedside clinics. In Dresden, Germany, she was house physician in the Royal Lying-in and Gynæcological Hospital, under Prof. F. Winckel. From there she was called back to America, where she was appointed by Gov. Talbot, of Massachusetts, to the responsible position of physician to the State Reformatory for Women in Sherborn. Connected with the prison was a hospital of one-hundred-fifty beds, likely to be filled from a body of from three to four hundred

inmates, bringing with them all the ills and diseases following the train of ignorance, vice and crime. "Four years later," writes Clara Barton, "it became my privilege, as superintendent of that prison, to observe how that duty was discharged by its resident physician. Perfect system prevailed. No prisoner could enter upon her term without a careful diagnosis of her physical condition and administration of the needful treatment. If any trace of mental trouble manifested itself, the case was closely watched and tenderly cared for. The most difficult surgical operations were performed, not only without loss of life, but with marked success. The control of the doctor over her patients, and these included from time to time nearly every inmate, was simply marvelous, and her influence throughout the entire institution not less remarkable. Among all classes she moved as one born to command, that most successful of all command, the secret of which lies in tact, conscious ability and sympathy with mankind. So long as that prison remains a success, so long will the influence of Dr. Hall's early administration and example for good be felt there." After nearly five years of service there, she was appointed superintendent by acclamation of the governor and his council. Though grateful for the honor, she declined the position, as its acceptance would necessitate the giving up of her medical work. Soon after that she formed a partnership with her distinguished colleague, Dr. Eliza M. Mosher, and together they began to practice in the city of Brooklyn, N. Y., where they still reside. In the autumn of 1884 they were appointed associate professors of physiology and hygiene and physicians to Vassar College, resigning in 1887, very much to the regret of all

LUCY M. HALL.

concerned. During the same year, upon the occasion of the semi-centennial commencement of the University of Michigan, Dr. Hall, as first vice-president of the Department of Medicine and

Surgery, was called upon to preside at the meeting of that body. As her colleagues many of the most eminent physicians and professors of the land were present. Afterward one of them remarked: "I

MARGARET THOMPSON HALL.

had predicted that fifty years after the admission of women a scene like this might occur. My prophecy has been anticipated by more than thirty years." As a writer Dr. Hall has contributed many articles upon health topics to the best magazines and other periodicals of the day. Her writings are characterized by a strength of thought, knowledge of her subject and a certain vividness of expression which holds the attention of the reader. Dr. Hall is a member of the Kings County Medical Society, of Brooklyn; of the Pathological Society; of the New York Medico-Legal Society, of which she has been treasurer; of the New York Academy of Anthropology; of the American Social Science Association, of which she is also vice-president, and a large number of other organizations, both in New York and Brooklyn. In the fall of 1887 she was appointed central committee delegate to the fourth International Conference of the Red Cross, of Geneva, held in Carlsruhe, Germany. By invitation she was a guest at the court of their Royal Highnesses, the Grand Duke and Grand Duchess of Baden. The latter will be remembered as the only daughter of the revered old Kaiser William and Empress Augusta. That high conference brought Dr. Hall into contact with very many of the most noted personages of the European courts, and that for a series of royal occasions and a length of time sufficient to challenge the scrutiny of the most critical. She passed not only unscathed, but with the highest commendations, everywhere doing honor to America and to American womanhood. Her elegance of bearing was a subject of personal remark. The respect of Her Royal Highness, the Grand Duchess, was marked and thoughtfully manifested by the appreciative gifts bestowed as

tokens of remembrance. Dr. Hall became the wife of Robert George Brown, of New York, on 29th December, 1891.

HALL, Mrs. Margaret Thompson, educator and newspaper correspondent, born in Dayton, Ohio, 28th March, 1854. Great care was taken with her early education by her father, the late Dr. Thompson, who was a member of the Medical Board in Nashville, Tenn., during the latter part of the Civil War. As a child she showed a keen desire for learning, and at the age of fifteen she was graduated, but continued her studies under Professor A. Reily, D.D., of Michigan. Being a natural musician, she accompanied her father through central Ohio on his recruiting expeditions for the Union Army. After the war, with her widowed mother and gallant brother, Capt. J. A. Thompson, she settled in Iowa, and then took up her vocation as a teacher, continuing her labors there and in Illinois until her marriage to J. Charles Hall, the publisher of the "Pacific Veteran," of San Francisco, Cal. She was the associate editor of that paper as long as it continued publication. She also organized and formed a department of the Loyal Ladies' League, and was publicly decorated for her services to the Grand Army of the Republic by the late General Sullivan. From time to time her little sketches and letters have appeared in different papers, among which are the "National Tribune," of Washington, D. C., the "American Tribune," the "Golden Gate" and Healdsburg "Enterprise," of California. Literary work of varied kinds has been her occupation for the last two years.

HALL, Miss Mary, lawyer, born in Marlborough, Conn., in 185-. She was the oldest

MARY HALL.

daughter of Gustavus Ezra Hall, of Marlborough. The original Hall ancestor was John Hall, of Coventry, Warwickshire, England, who came to this country with Governor Winthrop in 1630.

Her girlhood was spent in the old homestead with one sister and five brothers. Miss Hall was graduated in the Wesleyan Academy, Wilbraham, Mass., in 1866, and taught in that institution for several years, later filling the chair of mathematics in Lasell Seminary. During a summer vacation in July, 1877, she began her legal studies. Her intention was to enter her brother Ezra's office as a student, but his sudden death, in November, 1877, frustrated all her plans. John Hooker, reporter of the Supreme Court of Errors for Connecticut, at that time became interested in her career, and in April, 1878, she entered his office to continue her studies. In 1879 Miss Hall was appointed a commissioner of the Superior Court, and for this her papers were endorsed by the late Governor Hubbard, United States Judge Shipman, and other eminent men. It was the first time such an honorable appointment had been given to a woman in Connecticut. In March, 1882, Miss Hall formally applied for admission to the bar. The affair made a sensation. She took her examination in an open court-room, and not under the most favorable circumstances, but went through the ordeal with credit. The question of her eligibility was then submitted to the Supreme Court, and in July, 1882, a decision was rendered in her favor. She took her attorney's oath 3rd October, 1882, and was also made a notary public in the same year. Miss Hall's clients are usually women. She dislikes court practice and usually turns this work over to her brothers in the profession. For eight years she has been the sole woman lawyer in the State of Connecticut. The philanthropic work of Miss Hall deserves mention. During the winter of 1880 she gathered a few boys from the streets and read them stories, played games, or talked upon natural history, geology, or some other topic calculated to arouse interest and inspire observation and investigation. The boys were delighted, and she met them once a week, the number gradually increasing. They soon had to seek larger quarters, and in April, under her supervision, they organized, selected officers, and adopted a constitution and by-laws. The work widened, and several women came to her assistance. The plan had nothing in it of the day-school or Sunday-school, but simply to afford them entertainment and draw them from the bad life of the streets. They were instructed in good morals and the courtesies of life. The evenings had such attractions for the boys that they came with reinforcements, until again and again they had to seek for more commodious rooms. The name "Good Will Club" was adopted in 1880, with a badge having for a design a star and crescent. The work attracted the attention of gentlemen of wealth and influence, who contributed of their means, until now it stands upon a firm foundation. The Hartford Female Seminary building was purchased and fitted up at a cost of more than $25,000, and was dedicated on 22nd February, 1889. In 1890 the number enrolled was 846, and the largest attendance at any one time was 500. Miss Hall devotes her evenings to this work. She is a member of the First Congregational Church of Hartford.

HALL, Miss Pauline, opera singer, born in Cincinnati, O., in 1862. In private life she is known by her family name, Schmitgall. She early showed talent for singing and acting, and in her early years she sang in choruses. Being left to care for herself, Miss Hall concluded to go on the stage. Her first venture was made with the Alice Oates Company, in 1879, in which she appeared in the chorus and in minor parts. The company made a tour of the country, going to California.

In 1882 Miss Hall went to New York City, where she has made her permanent home. In New York she made her début as Venus with "Orpheus and Eurydice," and then she first attracted general attention. She joined the Casino Company and sang with great success for five consecutive seasons, becoming one of the most popular of the metropolitan singers. Her most notable success was in "Erminie," which ran for three years. During the past three years Miss Hall has traveled with a company of her own, and she has displayed great business capacity in her double rôle of star and manager. She has acquired a large fortune. Her repertory includes "Amorita," "Erminie," "La Belle Hélène," "Madame Favart" and many other operettas. She is known as a beautiful woman, of medium size, with black hair and brown eyes, and a quiet, reposeful manner on the stage. She is one of the few actors who "make up" very

PAULINE HALL.

little for their rôles. She has introduced a new method of acting and singing and demonstrated its success. The key-note of her artistic performance is naturalness.

HALL, Mrs. Sarah C., physician, born on a farm in Madison county, N. Y., 15th August, 1832, of parents of mixed English and Irish extraction. Her maiden name was Larkin. She is collaterally related to Commodore Perry. Her family were Quakers, and she was educated in the society and wore its peculiar dress until she was a young woman. At the age of sixteen years she began to teach school and board round, which she continued to do till her marriage with E. J. Hall, in 1853. After marriage they moved to Indianapolis, Ind., where she took a prominent part in organized charity work. She also taught in city schools at times till she took up the study of medicine. Her own tastes would have led her to the law, but the influence of her family doctor, J. T. Boyd, who urged upon her the great necessity for women physicians and offered his services as her preceptor, decided her course. Except from him she received but little encouragement in her new departure. Her preparatory

SARAH C. HALL.

studies were made while caring for her two children and doing all her own house-work and sewing, and in 1867 she entered the Woman's Medical College of Pennsylvania, from which she was graduated in 1870. She was one of the class which, in November, 1869, was hissed and insulted by the male students at the first Pennsylvania hospital clinic to which women were admitted, ignored by the lecturers, and followed and almost mobbed on the streets. The mere mention of such an occurrence now serves to show the advance of public opinion, but even at the time it caused a reaction in favor of women in medicine. In 1870 Dr. Hall went with her family to Fort Scott, Kans., where they now reside. She was one of the very first regularly qualified women physicians to practice in that State. At first pointed out to the curious on the street as "that woman doctor," frequently asked if her fees were not lower than a man's "because she was a woman," and for the same excellent reason rejected as a proposed charter member of the County Medical Society, she has met with sufficient success to see those things changed. After invitations repeated for several years, she lately became a member of the present County Medical Society, chiefly to countenance with her company a young woman doctor, who had just begun practice in the city and wished to join the society. She has long been a member of the State Medical Society, holds the position of medical examiner to several insurance orders of standing, and lately became a member of the American Medical Association. Although necessarily making her profession her chief task, Dr. Hall is an active member of the Eastern Star and Woman's Relief Corps, in both of which she has held high

office, while her heart and soul are especially given to her labors for equal rights. Her Quaker ancestry gave her a hereditary bias toward the equality of women, and her up-bringing never taught her that it could be even questioned. Her attention was first called to the need for its public recognition, when she received eight dollars a month and board for teaching the same school for which a man had the season before received twenty-four dollars a month and board, although the whole district declared her work to be better than his. Later and wider experience has only deepened her conviction of the necessity and justice of women standing men's equal in all things before the law. She attended many of the early suffrage conventions, both national and local. After moving to Kansas she was at first identified with suffrage work only in her own city, but during the campaign for municipal suffrage, in 1886 and 1887, she came prominently forward in the State councils, and she has seldom since lost an opportunity to aid wherever possible. She has also been several times on the executive committee of the National and National American Woman's Suffrage Associations. In 1888 she was elected to serve a three-year term on the Fort Scott school board. The suffragists of Kansas greatly desired that she should be one of their State's Lady Managers of the Columbian Exposition, but the matter was unfortunately not brought forward till too late.

HALL, Mrs. Sarah Elizabeth, educator, was born in New York City. She is the third daughter of John George Heybeck, who came to this country from the south of Germany about sixty-five years ago, and who lived to a very old age. Miss Heybeck began to teach when very young,

SARAH ELIZABETH HALL.

having distinguished herself in school and early shown special talent for that vocation. After graduating from the Saturday Normal School, the only institution in those days for the improvement of teachers in New York City, she received a State certificate, the highest honor conferred on teachers of the public schools. After teaching about three years in the lower part of the city, she was appointed, in 1858, to grammar-school No. 35, under Thomas Hunter, which for many years was known as the best boys' school of the city, and there she acquired the particular esteem of the principal. It was her influence in that school that induced the principal to abolish corporal punishment and to rule by moral suasion. When the Normal College was established, in February, 1870, she accepted the position of assistant to the president in preference to that of principal of a grammar-school which was offered her. In the past twenty-two years' service in the Normal College she has filled her place with zeal and executive ability.

HAMILTON, Miss Anna J., educator and journalist, born in Louisville, Ky., 20th April, 1860. She is descended on the maternal side from the old Kentucky family of Caldwells, and on the paternal side from the Hamiltons, of Pennsylvania. She inherits the marked intellectual traits which distinguished her ancestors. She was educated in the public schools of Louisville and was graduated from the girls' high school. She is now occupying a commercial chair in the Normal School, which she fills with success. She is known as an enthusiastic educator. She is a member of the Filson Club, which is the State historical club, and is a member of the Daughters of the Revolution. She is a writer of both prose and poetry. Her poems have been published in the local journals and in various periodicals. Much of her time has been given to editorial work. For a year she edited the children's column in a prominent educational

Encyclopedia of America." She is a member of the library committee from Kentucky for the World's Fair. The committee purpose to establish a woman's library, and she will collect and contribute all the volumes written by the women of Kentucky.

HAMM, Miss Margherita Arlina, journalist, born in Montreal, Canada, 29th, April, 1871.

MARGHERITA ARLINA HAMM.

She is a descendant from a long line of scholarly ancestors. Among her forefathers were literary men, theologians and soldiers. She has in her veins the best blood of southern France. Her maternal grandfather was Rev. Harold Jean Spencer, a prominent Episcopal clergyman, who was the author of several widely known pamphlets of the controversial order. Her paternal grandfather was General Pierre Hamm, a leader in the Liberal party in Montreal, Canada. Miss Hamm was only thirteen years old when she began to write for the newspapers. She found her first regular position on the Boston "Herald," and for four years she did all kinds of work on that journal. She then went to New York and joined the staff of the "World." Among her notable work was her interview with Mr. Cleveland on the tariff question, in 1889, which was cabled to the London, England, "Times." Another well-known achievement was her Bar Harbor interview with Mr. Blaine. She has done much "special" work for most of the New York dailies and at the same time corresponded for a number of western journals. She conducted the woman's department of the "United Press Literary Budget." Besides her prose work, covering everything in the line of daily journalism, Miss Hamm is a writer of much graceful verse, and her poems have appeared in "Current Literature," "Youth's Companion," "New England Magazine" and other leading periodicals. Her work is noted for its clear-cut, scholarly character, and there is nothing in the line of journalism that is not within the easy command of her pen. Wherever

ANNA J. HAMILTON.

journal, and wrote many entertaining lesson stories for the children. She is one of the editors for Kentucky on "A Woman of the Century" and is engaged in editorial work on the "National

and whenever brought into direct rivalry with male journalists, she has shown her ability to do the work far better than most of the men, and as well as the best of them. In political work she has been very successful.

HAMMER, Mrs. Anna Maria Nichols, temperance worker, born in Pottsvtlle, Pa., 14th September, 1840. Her father was Alfred Lawton, one of the pioneers of the coal region. On both sides of the house Mrs. Hammer is descended from Revolutionary stock. Her mother's great-grandfather was Michael Hillegas, the confidential friend of Washington and the first Continental Treasurer of the United States. Mrs. Hammer's great-grandfathers, General Francis and General William Nichols, distinguished themselves in the Revolutionary War, as did also her great-grandfather Lawton, who was a surgeon in the army and for many years was surgeon at West Point. Her grandfather Nichols was an officer in the war of 1812. Anna was educated in Philadelphia, Pottsville and Wilkes-Barré, Pa. In the former city she became the wife of William A. Hammer, and returned with him to Schuylkill county. After several years they removed to Newark, N. J. There a great spiritual awakening came to her, followed by her entrance into temperance work as a member of the Woman's Christian Temperance Union, very soon after the inauguration of that movement. Her national connection with the work has been as superintendent of three departments, work among the reformed, juvenile work and her present work, social or parlor work. She is also vice-president of the Woman's Christian Temperance Union for the State of Pennsylvania. Mrs. Hammer ranks high as a clear, forceful and ready speaker. At present her home

ANNA MARIA NICHOLS HAMMER.

is in Philadelphia, where her husband is in charge of the Reformed Episcopal Theological Seminary. She is a cultured woman of strong individuality, an earnest expounder of the work in Bible readings,

and greatly interested in the instruction and training of the young.

HAMMOND, Mrs. Loretta Mann, physician, born in Rome, Mich., 4th April, 1842. Her

LORETTA MANN HAMMOND.

parents were Daniel and Anna Stoddard Mann. Her mother came from the Stoddards, of Litchfield, Conn., a family of preachers, teachers and editors. Her father is descended from the Pilgrims of the Mayflower, and from the same Plymouth progenitor came the Hon. Horace Mann. Early in life Loretta showed tendencies towards her later study. At the age of nine she decided to study medicine, but in that she received no sympathy. Her father, though intelligent and valuing education in a man, was prejudiced against the education of women. When she was fourteen, she walked three miles, went before the school board, and on examination received a first-grade certificate. The first intimation her parents had of her ambition in that direction was when she walked in with the document in her hand. After that she had an hour a day for study, and her father began to say that they might as well let Loretta get an education, as she was so queer no man would ever want to marry her. At sixteen she was sent to Hillsdale College, and she never heard any more laments that she was a girl. After finishing the preparatory and junior years, she decided to study medicine. To be self-supporting, she learned printing, in Peru, Ind., and was an object of curiosity and remark for doing work out of woman's sphere. She began to set type in Hillsdale, Mich., at the sum of twelve cents per thousand, but her wages increased until, as compositor and reporter in Kalamazoo, she received the same wages as a man. While there, on invitation, she joined the State Typographical Union, the only woman in that body. Later she was the only female compositor in Philadelphia, Pa. The Typographical Union there did not admit women, but, being national, her card from Michigan had to be recognized. The book firm of Carey & Baird employed her at men's wages, despite the protests of their employés. There she earned the money for her medical

MARY VIRGINIA SPITLER HAMMOND.

course, graduating in 1872 from the Woman's Medical College of Pennsylvania. She soon after went to California and, during her eight years of practice, introduced to the profession a new remedy, California laurel. She wrote copious articles for the "Therapeutic Gazette," of Detroit, which were copied into the London journals, and the medicine was sampled all over America and England, before the manufacturers knew they were dealing with a woman. While in California she became the wife of Dr. W. M. Hammond, of Kansas City, Mo. Removing thence, they became proprietors and physicians of the "Fountain of Health," a mineral spring resort, where they now reside. One child, a daughter, Pansy, blesses their home. As a physician Dr. Hammond is hopeful, cheerful, painstaking and foreseeing. She believes stimulants are neither curative nor nutrient, but benumbing to the nerve centers, which is incipient death. She never gives morphine as a sedative. She was always an advocate of physical culture and while in college often walked twelve miles before breakfast, without fatigue. As a child, as soon as she knew the inequalities of human conditions, she was an active abolitionist and a woman suffragist. She has allied herself with the Socialist Labor Party movement and, although a capitalist, sympathizes with the laboring classes. With all her positiveness, she never antagonizes.

HAMMOND, Mrs. Mary Virginia Spitler, World's Fair Manager, born in Rensselaer, Jasper county, Ind., 12th March, 1847, where she has always resided. She is a member of the Board of World's Fair Managers of Indiana, a member of the committee on machinery and manufactures, and secretary of the committee on woman's work.

Her father, Col. George W. Spitler, was a pioneer settler and prominent citizen of Jasper county, and during his life held many positions of trust and honor. The rudiments of her education were obtained in the common schools in her native town. She attended the seminary in Crawfordsville, Ind., under the superintendency of Miss Catherine Merrill, and then spent a year near the early home of her father and mother, in Virginia. She next became a student in St. Mary's Academy, near South Bend, Ind., then under the charge of Mother Angela. She was graduated in that institution with the highest honors of her class. Her husband, Hon. Edwin P. Hammond, was in the Union service during the Civil War, before its close becoming Lieutenant Colonel and Commandant of the 87th Indiana Volunteers. He is an ex-judge of the supreme court of his State and is now serving his third term as judge of the thirtieth circuit. Their family consists of five children, four daughters and a son. She is a typical representative of the intelligent cultured Hoosier wife and matron. Her heart is always open for charitable work and deeds of benevolence. She takes great interest in the work of the World's Fair. Her acquaintance with general literature is broad.

HANAFORD, Rev. Phebe Anne, Universalist minister and author, born in Nantucket, Mass.,

PHEBE ANNE HANAFORD.

6th May, 1829. Her father, George W. Coffin, was a merchant and ship-owner. Phebe was reared in the doctrines and discipline of the Society of Friends. She was educated in the schools of her native town. From childhood she was ambitious to become a preacher. With advancing years her religious belief changed. She joined the Baptist Church first, and afterward became a member of the Universalist Church. In 1849 she became the wife of Joseph H. Hanaford, a teacher. Her domestic and literary pursuits for a time kept her ministerial ambitions in check. She taught for several years in Massachusetts schools. From 1866 to 1868 she edited the "Ladies' Repository" and the "Myrtle." In 1865, while visiting in Nantucket, she preached twice in the schoolhouse in Siasconset, at the request of her father. In 1866 she was invited to preach in South Canton, Mass., as a substitute for Rev. Olympia Brown. Miss Brown urged her to enter the ministry, and in 1868 she was ordained in Hingham, Mass. Her long ministerial career has been uniformly successful. She preached and lectured throughout New England and the Western and Middle States. She was the first woman to serve as chaplain in a State legislature, serving in the Connecticut House and Senate in 1870 and 1872. She has had pastoral charges in Hingham and Waltham, Mass., New Haven, Conn., and Jersey City, N. J. In 1887 she was pastor of the Church of the Holy Spirit in New Haven, Conn. She was conspicuous in temperance work, serving as grand chaplain of the Good Templars. In 1867 she represented her State grand lodge in the right worthy lodge in Detroit, Mich. Her literary work includes poems, essays, addresses and stories. Her published books are: "Lucretia the Quakeress" (1853); "Leonette, or Truth Sought and Found" (1857); "The Best of Books, and its History" (1857); "Abraham Lincoln" (1865); "Frank Nelson, the Runaway Boy" (1865); "The Soldier's Daughter" (1866); "The Captive Boy of Tierra del Fuego" (1867); "Field, Gunboat, Hospital and Prison" (1867); "The Young Captain" (1868); "George Peabody" (1870); "From Shore to Shore and Other Poems" (1870); "Charles Dickens" (1870); "Women of the Century" (1877), and "Ordination Book" (1887). She is the mother of several children.

SARAH JACKSON HANNA.

One son is a clergyman. Her life has been full of hard, earnest, conscientious and exalting work.

HANNA, Miss Sarah Jackson, musical educator, born on her father's sugar plantation,

near New Orleans, La., 4th December, 1847. She is the oldest daughter of James Jackson Hanna and Ellen Cooper. Her father was born in Ireland. The family comes of Scotch-Irish lineage of noble birth. The mother of James Jackson Hanna belonged to the same Scotch-Irish stock. She, and her brothers and sisters, after being actively interested in the Irish rebellion of 1803, sought refuge in the United States. Coming to this country in 1810, they settled in Tennessee, and then went to the rich cotton belt of Florence, Ala. From there Mrs. Hanna, the grandmother of Miss Sarah Hanna removed to southwestern Louisiana, where she devoted all her energies to the culture of sugar, in which she succeeded, leaving a valuable property to her heirs. On her mother's side Miss Hanna is the granddaughter of Dr. Thomas Cooper, a native of Manchester, England. He was a distinguished scientist and man of letters, and for many years before and at the time of his death president of South Carolina College, in Columbia, S. C. In 1860 Miss Hanna resided in New Orleans. Having shown in early childhood unusual musical talent, her father gave her every advantage. The last few years of her student life she spent under the instruction of Madame Francoise Lacquer. Her father's fortune having been swept away by war and lost in litigation, when he died, in 1867, she resolved to support herself as a teacher of the piano. She first went to Florence, Ala. Later she accepted a position in Ward's Seminary, Nashville, Tenn. There she met Thomas B. Binyon, to whom she was married in 1870. They went to Atlanta, Ga., where she has since resided. Later domestic and financial troubles compelled her to adopt again the teaching of music as a profession, which she has followed since, uninterruptedly and with marked success. For three years she was organist of St. Luke's Cathedral, organizing the first surpliced choir in Atlanta. Her health failing, she resigned that position and devoted herself exclusively to teaching. In 1885, by permission of the Superior Court of Fulton county, Ga., she resumed her maiden name.

HAPGOOD, Miss Isabel F., translator and author, born in Boston, Mass., 2nd November, 1850. She lived in Worcester, Mass., until 1880, when she became a resident of Boston. Miss Hapgood received a liberal education, and her talent for language has been developed to a remarkable degree. She has utilized her knowledge of the leading modern languages in the translation of standard authors' works into English. She is known wherever English is spoken by her work in Russian literature. Her "Epic Songs of Russia" is a standard classic and the only rendering of those productions in English that has ever been made. Her translations from the Russian include the works of Tolstoi, Gogol, Verestchagin and many others of the highest grade. She has written for various magazines a number of valuable articles on Russian subjects. Her translations of Victor Hugo's "Les Misérables," "Les Travailleurs de la Mer," "Notre Dame" and "L' Homme qui Rit" are pronounced the standards by the critics. She has translated many works, prose and verse, long and short, from the French, the Spanish and the Italian languages, with which she is perfectly familiar. Besides her work in translations, She has written much signed and unsigned critical work and articles in publications of the highest order in the United States. She is an industrious worker. Her home is now in New York City.

HARBERT, Mrs. Elizabeth Boynton, author, lecturer and reformer, born in Crawfordsville, Ind., 15th April, 1843. She is a daughter of

William H. Boynton, formerly of Nashua, N. H. Her mother was Abigail Sweetser, a native of Boston. Elizabeth was educated in the female seminary in Oxford, Ohio and in the Terre Haute Female College, graduating from the latter institution with honors in 1862. She published her first book, "The Golden Fleece," in 1867, and delivered her first lecture in Crawfordsville in 1869. She became the wife, in 1870, of Capt. W. S. Harbert, a brave soldier and now a successful lawyer. After their marriage they lived in Des Moines, Iowa, and there Mrs. Harbert published her second book, entitled "Out of Her Sphere." While living in Des Moines, Mrs. Harbert took an active part in the woman suffrage movement. She succeeded in inducing the Republicans of Iowa to put into their State platform a purely woman's plank, winning the members of the committee appointed to prepare a platform for the State convention by her earnest and dignified presentation of the claims of

ELIZABETH BOYNTON HARBERT.

woman. Thus Mrs. Harbert earned the distinction of being the first women to design a woman's plank and secure its adoption by a great political party in a great State. In the winter of 1874 Mr. and Mrs. Harbert removed to Chicago, and soon afterwards they made their home in the suburb of that city called Evanston, where they now live. Mrs. Harbert was engaged to edit the woman's department of the Chicago "Inter-Ocean." She held that arduous position for eight years, and her name was made a household word throughout the West. Their family consists of one son and two daughters. Mrs. Harbert is an earnest worker in the cause of woman suffrage and is interested deeply in philanthropic and charitable enterprises. For two years she served as president of the Social Science Association of Illinois, an organization formed "to suggest plans for the advancement of industrial, intellectual, social, educational and philanthropic interests, to the end that there may be better homes,

schools, churches, charities, laws, and better service for humanity and God." She served as vice-president of the Woman's Suffrage Association of Indiana, as president of the Woman's Suffrage Association of Iowa, and twelve years as president of the Illinois Woman's Suffrage Association. She has been one of the board of managers of the Girl's Industrial School in South Evanston. She is connected with the association for the advancement of women known as the Woman's Congress. She is president of the Woman's Club, of Evanston. Notwithstanding all the work implied in filling so many important offices, she finds her greatest pleasure in her pleasant home and her interesting family. Besides their Evanston home, they have a summer cottage in Geneva Lake, Wisconsin, where they pass the summers. Mrs. Harbert is versatile to a rare degree. Her love of nature finds expression in music and poetry, and her interest in the unfortunate members of the community shows in her many charitable and philanthropic works. Throughout her career she has been self-forgetful in her desire to do for others. Her pen and voice have been ready to render praise and encouragement, and her eyes have been closed to ingratitude on the part of those for whom she has unselfishly labored, that a better spirit of coöperation might spring up among womankind. The crowning excellence and most prominent characteristic of Mrs. Harbert is her deep sense of patriotism. As a writer she is pointed, vigorous, convincing. She has now in press a third book, entitled "Amore."

HARBY, Mrs. Lee C., author, born in Charleston, S. C., 7th September, 1849. She is a descendant of two families well-known in the South for the number of distinguished soldiers and authors they have produced, the Harbys and Cohens. The Harbys were soldiers in the Revolution, in which contest both of Mrs. Harby's great-grandfathers fought. Her father-in-law, L. C. Harby, who is also her granduncle, was a midshipman in the war of 1812, served in the Mexican war and in several other minor wars. At the outbreak of the late Civil War, in 1861, he held the rank of captain in the United States navy, but resigned and espoused the Confederate cause and served with distinction during the four years of that war. His son, J. D. Harby, the husband of Mrs. Harby, served in the same army. Mrs. Harby's maiden name was Cohen. She is a daughter of Marx E. Cohen, a native of Charleston and a graduate of the University of Glasgow, Scotland. Her mother was Miss Armida Harby, a great-granddaughter of Solomon Harby who was a grandson of Sir Clement Harby of the Harbys of Adston, an old English family; her father, Isaac Harby, of Charleston, S. C., was distinguished as a critic, essayist and dramatist, and his granddaughter, Mrs. Lee C. Harby, has inherited his literary talent. Mr. Cohen's family numbered six children, of whom Mrs. Harby was the fifth. Her early life was passed amid romantic city and plantation surroundings, which developed the vein of poetical thought in her nature. She was never a regular student in school, but was educated mainly by her scholarly father and her great-aunt, a refined and cultured woman, and their training was such as to turn her to literature at an early age. Arrived at maturity, she became the wife of her second cousin, J. D. Harby. They made their home in Galveston, Tex., and while living in that city Mrs. Harby published one of her first important compositions, "Christmas Before the War" (1873). In 1879 Mrs. Harby removed to Houston, Tex. In 1880 she became known as a poet of superior powers through a poem of welcome to the Texas Press Association, which met in Houston in the spring of that year. Her reputation as a writer, of both prose and verse, grew rapidly. While living in Houston she became a contributor to many of the most prominent periodicals of the eastern cities, among them "Harper's Magazine" and the "Magazine of American History." To the latter periodical she contributed in the numbers of October and November, 1888, a striking paper entitled "The City of a Prince," a historical sketch of a colony of Germans established in Texas by Prince Solms-Braunfels, of Austria. That paper made her reputation as a historical writer, and it secured for her at once the unusual honor of an unsolicited election to membership in the American Historical Association, before which she read a paper upon "The Earliest Texas," in its last annual meeting in Washington, in December, 1891. The larger portion of her historical work deals with the interesting subject of Texas, and she has achieved an important and valuable task in making a permanent

LEE C. HARBY.

record of many events connected with the settlement of the State, which would have been lost to future historians. Her portrayals of the life, the types and the peculiarities of that part of the Republic have been given to the public in a series of illustrated articles in "Frank Leslie's Illustrated Paper." Besides her historical work, she has contributed to leading periodicals a series of poems, essays and stories, all of which have found wide favor. Among other societies of which Mrs. Harby is a member is Sorosis, which elected her to membership while she was yet a resident of the South. She now resides in New York City.

HARPER, Mrs. Ida A., journalist, was born in Indiana, of New England parentage. She showed in childhood a remarkable memory and marked literary talent. Her education was almost wholly received in private schools, although she was graduated in the public high school. She entered the State University in Bloomington, but was married before completing the course. For a number of years after marriage she did a considerable amount of writing. Her work was of a character that always commanded excellent pay. For a dozen years she conducted a department in the Terre Haute "Saturday Evening Mail," that discussed all of the questions of the day and was widely copied. During that time Mrs. Harper traveled extensively and corresponded for a large number of papers, including the "Christian Union," "Western Christian Advocate," "Advance," Chicago "Inter-Ocean," Chicago "Times," the Detroit "Free Press," the Toledo "Blade," the Boston "Traveller," the Cleveland "Leader," the Indianapolis "Journal" and the Terre Haute "Gazette and Express." For the past ten years she has edited a woman's department in the "Locomotive Firemen's Magazine." In 1889 she decided to make literature a profession. She was at once invited to an editorial position on the Terre Haute "Evening News." In a short time she was made managing editor by the directors, one of the first instance on record of a woman occupying the position of managing editor on a political daily paper. She carried the paper through the hottest municipal campaign ever known in that city, making up an independent ticket from the best men on the other tickets. She wrote every line of the editorials and dictated the policy of the paper throughout the canvass, and every man on the ticket was elected. At the end of a year she was called to a place on the editorial staff of the Indianapolis "News," which she has filled for two years, going to her office regularly each morning. Socially, Mrs. Harper is very popular. Her family consists of one daughter. She believes thoroughly in opening all the departments of life and activity to women. She is conspicuous among the advocates of woman suffrage, being secretary of the Indiana National Woman Suffrage Association.

HARRELL, Mrs. Sarah Carmichael, educator and reformer, born in Brookville, Ind., 8th January, 1844. Her maiden name was Sarah Carmichael. In 1859 she began to teach in the public schools of Indiana, and for twelve years was remarkably successful, being the first woman teacher to receive equal wages with male teachers in southeast Indiana. Mrs. Harrell entered the primary class in Brookville College when eight years of age, and while still in the intermediate class she left college to take charge of her first school. She has always felt a deep interest in educational matters, especially in the splendid public schools of her native State, whose plans and curriculum have been enriched by many valuable original suggestions from her. In literature her work has been excellent. Under various pen-names she has written articles on floriculture, educational items and letters of travel. She became the wife, in 1872, of Hon. S. S. Harrell, a successful lawyer, now serving his fourth term in the State legislature. Her family consists of two daughters. She was appointed one of the Board of World's Fair Managers of Indiana by Governor Hovey. She is a member and the secretary of the educational committee and one of the committee on woman's work. Her efficiency in each of these responsible positions is well known, but her greatest work is the origination and carrying to a successful completion of the plan known as the "Penny School Collection Fund of Indiana," to be used in the educational exhibit in the Columbian Exposition. Besides these positions, she is superintendent of scientific temperance instruction for Indiana, and is preparing to secure the enactment of a law to regulate the study of temperance in the public schools.

HARRIS, Mrs. Ethel Hillyer, author, was born and reared in Rome, Ga. She was educated in Shorter College, and while still a student was regarded as an unusually bright and original writer.

SARAH CARMICHAEL HARRELL.

She graduated after taking the full course, including music, Latin and French. Her love for Rome, her "hill-girt city," is one of her strongest characteristics, and her enthusiastic devotion to her native land is deep-rooted. A daughter of Dr. Eben Hillyer and a granddaughter of Judge Junius Hillyer, she comes from one of the best families in the State. Her grandfather served five years in Congress and was the friend of such men as Stephens, Toombs, Hill and Cobb. Mrs. Harris is a niece of Judge George Hillyer, of Atlanta, a prominent member of the Georgia bar. On her grandmother's side she is a lineal descendant of Lyman Hall and George Walton, two of the signers of the Declaration of Independence, and consequently she is a "Daughter of the Revolution." After a happy girlhood she became the wife of T. W. Hamilton Harris, a young lawyer, of Cartersville, Ga., and two children blessed their union. One of these, a son, died young, the other, a yellow-haired little girl, survives. Mrs. Harris has contributed to some of the leading papers of the country, and many of her negro dialect and pathetic sketches have been praised by eminent critics. Her friends number a charming coterie of literary people, who honor and appreciate all that comes from her pen, and in society she ever finds a warm welcome.

HARRISON, Mrs. Anna Symmes, wife of William Henry Harrison, the ninth president of the United States, was born near Morristown, N. J., 25th July, 1775, and died near North Bend, Ohio, 25th February, 1864. She was a daughter of John Cleve Symmes. She received a thorough education and was a woman of marked mental powers along many lines. She became General Harrison's wife 22nd November, 1795, without the consent of her father. The marriage was performed during Mr. Symmes' absence from home. The father was soon reconciled to the marriage. During her husband's illustrious career as soldier, as secretary of the Northwest Territory, as territorial delegate in Congress, as governor of the Territory of Indiana, as a leader in the war of 1812 and 1813, as commissioner to the Indians, as a member of the House of Representatives, as a United States Senator, as minister to the United States of Columbia, as county court and state official in Indiana, and finally as President of the United States, Mrs. Harrison was his helper and guide. She was well informed on political affairs. Her husband was inaugurated President 4th March, 1841, and died on the 4th of the next month. Mrs. Harrison had remained in North Bend, Ohio, on account of sickness, and was unable to attend him in his last hours. She remained in North Bend until 1855, when she went to the home of her son. Her children were John Scott Harrison, born in 1804 and died in 1878 and Lucy B. Harrison, afterwards Mrs. David K. Este, born in Richmond, Va., and died in 1826.

ETHEL HILLYER HARRIS.

Her grandson, Benjamin Harrison, born in 1833, was elected President of the United States in 1888.

HARRISON, Mrs. Caroline Lavinia Scott, wife of Benjamin Harrison, twenty-third President of the United States, was born in Oxford, Ohio, 1st October, 1832. She is the daughter of the Rev. John Witherspoon Scott and Mary Neal Scott. She was educated in the Female Institute of Oxford, where her father was a professor and teacher. Carrie Scott became the wife of Benjamin Harrison, a rising young lawyer and former fellow-pupil, in Oxford, 20th October, 1853. In 1854 they removed to Indianapolis, Ind., and began housekeeping in a very modest way, while Mr. Harrison devoted himself to the practice of the law in such a vigorous and manly fashion as soon to attract the attention of the bar in the community. Two children are the offspring of their union, Russell B., and Mary Scott Harrison, now Mrs. McKee. Mrs. Harrison has always been a home-loving woman, of a

CAROLINE LAVINIA SCOTT HARRISON.

decidedly domestic turn, and noted for her perfect housekeeping. Well born and educated, she has kept pace with her husband intellectually, and has always taken an intelligent interest in all that pertained to his business or success in life. Since her husband's inauguration as President and her installation as mistress, the White House has gone through a thorough course of repairs, such as it never experienced before, notable as were several of its former occupants for good housekeeping. The results are very gratifying and greatly enhance the convenience and comfort of the household. Mrs. Harrison will go on record as the warm advocate of the extension of the family part of the executive buildings, which have long since ceased to equal the residences of wealthy representative citizens in Washington and other places. Mrs. Harrison comes of good Revolutionary stock, and she is the first president chosen to preside over the Society of the Daughters of the American Revolution, which she does with much grace and dignity. Mrs. Harrison's administration will be remembered for her patronage of art. While not highly gifted with artistic ability herself, she does very clever work in both water-color and on china, and several struggling young artists owe much of their success to her patronage. She is not fond of public and official social life, its responsibilities being somewhat onerous to her, but she enjoys the society of her friends. In religion she is a Presbyterian. She is quietly interested in all that tends to build up the interests of the Church of the Covenant, where the family attend. Mrs. Harrison's character can be summed up in a few words. She is a well born, well educated woman of the domestic type, an interested patron of art, who also numbers among her chosen

friends many persons distinguished for literary ability or high personal character. While she has enjoyed living in the White House, it has been as a woman of conservative character, who felt the responsibilities of her station more than she was uplifted by its honors and privileges.

HARRISON, Mrs. Constance Cary, author, born in Vaucluse, Fairfax county, Va., in 1835. She comes of an old Virginian family, related to the Fairfaxes and to Thomas Jefferson. Her youth was spent on the Vaucluse homestead, in a mansion that was destroyed during the Civil War to make place for a fort for the defense of the city of Washington. She saw much of the horrors of the war. After the restoration of peace, Miss Cary went to Europe with her mother. She witnessed the closing scenes of the reign of Louis Napoleon. Returning to the United States in 1867, she became the wife of Burton Harrison, a lawyer of Virginia. Several years after their marriage they removed to New York, where they now live. Mrs. Harrison began to write stories while she was yet a mere girl. In 1876 she published her first magazine story, "A Little Centennial Lady," which attracted attention, and since then she has written much and well. Her published books are "Golden Rod" (New York, 1880); "Helen of Troy" (1881); "Woman's Handiwork in Modern Homes" (1881); "Old-Fashioned Fairy Book" (1885), and "Bric-a-Brac Stories" (1886). She has written more recently "Flower de Hundred," a curious history of a Virginia family and plantation since 1650. She is the author of "My Lord Fairfax, of Greenway Court, in Virginia," and of "The Home and Haunts of Washington." She has produced several plays, chiefly adaptations from the French.

CONSTANCE CARY HARRISON.

One of these, "The Russian Honeymoon," was successfully produced in New York City in 1883. In 1890 her anonymous story, "The Anglomaniacs," appeared in the "Century Magazine," and the authorship was not revealed until the story was published in book form. That story won for her recognition abroad, and she is now ranked among the leading novelists of the day. Her home in New York City is a social and literary center.

HASKELL, Miss Harriet Newell, educator, born in Waldborough, Maine, 14th January, 1835.

HARRIET NEWELL HASKELL.

Her father was Bela B. Haskell, a banker and ship-builder and a conspicuous citizen of Lincoln county. He served two terms in the Maine legislature and was collector of customs of his district under President Taylor. Miss Haskell was educated in Castleton Collegiate Seminary, Vermont, and Mount Holyoke Seminary, Massachusetts, from which school she was graduated with honor in 1855. An unlimited capacity for fun is one of Miss Haskell's prominent traits, and is one of the points in which her nature touches that of a school-girl, making her relation to them one of unbounded sympathy. She has never lost this characteristic in all the serious responsibilities of her life, and therefore she holds the very key to the school-girl's heart. She is a fine scholar, an able critic and also preëminently a Christian woman. Her first experience in teaching was in Boston, in the Franklin school. Afterwards she was principal of the high school in her own town, and later in Castleton Collegiate School. It was while in that school the Rev. Truman Post, D.D., president of the board of trustees of Monticello Seminary wrote to a friend in Maine, asking him if he could recommend to him a woman to take the then vacant place of principal of Monticello, who was a scholar and a Christian, a woman of good business capacity and a good educator as well. The friend replied that there was only one such woman in the world, and that was Miss Haskell, of Castleton College, but that she could not be removed from the State of Vermont. After three years of solicitation, Miss Haskell became principal of Monticello, in 1868. The last years of

her father's life were passed with her in the seminary. He died in 1887. The Monticello Seminary was destroyed by fire in November, 1888, just as the institution was beginning its second half-century. Through Miss Haskell's energetic efforts a temporary building was put up, and the school was re-opened with eighty-nine of the one-hundred-thirty young women who were in the institution when the fire came. In less than two years the present fine buildings were erected. The corner-stone of the new building was laid on 10th June, 1889. The Post Library was given by friends of Dr. Post, of St. Louis, Mo., who was for thirty-six years the president of the board of trustees of the seminary. The Eleanor Irwin Reid Memorial Chapel was given by William H. Reid, of Chicago, Ill., in memory of his wife. The new seminary was opened in 1890 with one-hundred-fifty students, and is now in successful operation, equipped with every modern appliance, and managed by Miss Haskell, whose ideas dominate the institution in every detail.

HASWIN, Mrs. Frances R., musician, composer, poet and actor, born in Ripon, Wis., 14th May, 1852. She is descended from a notable ancestry. Gen. Isaac Clark, the Indian fighter and Revolutionary officer, of Vermont, was her great-grandfather. Her grandfather, Major Satterlee Clark, was graduated in the first West Point class in 1807. Her father, Col. Temple Clark, was a gallant officer in the Civil War. Her mother, now Mrs. Annie Starr, born Strong, was descended from noted New England Puritans. Mrs. Haswin's education was directed by her mother, a woman of marked characteristics in many ways, and from whom she inherits sterling traits of character as

FRANCES R. HASWIN.

well as her love of the ideal. She was a proud-spirited, sensitive girl, and showed her strong talent in music and histrionics at a very early age. She has composed and published music of a superior order, both vocal and instrumental. She has written many poems, both tender and heroic, all possessing a strong virility of touch, that have been widely copied and admired. She is the wife of Carl A. Haswin, a man of broad culture and a gifted and well-known actor. With him she has appeared in most of the prominent theaters of the United States, playing successfully leading rôles in his support. With all her talent and versatility, Mrs. Haswin is a woman of domestic tastes, which find full play in her ideal married life. Her home is in Holly Beach, N. J.

HATCH, Mrs. Mary R. P., poet and story writer, born in the town of Stratford, N. H., 19th

MARY R. P. HATCH.

June, 1848. She is the daughter of Charles G., and Mary Blake Platt. Her ancestors were English. The Blakes settled in Dorchester, Mass., in 1620, and the Platts in Stratford, Conn., the families presenting a long line of illustrious names, from Admiral Blake, the naval hero, to Senator Platt, who managed the Copyright Bill in Congress. The list includes the Blakes, Judsons and McLellans, of literary fame. Mrs. Hatch's life has been spent in the Connecticut valley. In childhood she possessed a quiet manner and a sensitive disposition, was a close observer, and a student of nature. She early developed scholarly and literary tastes. At the age of fifteen she left the common schools and attended the academy in Lancaster, eighteen miles from her home. There she studied the higher mathematics, rhetoric, Latin and French, and there her ability as a writer was discovered and recognized. From that time she contributed sketches on various subjects for the county papers, and articles under her pen-name, "Mabel Percy," from time to time appeared in the Portland "Transcript," "Peterson's Magazine," "Saturday Evening Post" and other papers and periodicals. Since then, under her true name, she has written for "Zion's Herald," Springfield "Republican," Chicago

"Inter-Ocean," the "Writer," the "Epoch," "Frank Leslie's Illustrated Newspaper" and others. After leaving school she became the wife of Antipas M. Hatch. Their family consists of two sons, and as the wife of an extensive farmer she has been a busy woman. Her management of her home has left her some time to devote to literature, and her versatility has enabled her to do creditable work in the wide realm of short stories, dialect sketches, essays and poems, grave and gay, society verses and verses in dialect. "The Bank Tragedy," published serially in the Portland "Transcript" and issued in book form, was a great success. Other stories from her pen are "Quicksands," "The Missing Man" and "A Psychical Study."

HAUK, Minnie, operatic singer, born in New York City, 16th November, 1852. Her father, Professor Hauk, was a German, and her mother was an American. She retains her maiden name on the stage. In private life she is known as the wife of Chevalier Ernst Von Hesse-Wartegg, the well-known traveler, to whom she was married in 1881. When she was a child, her parents moved to the West, settling in Kansas, near Leavenworth. They made their home in New Orleans, La., in 1855, where they lived during the Civil War. Minnie early showed her musical talent and inclination. A wealthy friend made it possible for her to receive a thorough musical education. Her first public appearance was in a charity concert in New Orleans, in 1865. In 1867 she went to New York City, where she sang in the choir in Christ Church and studied with Errani. In 1868 she made her début as Amina in "La Sonnambula," in New York City, and her success was complete. She won the critics and the public, and ever since that year she has ranked

MINNIE HAUK.

among the most popular of American singers. She made a successful tour of the United States, and then went to London, England, where she sang with brilliant success in Covent Garden, in October,

1868. In 1869 she sang in the Grand Opera, Vienna, and she repeated her triumphs in Moscow, Berlin, Brussels and Paris for several successive seasons. In Brussels, 2nd January, 1878, she created her famous rôle of Carmen. She studied with Richard Wagner, learning two rôles, Elsa and Senta, from him. Her repertory is an extensive one. She is both a superb singer and a powerful actor. Her impersonations have the force and truth of life. Madame Hauk is as happy in her domestic life as she is successful in her profession.

HAVEN, Mrs. Mary Emerson, educator, born in Norfolk, Conn., 22nd November, 1819,

MARY EMERSON HAVEN.

where her father, Rev. Ralph Emerson, subsequently professor in Andover Seminary, was then pastor. He was a relative of Ralph Waldo Emerson, and many of the family were noted educators. Her uncle, Joseph Emerson, was celebrated as a pioneer in female education, having given a life-long inspiration to such pupils as Mary Lyon and Miss Z. P. Grant, which resulted in their founding such institutions as those in Ipswich and Mt. Holyoke. Mary was educated in her uncle's school and in Ipswich, Andover and Boston. She became the wife of Rev. Joseph Haven, D. D., LL. D., pastor successively in Ashland and Brookline, Mass., and afterwards professor, first in Amherst College, and then called to the chair of systematic theology in the Chicago Theological Seminary. He was the author of text-books on "Mental and Moral Philosophy," standard in various colleges and schools in this and other countries. Mrs. Haven's position has given her large acquaintance with the literary world. Since her husband's death, in 1874, she has continued to reside in Chicago and has carried on work for the intellectual upbuilding in social life, for which she is admirably fitted by education, experience and extensive travel in this and foreign countries. She has been president of various clubs, of the Haven

Class in English literature, of art and history classes, of the "Athena" and of the "Heliades," or Daughters of the Sun, who are following his course around the world, studying all lands he shines upon. Mrs. Haven is a member of the Fortnightly of Chicago, the Woman's Board of Missions of the Interior, and of other associations. Her daughter, Miss Elizabeth Haven, was a teacher in Rockford Female Seminary. Another daughter, Mrs. Alice Haven Danforth, is the wife of Rev. J. R. Danforth, D. D. A third daughter, Miss Ada Haven, has been a missionary under the American Board of Foreign Missions in Pekin, China, since 1879. Mrs. Haven resides with her son, Joseph Haven, a physician, in Chicago.

HAWES, Miss Charlotte W., composer, lecturer and musical educator, born in Wrentham, Mass. She comes of old Puritan stock, her ancestors on the father's side having settled in Massachusetts in 1635. A large part of her early education was received in a good and cultivated home. She was the oldest daughter of a large family and became a close companion of her father, from whom she inherited her musical gift. She had her preliminary musical training in Boston and New York, continuing her studies in Germany, in Berlin and Dresden, under the direction of the father of Robert and Clara Schumann. During her stay in Dresden she formed the acquaintance of many eminent musicians, among them the famous Liszt. In 1877 she returned to Boston, where she has since made her home. She holds a high place as a composer of music, a musical lecturer and critic, and a teacher of music. She is well versed in the literature of music. One of her popular achievements in the double rôle of composer and poet is

CHARLOTTE W. HAWES.

her song, "God Bless the Soldier," written for the National Encampment in Boston in August, 1890, and dedicated to the Grand Army of the Republic. During the week of the encampment it was often played by the bands in the processions. Others of her popular songs are "Cradle Song," "Greeting," and "Nannie's Sailor Lad." She has filled engagements as a musical lecturer throughout the United States. In 1878 she was publicly invited by a number of men and women most distinguished in Boston's musical, literary and social circles to repeat the course consisting of "Nature's Music," "National Music, Hymns and Ballads," "The Influence of Music," and "Liszt." Miss Hawes is a frequent contributor of critical and biographical sketches to musical publications. She is the editor of "Famous Themes of Great Composers," which has gone through four editions. She is a prolific and successful composer, a faithful interpreter of the music of the great masters, a true poet, and a keen, though kindly, critic.

HAWES, Mrs. Flora Harrod, postmaster, born in Salem, Ind., in 1863, where she was educated. Her maiden name was Flora New Harrod. She is a daughter of the late Dr. Sandford H. Harrod, a physician well known throughout southern Indiana. The Harrods, after whom Harrodsburg, Ky., was named, went to that State with the pioneer, Daniel Boone. Miss Harrod, at an early age, became the wife of Professor Edgar P. Hawes, of Louisville, Ky. After a brief married life, her husband died, and she was left upon her own resources. She turned to teaching, and became a successful instructor in elocution, an art in which she excelled and had earned the honors in her school-days. She applied to President Harrison for the post-office in Hot Springs, Ark., going in person to urge her own appointment. She received the commission 16th August, 1889, took charge of the office 15th September, 1889, and was confirmed

FLORA HARROD HAWES.

by the Senate 19th December of the same year. Mrs. Hawes receives a salary of $2,600 a year and has a force of thirteen employés, four of whom are women. As postmaster, she is a rigid disciplinarian,

and she keeps the business of her office in the most satisfactory shape in every department. She is the youngest woman in the United States holding so important a position, and her office is the second largest one in the Union controlled by a woman. Her administration has been thoroughly satisfactory and successful.

HAWES, Miss Franc P., artist, was born near Chicago, Ill. She spent the larger portion of

FRANC P. HAWES.

her life in the East, and returned to Chicago in 1886, where she now resides. She comes of good ancestry and claims descent from Queen Anne of England. She is a daughter of John Hughes Hawes, a Virginian, and is related to the Lees and other noted Virginian families. The first wife of Mr. Hawes was a cousin of Jefferson Davis. He was a benevolent, liberal, public-spirited man, and a lawyer by profession. His second wife, the mother of Miss Franc, was a native of Cincinnati, O., and from her the daughter inherited her artistic talents. Miss Hawes, both as woman and artist, is a person of marked individuality. She has been an artist from her infancy. In childhood she painted whatever she saw, and frequently what her imagination saw. There are treasured still in her family several quaint landscapes and animal studies, painted by the eight-year-old girl before she had had a lesson, either in painting or drawing. The first landscape she painted under the eye of a teacher illustrates her singular gifts. It was scarcely "laid in" before the teacher was called away on some errand. He was gone three hours, and at last returned, with apologies for his absence, but they were unuttered, because in amazement he saw the picture finished, and finished so well that he had no suggestion to make, and it was never touched afterward. One artist, to whom she went for lessons, set her at work in drawing from the cast, but she declined to do that; her wish was to paint directly from nature, and she required instruction only in the intricacies of coloring. She has an intense earnestness, combined with a natural woman's gift of understanding without analysis From a delicate water-color of Venetian landscape with local color and atmosphere to a study of lions, her range is seen. A striking characteristic possessed by Miss Hawes is her memory. An idea once worked out never leaves her remembrance. While she prefers landscape, with an occasional excursion into the field of still life, as evidenced by her lion pictures, she yet has done a great deal in decorative work. She has received orders from Marshall Field, of Chicago, and others, receiving $5,000 for a single commission. Many of her tapestries and screens are exquisite, and all of them show originality and artistic merit. Though she has given the greater part of her life to art, she is distinguished for achievements in other fields. She has been a contributor to various publications in the East, furnishing articles on philosophical subjects which show much research. She has also acquired an enviable reputation as an organizer of clubs for philanthropical and literary study.

HAWKS, Mrs. Annie Sherwood, poet and hymn writer, born in Hoosick, N. Y., 28th May, 1835. Her maiden name was Sherwood. Her ancestry on her father's side was English, and on her mother's side, remotely, Holland Dutch. She was never graduated from any school, but she always had a passion for books and read widely. In her fourteenth year her genius began to find expression in verse. The first poem which she published appeared in a Troy, N. Y., newspaper. That poem at once attracted attention and was followed by others which were printed in various local

ANNIE SHERWOOD HAWKS.

papers. Miss Sherwood became the wife, in 1859, of Charles Hial Hawks, a resident of Hoosick. Mr. Hawks was a man of culture and intelligence, and he understood and appreciated his wife. In January,

1865, Mr. and Mrs. Hawks removed to Brooklyn, N. Y., in which city Mrs. Hawks still makes her home. Her husband died there in 1888. They had three children, one of whom, a daughter, is now living. Mrs. Hawks has always been identified with the Baptist denomination. In 1868 her pastor and friend, Rev. Dr. Robert Lowry, requested her to turn her attention to hymn writing. She did so, and wrote, among many others, "In the Valley," "Good Night," and "Why Weepest Thou?" In 1872 the hymn by which she is most widely known, "I Need Thee Every Hour," was written. Dr. Lowry sets all her hymns to music. Though Mrs. Hawks is chiefly known as a writer of hymns, she has by no means put her best work into them alone. She has written many noble poems.

HAWLEY, Mrs. Frances Mallette, poet and author, born in Bridgeport, Conn., 30th

FRANCES MALLETTE HAWLEY.

January, 1843. Her father, Prof. Rich, was a well-known teacher of vocal music. Frances possessed the gift of music in a remarkable degree. From the time she could speak plainly, she delighted in telling stories to her young companions. On 1st September, 1864, she became the wife of Wheeler Hawley, in Bridgeport, Conn., where she has resided since. Mrs. Hawley has a family of three sons and one young daughter. A fourth and youngest son died in youth. Her later stories and poems show deepening and widening powers.

HAYES, Mrs. Lucy Ware Webb, wife of Rutherford B. Hayes, the nineteenth President of the United States, born in Chillicothe, Ohio, 28th August, 1831, and died in Fremont, Ohio, 25th June, 1879. She was the daughter of Dr. James Webb and Maria Cook Webb, and the granddaughter of Judge Isaac Cook, of Connecticut. She was educated in the Wesleyan Female Seminary, in Cincinnati, Ohio, and was graduated in 1852. She became the wife of Mr. Hayes in 1853. Her husband and all her brothers served in the Union army during the Civil War, and her home was the shelter of soldiers sick and wounded. She spent two winters in camp in Virginia with her husband, and also served in the hospital for soldiers in Frederick

LUCY WARE WEBB HAYES.

City, Md. While her husband was a member of Congress from Ohio and Governor of that State, Mrs. Hayes actively promoted State charities. She was one of the organizers of the Ohio Soldiers' and Sailors' Orphans' Home, and served on its board of directors until it was made a State institution. She became mistress of the White House when Mr. Hayes was inaugurated, in March, 1877, and she presided throughout his term of office. Her régime was a decided departure from all former ones. While performing her duties in the most queenly manner and in accordance with every proper demand of the situation, she made the White House a religious and temperance home. She was a woman in whom the religious and moral elements predominated. While she presided in the White House, she would not permit wine to be served on the table. The innovation called down upon her much censure from certain quarters, but her action was highly commended by all temperance workers. At the close of her term in the White House she received a large album and other testimonials of approval from prominent persons. Retiring from the White House in 1881, Mr. and Mrs. Hayes returned to their home in Fremont, Ohio. Mrs. Hayes became deeply interested in the Woman's Relief Corps. She served for several years as president of the Woman's Home Missionary Society of the Methodist Episcopal Church. She was elected an honorary member of the Society of the Army of West Virginia, in recognition of her services to the soldiers during the Civil War. Mrs. Hayes was a woman of broad mind, liberal culture, exalted views and strong and positive character.

HAYNES, Miss Lorenza, minister, born in Waltham, Mass., 15th April, 1820. She is a direct descendant on the paternal side of Walter Haynes, who came from England with his family in 1638. The next year he bought of Cato, an Indian, for the sum of five pounds, a tract of land, now the town of Sudbury, near Boston. Lorenza is of the seventh generation, all of whom, including her father's family, except herself, were born in Sudbury. The maternal side is descended from the Scotch. From childhood Lorenza showed an unusual interest in books, and, born in a town which had a library and an annual course of lectures, she became a constant reader and student. Miss Haynes passed through the grades of the public schools, and then attended the Waltham Academy of Louis Smith. She taught one of the public schools in her native town for nearly two years, but love of study was so strong that she went for a time to the old academy in Leicester, Mass. Afterward she taught a public school for six years in the city of Lowell, and there made the acquaintance of Margaret Foley, a cameo cutter. Then began a friendship which continued for nearly thirty years and ended only at the death of Miss Foley, who had become an eminent sculptor in Rome. Miss Haynes afterwards held the position of lady principal in the Academy in Chester, N. H. She subsequently established a young ladies' seminary in Rochester, N. Y. After four years of intense labor she was compelled to return to her home for rest and restoration. Passing through many years of invalidism, she then accepted the position of librarian of the public library which Waltham was to establish, having entire charge of the cataloguing and work of organizing the library. After six-and-a-half years of service, she resigned her office in order to enter the Universalist Theological school of St.

LORENZA HAYNES.

Lawrence University, Canton, N. Y. Frequently, while librarian, she has been upon the platform as a lecturer. For a year before leaving the library she read and studied under the direction of Rev.

Olympia Brown, who wished her at once to take charge of a parish which was open to her. Miss Haynes was not willing to enter the work less equipped theologically than young men graduates. Two months before her course of study was finished in Canton, she received a call from the Universalist Church in Hallowell, Maine, to become its pastor when she left Canton. She had never preached before the society. She accepted the call, and was there ordained on 10th February, 1875. She officiated as chaplain in the House of Representatives and also in the Senate, in Augusta, Maine. This was the first instance of a woman acting in that capacity in that State. She was chaplain for two terms in the National Soldiers' Home near Augusta, the first woman who had filled that place, and had an invitation for a third term, when she resigned her pastorate in Hallowell for one in Marlborough, Mass. While preaching in the latter place she was invited by Post 43, Grand Army of the Republic, to make some remarks in the exercises of Memorial Day, 1876. The following year she was unanimously invited to deliver the oration of the day. It was the first time a woman in Massachusetts had filled that position. Miss Haynes has been settled over parishes in Fairfield, Me., Rockport, Mass., and Skowhegan, Me. She has often found her labors exceedingly arduous, especially during Maine winters, preaching sometimes in two or three places the same day. She has ridden ten and twelve miles in an open sleigh, with the mercury below zero, to officiate at a funeral. She left her parish in Fairfield, Me., in 1883, for a European tour. She has been from its organization a member and first vice-president of the Woman's Ministerial Conference. Miss Haynes has been a worker in various reformatory societies. She has always been a woman suffragist. She has often spoken upon platforms and before legislative committees in the State Houses of Massachusetts and Maine. Greatly to the regret of her society as of herself, in 1889, she was obliged to leave her last pastorate, which was in Skowhegan, Me., on account of over-worked eyes. Having previously bought herself a home in Waltham, but a few rods from the family homestead, where her only sister resides, she became the occupant of her cottage in July, 1889, where she now resides.

HAYWARD, Mrs. Mary E. Smith, business woman, born in Franklin, Pa., 9th July, 1849. Her maiden name was Mary E. Smith. When she was twelve years old, her father died. Her mother's determined efforts secured for her a good education. Imbued with the desire of being a useful member of the commonwealth, and endowed with natural abilities for a practical business life, she, after a season of teaching, entered into the oil and mercantile business till 1885, when she removed to Dawes county, Neb., then but sparsely settled, and took up some land claims. When the town of Chadron was located, she was one of the first to go into business there. She has been very successful. Tender toward all life, though her business includes a large millinery department, she never sells a bird or wing. On 29th December, 1887, she became the wife of W. F. Hayward. For years she has been one of the most prominent woman suffragists of Nebraska and has been identified with all humane work and reforms. She believes the church is responsible for the subservient condition of women. She is an agnostic and believes in "one world at a time." Mrs. Hayward is an embodiment of energy, push, perseverance and industry, and a fair example of woman's ability to succeed in practical life. She is a State member of the Nebraska Woman Suffrage Association.

HAZARD, Mrs. Rebecca N., philanthropist and woman suffragist, born in Woodsfield, Ohio, 10th November, 1826. With her parents, at an early age, she removed to Cincinnati, Ohio, and thence to Quincy, Ill., where, in 1844, she became the wife of William T. Hazard, of Newport, R. I. Five children were born to this union. In 1850 the family removed to St. Louis, Mo. For many years domestic affairs claimed the attention of Mrs. Hazard, but, being deeply imbued with religious principles, the wants and woes of humanity everywhere manifested received a share of her activities. In 1854 she united with other women in establishing an Industrial Home for Girls in St. Louis. For five years she was on the board of managers of that institution, which has sheltered thousands of homeless children. At the breaking out of the war Mrs. Hazard, who was an ardent Unionist, engaged in hospital work, giving all the time she could spare from her family to the care of

MARY E. SMITH HAYWARD.

sick and wounded soldiers. She helped to organize the Union Aid Society and served as a member of the executive committee in the great Western Sanitary Fair. Finding that large numbers of negro women and children were by the exigencies of war helplessly stranded in the city, Mrs. Hazard sought means for their relief. They were in a deplorable condition, and, as the supplies contributed to the soldiers could not be used for them, she organized a society known as the Freedmen's Aid Society, for their special benefit. At the close of the war that society was merged in an orphan asylum. Closely following that work came the establishment of a home for fallen women, promoted and managed chiefly by the same workers. It was maintained under great difficulties for some years, and was finally abandoned. Deeply impressed with the disabilities under which women labor in being deprived of political rights, Mrs. Hazard with a few other earnest women met one May day in 1867, and formed the Woman Suffrage Association of Missouri, the first society bearing the name, and having for its sole object the ballot for woman. To this cause Mrs. Hazard gave devoted service for many years,

REBECCA N. HAZARD.

filling the various offices of the association, and also serving one term as president of the American Woman Suffrage Association. In 1870 the city of St. Louis, falling under evil counsels, framed into law man's lowest thought concerning woman. Realizing the danger to good morals, Mrs. Hazard at once engaged in the conflict for the overthrow of that iniquity, a conflict more distasteful than any she had ever been called to share. Victory was with the right, and the law was repealed by the Missouri Legislature in 1874, one member only voting against repeal. The call for the formation of the association for the advancement of women, known as the Woman's Congress, was signed by Mrs. Hazard, and she has ever since been a member of that body, contributing at various times to its sessions the following papers: "Home Studies for Women," "Business Opportunities for Women," and "Crime and its Punishment." Mrs. Hazard is a member of the Woman's Christian Temperance Union and of the American Akadêmê, a philosophical society having headquarters in Jacksonville, Ill. Since the death of her husband, in 1879, she has practically retired from public work, but at her home in Kirkwood, a suburb of St. Louis, a class of women meets each week for study and mutual improvement. As a result of these studies Mrs. Hazard has published two papers on the "Divina Commedia." She has also written a volume on the war period in St. Louis, not yet published, and her contributions to local and other papers have been numerous.

HAZELRIGG, Mrs. Clara H., author, educator and reformer, born in Council Grove, Kans., 23rd November, 1861. She is the youngest living daughter of Col. H. J. Espy. Her mother was

Melora E. Cook, teacher in the schools of Sandusky, Ohio. Her father was apprenticed to learn a trade, but ran away at the age of thirteen to become a soldier. For more than ten years he was a member of the standing army of the United States. He served with distinction in the Mexican war and was Colonel of the 68th Indiana Volunteers during the Civil War. Wounded several times, carried off the field of Chickamauga for dead, his injuries caused his death shortly after the close of the war, and his four children were left orphans, their mother having died several years before his decease. With an only sister, Clara returned to Indiana, where she had resided during the war, and remained there until after her marriage. At the time of her birth Kansas was undergoing her early struggles for freedom, and the spirit of the times stamped itself on the mind of the child. From the age of eleven she supported herself. Fitting herself for teaching, she began to teach when a young girl, and that occupation she has followed almost without cessation for sixteen years. When twelve years old, she wrote for the press, but, being of a sensitive, retiring disposition, she shrank from public criticism and seldom wrote over her own name. In 1877 she became the wife of W. A. Hazelrigg, of Greensburg, Ind. They have one child, a girl. They removed to Kansas in 1884, and Mrs. Hazelrigg has taught every year since. She is principal of one of the city schools in El Dorado. She has traveled much during her vacations, and writes constantly during the entire year for the press. She has written for many prominent periodicals in various States. She is the editor of a department in a prominent Chicago paper, and is a regular contributor to the

CLARA H. HAZELRIGG.

Topeka "Lancet." She has labored in the silver-medal work for the Woman's Christian Temperance Union and in the public work of the Woman's Relief Corps. An active member of the Christian

Church since childhood, her work has always been with young people, with whom she is very popular.

HEAD, Mrs. Ozella Shields, author, born in Macon, Ga., 19th October, 1869. Her maiden

OZELLA SHIELDS HEAD.

name was Shields. She was reared and educated in Atlanta, Ga., and she is a thorough Georgian in heart as well as by birth. Her taste for literature and her talent for production were shown in childhood, when she wrote a number of love stories. Her first published work, a sensational love story of thirty chapters, was "Sundered Hearts," published in the Philadelphia "Saturday Night," when Miss Shields was eighteen years old. Her next works were "Verona's Mistake" and "A Sinless Crime," published in the same journal. Other stories followed in quick succession. In 1889 she brought out her "Izma" through a New York house. In November, 1889, she became the wife of Daliel B. Head, of Greenville, Miss., and her home is now in that town.

HEARNE, Miss Mercedes Leigh, actor, was born in Atlanta, Ga., 20th March, 1867. She is widely known by her stage name, Mercedes Leigh, which she chose when she began her professional career. Miss Leigh was born into the changed conditions that followed the Civil War in the South, and her early life was full of the echoes of the great struggle. She was educated in a private school in Philadelphia, Pa. At an early age she developed marked dramatic talent, which was carefully cultivated. Her histrionic powers and her emotional nature fitted her for stage work. She went to England, and while there achieved a brilliant success in London drawing-rooms as a dramatic reader. The critics abroad gave her high rank, and at home she has repeated her successes on an even greater scale. Besides her dramatic talents, Miss Leigh is the possessor of poetic talent of a fine order. Her work in verse bears every mark of culture. Her home is now in New York.

HEATON, Mrs. Eliza Putnam, journalist and editor, born in Danvers, Mass., 8th August, 1860. She is the daughter of the late Rev. James W. Putnam, a Universalist minister. She comes from Revolutionary ancestry. She was in youth a delicate girl and attended school irregularly. In 1882 she was graduated from the Boston University with the first honors of her class. In that year she became the wife of John L. Heaton, then associate-editor of the Brooklyn "Daily Times." Her newspaper work as an occasional contributor to the columns of that paper began almost immediately. In 1886 she took an office desk and position upon the editorial staff of the "Times." For four years her pen was busy in nearly every department of the paper, her work appearing mostly on the editorial page and in the special sheets of the Saturday edition, and ranging from politics to illustrated city sketches, for which her camera furnished the pictures. She handled the exchange editor's scissors and did a vast deal of descriptive writing and interviewing. Almost coincident with her engagement upon the "Times" was her entrance into the syndicate field. Through a prominent syndicate publishing firm of New York she sent out an average of three New York letters per week, illustrated from photographs taken by herself, and dealing with men, women and current topics of the day. In September, 1888, she took passage from Liverpool to New York in the steerage of the Cunarder "Aurania," for the purpose of studying life among the emigrants. She not only landed with her fellow-travelers at Castle Garden, but accompanied them as far west as Chicago in an emigrant train. When the New York "Recorder" was started in 1891, she undertook a task never before

MERCEDES LEIGH HEARNE.

attempted by any New York daily, to run a daily news page dealing with women's movements. The experiment was successful and had become recognized as the unique and especially attractive feature of the paper, when she resigned her charge to join her husband on the Providence "News," which he established in September of that year. From the first issue of the new daily Mr. and Mrs. Heaton were associated as joint-editors, and during a long and critical illness, into which Mr. Heaton fell at the end of the first few weeks of its existence, Mrs. Heaton was for months sole responsible editor. She has one child, a boy of eight years. She is a member of Sorosis and other women's clubs.

HEINSOHN, Mrs. Dora Henninges, opera singer, born in Mansfield, Ohio, 2d August, 1861. Mrs. Heinsohn comes from a very musical family. She began her studies when but seven years old, both vocal and instrumental, with her father, R. E. Henninges. She sang in concerts and operettas at fourteen, and her advancement was so rapid that she soon entered the Cincinnati College of Music, where she advanced to the highest position among vocal pupils, attracting not only the attention of the faculty, but also of persons generally interested in music. Her teachers up to that time had been Signor La Villa and Signor Stefanone. Later she became a pupil of Max Maretzek, under whose guidance she began to study Italian opera. Her first appearance in opera, after having sung many times in oratorios and concerts under Theodore Thomas, was under Mapleson, when she appeared as Leonora in Beethoven's "Fidelio." Soon after, she went to Paris, where she became a pupil of Mme. Lagrange, under whose direction she completed her studies. After her return to this country, Miss Henninges appeared in German opera in the Metropolitan Opera House, New York, and in many concerts, both in the East and the West. She possesses a powerful dramatic

DORA HENNINGES HEINSOHN.

soprano voice, which she uses with intelligence. Her repertory is a large one, consisting of hundreds of songs and dozens of operatic rôles. In 1888 Miss Henninges became the wife of G. W. Heinsohn,

of Cleveland, Ohio, and has since been devoting her time to teaching and to church and concert singing in St. Louis, Mo.

HELM, Miss Lucinda Barbour, author, born in Helm Place, near Elizabethtown, Ky., 23rd

LUCINDA BARBOUR HELM.

December, 1839. She is the granddaughter of Ben. Hardin, the satirist, humorist and jurist of Kentucky, and the daughter of John L. Helm, twice governor of Kentucky. He was the first governor after the Civil War. Her paternal grandfather, Thomas Helm, went to Kentucky in Revolutionary times and settled near Elizabethtown. That place, known as Helm Place, is still in the possession of the family. Her mother, Lucinda B. Hardin, the oldest daughter of Ben. Hardin, was a woman of culture. She early trained her children to a love for books. Miss Helm inherited from her mother a love for reading and a deep religious faith. At an early age she commenced to write poetry and prose under the pen-name "Lucile." When she was eighteen years old, she published a strong article on the "Divinity of the Savior." During the Civil War she wrote sketches for the English papers, which were received very favorably and were widely copied in England. While George D. Prentice was editor of the Louisville "Journal," she wrote many sketches for that paper. She afterwards wrote short stories for the "Courier" and the "Courier-Journal," and articles in the "Christian Advocate." She has published one volume, "Gerard: The Call of the Church Bell" (Nashville, Tenn., 1884). Miss Helm has written many leaflets for both home and foreign missions, which have been widely circulated. In May, 1886, the General Conference of the Methodist Episcopal Church South authorized the Board of Church Extension to organize the woman's organization known as the Woman's Department of Church Extension, until 1890, when it received a more definite title, Woman's Parsonage and Home Mission Society. Miss Helm was made the general secretary, and to her endeavors is due much of its success. The society, hoping to enlarge its power of good, decided to publish a paper, "Our Homes." Miss Helm was made the editor, and its success is assured. Miss Helm is also a member of the Woman's Foreign Missionary Society and of the International Christian Workers' Association.

HENDERSON, Mrs. Augusta A. Fox, social leader, born near Tiffin City, Ohio, 17th

AUGUSTA A. FOX HENDERSON.

May, 1843. She is the daughter of Alonzo H. Fox and Caroline A. Brownell, originally of New York, now of California. Mr. Fox was a successful "Forty-niner" and removed to Iowa with his family in 1853. Mrs. Henderson was a student in the Upper Iowa University, where she met her future husband, David B. Henderson, the able and brilliant representative of the 3rd District of Iowa since 1883. In 1866 she became Mr. Henderson's wife in West Union, the home of her parents. From there they went to Dubuque, where they now live. Alive to all the interests of the day and their ever increasing demands for attention, she has the qualities of mind and heart, a true sympathy, clear discernment and sound decision, that belong to those whom fate and fortune call out as leaders.

HENDERSON, Mrs. Frances Cox, linguist, traveler, author and philanthropist, born in Philadelphia, Pa., 21st July, 1820. She was educated abroad and spent twenty-one years in Europe, excepting Russia, associating always with persons speaking the language of the country. Her talent for languages was shown early by her translating, at the age of fourteen, from English into French two books, which were published in Paris by a well-known bookseller. In 1882 she published her "Epitome of Modern European Literature," comprising translations from nineteen European languages, the Swedish, Hungarian, Italian, Russian, Slovack, Spanish, Dutch, German, Polish, Czeck, Flemish, Portuguese, French, Croatian, Danish, Serbian, Slavonian, Norwegian and Roumanian. The first edition, published in 1881, of this work contained only seventeen translations. In its preparation she did not receive the slightest assistance. She has written numbers of short stories for periodicals, among others, sketches of southern life as it was before the abolition of slavery, but the "Epitome" is the only work to which she has ever affixed her name. Very much of her writing has been for purposes of immediate use, to awaken interest in local needs, or for household purposes, or in aid of progressive opinions, especially those which affect the status of woman. She claims to be the first person who understood that the Bible is the stronghold of "woman's rights." In 1848, when the two or three who dared to speak in favor of women were tempted to renounce their belief in revelation, she wrote to the leaders of the movement, proving to them that they would be forsaking their surest stronghold. Mrs. Henderson is a pronounced advocate of female suffrage, though she is not a platform speaker and takes no public part in their meetings. Like many others unknown to the public, she keeps up a guerrilla warfare as opportunity offers. She has published, at various times, very pronounced views upon the scattered race of the Hebrews, with ingenious arguments to sustain the position which she takes. She gives a generous portion of her time as well as means to looking after the welfare and comfort of those in her vicinity who are in need of any kind of help. Her affiliations are with the Episcopal Church. Mrs. Henderson is the widow of Gen. James Pinckney Henderson, U. S. A. Gen. Henderson is best

FRANCES COX HENDERSON.

remembered as the first Governor of Texas, after the admission of that State to the Union in 1845.

HENDRICKS, Mrs. Eliza C. Morgan, social leader and philanthropist, born near North Bend, a suburb of Cincinnati, Ohio, 22nd

November, 1823. She is the widow of the late Vice-President Thomas A. Hendricks. Her father was Hon. Isaac Morgan. The love of nature, which is one of Mrs. Hendricks' characteristics, was fostered

ELIZA C. MORGAN HENDRICKS.

by her early surroundings. The large and attractive homestead, in which she first saw the light, adjoined that of Gen. William Henry Harrison, and both dwellings were noted for their fine outlook. Mrs. Hendricks is connected with some of the leading families of Cincinnati, and it was in that city she made her début in the social world. She was married 26th September, 1845, and since that time she has resided in Indiana. Her first Hoosier home was in Shelbyville, in which place her husband was then engaged in the practice of law. They removed to Indianapolis in 1860, where he practiced for some years as a member of the law firm of Hendricks, Hord & Hendricks. Mrs. Hendricks was fond of domestic life and was the administrator of the household, saving her husband from all unnecessary annoyance or responsibility, and in many other ways was she his true help-meet. Her husband depended much upon her judgment. Often, while an occupant of the gubernatorial chair, when perplexed over applications for the pardon of criminals, did he call her into the conference, in order to avail himself of her intuitive perception of the merits of the case. Mrs. Hendricks' love of nature leads her to spend much time in the culture of flowers, in which she has much success. She has a great penchant for pets. Her fondness for horses led to that close observation of them which made her a good judge of their qualities, and it was she, not her husband, who always selected the carriage horses. A few years after her marriage, her only child, a bright and beautiful boy, died. Mrs. Hendricks was not only the light of her husband's home life, but, wherever nis official duties called him, he was accompanied by her, and when he twice visited the Old World, in quest of health, she was his

faithful companion. The great sorrow of her life was his death, which occurred in November, 1884. Since that event she has sought assuagement for grief and loneliness in a quickening of activities, especially in the lines of charity. Her most prominent philanthropic work was her persevering efforts, with other earnest women, to establish a "Prison for Women and Reform School for Girls." In answer to earnest and persistent solicitation on their part, the State Legislature made an appropriation, and in 1883 the building was erected. That institution has, from its beginning, been under the entire control and management of women. For some years it was the only one of its kind in the country. Mrs. Hendricks has, from its beginning, been the president of its board of managers. Before her marriage she connected herself with the Methodist Church. Her husband, the son of an elder in the Presbyterian Church, was strongly Calvinistic in faith. They both had a leaning toward the Episcopal form of worship, and together they entered that communion. Mrs. Hendricks is now living in Indianapolis.

HENRY, Mrs. Josephine Kirby Williamson, woman suffragist, born in Newport, Ky., 22nd February, 1846. After receiving a liberal education she became the wife, in 1868, of Captain William Henry, a Confederate soldier, a distinguished scholar and one of the most noted educators in the South. Their only child, Frederick Williamson Henry, who was killed in the terrible railroad disaster in Crete, Ill., inherited the genius of his mother and the talent of his father. Mrs. Henry enjoys the distinction of being the leader in her State of the most advanced political and social reform party in the country, the Equal Rights or

JOSEPHINE KIRBY WILLIAMSON HENRY.

Woman Suffrage party. She knows human nature and history well enough to realize that "human virtue demands her champions and martyrs." With courage, zeal and industry Mrs. Henry has for years been struggling with "supreme prejudice and sublime mediocrity" in her efforts to awaken in the breasts of her countrymen a sentiment of justice toward women, and in her countrywomen a sense of the dignity of true womanhood. What she has already accomplished marks an advance in the political and social history, not only of Kentucky, but of the Southern States. She is the only woman in the South who ever ran for a State office. She was a candidate of the Prohibition party of Kentucky, in 1890, for clerk of the Court of Appeals, receiving nearly five-thousand votes, and that in a State where, perhaps, the popular prejudice is stronger against "Woman's Rights" than in any other in the Union. She has spoken before the legislature and the constitutional convention and has addressed large audiences all over the State on woman's suffrage. Although she is physically frail and delicate, she can address a public meeting for an hour or more with the force of true eloquence and with happy touches of humor and quiet sarcasm. She is a woman of literary talent. She has written several poems of merit, and her prose is clear, bold and incisive. Over three-hundred articles of hers on the subject of "Married Women's Property Rights" have been published. Her leaflet on "Kentucky Women and the Constitution" and her editorials in the "Clarion," published in Versailles, attracted general attention and were copied into papers all over the country. She is superintendent of legislative and petition work of the Kentucky Equal Rights Association. She is an accomplished musician and pianist. As a vocalist she has achieved success. Her home is in Versailles, Ky.

HENRY, Mrs. Sarepta M. I., evangelist, temperance reformer, poet and author, born in Albion, Pa., 4th November, 1839. Her father, Rev. H. Nelson Irish, was a Methodist clergyman of the old style. He was preaching in Albion at the time of the daughter's birth. In 1841 he was sent to Illinois as a missionary, where he did heroic pioneer work and where he ended his days. In 1859 Miss Irish entered the Rock River Seminary, in Mt. Morris, Ill., when she had for her pastor Rev. J. H. Vincent, then just coming into his life work. Recognition had been given to her literary ability, and during her school days she won many honors in composition. On 7th March, 1861, Miss Irish became the wife of James W. Henry, of East Homer, N. Y. The Civil War broke in upon the plans of the young couple and left Mrs. Henry, in 1871, a soldier's widow. The trio of children born from this union are just such as would be expected from so true a marriage. Mary, an alumna of the Northwestern University in Evanston, Ill., is already a writer of acknowledged ability in both prose and verse, and at the national convention of the Woman's Christian Temperance Union in New York, in 1888, she was elected to the position of superintendent of the press department. Alfred, the oldest son, is a faithful and eloquent clergyman, and Arthur is an author. Mrs. Henry was among the first to join the crusade against rum. From the beginning of the organization of the Woman's Christian Temperance Union she has been associated with the national body as superintendent of evangelical work and as evangelist. The result of her seven years of service in gospel temperance in Rockford, Ill., would alone suffice to crown the labors of any ordinary life-time. A partial record of this work is found in her book "Pledge and Cross." Her published books number fourteen, of which two, "Victoria," written during the first year of her daughter's life, and "Marble Cross," are poems. The prose works are "After the

Truth," in four volumes, "Pledge and Cross," "Voice of the Home and its Legend," "Mabel's Work." "One More Chance," "Beforehand," "Afterward," "Unanswered Prayer," and "Frances Raymond's Investment." Mrs. Henry has long occupied pulpits among all denominations throughout the land. Through her evangelistic work saloons have been closed, churches built and hun-

SAREPTA M. I. HENRY.

dreds converted. Her home is now in Evanston, Illinois.

HENSCHEL, Mrs. Lillian Bailey, vocalist, born in Columbus, Ohio, 17th January, 1860. Her musical talent manifested itself very early in life, as, when she was fifteen months old, she plainly showed her choice of different tunes, crying and refusing to sleep if her mother sang one song, and at once remaining quiet when she heard another air. At the age of eighteen months the little one could sing the different tunes she had been accustomed to hear. From that point her whole life has been devoted to the study of music. She began to take piano lessons at the age of seven. Her mother, who was also a singer and had received vocal instruction in Boston, Mass., from the best teachers of her time, directed the daughter's vocal studies. At the age of fifteen the family removed to Boston, and she continued her studies with her uncle, Charles Hayden, a well-known vocal teacher. Later she became a pupil of Madame Rudersdorf, with whom she studied two years. In 1876 Lillian Bailey made her first public appearance in one of B. J. Lang's concerts, given in Boston, meeting with success. After her début she continued to be a favorite singer in Boston, and her services were in constant demand during the concert season, until, in 1877, she went to Paris to study with Madame Viardot, with whom she remained for some time. In the spring of 1878 she went to London, where she made her first appearance in England with the London Philharmonic

Society. In that concert she sang for the first time one of those duets with Mr. Henschel, which have since become so famous. She returned to America in the autumn of 1880 and became the wife of

LILLIAN BAILEY HENSCHEL.

George Henschel, the musician, in the spring of 1881. They remained in Boston three years, Mr. Henschel having charge of the Boston Symphony Orchestra. They removed to London in 1884, which is now their permanent home. There Mr. Henschel holds the position of a leading musician. Mrs. Henschel's fame as a singer is world-wide, as she has been heard in all the principal cities of Europe. At the time of the Ohio Centennial, held in Columbus, she was represented as being one of the celebrated women of that State. Mr. and Mrs. Henschel receive their friends with great hospitality in their beautiful home. Many a homesick American, having located in London to study music with Mr. Henschel, has found in these successful musicians true friends and helpers, who were ready and willing to dissipate the feeling of unrest and to assist in showing the way onward to success.

HERRICK, Mrs. Christine Terhune, author and editor, born in Newark, N. J., 13th June, 1859, where her father was settled as pastor of a Dutch Reformed Church. Her mother is the well-known author, "Marion Harland." In 1876 she went abroad with her parents and spent two years in some of the principal cities of Europe, acquiring a knowledge of foreign languages and continuing an education which had been previously carried on under private teachers at home. After returning to this country, Miss Terhune lived for several years in Springfield, Mass., perfecting herself in English literature, Anglo-Saxon and philology. Her ambition was to teach her favorite branches, and for a time she had a class in a private school for girls. About that time she met and became the wife of James Frederick Herrick, a member of the editorial staff of the Springfield

"Republican." Early in her married life Mrs. Herrick began to write on home topics, developing the talent which has made her so well known. She has contributed to many leading periodicals and newspapers, and has published five books, four of them on home topics, and the other a compilation of correspondence between the late Duke of Wellington and a young woman known as "Miss J." At present Mrs. Herrick lives in New York. She edits the woman's page of the New York "Recorder." Her husband is connected with another metropolitan daily newspaper. While kept very busy by her literary engagements, she does not neglect her household cares, the precepts which she teaches finding practical illustration in her pretty and well-regulated home. She has had four children, and two little boys survive. The rapidity and ease with which Mrs. Herrick turns off her literary work enables her to pay some attention to the obligations and pleasures of society. She is as clever a talker as she is a writer, and is an active member of Sorosis. Her health is unusually good and her activity and good spirits unfailing. She

CHRISTINE TERHUNE HERRICK.

spends her summers in her country home, "Outlook," among the hills of northern New Jersey.

HERSOM, Mrs. Jane Lord, physician, born in Sanford, Me., 6th August, 1840. Her father and mother were of good English descent. She was educated in Springvale, Me., whither the family had removed. She began to teach before she was sixteen, going to school in the fall and winter and teaching in the summer. In 1865, when twenty-five years of age, she became the wife of Dr. N. A. Hersom. He took his bride to Farmington, N. H., where they settled. In 1862 Dr. Hersom had entered the army as an assistant surgeon, was promoted to first surgeon, and afterwards had charge of a field hospital. After the war he began a laborious country practice. His strength soon gave way so as to necessitate a vacation of five years.

He then resumed work and established himself in Portland, Me., where he soon acquired a practice which demanded all his time and energies. In 1881 Dr. Hersom went abroad for needed rest and died

JANE LORD HERSOM.

in Dublin, Ireland, one week after landing. Mrs. Hersom had read medical works to her husband during his sickness, and, enjoying them, continued to read when the need was past. Her husband had been aware of her special fitness, and had often told her she would make a fine physician. The knowledge of his confidence in her abilities acted as a stimulus, and with characteristic energy she began her studies with Prof. S. H. Weeks, of Portland, Me. In 1883 she entered the Woman's Medical College in Philadelphia. After her graduation from that institution she began work in Portland, planning only for a small office practice. Her desires have been far more than realized. She has had a large and increasing practice from the first. She was elected physician of the Temporary Home for Women and Children, in Portland, which position she held for four years, until she was obliged to resign in order to attend properly to her other duties. She is a member of the American Medical Association, the State and County Medical Societies and also of the Practitioner's Club, of which she was elected president for 1892. She is an active member of the Woman's Suffrage Association. She became a woman suffragist through her experience as a student and physician. One of her children died in infancy, and one daughter is living.

HEWITT, Mrs. Emma Churchman, author and journalist, born in New Orleans, La., 1st February, 1850. At three years of age she moved north with her parents, who settled on a farm in Rahway, N. J., afterward moving to Burlington, N. J., and later to Camden, in the same State, where she resided until several years ago, when she moved to West Philadelphia, Pa. She comes of a long line of cultured and educated people, and

is a direct descendant of old John Churchman, who was prominent in the sect of Friends in his day. Mrs. Hewitt is a fluent French scholar, with a knowledge of several other modern languages. She began to write short stories at such a very early age that it has been quaintly remarked that she was "born with a pen in her hand." In 1884 she became a journalist and engaged with the "Daily Evening Reporter" of Burlington, N. J., where she labored until its change of management. In 1885, at the solicitation of the publisher of the "Ladies' Home Journal," she began a series of articles with the unique title "Scribbler's Letters to Gustavus Adolphus." The next year she received a call from the same publisher to the associate-editorship of the journal, which position she filled for four years. Notwithstanding her arduous and exacting work while occupying the editor's chair, she contributed regularly sketches, short stories and articles on domestic topics to at least a dozen other periodicals. Her "Ease in Conversation" first appeared in the "Ladies' Home Journal" under the title of "Mildred's Conversation Class." These articles have been published in book form (Philadelphia, 1887), and the volume, entitled "Ease in Conversation," has gone into its third edition, and her "Hints to Ballad Singers" (Philadelphia, 1889) has had an extended sale. Her chief literary work is the "Queen of Home," (Philadelphia, 1889) treating in an exhaustive and masterly manner subjects of household interest from attic to cellar. She has contributed from time to time to the Philadelphia "Press," the "Christian-at-Work," the "Sunday School Times," the "Weekly Wisconsin," the "Housekeeper," the "Ladies' Home Journal," "Babyhood," the "Home

EMMA CHURCHMAN HEWITT.

Guard," "Golden Days," "Our Girls and Boys," "Our Young Men," "Wide Awake," "Munyon's Illustrated World," "Lippincott's Magazine," and a number of others. She is a regular contributor to several English home magazines and has lately completed a series of papers on household topics for a London periodical. Mrs. Hewitt has a son, a young man of eighteen years, and a daughter in her sixteenth year. About two years ago Mrs. Hewitt severed her connection with the "Ladies' Home Journal'" and accepted a position on the editorial staff of the "Home Magazine," published in Washington, D. C., which she was obliged to resign on account of the death of her sister, which compelled her to live in Philadelphia. She is now connected with "Leisure Hours," a monthly publication in Philadelphia.

HIBBARD, Mrs. Grace, author, born in a suburb of Boston, Mass., and there received her education. She is the daughter of the late Dr. Porter, a Massachusetts clergyman, and a descendant of an old English family. Her early life was spent in New England, where, at her father's knee, when still a child, she learned the Hebrew and Greek alphabets long before she learned the English. At an early age she was graduated from a young ladies' college near Boston. Soon after she graduated her father removed to Chicago, where after a short time he died. Mrs. Hibbard has spent the last few years in Colorado and California, and she has made a number of trips to Mexico, where she studied the Mexican character, which she has portrayed in her writings. Her first literary work appeared in the Springfield, Mass., "Republican," and since then she has been a contributor to many of the leading magazines and papers of America. In short stories and ballads she excels. One short sketch, "Bummer and Lazarus," a story of San Francisco, was translated into the German and printed in one of the leading papers published in

GRACE HIBBARD.

the German language. She has contributed to "Belford's Magazine," the San Francisco "Morning Call" and other journals. About three years ago she became the wife, in Colorado Springs, Col.,

of Dr. Hibbard, of Denver, Col., and now lives in the last named city.

HIBLER, Mrs. Nellie, musical educator, born in Utica, N. Y., 10th September, 1858. Her

NELLIE HIBLER.

parents, Mr. and Mrs. John R. Owen, are Welsh, and members of families of culture. Nellie from her early childhood was noted for her love of music. When quite young, she was graduated from the Utica advanced school and entered the academy. When in her sixteenth year, she accompanied her parents to Wales, and for three years they lived in the town of Aberystwyth. There Nellie received a scholarship for piano and harmony. By extraordinary diligence she was graduated in two-and-a-half years instead of three. She received the title Associate in Music of the University College of Wales. While abroad, her studies were under the direction of Dr. Parry, the famous Welsh composer. Not long after her graduation she returned with her parents to Utica, where she was for a time the organist of the South Street Methodist Episcopal Church. Afterward the family moved to Parker's Landing, Pa., where the daughter sang in the Presbyterian Church. She gathered a large class in music, which she taught with much success until she became the wife of Mr. Hibler, of Parker's Landing, who was then teller of the Exchange Bank. In less than three years after her marriage her husband and infant son died, within a few days of each other. Again she took up her profession and concluded to make a specialty of voice culture. She has been instructed by some of the best teachers in America. In Bradford, Pa., where she now resides, she was a leading soprano for two years in the Presbyterian Church, and for two more years the leader of the choir. Owing to the increased number of her private students, she resigned her position as a leader. She often sings in concerts and some of her compositions have been lately published.